ISBN 978-1-5284-6656-1
PIBN 10929871

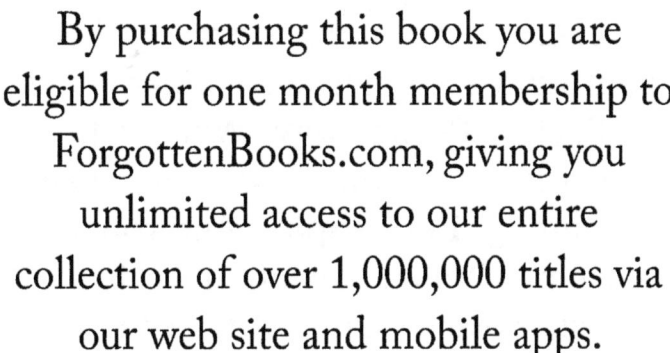

REPORTS

OF

CASES AT LAW AND IN EQUITY

DETERMINED BY THE

SUPREME COURT

OF THE

STATE OF IOWA.

———

MAY 25, 1898—DECEMBER 16, 1898.

———

BY

Benj. I. Salinger.

———

VOLUME XVII,

BEING VOLUME CVI. OF THE SERIES.

DES MOINES, IOWA:
GEO. H. RAGSDALE, PUBLISHER.
1899.

JUDGES OF THE SUPREME COURT

DURING THE TIME OF THESE REPORTS.

HORACE E. DEEMER, RED OAK, *Chief Justice*.
GIFFORD S. ROBINSON, SIOUX CITY.
CHAS. T. GRANGER, WAUKON.
JOSIAH GIVEN, DES MOINES.
SCOTT M. LADD, SHELDON.
CHARLES M. WATERMAN, DAVENPORT.

OFFICERS OF THE COURT.

MILTON REMLEY, IOWA CITY, *Attorney General*.
C. T. JONES, WASHINGTON, *Clerk*.
BENJ. I. SALINGER, CARROLL, *Reporter*.

JUDGES OF THE COURTS

FROM WHICH APPEALS MAY BE TAKEN TO THE SUPREME COURT.

DISTRICT COURTS.

First District—HENRY BANK, JR., Keokuk.

Second District—M. A. ROBERTS, Ottumwa; T. M. FEE, Centerville.
F. W. EICHELBERGER, Bloomfield; ROBERT SLOAN, Keosauqua.

Third District—H. M. TOWNER, Corning; W. H. TEDFORD, Corydon

Fourth District—WM. HUTCHINSON, Orange City; GEO. W. WAKE-
FIELD, Sioux City; F. R. GAYNOR, Le Mars; JOHN F. OLIVER,
Onawa.

Fifth District—J. H. APPLEGATE, Guthrie Center; A. W. WILKINSON,
Winterset; JAMES D. GAMBLE, Knoxville.

Sixth District—DAVID RYAN, Newton; BEN MCCOY, Oskaloosa; A. R.
DEWEY, Washington.

Seventh District—JAMES W. BOLLINGER, Davenport; W. F. BRANNAN,
Muscatine; P. B. WOLFE, Clinton; A. J. HOUSE, Maquoketa.

Eighth District—MARTIN J. WADE, Iowa City.

Ninth District—W. F. CONRAD, CALVIN P. HOLMES, THOMAS F.
STEVENSON, CHARLES A. BISHOP, Des Moines.

Tenth District—FRANK C. PLATT, Waterloo; A. S. BLAIR, Manchester.

Eleventh District—D. R. HINDMAN, Boone; S. M. WEAVER, Iowa
Falls; BENJAMIN P. BIRDSALL, Clarion.

Twelfth District—JOHN C. SHERWIN, Mason City; J. F. CLYDE, Osage,
C. H. KELLEY, Forest City.

Thirteenth District—L. E. FELLOWS, Lansing; A. N. HOBSON, West
Union.

Fourteenth District—LOT THOMAS, Storm Lake; WILLIAM B. QUAR-
TON, Algona.

Fifteenth District—A. B. THORNELL, Sidney; WALTER I. SMITH,
Council Bluffs; N. W. MACY, Harlan; W. R. GREEN, Audubon.

Sixteenth District—S. M. ELWOOD, Sac City; Z. A. CHURCH, Jefferson.

Seventeenth District—GEORGE W. BURNHAM, Vinton; OBED CASWELL,
Marshalltown.

Eighteenth District—H. M. REMLEY, Anamosa; WILLIAM G. THOMP-
SON, Marion.

Nineteenth District—FRED O'DONNELL, Dubuque; JAMES L. HUSTED,
Dubuque.

Twentieth District—JAMES D. SMYTH, Burlington; WINFIELD S. WITH-
ROW, Mt. Pleasant.

SUPERIOR COURTS.

Cedar Rapids—THOMAS M. GIBERSON.

Council Bluffs—J. E. F. MCGEE.

Keokuk—RICE H. BELL.

TABLE OF CASES REPORTED

IN THIS VOLUME.

(v)

viii

CASES REPORTED.

REPORTS

OF

CASES AT LAW AND IN EQUITY

DETERMINED BY THE

SUPREME COURT

OF

THE STATE OF IOWA

AT

DES MOINES, MAY TERM, A. D. 1898,

|106
|127

106
f132

AND IN THE FIFTY-SECOND YEAR OF THE STATE.

F. A. TISDALE v. C. W. MAJOR, Assignee, Appellant.*

Attachment of Real Property: DAMAGES. The depreciation of real property upon which a writ of attachment has been levied, occurring while the levy remains in force, if there is no change of possession, is not the immediate result of the attachment, and recovery therefor cannot be had in an action upon the attachment bond.

SAME. Mental suffering resulting from the wrongful and malicious suing out of a writ of attachment does not afford a ground for the recovery of compensatory damages.

PLEADING: *Ultimate facts.* The averments in a petition in an action upon an attachment bond as to the purpose for which the property levied upon was used and that it was the only mill machinery and equipment of the kind located in the town and doing a substantial business, are properly stricken out, as they do not present ultimate and material facts.

---

*The figures on the left of the syllabi refer to corresponding figures placed on the margin of the case at the place where the point of the syllabus is decided.

Appeal from Wapello District Court.—HON. T. M. FEE, Judge.

WEDNESDAY, MAY 25, 1898.

ACTION at law, aided by attachment, to recover an amount alleged to be due from the defendants Deitrich & Capell, and the members of that firm, on a promissory note and on accounts. C. W. Major, as assignee of the defendants, intervened. There was a trial by the court without a jury, and a judgment in favor of the plaintiff. The intervener appeals.—*Affirmed.*

McElroy & Heindel for appellant.

McNett & Tisdale for appellee.

ROBINSON, J.—The writ of attachment was issued on the alleged grounds that the defendants were about to dispose of their property with intent to defraud their creditors, and that they had disposed of their property, in whole or in part, with intent to defraud their creditors. The writ was levied upon certain real estate in the city of Ottumwa. The defendants appeared to the action, and filed an answer, in which they admitted that they were indebted to the plaintiff on the note and accounts in suit to the amount claimed, but alleged that the attachment was wrongfully and maliciously sued out, and that on the day it was levied they made to C. W. Major an assignment of all their property not exempt from execution for the benefit of their creditors. On the same day the assignee filed a petition of intervention, in which he admitted the indebtedness of the defendants as alleged by the plaintiff, and sought to recover on the attachment bond, by virtue of the assignment by the defendants to him, for damages alleged to have been sustained by the defendants, in consequence of the alleged wrongful and malicious suing out and levying of the writ of attachment. A motion to strike out portions of the petition of intervention was sustained in part, the intervener thereafter filed an "amended and supplemental petition," and a motion to strike out portions of that petition was sustained. No evidence was offered on the trial in behalf of the defendants and the intervener, and the questions presented by the appeal for our consideration grow out of the sustaining of the motions.

I. One of the paragraphs of the petition of intervention which was stricken out purports to state a part of the damages alleged to have been sustained by the defendants, and is as follows: "In the depreciation in the market value of said attached property, caused by the issuance and levy of said writ of attachment in the sum of $2,000."

1   It is stated in the petition that the property levied upon was a mill used in manufacturing doors, sash, blinds, counters, book cases, and other articles, and that it was equipped with a large quantity of valuable machinery, which was a part of the mill and of the property upon which the attachment was levied. It does not appear that possession of any part of the property levied upon was taken under the writ, nor that the right of the defendants and their assignee to use it was interfered with in any manner. The question to be determined is whether an attaching creditor is liable for the depreciation in value of real estate levied upon, which occurs while the attachment is in force. The mere issuing and levying of a writ of attachment upon real estate cannot ordinarily cause it to depreciate in value. The appellant suggests that some portion of the machinery might become worthless, or out of date, and in that case it could not be exchanged for new and improved machinery. Nothing of that character is suggested by the portion of the petition stricken out, nor would proof of damage by reason of inability to make improvements, or by loss of a sale, be material under it. It is the general rule that the depreciation of real property upon which a writ of attachment has been levied, which occurs while the levy remains in force, if there be no change of possession, is not the immediate result of the

attachment, and recovery therefor cannot be had of the attaching creditor. *Heath v. Lent,* 1 Cal. 410; *Trawick v. Martin-Brown Co.,* 79 Tex. 460 (14 S. W. Rep. 564); *Brandon v. Allen,* 28 La. Ann. 60; *Muldoon v. Rickey,* 103 Pa. St. 110; Drake Attachments, section 179; Wade Attachments, section 301; 2 Sutherland Damages, section 512. The only cases cited by the appellant as holding a contrary doctrine is that of *Lowenstein v. Monroe,* 55 Iowa, 82, but that involved a levy upon personal property, which is subject to a different rule.

II. One of the paragraphs of the petition of intervention stricken out described the purposes for which the property levied upon was used, and that it was the only

2   mill, machinery, and equipment of the kind located in Ottumwa, and it was doing a substantial business.

The paragraph was in the nature of a statement of evidence not relevant to any issue in the case, and not of ultimate and material facts, and it was properly stricken out.

III. The amended and supplemental petition contained a paragraph of which the following is a copy: "That the suing out of said attachment on said false grounds caused great shame, degradation, humiliation, wounded pride, and mental suffering to the defendants, and each of them, to their actual damage in the sum of three thousand

3   dollars." That was stricken out on motion, and of that ruling the appellant complains. The question thus presented is whether there can be a recovery as of actual damages for mental anguish, including the feelings of shame, degradation, humiliation, and wounded pride. In *Stevenson v. Belknap,* 6 Iowa, 97, a recovery by a father for his anxiety and wounded feelings because of the seduction of his daughter was held to be authorized. In *Muldowney v. Railway Co.,* 36 Iowa, 402, a recovery was permitted for mental anguish suffered by a person who was injured in a railway accident. In *McKinley v. Railroad Co.,* 44 Iowa, 314, it was held that "mental anguish arising from the nature and character of an

assault is an element of compensatory damages." In *Parkhurst v. Masteller,* 57 Iowa, 474, it was held that a person might recover compensation for mental suffering caused by a malicious prosecution. In *Shepard v. Railway Co.,* 77 Iowa, 54, it was held that compensatory damages might be recovered for the mental suffering of a passenger, caused by her being wrongfully compelled, with insult and abuse, to leave a train; and the same rule was applied in *Curtis v. Railway Co.,* 87 Iowa, 622. It will be observed that each of these cases involved an injury to the person, or a violation of personal rights, as distinguished from injury to tangible property, or to the rights of such property. In *Mentzer v. Telegraph Co.,* 93 Iowa, 752, the right of the sender of a telegram to recover for mental suffering which resulted from negligence in the delivery of the telegram was involved, and many authorities upon the right of recovery for mental anguish were reviewed. It was there said that, to authorize such a recovery, "there must be some direct and proximate connection between the wrong done and the injury to the feelings, to justify a recovery for mental anguish." Also: "Every breach of contract is likely to cause some pain, but some of these contracts relate to property and pecuniary matters, and in such case the law furnishes what has always been held to be an adequate remedy for pecuniary loss sustained." In the case of *Campbell v. Chamberlain,* 10 Iowa, 337, in which recovery was sought on an attachment bond, it was held that injuries to credit and character were too remote to be considered in such an action, and that rule was approved in *Lowenstein v. Monroe,* 55 Iowa, 82. See, also, 1 Sutherland Damages (2d ed.), section 55; 2 Sutherland Damages (2d ed.), section 512. Although none of the cases last cited are precisely in point, yet they tend strongly to support the conclusion we reach that mental suffering resulting from the wrongful and malicious suing out and levying of a writ of attachment does not afford ground for the recovery of compensatory damages. We think that the district court was right in striking out the paragraph of the amended and supplemental petition which we have been considering. A careful examination of the entire record fails to disclose any error prejudicial to the defendant, and the judgment of the district court is AFFIRMED.

MARY CHAMBERS v. JOHN JACKSON and CHRISTIAN TRUMP, Appellants.

Homesteads: ABANDONMENT. Certain judgments rendered were not liens upon realty owned by defendant because of its being a homestead. He left it to reside with his daughter without intending to return, neither did he return. Within three days *after* leaving, he deeded the said property to the daughter in consideration of her agreement to furnish him a home and support for life. *Held*, in the absence of a showing that the deed was in pursuance of an agreement made before grantor left the realty, the homestead was abandoned and the lien of the judgments attached before said transfer by deed.

Appeal from Lee District Court.—HON. A. J. MCCRARY, Judge.

WEDNESDAY, MAY 25, 1898.

ACTION in equity to restrain the sale of certain real estate on execution. There was a trial on issues joined, and a decree for plaintiff. Defendants appeal.—*Reversed.*

Watson & Weber and *T. B. Snyder* for appellants.

T. H. Johnson for appellee.

WATERMAN, J.—One F. H. Brewer was the owner of certain real estate in the city of Ft. Madison, in this state, which he occupied with his wife as a homestead. On February 26, 1895, defendant Jackson recovered two judgments against said Brewer and another in the district court of Lee county for the sum of two hundred and thirty-six dollars and eighty-six cents each, with costs. These judgments when rendered, were not liens on the real estate in controversy. On August 20, 1895, executions were issued on said judgments, and levied on said real estate. Plaintiff then instituted this action, claiming that the property so levied upon was the homestead of Brewer, who was the father of plaintiff, and that she is the owner thereof by purchase.

The evidence discloses the following facts: Brewer was a man eighty-four years of age. His wife died in February, 1895, and he continued alone in the occupancy of his homestead until April 1st following. On that day he left his property, and went to reside with his daughter. On April 3d, father and daughter entered into a written agreement, by the terms of which the latter was to furnish her father with a home and support during the remainder of his life, and in consideration therefor was to receive a deed of the homestead property. Such a deed was executed and delivered on April 3d. The father testified that when he left the homestead on April 1st he had no intention of returning. He did not, in fact, return, but still resides with his daughter, so far as disclosed by the record. There is no evidence of any agreement between the father and daughter prior to the contract of April 3d, of which we have made mention. We are constrained to hold that the homestead was abandoned by Brewer on April 1st, that the lien of the judgments attached, and the decree of the trial court was erroneous in holding otherwise.—REVERSED.

N. C. FIELD, Petitioner, v. A. B. THORNELL, Judge.

106
126

Contempt: NEWSPAPER ARTICLE. During an *adjournment* in a cause on trial, an editor handed two jurors a copy of his paper to which one of the jurors was a subscriber. It had an article on the pend-
1   ing trial, headed "A put up job;" and in which the arrest, the apparent conclusiveness of the evidence and public indignation were referred to. It then stated that a revulsion of feeling had set in and that, now, "the majority of the sensible, thinking people took very little stock in the story told by the parties chiefly interested." It named the jurors, belittled the talk of the county attorney, and exalted that of defendant's counsel. It then proceeded to attack the standing, character, and intelligence of the state's

5   witnesses, and to say that while the action of a jury is uncertain,
1   there is no doubt in the minds of intelligent men as to what the
verdict ought to be. Neither the proceedings nor the evidence
were given but a set of derogatory innuendoes and an inferential
statement that the witnesses were in a deal to convict defendant.
The two jurors read the article and one of them read part of it
aloud in the jury room while the jury was deliberating. *Held*,
a   This was contempt within Code, 4460, which inhibits contempt-
2-5   uous and insolent behavior towards a court "while engaged in the
discharge of a judicial duty."
b   The judicial duty is not ended by an adjournment and is not
3-5   performed until the particular case is disposed of.

Motion to Discharge: WAIVER. Where defendant moves a discharge,
at the conclusion of the state's evidence, the court declines to
4   decide it "off hand" and the defendant introduces evidence without insisting on a ruling or saving an exception, he will be deemed
to have acquiesced in the conduct of the trial.

CERTIORARI *to* HON. A. B. THORNELL, Judge of the Fifteenth
Judicial District of Iowa.

WEDNESDAY, MAY 25, 1898.

ON June 8, 1896, the county attorney filed an information accusing the petitioner of contempt of court, in that he
published in the *Mills County Tribune* a false and scurrilous
article concerning the trial of the State of Iowa against William De Ford, entitled "A Put-Up Job," and willfully and
corruptly, and with the malicious intent of influencing the
jury in said cause, and thereby preventing the decent and
orderly administration of justice, handed a copy of said paper
to each of two jurors in said cause. The petitioner entered a
plea of not guilty. There was a hearing on the following
day, when he was found guilty and a fine of thirty dollars
imposed. Petition *dismissed*.

P. P. Kelly and *O. R. Patrick* for petitioner.

LADD, J.—The case of the state against William De
Ford, accused of the crime of incest, was on trial in the district
court of Mills county. Nearly all the evidence had been
introduced, and the court had adjourned until the following

morning. Two of the jurors, William Van Doren and James Galbraith, went to the petitioner's place of business; and he handed each of them a copy of the *Mills County Tribune,* a newspaper of general circulation in that community, and of which he was publisher. Galbraith was a subscriber, but Van Doren was not. This paper contained an article headed "A Put-Up-Job," concerning the trial, in which the arrest of the defendant, the apparent conclusiveness of the evidence, and the public indignation are referred to. It then proceeds: "But it wasn't long before there came a reaction. Curious facts and unaccountable incidents came to mind, that began to throw a shadow of doubt on the whole transaction, and very many good people became convinced that the whole thing was a farce and a put-up job. As this wore on, this conviction became stronger; and, when the case came up for trial, the majority of the sensible, thinking people of the locality where the reputed crime occurred took very little stock in the story as told by the parties chiefly interested." The names of the jurors are then given, the talk of the county attorney belittled, and that of the attorney for the defense pronounced "one of the most notable speeches we ever heard in the court room." One witness is said to be conceded a jail bird by the county attorney, and to belong to the penitentiary. It continues: "After the opening statements to the jury, the first witness for the state was called, it being the fellow Hobbes. His testimony was about what might be expected, coming as it did from one of the four men in the deal. Mrs. Harmer was then put on the stand, and told, of course, the story that she had been expected to tell. She told just what her husband wanted her to tell, and admitted (?) that everything had happened just as her husband said it did. Poor, silly thing! Everybody felt sorry for her, and there was not a few that felt she ought to be in the insane asylum instead of on the witness stand. At the conclusion of the woman's testimony the case was adjourned until yesterday, when it was again resumed. 'Doc' Lemonds, Alec McCrary, and Frank Harmer were put on the stand when the trial was resumed, and told their little story fairly well; but, as might be expected, on cross-examination they contradicted and tangled themselves up in bad shape. The defense began its testimony yesterday afternoon and the evidence is being heard to-day. It is expected that the case will go to the jury to-night or in the morning. Of course, there is no telling what the jury's verdict will be, as juries are an uncertain quantity sometimes; but there is no doubt in our mind what it ought to be, nor do we think there is any doubt in the mind of every intelligent man who has familiarized himself with the facts in the case." The petitioner had been in attendance at court during the trial, knew the jurors and was much interested in the case. He wrote the article naming them on the day he delivered the papers. His explanation is that he published the article as a matter of news, and did not think at the time of the case, or that Galbraith and Van Doren were jurors. The article was read by these jurors, and Galbraith gave his paper to another juror, and Van Doren read a part of the article aloud in the jury room when the jurors were deliberating on their verdict.

I. The petitioner first insists that the particular offense of which he was adjudged guilty is not included in the terms of the statute. We think it comes within the purview of subdivision 1 of section 4460 of the Code which provides for the punishment of "contemptuous or insolent behavior toward such court while engaged in the discharge of a judicial duty which may tend to impair the respect due to its authority."

2   Coke once said: "We shall never know the true reason of the interpretation of the statutes if we know not the law before the making of them." The power to punish for contempt is recognized as inherent in all courts, and essential to the preservation of order in judicial proceedings, and to the due administration of justice. The exercise of such power may be traced as far back in antiquity as the trial by jury; and it has been well said that the experience of ages has demonstrated its compatability with civil liberty and the purest ends of justice. "It is a trust given to the courts,

not for themselves, but for the people, whose laws they enforce
and whose authority they exercise." *Watson v. Williams,*
36 Miss. 331. Unless the court may protect itself in the
fulfillment of its important and responsible duties for the
public good, it becomes impotent and contemptible. To deprive
it of that power would be equivalent to ending its useful
existence. If it may not repel and punish those who impede,
obstruct, or embarrass the administration of law, then no
litigant may rely with any assurance upon the ability of the
court to insure him a fair and impartial trial. Of what value
is the right of trial by jury or of cross-examination of witnesses, if the result be controlled by inimical influences,
against which there is no opportunity to contend? The
language of the statute does not require us to adopt a construction which will cripple the administration of justice,
and deprive parties and the state of the hearing of causes
unmolested by extrinsic influences, whether within or without the actual presence of the court. That maliciously
attempting to influence a juror in reaching his verdict, or in
any way attempting to prevent the decent and orderly administration of justice, as charged in this case, is contemptuous
behavior towards the court, tending to impair the respect due
to its authority, is not questioned, nor could it be, in the light
of the authorities. But it is asserted that the words "while
engaged in the discharge of a judicial duty" limit such
behavior to the time the court is actually in session, and to
acts committed in its presence. If so, then during the inter-
mission of court, while the trial is in progress, the jurors may
be approached by friend or foe of the litigant parties, witnesses, and officers denounced or intimidated, and the judge
threatened or insulted with impunity. We shall not inquire
whether the legislature may thus deprive the judiciary of
powers necessary to enable it to perform the duties conferred
by the constitution, because such an intention will not be
imputed to that body. If the statute may be said to be
subject to two constructions, that in harmony with the dic-
tates of sound public policy will always be preferred to one

inimical to the public good. The court throughout a trial is "engaged in the discharge of a judicial duty." The necessities of nature require temporary suspension of the proceedings, for all must eat and sleep. But the judicial

3   duty is not performed until the particular case is disposed of. The purpose of the statute is that during the pendency of specific legal proceedings the court shall be permitted to administer the law according to approved rules and precedents, without molestation or interference.

II. Upon the conclusion of the evidence in behalf of the state, the petitioner moved that he be discharged. The court remarked: "I shall not decide this motion offhand. If

you want to introduce any evidence, why do so;

4   because this motion involves the case." Without insisting upon a ruling or saving an exception, the petitioner proceeded with the introduction of his evidence. With the record in this condition, he is not in a situation to complain, and will be deemed to have acquiesced in the manner of conducting the trial.

III. The article is not a fair account of the trial, but rather, as admitted, a statement of the petitioner's convictions. Neither the proceedings of the court nor the evidence

is given, but comments thereon charging, in effect

5   or by inuendo, that one witness for the state was a jailbird; another, silly and suitable for the insane asylum; that four of them were in a deal to convict the defendant; and that, whatever the jury might do, there was no doubt in the mind of every intelligent man, familiar with the facts, that it should acquit him. This was while the case was on trial, and, as the paper was published and distributed at the county seat, the petitioner must be presumed to know that the article would be likely to fall into the hands of the witnesses and jurors in attendance. The question arises, then, whether the court may, by contempt proceedings, protect witnesses from denunciation and intimidation by the public press, and the jurors from the influence created thereby, and suggestions of their proper course during the

progress of a trial. It was remarked by Lord Hardwick, in 2. Atk. 471, that "there cannot be anything of greater consequence than to keep the streams of justice clear and pure, that parties may proceed with safety both to themselves and their characters." Mr. Cooley, in his work on Torts (page 424) says: "It has also been held in many cases that the publication of an article in a newspaper commenting on proceedings in court then pending and undetermined, or upon the court in its relation thereto, made at a time and under circumstances calculated to affect the course of justice in such proceedings, and obviously intended for that purpose, may be punished as a contempt, even though the court was not in session when the publication was made." *In Re Sturoc,* 48 N. H., 428, the accused published an article referring to the prosecution and "smelling committees" in going beyond the limits of their towns, and inquiring: "How does it look to you taxpayers of New Hampshire, that your hard-won earnings should be squandered by bigots or demagogues in this way? Yet such must inevitably be the effect if certain outrageous proceedings lately instituted in the town of Sunapee are to be tolerated and sustained." The article was published in the village where the court was in session, and during the term at which the case was likely to be called for trial. The court says: "It is not, however, open to doubt that the article has an obvious tendency to bring the prosecution and the promoters of it into odium and contempt. The whole tone of the article assumes that the prosecution was illegal, oppressive, and unjust; and, in particular passages, it denounces the prosecution in opprobious and abusive terms. It must have been intended to persuade those who read it that the prosecution ought not to be maintained. If jurors, who might read the article, should adopt such views of the cause they would be improper persons to try it, and the direct effect would be to obstruct and corrupt the administration of the law. The character of the article, and the time and circumstances of the publication oblige us to find that as this was the natural, so it must have been the intended, effect of the publication. The natural consequences of his act being to corrupt the administration of the law, the defendant cannot discharge himself by alleging that he meant no harm, and did not suppose that he was doing anything illegal." In *Littler v. Thompson,* 2 Beav. 129, a published article representing the proceedings as vexatious and the witnesses as guilty of perjury, was adjudged contemptuous. The general doctrine is stated in 2 Bishop, Criminal Law, section 259, to be that any publication, whether by parties or strangers, relating to a cause in court, which tends to prejudice the public as to its merits, and to corrupt or embarrass the administration of justice, may be visited as a contempt; and this includes reflections on the tribunal or its proceedings, or on the parties, the jurors, the witnesses, or the counsel.

We have discovered no authority denying the power of a court to punish as contempt an act which tends to impede, embarrass, or obstruct it in the discharge of its duties. The necessity for this power is that the law may be fairly and impartially administered, uninterrupted by any influence affecting the safety or tending to direct the conclusion of the judge or jurors, or preventing or interfering with the officers of the court, or intimidating or coercing witnesses in giving their testimony. Can it be that a court has no power to protect counsel from publications calculated to intimidate and prevent them from a proper defense of suitors? Is it possible that jurors, while in the discharge of their duties, may be held up before the public as without intelligence, and not reliable when forced to sit upon the trial of causes? May witnesses who are required to attend trials by compulsory process be denounced as jail birds, conspirators, and fit subjects for the lunatic asylum during the progress, because, forsooth, they may not testify in accordance with the whim or judgment of some editor? If so, then attorneys, jurors, and witnesses in attending courts must not pay heed to the fearless discharge of their duties, if they would avoid excoriation of the newspapers, but conform their conduct and testimony to the intimations which may be thrown out in advance. Such is not law. The courts must be left free during the progress of trials to investigate, untrammeled by such influences. Newspapers cannot be permitted to invade the sanctity of the courts of justice, assail litigants, intimidate witnesses, and dictate the verdicts of jurors or the judgments of the court. The trial of De Ford was pending when the article in question was published. The petitioner had every reason to believe it would fall into the hands of the witnesses and jurors. Its natural tendency was to intimidate the witnesses in attendance of court, and to influence the jury in reaching their verdict. The judgment imposed was fully warranted by the evidence and the law. *State v. Judge Civil Dist. Ct.* (La.), 14 South. Rep. 310. It must be added, however, that the courts have no power or desire to control the press in its legitimate sphere. Its freedom is jealously guarded by the law, and made secure in the constitution. It enjoys the utmost latitude in reviewing the action of the courts, and may, after the particular litigation is ended, assail, with just criticism, opinion, rulings, and judgments with the weapons of reason, ridicule, or sarcasm. "But the liberty of the press must not be confounded with mere license. Liberty of the press stops where a further exercise would invade the rights of others. This provision of the constitution does not authorize a usurpation of the functions of the courts. Under a plea of the liberty of the press, a newspaper has no right to assail litigants during the progress of a trial, intimidate witnesses, dictate verdicts or judgments, or spread before juries its opinion of the merits of cases which are on trial." *In re Shortridge,* 99 Cal. 526 (34 Pac. Rep. 227). It is seldom, however, that an honorable journalist so far forgets his self-respect as to trespass upon the rights of the judiciary, or seek to control or improperly influence its conclusions. Courts are constantly passing on questions affecting the life and liberty of the citizen, as well as the rights of property; and the freedom of the judiciary to investigate and decide is quite as important to the well-being of society as the freedom of the press. Let the

courts perform their duties unmolested, but their final judgments, as well as the manner of reaching them, are thereafter
open to the world for such criticism or condemnation as taste
or necessity may require. As supporting the views expressed,
see *People v. Wilson*, 64 Ill. 195; *Fishback v. State*, 131 Ind.
304 (30 N. E. Rep. 1088); *Myers v. State*, 46 Ohio St. 473
(22 N. E. Rep. 43); *Ex parte Barry*, 87 Cal. 109 (25 Pac.
Rep. 256); *State v. Doty*, 90 Am. Dec. 671; *State v. Judge of
Civil District Court*, 45 La. Am. 1250 (14 South. Rep. 310;
State v. Galloway, 98 Am Dec. 404, and note; *Cooper v.
People*, 13 Col. 337, 373 (22 Pac. Rep. 790); *State v. Kaiser,*
8 Lawyers Rep. Ann. (Or.) 584, and note (s. c. 23 Pac. 964);
State v. Morrill, 16 Ark. 384.—DISMISSED.

GEORGE LACY v. THE COUNTY OF KOSSUTH IN THE STATE OF
IOWA, Appellant.

Paupers: MEDICAL AID: *Liability.* It is provided that township
trustees may furnish medical attendance to paupers who they
1   think ought not to be sent to the poor house (Code, 1873, amended
by Eighteenth General Assembly, chapter 133,); that the expense
shall be audited and paid by the county (section 1368); that such
relief is subject to the approval of the county board which may
8   reject or diminish claims therefor allowed by the trustees, and
that the county board has power to contract for the support of the
poor, with the lowest bidder. *Held*, the board has power to contract with a physician for attendance upon the county poor; that
the trustees cannot employ a physician other than the one contracted with by the board and charge the county with his services
to a pauper without proof that the county physician was either
incompetent or inconvenient of access.

INFECTIOUS DISEASE. Acts Eighteenth General Assembly, chapter 151,
section 21, makes it the duty of the board of health of a township
to provide assistance for a resident thereof affected with a disease
1   dangerous to the public health; the expense to be charged to the
person so affected, or other person liable for his support, if able;
otherwise to the county to which he belongs. Section 14 provides
that, "every local board of health shall obtain a competent physi-
8   cian who shall be the health officer within its jurisdiction;" also
that such board shall regulate all fees and charges of persons
employed by it in the execution of the health law. *Held*, that the

health physician is not required by virtue of his appointment to treat persons professionally, but that the board has power to employ a physician to treat an infected person; and such physician may recover, if the patient be a pauper, for the services so performed, from the county, even though the board of supervisors may have a contract with another physician to treat all paupers of the county.

Evidence: HARMLESS ERROR. The contract between a county and a
12 physician employed by it to treat the paupers of the county is properly excluded in an action against the county for medical service rendered by another physician, where the fact of the former physician's employment is admitted.

CLAIM AGAINST COUNTY: *Certificate.* Certificate of the board of health, attached to the statement of account for medical services presented
7 to the county board of supervisors, to the effect that the claimant was employed by the board and that he performed the service stated, and that the bill was correct and in accord with the contract made with him, is admissible as part of the claim, in the action against the county.

SAME. A certificate of the board of health attached to the bill of a physician employed by it, reciting such employment, that the
11 service was rendered as stated, and that the charges were in accordance with the contract, is proper evidence of such facts in an action on the account.

COMPETENCY OF PHYSICIAN. Evidence of particular acts is not admissible to prove the incompetency of the physician. His gen-
10 eral reputation of skill is alone relevant and can be proved only by persons knowing such reputation in the community where he is engaged in practice who do not base their testimony on mere rumor.

OPINIONS: *Insolvency.* Witnesses who, from inquiry and observation, know the financial ability of a person, are competent to testify as
6 to such facts; and after stating the facts, their evidence that the execution against him could not be collected, and that he had no property out of which a bill could be collected, is competent.

DOCTOR'S LICENSE: *Burden of proof.* It will be presumed that a physician has been duly authorized to practice, where the question
5 arises collaterally in a *civil* action between the physician and one who employed him; and the burden of proving a want of license is on him who denies the license.

Appeal: OBJECTIONS BELOW: *Waiver of pleadings.* In a suit to charge a county for treating a patient it was not pleaded that his relatives were unable to pay. This defect was not objected to below, except it be in manner following: The defendant objected
4 to evidence offered to prove the financial condition of the relatives and moved a directed verdict, alleging absence of evidence showing their inability to pay. The court charged that there could be

no recovery without such evidence. *Held*, such defect in pleading is not available on appeal, though it rendered the petition vulnerable to demurrer or motion in arrest of judgment, if not to answer, and this, though it is provided by statute that no pleading shall be held sufficient on account of failure to demur thereto. (Chapter 96, Twenty-fifth General Assembly.)

Appeal: ASSIGNMENT OF ERRORS. A ground for exception to an
9 instruction that it is not authorized by law is too general for consideration.

Appeal from the Palo Alto District Court.—Hon. W. B. QUARTON, Judge.

WEDNESDAY, MAY 25, 1898.

ACTION at law to recover compensation for medical services rendered a pauper at the instance of the township trustees, and for like services rendered to one afflicted with a contagious disease, at the instance of a local board of health. The defense was a general denial and an affirmative plea that defendant employed a regular physician, whose duty it was to look after such patients on behalf of the county. The authority of the township trustees and of the board of health to bind the county is also put in issue. The case was tried to a jury, resulting in a verdict and judgment for plaintiff, and defendant appeals.—*Reversed.*

Raymond & Raymond and *Carr & Parker* for appellant.

Clarke & Cohenour for appellee.

DEEMER, C. J.—The acts of the legislature material to a determination of the main questions in the case are as follows: "When any person * * * residing within
       any * * * township within this state shall be
1   infected * * * with * * * sickness
       dangerous to the public health, the board of health of
the * * * township where said persons may be, shall make effectual provisions in the manner in which they shall judge best, for the safety of the inhabitants, * * * by providing nurses and other assistance and supplies, which

shall be charged to the person himself, his parents or other person who may be liable for his support if able; otherwise at the expense of the county to which he belongs." Acts Eighteenth General Assembly, chapter 151, section 21. Section 14 of the same chapter also provides that "every local board of health shall appoint a competent physician of the board, who shall be the health officer within its jurisdiction;" also, "that local boards shall also regulate all fees and charges employed by them in the execution of the health laws, and of their own regulations." Section 303 of the Code of 1873 vests in the board of supervisors of the respective counties the "exercise of all the powers in relation to the poor given by law to the county authorities." Section 1361 of the Code of 1873, as amended by chapter 133, Acts Eighteenth General Assembly, provides that "the township trustees shall provide for the relief of such poor persons in their respective townships as should not in their judgment be sent to the county poor house. * * * The relief thus furnished may be in the form of * * * medical attendance." Section 1363: "All moneys expended (as contemplated in section 1361) shall be paid out of the county treasury after the proper account rendered thereof shall have been approved by the board of supervisors. * * * But the board * * * may limit the amount of relief thus to be furnished." Section 1365, as amended by Acts Twenty-second General Assembly, chapter 101, so far as material, is as follows: "The poor must make application for relief to the township trustees, * * * and if the trustees are satisfied that the applicant is in such a state of want as requires relief at the public expense, they may afford such relief, subject to the approval of the board of supervisors, as the necessities of the person require. * * * The board * * * may examine into all claims * * * for medical attendance allowed by the * * * trustee, * * * and if they find the amount allowed * * * unreasonable or exhorbitant * * * they may reject or diminish the claim as in their judgment would be right and just. * * *" Section

1366: "All claims and bills for the support of the poor shall be certified to be correct by the proper trustees and presented to the board of supervisors, and if they are satisfied that they are reasonable and proper they are to be paid out of the county treasury." Section 1369 provides that "the board of supervisors may enter into contract with the lowest bidder * * * for the support of all the poor of the county for one year at a time. * * *"

We have held that the board of supervisors has authority under these sections to employ a competent physician to attend to all the poor of the county, and that the township trustees cannot disregard such employment and engage other physicians to render such service at the expense of the county. *Mansfield v. Sac County,* 59 Iowa, 694; *Gawley v. Jones County,* 60 Iowa, 159. To the first count of plaintiff's petition, which was for services rendered at the instance of the board of health to a pauper sick with a contagious disease, defendant filed answer, in which it pleaded that the local board of health had in its employ one Dr. Armstrong, who was the health officer of the board, and that said board had no authority to employ another physician. It also pleaded that it had employed a qualified physician to attend to all the poor persons of the county, who was willing and able to perform the services for which plaintiff seeks compensation, and that neither the board of health nor any one for the patient requested the attendance of the county physician. A demurrer to each of these pleas was sustained, and the error assigned upon this ruling presents the first question for our consideration. The law provides, as we have seen, that each local board shall appoint a competent physician who shall be the health officer within its jurisdiction. By such appointment he becomes simply an officer to assist in the administration of the law and the enforcement of the regulations of the board. As such, he is not required to treat the sick in his professional capacity. Whatever the board deems best for the safety of the inhabitants, in the matter of assistance and supplies, they may order, under the provisions of the Acts of the Twenty-second General Assembly, before quoted; and compensation for such service is to be had under the provisions of that enactment. The health officer could not be compelled to render assistance to infected persons simply because he was appointed physician to the board. As plaintiff was called to the service by the board of health to treat an infected person, he is entitled to his compensation, although the county may have had a contract with a physician by which such physician undertook to treat all the paupers of the county. The fact that the patient is a pauper is material to the inquiry as to who shall pay the bill, and not to who shall perform the service. The demurrer was properly sustained. As sustaining our conclusions, see *Village of St. Johns v. Board of Sup'rs of Clinton County,* 111 Mich. 609 (70 N. W. Rep. 131); *City of Clinton v. Clinton County,* 61 Iowa, 205.

II. Plaintiff did not plead the inability to pay of any other relative that the father of the patient, and appellant insists that the petition does not state a cause of action. It relies upon the statute before quoted, and the case of *Tweedy v. Fremont County,* 99 Iowa, 721. That the petition was demurrable must be conceded; and it may be, although we do not decide the point, that the question might have been made in answer. A motion in arrest of judgment might also have been based upon the plaintiff's failure to state a cause of action. But the point was not raised in any such manner. There is no reference in any of the proceedings to this defect. True it is that defendant moved that the court direct a verdict for defendant as to the first count of the petition, for the reason that there was no evidence that the parents and grandparents of the person for whom the services were rendered were not able to pay, which motion was overruled. But this did not go to the defect in the pleading. It is also true that defendant objected to the evidence offered by plaintiff as to the financial condition of the parents and grandparents; and it further appears that the court instructed that the jury must find that neither the parents nor the grand-parents of the patient were able to pay. In view of the state of the pleadings, the rulings excepted to were, no doubt erroneous; but the error was without prejudice to the appellant. The effect was to cast an unnecessary burden upon the appellee. These instructions, which were not excepted to by appellee, constituted the law of the case; and it was the duty of the jury to follow them, whether right or wrong. It may be there was not sufficient evidence to justify the finding as to the responsibility of the grandparents; but this question was not presented to the trial court. No motion for a new trial was filed. Appellant did nothing after verdict but except to some of the instructions. Appellant argues, however that it was not bound to present the question of the sufficiency of the pleading to the trial court, and it relies upon chapter 96 of the Acts of the Twenty-fifth General Assembly. We need not set out this statute. It is sufficient to say that we have frequently held that the insufficiency of the pleading cannot be presented for the first time in this court. See *Boyd v. Watson,* 101 Iowa, 214; *Weis v. Morris,* 102 Iowa, 327; *Reed v. City of Muscatine,* 104 Iowa, 183. The case of *Weis v. Morris* is decisive of the question here presented. There was no error of which appellant may complain.

III. Appellant contends that there is no evidence that appellee was authorized to practice his profession in this state. The evidence shows that appellee is a physician and surgeon; that he is a graduate of a medical college, and has practiced his profession in Kossuth county for over eleven years. The rule seems to be that when the question of license arises collaterally in a civil action between the physician and one who employs him, due qualification under the statute will be presumed, and the burden is upon him who denies such license. *Brown v. Young,* 2 B. Mon. 26; *City of Chicago v. Wood,* 24 Ill. App. 42; *Thompson v. Sayre,* 1 Denio, 175. In case of public prosecution the rule is the other way.

IV. To prove the inability of the father of the patient to pay the bill, appellee was permitted to introduce in evidence

the testimony of several parties who had made investigation and inquiries in regard to the amount of property owned by him; and, after narrating these facts, they were allowed to state whether a bill could be collected by execution or otherwise.   Other witnesses who stated they had made
6   investigation were permitted to testify that he had
no property out of which the plaintiff's bill could be collected.   The objection was that it was hearsay and an opinion based on hearsay, not the best evidence, and no foundation laid for secondary evidence.   The objection was properly overruled.   *Hard v. Brown,* 18 Vt. 87; *Sherman v. Blodgett,* 28 Vt. 149; *Crawford v. Andrews,* 6 Ga. 244.   We have held, in the case of *Hall v. Ballou,* 58 Iowa, 585, that a witness could not state whether another person was solvent or insolvent.   But it appears that the witness in that case did not know of the financial condition of the person inquired about, "except by general reputation."   See, also, *Fairchild v. Case,* 24 Wend. 381.   Some of the evidence offered to show the financial responsibility of the mother and grand parents was perhaps incompetent, under the rule stated in the *Hall Case.*   See, however, *Nininger v. Knox,* 8 Minn. 140 (Gil. 110).   But, as we have already said, the error, if any, was without prejudice.

V.   A certificate of the board of health, attached to appellee's statement of account which was presented to the board of supervisors, stating that plaintiff was employed by the board, that he performed the services stated, and that the bill was correct and in accord with the contract made with him, and that the father of the patient was not responsible, was
offered in evidence, together with the statement of
7   account.   That part of this certificate referring to the
responsibility of the father and to the contract price of the work was rejected; the remainder of it was received.   In this there was no error.   The certificate was properly attached to the bill and presented to the board.   When so attached, it became a part of the claim, and, as such, was admissible in evidence.   See *Tweedy v. Fremont County, supra*

VI. We have now disposed of all the controlling assignments of error relating to the first count of the petition, and we turn our attention to the second, which is for medical
8   services rendered a poor person under employment by the township trustees. It is conceded by appellee that, as the board of supervisors had employed a physician to furnish medicine and medical aid to all poor persons in the county, he cannot recover unless he shows that the person so employed was incompetent or inconvenient of access. The county entered into a contract with one Dr. McCormack to care for the poor during the year in which plaintiff performed his services. And plaintiff attempted to prove, not only that he was incompetent, but that he was so located as to be inconvenient to the poor of the township in which the patient treated by plaintiff resided. The argument presents but two questions relating to this matter: *First,* the correctness of the instructions; and, *second,* the rulings on the admission and rejection of evidence. No motion for a new trial was filed, and the sufficiency of the evidence is not presented. The exceptions to the instructions were in writing, filed on the same day they were given, but not at the time they were read, as we understand the record. These grounds of excep-
9   tion were: *First,* that said charge was not authorized by law; and, *second,* that it "includes trustees, nurses, and others interested therein." These ground are entirely too general, and the objections now urged in argument cannot be considered. *Patterson v. Railway Co.,* 70 Iowa, 593; *Benson v. Lundy,* 52 Iowa, 265; *Price v. Railroad Co.,* 42 Iowa, 16.

VII. To prove the incompetency of McCormack, appellee introduced evidence as to his immoderate use of liquors, how he stood in the profession, his neglect of patients,
10   and particularly of pauper patients; and one witness was permitted to testify as to his reputation for neglecting cases and incompetency in general. This witness did not pretend to know anything of his capacity except a rumor that he neglected his cases and was incompetent. Another was permitted to state that his standing with the

medical profession was not good. And still others gave evidence as to a particular instance of neglect. All this evidence was objected to, and allowed over defendant's objection. When the character or competency of a person is directly in issue, it is no doubt true that one familiar with his character or ability may give evidence of the fact; and it is also a general rule that evidence of character must be confined to general reputation, and that particular acts or specific facts are not admissible. *Forshee v. Abrams,* 2 Iowa, 571; *Frazier v. Railroad Co.,* 38 Pa. St. 104; *Utley v. Merrick,* 11 Metc. (Mass.) 302. This must also be the rule as to competency. Surely, the court cannot try collaterally each and every case tending to show the ability or competency of the person whose skill is the subject of inquiry. Again, before one is permitted to speak as to the character or reputation of another, knowledge must appear. The mere individual opinion of the witness is not admissible. No one will be permitted to speak affirmatively to the character or competency of another as distinguished from general reputation solely from rumors or reports. *Haley v. State,* 63 Ala. 83. Applying these well-settled rules to the case at bar, it will be seen that much incompetent evidence as to the competency of Dr. McCormack was admitted. The particular case inquired about happened some five years prior to the time plaintiff was called upon to perform his services, and the evidence shows that the fault was neglect or inattention. Surely, the defendant could not be expected to meet any such evidence. Moreover, if such evidence was competent, then it was proper for the parties to introduce evidence regarding each and every case treated by Dr. McCormack since he commenced the practice of his profession. We do not overlook the fact that the evidence shows that one of the trustees who employed the plaintiff had knowledge of the treatment in this particular case, but this circumstance is no justification for the evidence. The belief of the trustee is not the test. The fact only was material to the inquiry. If the board in fact employed a competent and convenient physician to care for the poor, the trustees were not authorized to employ another simply because they believed the county physician was inattentive, neglectful, or incompetent.

VIII.   A certificate from the township trustees attached to the account presented to the board of supervisors was admitted in evidence.   That it was properly received, 11   see the authorities cited in the fifth paragraph of this opinion, and *Mussel v. Tama County,* 73 Iowa, 101.

IX.   We see no error in the cross-examination of Dr. McCormack, of which defendant may justly complain.

X.   The fact that Dr. McCormack was employed by 12   the county to furnish medical aid was admitted, and it was not error to exclude the contract itself.

For the errors pointed out, the judgment of the district court is REVERSED.

EWING & JEWETT, Appellants, v. W. E. STOCKWELL *et al.*

Mechanics' Liens: STATEMENT: *Mistake.* An inadvertent failure to give proper credits in a statement for a mechanic's lien does not 1   render it unjust and untrue within the contemplation of the Code of 1873, section 2133, requiring the filing of a just and true statement or account of the demand due after allowing for credits.

FILING. The filing of an insufficient statement for a mechanic's lien or a failure to file any statement will not defeat the lien except as 2   to purchasers or encumbrancers in good faith, without notice, whose rights accrued thirty or ninety days, as the case may be, before the claim was filed.

Appeal from the Polk District Court.—HON. W. F. CONRAD, Judge.

THURSDAY, MAY 26, 1898.

PLAINTIFFS bring this action for judgment against the defendant Stockwell, and for a decree establishing and foreclosing a mechanic's lien upon real estate described. The State Building & Loan Association of Indiana and L. E. Bolton were made defendants; and each answered, denying plaintiff's right to a lien, and asserting their rights respectively, to judgments against defendant Stockwell, and to foreclosure of liens in their favor on said premises. The defendant Stockwell made default and judgments were entered against him in favor of each of the other parties, and decrees in favor of said association and of defendant Bolton, as prayed. The court refused to establish and foreclose the mechanic's lien claimed by the plaintiffs, and from that refusal the plaintiffs appeal.—*Reversed.*

Dowell & Parrish for appellants.

B. F. Maricle for appellee State Building & Loan Ass'n. *B. Chavannes* for appellee L. E. Bolton.

GIVEN, J.—I. The only question to be determined on this appeal is whether the appellants are entitled to the establishment and foreclosure of the mechanic's lien claimed by them. Appellees contend that they are not, for the reason that the statement for a lien filed by them is not "a just and true statement or account of the demand due him [them] after allowing all credits," as required by section 2133 of the Code of 1873. On October 10, 1895, the plaintiffs filed a duly verified statement for a mechanic's lien, in the sum of five hundred and twenty-two dollars and six cents, for lumber furnished to the defendant Stockwell for the erection of certain improvements on the premises described; the first item being furnished March 29th, and the last, July 25, 1895. This action was commenced December 10, 1895, to establish and foreclose said lien; and on January 27, 1896, the case came on for hearing on the pleadings then on file, and the proofs offered by the parties. The evidence on behalf of the plaintiffs showed that said statement for a lien was not "a just and true statement or account of the demand due him [them] after allowing all credits," for that it was omitted to credit therein the defendant Stockwell with one hundred and thirty-nine dollars and twenty-one cents discount on list prices, as per contract, and there was omitted a further credit of forty-

five dollars on account of insurance furnished to plaintiffs by
said Stockwell. The evidence also showed that eight days after
filing said statement, to-wit, October 18, 1895, Stockwell, in
settlement of said claim, wherein he was allowed said credits,
executed to plaintiffs his promissory note for the balance of
three hundred and thirty-seven dollars and eighty-five cents.
On the eighth day of February, 1896, the plaintiffs filed an
amendment to their petition, alleging that their former statement for a lien, "because of certain unintentional errors
therein, did not contain an absolutely correct statement of the
account due and owing from the said W. E. Stockwell, in that
it failed to give the said Stockwell certain credits to which he
was entitled." They further allege that on the eighth day of
February, 1896, they filed in the office of the clerk "an amendment to the statement for mechanic's lien filed on the said
10th day of October, 1895, which contains a just, true, and
correct statement of the amount due and owing from the said
W. E. Stockwell to these appellants for the lumber and
material furnished as alleged in the original petition." The
amendment to the statement for a lien attached to this amendment of the petition shows the same as the former statement,
except that said credits are allowed, and a demand for
"$337.85, instead of $522.06." The abstract shows that on
the eighteenth day of February, 1896, the case came on for
further hearing, and that the plaintiff introduced evidence to
the effect that said amendment to the statement for lien was
a just, true, and correct statement of the amount due to appellants. The appellants also introduced said amendment in evidence. To this evidence appellees objected, for the reason
that the testimony was closed, and the case submitted; that
plaintiffs showed no reason entitling them to take further evidence; and for the reason that plaintiffs knew the facts before
said amendments, and that they gave no notice to appellees of
the filing of said additional statement for a lien. It cannot be
questioned that the first statement filed by appellants did not
allow all credits to which Stockwell was entitled.

II. It is apparent, however, that the omission was

unintentional, and without any purpose to defraud. It arose in this manner: By the contract, Stockwell was to have the lumber at a certain discount on list prices. The lumber was charged at list prices, as delivered, with the intention of giving credit for the discount at the close of the account. This was omitted, and the agent of appellants who verified and filed the first statement, overlooking the omission, verified and filed the statement without giving the credit. It was also agreed that Stockwell was to have credit for certain insurance which he was to, and did thereafter, furnish to appellants. For this no credit was given on appellants' books, either through oversight, or because the amount was not reported by Stockwell. The first statement for a lien being taken from the books, the credits for the discount and insurance were not given therein. That these omissions of credit were without any intention to defraud is evidenced by the fact that eight days after the statement was filed appellants and Stockwell had a settlement, in which said credits were allowed, and Stockwell executed his promissory note for the balance, three hundred and thirty-seven dollars and eighty-five cents. The case is unlike *Stubbs v. Railroad Co.,* 65 Iowa, 513, as in that case there was an intention to defraud. In *Lumber Co. v. Miller,* 98 Iowa, 468, it is said: "A statement or account of the demand, within the statute, that is made and verified in good faith, is just and true, within the meaning of section 2133, though unintentional errors may be found to exist therein." In *Chase v. Mining Co.,* 90 Iowa, 25, it is said: "There was no intentional wrong in the statement, and no sufficient reason for applying the rule announced in *Stubbs v. Railroad Co."* See, also, *Chicago Lumber Co. v. Des Moines Driving Park,* 97 Iowa, 25. It is true that in the cases cited the errors in the statements were not so directly as to the amount claimed as in this, but they were as to matters equally important, and in some instances affected the amount due.

Appellee Bolton's lien is for materials furnished for the same improvements; and the building and loan association

claim under a mortgage executed May 20, 1895, which was
during the period plaintiffs were furnishing the
2   materials. As against the owner, the filing of an
insufficient statement, or the failure to file any statement, will not defeat the lien. A failure to file it within the
time required will not defeat the lien, except as against purchasers or incumbrancers in good faith, without notice, whose
right accrued thirty or ninety days, as the case may be, and
before any claim for the lien was filed. *Chicago Lumber Co.
v. Des Moines Driving Park, supra.*

Our conclusion is that the plaintiffs are entitled to have
their lien established as prayed, and the case will be remanded
for a decree in harmony with this opinion.—REVERSED.

J. F. BROCK v. DES MOINES INSURANCE COMPANY, Appellant.

Insurance: PROOF OF LOSS: *Waiver.* Where an agent who has
1   power to appoint agents, make collections and to investigate and
5   settle losses, takes a paper which he calls proof of loss, telling
2   assured that no more is required, on which assured relied, and the
3   paper is submitted to the insurer who neither objects to its inform-
4   ality or notifies the assured that formal proofs are not waived,
formal proofs are waived, notwithstanding provisions in the policy
that none of the terms or conditions thereof can be waived except
by a writing of the secretary and that no agent has authority to
waive or modify any of the printed conditions.

SAME. An informal proof of loss taken by an authorized agent with
a statement that no more is required, which statement is relied on,
and which proof is submitted to the insurer, and to which he
6   makes no objections, waives formal proof, though the informal
proof recited that the insurer has "not waived any of its legal rights
or defenses by investigating my loss for the purpose of getting
facts relative to my fire, or amount of stock on hand at time of
loss."

Evidence: SECONDARY: *Discretion.* What is a reasonable time for
7   the production of a letter in possession of the adverse party to
authorize the admission of secondary evidence of its contents is
within the discretion of the trial court.

PRINCIPAL AND AGENT. In an action against an insurance company,
plaintiff testified to conversations he had with persons in the home
8   office of the company. He could not state positively that they

were officers or agents of the company, but the company acted in accordance with statements made by those persons to plaintiff. *Held*, that no prejudice resulted from admitting the testimony.

Appeal from Hamilton District Court.—HON D. R. HIND-MAN, Judge.

THURSDAY, MAY 26, 1898.

ACTION at law on a policy of fire insurance. There was a trial by jury, and a verdict and judgment for the plaintiff. The defendant appeals.—*Affirmed.*

McVey & McVey for appellant.

George Wambach and *Wesley Martin* for appellee.

ROBINSON, J.—The policy in suit was issued by the defendant in May, 1892, and purported to insure the plaintiff, for the term of one year, against loss or damage by fire, to the amount of two hundred dollars on his store building in Homer, and one thousand dollars on his stock of merchandise contained in the building. In January, 1893, the building and the merchandise contained therein were destroyed by fire, and the plaintiff seeks to recover for that loss, to the amount of the policy. This cause was before us on a former appeal, and the judgment of the district court was reversed because of insufficient proofs of loss. See 96 Iowa, 39. After the cause was remanded for further proceedings, an amendment to the petition was filed, setting out facts which were alleged to constitute a waiver of proofs of loss other than those furnished, and to estop the defendant to question their sufficiency. The defendant denies the alleged waiver and estoppel, and denies all liability.

I. There is conflict in the evidence respecting the facts upon which the alleged waiver and estoppel are based, but the jury was authorized to find such facts to be substantially as follows: When the fire occurred, the plaintiff was

1   visiting in Adair county. As soon as he was informed of the fire, he returned to Homer; calling on his way at the office of the defendant in Des Moines, and stating to

persons in the office what he knew of the fire. He was told to investigate the loss, and inform the defendant of its amount and origin, and that the company would send an adjuster to investigate it. The plaintiff, on the day of his arrival at Homer, wrote to the defendant that the building was burned and also his stock of merchandise, and that his loss on the latter was more than one thousand four hundred dollars.

An agent of the defendant, named Moody, testified as a witness, in regard to his duties, as follows: "I do most any-thing. I write insurance; make collections; appoint agents; inspect risks; investigate losses; sometimes settle matters." He also testified that he had done that kind of work for the defendant for six or seven years. A few days after the plaintiff wrote to the defendant as stated, Moody appeared at Homer and informed the plaintiff that he had come to adjust his loss, and that he understood the plaintiff had written a letter to the company. Moody spent several hours at Homer, investigating the loss; and then, at his request, the plaintiff went with him to Webster City, and together they went into Moody's room at an hotel, and there spent several hours in considering the loss. Moody asked for a statement of the merchandise destroyed, and the plaintiff submitted an inven-tory of it, prepared but a short time before the fire. Moody examined it, took a statement of all the plaintiff had lost, and said he would write out a proof of the loss, and have it acknowledged. Thereupon he wrote out the following:

"State of Iowa, Hamilton County—ss. I, J. F. Brock, being duly sworn, on oath depose and say:

"That on the 16th day of January, 1893, I made inven-tory of my stock of goods in my store at that date, including medicines; and some of the medicines was held by me for sale on commission; also, said inventory, including furniture and fixtures in my store. The said inventory, including above-mentioned medicines and furniture and fixtures, amounted to fourteen hundred forty-six 29-100 dollars ($1,446.29).

Medicine held on commission amounted to.........$ 36 01
Furniture and fixtures........................ 53 58
Goods sold after inventory, and prior to fire....... 80 42

Reducing my stock and inventory...........$170 01

"That my policy permits me to carry insurance on ¾ actual value of my stock of goods, in policy No. 58,275, Des Moines Insurance Company. That I refuse to allow any depreciation of value on my stock on account of age or damaged goods. I have been in the business since August, 1890. At the time I went into business, I purchased a stock of goods of Mr. J. E. Smith, at Homer, Iowa.

"It is agreed that the Des Moines Insurance Company has not waived any of its legal rights or defenses by investigating my loss for the purpose of getting facts relative to my fire, or amount of stock on hand at time of loss."

After the instrument was drawn, Moody and the plaintiff went to the office of a notary public. The plaintiff was there asked if he understood the paper; and Moody answered for him that he did, and also stated that it was a proof of loss. The plaintiff also said that he understood it, and he signed and swore to it. Moody then took it; said he would immediately mail it to the defendant. The plaintiff asked

3   him if that "was all that was required to know; if it
        was all right?" and Moody answered: "Yes; that
is all right."   The plaintiff relied upon what had been said and done as being sufficient, and did not make any further proof. The defendant did not make any objection to the proof, nor call for additional information. We held on the former appeal that the proof furnished failed to comply with the statutory requirements. In response to the claim

4   of waiver and estoppel, on which the plaintiff relies,
        the defendant calls attention to certain provisions of
the policy. One of those relates to notice and proof of loss, but, in view of the requirements of chapter 211 of the Acts of the Eighteenth General Assembly, need not be specially considered. Other provisions are as follows: "It is further

mutually agreed by the parties hereto that no condition, stipulation, covenant, or clause hereinbefore contained or referred to shall be altered, annulled, or waived, or clause added to these presents, except by writing endorsed hereon or annexed hereto by the secretary, with his signature affixed thereto; any contract by parol, or understanding with the agent, had before or after issuing the policy, to the contrary notwithstanding. It is further expressly agreed by the parties hereto that none of the terms or conditions of this policy can be waived by any person or persons whomsoever, except in writing by the secretary of the company. * . * * No agent of this company has any authority to waive, modify, erase, or strike out any of the printed conditions of this policy." It is insisted that, under these provisions, Moody had no authority to waive the formal proofs of loss which are required by the statute, and cases are cited in support of that claim. We had occasion to review those cases in the recent case of *Ruthven v. Insurance Co.,* 102 Iowa, 550, and need not repeat what was there said. The case of *Kirkman v. Insurance Co.,* 90 Iowa, 457, is especially relied upon by the appellant, but that lacked important and controlling facts which are involved

5   in this. Moody appears to have been something more than an adjusting agent. He had power to appoint agents, make contracts of insurance, and to settle losses. But as a mere adjusting agent, with authority to ascertain and settle losses, he had, of necessity, power to determine what proofs were satisfactory, and to waive those which were regarded as unimportant. He proceeded to obtain information in regard to the origin and extent of the loss, and was promptly furnished with all the information which he demanded. When he had procured all the information he desired, and had obtained the signature and oath of the plaintiff to the statement he had prepared, he, in substance and effect, told the plaintiff that the proof furnished was all that was required. In this respect the case is much like the *Ruthven Case,* in which we said: "The defendant must be charged with the knowledge which he [the adjuster] acquired

while acting for it.   *   *   *   He had all the proofs which
he asked for, and forwarded them to the defendant.   With
constructive, if not actual knowledge of all these facts, the
defendant did not inform the plaintiffs that formal proofs
were not waived, nor demand them.   We think the jury was
fully authorized to find that they were waived by Bliven, and
that he also waived the written indorsement required by the
terms of the policy." Bliven was the general western manager of the defendant in that case, and, in the adjustment of
all losses in his department, stood for and represented his
company, and had the power to waive any requirement in
regard to proofs of loss which it could have waived.   In this
case the company was called upon to act for itself directly,
and not through a general manager; yet it was silent when
it should have spoken, and must be held bound by the acts
and statements of Moody.   See, also, *Dyer v. Insurance Co.,*
103 Iowa, 524.   It does not appear that the adjuster in the
Kirkman Case made any attempt to take proofs of loss, and
what he said was in the nature of an expression of an opinion
respecting the effect of the information which had been sent to
the company, and as to what the company would do.

II.   It is said that the last paragraph of the instrument
prevents the plea of waiver from being effectual.   That is as
follows: "It is agreed that the Des Moines Insurance Company have not waived any of its legal rights or defenses
by investigating my loss for the purpose of getting
facts relative to my fire, or amount of stock on hand
at time of loss."   This provision must be construed in the
light of what was said and done on the day it was signed.   It
does not, in terms, refer to proofs of loss.   That it was not
understood by the plaintiff to refer in any manner to such
proofs is clear; and Moody must have known that fact, if the
evidence for the plaintiff be credible.   If Moody intended, by
the instrument, to reserve to the defendant the right to insist
upon the statutory proofs of loss, then he intended to perpe-
trate a fraud upon the plaintiff,—a conclusion we are not

inclined to adopt. The instrument provides that the defendant did not waive any of its legal rights or defenses by "investigating" the loss, but it does not provide that the taking of the proof furnished by the plaintiff, and the representations made to him as to its sufficiency, and the failure of the defendant to demand additional proof, should not have that effect. This interpretation is not only necessary to do justice, but it is authorized by the rules of interpretation which apply in such cases.

III. Error is alleged of certain rulings of the court on the admission of evidence, which we will now consider. The letter which the plaintiff claims to have written the defendant was not introduced in evidence. Before the trial of

7   the case was commenced, the plaintiff served upon the defendant notice to produce the letter, and that, if it were not produced, secondary evidence of its contents would be offered. As the letter was not produced, the plaintiff was permitted to testify as to its contents. The appellant contends that the notice was not served a sufficient length of time before the trial to require the production of the letter, or permit secondary evidence of its contents to be given. In ruling upon the admission of the secondary evidence, the court was authorized to consider the time which the defendant would require to obtain the letter from its Des Moines office, and whether a reasonable time for that purpose had been given. The record does not show any abuse of the discretion lodged in the court,

in holding that the notice given was sufficient, and

8   that secondary evidence was admissible. It is said that the court erred in permitting the plaintiff to testify to a conversation he had in the Des Moines office while on his way from Adair county to Homer after the fire. He was not able to state positively that the persons with whom he conversed were officers or other agents of the defendant, but it appears that the defendant acted in accordance with the statements which those persons made to the plaintiff; and, even if they were not authorized to act for it, no prejudice

could have resulted from admitting evidence as to the conversation with them.

IV. Portions of the charge given to the jury are criticised, and error in the refusal of the court to give certain instructions asked is claimed. We have examined all these matters, but without discovering any prejudicial error. The judgment of the district court is sustained by the evidence, and appears to be right, and it is AFFIRMED.

J. WALTER LEE, Appellee, v. J. C. GRIMM, Garnished at suit of plaintiff v. JOHN TEETER, Appellant.

Exemptions: PENSION MONEY. One seeking to establish an exemption in property alleged to be partly paid for with pension money must show, not only that such money was invested in the property, but also the exact amount invested.

SAME. One owning certain shares of loan association stock bought real property. For the purchase price he gave a mortgage on said property and pledged said stock. Some pension money was used in payments made on the stock and the buyer intended to mature the stock and pay the mortgage with pension money. *Held*, that the proceeds of selling the real property on execution were not exempt, where the purchaser agreed, as part of the purchase price, to pay the loan and remove all clouds and liens, and the seller still retains the stock. His exemption will be found there.

Appeal from Johnson District Court.—HON. M. J. WADE, Judge.

THURSDAY, MAY 26, 1898.

THIS is a garnishment proceeding in which plaintiff, Grimm, and others are seeking to subject to the payment of certain judgments against Teeter the amount owing by Grimm to Teeter as purchaser of certain real estate in the city of Iowa City. Teeter intervened, claiming that the property sold to Grimm was and is his homestead; that it had been purchased in part at least with pension money; and that the proceeds of the sale are exempt from execution. The garnishee denied that the proceeds were exempt, and further pleaded that, by arrangements between Grimm and Teeter, Grimm was to pay all judgments against Teeter. The cause was tried as an equitable one, resulting in a decree dismissing the intervener's petition; and from the order so made intervener appeals.—*Affirmed.*

Slater & Hunt for appellant.

Bailey & Murphy, Fred Cochran, and *Ira J. Miller* for appellees.

DEEMER, C. J.—Teeter purchased the lot sold to Grimm on or about the tenth day of June, 1893, and immediately went into possession and occupancy of the same. His possession continued until the sale to Grimm, in the early part of June, 1896. At the time of his purchase, Teeter had invested in stock of a building and loan association about eighty-four dollars. The consideration for the lot was nine hundred dollars. Seven hundred and fifty dollars of this he borrowed of the building and loan association in which he held stock, gave a mortgage upon the real estate, and pledged his ten shares of stock in the association as security for the loan. The remainder, to-wit, one hundred and fifty dollars, he borrowed on his individual note, which was renewed from time to time, and finally reduced to judgment. This judgment was of record at the time Grimm purchased, and it is conceded that Grimm was to pay the same as part of the consideration. The sale to Grimm was at public auction, and it was announced and agreed at this sale that all liens or clouds upon the title should be removed, and that the purchaser should satisfy the same. Grimm's bid of one thousand five hundred and twenty-five dollars was accepted, and it is agreed that of this amount he was to pay liens amounting to one thousand two hundred and forty-nine dollars. This sum included the judgment upon the one hundred and fifty dollar note, the mortgage to the building and loan association, and the taxes against the property. The controversy is over the remainder of the purchase price.

The plaintiffs in the garnishment proceedings had all recovered their judgments prior to the sale to Grimm, and the record shows that the debts upon which three of the judgments were obtained were contracted prior to the time Teeter acquired his title. Section 1992 of the Code of 1873 provides that the homestead may be sold on execution for debts contracted prior to the purchase thereof; and, as the debts so contracted amount to more than the balance of the purchase price of the lot now in dispute, it is clear that intervener is not entitled to hold this balance, because of the homestead character of the premises. With his pension money, appellant paid dues upon his stock and interest upon his loan of the building and loan association to the amount of four hundred and eighteen dollars and nine cents. He also claims to have paid thirty-five dollars of the pension money for an old house which he moved upon the premises. The record does not show the exact amount paid as interest upon the loan ; nor is there any means by which we can determine the value of the stock owned by Teeter. Grimm, however, agreed to, and did, pay the loan of the building and loan association, and no deductions appear to have been made on account of payments upon the stock.

The evidence clearly shows that Teeter retained his stock in the association, and that the purchaser paid the amount of the loan. As appellant is seeking to establish an exemption, it is incumbent on him to show, not only that he invested his pension money in the property, but the exact amount of such investment. This he has failed to do. At most, he has adduced evidence tending to show that he paid some interest upon the loan, but the exact amount of his payments are not established. His investment seems to have been in stock of the building and loan association, which he still retains, and in this will he find his exemption. The money invested in the lot was borrowed. True, appellant expected to pay the loan with the avails of his pension ; but, instead of so doing, he made a contract by the terms of which his vendee agreed to pay the loans as a part of the purchase price. Under such a state of facts, he cannot be heard to say that the avails of the homestead are exempt because of his purpose to pay the purchase price with pension money. There is no showing that any part of appellant's pension money was invested in the homestead. Aside from this, however, we are constrained to believe that it was agreed at the time of the auction sale that all judgments which might cast a cloud upon the title should be paid by Grimm as part of the purchase price. The judgments held by the appellees were all apparent liens, and were, as we think, in contemplation of the parties at the time the sale was made. This finding is alone sufficient to justify the decree.— AFFIRMED.

STATE OF IOWA v. FRANK DORLAND, Appellant.

Criminal Appeals: PRINTING: *Construction of statute.* The provision of Code, section 5462, that in case a judgment in a criminal case is reversed or modified in favor of defendant, on appeal, he shall be entitled to the cost of printing abstracts and briefs not exceeding 1 one dollar for each page, applies to a c:se decided on appeal after the section took effect, although the printing was done before that day. And Code, section 51, providing that the repeal of existing statutes shall not affect any suit or proceeding had or commenced, refers to *civil* cases only.

TAXATION. The cost of printing the abstract and briefs on appeal by defendant in a criminal case which Code, section 5462, provides 2 he shall recover in case the judgment is reversed or modified in his favor, may be taxed against the county, on motion, in the supreme court, in the main case.

Appeal from Fayette District Court.

THURSDAY, MAY 26, 1898.

On motion to tax costs.

Ainsworth & Ainsworth and *W. E. Fuller* for the motion.

DEEMER, C. J.—Frank Dorland was convicted of the crime of manslaughter, and appealed to this court. Here the judgment was reversed, and the case remanded. See 103

Iowa, 168.   Defendant now files a motion asking that the cause be redocketed, and that he recover from Fayette county the amount paid for printing abstracts, briefs, and arguments, in the sum of one hundred and fifty-one dollars.   He presents witḣ his motion a receipted bill from the printer, and, as we understand, asks that the amount so paid be taxed as costs against the county wherein the crime is said to have been committed.   The latter part of section 5462 of the Code, which took effect October 1, 1897, is as follows: "And, in case the judgment of the trial court is reversed or modified in favor of the defendant on the appeal of defendant, he shall be entitled to recover the cost of printing abstracts and briefs not exceeding one dollar for each page thereof, to be paid by the county from which the appeal was taken."   Sentence was pronounced upon defendant October 11, 1895, and he appealed to this court on the same day.   The printing was all done prior to the time the new Code went into effect, but the opinion was not filed until October 12, 1897.   Two questions are 1   involved in the determination of the motion: *First,* Does the statute apply to cases pending at the time it went into effect?   *Second.*   Should the cost of printing the abstract and briefs be taxed against the county in the main case, or is recovery to be had in an independent suit?

Prior to the enactment of the paragraph of the statute quoted the county was not liable for the cost of printing defendant's abstracts and briefs in a criminal case, although he secured a reversal or modification of the decision.   *Red v. Polk County,* 56 Iowa, 98; *State v. Rainsbarger,* 74 Iowa, 539.   The statute was undoubtedly enacted to supply this *casus omissus* referred to in the *Rainsbarger Case.*   It relates to the printing of abstracts and briefs for presentation of causes to this court, and makes an allowance for expenses incurred by defendant in prosecuting the appeal.   Such an allowance is clearly of costs; and, if so, there is no reason why it should not apply to pending suits.   While the statute relates to a criminal case, it does not affect the penalty, and is in no sense *ex post facto.*   It is not

asked to make it retroactive, for the case was decided on appeal
after the statute took effect. Section 51 of the Code, which says
that the repeal of existing statutes shall not affect any suit or
proceeding had or commenced, refers to civil cases only. And
section 53, which provides that no suit or prosecution pending
when the new Code went into effect shall be affected, has no
application; for it further provides that the proceedings may
be conformed to the provisions of the new Code as far as
consistent. The statute in question relates to the remedy, and
it is well settled that a particular mode of procedure is not a
vested right. On the contrary, the legislature may change or
abolish it at pleasure. See *Tilton v. Swift,* 40 Iowa, 78;
Kossuth County v. Wallace, 60 Iowa, 508; Cooley Consti-
titutional Limitations (5th ed.), 328. In the case of *Drake v.
Jordan,* 73 Iowa, 707, we held that a statute providing for
the taxation of an attorney's fee passed after an action was
commenced, but before its determination, related merely to
the remedy, and that attorney's fees should be taxed. See,
also, *Farley v. O'Malley,* 77 Iowa, 531; *Farley v. Geisheker,*
78 Iowa, 453. Again, costs are incident to a judgment, and
are no part of the relief sought; hence they do not become a
debt until judgment is rendered. It follows, therefore, that
they are to be taxed and regulated by the statute in force at
the time of the termination of the suit. *Meigs v. Parke,* 1
Morris (Iowa), 378; *Com. v. Cambridge,* 4 Metc. (Mass.) 35;
Billings v. Segar, 11 Mass. 340; *Pelham v. Aldrich.* 8 Gray
515; 5 Enc. Pl. & Prac. pp. 111-113.

    We come now to the second question. The statute says
defendant "shall be entitled to recover the cost of printing
abstracts and briefs." It is manifest, we think, that he is to
recover it upon a reversal or modification of the judg-
2   ment; and the only way in which he can do this is to
have them taxed as costs. When so taxed, they are to
be paid by the county from which the appeal is taken. The
only difficulty to be apprehended from this method of procedure lies in the fact that recovery is limited to the amount
actually paid, provided it does not exceed a certain amount.

This suggestion is met by the new rules of this court, which require the party to state and the attorney to certify the actual cost of printing abstracts and arguments. See rule 94. When the costs are taxed, the amount is to be paid by the county. If not so paid, they may undoubtedly be recovered by suit. The motion will be sustained, and the clerk ordered to tax the sum of one hundred and fifty-one dollars against the appellee.— SUSTAINED.

106
106
J106 4

CHICAGO, ROCK ISLAND & PACIFIC RAILWAY COMPANY v. H. C. MURPHY AS TREASURER OF POLK COUNTY, Appellant.

County Taxation: CITIES AND TOWNS. The authority given the board of supervisors (Section 1, Chapter 200, Acts Twentieth General Assembly) to levy a tax of not more than one mill on the dollar "of the assessed value of the taxable property in their county" for a county road fund, gives the right to so tax property in a city or town of the county, though no part of the sum raised is expended in said municipality or intended to be so expended.

Appeal from Polk District Court.—HON. C. P. HOLMES, Judge.

THURSDAY, MAY 26, 1898.

ACTION in equity to restrain the collection of a road tax levied upon property of the plaintiff. A demurrer to the petition was overruled, and, the defendant refusing to plead further, a decree was rendered in favor of the plaintiff for the relief demanded. The defendant appeals.—*Reversed.*

W. G. Harvison, C. A. Bishop and *C. C. Nourse* for appellant.

Carroll Wright for appellee.

ROBINSON, J.—The material facts shown by the pleadings are substantially as follows: The defendant is the treasurer of Polk county, and the defendant owns several lines of railway in that county, parts of which are within the city of Des Moines, and other parts are within certain incorporated towns. The assessed value of the portions of the plaintiff's railways within the city and towns referred to, as fixed by the executive council for the purposes of taxation, is two hundred and thirty-one thousand four hundred and fifty-two dollars. In the year 1895 the board of supervisors of Polk county levied a tax of one mill on the taxable property within the county for county road purposes; and that levy was carried into the tax lists of the county against the property of the plaintiff, including that within the city of Des Moines, and other towns of the county, and also against a lot of land within the city of Des Moines; and that tax is the one in controversy. The plaintiff has paid all the taxes levied upon its property, excepting the tax in controversy, and seeks to enjoin the collection of that, and to have it declared void and canceled, on the alleged ground that the board of supervisors had no authority to levy such a tax on any property located within the limits of a city or incorporated town. Whether such authority existed at the time the levy was made is the question we are required to determine.

I.   The authority to levy the tax is claimed by virtue of section 1 of chapter 200 of the Acts of the Twentieth General Assembly, which provided "that the board of supervisors of each county may at the time of levying taxes for other pur- poses, levy a tax of not more than one mill on the dollar of the assessed value of the taxable property in their county, which tax shall be collected at the same time and in the same manner as other taxes are collected and shall be known as the county road fund, and shall be paid out only on the order of the board of supervisors for work done on the highways of the county, in such places as the board shall determine. *   *   *" It is said in behalf of the appellee that a tax, to be valid, must inure to the benefit of the district or locality taxed, and there must be authority to expend the tax, or some portion thereof, within such district. It is further said that the board of supervisors of a county lacked the power, under the statute cited, to levy a tax on the property within a city or incorporated town for the benefit of the county road fund, for the reason that such fund can be paid out only on the order of the board, and it has no authority to expend any money in grading, repairing, or otherwise improving any street in a city or incorporated town. It was held in *Gallaher v. Head*, 72 Iowa, 173, that counties do not have the right to establish highways within cities and incorporated towns, for the reason that the latter have the right to establish, change, and improve streets within their limits, and to regulate their use, and that such power is inconsistent with a right in the county to establish and improve highways therein, and must be regarded as exclusive. In the case of *McCullom v. Black Hawk County,* 21 Iowa, 409, the liability of a county for a defective bridge within a city was considered; and it was held that although a county is liable in certain cases for defective bridges in highways of the county, and although the bridge there in controversy had been erected by the county upon a highway before the city was incorporated, yet, as it was afterwards included within that city, the liability of the county ended, and that of the city commenced, when the organization of the latter was completed. The decision was based largely upon the conclusion of the court that the city had jurisdiction of the streets and bridges therein, and that they could not be subject to the control of two independent sets of officers. In *Clark v. Town of Epworth*, 56 Iowa, 462 it was held that the defendant was liable for a ditch which was dug by the road supervisor of the township in which the town was situated, and negligently left without barrier or signal to indicate danger. It was said that the statute which authorized township trustees to divide their townships into such number of highway district as they might deem necessary for the public good was broad enough to confer upon the trustees unrestricted control over the establishment of highway districts in their townships; yet it was held that the power granted to cities and incorporated towns over their streets, including the power to grade and keep them in repair, was inconsistent with any right on the part of the township officers to exercise control of the streets. That case was based in part upon *Marks v. Woodbury County,* 47 Iowa, 452, on which the appellee especially relies. That case involved the validity of a road tax levied by the trustees of the township of Sioux City upon real estate within that township, which was also within the city of Sioux City, and the interpretation of that portion of section 969 of the Code of 1873 relating to the powers of township trustees to levy road taxes, which was as follows: "At the April meeting said trustees shall determine upon the amount of property tax to be levied for highways, bridges, guide boards, plows, scrapers, tools and machinery adapted to the construction and repair of highways, and for the payment of any indebtedness previously incurred for highway purposes, and levy the same, which shall not be less than one nor more than five mills on the dollar on the amount of the township assessment for that year." It was argued that the tax was to be levied upon the township assessment, which included the assessment for the whole township, but this court held that such was not the purpose of the statute; that it was not designed to point out the property upon which the tax was to be levied, but that it meant that the tax should not be less than one nor more than five mills on the dollar on the amount of the township assessment for the year for which the levy was made, or, in other words, to designate the assessed valuation upon which the tax should be levied. It was said, in effect, that the property to be taxed must be ascertained from other provisions of the law, which were referred to; that township trustees were not authorized to include a city within their township, in a road district; and that, although it was the duty of a road supervisor to collect and expend the road tax within his district, he was not authorized to collect or expend it within a city. The conclusion was reached that the power of the trustees to levy a tax extended only to property within the territory over which they had jurisdiction for road purposes. It may be regarded as established that, under the law as it existed when the levy in question was made, township officers had no jurisdiction of the streets of cities and towns within their respective townships, and no authority to levy or collect road taxes on property within such corporations. A careful analysis of the two statutes shows that there is a difference between the meaning and legal effect of section 969 of the Code of 1873 and the statute in question, in regard to the assessment upon which the taxes for which they provide shall be levied. The language of section 969 is that the tax shall be levied "on the amount of the township assessment," and the language of the act in question is that the board of supervisors shall "levy a tax of not more than one mill on the dollar of the assessed value of the taxable property in their county." We are of the opinion that the phrase, "of the taxable property in their county," enlarges the scope of the words preceding, and that the language of the section is sufficiently comprehensive to include all of the property of the county which is taxable when the levy is made. It is precisely the same, in legal effect, as was the corresponding provision of section 796 of the Code of 1873, in regard to the levying of taxes for state revenue, for support of schools, and for making and repairing bridges, which required the board of supervisors of each county to levy taxes for the purposes specified "upon the assessed value of the taxable property in the county." There is not the slightest ground for claiming that any of the taxable property in any county was exempt from taxation for the purposes designated in that section, and it is clear that all taxable property was intended to be so taxed. Hence the use of language in the statute in question having precisely the same meaning is very satisfactory evidence that the general assembly intended to make all taxable property in a county, whether within or without its cities and towns, subject to taxation for the county road fund. It is well settled that counties may construct, or aid in constructing, bridges within the limits of cities and incorporated towns. *Oskaloosa Steam-Engine Works v. Pottawattamie County,* 72 Iowa, 134; *Bell v. Foutch,* 21 Iowa, 119; *Barrett v. Brooks,* 21 Iowa, 144; Code 1873, section

527. It is suggested that the use of the word "taxable" in
the statute in question indicates a legislative intent not to
authorize the taxing of all property within a county for the
benefit of the county road fund, and therefore it may be presumed that the property within cities and incorporated towns
was intended to be exempt from taxation for that purpose.
But the word is used in the same connection and with the
same force that it was used in section 796 of the Code of 1873,
and means no more than that the taxes provided for shall not
be levied upon property exempt from taxation, as property of
the United States and of this state, property of a county,
township, city, incorporated town, or school district, when
devoted entirely to the public use and not held for pecuniary
profit, and other classes of property which were by law
exempt from taxation. See section 797 of the Code of 1873,
as amended.

II.   It is insisted that the tax in question is not valid
because no part of it can be expended in the city and towns
within which the property sought to be taxed is situated. The
law has been stated to be that: "The burden of a tax must
be made to rest upon the state at large, or upon any particular
district of the state, according as the purpose for which it
is levied is of general concern to the whole state, or, on the
other hand, pertains only to the particular district. A state
purpose must be accomplished by state taxation, a county
purpose by county taxation, or a public purpose for any
inferior district by taxation of such district. This is not only
just, but it is essential." Cooley Taxation, 141. The same
author also states that: "There are same cases in which the
character of a proposed public expenditure is such that there
may be a difference of opinion as to the propriety or justice
of its being provided for by a small district, or a larger one.
Cases of highways afford an illustration. In many of the
states the cost of these is usually borne by the towns, and it is
not surprising to find a general impression prevailing in
some quarters that the towns must always, and ought always
to, bear it. But there is probably no state that does not pro-

vide for highways of more general importance than the ordinary townways,—highways that are very properly called and treated as state or county roads, and which are made and kept in repair by an expenditure of state or county money. In such a case the state or county is the proper taxing district, and the town will not be taxed for the purpose of the road, except as a part of the larger district to which it belongs. The state or the county might possibly be the proper taxing district, even though the work were wholly within the town; the importance and cost of the work, and not its locality, being in many cases the controlling consideration. In all such cases legislation must determine what the district shall be." Cooley Taxation, 144. The general assembly of this state has deemed it proper to make each county a district for the purpose of obtaining a county road fund. No doubt, the purpose was to enable the board of supervisors to make improvements in the highways within its county which could not be made with the township funds available for the purpose, and a discretion as to the improvements which should be made was vested in the board. Whether it be true, as claimed by the appellant, that a part of the tax may, with the concurrence of the proper authorities, be expended in the cities and incorporated towns of the county, we do not find it necessary to determine; for, if it be conceded that no part of the tax could be so expended, that fact would not make the tax on property within such corporations void. Good highways are of general benefit, not only to the territory through which they pass, but to the inhabitants of cities and towns, by facilitating travel, and thus promoting intercourse and trade. That fact is well known, and was recognized by chapter 52 of the Acts of the Eighteenth General Assembly, which permitted the expenditure in certain cases of a portion of the highway taxes of cities and incorporated towns to aid in the construction and repair of highways outside, and within three miles, of their corporate limits. A provision of a similar character is found in section 899 of the Code of 1897. Whether, in the enactment of the statute in question, the general assembly adopted

the means best calculated to secure good roads and do justice
between the different parts of each county is a question of
public policy, which we are not authorized to determine. It
is enough to say that the taxing district for the purposes of
the county road fund is the county, and that all taxable property in the county, whether within or without cities and incorporated towns, is subject to taxation for the benefit of that
fund. It follows from what we have said that the demurrer
filed in this case should have been sustained, and the judgment of the district court is therefore REVERSED.

MARY A. MORTON v. THE CITY OF BURLINGTON, Appellant.

Grade: IMPLIED EXTENSION. While it may be true that changing grade
at a corner, of necessity, amounts to a change for some distance
1 from the corner, such rule creates a liability and not a right, and
it will not be extended to a holding, that where a grade is established on two streets which cross a third, the same grade is made
by implication on that portion of the street crossed which lies
between the two said streets which cross it. *Conklin v. City*, 73
Iowa, 343, *limited and questioned*.

Evidence: DAMAGE: *Change of grade.* The immediate surroundings
of plaintiff in an action against a city for damages from a change
4 of grade in the street in front of it, and the effect upon it, if any,
of bringing the streets on either side to grade, may be considered
by the jury in determining how much and in what way the work
complained of affects the property. If there is any benefit, it bears
on recovery

Pleading: PROOF: *Objections.* Where plaintiff pleads that a grade
fixed by an ordinance was wrongfully changed, the court will not
assume that a later ordinance authorized the grade change com-
1 plained of, by sustaining objections to evidence tending to show
that the grade was changed after improvements were built with
reference to it. If the first ordinance was superseded, it was a fact
for defendant to show.

Instructions: CONSTRUED. An instruction which explains that an
ordinance adopted prior to a change of grade complained of, was
admitted in evidence to show whether or not the plaintiff's means
of convenient access to his property were increased by grades which
3 that ordinance established, does not tell the jury, in effect, that
the means of access were increased, and that only the extent of
the increase is to be determined.

Appeal from Des Moines District Court.—Hon. **W. S.** WITHROW, Judge.

THURSDAY, MAY 26, 1898.

THIS is an action for damages on account of injury done to real estate by an alleged change in the grade of the street upon which the property abuts. From a verdict and judgment in plaintiffs favor, the defendant appeals.—*Reversed.*

La Monte Cowles for appellant.

Stutsman & Stutsman for appellee.

WATERMAN, J.—Plaintiff owns a lot on North street, in the defendant city. On either side of her property, and about three hundred and twenty feet apart, Ninth street and Central avenue intersect North street. The grade of North street was established by ordinance in 1858. In 1873 the grade at the intersections of North street with Ninth street and with Central avenue was changed and established about six feet lower at Central avenue and about four feet lower at Ninth street than that fixed by the ordinance of 1858. In 1878 plaintiff erected buildings and made other improvements on her property. By an ordinance passed in 1892, the grade of North street was again changed, but nothing is claimed on account of this action by plaintiff. As a matter of fact, it did not change the street in front of her property from the level fixed by the ordinance of 1873.

II. A number of the assignments of error are based upon rulings on evidence, and these can be disposed of by calling attention to an evident misapprehension of counsel for appellant. Plaintiff had a right to make her case upon her own theory, and introduce any legitimate evidence which tended to sustain it. She claimed that the grade of North street was established in 1858, and that there was an attempt to change it by resolution in 1894, and that under this resolution the work was done of which she complains. Whether what was attempted by this resolution would amount to a change of grade, may well be questioned; but the point is not made here. We take the same cause of action as stated.   Plaintiff surely

1   had the right to prove what she alleged.   The ordinance of 1858 was admissible.   If, as defendant claims, it was superseded by a later ordinance, that was matter for the defense to show.   It could not be assumed in objections to evidence.   At least the court was not called upon to accept and adopt any such assumption in ruling upon the admissibility of testimony.   We find no error in the court's rulings on these matters.

III.   Defendant offered in evidence the ordinance of 1873, which established the grade at the intersections of North street with Central avenue and with Ninth street. This

2   evidence was offered to show that it must have been the intention of the city to change the grade of North street between these two corners; and to support this theory *Conklin v. City of Keokuk*, 73 Iowa, 343, is relied upon.   We are not inclined to extend the rule in that case.   It was there held, in favor of the property owner, that where the city changed the grade of a street at a certain corner it amounted of necessity to a change for some distance back from the corner on the intersecting streets.   While we held in that case that the city might thus incur a liability, we have no disposition to say that it may so acquire a right.   A grade, in this state, can be neither established nor changed save by ordinance.   *Blanden v. City of Ft. Dodge,* 102 Iowa, 441; *Kepple v. City of Keokuk*, 61 Iowa, 653.   And yet we are asked here to hold that it may be done by mere implication; that in places unmentioned in the ordinance, and to levels undetermined, the grade may be changed, and the city thus acquire rights against the property owners.   We must say that this cannot be done.   If this holding and that in *Conklin v. City of Keokuk* cannot stand together, this must prevail.

IV.   We say this much on this subject, although the ordinance was in fact admitted later by the court, when offered for another purpose, because the court in an instruction lim-

ited its scope and bearing, and this instruction is excepted
to by defendant. The instruction is paragraph 7 of the
court's charge, and the portion material is as follows:
3   "Evidence has been introduced showing the grades
established in 1873 on other streets connecting with
and intersecting North street. You are instructed that such
evidence is received for the sole purpose of showing whether
or not the means of convenient access to plaintiff's property
were increased." Defendant's objection is grounded on tho
idea that this instruction tells the jury, in effect, that means
of access to plaintiff's land were, in fact, increased, and leaves
them to determine only to what extent. We do not so understand it. The jury is told to find whether or not the property was made more accessible, and this would naturally be
taken to mean that the question to be determined was, how
did the ordinance of 1873 affect the property in the respect
mentioned?

V. Two witnesses were introduced by defendant, and
asked, in substance, to state the levels of the two streets at
the corners where the grade was established in 1873, and
the depth of the cut there if those streets were brought to that
grade. On plaintiff's objection this evidence was
4   excluded. It should have been admitted. The defendant should have had an opportunity to show the
immediate surroundings of plaintiff's property, and the effect
upon it, if any, of bringing Ninth street and Central avenue
to grade, in order to enable the jury to determine how much
and in what way the work complained of affected plaintiff's
land. If her land was in fact benefited thereby through
improving the means of access to it, this fact should have been
considered in fixing the amount of her recovery. *McCash
v. City of Burlington,* 72 Iowa, 26; *Stewart v. City of Council
Bluffs,* 84 Iowa, 61. For the error just pointed out, the judgment will be REVERSED.

PETER AKESON v. THE CHICAGO, BURLINGTON & QUINCY
RAILWAY COMPANY, Appellant.

Master and Servant: NEGLIGENCE: *Fellow servant.* It being the
duty of two railroad employes to fill tenders with coal from an
adjoining track, the negligent act of one of them which injured
the other by pushing a plank used as a bridge between coal car
and tender into the car after the work was done and the engine
about to start, was connected with the use and operation of a railroad, within Code, section 2071, abrogating the fellow servant rule
as to acts of negligence connected with such use and operation.

Appeal from Montgomery District Court.—HON. W. R.
GREEN, Judge.

THURSDAY, MAY 26, 1898.

ACTION at law to recover for personal injuries alleged
to have been caused by negligence on the part of the defendant. There was a trial by jury, and a verdict and judgment
for the plaintiff. The defendant appeals.—*Affirmed.*

Smith McPherson for appellant.

J. M. Junkin for appellee.

LADD, J.—For about two and a half years before the
month of August, A. D. 1892, when the accident in question
occurred, the plaintiff had worked for the defendant in its
coal house at Red Oak. His duties required him to shovel
coal from the cars into chutes, to break the coal and wet it
for use, and to assist in filling the tenders of locomotive
engines with coal. In the month referred to, the coal house
was rebuilt; and, while that was being done, tenders were
supplied with coal from cars which were placed on the coach
track next to the main line. The sides of the coal cars were
about four feet high, and, when a tender was to be loaded, it
was run onto the main line track, opposite the coal car. A

bridge was made by placing together two planks, each of which was about ten feet in length, one foot in width, and two inches in thickness, in such manner that one end of each plank rested on top of the coal car, and the other on top of the tender. The bridge thus made was nearly level, and was used by plaintiff and a co-employe in passing from the car, with a box which was provided with handles at each end, and was filled with coal, and in returning with the empty box after its contents had been dumped into the tender. On the day of the accident, a locomotive engine in charge of an engineer and fireman was run up to the coal car for coal, and a bridge was made, and the tender filled by the plaintiff and his co-employe, Forshay, in the manner described. When that work was finished Forshay remained on the tender, as he frequently did, for the purpose of riding on it to the water tank, to get water for the engine, while the plaintiff returned over the bridge to the coal car. As he was about to step from the bridge to the car, Forshay picked up a plank, and shoved it into the car. The plantiff claims that the plank caught one of his feet, and made him fall or jump into the car in such a manner as to cause a double hernia, and the evidence tends to sustain the claim. The verdict and judgment in his favor were for the sum of one thousand five hundred dollars. The assignment of the claim in suit to Carrie Akeson has been shown, and she has been substituted as party plaintiff.

The liability of the defendant depends upon the meaning and application of section 2071 of the Code (section 1307, Code 1873), which is as follows: "Every corporation operating a railway shall be liable for all damages sustained by any person, including employes of such corporation, in consequence of the negligence of agents or by any mismanagement of the engineers or other employes of the corporation, and in consequence of the willful wrongs, whether of commission or omission, of such agents, engineers, or other employes, when such wrongs are in any manner connected with the use and operation of any railway, on or about which they shall be employed, and no contract which restricts such liability shall be legal or binding."

The evidence tends to show that the accident was occasioned by the negligence of Forshay. It is said, howerever that this was in no manner connected with the use and operation of the railway. The court instructed the jury "that, at the time the injury complained of occurred, the plaintiff was working for defendant, loading coal into the tender of what is called a 'live engine,' with the help of some co-employes. When so doing, he and his co-employes were engaged in operating defendant's railway." In argument, nearly all of the authorities construing the statute set out are reviewed, and it is respectively contended that, under previous decisions, this case falls within and without its purview. For the purpose of determining this controversy, and in order to deduce a rule, if possible, in harmony with the meaning of the legislature, we shall consider somewhat in detail what has heretofore been said in construing this statute. In 1862 the first act modifying the common law was adopted. It provided that "every railroad company shall be liable for all damages sustained by any person, including employes of the company, in consequence of any neglect of the agents, or by any mismanagement of the engineer or other employes of the corporation to any person sustaining such damage." Laws 1862, p. 198. Prior to this, an employe could not recover from the company damages occasioned by the negligence of a co-employe in the same service. *Sullivan v. Railroad Co.,* 11 Iowa, 421; *Jones v. Railroad Co.,* 16 Iowa, 6; *Hunt v. Railroad Co.,* 26 Iowa, 363. The constitutionality of this statute was passed upon in *McAunich v. Railroad Co.,* 20 Iowa, 338, and there placed upon precisely the same ground as stated by Chief Justice Fuller in *Railroad Co. v. Pontius,* 157 U. S. 209 (15 Sup. Ct. Rep. 585), when construing a similar statute of the state of Kansas. In *Ney v. Railroad Co.,* 20 Iowa, 347, contractors and persons engaged in constructing the roadbed and in laying down ties and rails are held not to be engaged as employes in operating the road. The court, in order to uphold the constitutionality of the law in *Deppe v. Railroad Co.,* 36 Iowa, 52, limited the term "employes" to those engaged in operating

the railroad, saying, through Cole, J.: "The manifest purpose of the statute was to give its benefits to employes engaged
in the hazardous business of operating railroads. When thus
limited it is constitutional; when extended further, it becomes
unconstitutional." *Johnson v. Railway Co.*, 43 Minn. 222
(45 N. W. Rep. 156; *Railway Co. v. Mackey*, 127 U. S. 205
8 Sup. Ct. Rep. 1161); *Railroad v. Pontius*, 157 U. S. 209
(15 Sup. Ct. Rep. 585); *Bucklew v. Railway Co.*, 64 Iowa.
603. The *Deppe Case* was decided under the act of 1862.
Deppe was engaged in shoveling dirt on mud cars, and sometimes went with the train to unload, and at other times
remained at the bank to undermine with a pickax. The bank
was about twenty feet high from the rock on which he stood to
shovel. While shoveling loose dirt, the bank caved down, and
injured him. In holding that he was entitled to recover, this
language is used: "It is true, he was not injured while or by
operating the train; but neither the act itself nor the constitutional limitation requires us to put this very narrow construction upon it. The plaintiff was employed for the discharge of a
duty which exposed him to the perils and hazards of the business of railroads; and, although the injuries did not arise from
such hazards, they cannot be separated from the employment.
If the plaintiff had been employed exclusively for shoveling or
loading the dirt, he could not recover, although he might have
ridden to and from his work on the cars. The ground we rest
our affirmance upon is that where the employment is entire,
and a part of the continuous service relates to the perilous
business of railroading, it brings the case within the meaning
of the statute and its constitutional limit." The soundness of
this decision is questioned in *Malone v. Railway Co.*, 61 Iowa,
326, and is upheld in the same case reported in 65 Iowa, 422,
wherein it is said: "To meet the objection that the act of
1862 created a rule of liability which was applicable to railroad companies alone, and did not affect other employes under
precisely the same circumstances, and that it was therefore
class legislation, and in violation of the state constitution,
the court, in *Deppe's Case*, construed the act as creating a

remedy only in favor of that class of employed who were
engaged in the hazardous business of operating railroads;
and the correctness of the holding of that case on that question
is not doubted. But the subsequent legislation has established
a new rule as to the class of acts for which the companies are
liable. So that, to entitle an employe now to recover against
the company for injuries which he has sustained in consequence of the negligence or mismanagement or wilfulness of a
co-employe, he must show (1) that he belonged to the class of
employes to whom the statute affords a remedy, and (2) that
the act which occasioned the injury was of the class of acts
for which a remedy is given. We think it very clear that the
plaintiff has failed to establish the latter fact." *Deppe's Case*
may, then, not be deemed controlling in determining what is
meant by the use and operation of a railroad. Discrimination
has not been made in citing this case in subsequent opinions.
It has been referred to as holding that the negligence occasion-
ing the injury need not necessarily be connected with the
movement of trains, cars, or machinery on the tracks without
calling attention to the change in the statute. That the
employment at the time of the injury must have exposed the
complainant to the hazards of railroading, without reference
to what he may be required to do at other times, is no longer
questioned. *Butler v. Railroad Co.,* 87 Iowa, 206; *Keatley v.
Railroad Co.,* 94 Iowa, 685; *Canon v. Railway Co.,* 101
Iowa, 613. It may be well to say, however, that the statutes of
Minnesota and Kansas are like that construed in *Deppe's
Case.* See *Lavalle v. Railway Co.,* 40 Minn. 249 (41 N. W.
Rep. 974); *Railroad Co. v. Pontius,* 52 Kan. 264
(34 Pac. Rep. 739). In *Johnson v. Railway Co.,* 43
Minn. 222 (45 N. W. Rep. 156), the supreme court
of Minnesota, after mature consideration, held that the
statute "only applies to those employes who are exposed
to the peculiar hazards incident to the use and operation of railroads, and whose injuries are the result of such
dangers." With one exception, recovery has not been permitted in any case in this state, other than *Deppe's,* where the
wrongful act causing the injury was not occasioned by the

actual movement of trains, cars, or machinery on the track. *McKnight v. Construction Co.,* 43 Iowa, 406; *Frandsen v. Railroad Co.,* 36 Iowa, 372; *Handelun v. Railway Co.,* 72 Iowa, 709; *Nelson v. Railway Co.,* 73 Iowa, 570; *Larson v. Railway Co.,* 91 Iowa, 81; *Haden v. Railway Co.,* 92 Iowa, 226; *Pierce v. Railway Co.,* 73 Iowa, 140. On the other hand, there are numerous cases holding that, although the complainant was engaged in work on a railroad, he may not recover. In *Potter v. Railway Co.,* 46 Iowa, 399, a person injured while moving an engine driver in the shop was held not to have been injured in the operation of the road. *Smith v. Railroad Co.,* 59 Iowa, 73. The plaintiff was not entitled to recover when injured while engaged in loading a car on the track with timber. To the same effect, see *Schroeder v. Railway Co.,* 41 Iowa, 344. In the same case reported in 47 Iowa, 375, it appeared the plaintiff was injured by the movement of cars, and he was permitted to recover. In *Malone v. Railway Co., supra,* it was held that assisting in closing the door of the roundhouse after the engine had entered was not included in operating a road. *Luce v. Railway Co.,* 67 Iowa, 75. The plaintiff, in hoisting coal for the purpose of filling a car by means of a crane, was not engaged in the operation of the road. In *Stroble v. Railway Co.,* 70 Iowa, 560, the court, speaking through Beck, J., said: "This negligence, to render a corporation liable, must be of an employe, and affect a co-employe, who are in some manner performing work for the purpose of moving a train, as loading or unloading it, superintending, directing, or aiding its movement. The persons must be connected in some manner with the moving of trains. Work preparatory thereto, which may be done away from a train, is not connected with its movement. The statute, it will be observed, holds the corporation liable for the negligence of a co-employe which is 'in any manner connected with the use and operation of any railway.' What is the use and operation of a railway? It is constructed for the sole purpose of the movement of trains. That is its sole use. What is the operation of a railway? They can be operated in no other

way than by the movements of trains." The first three
sentences were quoted with approval in *Butler v. Railroad Co.,*
supra, as holding that the party injured must be exposed to
the hazards of railroading. Rothrock, J., in *Pyne v. Railway*
Co., 54 Iowa, 223, said: "We think the proper test in determining the question is: Does the duty of the employe require
him to perform services which expose him to hazards peculiar
to the business of using and operating a railroad? If it does,
and while in the line of his duty, he, by the negligence of a
co-employe, receives an injury from a passing train or from
other appliances used in the use and operation of the road, he
may recover." In *Foley v. Railway Co.,* 64 Iowa, 644, the
same judge used this language: "With the exception of
Deppe's Case, all the actions in which this court has determined that railroad companies are liable in this class of cases
are those where the injury was received by the movement of
cars or engines upon the track. In *Larson v. Railway Co.,*
91 Iowa, 81, the court, through Given, J., said that "an examination of the cases preceding that of Stroble will show that in
none of them was it held that the use and operation of a railroad were limited to the movement of what are commonly
known as 'trains.' The cases are all grounded upon the view
that the statute applies when the employment and the wrong
are connected with the handling of railroad machinery moved
upon railroad tracks." In that case the injury was occasioned
by the moving of a hand car. See *Railroad Co. v. Artery,* 137
U. S. 507 (11 Sup. Ct. Rep. 129). In *Nelson v. Railway Co.,*
supra, the plaintiff was injured while operating a ditching
machine on a railroad. The use and operation of a railroad
does not consist in the movement of trains alone. It is within
the statute if the injury is occasioned, as said in *Larson's Case,*
"in handling the railroad machinery moved upon a railroad
track." In *Butler's Case* it is said by Kinne, J., after reviewing many previous decisions: "In the cases heretofore cited,
it has repeatedly been held that this statute was intended for
the protection and benefit of employes, who, from the very
nature of their employment, are exposed to the hazards

peculiar to the business of using and operating a railroad."
The only dangers peculiar to railroading are those occasioned
by the movement of the engines, cars, and machinery on the
track, or directly connected therewith.   It is evident that
the statute contemplates such injuries only as are caused by
the negligent acts of employes so engaged.   In no other proper
sense is a railroad used and operated.   The exception referred
to is that of *Smith v. Railway Co.,* 78 Iowa, 583.   There the
plaintiff was a snow shoveler, and, while not shoveling, rode
in the caboose. The water-closet of this was filled with shovels
and picks. The light of the engine faced towards the caboose.
In pressing necessity, the plaintiff, finding the closet in this
condition, went on the platform to relieve himself. This was
covered with snow and ice, and, being for the moment blinded
by the headlight, he was unable to see the bridge. He slipped
and fell to the ground below. The court, through Robinson,
J., said: "The placing of the tools in the water-closet,
the stopping of the caboose on the bridge, the failure to notify
the occupants of its position, and permitting ice and snow to
accumulate on the platform, were matters connected with the
use and operation of the train, and hence of the railway. He
would not have been hurt had he not been on the train in the
discharge of his duties. The services of himself and others
were required, and, in order that the train might be moved,
and when the tracks were cleared of obstructions, he was
obliged to ride on the train. We think he was within the
statute." To hold that the injury must have been caused by
the actual movement of the cars, engines, or machinery, to
come within the protection of the statute, would be giving too
narrow a construction to the words "in any manner connected
with the use and operation of any railway." Besides, as
shown, such a conclusion would be contrary to previous adjudi-
cations, repeatedly cited and approved by this court. The
rule in Minnesota, with a statute by construction like ours, is
that "if there is any substantial element of hazard or condition of danger which contributed to the injury, and which is
peculiar to the railroad business, the statute applies." *Nichols*

v. Railway Co., 60 Minn. 319 (62 N. W. Rep. 386); *Leier
v. Transfer Co.,* 63 Minn. 203 (65 N. W. Rep. 269); *Blom-
quist v. Railway Co.,* 65 Minn. 69 (67 N. W. Rep. 804).

The peculiarity of the railroad business, which distinguishes it from any other, is the movement of vehicles or
machinery of great weight on the track by steam or other
power, and the dangers incident to such movement are those
the statute was intended to guard against. If, then, the injury
is received by an employe whose work exposes him to the
hazards of moving trains, cars, engines, or machinery on the
track, and is caused by the negligence of a co-employe in the
actual movement thereof, or in any manner directly connected
therewith, the statute applies, and recovery may be had.
Beyond this, the statute affords no protection. The purpose
of the lawmakers was evidently not to make men, because
employed by railroad companies, favorites of the law, but to
afford protection owing to the peculiar hazards of their situation. That the plaintiff's employment exposed him to the
peculiar dangers of railroading admits of no doubt. The
important question is whether the negligence of Forshay,
causing the injury, was so immediately connected with and
incident to the movement of the engine and tender as to come
within the statute. We think it was. The engine had been
detached from an incoming freight train, and was moved opposite the coal car, for the purpose of filling the tender with
coal to be used as fuel, and, this done, by running two planks
from the tender to the coal car. Over these the coal was carried
in boxes, and, when this work was done, these were necessarily
taken from the tender to enable the engine to move from the
main track. In doing this, Forshay picked up and pushed one
of the planks just as the plaintiff was about to step on the coal
car, and, to save himself, the latter was compelled, in order to
avoid this plank, to jump sidewise among some boxes below.
The very purpose of removing the plank was to enable the
engine to move, and if, in doing this, Forshay was negligent,
such negligence was so closely connected with the movement as
to come within the terms of the statute. Indeed, it is diffi-

cult to conceive of a case where negligence not in the actual movement of an engine is more directly connected therewith. The other issues were properly submitted to the jury. We discover no error in the record, and the judgment is AFFIRMED.

H. B. STOCKWELL, Appellant, v. THE CHICAGO & NORTH-WESTERN RAILWAY COMPANY.

Master and Servant: RISKS OF EMPLOYMENT. A locomotive fireman
1 assumes the risk of being overcome by the heat while in a position
2 over the boiler for the purpose of oiling the machinery, which
3 position he is obliged to assume because of the defective condition of the automatic lubricator.

SAME. What will constitute the ordinary care which a master is bound to exercise in inspecting and repairing appliances furnished to his
2 servants depends somewhat upon the danger to be reasonably apprehended from the defective condition of such appliances and the opportunity which the servant has of discovering such condition.

RULE APPLIED: *Proximate injury.* Plaintiff was a fireman on a locomotive equipped with an automatic lubricator, so arranged that oil was forced through a glass tube in the cab. This tube, as sometimes occurs, broke, when it became necessary to shut off the steam
1 forcing the oil and to pour oil into the cups, from over the boiler, until a new tube could be inserted. Because of a defective T, plaintiff, after closing the valve, was unable to reopen it again,
3 after replacing the tube, and was therefore obliged to oil the engine by climbing on top of the boiler and pouring oil into the cups, and, while so engaged, he was overcome by heat and injured. *Held,* that the breaking of the tube and the T were not the reasonable and probable cause of plaintiff's injury, and that, since it was his duty to oil the engine in this way, on the breaking of the tube, the heat was a risk incident to the employment, and he could not recover.

Appeal from Clinton District Court.—HON. P. B. WOLFE. Judge.

THURSDAY, MAY 26, 1898.

ACTION to recover for personal injuries sustained by plaintiff while in the employment of the defendant as a locomotive fireman, because of certain alleged acts of negligence on the part of the defendant. The defendant answered, denying generally, and alleging that the conditions complained of were known to the plaintiff; that he continued in service without complaining thereof, and thereby assumed the risk, and waived the right to complain of injuries that might be caused thereby. At the close of the evidence, the court, on motion of the defendant, directed a verdict for the defendant, and rendered judgment thereon. Plaintiff appeals.—*Affirmed.*

Chas. A. Clark and *C. H. George* for appellant.

Hubbard & Dawley for appellee.

GIVEN, J.—I. There is no dispute as to the facts, and they are substantially as follows: On and for a long time prior to July 13, 1892, the plaintiff was employed by the defendant as a locomotive fireman, and on that day, and for some time previous, he was firing engine No. 749, Mr. Yule being the engineer. On the morning of the thirteenth they started east from Belle Plaine for Clinton, the engine drawing a train of freight cars. This engine was equipped with an automatic lubricator, attached to the end of the boiler in the cab, so arranged that, when open to the pressure of the steam and water, oil, supplied from an oil cup, was continually forced through a glass tube, and thence through pipe to the cylinders, the passage of the oil being observable through the glass tubes. It was provided with valves by which the oil and the steam and water pressure could be shut off and turned on. It sometimes occurred that from heat or other cause the glass tube would unexpectedly collapse, and in such instances it was necessary to immediately shut off the steam and oil from the lubricator, until another glass tube, a supply of which was carried on the engine, could be put in place. As the train was leaving Belle Plaine that morning, the tube in the lubricator on the left-hand side of the engine broke, whereupon plaintiff immediately closed the valves, so as to prevent a flow of steam and hot oil into the cab, and for the purpose of putting in another tube. The T, or handle, to these valves being very hot, it was necessary to quickly give them a turn, let go, grab, and turn again, and so on until the valve was closed. In thus closing one of these valves, the stem broke off, so that the valve could not be opened; and therefore a new tube could not be inserted, thus rendering it necessary, in oiling the engine, that oil should be poured into the cup by hand, at frequent intervals. This could only be done when the engine was in motion, and not working steam, and was usually done after steam had been shut off, in coming into stations. It was the duty of the plaintiff, when the lubricators were not operating, to put oil into the cup. To do this, he had to get up over the end of the boiler, with his head near the top of the cab, and remain there for several minutes, gradually putting oil into the cup. This duty plaintiff had performed eight or nine times after leaving Belle Plaine before reaching Stanwood, and had put oil into the cup on coming into Stanwood. The day was very hot, and the position which plaintiff had to take in putting oil into the cup exposed him to a great heat from the boiler. After oiling on approaching Stanwood, the plaintiff, though a strong man, was overcome by the heat to which he had been exposed, and, there can be no doubt, was seriously injured thereby. At the time the T or handle to the valve broke off, it fell to the floor of the cab, and plaintiff testifies: "I got down, and picked it up, and looked at it, and it was half broken off. I could tell that by the grease, the corroding on it; it was two-thirds broken off. That was the rod itself, right under the T. I thought no more of it, but just threw it out of the cab." He further testified: "I had never observed or known before that it was broken or weak, only it was the least little bit bent, but almost everything in the cab was bent some. The T was what was bent a little bit. If an inspection had been made, it could have been determined by an examination whether it was defective or not; if a man had closed it off, for it broke off with my turning it with my fingers. It could have been tested by tapping it with a hammer. It would not have taken but a very light tap. Or it could have been tested by closing it or opening it."

VOL. 106 Ia—5

II.   Counsel have discussed this case with much elaboration and many citations of authorities, but, as we view it, it
involves only the application of a few well-established and
undisputed principles of law.   The charge is that the defendant negligently and carelessly failed to inspect said apparatus
and keep the same in repair, in consequence of which negligence plaintiff was injured without fault on his part.   Defendant's motion for a verdict was upon the grounds that there
is not sufficient evidence to support the charge of negligence,
nor a finding that the negligence charged was the proximate
cause of the injuries complained of ; also upon the grounds
that plaintiff knew of and voluntarily assumed the dangers,
that he was guilty of contributory negligence, that the injuries
were not the natural and probable result of the negligence
charged, nor such as could have been reasonably foreseen, and
that the evidence is not sufficient to sustain a verdict for the
plaintiff.   The learned district judge held that the plaintiff,
having accepted the employment knowing that he might be
required to use the cups, and oil the engine through them,
assumed the risk of so doing, and therefore sustained the
motion for a verdict.   The principles of law applicable to this
case are laid down in *Brann v. Railroad Co.,* 53 Iowa, 596, are
fully sustained by the cases cited therein, have ever since been
followed, and are undisputed in this case.   Under the law as
there announced, this defendant was bound to use ordinary
care in selecting this lubricator, so as not to subject its
employes to unreasonable danger, but no complaint is made
         of the selection.   As such appliances may in time
2   become out of repair, defendant was also bound to
         exercise ordinary care in inspecting and repairing the
appliance, so as to keep it fit to be used.   "What is such care
must be measured by the character of the business and risk
attending its prosecution."   "Ordinary care does not require
that every possible contingency must be anticipated and
guarded against, but only such as are likely to occur.   The
duty imposed does not require the use of every possible pre-
caution to avoid injury to individuals, nor that the company

should have employed any particular means which it may appear, after the accident, would have avoided it. It is only required to have used such reasonable precautions to prevent accidents as would have been adopted by prudent persons prior to the accident." *McKee v. Railway Co.,* 83 Iowa, 622. The only consequences that could reasonably have been anticipated to follow a break of the valve stem were these: That if broken when the valve was open, and so that it could not be closed, steam and oil would be injected into the cab until the steam was shut off from the engine; and, if broken, as it was, when the valve was closed and out on the road, the oiling would have to be done by hand, through the cups. Surely, the most prudent person would not have anticipated that the occasional occurrence of the break of the glass tube and the breaking of the valve stem would have occurred at a time when the combined heat of the day and that from the boiler would have rendered oiling by hand dangerous. Where only such consequences as we have named were to be expected, ordinary care did not require the same diligence in inspecting as where defects were more liable to occur, and where actual danger might reasonably be expected. This lubricator was under the constant observation of the plaintiff, and, in part at least, under his care, and he could have discovered the defect in the valve stem as readily as any other person. Though it be conceded that he was not charged with the duties of inspecting the lubricator, yet certainly the defendant had a right to assume that he would report any defects therein observed by him, and that, none being reported, he had not seen any. We think it cannot be said that, as to the plaintiff, the defendant was negligent in not discovering and repairing the stem of this valve.

III. It is also laid down as the law in the case of *Brann v. Railroad Co., supra,* that, in accepting employment as a fireman, the plaintiff assumed the ordinary risks incident to that employment. The lubricator was so constructed as that, in the event of its failing to operate as intended, the oiling of the engine could be done by hand, through the cups. Plaintiff concedes that when, from any cause, the lubricator failed to operate, it was his duty to do the oiling by hand, just as he did it on the thirteenth day of July, 1892, and therefore, under the rule, he assumed all the ordinary risks of oiling in that manner. The injury is said to have resulted from the excessive heat to which the plaintiff was exposed. But exposure to the heat was one of the ordinary risks of the employment. He assumed the duty of oiling by hand whenever occasion required it, whether the day was hot or cool.

IV. It being plaintiff's duty to oil by hand, and he having done so in the proper manner, he was not guilty of any negligence contributing to his injury in doing the oiling. We have seen, however, that he knew that the T of the valve had been bent for some time, and that he did not report that fact, nor examine it to see whether or not the stem was broken. Whether this failure on his part was such negligence as to defeat recovery we need not determine, as, for the reasons already stated, the court correctly sustained defendant's motion for a verdict.—AFFIRMED.

S. W. KERR v. C. W. EDGINGTON, Garnishee, Appellant.

Garnishment. A judgment will not be rendered against a garnishee upon his answer where it is left in reasonable doubt whether he is chargeable or not, and his debt or possession of property must be clear.

Appeal from Humboldt District Court.—HON. W. B. QUARTON, Judge.

FRIDAY, MAY 27, 1898.

C. W. EDGINGTON was garnished on execution at the suit of S. H. Kerr against W. H. Kennedy. He gave his answers in court, in which he admitted having received from Kennedy one thousand eight hundred dollars. He stated that the money was handed him by Mrs. Kennedy in the presence of her husband, to keep until they settled up their bills; that he was to keep the money, and they would use it as they wanted it to pay their bills where they owed them. He stated that Kennedy was owing him, and we understand him to have claimed that he was to take out of the amount what Kennedy was owing him. He stated that Kennedy drew out, on checks and otherwise, five hundred and sixty-nine dollars and sixty cents, leaving a balance of one thousand two hundred and thirty dollars and forty cents of the amount deposited. The items of Kennedy's indebtedness to him are indefinite and confused. He seems to have been without counsel, and his conclusions are not clear, but items are presented aggregating one thousand nine hundred and seventy-five dollars and sixty cents. The district court entered judgment against the garnishee in favor of plaintiff for nine hundred and forty-eight dollars and seventy-five cents and costs, from which the garnishee appeals.—*Reversed.*

L. E. England and *P. Finch* for appellant.

F. H. Helsell for appellee.

G**RANGER**, J.—The judgment in this case should not have been entered. The proceeding was the mere taking of the answers of the garnishee. That he intended to deny that he had any money belonging to Kennedy or was indebted to him is clear. Nothing more can be said of the facts than that they leave the conclusion doubtful. There is no way to account for the conclusion of the court below, except to disregard the intention of the garnishee to deny a liability, as it appears from his answers, and, by construing his statements, reach a different conclusion. Such a course is not authorized in such a proceeding. No issue is formed, and, in a sufficient sense, no trial is had. The object of such a proceeding is to see if the garnishee acknowledges a liability in some form, or states facts to clearly authorize such a finding. It is said in *Hibbard v. Everett,* 65 Iowa, 372, in such a proceeding, speaking of a garnishee, that, "to hold him liable,

his answer must contain a clear admission to that effect." In
Morse v. Marshall, 22 Iowa, 290, where an issue was taken
on the answer filed, and the issue was tried upon the answer,
the other evidence not conflicting with it, it is said: "In
order to charge the garnishee on his answer alone, there must
be in it a clear admission of a debt due to, or the possession of
money or attachable property of, the defendant." It is also
said in that case: "If it be left in reasonable doubt whether
he is chargeable or not, he is entitled to judgment in his
favor." There are several quite similar holdings in this
state, and the rule has general support on authority. In
such a proceeding, if the answer does not authorize a judgment, under such a rule, the plaintiff in execution, if not content with a judgment discharging the garnishee, should take
issue on his answer, so that a trial can be had, and the rights
of parties determined thereunder. The judgment is
REVERSED.

MARGARET F. KLINKER, Appellant, v. JOHN SCHMIDT, *et al.*

Action: PARTIES. The possibility that controversies respecting boundary lines may arise between the owners of other lots of the tier,
similar to that involved in the action, does not make them proper
parties to an action respecting boundary lines, between the owners
of two adjoining lots of the tier

RULE APPLIED. An action was brought for the recovery of a strip of
land claimed to belong to plaintiff's lot adjoining that of defendant. Defendant, by amendment and cross petition, pleaded adverse
possession for over ten years, and that he, as well as the other
owners of the lots in the block, who were made co-defendants by
his petition, are holding their land, as marked by fences and other
visible monuments accepted as the true boundary line, regardless
of the lot lines and the descriptions contained in their deeds, and
asked that the question as to all the boundaries be decided. It
appeared that all the lots overlapped on their neighbor's land some
fourteen feet on the east. *Held,* that the cross petition did not
raise any issue in which co-defendants were interested, since the
defenses would not necessarily be the same, and hence such owners should not have been made defendants.

TRANSFER TO EQUITY. It was error to transfer the cause to the equity
side of the court.

Appeal from Dubuque District Court.—HON. J. L. HUSTED,
Judge.

FRIDAY, MAY 27, 1898.

ACTION against John Schmidt for recovery of real
property. In an amendment to his answer and cross petition
he made other parties defendants, and upon his motion the
cause was transferred to the equity side of the calendar.
Decree was entered for Schmidt as prayed, and dismissing
plaintiff's petition, and also the cross petition of the defendants. The plaintiff and Schmidt appeal; that of the former
being first perfected.—*Reversed.*

William Graham, Lyon & Lenehan, and *Horatio B.
Smith* for appellant.

Henderson, Hurd & Kiesel for appellee.

LADD, J.—The petition contains the averments usual in
an action for the recovery of real property, and as required by
section 4187 of the Code. John Schmidt alone is made
defendant, and is alleged to be in the wrongful possession
of a strip of land fourteen feet wide along the westerly side of
the east thirty-five feet of lot 12, in block 1, of West Cascade.
The ownership of the east thirty-five feet of this lot is alleged
to be in plaintiff, and the west twenty-five feet in Schmidt.
The answer of the latter was a general denial. Lot 12 is
sixty feet wide and one hundred and twenty feet long. It
faces National street on the south, and is at the corner border-
ing East street. West of this lot, and, with it, constituting the
south half of block 1, are lots 11, 10, 9, and 8, in the order
named. The defendant filed an amendment to his answer
and a cross petition, in which he made the owners of all these
lots parties defendant, and alleged his ownership of a portion
of lot 12, describing the same by objects and localities; that
his possession had been adverse for more than ten years under
color of title and claim of right; that for more than ten years

the boundary lines between him and plaintiff had been indicated by a fence and buildings, and during that time accepted as and considered the true line. He also alleged that he was unable to describe his lines better because the owners of the block have held it in disregard of the lines; that each of the co-defendants is the owner in severalty of some portion of the block; that the land so owned is marked by fences, walls, buildings, or other visible monuments which have been accepted as indicating the true boundary lines regardless of lot lines and descriptions contained in the deeds; that granting the plaintiff's petition will compel the defendant and each of his co-defendants, if they shall desire to hold portions of said block, to bring and maintain actions against his neighbor. The prayer is for the dismissal of plaintiff's petition, that inquiry be made as to the respective ownerships of the several defendants, and the respective interests of all parties be ascertained and described, and for such other equitable relief as may be proper. On motion the cause was then transferred to the equity side of the calendar, and each of the co-defendant filed answers, asking relief peculiar to his particular case. The plaintiff objected to the filing of the amendment to the petition bringing in new parties defendant, and also resisted the motion to transfer to the equity side of the calendar.

I. The plaintiff filed an assignment of errors to the effect that the court erred in permitting the defendants other than Schmidt to be brought in by Schmidt, and also in transferring the cause to the equity side of the calendar. It may be well to say by way of explanation, although this does not clearly appear in the petition or amendment, that the building of plaintiff extends in East street about fourteen feet, and that each lot owner to the west is apparently over fourteen feet on his neighbor's land to the east; and the owners of lot 8, instead of thirty-two feet, the width of their lot, occupy about forty-six feet front. Now, the question arises whether the other lot owners are so interested in fixing the line between plaintiff and defendant Schmidt that they are proper or necessary parties. No other actions were pending, and none threatened. Merely the possibility of controversies between other lot owners is made the ground for bringing them into this case. The answer and amendment thereto did not raise any issue in which the co-defendants of Schmidt were interested. If the other owners were occupying the block regardless of boundary lines, in what way would that justify Schmidt in retaining land belonging to the plaintiff? Unless he established one of the defenses interposed by him, the record title of Klinker must prevail. The mere fact that the plaintiff might recover of Schmidt would not indicate that he in turn would be entitled to recover a similar amount of land from his neighbor beyond. If the owners of lot 10 were occupying fourteen feet of lot 11, it would not follow that because of the recovery of the fourteen feet by Klinker, the owner of lot 11 would be entitled to maintain an action for a similar amount of land from the owners of lot 10. As well say, when the line between the north quarters of section 6 is in controversy, all the owners of land in the north half of the upper tier of sections across the township or county must be made parties to the action. The defenses would not necessarily be the same. One might plead adverse possession, another an agreement fixing the boundary, and still another settlement by conveyance or otherwise. It is not a case of avoiding a multiplicity of suits, but of forcing others to participate in litigation in which they are not directly concerned. The owners of other portions of the block were in no way interested in the subject-matter of the controversy between Schmidt and Klinker, nor was the latter concerned in the adjustment of the lines between owners on the west of him. Suppose separate actions were pending between owners of the adjoining lots, putting in issue the right to each strip of land overlapping, could such actions be consolidated? Certainly not, because the subject-matter in each would not be identical, nor would the parties or issues. We think the owners of the land in this block other than the plaintiff and defendant were not concerned in the con-

troversy, and ought not to have been made parties to
the suit. The litigation might settle the principles of law
applicable to their situation, but in other respects would not
be in any way controlling. The answer and amendment put
in issue plaintiff's title, and set up as affirmative defenses—
First, adverse possession; and, *second,* the establishment of
the line by acquiescence and agreement. These were matters
proper for the consideration of the jury, and the plaintiff had
the right to have the issue submitted for such determination.
After the introduction of the evidence, another amendment
to the petition was filed, pleading an estoppel, but this also
raised an issue at law. Because of the errors of the court in
permitting other parties not interested to be made defendants,
and in transferring the cause to the equity side of the calendar, and there hearing it as an action in equity, the decree
is reversed, and the cause remanded for proceedings in harmony with this opinion.—Reversed.

Henry McClelland v. William P. Bennett, Appellant,
Mary McClelland, Intervener.

Estoppel: ADJUDICATION: *Homesteads.* An action was brought to
restrain a sheriff's sale on the ground that the property to be sold
was a homestead. A temporary injunction ordered became ineffective through failure to file bond, and a permanent injunction
granted was set aside. But a finding in the decree that the propt
erty was a homestead was never set aside or appealed from. Notwithstanding this finding there was a sale after the permanent
injunction was set aside, and a sheriff's deed resulted. *Held,* the
finding of homestead concluded parties and privies and said decree
did not estop the setting up of the homestead right in an action
to set the deed aside, since no injunction was necessary to protect
the homestead right, the suit to establish it being notice of that
right, the modification of the decree which nullified the injunction
cannot affect that part of the decree which established the
homestead.

HARMLESS ERROR. Where a husband sued to set aside a sheriff's
deed and quiet title to premises, claiming a homestead right
therein. and, after all the evidence was introduced, it appeared
that the plaintiff was entitled to a decree, permitting his wife to

then intervene and set up a homestead right thereto, was harmless error.

Appeal from Polk District Court.—HON. THOMAS F. STEV-
ENSON, Judge.

FRIDAY, MAY 27, 1898.

ACTION to set aside a sheriff's deed, and quiet title to real
estate. Decree for plaintiff. Defendant Bennett appeals.—
Affirmed.

John McLennan and *Dowell & Parish* for appellant.

Balliet & Stahl for appellee.

WATERMAN, J.—On March 29, 1895, plaintiff began
this action, asking to have a sheriff's deed of the premises in
controversy, which was made to defendant Bennett, set aside,
and the title thereto quieted in him. Plaintiff sets up the
proceedings in a certain cause, which he styles "Equity Cause
No. 4,873," and claims that in that action his homestead right in said premises was established against one
William Wyant, who owned the judgment on which
defendant's title is based. Bennett filed an answer and
cross petition. He denies that the land in question is
the homestead of plaintiff; denies that plaintiff's homestead right was ever establish by decree of court against
said Wyant. He then sets up the judgment obtained
by Wyant against plaintiff; the sale, under execution issued
thereon, to him; and the execution of the sheriff's deed. He
prays that his title to the premises may be quieted, and that
he may be put in possession thereof. By an amendment filed
later, he alleges that plaintiff is estopped by the judgment in
equity cause No. 4,873 from setting up the claim of
homestead.

II. Plaintiff, in making his case, introduced the record
in equity cause No. 4,873; and as the proceedings in that case
were somewhat singular, and both parties found claims upon

the judgment therein rendered, we shall devote some attention to what was there done. The plaintiff here was the plaintiff in that action, and it was brought against William Wyant
and the sheriff of Polk county. The petition made the claim
of homestead, and recited that the sheriff was about to sell
the same under execution issued on a judgment obtained by
Wyant against plaintiff. The relief asked was that the
threatened sale be enjoined, and the judgment declared not a
lien on said property. That action was begun February 27,
1894. On April 7th of the same year, what is styled an
"order" was entered by the court. It is, in form, a decree.
It recites the facts showing the court's jurisdiction, and that
it has fully heard the case, and concludes as follows: "It is
therefore ordered, adjudged, and decreed by the court that
the judgment [describing the Wyant judgment] is not a
lien on [here the premises in question are set out], and that
J. D. McGarraugh, sheriff of Polk county, Iowa, and William
Wyant, be, and they are, forever enjoined from selling said
real estate under and by virtue of said execution.   *   *   *"
On April 18th, Wyant filed a motion to set aside this order or
decree. On July 5th following, the court entered what is
denominated "a decree" on this motion. It recites that on
March 7, 1894, the court gave plaintiff a temporary injunction restraining the sale of his homestead, on condition that he
file a bond in the sum of one thousand dollars; that he failed
to file such bond; that the property was sold by the sheriff on
March 20, 1894; and the sheriff is, by its terms, then ordered
to pay over to Wyant the money received on such sale, and
the order granting an injunction is set aside. Thereafter
plaintiff moved to set aside this order, as in conflict with the
decree of April 17th, and this motion was overruled. After
all the evidence was introduced in the case at bar, against
defendant's objection, Margaret McClelland, the wife of
plaintiff, was allowed to intervene and set up a homestead
right in the premises in controversy.

III. It will appear from what has been said that the
order for a temporary injunction in the case No. 4,873 did

not take effect, because of plaintiff's failure to file the bond
required, that the sale of the real estate was made under the
Wyant judgment to defendant, and that thereafter the decree
was rendered which in terms permanently enjoined the sale
of the same. On defendant's motion the decree was so far
modified as that the order for a permanent injunction was
set aside. Another matter not involved in the case, nor
necssarily incident to it, was also included in this motion;
and that was the disposition of the proceeds of the sale, which
seem to have been held by the sheriff. The finding of the
court, however, that the Wyant judgment was not a lien on
these premises, was never set aside, nor in any way modified.
No appeal was taken from that ruling, so it must be regarded
as final, both as to parties and privies. No serious question
is made here as to the fact that plaintiff has a homestead
right in the property. The only claim relied upon is that
he is estopped from setting it up, because of the judgment to
which we have referred. Plaintiff might have prosecuted
the action No. 4,873 to have the cloud caused by the apparent
lien of the Wyant judgment removed from his title, without
asking the aid of a writ of injunction. In such a case a purchaser at the execution sale, had on the judgment after such
action was commenced, would have taken subject to plaintiff's
rights as they might be established by the subsequent decree.
Code 1873, section 2628; *Ferrier v. Buzick,* 6 Iowa, 258;
Jackson v. Railway Co., 64 Iowa, 292; *Rider v. Kelso,* 53
Iowa, 367. The situation of the parties is not different in
the case at bar from what it would have been in that supposed. The injunction was not necessary to protect plaintiff's title as against the threatened sale. The purchaser at
the execution sale took with notice of plaintiff's right; and
this right, as expressed in the judgment entry, was to hold his
land free and clear from the lien of the Wyant judgment.

What we have said disposes of the claim that there was
error in permitting the wife of plaintiff to intervene after the
cause had been submitted for decision. The error was manifestly without prejudice. The decree of the trial court is
AFFIRMED.

Hopkins Fine Stock Company, Appellant, v. James Reid, Constable.

Mortgage: FUTURE INCREASE OF MARES. A chattel mortgage pur-
4 porting to cover certain mares and all increase of said mares,
includes foals born *after* the execution of the mortgage and not
alone those in existence at the time of its execution.

Appeal: APPEAL TO SUPREME COURT: *Presumptions.* Where a case
1 appealed to the district court involves a sum which is within the
jurisdiction of a justice, upon consent, the court will presume
that consent was given, no objection to the jurisdiction appearing,
and no question as to it being presented.

Bill of Exceptions: STRIKING. Where a bill of exceptions was not
2 signed until after the time given to prepare and file it, it will be
striken out.

SAME: *Shorthand report.* The evidence is properly preserved of record
on appeal if the shorthand notes certified by the judge and reporter
were filed within the time given to file bill of exceptions, although
3 the transcript is not filed until the time had elapsed. *Hirrison
vs. Snair,* 76 Iowa, 558, *distinguished.*

Appeal from Page District Court.—Hon. A. B. Thornell, Judge.

Friday, May 27, 1898.

THIS is an action in replevin, which originated in the
court of a justice of the peace. The value of the property was
fixed in the petition at one hundred and ten dollars. It was
taken by appeal to the district court, and was there tried,
without the intervention of a jury. From a judgment in
defendant's favor, the plaintiff appeals.—*Reversed.*

J. R. Good for appellant.

G. I. Miller for appellee.

WATERMAN, J.—No objection seems to have been made
to the jurisdiction of the justice and no such question is pre-

sented here. We are therefore authorized to presume that the parties gave their consent to the trial by the justice. *Chesmore v. Barker,* 101 Iowa, 577.

II. Appellee moves to strike from the record the bill of exceptions, because not signed or filed in time. The judgment of the district court was rendered April 4, 1896, and, by its terms, one hundred days were given in which to prepare and file a bill of exceptions. The bill of exceptions was signed July 31, 1896, and it was filed a few days later;

2 appellee says August 3, 1896. The abstract is prepared in such a confused and confusing way that we are not able to find in it the exact date. This, however, is immaterial. It was not filed before it was signed, and it was signed eighteen days after the time fixed by the court had expired. The motion to strike will be sustained.

3 *Barber v. Scott,* 92 Iowa, 52. It appears, however, that the original shorthand notes were certified by the judge and the reporter, and filed April 4, 1896. The transcript of these notes was not filed until July 28th, which was fifteen days after the expiration of the time fixed for the bill of exceptions. If the filing of the original notes, so certified, constitutes or takes the place of a bill of exceptions, then we may consider the case. In *Bunyan v. Loftus,* 90 Iowa, 122, it was held that the evidence was properly preserved of record, if the shorthand notes certified by the judge and reporter, were filed within the time limited, although the transcript was not filed until the time had elapsed. See, also, to same effect, *Fleming v. Stearns,* 79 Iowa, 256; *Hood v. Railway Co.,* 95 Iowa, 331. *Harrison v. Snair,* 76 Iowa, 558, seems to conflict with the rule of these cases, but it will be noted that in that case the transcribed notes were never filed.

III. Plaintiff claims possession of the property in question,—certain horses,—under a chattel mortgage executed by one B. J. McKie to one F. Larabe, and by the latter assigned to plaintiff. The claim of defendant is founded on the levy of a general execution issued on a judgment against

McKie. The mortgage was made in the state of Missouri, and counsel devote no small portion of their arguments to a discussion of its validity. We need not follow them further than as to a single matter, of which we will presently speak. The trial court held the mortgage valid as to the animals described, and which were in existence at the time the mortgage was made, and gave possession of one horse to plaintiff. Defendant has not appealed, so this finding of the district court must stand. The mortgage, after describing certain horses and mares by color, age, and name, says, "and all increase of said mares and the increase of increase." It is admitted that the animals in controversy are the increase of said mares, and their ages, as given in the judgment entry, show that they were foaled since the mortgage was made. The question we have to consider is whether the descriptive clause which we have set out is sufficient to give a lien on the colts of the mortgaged mares, as against defendant.

4

IV. The claim of the appellee is that the description does not expressly cover the future increase, and that it might well be held to mean only such foals of the mares as were in existence at the time the mortgage was made. Defendant, as we have said, seized this stock on an execution issued upon a judgment against McKie, and he is claiming the property under this levy. He is held to notice of the instrument and its recitals. Now, what impression or knowledge would he naturally get from this description? Would one suppose from reading it that the mortgage covered the animals described, and others,—neither kind or number mentioned,—that were in existence at time; or would he reasonably conclude that the mares and any addition or augmentation to their number they might thereafter make, by giving birth to foals were intended to be included? It is not a question whether one can, by a refinement of reasoning, extract a particular dubious meaning from the language used here, but rather, what is its plain common sense signification? We have held that a chattel mortgage will not cover after-acquired property unless the intention so to do is clearly expressed. Following this rule, it was decided in *McArthur v. Garman,* 71 Iowa, 34, that a mortgage of a horse and "all earnings, whether by premium or otherwise," would not cover future earnings. And in *Lormer v. Allyn,* 64 Iowa, 725, we held that a description of "all books of account and rights of credit arising out of said business would not include 'rights of credit' arising or accruing after the execution of the mortgage. We are asked to go further in this case than in either of those cited, and this we have no disposition to do. In *Thompson v. Anderson,* 94 Iowa, 554, in which we held the description in the mortgage to include the future increase of animals, the language of the instrument was 'all the horses, colts, cattle, hogs, together with all increase of the above until the obligation named below is fully paid.' " Reasoning not as subtle as that indulged in by appellee would warrant a construction that the words "until the obligation below is fully paid" qualified the right of the mortgagee to hold the property conveyed, rather than fixed a future period, during which the accessions by birth were to be made. If this construction is correct, the case last cited affords direct support for our holding that the description in the mortgage in dispute was sufficient to include the future increase of the animals described. We are content, however, to rest our decision on principle alone. The court below, in holding the description in the mortgage insufficient to cover and include the animals in dispute, was in error; and, because of this, its judgment is ʀᴇᴠᴇʀsᴇᴅ.

Sᴛᴇᴘʜᴇɴ MᴄKɪɴʟᴇʏ ᴠ. Bᴀɴᴋᴇʀ's Aᴄᴄɪᴅᴇɴᴛ Iɴsᴜʀᴀɴᴄᴇ Cᴏᴍᴘᴀɴʏ ᴏꜰ Dᴇs Mᴏɪɴᴇs, Iᴏᴡᴀ, Appellant.

Iɴsᴜʀᴀɴᴄᴇ: ᴄᴏɴsᴛʀᴜᴄᴛɪᴏɴ ᴏꜰ ᴀᴄᴄɪᴅᴇɴᴛ ᴘᴏʟɪᴄʏ. The insured in a policy of accident insurance providing indemnity for injuries "immediately, wholly and continuously disabling (him) from transacting any of the duties pertaining to his occupation as a merchant" is not entitled to indemnity during the time he was able to perform some of the work pertaining to such occupation,.

although there were many of the duties incident to it that he could
not perform.

Review of Verdict: COURT AND JURY: *Objections below.* Where the
question whether plaintiff was engaged in work, during the doing
1 of which the accident policy did not afford indemnity, is submitted
to the jury, without objection, a finding that the work done was
not of that character, will not be disturbed, if there is evidence to
sustain it.

Appeal from Louisa District Court.—HON. W. S. WITHROW,
Judge.

FRIDAY, MAY 27, 1898.

ACTION upon a policy of insurance by the defendant to
the plaintiff, insuring him against the effects of personal
bodily injuries caused solely by external, violent, or accidental means.   Verdict and judgment were rendered in favor
of the plaintiff for two hundred dollars.   Defendant appeals.
—*Affirmed* conditionally.

H. O. Weaver and *N. T. Guernsey* for appellant.

Fred Courts for appellee.

GIVEN, J.—I.   The policy insured the plaintiff against
the effects of personal bodily injuries, caused solely by
external, violent, or accidental means.   The policy provides
that it should not cover the insured while engaged in the
physical labor of handling heavy hardware, stoves, or any kind
of machinery.   The plaintiff testified that he was engaged in
the hardware and implement business; that he went into the
country to the farm of a Mr. Wheeler, to put a pump in order
that was out of repair; and, as to the cause and manner of
the injury, testifies as follows: "I went out, and took the
pump out, and took the casing out of the well (the tubing, we
call it), and fixed the pump, and was putting the tubing back
in the well again (the gas-pipe; we call it tubing).   And we
had perhaps two or three lengths of the pipe down,—sixteen
or eighteen feet long,—and there were two men holding it

with a chain, and I was down in the well with a clamp; and I would loosen up the clamp, and let it slide down, and then catch it; and, as they started a piece down, the chain slipped, and it caught these two fingers between the chain and the clamp. The flesh was all torn off of these fingers, and this finger was cut clean up here on the left hand, and the thumb was cut on the left hand, and this finger never got well yet, and is numb. As soon as I was hurt, I got right up out of the well, and untied my horse, and got into the buggy, and came home, and went to the doctor's, and had it dressed. I went to Dr. Allen. I notified the company about the second day after the injury. I was under the doctor's treatment for about eight weeks before he quit treating me."

Appellant's contention is that the injury was received while appellee was engaged in the physical labor of handling heavy hardware and machinery, while appellee contends that he was not so engaged. Considerable testimony was taken as to whether the piping and appliances with which plaintiff was working are classed by the hardware trade as heavy hardware or machinery. The court submitted this question to the jury, and instructed that, if plaintiff was at the time of the injury engaged in the occupation of handling either heavy hardware, stoves, or other machinery, he would not be entitled to recover, and that the meaning or definition of these terms is that used and commonly accepted in the business in which plaintiff was engaged at the time the contract of insurance was entered into. No complaint is made of this instruction, and we cannot say that, under the evidence and this instruction, the jury was not warranted in finding that the plaintiff was not engaged, at the time of his injury, in the occupation of handling heavy hardware or machinery.

II. The indemnity provided in the policy is only as to injuries immediately, wholly, and continuously disabling the plaintiff from transacting any of the duties pertaining to

his occupation as a merchant. The agreement is to pay
2   twenty-five dollars per week, not exceeding fifty-two
consecutive weeks, during such disability. Plaintiff
claims that he was thus disabled for eight weeks immediately
following the accident, while appellant cõntends that the evidence shows that during the latter part of said eight weeks
plaintiff was able to and did perform his duties as a merchant.
It will be observed that the indemnity is for injuries "immediately, wholly, and continuously disabling the plaintiff from
transacting any of the duties pertaining to his occupation as
a merchant." It clearly appears from the evidence that the
plaintiff was not thus disabled to exceed four weeks. In his
proofs of the injury made to the defendant, he says: "I was
totally disabled from the 14th day of August, 1895, to the
18th of September, 1895. Between said times I transacted no
part of my occupation." The affidavit of his attending physician in support of the claim states that plaintiff was totally
disabled from the fourteenth of August to the eighteenth day
of September, and but partially from the eighteenth of September to the eighteenth of October. While plaintiff states
in his testimony that for about eight weeks he was not able
to do anything, he states on further examination that, during
the eight weeks following the injury, he was about the store.
"At first I could not perform the light work about the store.
I did not pretend to do anything at all until the 8th day of
September, I believe. That was the first time I undertook to
do anything about the store. Then I could sell small goods,
or anything that did not have to be tied up; anything that I
could handle with one hand I could sell." There is no evidence upon which to base a finding that the plaintiff was
totally and continuosly disabled for more than four weeks,
and, under the terms of the contract, it is only for that period
that he is entitled to recover. The verdict is manifestly
excessive to the amount of one hundred dollars, and, unless
plaintiff files a remittitur in writing of one hundred dollars

within thirty days from the filing of this opinion, the judgment will stand REVERSED.

Mary Ford, Administratrix of the Estate of H. P. Ford, Deceased, v. The Chicago, Rock Island & Pacific Railway Company, Appellant.

Negligence: COURT AND JURY. A railway employe who knew of the location and condition of an unsafe cattle guard, was, as a matter
9 of law, guilty of contributary negligence where, while attempting to pull a coupling pin he walked between two moving cars and fell into the cattle guard and was run over and killed.

Instructions. An instruction which contains an unqualified statement that if an employee was killed by reason of a defective appliance
8 the master is liable, is erroneous where it ignores the defense of contributory negligence and waiver interposed by the master.

Plea and Proof: INSTRUCTIONS. In an action for injury by a defective cattle guard, contributory negligence is an affirmative defense and plaintiff need not plead or prove freedom from contributory negligence. Plaintiff may rely on the denial interposed by law, or
6 he may deny the contribution or confess and avoid, with or without denial. And where plaintiff simply files denial, it is error to submit whether defendant could have avoided the injury by reasonable care after discovering the contributory negligence of plaintiff. Such issue should have been expressly pleaded by plaintiff, after defendant asserted contributory negligence.

Crowley v. Railway, 65 Iowa, 658, *distinguished.*

:SAME. An allegation that plaintiff's intestate "dropped into the cattle guard while he was in such position that he could not see it (cattle
7 guard), with the knowledge of the engineer, fireman and watchman that he could not see it" is not sufficient to raise that issue.

Pleading: BURDEN OF PROOF: *Instruction construed.* Plaintiff averred an injury caused by a defective cattle guard. Defendant pleaded contributory negligence and a waiver of the defect. There
1 was a reply which admitted continuing at work with knowledge of said defect, and of its being dangerous, but it pleaded protest and promise to repair, in avoidance. The court put the burden on plaintiff to prove the alleged negligence and resulting injury and damage and also charged that defendant should establish the contributory negligence and waiver asserted by it. *Held,*

a. An admission that deceased continued at work with knowledge that the guard was defective, standing alone, admits a waiver of _that defect. Hence it was error to oblige defendant to prove an admitted fact.

b. As protest and promise to repair would overcome the said admitted facts, these were properly pleaded in avoidance, but it was for plaintiff to prove that allegation and not for defendant to negative it.

Worden v. Railway Co., 72 Iowa, 301, *distinguished.*

c. While the jury is also told that knowledge of danger is admitted and that this constitutes a waiver, this is not said with reference
2 to burden of proof; nor is it said to be admitted that such knowl-
4 edge existed without objection and promise of amendment, and therefor, it cannot be known but that the jury held such knowledge not to constitute a waiver because defendant had failed to prove the absence of protest and promise to repair.

d. If the jury did not so understand it, the charge was contradictory.
5 It said, then, that defendant should prove a fact, and also, that the same fact was admitted.

Appeal: PRESUMPTIONS. The appellate court will presume that prej-
5 udice resulted from error of the trial court unless the contrary affirmatively appears.

INSTRUCTIONS. An affirmative error in an instruction respecting the
8 burden of broof is available on appeal although the appellant did not request an instruction on that subject.

Appeal from Cedar District Court.—HON. W. G. THOMPSON, Judge.

FRIDAY, MAY 27, 1898.

ACTION at law to recover damages resulting from the death of H. P. Ford. The negligence alleged is failure to erect a safe and sufficient cattle guard at a place where the railroad crosses a public street in the town of West Liberty. The defendant denied the alleged negligence, and pleaded contributory negligence and waiver of the defects. The plaintiff, in reply, pleaded protest and promise of repair. The case was tried to a jury, resulting in a verdict and judgment for plaintiff. Defendant appeals.—*Reversed.*

Robert Mather, Cook & Dodge, and *T. B. Hanley* for appellant.

Preston, Wheeler & Moffit for appellee.

DEEMER, C. J.—This is the third time this case has been before us. The first opinion will be found in 91 Iowa, 179, the second in 71 N. W. Rep. 332. A re-hearing was granted on the second appeal, and the case has again received most careful consideration. The facts are fully set out in the first opinion, and need not be repeated, except in so far as they may be necessary to a full understanding of the points decided upon this appeal.

The court instructed that under the issues the burden was on the plaintiff to establish the alleged negligence, the injury to the estate and consequent damage; and on defendant "to establish by a fair preponderance of 1   the evidence the allegations which it makes against plaintiff's intestate, and which it charges contributed to his injury, as well as to establish any waiver claimed by it." This was the only instruction relating to the burden of proof which was given. The reply filed by plaintiff admitted that her intestate knew of the cattle guard, and that it was dangerous, and with such knowledge continued in the employment of the defendant. But, in avoidance, plaintiff pleaded protest and promise of repair. It is evident that the court was in error in placing the burden on defendant of proving a matter which was admitted in the pleadings. Appellee contends, however, that waiver consists of four ingredients, viz.: knowledge of danger, continuance in employment, absence of protest, and absence of promise to repair; and that the burden was on defendant to prove each and all of these propositions. The case of *Worden v. Railway Co.,* 72 Iowa, 201, is cited in support of this position. In that case the defendant alleged that deceased, long prior to the injury, had full knowledge of the condition of the track, and continued in the service without objection, and without promise of change. The question here presented does not seem to have been argued in that case, for the reason, no doubt, that defendant pleaded absence of protest and promise to repair. It is true, we said "that the instruction, standing by itself, does not express the law, because it omits the element of waiver, which consists in remaining, after knowledge, without objection, and without promise of amendment." This is a correct statement of the law, but it does not support the appellee's contention in this case. No reference is made to the burden of proof, and no attempt was made to determine where it should be placed. The question was determined adversely to appellee in the case of *Coates v. Railway Co.,* 62 Iowa, 486. In that case it is said, after referring to the case of *Wells v. Railroad Co.,* 56 Iowa, 520, which requires the defendant to prove that the person injured had knowledge of the danger: "We think that, when the defendant has shown that fact, it may well rest upon it as a defense, and that, in the absence of some excuse from the plaintiff for exposing himself to dangers known to him, there can be no recovery. It is a general rule (subject, of course, to some exceptions) that a party to an action is not required to establish the negative of a proposition. When the defendant shows that the plaintiff knew of the dangerous condition of the road or machinery which he aided to operate, it is then incumbent on the plaintiff to show that he was in some manner justifiable in exposing himself to the danger. The fact that such proof cannot be made in some cases, where the injury results in death, is no reason why the rule that the party who holds the affirmative of an issue is required to assume the burden of proof should not be enforced. If the burden had been held to rest on the defendant to prove the negative, it would have been required to introduce as witnesses all of its officers and employes to whom such notice might be properly given, and prove by them that no complaint was made." This is a correct statement of the rule as we understand it, and is a complete answer to appellee's argument. In the

2   argument upon re-hearing, appellee concedes the error in the instruction, but argues that it was without prejudice, for the reason that in another instruction, to-wit, the eighth, the court told the jury that plaintiff conceded that

deceased knew of the location and construction of the cattle guard when he entered defendant's service as a switchman. It is true, such a statement is found in the eight paragraph of the charge, but it has no reference to the question as to the burden of proof. It relates simply to the matter of waiver, and is a correct statement of the law upon that subject. But how are we to know but that the jury understood the word "waiver," as used in instruction 4, as appellee's counsel understood it? As said in the *Worden Case,* "waiver consists in remaining, after knowledge, without objection, and without promise of amendment." So counsel understood it, and the jury, no doubt, had the same idea. If they did, then the fourth instruction cast upon defendant the burden of proving absence of protest, and promise of repair.

3   Again, it is suggested that, as defendant asked no instruction with reference to the burden of proof, it is not in position to complain. It is true, no instruction was asked; but the court, in the absence of a request, undertook to state where the burden was as to each and every issue presented by the pleadings; and the rule is well settled that, when the court attempts to so instruct, it must do so correctly, whether request be made or not. *State v. Pennell,* 56 Iowa, 29. As the reply admitted knowledge of the defect, and continuance in the employment, plaintiff was not entitled to recover without proving affirmatively that deceased protested against the defect, and was promised that it should be repaired. No such instruction was given. On the contrary, the court said that, under the issues as tendered, the plaintiff need only prove the alleged negligence, the injury to the estate she represented, and the consequent damage. Surely, this was error of the most prejudicial kind. More-

4   over, as the court instructed that the burden was upon the defendant to establish the allegations which it made against the plaintiff's intestate, as well as to establish any waiver claimed by it, and at the same time instructed that plaintiff had admitted that her intestate had knowledge of the

defect and the dangers incident thereto, it is evident that something more was intended by the use of the word "waiver" than mere knowledge and continuance in employment. Counsel for appellee certainly had this idea upon the original submission, and it is strange if the jury did not reach the

5   same conclusion. When error appears, prejudice will be presumed, unless the contrary affirmatively appears.

With this rule in mind, it seems quite clear that there was not only error, but that the error was prejudicial. But it is said the instructions, taken as a whole, are not erroneous. This argument is based upon the thought that the jury understood the term "waiver" to mean no more than knowledge of the defect, and continuance in the employment, and further proceeds upon the idea that, as the eighth instruction states that these matters were admitted, there was no prejudice. The fault in this argument lies in the fact that, if the instructions are so construed, they are in direct conflict; one saying that the burden was upon defendant to prove a certain state of facts; and others, that this same state of facts was admitted by the plaintiff. Contradictory and conflicting instructions are almost universally held to be erroneous, except in cases where the court can say there was no prejudice. See *Carlin v. Railroad Co.,* 31 Iowa, 371; *Potter v. Railroad Co.,* 46 Iowa, 399; *Roby v. Appanoose County,* 63 Iowa, 113; *Blaul v. Tharp,* 83 Iowa, 665. From any point of view, the instruction was erroneous, and, as the error does not affirmatively appear to have been without prejudice, the case must be reversed.

II.   .The negligence charged was the failure to construct and maintain a good, safe, and sufficient cattle guard. The defendant, as we have seen, pleaded contributory negligence. To this plaintiff responded by a general denial. The twelfth

6   instruction given by the court was as follows: "If you should find from the evidence, and under the foregoing instructions, that the plaintiff's intestate, H. P. Ford was negligent, still defendant could not escape liability if the act which caused the injury was done by defendant after

it discovered said Ford's negligence, if you find from the evidence that defendant could have avoided the injury in the exercise of reasonable care." This instruction is challenged because it is said there was neither pleading nor proof to sustain it. A careful examination of the evidence leads us to the conclusion that there was sufficient to take the case to the jury, provided the question is properly made in the pleadings. It must be remembered that this is not a case where plaintiff must plead and prove freedom from contributory negligence. Such negligence is a defense which the defendant must plead and prove. See 91 Iowa, 179. When such an issue is tendered, plaintiff may rely upon the denial interposed by law, or he may file a written denial, or he may confess and avoid with or without a denial. *McDermott v. Railway Co.,* 85 Iowa, 180; *Stanbrough v. Daniels,* 77 Iowa, 561; *Day v. Insurance Co.,* 75 Iowa, 694; *Schulte v. Colthurst,* 94 Iowa, 418; *Nichols v. Railway Co.,* 94 Iowa, 202. These rules are so elementary that they scarcely need the citation of authorities in their support. But appellee insists that, when contributory negligence is pleaded, the rule does not apply; and she relies upon the case of *Crowley v. Railway Co.,* 65 Iowa, 658. That was a case where plaintiff was injured by a moving train negligently run with great force, and at a speed in violation of the ordinances of the City of Cedar Rapids. The plaintiff pleaded freedom from contributory negligence, which the defendant denied. In passing upon an instruction very similar to the one above set forth, the court said: "It is insisted that there is neither averment nor proof that the defendant could have prevented the injury after the discovery of plaintiff's negligence. We do not think such an allegation is necessary to be made in the petition. It is a phase of the rights and obligations of the parties, which arises upon the proof, rather than by pleading. We know of no rule of pleading which requires the plaintiff, in actions of this character, to confess negligence on his part, and avoid it by alleging that the defendant might have averted the injury by using proper care after the discovery of plaintiff's peril." As applied to the facts in that case, this statement of the law is correct. In other words, recovery in such a case is not upon the ground that defendant has been guilty of a second and independent act of negligence, which must be charged as a separate and independent cause of action, but upon the ground that defendant's recklessness and wantonness cannot be excused by plaintiff's contributory negligence. In the case at bar the negligence charged was the failure to maintain a safe and sufficient cattle guard. All that plaintiff needed to do in the first instance was to plead and prove the neglect of the defendant, and the consequent injury. Defendant had the right to plead in defense that the injury was the result of the intestate's contributory negligence, independent negligence, or any other matter or thing which would defeat the plaintiff's action. If plaintiff desired to avoid this defense by any new matter, as that the defendant negligently ran the train upon him after discovering his peril, he should have pleaded it. A plea of contributory negligence as a defense to an action under section 1288 of the Code of 1873 is or may be quite different from an allegation in a petition that plaintiff was free from contributory negligence. In the latter case it is "a phase of the rights and obligations of the parties which arises rather upon the proofs than by the pleadings," and it is not necessary for plaintiff to do more than state, in a general way, freedom from contributory negligence. In the former, contributory negligence is purely a defense, which plaintiff should meet by proper averment and proof. Any other rule would require the defendant to meet an issue not tendered by the pleadings, and of which he could not possibly be advised. The case at bar is a good illustration of the rule. The cause of action which the defendant was called upon to meet was failure to construct and maintain a good, safe, and sufficient cattle guard. The defendant pleaded in defense that plaintiff's intestate was guilty of contributory negligence in walking into the guard. Plaintiff denied this. It was practically admitted at the trial, however, that the deceased did know of the defective guard, and that he walked into it with this knowledge. Whether or not his act in so doing was negligence, was properly submitted to the jury. But the court also gave the instruction now complained of, which related, not to the negligence charged in the petition, but to the negligence of the engineer and trainmen in charge of the train after they knew of the peril deceased was in. Surely, this is not a phase of the negligence charged. Under section 2665 of the Code of 1873, which provides, in substance, that there may be a reply "where some matter is alleged in the answer to which plaintiff claims to have a defense by reason of the existence of some fact which avoids the matter alleged in the answer," it was held in the case of *Hay v. Frazier,* 49 Iowa, 454, that, if plaintiff expects to introduce evidence of matter to avoid the facts pleaded in the answer, he should plead such matter by way of reply. See, also, *Zinck v. Insurance Co.,* 60 Iowa, 266; *Kervick v. Mitchell,* 68 Iowa, 273; *Smith v. Griswold,* 95 Iowa, 684; *Willits v. Railway Co.,* 80 Iowa, 531; *Bank v. Wright,* 84 Iowa, 728. Appellee contends that the petition charges negligence of defendant's agents and servants after the peril of deceased was discovered. We need not set out the allegation relied upon. It is sufficient to say that, in our judgment, it does not go to the extent claimed. True, it says that plaintiff's intestate "dropped into the cattle guard while he was in such position that he could not see it, with the knowledge of the engineer, fireman, and watchman that he could not see it;" but this is far from charging actual negligence on the part of the defendant's agents after they discovered the peril deceased was in. As there was no issue justifying the giving of the twelfth instruction, it must be held to be erroneous.

III. In the fifth instruction the court said to the jury, in effect, that if plaintiff had proved that the cattle guard was not good, sufficient, and safe, and that H. P. Ford sustained

injury and death by reason thereof, then plaintiff was entitled
to recover. Complaint is made of this unqualified
8   statement of the law, because it overlooks the defenses
of contributory negligence and waiver. The instruction should have had some such qualification. *Hoben v. Railroad Co.,* 20 Iowa, 562. Under the issues as presented,
instruction No. 4 asked by the defendant should have been
given. It is as follows: "If you find from the evi-
9   dence that the intestate, H. P. Ford, went between two
of the moving cars, at a distance of about seventy-five
feet east of the cattle guard in question, for the purpose of
pulling a pin to uncouple said cars, and found that the pin
which he intended to pull was sticking fast, so that he could
not pull it out with his hand, and that he thereupon took the
other coupling pin, and attempted to loosen the fastened pin
by pounding it, and, while so engaged continued to walk
between the moving cars, towards the said cattle guard; and if
the jury further find that said H. P. Ford knew of the location of said cattle guard and might have avoided it by
stepping from between said cars, but failed to do so,—then
the said H. P. Ford was guilty of contributory negligence,
and your verdict must be for the defendant." As sustaining
this view, see *Pieart v. Railway Co.,* 82 Iowa, 148.

Some other matters are discussed by counsel, but, as
they will not arise upon a re-trial, they will not be considered.
For the errors pointed out, the judgment is REVERSED.

HATTIE FORD v. THE CITY OF DES MOINES, Appellant.

Negligence: SIDEWALKS: *Jury question.* Evidence is admissible that
a walk sloped five feet in forty and that it had no cleats or handrail, and where it also appears that the walk was not constructed
1   according to any plan adopted by the city, but built as a temporary expedient to be used until the street was brought to grade, it
becomes a jury question whether the city was negligent in constructing and permitting the walk to remain as it was at the time
of an accident.

SAME. *Several causes of injury.* A city is not relieved from liability
   for injuries sustained by falling upon a sidewalk which was estab-
3 lished at too steep a grade, because the icy condition of the walk,
   for which it was not responsible, contributed to the accident. It
   was for the jury to say whether danger from snow should have
   been provided for when a sloping walk was built.

DAMAGES: *Future suffering.* To authorize an allowance for future
2 pain, inconvenience and impairment of enjoyment, in an action
   for personal injuries, the evidence must show that such consequences are reasonably certain to continue, and evidence which
   merely shows that they may continue is not sufficient.

Appeal from Polk District Court.—HON. T. F. STEVENSON,
Judge.

SATURDAY, MAY 28, 1898.

ACTION at law to recover for personal injuries sustained from a fall on a sidewalk, for which the defendant is
alleged to have been responsible. There was a trial by jury,
and a verdict and judgment for the plaintiff. The defendant
appeals.—*Reversed.*

J. K. Macomber for appellant.

Balliet & Stahl for appellee.

ROBINSON, J.—In the year 1895 an officer of the defendant constructed on Fifteenth street, from an alley to Center
street, a temporary sidewalk. It was placed in a trench cut
for that purpose, was about forty feet in length and three feet
in width, and was made by placing together planks lengthwise
of the trench. The walk was sloping, the difference in height
between the highest and lowest parts of the walk being about
five feet; but cleats were not fastened on the walk, nor were
there hand rails at the sides. While the walk was in that condition, the plaintiff attempted to pass down it, and in so doing
slipped and fell, and received the injuries of which she complains. The verdict and judgment were for the sum of five
hundred dollars, exclusive of costs.

I.   The defendant objected to the introduction of evidence which showed that the walk was sloping, and now claims that it was erroneously admitted, for the alleged reason that, if the walk was too steep, it was due to a fault in the plans, and to an error in judgment, and not to neglect of duty.   A sufficient answer to this claim is that the walk was not

1   constructed according to any plan adopted by the defendant.   It was a mere temporary expedient, apparently intended to be used until the street should be brought to the established grade; and, if it was improperly constructed or lacked appurtenances it should have had to make it reasonably safe for the use for which it was designed, the city was negligent in permitting it to remain in that condition.   *Clemence v. City of Auburn,* 66 N. Y. 334.   It was, therefore, proper for the plaintiff to show that the walk was sloping, and also to show that it lacked appurtenances which were required to make it safe.   Whether the defendant was negligent in constructing the walk and in permitting it to remain as it was at the time of the accident was a question for the determination of the jury.   *Baxter v. City of Cedar Rapids,* 103 Iowa, 599, and *Graham v. Ttown of Oxford,* 105 Iowa, 705.

II.   The district court charged the jury as follows: "If you find that the plaintiff is entitled to recover, the next inquiry will be as to the amount of her recovery.   *   *   * The damages to which she is entitled, if any, are such as are caused by the bodily pain and suffering, distress and mental anguish and inconvenience, and the impaired enjoyment of life by reason of the injury, and for such pain and inconvenience and impairment of enjoyment for such

2   time as the same has been or may continue, as shown by the evidence, in the future, if any.   *   *   *" This is similar to an instruction considered in *Fry v. Railway Co.,* 45 Iowa, 416, which was as follows: "If you find from the evidence, as hereinbefore stated, the plaintiff is entitled to recover, then you will take into consideration the nature and character of the wound or injury, the present situation

and condition of her limb, the pain she has suffered, or which from the evidence she will suffer, and you will give her such damages as will fairly compensate her for all past, present, or future physical suffering or anguish, which is, has been, or may be caused by said injury." We said of that instruction that it was too broad; that it was of a nature to allow the jury to enter the domain of conjecture, and indulge in speculation to a greater extent than was allowable; that the jury should have been directed that it might give the plaintiff damages for such future pain as it was reasonably certain from the evidence she would suffer, and that the jury should have been clearly and positively instructed that it should determine as to the future suffering from the evidence alone. The portion of the charge under consideration authorized the jury to allow for "pain and inconvenience and impairment of enjoyment for such time as the same   *   *   *   may continue, as shown by the evidence, in the future.   *   *   *" In other words, the jury was authorized to allow the plaintiff for pain, inconvenience, and impairment of enjoyment which the evidence showed might continue in the future, which was merely possible, not for what the evidence showed was reasonably certain to continue. In this respect the charge was erroneous.

III. Some of the evidence tends to show that the walk in question was made slippery by snow which fell during the afternoon of the accident, and which was partially melted and slushy, and that the plaintiff slipped and fell in consequence of that condition of the walk. It is insisted by the appellant that it is not liable for injuries caused by fresh snow or ice. That would be true in many cases; as, where snow has fallen or ice has accumulated on a walk which is properly constructed, and a reasonable time for its removal has not elapsed when injury is caused by it. See *Huston v. City of Council Bluffs,* 101 Iowa, 33; *Lindsay v. City of Des Moines,* 68 Iowa, 368. But that walks are made slippery by melting snow is a fact of common knowledge, and should be considered in constructing walks, especially those which have

sloping surfaces, and, in consequence are liable to be dangerous when slippery.   See *Grossenbach v. City of Milwaukee,*
65 Wis. 31; *Perkins v. City of Fon du Lac,* 34 Wis. 435.   It
cannot be said, as a matter of law, that the defendant is not
liable for the accident in question, even though the snow had
fallen so short a time before the accident occurred that there
had not been a reasonable time for the removal of the snow.
Whether it should have been provided against in the construction of the walk was a question for·the determination of the
jury.

IV.   We find it unnecessary, in view of the disposition
which must be made of the case, to determine other questions
presented in argument.   For the error of the district court in
giving the part of its charge which we have considered, its
judgment is REVERSED.

REPORTS

OF

CASES AT LAW AND IN EQUITY

DETERMINED BY THE

SUPREME COURT

OF

THE STATE OF IOWA

AT

DES MOINES, OCTOBER TERM, A. D., 1898.

AND IN THE FIFTY-SECOND YEAR OF THE STATE.

STATE OF IOWA v. JOHN BAKER, Appellant.

Rape: EVIDENCE OF COMPLAINTS. It was testified that the victim of an attempted rape soon after told her mother and another of a
2 pain in the stomach, across her back, and in her throat. *Held* that this did not relate to the details of the assault.

SAME: *Harmless error.* Admission of the statement of the victim of an attempted rape, attributing pain in her stomach to the posi-
2 tion of the man's knees on her abdomen, was harmless, where it was not denied that some one committed the assault, since it did connect accused with it.

CURING ERROR Testimony of a constable, arresting one accused of attempted rape, as to what others said to him while in pursuit,
8 went in without objection, and motion to exclude it was overruled. At the close of the examination all such testimony was stricken, and the jury cautioned to disregard it. *Held*, that the error was cured.

Identification: CORROBORATION. An attempted rape was committed near a school house a few minutes past 8, A. M. Accused left a

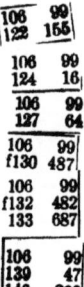

(99)

1 house one and one-half miles west at 7:40. A man was seen about a mile east of the school house about 8:40. The victim testified that her assailant wore striped pants and a checkered shirt, and that she scratched his face and hurt his eye When arrested the same day, accused was so clothed, and his face was scratched and his eye bruised. He pretended ignorance at the time, of the condition of his face and eye, but on the trial explained that a stick struck him while chopping wood that morning. Evidence tended to show that he washed his face after the chopping, and it was uninjured. *Held*, sufficient to corroborate his identification by her.

Appeal from Story District Court.—HON. B. P. BIRDSALL, Judge.

TUESDAY, OCTOBER 4, 1898.

THE defendant, having been accused and convicted of assault with intent to commit rape, appeals.—*Affirmed.*

J. F. Martin and *Funston & Gifford* for appellant.

Milton Remley, Attorney General, and *Hubert Remley* for the State.

LADD, J.—The evidence warranted the jury in finding that some one assaulted Bertha McVey, with the purpose of committing rape, on the morning of May 28, 1896. She
1 identified the defendant as the guilty party. He insists, however, that she is not corroborated by other evidence tending to connect him with the commission of the offense. The statute does not fix the *quantum* or kind of evidence required, nor is its sufficiency to be determined by excluding the evidence of the injured party. *State v. McLaughlin,* 44 Iowa, 85. If, considered in connection therewith, the other evidence tends to identify and single out the accused as the perpetrator of the crime, it is of that character contemplated by the statute, and its sufficiency is to be passed upon by the jury. *State v. Watson,* 81 Iowa, 380; *State v. French,* 96 Iowa, 255; *State v. Moore,* 81 Iowa, 578; *State v. Mitchell* 68 Iowa, 116; *State v. McLaughlin,* 44 Iowa, 82. The assault was committed near a school house, a few minutes

after 8 o'clock A. M., and the defendant left the farm house of Halteman, where he ate breakfast, one and a half miles west, twenty minutes before eight. A man was seen on the track about a mile east of the school house about one-half hour later. The defendant might have reached the scene of the crime, attempted the outrage, and gone east, as stated by Bertha McVey. He is shown to have taken dinner with Myers about five miles north, at 2 o'clock P. M., and an hour later to have hired out to work for Mortz one month. The prosecutrix, a girl of thirteen years, testified that the man who assaulted her wore striped pants and checkered shirt, and that she scratched his face and hurt his eye. When arrested on the same day, other witnesses testify the defendant was so clothed, and that his face appeared to have been recently scratched and his eye bruised. He manifested ignorance of the condition of his face and eye when his attention was called to it, but explained on the trial, that, in chopping wood for his breakfast that morning, a stick flew and struck him in the face. Other evidence tended to show that, after he finished chopping and before eating, he washed his face and it was uninjured. These circumstances tended to identify and point out the defendant as the perpetrator of the crime. The weight to be given the explanation of the telltale marks was for the jury. If not accepted, these might well, in connection with the other circumstances mentioned, be deemed corroboration sufficient to meet the requirement of the statute.

II. The record fails to show, as contended, that witnesses testified to the particulars of the complaint made by the prosecutrix. Soon after the assault she told her stepmother and another of a pain in the stomach, across the back and in the throat. This related to her condition, and not to the details of the assault. True, she attributed the pain in the stomach to the position of the man's knees on her abdomen; otherwise no details were given, and this statement alone could not have worked prejudice to the defendant. That an assault had been committed by some one was not controverted.   The main issue was whether the defendant or some one else was the assailant.

III.   The constable making the arrest testified to what different persons said to him when in pursuit of the accused. Whether this evidence was given in narrative or in response to questions is not disclosed by the record.   Objections were not interposed, but the defendant sought to have the answers, after given, excluded.   His motions for that purpose 3 were overruled, but, when the examination had been concluded, all such evidence was stricken, and the jury cautioned to disregard it.   We are unable to discover any just ground of complaint in these rulings.   The evidence, while it had little or no bearing on the case, was hearsay, and the court might well have sustained the motions when made, but, as the final ruling had this effect, the appellant is not in a position to complain.   The judgment is AFFIRMED.

STATE OF IOWA v. JAKE COPELAND, Appellant.

Manslaughter: EVIDENCE: *Sentence.* Deceased was insulting, threatening and violent towards accused, and was endeavoring to provoke a quarrel, which accused tried to avoid.   Deceased pressed the quarrel so that they came together, and accused stabbed 2 deceased four times with a pocket knife, causing death.   There was some evidence that deceased had a razor, but none that he 3 used it.   Both were drunk, but had been friendly and on good terms, and accused assisted to carry deceased to his home.   *Held*, that a verdict of manslaughter was warranted, but that sentence should be reduced from six to three years.

Conduct of Jury: NEW TRIAL.   Statements of jurors, while deliberating, that accused "was a tough boy" and that his only witness 1 was a "pretty bad boy, a hard drinker and a bad character," do not indicate prejudice, where the evidence shows their truth.

Appeal from Fremont District Court.—HON. A. B. THORNELL, Judge.

TUESDAY, OCTOBER 4, 1898.

THE defendant was indicted for the crime of murder in the first degree for the killing of one Albert McFarland on the tenth day of December, 1896, and on the trial was convicted of the crime of manslaughter, and judgment of imprisonment in the penitentiary at Fort Madison for the period of six years rendered against him, from which judgment the defendant appeals.—*Modified*.

W. E. Mitchell for appellant.

Milton Remley, Attorney General, and *Jesse A. Miller* for the State.

GIVEN, J.—I.   Defendant's counsel, appointed by the court, being unprovided with means to prosecute this appeal, and having submitted the case upon what seemed to be a brief abstract and argument, we have resorted to the transcript of the record and the evidence to find, after careful reading, that the abstract, with that of the appellee, presents quite fully the record in the case, and that the argument of counsel for defendant presents all that may fairly be urged in his behalf. It is first argued in behalf of the defendant that the court erred in overruling his motion for a new trial upon the ground of misconduct of the jury.   The conduct complained

1   of is that while the jury was deliberating a juror remarked of the defendant that he was a tough boy, and another juror said of defendant's only witness that he was a pretty bad boy, a hard drinker, and bad character.   The evidence leaves no doubt as to the truth of these statements.   They were legitimate deductions from the evidence, and do not even indicate prejudice on the part of the jury.

II.   It is next urged that the evidence is insufficient to support the verdict.   It shows that on the evening of December 10, 1896, the deceased, the defendant, and one other person, while in a state of intoxication, went into a

2   restaurant in Hamburg; that deceased was insulting, threatening and violent in his manner towards the defendant, and was endeavoring to provoke a quarrel with the

defendant, which the defendant endeavored to avoid. The deceased pressed the quarrel so that he and defendant came together, and during the altercation the defendant inflicted four wounds on the deceased with a common pocketknife, one of which wounds punctured the intestines at four different places, which caused the death of the deceased the following morning. There is some evidence tending to show that deceased had a razor in his pocket but none that he attempted to use it. There is also testimony tending to show previous threats made by the deceased against the defendant, and which were communicated to the defendant some time prior to the altercation. We doubt the truth of this testimony, as it is apparent that the men were on friendly terms up to, and even after, the altercation. The defendant assisted in taking the deceased to his home after the wounds were inflicted. We are in no doubt that it was the drunken condition of the men, especially of the deceased, that prompted the quarrel, and not any previous hatred or animosity. While there is much to be said in mitigation of the conduct of the defendant, it cannot be justified under the law. He was not so pressed by his assailant as to be justified in using his knife as he did, knowing, as he must, that so using it was likely to cause death. The jury was fully warranted in returning the verdict that it did.

III. It is urged on behalf of the defendant that the penalty imposed, namely, six years' imprisonment in the penitentiary, is too severe, and should be reduced by this court. In view of the provocation under which the defendant acted, his effort to avoid the quarrel, and the manner in which it was pressed, we are of the opinion that the penalty should be modified to imprisonment for a term of three years.—MODIFIED and AFFIRMED.

WILLIAM BRADLEY, by his Executors, J. A. and D. C. Bradley, Appellants, v. APPANOOSE COUNTY, et al.

Highway: ABANDONMENT: *Estoppel.* Non-user will not operate to discontinue a lawfully established highway unless accompanied
1   by such long continued adverse possession or transfer of the land by purchase and sale as to demand that the public should be estopped from asserting the right to reopen it.

SAME. One who has agreed that a highway which he has fenced up
2   and cultivated may be reopened is estopped from asserting any right to the land, where public expenditures have been made upon it in reliance on such agreement.

Appeal from Appanoose District Court.—HON. ROBERT SLOAN, Judge.

TUESDAY, OCTOBER 4, 1898.

SUIT in equity to enjoin defendants from opening up a road through land belonging to the decedent. Defense, a general denial, and a plea of estoppel. Decree dismissing the petition, and plaintiffs appeal.—*Affirmed.*

C. F. Howell for appellants.

Baker & Moore and *J. M. Wilson* for appellee.

DEEMER, C. J.—William Bradley commenced this suit to enjoin defendants from opening up and improving a highway running through his land, which was duly established by act of the legislature in the year 1847. After the suit was commenced, Bradley died, and his executors were substituted as parties plaintiff. The appeal is from the order dismissing plaintiff's petition, and the two propositions relied upon for reversal are: *First,* that the highway, while duly established, has been abandoned; and, *second,* that appellants have gained title thereto by adverse possession.

As the highway was duly established, the burden of showing adverse possession or abandonment is upon the plaintiffs. In what follows it must not be understood that we are announcing the doctrine that ten years' adverse user will of itself defeat a regularly established public road, for we have distinctly held in many cases that as a general rule mere non-user will not operate to defeat public rights. In other cases we have said, however, that where there has been non-user, and private rights have been acquired by long-continued adverse possession and consequent transfer of the lands, the public will be estopped from asserting the right to open the highway. The road in question has not been used to any great extent since it was established by the legislature. For a considerable period of time, when the country was new, and the lands unfenced, the public traveled along or near the established road, departing from the lines of the highway, and passing over the ground which was the more easily traveled by reason of its contour; but no work was done upon it except to build one bridge, and partially erect another. Finally, the travel seemed to concentrate upon a line running north and west from the highway in question, to a ford crossing a creek which intersects the highway. A bridge was afterwards built over the creek, at or near the ford; and the public crossed this bridge, and diverting their course to the southwest, came again upon the established road. The road in question has not been used except as stated, since it was first established; but, as we have seen, mere non-user will not operate to discontinue a legally established highway, unless there has been such long-continued adverse possession or transfer of the lands by purchase and sale as that justice demands the public should be estopped from asserting the right to open it up.

The evidence as to adverse possession is in hopeless conflict. But we are constrained to hold that plaintiffs have failed to establish adverse user for the time required by statute. Decedent's grantor recognized the existence

2   of the highway, and fenced with reference thereto. True it is that soon after Bradley purchased he fenced up the road and cultivated the ground upon which it is located. But this was done within the ten years just prior to the commencement of this suit. Moreover, the deceased recognized the existence of the highway shortly before he brought this action, and agreed that it might be opened and improved. On the strength of this agreement, the county commenced grading the road, and had expended more than seventy-five dollars in the erection of a bridge, across the stream of which we have spoken in the line of the established road, before this action was commenced, and, but for the issuance of a temporary writ of injunction, would have had the road in condition for public travel. As this expenditure was made upon the faith of Bradley's agreement not to oppose the opening of the road, his executors should not now be permitted to stop the work, and render unfruitful the expenditure of the money. They are clearly estopped from asserting any rights in or to the established highway. The decree of the district court is right, and it is AFFIRMED.

STATE OF IOWA v. A. M. BAUGUESS, Appellant.

Indictment: INDECENT EXPOSURE. An indictment for lewdness
1   under Code, 1873, section 4012, for indecently exposing one's person is not defective for failure to particularly specify the portion of the body so exposed.

SAME. The persons to whom the accused male an indecent exposure
2   of his person need not be specified in an indictment for lewdness under Code, 1873, section 4012. It is not necessary that any person should witness the exposure.

Appeal from Lee District Court.—HON. HENRY BANK, Judge.

TUESDAY, OCTOBER 4, 1898.

DEFENDANT was indicted and tried for the crime of lewdness and from a judgment of conviction prosecutes this appeal.—*Affirmed.*

T. B. Snyder and *Watson & Weber* for appellant.

Milton Remley, Attorney General, and *Jesse A. Miller* for the State.

WATERMAN, J.—I.   The only matters seriously urged relate to the sufficiency of the indictment.   The material portion of that instrument is as follows: "That A. M. Bauguess, on the 28th day of June, 1897, at the township of Madison, in the county of Lee and state aforesaid, did willfully, unlawfully, and designedly make an open, indecent, and obscene exposure of his person in a public place, to-wit, at or near Pine street, on the north side of Sixth street, in the city of Fort Madison," etc.

II.   The first point sought to be made by appellant is that the indictment is fatally defective in not particularly specifying the part of the body that was expose'.   It is said that no crime is charged, since the offense is not described, but only named.   The indictment was found under section 4012, Code 1873.   The offense is designated as "lewdness," and the different forms of lewdness that are made punishable are described.   The portion of the section that has application here is in these terms: "If any man or woman, married or unmarried, is guilty of open and gross lewdness and designedly make open and indecent or obscene exposure of his or her person or of the person of another, every such person shall be punished," etc.   The offense, we think, is here both named and described.   The phrase, "an indecent exposure of the person," in our opinion, has a well-settled and commonly accepted signification.   It means the exhibition of such parts of the person as modesty or a sense of self-respect requires to be kept usually covered.

Appellant argues that, so far as appears, the exposure might have been of the hand or foot. But the charge is that it was an indecent and obscene exhibition, and this precludes any such idea as that suggested. It has been repeatedly held that an indictment is sufficient if it charges the offense in the language of the statute, when that shows the material facts which constitute the offense. *State v. Whalen,* 98 Iowa, 662, and cases cited. See, also, the more recent case of *State v. Porter,* 105 Iowa, 677. It is thought by counsel for appellant that this case falls within the rule announced in *State v. Butcher,* 79 Iowa, 111, but we think not. The distinction appears clear. In the latter case the offense, while named in the statute, was not described. The crime there charged was "willfully and unlawfully interrupting and disturbing a public school." This language is evidently not intended as a description of the forbidden act. One might "interrupt and disturb" a school by writing threatening letters to a timid or nervous teacher, and yet, we take it, such acts would not be violative of this section. It was therefore held that the acts constituting the offense should be set out in the information, in order that it might appear whether they amounted to a crime. In the statute governing the case at bar, as we have already said, the offense is not only named, but described, and the indictment follows the statute. This is sufficient. See, in addition to the decisions cited from this court, *State v. Griffin,* 43 Tex. 538; *State v. Hazle,* 20 Ark. 156.

III. Another objection made to the indictment is that it does not charge to whom the defendant exposed his person. We know of no rule requiring this to be done. Indeed,
2   we feel confident that, if a case should be made on a confession corroborated by circumstances, a defendant might properly be convicted of this offense, although no person witnessed the indecent act.

IV. It is conceded that the instructions, as abstract propositions of law, are correct; that if the indictment properly charges the offense they should be sustained. But it is contended that they contain elements that are not found in the offense as described in the indictment, and therefore they are erroneous. We have held the indictment sufficient, and a careful reading of the charge convinces us that it is unobjectionable.—AFFIRMED.

$\frac{11}{7}$

STATE OF IOWA v. J. K. OLDS, Appellant.

Forgery: CROSS-EXAMINATION OF PROSECUTOR. The complaining witness in a prosecution for forgery who has testified that he drew a check for the money advanced to defendant on the alleged
1 forged note and also drew a check for other purposes and that he generally destroyed his checks when returned to him cannot properly be asked on cross-examination why he destroyed them, where the question is not confined to the check in controversy and there is no suggestion that it was destroyed for an improper purpose.

Confronting: WAIVER: *Judicial notice.* Where, at defendant's request, the trial was continued on condition that the evidence of witnesses given at previous trials should be admissible, such evi-
2 dence was admissible without formal proof of the agreement for
8 its admission, the court taking judicial notice thereof; and the right of defendant in a criminal case to be confronted by the witnesses against him may be waived.

Instruction on Impeachment. There was testimony tending to impeach and sustain defendant's reputation for truth and veracity
4 and his moral character, and similar testimony concerning other witnesses. The jury was told to consider it as bearing on credibility, and that the evidence of any witness should not be disregarded for this alone, especially in corroborated particulars. *Held,*

a. This was not erroneous as limiting the bearing of the testimony on defendant's character to his credibility and excluding it on his guilt or innocence

b. Defendant not having asked an instruction on the effect of this evidence, the failure to instruct more fully than this is not erroneous.

c. The instruction did not authorize the jury to disregard testimony.

Misconduct of Judge: JURY. An affidavit showed that while the jury was deliberating the judge entered the jury room, and engaged in
5 a conversation with two jurors, which was not disclosed. Another affidavit stated that he had so entered, and, on being informed

that the jury could not agree, told them that he could not communicate with them there, and that they would have to be brought into court. *Held*, that no conduct prejudicial to defendant was shown.

SAME. Where the jury were brought into court in the absence of defendant and his counsel, and stated to the court that they could
7   not agree, and the judge told them that he could not give them any light, and sent them back, defendant was not prejudiced.

SAME. It is not improper for the court to state to the jury in a criminal case on its third trial, after they have been out some time and have reported that they cannot agree, that it is very import-
8   ant that a verdict should be arrived at and that they should retire again and make an earnest effort to reach a verdict, and that in the meantime the court will consider the matter and see if there are additional instructions he can give them

Misconduct of Jurors: NEW TRIAL. Improper statements made by some of the jurors while they were deliberating upon their verdict in a criminal case are not alone sufficient to authorize a new trial, but it must appear that prejudice resulted therefrom, or that the
9   statements were of a character to cause prejudice and that the presumption that they were prejudicial has not been overcome, especially where the affidavits are in conflict both as to what occurred and as to whether it was prejudical, and the trial judge refuses a new trial.

Appeal: AFFIDAVITS It is not competent to show on appeal, by affidavits, what transpired in the presence of the court or judge
6   unless the judge refuses to certify the facts as they are claimed to be by the party desiring his certificate.

Appeal from Dallas District Court.—HON. J. A. STORY, Judge.

TUESDAY, OCTOBER 4, 1898.

THE defendant was convicted of the crime of forgery, and from a judgment which required that he be imprisoned in the state penitentiary at Fort Madison for the term of three years, and pay the costs taxed in the case he appeals.—*Affirmed.*

Shortley & Harpel, White & Clark, and *H. A. Hoyt* for appellant.

Milton Remley, Attorney General, and *Edmund Nichols* for the State.

ROBINSON, J.—The defendant is accused of the crime of forging a negotiable promissory note for the sum of five hundred dollars, which purported to be the note of J. K. Myers and Myer E. Myers. It is averred that by the name last given the defendant meant Mary E. Myers, the wife of J. K. Myers.

I.   It was claimed in behalf of the state that the defendant made several loans of money for one A. Bohner, and that he applied to Bohner to make a loan to J. K. Myers, and stated that Myers and his wife would give their note for that amount; that Bohner agreed to make the loan, drew the required amount of money from a bank, and paid it to the defendant, receiving from him in exchange the note in question. Bohner, having testified that he loaned money and bought horses, checking the money from the bank, sometimes making the checks payable to himself and sometimes to others; that he did not have the check on which he drew the money for the note in question; and that the checks were returned to him,

and generally destroyed,—was asked: "Why did
1   you destroy them?" An objection to the question was
sustained, and of that ruling the appellant complains. We think it was correct. Bohner's reasons for destroying the checks after they had been paid and returned to him were wholly immaterial. The question was not confined to the check used to procure money for the note in controversy, and there is no suggestion in the record that it was destroyed for an improper purpose.

II.   During the trial of the cause the state offered in evidence a transcript of the official shorthand reporter's notes of the testimony given on a former trial of the cause by Marshall D. Ewell. In connection with the offer the statement was made that the "evidence is offered under the stipulation and terms provided in the continuance of this cause at the last term of court." The defendant objected to the introduction of the evidence, "for the reason that it is incompetent, the stipulation referred to not relating to any use of the testimony in this case, and the statute provides that the defendant shall be confronted with the witnesses on his trial." The objection was overruled, and the evidence was admitted. It appears that there have been several trials of this cause. The last one was commenced in April, 1896. At the November term, 1895, the defendant applied for a continuance of the cause. The court found the application to be insufficient in law, but in consideration of the condition of the defendant, the engagement of counsel in other courts, the business of the court, and the early day at which it was required to adjourn, and in the furtherance of justice, continued the cause upon the following, among other, terms and conditions, to-wit: "That the personal presence of any witness or witnesses who were examined and testified on the trial of the cause of the State of Iowa against J. K. Olds, No. 739, criminal, in this court, which was tried at the November term, A. D. 1894, of this court, is waived by the defendant, and defendant expressly consents that upon the trial of this cause at any time hereafter the testimony of any such witness or witnesses as taken by and reduced to writing by the official shorthand reporter at the time thereof may be read in evidence on the trial of this cause, and shall have the same force and effect as if such witness or witnesses were personally present at the time of the trial, and orally examined before the jury, and such testimony may be read to the jury, either from a certified transcript of the testimony of such witness or witnesses, or may be read by the official shorthand reporter taking the same from the notes.   *   *   * To all which the defendant in person and by counsel, in open court, voluntarily agrees thereto, and accepts such terms, and upon the acceptance of the conditions imposed it is ordered that this cause be continued until the next term of this court. *   *   *" The record we have set out is signed by one of the judges of the judicial district of which Dallas county was a part, and is contained in an additional abstract filed by the state, and is shown by the transcript. The appellant

3   contends in this court that the record we have set out was not introduced in evidence in the district court, and denies that any evidence was offered to show that the

transcript read was a transcript of the testimony of Ewell given on a trial of this cause. It is evident that the objections thus urged are purely technical, and made for the first time in this court. The appellant now relies upon the failure of the record to show that the matter we have set out was formally introduced in evidence, or that formal proof was offered to show that the transcript read was a transcript of the evidence which Ewell gave on a trial to this cause. It will be noticed that these alleged defects were not presented by the objection made in the district court. That objection was based upon the alleged ground that the transcript offered was incompetent, that the statute provided that the defendant should be confronted on the trial by the witnesses against him, and that the stipulation did not provide for the use of the testimony in this case. Whether the transcript was admissible in evidence was a preliminary matter, to be determined by the court. For that purpose the court was authorized to take judicial notice of the record in this case, and of the stipulation thereby shown, and it was not necessary to make formal proof of such record and stipulation. It is true that it is the right of the defendant in a criminal prosecution to be confronted on the trial by the witnesses against him, but it is a right which may be waived by him, and the testimony of the witnesses, in writing, be received. *State v. Fooks,* 65 Iowa, 452; *State v. Polson,* 29 Iowa, 133. The order of the court to which the parties agreed provided for the transcript of testimony which was received in evidence, and the court did not err in receiving it.

III. The sixth paragraph of the charge to the jury is as follows: "Testimony has been introduced to impeach certain witnesses in this case, tending to show that their reputation for truth and veracity is bad; also that their general moral character is bad. Testimony has also been introduced tending to sustain their reputation for truth and veracity, and their general moral character. You are to consider such testimony as bearing on the credibility of such witnesses, but you should not, for such reason alone, disregard their testimony, especially in those particulars, if any, where they are corroborated by other credible witnesses, or by facts and circumstances proven by the evidence in the case. You are to consider all their testimony in the light of, and in connection with, all the other evidence and circumstances disclosed in the case, and give to the evidence of said witnesses such credibility as you may deem it entitled to receive."

4   The defendant testified as a witness, and testimony was introduced which tended to show that his reputation for truth and veracity and his moral character were bad, while other testimony tended to show that they were good. Similar testimony was given respecting other witnesses. The appellant complains of the portion of the charge quoted, and alleges that it erroneously limited the effect of the proof of his general moral character to his credibility, whereas it should have been given weight in determining the fact of his guilt, and, further, that it licensed the jury to disregard testimony. We do not think either of the objections is well founded. The testimony offered by the state was given after the defendant had testified, for the purpose of affecting his credibility as a witness. The portion of the charge in question did not designate the defendant specifically, but was general in its terms, and applied to all of the witnesses whose credibility had been assailed. It did not in any manner refer to the weight which should be given to proof of moral character as tending to prove or disprove the innocence of the defendant. In view of the character of the testimony given, and the purpose which the court designed to accomplish by the portion of the charge in question, it was the duty of the defendant to ask such further instruction as he desired in regard to the effect of the evidence in controversy, and the court did not err, in the absence of a request of that kind, in not instructing more fully respecting such evidence. We do not find any ground for the claim that the charge authorized the jury to disregard testimony.

IV.   It is insisted with great earnestness that the evidence does not sustain the verdict.   Much evidence, including the testimony of numerous expert witnesses, was given to establish the guilt of the defendant, and to disprove it, and it is evident that the case was not only warmly contested, but that it was thoroughly tried.   Much evidence tended strongly to show that the defendant was guilty as charged ; and, while it was contradicted in the most direct and positive manner, we cannot say that the evidence of guilt was not sufficient to sustain the conviction.

V.   The affidavits of jurors were used in support of a motion for a new trial.   One of them avers that, after the jury had been deliberating about three hours, the trial judge entered the jury room, and engaged in conversation with two jurors, but that the conversation was not heard by the affiant.   Another affidavit states that the judge entered the jury room while the jury was there; that he was informed that the jurors had difficulty in agreeing as to some of the evidence, and a juror named Higgs said he could not agree with the others; that the judge, in response, said he could not communicate with the jury in its room, and that it would have to be brought into court.   If the affidavits be accepted as competent proof of what occurred, it does not appear that anything was said or done by the judge which could have prejudiced the defendant.   It is not competent, however, to show by affidavits what transpires in the presence of the court or judge, unless the judge refuses to certify the facts as they are claimed to be by the party desiring his certificate.   See *State v. La Grange*, 99 Iowa, 10.   It appears from a certificate of the trial judge that the jury was brought into court in the absence of the defendant and his attorney; that the jury then informed the court that an agreement had not been reached, and that the cause of the disagreement was a question of fact; that the court thereupon stated that it could not give the jury any light, and it was returned to the jury room.

What was thus done and said was entirely proper, and without prejudice to the defendant. Nothing in the record, excepting the affidavits already referred to, shows that the judge
entered the jury room. It appears from a statement
8   in the record, not found in the judge's certificate, that
on one occasion when the jury was brought before the
court and reported that it had not been able to agree on
account of a difference respecting a question of fact the court
said to the jurors: "This is a case that it is very important
that a verdict should be arrived at; and, while you have been
out for quite a long while, I feel that it is the duty of the court
to ask you to retire again, and make an earnest effort on the
part of each one of you to arrive at a verdict, and in the meantime I shall consider the matter, and see if there is some additional instructions that I may be able to give you, that may
help you some in arriving at a verdict. You may retire with
your bailiff." There was nothing in what was thus said and
done of which the defendant can justly complain. It appears
that there had been two pervious trials of the cause, and that
fact and the character of the case made an agreement by the
jury especially desirable.

VI.   The appellant complains of misconduct on the part
of some of the jurors. It appears that for a considerable time
preceding the agreement eleven of the jurors favored a verdict
of guilty, and that Juror Higgs alone favored a verdict of not
guilty. Affidavits of several of the jurors have been
9   filed, which state, in substance, that while the jury was
considering the case, and while Higgs was contending
for a verdict for the defendant, some of the jurors told him,
in order to induce him to agree to a verdict of guilty, that,
counting jurors who had favored conviction on the former
trials, twenty-five or thirty jurors believed the defendant
guilty; that defendant had been caught with a woman or
women in a block in the town of Perry, suggesting that he
had been guilty of immoral sexual relations with the woman
or women; that he had been in several "scrapes" in Perry

before, although the nature of the "scrapes" was not stated, excepting that they were dishonorable; that the defendant had been in at least two other "scrapes" of the same nature as that involved in this case; that he was generally crooked; that he was a bad man generally, and ought to be convicted, and that the general outside opinion was that he was guilty. Some of the affidavits state that while the jury was deliberating some of the jurors had a conversation in the hall adjoining the jury room, with the sheriff, who was acting as bailiff in charge of the jury; that the sheriff was then told that there was "no way of bringing Higgs over unless we freeze him out," and the sheriff answered, "You will have to freeze him out, then, as the judge says there will have to be a verdict;" that the statement of the sheriff was repeated to Higgs; that Higgs was asked by the jurors how much he was getting for hanging the jury, and he was accused of having improper motives in doing so, and it was suggested that he had received money for that purpose; that it was repeatedly said in the presence of Higgs that the other jurors would freeze him out; that they could stand it longer than he could. Other statements of an improper nature are alleged to have been made during the deliberations of the jury. An affidavit made by Higgs states that from what the judge said about having a verdict he became strongly impressed with the idea that a verdict would have to be rendered; that he did not believe that the evidence showed that the defendant was guilty; that the other jurors insisted on a verdict for the state; that the sheriff had informed him that the defendant would get a re-hearing in the supreme court, and would not have to go to jail; that the affiant believed he could not hold out much longer against younger and more robust men, and, not caring to endure longer the insinuations and covert abuse to which he had been subjected for hours, he finally agreed to the verdict which was rendered. The larger part of the affidavit of Higgs is devoted to matters which inhere in the verdict, and is, therefore, of no force. However, the competent allegations of misconduct contained in affidavits filed by the defendant would have been ample, had they not been controverted, to require a new trial. *State v. La Grange*, 99 Iowa, 10. But the counter affidavits filed by the state show that many of the claims made by the defendant are without sufficient grounds, and that prejudice could not have resulted to him from the matter of which he complains. It is shown that the insinuations respecting the motives and conduct of Higgs were spoken in jest, and were so understood by him; that before the agreement was reached it was stated by different jurors, and agreed to by all, that all remarks which had been made, and which were not based upon the evidence, should be disregarded, and the case determined solely upon its merits, and that thereafter no remarks were made not based upon the evidence offered in court; that it was said the case would probably be appealed to the supreme court, but it was agreed that the determination of the case by the jury could not be affected by that fact, and that it was agreed by all, especially by Higgs, that no weight could be given to the result of any former trial, and that Higgs was treated kindly and with respect, by his fellow jurors. The sheriff, in an affidavit made by him, denies explicitly having made the statements attributed to him, and recites what was said and done by him; and, if his statement be correct, he was not guilty of any misconduct. It is no doubt true that improper statements were made by some jurors while they were deliberating upon their verdict, but that alone is not sufficient to authorize a new trial. It must appear that prejudice resulted from the statements, or that they were of a character to cause prejudice, and that the presumption that they were prejudiced has not been overcome. In *Foedisch v. Railway Co.*, 100 Iowa, 728, it was said: "A verdict will not be set aside merely because a jury member has, in violation of his sworn duty, talked to persons about the case. It must appear that the misconduct was such as to materially affect the substantial rights of the complaining party." In *Carbon v. City of Ottumwa*, 95 Iowa, 524, it

was said: "It is not, however, every act of misconduct of a
juror which will warrant a court in setting aside a verdict. It
should be made to appear that the misconduct prejudiced the
complaining party. The circumstances disclosed should be
such as to satisfy the trial court that a fair and impartial trial
has not been had." The cases cited were civil, but the rules
stated are applicable in criminal cases, although it is true that
on some grounds the courts will set aside verdicts more readily
in criminal than in civil cases. *State v. Wise,* 83 Iowa, 596.
Among the cases which tend to support the rule we have
announced in this case are *State v. Woodson,* 41 Iowa, 425;
State v. Beste, 91 Iowa, 565. A careful examination of the
case satisfies us that the misconduct of the jurors to which we
have referred, so far as it is shown, was not prejudicial.
What we have said disposes of the controlling questions in the
case. We have considered all questions presented in argument, but some are not of sufficient importance to justify
special mention of them. It is sufficient to say that we do
not find any ground for disturbing the judgment of the district court, and it is AFFIRMED.

STATE OF IOWA, Appellant, v. J. A. GUNN and R. J. BOAT-
MAN.

Appeal by State: REVIEW: *Rulings on evidence.* Where the objections to certain questions asked by the state in a criminal prosecution, on the ground that they were "incompetent, irrelevant, and
1   immaterial, privileged and hearsay," were sustained without stating the ground for the ruling, the question whether the objections
were properly sustained on the ground that the question called
for confidential communications will not be considered on an
appeal *by the state,* where the rulings of the court were mostly
sustainable on other grounds.

Evidence. In a prosecution of B. for committing an abortion by the
use of drugs and instruments, on a woman, causing her death, a
druggist testified for the defense that deceased came to his store
a short time before she was sick, with a prescription which she
stated a Dr. S. had given her, which witness had refused to fill.

2   Evidence was then given over objection that the drug prescribed
would produce an abortion, and of other facts to show Dr. S. was
the author of the prescription. *Held,* that the evidence was inadmissible, on account of its immateriality. The evidence was not
admissible on the ground that it contradicted her dying declaration, that the abortion was produced by a doctor who was one of
the defendants, since the fact that the deceased attempted it in the
way described would not tend to prove that she would not afterwards permit it to be done by drugs and instruments in the hands
of defendant, as charged in the indictment.

Appeal from Mahaska District Court.—HON. BEN McCOY,
Judge.

TUESDAY, OCTOBER 4, 1898.

INDICTMENT for murder in the second degree. Verdict
of acquittal, and the state appealed.—*Reversed.*

Milton Remley, Attorney General, and *Jesse A. Miller*
for the State.

No appearance for appellee.

GRANGER, J.—The indictment charges the offense to
have been committed upon one Irene Severt, a woman then
pregnant, in an attempt to produce abortion by the use of
drugs and instruments. The death occurred September 17,
1895. The following written statement was signed by her
September 14, 1895:

"(1) The man that seduced me was Mr. J. A. Gunn.
(2) He was present when Dr. R. J. Boatman committed the
abortion. The doctor used instruments four or five times. I
also took four or five capsuls prior to the forceps or the instruments. (3) Mr. Gunn came to my room several times, and
came into bed to me, and got me in the family way. (4) Mr.
Gunn employed Dr. Boatman to produce the abortion. Irene
Severt.

"The above was taken September the 14, 1895. Ira
Barr. Josie Rankin."

"(Exhibit B.)"

The court admitted in evidence the following part of the statement, and rejected the balance: "He (Mr. J. A. Gunn) was present when Dr. R. J. Boatman committed the abortion. The doctor used instruments four or five times. I also took four capsules prior to the use of the forceps or instruments." The part of the statement excluded is as follows: "The man that seduced me was Mr. J. A. Gunn. Mr. Gunn came to my room several times, and came into bed to me, and got me in the family way. Mr. Gunn employed Dr. Boatman to produce the abortion."

It seems to have been the purpose, largely, in taking this appeal, to obtain a construction of section 3643, Code 1873, as to confidential communications between a physician and his patient. One Dr. Sigafoos was the attending physician before the death of Irene Severt, and wrote the statement that was signed by her. He was a witness for the state; and the complaints, in argument, on this branch of the case, are as to rulings of the court excluding questions to him as a witness. The following is appellant's statement, in argument, of the questions refused by the court, wherein the court is thought to be in error: "The doctor was asked in separate questions who suggested the making of the statement; whether the question of having a witness to the paper was discussed between them; whether Irene said when she made the statement that she wanted people to know its contents after she died; whether she objected to the calling of a certain witness; and whether or not, at the time the statement was made, she requested the doctor to get paper and write what she wanted to say, and she would sign it; whether he read Exhibit B to her, and whether she said it was all right or not, and true; whether, as a physician, he considered her in her right mind at the time the statement was made; whether there was anything in connection with the execution of Exhibit B or the conversation between them which was necessary for him to know in order to treat her case; whether it

1

was necessary for him to know, in order to treat her, who committed the abortion; whether, at any time prior to the making
of the statement, she stated voluntarily to him that she
wanted to make a statement; whether he asked her to make
the statement; whether at the time the statement was made
she wanted to make the statement, and stated that she wanted
to make it before witnesses." It is said that the court sustained objections to each of these questions, on the ground
that they called for confidential communications between a
physician and his patient. The argument refers to a part of
the record to show the fact. It seems to be a misapprehension. To all of the questions in that part of the record
objected to, the grounds of objection are "incompetent, irrelevant, and immaterial, privileged and hearsay." The record
does not disclose that a single ruling is based on the ground
that the question calls for a confidential communication. The
ground of the ruling is stated in but a single case, and then it
is because the question calls for hearsay evidence. It may be
said that, with slight exceptions, we think the rulings of the
court sustainable on other grounds than the one argued. The
case is before us on the state's appeal merely to settle the law;
and, with no argument for appellees, we are not disposed to
consider questions of grave importance that do not affirmatively arise on the record. It is to be remembered that the
statement, as a dying declaration, was admitted in evidence,
with the exceptions stated, so that the evidence in question
was not to lay the foundation for the admission of the statement, but only as bearing on its credibility and weight as
evidence; and it is on this theory that the case is argued.
Before we can say that the court erred as to any of these
questions, we must be prepared to hold that no one of the
objections made to a particular question was good, and no
complaint is made to justify such a conclusion. The case
is not before us as it would be on an appeal by the defendants,
when it would be our duty to examine the record, and protect
the defendants from prejudice because of error. It seems

unnecessary to say more on this branch of the case. The law as to appeals by the state in such cases does not contemplate that we shall deal with imaginary questions; and it is to be said of the questions argued that they arise only upon a supposition that, of several grounds stated in support of our objection, the court based its ruling on the particular one argued.

II.   Mr. Dale was a witness for the defense. He is a druggist, and was permitted to give evidence, against objections, that Irene Severt, before she was sick, a short time, came to his store with a prescription, saying that Dr. Sigafoos gave it to her. The following appears: "You may state what further she said to you at that time in relation to Dr. Sigafoos and the prescription. A. Why, she handed me the prescription and told me she wanted it filled. I took the prescription, and walked back of the case, and studied it about three minutes. I turned around, and said, 'Who wrote this?' She said, 'Dr. Sigafoos.' I said I couldn't fill it. She made a motion, and said, 'I guess Dr. Sigafoos knows his business.' I said, 'I guess I know mine; I can't fill it.' She kind of laughed, and walked out. That is the substance of it." . It appears from the testimony of the witness that he declined to fill the prescription. This fact appeared quite early in his testimony. After it appeared that the prescription was not filled, so that it was apparent that the abortion was not attempted in that way,—that is, by the taking of that drug,—considerably other testimony, including what we have set out, was taken to show the nature of the drug; as, that it would produce abortion, what physicians were in Fremont, and other testimony tending to show that Dr. Sigafoos was the author of the prescription. It is urged that it was error to admit such testimony. Had Irene Severt at that time procured a drug of that nature, it would, of proper to have shown the fact as bearing on of what produced the condition she was in ath. an attempted abortion in some form being the evident cause of her death. But, with the conclusive statement that she did not get the drug we are not able to imagine a reason for the admission of the evidence on that subject that followed the statement, including what is above set out. Among the objections to questions was that of their being immaterial, and we think such objections well taken. We cannot well argue the proposition, for we have no reasoning in support of the holding. In the record, we find a statement of counsel for defendant, to the court, in favor of the admission of the evidence, that it was to contradict her dying declaration; but it does not have that effect. The evidence would only prove that she desired and was attempting to produce abortion; and that she was so attempting was not in dispute. That she attempted it in that way, and failed, would not tend to prove that she did not afterwards permit it to be done in the way charged in the indictment. We need not consider the question whether or not such evidence would be proper if it did tend to contradict the dying declarations. The judgment of acquittal must stand, under the statute. The ruling by which the improper testimony was admitted, as suggested, must be REVERSED.

STATE OF IOWA v. ZELMAR HUGHES, Appellant.

Seduction: WHAT CONSTITUTES. Prosecutrix was a country girl, seventeen years of age, and defendant was several years her senior. He
1 was her suitor and he flattered and caressed her, and promised that if she would submit to him, no conception should result and if it did he would marry her. *Held,* she having submitted, a conviction was warranted.

EVIDENCE: *Curing error.* Where, in a prosecution for seduction, prosecutrix testified that she told her mother of her condition soon after the act, and the mother testified that she had discovered her
4 daughter's condition at that time, error in admitting the mother's testimony because it was based on what prosecutrix told her was cured by withdrawing prosecutrix testimony from the jury.

CORROBORATION. Evidence that defendant, though engaged to another, waited on prosecutrix as a suitor and said that he "was

going to show her a hot time" and that he said, after the act, not
8   having seen her for a week, that he was going to her house for
sexual intercourse, corroborates prosecutrix. Such statements
are rebuttal where intercourse is denied, and harmless, if not
strictly rebuttal.

COMPETENCY: *Objection.* The testimony of the mother of the prosecutrix that she discovered that her daughter was pregnant about
5   four weeks after the alleged seduction is admissible, where the
objection raised was only to the competency of the evidence and
not of the witness.

SEDUCTION. A sentence of two years and six months imprisonment
for the crime of seduction is not excessive where the evidence
6   tended to show that the defendant paid his attentions to the
prosecutrix with the deliberate purpose of accomplishing her ruin.

Appeal from Pottawattamie District Court.—HON. W. N.
MACY, Judge.

WEDNESDAY, OCTOBER 5, 1898.

THE defendant having been accused and convicted of the
crime of seduction, appeals.—*Affirmed.*

Benjamin & Preston and *L. T. Genung* for appellant.

Milton Remley, Attorney General, and *Jesse A. Miller*
for the State.

LADD, J.—That some man had sexual intercourse with
the prosecutrix about March 30, 1896, is put beyond dispute
by the birth of a fully-developed child, December 18th of
the same year. As to whether the defendant is that man, the
evidence is in conflict, she affirming and he denying. Her
previous chastity is not questioned, nor is the fact that she
was then unmarried. But the defendant insists the evidence
utterly fails to show that intercourse, if had, was procured
      through artifice, flattery, or deception. That he paid
1   his attentions to the prosecutrix, by taking her to
      church several times, to a literary society, a theater,
and a dancing party, during February and March, 1896, is
admitted; and she testified that he hugged and kissed her

repeatedly, told her she was pretty and sweet, and on the night in question addressed her as his "pretty sweetness." On the way home from the dancing party, according to her testimony, after some caressing, he took liberties with her person, and told her what he wanted, and that he was going to have it. She responded that he was not. He then said he would not harm her, and would be careful, and remarked: "You don't need to be afraid of me knocking you up. If I was ornery enough to do the like, and get a woman in a fix, I would marry her. I know my sweet little girl won't refuse me." He also promised her that he would not get her in a family way. He then helped her from the buggy to the robe laid on the ground by the roadside, and the act complained of occurred. All of this he denies. The evidence tends to show that the prosecutrix submitted to the embraces of the defendant, if at all, by reason of his promises that he would not get her in a family way, and that, if he did, he would marry her. While the statement, if made, was not direct, it was meant to be so understood by her, and she so accepted it. His assurances that no harm would be done evidently related to physical injury, and were not representations as to the character of the act. But it cannot be said that she relied upon these promises entirely freed from the flattery and arts he had been previously and was then practicing. Indeed, it was held in *Wilson v. State,* 73 Ala. 527, that the prosecutrix will not be permitted to testify that she yielded in consequence of a promise of marriage or of any act or declaration of the defendant, because that is a matter of inference to be drawn by the jury from the facts and circumstances proven or presumed. While such is not the rule in this state, it is yet true that the jury may and should consider all the influences exerted by the defendant in overcoming the objections of the prosecutrix. Here she says the promises caused her to yield, but she does not state that these were the only influences operating on her will. What she doubtless meant was that but for these promises she would

not have submitted. As said in *State v. Higdon,* 32 Iowa,
262: "The exact amount or what kind of seductive arts is
necessary to establish the offense charged cannot be defined.
Every case must depend upon its own peculiar circumstances,
together with the condition in life, advantages, age, and intelligence of the parties. All these circumstances, it must be
presumed, were observed and duly considered by the jury and
court below. From her demeanor they could tell whether her
story went beyond or fell short of the real facts." It was
held in *State v. Knutson,* 91 Iowa, 549, that to induce intercourse by a promise to marry the prosecutrix if anything
went wrong might constitute seduction, the court remarking:
"It is said that the promise of defendant, which caused her
to yield to him the last time, was conditional, and wholly
insufficient to induce a chaste woman to submit to sexual
intercourse. It appears that several promises were made,
and their effect upon the prosecutrix was for the jury to
determine." In *State v. Hemm,* 82 Iowa, 609, an instruction
to the effect that procuring intercourse "by representing that
there was nothing wrong in the act, and that no one would
find it out," constituted seduction, is approved, and it is there
said: "By the act of intercourse in this case, the prosecutrix
became a mother, and his representations were false. If she
yielded because of his representations, it was a case of deception or fraud, for he was the means of her public exposure.
His representations were no less than a promise that it would
not be known, which he rendered false. See *State v. Prizer,*
49 Iowa, 534. But it is said that a woman with chaste character would not yield because of such representations. That
was a question for the jury. The law does not determine that
she would not." The reasoning of these cases leads to the
inevitable conclusion that to induce an unmarried woman of
previous chastity to yield her virtue by a promise of marriage
in event she becomes pregnant may be seduction. Whether
a woman of chaste character would so yield, and whether, if
she so does, it is voluntary, and to gratify her desires, rather

than because of such conditional promise, may well be considered in connection with all the facts and circumstances shown upon the trial. But it cannot be said as a matter of law that an unsophisticated country girl of seventeen years, when addressed by a young man of five or six years her senior, with possibly a greater knowledge of the world, as in this case, and under the circumstances disclosed, would necessarily be of previous unchastity in yielding on the strength of such a promise, or that she submitted as a result of passion, rather than the false promises of the defendant. The question is not determined in *State v. Reilly*, 104 Iowa, 13. Where a promise of marriage must be the inducing cause, as in New York and Oregon, intercourse procured by conditional agreement to marry in event of conception is adjudged not to be within the statute. *People v. Van Alstyne*, 144 N. Y. 361 (39 N. E. Rep. 343); *State v. Adams*, 25 Or. 172 (35 Pac. Rep. 36). As applied to our statute, the reasoning of these authorities is not controlling, but important in passing on the facts of each particular case.

II. Proof of acquaintance and of opportunity is not alone sufficient corroboration of the prosecuting witness. *State v. Painter*, 50 Iowa, 317; *State v. Smith*, 54 Iowa, 743; *State v. Araah*, 55 Iowa, 258. The evidence in

2   this case, however, tends to show that the defendant was waiting on the prosecutrix as a suitor. If this were not true, how, then, shall the fact that he was with her, attending church or entertainments, taking long drives, seven or eight times in as many weeks, be explained? There are some circumstances indicating the deliberate purpose on his part of accomplishing her ruin. He was engaged at the time, and was married to another within two weeks after the alleged seduction. Besides, one witness testified that the defendant told him prior to the offense that he was going to go with the prosecutrix, and was going "to show her a hot time." To another witness, on the Sunday after that event, he stated that he was going to the home of prosecutrix for sexual inter

course. If the jurors believed he was waiting on Cyrene only ostensibly as a suitor, and relied on the testimony of the other witnesses referred to, then they might well find that evidence other than that of the injured party tended to connect the defendant with the commission of the offense.

III. It is said that the evidence of defendant's statement that he was going to the house of prosecutrix for sexual intercourse was not admissible. This occurred within a week after the alleged seduction. The defendant had not seen the prosecutrix in the meantime. The only fair inference

3   to be drawn from the statement was that such a relation existed between them. He had denied on examination any illicit connection with the girl, and this tended directly to rebut such evidence. Moreover, it tended to corroborate, as before stated, the story of the prosecutrix. See *State v. Hill,* 91 Mo. 423 (4 S. W. Rep. 121). Even if the evidence was not strictly in rebuttal, this was without any prejudice to the defendant.

IV. The mother of the prosecuting witness, over the objection of the defendant, testified that she discovered her daughter's condition two weeks after the defendant's wedding, which occurred thirteen days after the alleged seduc-

4   tion. The court had allowed Cyrene to state that she informed her mother of her condition at that time, but afterwards withdrew such evidence from the jury. The defendant insists that this information could alone be derived from the statements made by the daughter. If so, then the court, in withdrawing the evidence of the daughter

5   from the jury, cured the alleged error. But the existence of pregnancy was a fact proper to be proven on such a trial, and no objection was made to the competency of the witness. The evidence was competent; the witness may have been incompetent. But the objection of incompetency went to the evidence only, and not to the witness. *White v. Smith,* 54 Iowa, 233; *Ball v. Railway Co.,* 74 Iowa, 132.

V.   The claim that the evidence established the crime of rape rather than seduction, and the exception to the eleventh paragraph of the court's charge to the jury, are

6
without merit; and require no consideration.   The defendant was sentenced to serve a term of two years and six months in the penitentiary.   As said, there are circumstances tending to show that he paid his attentions to the prosecutrix for the deliberate purpose of accomplishing her ruin.   In view of this state of the record, we cannot say the judgment is excessive.—AFFIRMED.

E. M. HEATH V. WILLIAM HALFHILL, G. W. ASH and B. D. NICHOLS, Appellants.

Jurisdiction: JUSTICE OF THE PEACE.   A justice of the peace does
2   not acquire jurisdiction of a defendant, residing in another county, although the latter appears and files a counter claim.

CONSTABLES: *Liability.*   An officer is not liable for a levy under an
1   execution regular on its face, issued on a judgment void only for
4   want of jurisdiction of defendant, even where he had notice of the defect when making the levy, unless he acted with improper motives.

SAME: *Justices.*   A justice is not liable for renewing in good faith an
1-3 execution on a judgment void only for want of jurisdiction of
4-5 defendant, even where he made the renewal with notice of the defect.

Equity: RELIEF BY INJUNCTION.   The fact that a void judgment has
7   been satisfied by execution will not prevent the restraining of the enforcement of such judgment.

SAME.   Where a judgment is restrained and the judgment defendant
1   awarded damages, the court has no power, over the objection of
6   the judgment creditor, to order money collected on the judgment by garnishment to be refunded to a garnishee who was not a party to the suit to restrain.

Appeal from Clayton District Court.—HON. A. N. HOBSON, Judge.

WEDNESDAY, OCTOBER 5, 1898.

ACTION to enjoin the enforcement of a judgment. From a decree in plaintiff's favor the defendants appeal.—*Modified.*

S. T. Richards for appellants.

Newberry Bros. and *J. E. Corlett* for appellee.

WATERMAN, J.—We may say in the beginning that the undisputed testimony shows that the plaintiff, Heath, was, at the time of the proceedings complained of, a resident of Delaware county. In July, 1896, the defendant Halfhill

1   instituted an action against plaintiff for the recovery
         of money, before a justice of the peace in and for
Clayton county. Defendant Ash is the justice before whom such action was brought, and the other defendant, Nichols, is the constable who executed certain process, of which more will be said later. The action proceeded to judgment. Execution was afterwards levied by garnishing one Ringer, and seizing a certain buggy belonging to plaintiff. The sum of forty-two dollars was collected under the Ringer garnishment, and the buggy, which the evidence shows was of the value of seventy-five dollars, was sold on execution. The relief asked in the case at bar is that the enforcement of said judgment be enjoined. The execution spoken of was levied after this action was begun, and the amounts collected thereon were sufficient to satisfy the judgment. The district court, on finding in plaintiff's favor, rendered a decree restraining, in terms, the collection of the judgment, and also allowed a recovery for the amount that had been collected on execution. The action before the justice was based upon an open account. It is clear that he had no jurisdiction. Code 1873, section 3507; *McMeans v. Cameron,* 51 Iowa,

         691; *Boyer v. Moore,* 42 Iowa, 544. Appellants seem to
2   think this case is not governed by the authorities cited,
         for the reason, as they insist, the defendant in the
action before the justice appeared and filed a counterclaim. In response to this it is enough for us to say that there is no

evidence that any counterclaim was filed; and in the first
of the cases we have just cited it is held that the justice does
not acquire jurisdiction of a nonresident defendant, even
though the latter appears, and goes to trial without objection.

II. Appellants insist that in no event can the justice
and constable be held liable, under the testimony. The rule
is that a justice of the peace is not liable for his judicial conduct, unless he acts corruptly. *Gowing v. Gowgill,*
3   12 Iowa, 495; *Londegan v. Hammer,* 30 Iowa, 508;
Henke v. McCord, 55 Iowa, 378. There is no evidence of improper motive in this case. As to the constable,
the law is that he is protected when acting under a writ, regular on its face. *Henke v. McCord, supra.* If the court has
jurisdiction of the subject-matter (and it had in the case
complained of), but has failed to get jurisdiction of the person, an execution regular on its face will protect the officer.
Savacool v. Boughton, 5 Wend. 170; *Howard v. Clark,* 43
Mo. 344. Indeed, we think the point is ruled in favor of said
officers by the case of *Thompson v. Jackson,* 93 Iowa, 376,
which, in its facts, is almost identical with the case at bar.

An attempt, however, is made to distinguish the cases
4   in two particulars. It is said, first, that the officers
here had notice of plaintiff's claim of want of jurisdiction before they acted. We do not perceive that this affects
the matter. If defendant had appeared in the justice court,
and set up the want of jurisdiction, and the court in good faith
had found against him, it could not well be claimed that the
justice would be liable for his erroneous ruling. If the justice
would be protected in such case in issuing the writ, certainly
the constable would be in executing it. Again, it said that,
while some of the acts of a justice of the peace are judicial,
for an error in which he is not liable, others—such as the issuance of process—are purely ministerial, and for these
5   he may be held when he acts illegally. This position
may be granted. The facts here are that the justice
renewed the execution against defendant after he had notice

that defendant claimed residence in another county. While
the act of issuing process of some kind is ministerial, we are
not prepared to say that the renewal of this execution, which
was issued on a judgment rendered by the justice himself,
comes within that term. We are certainly not going to hold
that the justice is protected from all liability in deciding that
Halfhill was entitled to an execution, but is liable because he
issued the writ. This point, though not expressly raised in
Thompson v. Jackson, was necessarily involved in that case,
and our holding is in accord with what is there said. The
money judgment must be reversed as to Ash and Nicols.

III. Halfhill's liability, we think, must be restricted
to the value of the buggy alone, because of certain features
of the decree. The trial court, instead of giving plaintiff
judgment for the amount collected under the garnish-
6 ment, ordered that sum returned to Ringer, the garnishee, and rendered judgment in plaintiff's favor for
only the value of the buggy, seventy-five dollars. Ringer was
not a party to this action, and no lawful order could be made
giving him any right against the defendants. This provision
of the decree is invalid. Plaintiff, not having appealed from
the judgment, can have no more favorable finding in this
court.

IV. Appellants urge the claim that the case is not of
equitable cognizance, because the judgment was satisfied
before the decree was rendered. This complaint is first made
in this court. But, waiving this fact, we have to say
7 that the satisfaction of the judgment was enforced.
The cause, when commenced, was well founded, and
presented an issue properly triable in equity. The trial court
rightly retained it for such judgment as would protect plaintiff. The decree against Halfhill, modified as we have suggested, will be permitted to stand. The entry will therefore
be, judgment in favor of Ash and Nicols for costs, and as
further modified by what we have herein said, the decree to
stand AFFIRMED.

F. F. FAVILLE, Administrator of the Estate of P. Howes, Deceased, Appellant, v. LUNDVALL & COMPANY.

Principal and Agent: LANDLORD AND TENANT. The authority of an agent to make a lease does not imply an authority from his principal or principal's assignee, to cancel it.

Appeal from Buena Vista District Court.—HON. W. B. QUARTON, Judge.

WEDNESDAY, OCTOBER 5, 1898.

THIS action was commenced September 20, 1894, by P. Howes, since deceased, as assignee of a certain lease of real estate by L. B. Gregory, by F. F. Faville, his agent, and the defendant company, lessee, to recover ninety dollars and interest as rent from April 1 to September 30, 1894. A landlord's attachment was asked and issued. On October 23, 1894, the defendant answered in substance as follows: They admitted that they rented the premises as stated, and that under the lease there were one hundred and eight dollars due the lessor. They deny that Gregory assigned his rights under the lease to the plaintiff. They allege that they have been ready to pay the rent until after the twenty-eighth of September, 1894; that some two months previous to that time one Mills demanded the rent, and served notice on them demanding possession of the premises. They allege that they are ready and willing to pay the rent due under the lease to the party entitled to receive the same, and ask that Mills be made a party to this suit. Thereafter plaintiff died, and Faville, administrator, was substituted as party plaintiff, and on January 10, 1896, filed an amendment to the petition, alleging that since the commencement of this action the rent has accrued under the lease for the full term, and asking to recover three hundred and sixty dollars, with interest. March

25, 1896, the defendants amended their answer, alleging that,
on or about the twentieth day of April, 1894, said lease was,
by oral agreement with the plaintiff, or his agent or
attorney, F. F. Faville, canceled, and that the defendants
vacated the premises, and were released from further responsibility in connection with the lease; that at the time defendants
vacated the premises there was due to the proper owner
thereof one hundred and twenty dollars, which sum defendants produced in court, and asked to be discharged, with costs.
Plaintiff replied, denying that there was any agreement to
cancel said lease; denying that Faville, as agent for the plaintiff, had any power or authority to cancel it; and alleging that
there was no consideration for such an agreement. A jury
being waived, the case was tried to the court, and, C. B. Mills
having dismissed his petition of intervention, $17.10 of the
costs were taxed to him. On the issues joined between the
plaintiff and defendants the court found with the defendants
and ordered one hundred and twenty dollars held by the clerk
to be paid to the plaintiff, and rendered judgment against the
plaintiff for the remaining costs. Plaintiff appeals.—
Reversed.

M. J. Sweeley and *F. F. Faville* for appellant.

GIVEN, J.—I. We have no argument for appellees.
There was no dispute as to Faville's authority to execute the
lease, but whether authorized or not, both parties recognized
the lease by giving and taking possession and by paying and
receiving rent under it. The defense relied upon is the
alleged cancellation of the lease. The burden was on the
defendant to establish that allegation, and this, we think, they
failed to do. Authority to Faville to make the lease did not
carry with it authority from Gregory to cancel it; much less
would authority from Gregory to make the lease carry with
it authority from Howes' assignee of the lessee, to cancel it.
The allegation is that "the lease set out in plaintiff's petition

was by oral agreement canceled, and by agreement with the plaintiff, or his agent and attorney, F. F. Faville, the defendants vacated said premises, and were released from further responsibility in connection with the lease contract." There is not a syllable of evidence that Howes ever agreed to a cancellation of the lease or vacation of the premises, nor that he ever authorized Faville to make such an agreement. Neither is there any evidence that Gregory ever authorized such an agreement. The defendants Lundvall and Nordstrum testified to a conversation with Faville in which they asked him if he would cancel the lease, as they had a chance to rent the new building, and that he said that, if it was a favor to them, he would see that the lease was cancelled at the time they were ready to move, and that they did not pay him anything for the release. It may well be questioned whether this shows an agreement to release, but, in view of what we have said to Faville's want of authority, we think there was no evidence to sustain the allegation of a release.—*Reversed.*

GEORGE R. STREVER v. CHICAGO & NORTHWESTERN RAILWAY COMPANY, Appellant.

Stock Killing: LIABILITY: *Prejudicial error.* An instruction which allows a recovery for the killing of cattle on unfenced depot grounds, by a train running faster than eight miles an hour, is erroneous because it failed to require that the cattle injured should be "running at large" (Code, 1873, section 1289,) and prejudice will be presumed from such error in the absence of a showing that the verdict was based on other grounds of negligence.

Appeal from Hamilton District Court.—HON. D. R. HINDMAN, Judge.

WEDNESDAY, OCTOBER 5, 1898.

THE petition is in four counts, in the first three of which damages are sought because of fires set out or caused by defendant's locomotives. In the fourth count recovery is sought for cattle killed and injured on one of defendant's depot grounds by one of its trains, negligence being charged in the operation of the train. There was a recovery on each of the four counts, the general verdict being for plaintiff in the sum of one hundred and seventy-five dollars and ninety-one cents. From the judgment the defendant appealed.—*Reversed.*

Hubbard, Dawley & Wheeler for appellant.

A. N. Boeye for appellee.

Granger, J.—On this appeal, no question is made as to the recovery on the first three counts of the petition. As said in the statement of the case, the cattle were injured on one of the defendant's depot grounds, and the negligence charged is that the train was being run at a rate of speed exceeding eight miles an hour, and also a failure to ring the bell and sound the whistle as by law required. It may be conceded that the averments of the petition are such that a recovery might be had because of the negligence charged in either respect upon sufficient proof, and the court so charged the jury. Upon the issue of the right of plaintiff to recover because of negligence in operating the train at an unlawful rate of speed the court gave the following instruction: "It is the law of this state that the operating of trains upon depot grounds necessarily used by the company, and public, where the railroad has not fenced its track, at a greater rate of speed than eight miles per hour, shall be deemed negligence; and it is for you to determine, from the evidence, whether or not the crossing at the alleged place of injury to the cattle was upon the defendant's depot grounds necessarily used by the defendant and the public; also whether or not defendant's track at that point was fenced, and whether or not the defendant's train that ran into plaintiff's cattle was then running at a greater rate of speed than eight miles an hour." The complaint as to the instruction is that it does not appear that the cattle when, injured, were running at large. While there is a slight contention, in argument, as to the fact, it may be set at rest by a statement that it affirmatively appears that the cattle were not running at large, but were being driven by, and under control of, a son of plaintiff. A recovery for such negligence must be under section 1289, Code 1873, which makes the act of running trains at a speed exceeding eight miles per hour, through depot grounds, negligence, and renders the company liable, under the section, for live stock running at large. The section, in respect to liability for excessive speed of trains, has been construed by this court, and liability limited to stock running at large. See *Cohoon v. Railway Co.*, 90 Iowa, 169; *Johnson v. Railway Co.*, 75 Iowa, 157. The legal proposition is, by the cases cited, so conclusively settled that comment is unnecessary. It follows that the instruction is erroneous.

It is said, however, that the error is without prejudice because of a right of recovery under the other averments of the petition. This leads to a consideration of what presumptions follow an erroneous instruction. With the error established, the rule is to regard it as prejudicial. In *Reynolds v. City of Keokuk,* 72 Iowa, 371, it is said: "The rule is that, where there is an error, a presumption of prejudice arises which cannot be disregarded, unless the record discloses affirmatively, and the court is satisfied, that the error was not prejudicial." To the same effect, see *Hall v. Railway Co.,* 84 Iowa, .311, and cases there cited. The evidence in the case would, unmistakably, sustain a finding that the speed of the train exceeded eight miles per hour, and, with that fact found, the instruction conclusively gave to plaintiff a right of recovery because of such negligence, notwithstanding the cattle were not running at large. Such a recovery would be, of course, unwarranted, and it is as presumable as a recovery upon any other ground. To say, under the rule, that the instruction is not prejudicial, it must affirmatively appear that the verdict was based on other grounds of negligence.

Such a conclusion is not deducible from the record. Because of this error the judgment must be **REVERSED**.

HARRY NEWBURY v. GETCHELL & MARTIN LUMBER AND MANUFACTURING COMPANY, Appellant.

Appeal: FILING ABSTRACT: *Affirmance on motion.* Rule 28 provides that an appeal may be dismissed or the order or judgment
1   appealed from affirmed, upon motion of appellee, where appellant does not file abstract thirty days before the second term after appeal is taken, unless further time is given by the supreme court
4   or a judge thereof. The rules of the court regarding the preparation and submission of causes have the force of law, and the Code provides that abstracts shall be filed in accordance with rules so established. *Held,*

a-2   Rule 28 is a copy of the statute and Rule 20 is a creation of the court.

b-3, 4   If the two conflicted, and they do not, the statutory one rules.

c-5   The court cannot waive a statutory rule which the statute does not authorize it to waive.

d-13   Rule 28 is mandatory; Rule 20 provides only that, at least thirty days before the day assigned for the hearing of a cause, appellant shall serve abstract and shall file the same at least fifteen
4   days before the first day of the term for which the cause is to be docketed for trial. It does not govern where the thirty days before hearing and said time before docketing reach a time later than thirty days before the second term after appeal is taken. Neither is the period fixed at thirty days before the second term a license to delay till then. It is, instead, a limit to delay, and if the abstract should be filed sooner, under other rules, Rule 28 does not extend the time as fixed by these other rules   Rule 20 simply authorizes the court, or judge thereof, under peculiar circumstances, to waive or modify the rules relating to abstracts.

RELIEF ON MOTION: *Affirmance or dismissal.* Where appellee has the right to have an appeal "dismissed or the judgment or order
13   affirmed" for failure of appellant to file an abstract within a specified time, the court will grant that form of relief best calculated to do justice; which, in most cases, will be the relief first asked.

WAIVER. The right to dismissal or affirmance on motion may be waived by agreement or consent, by failure to insist upon it and
8   perhaps in other ways; or appellee may be estopped by his conduct to assert the right. But where no such matters intervene the right exists though the abstract is on file when the motion is made.

Second Appeal. A second appeal taken while the first is pending,
13 and within six months after judgment, is without effect and will,
13 on motion, be dismissed, as a matter of form, on the affirmance
of the judgment.

EXTENSION OF TIME: *Grounds.* An extension of time in which to
prepare a case for submission to the supreme court will be granted
2 where the delay is occasioned by unforeseen demands upon an
attorney's time and no injury will be caused the other party; but
where he has no reasonable grounds for believing he can submit
the case in time or knows that he cannot do so, it is his duty to so
inform his client, or obtain assistance

Notice of application. Notice of an application to extend the time for
9 filing an abstract of record should be served on the adverse party
or his attorney.

Time of application. The extension of time wherein to file abstract,
6 provided for by Rule 28 cannot be granted after the time for filing,
13 allowed by that rule, has expired.

Nunc pro tunc order. The supreme court has no authority to make
11 an order *nunc pro tunc,* to the effect that an abstract filed after
13 the expiration of the time prescribed by Code, 1873, section 4120,
be considered as filed in time.

BILL OF EXCEPTIONS: *Jurisdiction.* The filing of a bill of exceptions
7 is not necessarily jurisdictional, as is the service of a notice of
appeal.

Appeal from Polk District Court.—HON. T. F. STEVENSON,
Judge.

WEDNESDAY, OCTOBER 5, 1898.

ACTION at law submitted on motions and applications
for a modification of the rules.—Judgment *affirmed.*

N. T. Guernsey for appellant.

Thos. A. Cheshire for appellee.

ROBINSON, J.—The final judgment from which the
appeal in this case was taken was rendered against the defendant on the sixth day of November, 1897. On the ninth day
of the same month the defendant served notice of appeal, and
secured the clerk of the district court his fees for a transcript.

On the twelfth day of April, 1898, the appellee served upon the appellant a motion to affirm the judgment of the district court on the ground that the appellant had not filed in the office of the clerk of this court, thirty days before the second term after the appeal was taken, an abstract of the record. The appellee had the case docketed, and filed with his motion a certified copy of the judgment, *supersedeas* bond, notice of appeal, and proof of service thereof. On the same day the appellant filed an application for an extension of time in which to file an abstract, and two days later filed its abstract. On the twenty-seventh day of that month the appellant applied to a judge of this court for an order that the filing of the abstract should stand as a sufficient compliance with the rules of this court, and that the rules be waived or modified for that purpose. There has not been a ruling upon either application. On the fifth day of May, 1898, the defendant caused to be served a second notice of appeal, and six days later the appellee served, and on the next day filed, a motion to dismiss that appeal. Resistance has been made to the several motions and applications mentioned, and written arguments have been filed.

I.   The motion of the appellee to affirm is based upon section 28 of the statutes and rules regulating the practice in this court, which is as follows:

"Sec. 28.   If an abstract of the record is not filed by appellant thirty days before the second term after the appeal was taken, unless further time is given by the court, or a judge thereof for cause shown, the appellee may file an abstract of such matters of record as are necessary, or may file a copy of the final judgment or order appealed from, notice of appeal and return of service thereof, certified by the clerk of the trial court, and cause the case to be docketed, and the appeal upon motion shall be dismissed, or the judgment or order affirmed."

So much of that section as is involved in the question before us is a copy of section 4120 of the Code.

In support of the application for further time in which
to file an abstract, the appellant filed an affidavit of its president, which shows that the appeal was taken in good faith,
and that Mr. Guernsey, the attorney for the appel-
2   lant, had been instructed to perfect the appeal, and
present the cause in this court. The application was
also accompanied by the affidavit of Mr. George R. Sanderson, an attorney engaged as an assistant in the office of Mr.
Guernsey.   Mr. Sanderson's affidavit states, in effect, that
preparation of the abstract was commenced by Mr. Guernsey
about the first of January, 1898, and that he worked upon it
from time to time, as his other engagements would permit,
and completed a copy thereof for the printer on or about
April 7, 1898; that since the taking of the appeal Mr.
Guernsey had been engaged "in the preparation for submission and in the actual trial of many important cases in the
United States supreme court, supreme court of the state of
Iowa, United States circuit courts in Iowa and other states,
and in the state courts of Iowa and other states, and has
been frequently absent for several days at a time from his
office in giving attention to said cases and other professional
engagements." The showing made by these affidavits and by
others attached to the second application fully establishes
the fact that the appeal was not taken for delay, but in good
faith, because Mr. Guernsey believed that the judgment
should be reversed for substantial reason affecting the merits
of the case.

One of the questions presented by the first application,
although not controlling, in the view we take of the case, is
important because of its frequent recurrence in motions to
dismiss or affirm in this court. It is, what will excuse an
appellant for failure, by reason of demands upon the time of
his attorney, to have his cause ready for submission at the
time fixed by the rules or order of the court? To do justice is
a chief object of litigation, and when instituted it should be
prosecuted with reasonable diligence. A party should not

be permitted to delay it without satisfactory cause. It is our practice to make due allowance for unexpected and unavoidable demands upon the time of attorneys, whether due to business or sickness or other cause. But unnecessary delay in the prosecution of a cause may operate as a denial of justice, and the rights of all parties must be kept steadily in view. An attorney having charge of a case, in consequence of unforeseen demands upon his time and without fault on his part, may be unable to prepare his side of a cause for submission within the time prescribed by the rules; and in such cases, where we have the power to grant an extension of time, and injury to other parties will not result from such an extension, we do not hesitate to grant it if asked. But if the business of an attorney is so large that he has no reasonable grounds for believing that he can submit his cases within the time prescribed by the rules, or if he knows that he cannot do so by reason of long-continued sickness or other cause, it is his duty, if the adverse party will not consent to delay, to obtain the assistance of another attorney, if he be authorized to do so, or to inform his client of the emergency, in order that arrangements may be made for a timely submission. It does not appear from the affidavit of Mr. Sanderson that Mr. Guernsey had any unexpected demands upon his time which caused the delay in the completion of the abstract. So far as is shown, the business he was called upon to transact during the time in question, although seemingly large, was no more than he was ordinarily required to do.

II. The second application was made under section 90 of the rules of this court, for a waiver or modification of the rules respecting the time of filing abstracts. Section 90 provides that "when, by reason of peculiar circumstances, the foregoing rules relating to abstract, preparation and argument of causes, ought to be waived or modified in any case," an order to that effect may be made by any judge of this court in vacation, upon due application

and notice. The showing made in support of the second application is that the appeal was taken in good faith, and not
for delay; that Mr. Guernsey was exceedingly busy with professional work, but intended to complete and file the abstract
within the time required by the rules; that he knew that
changes in the rules were made in the year 1897, and, in order
to be certain to have the abstract filed in time, he requested
Mr. Sanderson, at several different times, to examine the rules,
and ascertain and inform him when they required that the
abstract be filed; that the abstract was ready for the printer
on the seventh day of April, when, in order to be certain of
the date, he again asked Mr. Sanderson when the abstract
should be filed under the new rules, and was informed by him
that it was not necessary to file it before April 21st; that the
abstract could have been printed and filed by April 9th, which
would have been in time, but, in consequence of the information given by Mr. Sanderson, was not filed until April 14th,
or less than thirty days before the next term of this court.
It is further shown that Mr. Sanderson had practiced law
for eighteen years, and was regarded by Mr. Guernsey as competent and reliable; that Mr. Sanderson, in giving the information which caused the delay in filing the abstract, had not
observed section 28 of the rules, but had examined and relied
upon section 20, which provides that, "at least thirty days
before the day assigned for the hearing of a cause, the appellant shall serve upon each appellee, or his attorney," a printed
copy of the abstract, and that "the appellant shall also, fifteen
days before the first day of the term for which the cause is
to be docketed for trial, file with the clerk, twelve copies of
said abstract." The first day of the May term of this court
commenced on the tenth day of May, and the causes from Polk
county were assigned for hearing on the twenty-third day of
the month. Therefore, if section 20 of the rules had alone
governed the time of filing, Mr. Sanderson's statement to
Mr. Guernsey would have been correct. But section 20 must

be construed with section 28. If there were conflict between
the two sections, so much of section 28 as is
copied from section 4120 of the Code would
necessarily prevail, for the reason that section
20 is not statutory. It is true that rules of this
court in regard to the preparation and submission of
causes have the force of laws duly enacted. *State v. Day*, 68
Iowa, 213. It is also true that section 4118 of the Code
provides that "printed abstracts of the record shall be filed
in accordance with rules established by the supreme court,"
but the authority thus given must be so exercised as to conform
to the statute. We do not think, however, that there is any
conflict between sections 20 and 28 of the rules. Section 28
does not give to the appellant the right to delay the filing
of an abstract until thirty days before the second term after
the appeal was taken, but merely provides that if not filed
thirty days before such term, and further time is not given,
the appellee may have the appeal dismissed, or the judgment
or order from which it was taken affirmed, by pursuing the
method pointed out. Many cases, however, are submitted at
the first term of this court after the appeal is taken. That is
true of criminal cases and of cases advanced, and would be
true of most cases if the business of the court permitted it to
receive, at each term, all the cases which could be made ready
for submission. The waiver or modification of rules
for which section 90 provides cannot be construed to
apply to statutory requirements, which the court is
not authorized by statute to waive, for the reason that the
section is not statutory. So much of section 28 as is involved
in this case is, as we have seen, a part of the Code, and there
is no statutory provision which authorizes this court to
waive or modify it. The affidavits filed in support of the
second application show that the failure to file the abstract
within the time required by the rules was not primarily due
to the demands of business, but to a mistake respecting the
requirement of the rules. However, the judgment was for

four thousand three hundred dollars, besides costs, and, in view of the showing of merits and good faith made, the short time which elapsed after the expiration of the time for filing the abstract before it was filed, the fact that the condition of the business of the court was such that the case could not have been submitted on its merits before the October term of court for 1898, and the further fact that the mistake, although of law, was not an unnatural one, we should be disposed to overrule the motion to affirm, and require a submission on the merits, had we the power to do so.

III.   We are next required to consider the proper interpretation of section 28 and the effect which should be given to it.   That it gives to this court, or to any of the judges thereof, the right to give an extension of time in which to file an abstract, for cause shown, provided an application therefor be made before the right to file the abstract has expired, is clear, and not questioned.   But can an application not made thirty days before the second term after the appeal is taken be granted?   It is claimed by the appellee that the section is mandatory, and that, by filing his motion to affirm and transcript, he acquired a substantial right under the statute, of which he cannot be deprived.   The appellant contends that the section is directory.   No cases precisely in point have been called to our attention, but we may be helped to a correct conclusion by examining cases decided under statutes which involved the application of somewhat similar rules of interpretation.   Section 3180 of the Code of 1873 provided that the notice of appeal must be served at least thirty days, and the cause filed and docketed at least fifteen days, before the first day of the next term of this court, or the same should not be tried unless by consent of parties, and that, if the appeal was taken less than thirty days before the term, it should be filed and docketed before the next succeeding term.   Section 3181 provided that, if the appellant failed to file the transcript and have the cause docketed as required by section 3180, or failed to file, at the

time the transcript should be filed, the certificate of the clerk
of the inferior court, stating when he was served with notice,
and that he had not had sufficient time in which to prepare the
transcript, the appellee might file a certified copy of the judgment or order appealed from, and of the notice served on the
clerk, and have the appeal dismissed, or the judgment or order
appealed from affirmed. Rules of this court contained similar
requirements in regard to abstracts. It was held, under these
provisions, in *Turner v. Hine,* 37 Iowa, 500, that they were
not merely directory, and a motion to affirm the judgment
was sustained for failure to file the transcript and abstract
within the time required by the statute and rules, although the
transcript and abstract were on file before the motion to affirm
and transcript of judgment were filed by the appellee. An
important difference between the provisions considered in that
case and section 28 is that the latter contains authority for
the granting of further time for cause shown. The case is
authority for the conclusion that, if further time be not
granted, the filing of the abstract after the time fixed for
that purpose, without leave, will not defeat the right of the
appellee to demand a dismissal of the appeal or an affirmance
of the judgment or order appealed from, by motion filed after
the filing of the abstract, and that to that extent the section
is mandatory. Section 1805 of the Code of 1851 provided
for the taking of exceptions, and section 1806 provided that
"such exceptions must be in writing, but the court may allow
such time as may be deemed reasonable to settle and reduce
the same to form." It was held, under these provisions, that,
in the absence of an express agreement or consent to extend
the time for settling the exceptions, the judge did not have
any power to sign them after the adjournment of court.
Claggett v. Gray, 1 Iowa, 19.

Section 2831 of the Code of 1873, as amended by chapter 209 of the Acts of the Eighteenth General Assembly,
contained the following: "An exception is an objection taken
to a decision of the court or party acting as the court, on a

matter of law.   The party objecting to the decision must do
so at the time the same is made   *   *   *   and embody his
objection in a bill of exceptions to be filed during the term,
or within such time thereafter as the court may fix; but in no
event shall the time extend more than thirty days beyond the
expiration of the term, except by consent of parties or by order
of the judge.   *   *   *"   Numerous decisions have been
rendered under that statute.   In *Short v. Railway Co.,* 79
Iowa, 73, it appeared that the judgment gave to the defendant
sixty days in which to file a bill of exceptions.   No bill of
exceptions was filed within that time, but three months after
the judgment was rendered the defendant filed a motion in
court for leave to fill a bill of exceptions as of a time within
the sixty days, and, between seven and eight months after the
time for filing the bill of exceptions had expired, the court sustained the motion so far as to allow the defendant to file the
bill of exceptions as of the date of the order sustaining the
motion. This court held, in effect, that the order was unauthorized, but refrained from expressing an opinon as to the power
of the court to make a *nunc pro tunc* order.   In *Rosenbaum v.
Partch,* 85 Iowa, 410, ninety days were given each party in
which to file a bill of exceptions, and that time expired on the
twenty-fifth day of January, 1890.   No bill was filed within
the time thus given, but at the next term of court, on the
fifteenth day of the next March, a motion for leave and time to
file a bill of exceptions was filed and sustained, and an order
was made that the bill should be filed within ten days.   No
notice of the motion had been given.   This court held that
the court had no power to make the order, and said, in effect,
that, if there was any reason for extending the time for filing
a bill of exceptions by an application to the court or judge,
it ought to be discovered, and the order asked before the
original time given expires.   In *White v. Abstract Co.,* 96
Iowa, 343, that holding was approved, and it was said that
the statute did not permit the exercise of discretion, and
that "when the time for filing a bill of exceptions, as fixed

by law, the consent of parties, or the order of the court or judge, expires, so that the right must be revived rather than extended, neither the court nor the judge has that right. While either may possess the right, by proper order, to extend or continue the time for the exercise of such right, neither has the right, when it is once lost, to restore it." See, also, *Bennett v. City of Marion,* 101 Iowa, 112. It is suggested that the rule in regard to bills of exception is founded upon the lack of jurisdiction in courts to make orders in vacation. The lack of such jurisdiction was commented upon in *Claggett v. Gray, supra,* but the statue there construed gave to courts only, and not to judges, the power to allow time in which to settle exceptions, and that fact necessarily influenced the decision of the case.

It is also said that the filing of the bill of exceptions is essential to give this court jurisdiction of the exception sought to be reviewed. The office of the bill of exceptions is to make of record what would otherwise not be preserved as 7   a part of it, but we have refused to strike from the record a bill of exceptions which was designed to show the evidence taken on a trial, but which was not filed within the time limited by agreement of parties, where it appeared from an additional abstract that all of the evidence was before us. *Richardson v. Blinkiron,* 76 Iowa, 255. If parties agree as to the proceedings had in the trial of a cause, a bill of exceptions to show such proceedings is not necessary, and therefore is not essential to confer upon this court power to act upon matters which are admittted. It is not jurisdictional in the sense that the service of a notice of appeal is jurisdictional. Section 2831 of the Code of 1873, as amended, provided for the filing of a bill of exceptions during the term at which the exceptions were taken, "or within such time thereafter as the court may fix; but in no event shall the time extend more than thirty days beyond the expiration of the term, except by consent of parties or by order of the judge." As we have seen, these provisions did not authorize a court or

judge to extend the time for filing a bill of exceptions after
the time originally fixed for filing it had expired.   Section
4120 of the Code, as found in section 28 of the rules, gives to
an appellee the right to have the appeal dismissed, or the
judgment or order appealed from affirmed, "if an abstract
of the record is not filed by appellant thirty days before the
second term after the appeal was taken, unless further time is
given by the court or a judge thereof, for cause shown."   The
rule of interpretation which required the extension of time
for which section 2831 of the Code of 1873 provided, to be
granted before the right to file a bill of exceptions had expired,
requires us to hold that the extension of time authorized by
section 4120 of the Code, to be effectual, must be granted
before the right to file the abstract has expired.   In other
words, neither this court, nor a judge thereof, can grant to an
appellant the right, which has once been lost, to file an
abstract, but while that right exists the time for its exercise
may be extended by this court or by one of its judges.   This
conclusion accords with rulings already made by this court,
and will tend to secure diligence in the prosecution of appeals.

Our attention has been called to the fact that under rules
which were in force before October, 1897, we frequently
refused to dismiss appeals or affirm judgments and orders,
on motion founded upon the failure of the appellant to file
an abstract and argument within the time required by the
rules.   We said in *Fowler v. Town of Strawberry Hill,* 74
Iowa, 644, that "we are not accustomed to summarily affirm
causes, after they are prepared for submission on the part
of appellants, on the ground of delay in presenting abstracts
and arguments.   If prejudice has resulted to the other party
by such delay, redress must be sought in some other way."
The practice thus indicated was founded in large part upon
chapter 56 of the Public Acts of the Fifteenth General Assembly, which provided that no appeal to this court should be
dismissed, or judgment of the court below affirmed, because
the cause was not docketed or transcript filed in this court,

if it was made to appear that the appeal was taken in good faith, and not for delay, or if from the conduct of the appellee or his counsel the appellant was induced to believe that no motion to dismiss or affirm would be made. But that provision is not found in the Code, and has ceased to be the law. It is true that although section 19 of the rules of this court in force before October, 1897, required that additional abstracts be delivered to counsel for appellant within ten days after the abstract was received, we rarely sustained a motion to strike from the files an additional abstract served after the time specified. That rule was not statutory, however, but was adopted by this court, and was waived in the interest of justice, when prejudice would not result from the waiver. We are not to be understood as holding that the appellee, in all cases in which the appellant has failed to file an abstract within the time limited, and further time has not been granted, will be entitled to a dismissal or affirmance, on the filing of a motion, with the necessary abstract or transcript. It is undoubtedly true that the right to a dismissal or affirmance may be waived by agreement or consent, or by failing to insist upon it, and perhaps in other ways, and that the appellee may be estopped by his conduct to assert the right. But, where there is no waiver or estoppel, the appellee has the right to insist upon a dismissal or affirmance when he brings himself within the terms of the statute, and that would be true, even though the abstract be on file when the motion is made. In that respect the statute is mandatory. See *Turner v. Hine*, 37 Iowa, 500.

IV. For the purpose of avoiding some confusion in practice which has heretofore existed, we deem it proper to say that notice of an application to extend the time for filing an abstract should be served on the adverse party or his attorney.

V. It is insisted that section 28 of the rules does not require an affirmance on the application of the appellee, but that this court may, in its discretion, affirm the judgment or dismiss the appeal. In some cases there may be a material difference between the effect of dismissing the appeal and affirming the judgment or order from which the appeal is taken, but the appellee does not have the absolute right to elect which remedy he will have. It is the customary and approved practice for the appellee to ask in ·the alternative that the judgment or order appealed from be affirmed, or that the appeal be dismised, and when that is done, and the appellee is entitled to relief asked, this court grants that form of relief which seems to be best calculated to do justice, and in most cases that is the relief first asked. In this case the effect of an affirmance would be practically the same as that of a dismissal.

10

.   VI.   The appellant asks that an order *nunc pro tunc* be made to the effect that the abstract filed April 14th be considered as filed April 9th. An order of that character will be made to avoid the effects of a delay by the court or of a delay or omission of its clerk, but rarely, if ever, to remedy a delay or omission due to a party or his attorney. *Brignardello v. Gray,* 1 Wall. 627; *Shephard v. Brenton,* 20 Iowa, 41; 12 Am. & Eng. Enc. Law, 80; Freeman Judgments, sections 56-60; 1 Black Judgments, section 129. Such an order in this case would be an evasion of the statute and is unauthorized.

11

VII.   Within six months from the date of the judgment the appellant served a second notice of appeal, and secured the clerk his fees for a transcript. It is claimed by the appellant that the second appeal was properly taken, and that it furnishes a sufficient reason for overruling the motion to affirm the judgment. Numerous authorities are cited to show that a second appeal is not barred by the dismissal of the cause on the first appeal. But that is not the case before us. This case has not been dismissed. When the second notice of appeal was served the cause was pending in this court, and the second notice added nothing to the jurisdiction which this court then had of the case or to its

12

power to grant relief.   We have no occasion to determine
whether a second appeal may be taken after the dis-
13   missal of a cause on the first appeal.   It follows from
what we have said that the second appeal is without
effect; that we are not authorized to grant the applications of
the appellant' for additional time in which to file its abstract,
for a modification of rule 28, nor for an order *nunc pro tunc,*
and that the appellee is entitled to an affirmance-of the judgment.   The applications of the appellant will therefore be
denied; the motion to dismiss the second appeal will, as a
matter of form, be sustained; and the motion to AFFIRM the
judgment of the district court will also be sustained.   Orders
to that effect will be duly entered.—AFFIRMED.

GREEN BAY LUMBER COMPANY, Appellant, v. EDWIN THOMAS
et al.

Mechanic's Lien: SUB-CONTRACTOR.   The owner is not protected
against a sub-contractor's lien, to the extent of payments made
1   to the contractor in anticipation of the time of payment specified
in the contract, with knowledge of the sub-contractor's claim.

ESTOPPEL OF SUB-CONTRACTOR.   Where a sub-contractor represented
to the owner, before settlement with the principal contractor, that
he would not look to the owner for payment for materials fur-
2   nished, he is estopped from claiming a lien as to part of an installment due at that time to the principal contractor, which was paid
by the owner to other sub-contractors on the strength of such
representation.

Appeal from Jackson District Court.—HON. A. J. HOUSE,
Judge.

THURSDAY, OCTOBER 6, 1898.

SUIT in equity to establish and enforce a mechanic's lien.
Plaintiff is a subcontractor who furnished lumber and
material to defendant Thomas, the principal contractor, for
the erection of a house upon land belonging to defendant Dunham.   Defendants admit that lumber was furnished, but say

that plaintiff did not file its lien within the time required by statute; that the owner has paid the contractor in full; and that plaintiff, by reason of certain representations and statements is estopped from enforcing its lien. Decree for defendants, and plaintiff appeals.—*Reversed in part.*

D. A. Fletcher, G. L. Johnson, and *C. C. & C. L. Nourse* for appellant.

Levi Keck and *Wm. Graham* for appellees.

DEEMER, C. J.—The first question in the case is, did the plaintiff file its lien and serve notice upon the owner within thirty days after furnishing the last item of material? It filed its lien and served the notice on the twenty-second day of December, 1896. There is a serious dispute as to when the last item of material was furnished. Appellant claims it was on the twenty-third day of November, while appellees insist it was on the twenty-first. Careful consideration of the evidence leads us to the conclusion that it was on the twenty-third, and that the lien was filed and notice given in time.

Appellees insist, however, that the owner paid in strict accord with the terms of his contract, and that the lien, if any, can only be established for the amount remaining unpaid at the time the notice was served. The contract price
1   of the building was four thousand one hundred dollars, which was to be paid as follows: Seven hundred dollars when the foundation was completed and the lumber was on the ground; one thousand dollars when the roof was on; five hundred dollars when the building was ready for plastering; three hundred dollars when the plastering was completed; and the remainder, one thousand six hundred dollars when the entire building was completed. There was also an agreed bill of two hundred and forty-two dollars for extras which was to be paid upon the completion of the building. The owner did not pay according to the terms of his contract, for when the building was accepted, which was some time in

December, 1896, the balance found due on settlement was about three hundred and seventy-nine dollars. The owner knew plaintiff was furnishing material for the building, and also knew before she made settlement with Thomas that plaintiff's bill had not been paid. Under this state of facts it is clear that the plaintiff's lien should be established. *Simonson Bros. Mfg. Co. v. Citizens' Bank,* 105 Iowa, 246, and cases cited. The case of *Epeneter v. Montgomery County,* 98 Iowa, 159, is not in point, for the reason that in that case the payments were made in strict accord with the terms of the contract, while in this case they were made in disregard of its terms; and for the further reason that that case was made to turn upon the provisions of chapter 179, Acts Twentieth General Assembly.

Again, it is argued that plaintiff is estopped from asserting its lien by reason of certain representations made by its agents to the owner of the building before final settlement was made with the principal contractor. This argument is based upon the claim that the plaintiff's agent represented to defendant Dunham, prior to the time of the final settlment with Thomas, that it would not look to the owner for payment for the materials furnished, and that, relying upon this statement, the owner made a final settlement with the principal contractor. At the time it is claimed this conversation took place, the owner was owing the principal contractor three hundred and seventy-nine dollars and thirty-five cents. Thereafter she paid one hundred and twenty dollars of this amount to some plumbers, and sixty dollars to a painter, and the balance, to-wit, one hundred and ninety-nine dollars and thiry-five cents she turned over to plaintiff, leaving a balance due it of five hundred and thirty-eight dollars and thirty cents. We are satisfied that this one hundred and eighty dollars was paid upon the strength of certain statements and agreements made by plaintiff's agent, and that plaintiff is estopped from insisting upon re-payment of this amount. Our conclusion is that plaintiff is entitled to have its lien established against the property described in the petition as owned by defendant Julia B. Dunham, to the amount of three hundred and fifty-two dollars and twenty-eight cents, with six per cent. interest from December 22, 1896, and the costs of suit. At plaintiff's option, exercised within twenty days from the filing of this opinion, it may have a decree in this court; otherwise the cause will be remanded to the lower court for a decree in harmony with this opinion. As to the defendant Thomas the decree is AFFIRMED, and as to the defendant Dunham it is REVERSED.

STATE OF IOWA V. L. BERNHOLTZ, GEORGE B. FRAZIER, FRANK SALMEN, F. M. BAUGHMAN, B. UNGRUE, Appellants.

Elections: BALLOT: *Fault of officials.* Under Code, section 1122, providing that no ballot, properly marked by the voter, shall be rejected because of any discrepancy between it and the nomination paper, nor for any error in stamping or writing the indorsements thereon by the officers, nor because of any error in delivering the wrong ballots at the polling place, but that any ballot
1 delivered by the proper official to a voter shall be counted as cast for all candidates for whom the voter had a right to and did vote, an election of candidates for municipal offices, by a majority of ballots cast, is not invalidated by the fact that the mayor and council, without authority, changed one ticket on the ballot by heading it "democratic," which change was without fraud and deceived no one, where the election officers accepted those, and refused to use the ballots prepared by the recorder who was rightfully authorized to prepare them. The misconduct of election officers cannot overturn the voter's will.

SAME. Code, section 1121, prohibiting any "but ballots provided in accordance with the provisions of this chapter" from being
2 counted, intends that no ballot of the voter's choosing, but only those furnished by the proper officials to the voter, shall be counted.

Appeal from Carroll District Court.—HON. Z. A. CHURCH, Judge.

THURSDAY, OCTOBER 6, 1898.

THE defendants were mayor, treasurer, recorder, council-
man, and assessor of the incorporated town of Breda prior to
the election of March 28, 1898, and claim to hold over because
of no election on that day. A ticket was duly nominated by
petition, and candidates named for all of these offices, which
was designated on both printed ballots as "Citizens."   A
caucus, designated in the call printed in a local paper as
"Citizen's Caucus," was held on March 16, 1898, and B. K.
Jackson nominated for mayor, F. N. Bruning for treasurer,
Henry Bruning for recorder, A. H. Le Duc for assessor, and
J. H. Bohenkamp, II. Bruning, and Theo. Ewaldt for councilmen. The citizens present belonged to the democratic party,
though the certificate filed with the recorder did not indicate any party whatever. Two days before the election three
members of the council and citizens requested the mayor
to call a special meeting of that body in order to have "Democratic" placed over this ticket on the ballot, which he did on
four hours' notice. Three members met with the mayor,
appointed Joseph Dunck recorder pro tem., and directed him
to make the proposed change. By the town ordinance the
mayor was not permitted to convene the council on less than
twelve hours' notice. Dunck and the city marshal caused a
sample ticket to be posted, and also tickets to be printed for
use on election day, with candidates as stated,—the ticket
headed by Jackson for mayor under the designation "Democratic." Salmon, the recorder, had tickets printed without
this heading, and delivered them, as required by law, to the
election officers, by whom they were rejected. Those prepared
by Dunck were received, and, being properly endorsed, were
handed to the voters, and cast at the election. The candidates
on the ticket headed "Democratic" received a majority of the
votes cast, and were declared elected. The defendants, believing the election was illegal, refused to surrender their offices,
and this action was brought to oust them therefrom. The
relief prayed as granted, and the defendants appeal.—
Affirmed.

W. R. Lee for appellants.

A. T. Olerich and *Salinger & Korte* for appellee.

LADD, J.—The ballots cast at the election in the incorporated town of Breda, March 28, 1898, were not prepared and printed by any one authorized by law. The statute confers this duty on the recorder without any supervision on the part of the mayor or council. Section 1107, Code. It is only when objections are filed that the mayor and members of the council may act, and then only to pass upon the particular objections urged. Section 1103, Code. In this case no objections were filed, and the mayor and three councilmen, in assuming to correct the ballot, were mere intermeddlers. Whether the meeting of the council was lawful, or Dunck rightly appointed recorder pro tem., we need not inquire, for, as such, it had no authority whatever with reference to the preparation of the ballots, and could confer no such authority on him. His duties extended no further than the temporary purposes of that meeting, and in no way ousted the duly-elected recorder from the discharge of his duties in preparing and printing the ballots. The reason for rejecting those so prepared by the judges does not appear, unless it be their belief in the plenary powers of the council not only to ignore their own ordinances but the statutes of the state. They accepted those printed by Dunck, and these were voted by the electors. The two sets were identical, with this exception: That used had "Democratic" over the ticket headed by Jackson for mayor, while that designation was omitted from the other. As no objection to the certificate of nomination made by the caucus was filed, the propriety of printing that is not argued. But see *Schuler v. Hogan,* 168 Ill. Sup. 369 (48 N. E. Rep. 195); *Bowers v. Smith* (Mo. Sup.), 17 S. W. Rep. 761; *People v. Wood* (N. Y.), 42 N. E. Rep. 536. The point made is that, as the ballots cast were not prepared by any one authorized by law, the election was

invalid. With the statute as it was when *State v. Smith*, 94
Iowa, 616, was decided, this position would be sound. The
election law, however, was somewhat modified by the Code
which went into effect October 1, 1897. Section 1122 is as
follows: "No ballot properly marked by the voter shall be
rejected because of any discrepancy between the printed
ballot and the nomination paper or certificate of nomination,
and it shall be counted for the candidate or candidates for
such offices named in the nomination paper or certificate of
nomination. 'No ballot furnished by the proper officer shall
be rejected for any error in stamping or writing the endorse-
ments thereon by the officials charged with such duties, nor
because of any error on the part of the officer charged with
such duty in delivering the wrong ballot at any precinct or
polling place, but any ballot delivered by the proper official to
any voter shall, if properly marked by the voter, be counted
as cast for all candidates for whom the voter had a right to
vote, and for whom he has voted." It must be borne in mind
that the election law was enacted to aid the elector in expressing his free choice, and not, by technical obstructions, to
make the right of voting difficult and insecure. He has no
part in the preparation of the ballots, and the object of this
section is to prevent his disfranchisement without any fault
on his part because of some mistake or willful misconduct of
the election officers. The distinction between errors of such
officers which would have the effect to deprive voters of the
franchise, and a disregard of the law by the electors themselves, runs through all the cases. See *Lindstrom v. Board,*
94 Mich. 467 (54 N. W. Rep. 280); *Miller v. Pennoyer*, 23
Or. 364 (31 Pac. Rep. 830); *Kirk v. Rhoads,* 46 Cal. 399;
Cook v. Fisher, 100 Iowa, 31, and authorities cited. The
very evident purpose of section 1122 was the complete protection of the voter in the exercise of the right of suffrage, if
himself without fault, regardless of the errors of the
2   election officers. The clause in section 1121 prohibiting any "but ballots provided in accordance with the
provisions of this chapter" from being counted, evidently,

relates to ballots furnished the voter. He may not use a ballot of his own choosing, but must cast such as are provided by the proper officials. This is to be given him by the judges of election. Section 1114. When so received, he may rely upon it as genuine, and, when properly marked by him, have it counted as cast for all candidates for whom he had the right to vote and did vote. This is not a case where the electors have been deceived or misled by the mistake or fraud of the officers. The ballots were in all essential particulars like those prepared by the recorder. The use of the word "Democratic" on the ticket could have deceived no one. The voters had the right, under section 1122, to have the ballots counted as cast, and when this was done the result was not in doubt. While the officers are without excuse in violating the plain provisions of the statute, their misconduct cannot be permitted to overturn the expressed will of the people.— AFFIRMED.

JAMES W. TURLEY v. BRYON GRIFFIN, Appellant.

|106   1
|f111
106
128

Instructions: HARMLESS ERROR. An instruction that plaintiff could not recover on a certain state of facts because, as was erroneously
6   stated, such facts amounted to a "fraud," was not prejudicial where the jury was elsewhere correctly instructed, without reference to fraud, that, on substantially the same state of facts, plaintiff could not recover.

SAME. The provision of Code, 1873, section 2786, that instructions
7   allowed by the court, shall be marked "given" is directory only.

Exceptions: MOTION FOR NEW TRIAL: *Amendment.* Under Code, 1873, section 2789, providing that either party may take and file
1   exceptions to the instructions within three days after verdict, a party who does not except to instruction when given or within three days after verdict, waives objections, and cannot urge them by way of amendment to a motion for a new trial, filed by leave of court, after the expiration of the three days.

SUFFICIENCY. An exception to the granting of a new trial is sufficient
8   for a review of that ruling though the new trial was granted on a
4   ground presented in an amendment to the motion which was filed
5   by leave of court, without exception to the permission to file it.

SETTING OUT GROUNDS. Under Code, 1873, section 2789, requiring the grounds of objection to be set out where the exceptions to instruc-
1 tions are first taken in the motion for a new trial, an objection such as "contrary to law, not warranted by the facts and prejudicial to the plaintiff" does not sufficiently set out the grounds thereof.

Appeal: REVIEW: *Granting new trial.* The supreme court reluct-
2 antly interferes with the granting of a new trial by the trial court, but will not hesitate in determining whether or not the trial court abused its discretion, where the precise ground on which it based its action is known.

Appeal from Delaware District Court.—HON. FRED O'DONN-
ELL, Judge.

THURSDAY, OCTOBER 6, 1898.

ACTION to recover damages of defendant for negligence as bailee. There was a trial to jury, and verdict for defendant. Upon plaintiff's motion, the verdict was set aside and a new trial ordered. From this order defendant appeals.— *Reversed.*

Yoran & Arnold and *Dunham & Norris* for appellant.

Bronson & Carr and *B. J. Wellman* for appellee.

WATERMAN, J.—Plaintiff placed certain money and papers in an iron safe belonging to and in the custody of defendant. The safe was opened by some person, and the property stolen, and this action is to recover its value. We have none of the evidence before us. The instructions, how-ever, are in the record, and they comprehend, besides those given on the court's own motion, three paragraphs which were given at defendant's request, and which are numbered, respectively, 1, 2, and 2½. None of these instructions were
1   excepted to at the time they were given; neither was
any exception taken in the motion for a new trial which was filed within three days after the verdict. The date of the rendition of the verdict was February 28, 1893. The motion for a new trial was filed March 1, 1893. On

October 17, 1894, by leave of court, plaintiff filed an amendment to his motion for a new trial, the first ground of which is as follows: "The court erred in submitting to the jury the instructions asked by the defendant; that they are contrary to law, not warranted by the facts, and prejudicial to the plaintiff; and also because the court erred in failing to mark them 'given.'"

The ruling of the court on this motion, as it appears in the record entry, and so far as is material here, is in these words: "It is ordered that said motion be, and the same is, sustained on part of first ground thereof, which alleges error in giving instruction asked by defendant, marked 2½, to which defendant excepts," etc. It has been said quite

2   often that this court interferes reluctantly with the action of the trial court when a new trial is granted. Much latitude is allowed for the exercise of its discretion; but it is a legal discretion that should control, and when, as in this case, we know the precise ground on which the court based its action, we have no hesitation in determining whether its discretion was abused. *Stockwell v. Railway Co.,* 43 Iowa, 470; *Riley v. Monohan,* 26 Iowa, 507. In the case at bar the court rested its decision solely upon a conceived error in instruction No. 2½ given the jury at defendant's

3   request. Appellant's contention is that this instruction was never excepted to by plaintiff until the amendment to the motion for a new trial was filed, some eighteen months after the verdict, and that this amendment should not have been considered. This is met by appellee with the assertion that the amendment was filed with leave of court, and that appellant took no exception to the court's action in this respect. We do not think appellant is prejudiced by a failure to object to the ruling of the court granting leave to file this paper. A motion is always considered as a whole and upon its merits. Plaintiff was at liberty to present any matters that he desired in his motion;

but it does not follow that he was entitled to a favorable consideration by the court of anything that he was not legally authorized to urge. Appellant was not interested in what plaintiff put into his motion, but only in what matters the court considered. Proper exception was entered to the ruling of the court on the motion, and this, we think, was sufficient.

II. Any error in the instruction was waived by plaintiff through his failure to except thereto, unless the court was justified in permitting him to amend his motion at the time and in the manner he did. Section 2789, Code 1873, provides, in substance, that either party may take and file exceptions to the instructions within three days after the verdict. Under this section we have held that, where exceptions are not taken at the time the instructions are given, they can only be preserved in writing filed within three days after the rendition of the verdict. *Dean v. Zenor,* 96 Iowa, 752; *Hallenbeck v. Garst,* 96 Iowa, 509. If exceptions are not taken within the time specified, they should not be considered, even if incorporated in a bill of exceptions duly signed. *Bailey v. Anderson,* 61 Iowa, 749.

5   Where, by agreement of the parties, leave is granted for delay in filing the motion for a new trial, it does not authorize the incorporation in such motion of exceptions to the instructions, which were not taken at the proper time. *Bush v. Nichols,* 77 Iowa, 171; *Leach v. Hill,* 97 Iowa, 81. We think the instructions were not properly excepted to by plaintiff.

III. If it should be said that the court was justified in setting aside the verdict, if an erroneous instruction was given, even though no exception to it was preserved, we would respond that any such idea seems to be excluded by the terms of paragraph 8, section 2837, Code 1873; but no such terms tion is before us. Instruction No. 2½ does not differ in substance from No. 2 given at defendant's request, and the objection to the latter was overruled. The only discernible difference between these two instructions is that the word "fraud" is used in No. 2½. That the

4

6

word was improperly used may be conceded; but it is clear that no prejudice to plaintiff could have resulted. The jury was told in No. 2 that, on a certain state of facts, plaintiff could not recover; and in No. 2½, on the same state of facts repeated, it was said plaintiff could not recover because his conduct, as set out, would amount to a "fraud." The two instructions should stand or fall together. The trial court held the first to be good, and the plaintiff does not complain. The rule thus announced sustains the other instruction also. Moreover, we will add here that we think the abstract proposition of law contained in paragraph No. 2½, leaving out the reason the trial court gives for its conclusion, is correct.

IV. So far, we have treated the amendment to the motion for a new trial as presenting exceptions, proper in form, to the instructions. Section 2789, Code 1873, provides, in substance, that, where exceptions to instructions are

7   first taken in the motion for a new trial, the grounds of the objection must be set out. This is not done in the motion in this case, further than to say that the paragraphs under consideration were not marked "given" by the court, as required by section 2786, Code 1873. We regard this provision as directory only, and we may further say in this connection that the trial court seems to have held against plaintiff on this ground, and no exception was taken thereto. Our conclusion is that, even if the trial court had been warranted in considering this amendment to the motion, nothing therein contained afforded any basis for its action in setting aside the verdict.—REVERSED.

FRANK JONES, Appellant, v. CALVIN COOLEY.

Vendor and Purchaser: FIXTURES. A purchaser of land is not entitled to an injunction restraining a third person from removing a fence inclosing the land, where the fence was erected by the latter under an agreement with the vendor permitting its removal, and the purchaser knew of such agreement at the time he paid the purchase money.

106
126
106
130

Appeal from Clarke District Court.—Hon. W. H. TEDFORD, Judge.

THURSDAY, OCTOBER 6, 1898.

PLAINTIFF, the owner of a certain tract of land, brought this action to enjoin the defendant from removing the fence enclosing the same. Defendants answered, claiming that, under the terms of a written lease from the former owner of the land to him, he was the owner of the fence and had a right to remove it. In an amendment to his answer he alleged that plaintiff had converted the fence to his own use; that it was of the value of one hundred dollars, for which he asked judgment; that "this amendment is filed by leave of court and by consent of parties, in order that an adjustment of the whole dispute may be had." Judgment was rendered in favor of the defendant for one hundred dollars. Plaintiff appeals.—*Affirmed.*

John Chaney and *W. S. Hedrick* for appellant.

Temple & Hardinger for appellee.

GIVEN, J.—I. The defendant leased the land, then wild and unimproved, from the owner, William Stricker, for five years from March 1, 1886, under a written contract which provided that defendant should pay the taxes for the use of the same, "and to build a good and substantial fence enclosing said land, and at the end of his lease the said William Stricker should have the option of purchasing the said fence at its reasonable value, and, if he elected not to purchase the same, then the defendant was to have the privilege of removing the same, the fence to remain his property until purchased by said Stricker." William Stricker died testate, his will providing for the sale of the land by his executor. About the twenty-seventh day of March, 1891, an agreement was concluded between the plaintiff and the

executor by which plaintiff purchased the land for four
thousand six hundred dollars, he also agreeing to pay eighteen
dollars and twenty-one cents taxes then due for the previous
year, and which taxes the plaintiff then paid.   This action
was commenced on the seventeenth day of April, 1891, and in
September following the four thousand six hundred dollars
was paid.   Defendant fenced the land and paid the taxes as
he had agreed to do, and continued to occupy the land under
the contract up to the time the plaintiff purchased it.   There
is a conflict in the evidence as to whether plaintiff knew of
the defendant's claim to the fence at the time he made the
contract of purchase.   We think the weight of the evidence
is in favor of the conclusion that he did have such knowledge,
but, be that as it may, it is clear that he had that knowledge
before he paid the four thousand six hundred dollars, as this
action was commenced April 17, 1891.

II.   By the contract the fence was to remain the property of defendant, with the privilege of removing the same,
"until purchased by said Stricker."   Stricker did not purchase it; hence the ownership and right of removal remained
in the defendant.   Plaintiff did know of defendant's ownership of the fence and his right to remove it when he paid
the four thousand six hundred dollars, and could have protected himself to the extent of the value of the fence at that
time, if, under his contract of purchase, he was entitled to do
so.   The judgment of the district court is correct, and is
AFFIRMED.

GJEST HANSEN, Appellant, v. THE FARMERS CO-OPERATIVE
CREAMERY.

License as to Real Estate: WATERS: *Acquiescence*. Where, with the
    owner's acquiescence, waste waters from a leased portion of a
    · tract were conducted across the other part for eight years, first by
    being turned upon the lands, then through a ditch built by the
    lessee, who paid the owner an annual rental for the land occupied

by it, and then through an underground drain, the lessee had a
license for the term of the lease to conduct such waters across the
land which was not a mere right, revocable at the pleasure of the
lessor.

Appeal from Mitchell District Court.—HON. JOHN C. SHER-
WIN, Judge.

THURSDAY, OCTOBER 6, 1898.

IN March, 1887, the defendant company leased of the
plaintiff one acre of land, which was a part of a forty-acre
tract owned by him, for a term of twenty years, on which a
creamery was to be, and was, built and put in operation.
The lease was, on the eleventh of June following, reduced to
writing, and signed by the plaintiff. The waste water from
the creamery has been discharged over and through plaintiff's
land, adjacent to the creamery lot, since the creamery was
in operation, about the first of May, 1887. At first this
waste water passed over the surface, then through an open
ditch, and later through an underground drain. This action
was commenced in May, 1895, and is to enjoin the defendant
company from the further use of a ditch or drain across his
land and for damages. The use of the land for drainage
is admitted in the answer, and license and estoppel is pleaded
in defense. The district court dismissed the petition, and
the plaintiff appealed.—*Affirmed.*

Marsh & Hambrecht for appellant.

W. L. Eaton for appellee.

GRANGER, J.—The written lease is entirely silent as to
a right to pass waste water over plaintiff's land. Without
extended comment on the evidence, we find the facts, as
admitted and established, to be substantially as follows:
That, when the agreement was made to lease the lot for
creamery purposes, the question of disposing of the waste
water was talked of, and the parties understood that it must

be taken in some way across plaintiff's land, but made no definite agreement therefor; and when the creamery was started the water was turned over the surface of the land, and thus passed over it for about three years; that the water passing over the surface of the ground bred a nuisance, and the parties then agreed that an open ditch should be made and fenced one rod wide, and there should be paid for the strip of land so used five dollars per annum; that, prior to the open ditch, a cistern was made on the creamery lot, and the waste water turned into that, and, later, a hole was drilled through the rock from the bottom of the cistern to thus dispose of the water, but both methods proved unsatisfactory, and the open ditch was used; that about 1890, the open ditch being unsatisfactory to plaintiff, inverted plank troughs were placed in a ditch and covered, which makes the present drainage; that the cost of the present drainage was about three hundred dollars; that the drainage across plaintiff's land, in the different ways, was continued for about eight years, and until the spring of 1895; that the manner of the exercise of this right by the company, and the plaintiff's acquiescence therein, show quite clearly that the right was exercised in pursuance of an understanding between the parties to that effect.

Plaintiff had quite full knowledge of all the details as to work and expenditures during the entire time, and no question was made as to the right of the company to discharge the water across his land till the spring of 1895. A provision of the lease is to the effect that the company shall not create, permit, or maintain a nuisance on the leased premises, or on any part of plaintiff's premises lying adjacent thereto. Because of this provision, the right of flowage across the land must be so used as not to violate the provision. This likely had to do with the changes made from time to time. When we take the conflict of evidence, because of contradictory statements as to what was said when the agreement was made, which are, of the two, stronger in favor of defendant's claim, and then take the circumstances under which the right has been exercised, and the conclusion is not a doubtful one that defendant had a license or permission to flow the water across the land, and that the present method of doing it is one that he agreed to, not, however, to include any improper construction or keeping in repair of the drain. We are not to be understood as finding that the right of flowage across the land was a part of the contract to lease, for we think the written lease embraces what was then intended; but our finding is that independent conversations ripened into a consent or acquiescence by plaintiff in the use of the land for flowage, because of which money and labor have been expended under a mutual understanding that the right should continue during the leasehold period. In *Vannest v. Fleming,* 79 Iowa, 638, this court said: "The assent of the defendant to the construction of the ditch on his land is in the nature of a license, which, having been accepted, and the rights conferred assumed and exercised, cannot be set aside or disregarded." The case cites authorities to support the rule. The language seems clearly applicable to the facts of this case. Facts could hardly be nearer in line for the application of such a rule. It is not a mere naked license, revocable at pleasure. It amounts to a grant for a definite period, and when accepted and expenditures made to render it effective, it becomes irrevocable. 13 Am. & Eng. Enc. Law, 550; *Vannest v. Flemming, supra.* In the latter case it is said: "The parties have recognized the ditch, have plowed and farmed in accordance with it, and have expended money and labor in the performance of the contract. It can be set aside, disregarded, and annulled by neither without the consent of the other." Then follows the language we have before quoted. There is no such difference of facts in that case as to defeat it as an authority in this case. Here money and labor have been expended for years, and the plaintiff has, to some extent, at least, counseled in the doing of it. We think the judgment below is right, and it is AFFIRMED.

S. M. LEACH, Cashier, v. M. D. HILL, EXCHANGE BANK OF EARLHAM, and THOMAS EARLY, Appellants, and J. C. HILL and C. E. SISSON.

Indorsement in Blank: RIGHTS UNDER. Early told Sisson that S.
1 should buy cattle for him and that he would provide funds for the
   payment of checks for cattle, drawn by Sisson in the latter's name.
3 S. gave such a check to Hill, who endorsed it to plaintiff, in blank,
4 with intent thereby to transfer all his rights growing out of his
   selling the cattle. *Held*, this endorsement gave plaintiff the right
   to sue Early on said agreement with Sisson, and an oral agreement
   to that effect is admissible in evidence.

ORAL ACCEPTANCE. An oral agreement by a banker to accept checks
   drawn upon him by a certain person is binding as to checks drawn
1 within a reasonable time notwithstanding the drawer had no funds
   in the bank at the time of the promise or at the time the checks
5 in question were drawn, where a third person who did have funds
   in the bank had agreed to provide funds to meet such checks.

FUTURE CHECKS: *Jury question.* Plaintiff testified that he telephoned
   defendant, inquiring whether thereafter checks drawn by S., a
1 live stock buyer, would be paid, and the response was, "It will be
   all O. K. to cash checks from S. to the amount of stock he gets."
   Defendant testified that this response was an inquiry as to specific
5 checks. *Held*, that the jury was warranted in finding that it referred
   to future checks.

SAME. Where checks are given for the purchase of stock by stock
1 buyers, seventy days is not an unreasonable time for a promise to
6 accept future checks to be binding.

Parties: BANK AND CASHIER: *Trustee of express trust.* Where a
   cashier, for his bank, cashes a check upon the undertaking of
1 third persons that the check should be honored by the drawee, he
   may bring suit as cashier to recover on the check and said inci-
2 dental agreement without joining his bank as a plaintiff. In such
   suit he acts as the trustee of an express trust and may, under Code
   of 1873, section 2544, sue without joinder of him for whose benefit
   the contract sued on was made.

Appeal from Dallas District Court.—HON. JOHN A. STORY, Judge.

FRIDAY, OCTOBER 7, 1898.

IN this case verdict and judgment were rendered against
M. D. Hill, the Exchange Bank of Earlham, and Thomas
Early for one hundred and nineteen dollars and five cents, in
favor of the plaintiff, from which they appeal. The issues and
facts appear in the opinion.—*Affirmed.*

Cummins & Wright and *D. W. Woodin* for appellants.

White & Clark for appellee.

GIVEN, J.—I. The following facts, as shown by the
pleadings and proofs, are undisputed: On and for some time
prior to January 27, 1893, S. M. Leach was cashier of
the Adel Bank, of Adel, and M. D. Hill was pro-
1   prietor and cashier of the Exchange Bank of Earlham, at Earlham, Iowa. Thomas Early was a man
of ample means, residing at Earlham, and largely engaged in
buying, shipping, and selling live stock. He transacted the
principal part of his banking business in connection with
the buying and selling of stock through said Exchange Bank
of Earlham. C. E. Sisson, though possessed of no means,
was engaged in buying live stock for shipment, and purchased
stock from J. C. Hill to the amount of one hundred dollars,
which stock Hill delivered for shipment, at the agreed place,
on said twenty-seventh day of January, 1893. Sisson gave
to Hill a check on the Exchange Bank of Earlham for the
one hundred dollars, signed "C. E. Sisson." J. C. Hill
indorsed said check in blank, and delivered the same to S. M.
Leach, cashier, receiving therefor one hundred dollars of the
money of the Adel Bank. S. M. Leach, as cashier, sent said
check to the Exchange Bank of Earlham for payment, which
was refused and the check protested, at a cost to plaintiff of
two dollars and forty-eight cents. Sisson had no money in
the Bank of Earlham to his credit at that time, but Early had
credit largely above the amount of all outstanding checks
given by Sisson for stock purchased. The plaintiff's petition
is in two counts, in the first of which, in addition to the facts

above stated, it is alleged as follows: That it was verbally agreed between defendant Thomas Early and the said C. E. Sisson that the said C. E. Sisson should and would purchase live stock for and on account of the said Thomas Early, and that such stock, after its purchase by the said C. E. Sisson, as agent for the said Thomas Early, should be delivered to the said Thomas Early, and shipped either in the name of the said Thomas Early or of the defendant M. D. Hill; and that said stock should be paid for by checks drawn by the said C. E. Sisson upon the said Exchange Bank of Earlham or M. D. Hill, in favor of the person of whom said stock should be purchased; and that the said Thomas Early should and would pay and provide for the payment of said checks by the said Exchange Bank of Earlham or M. D. Hill; that the said checks should be drawn in the name of said C. E. Sisson as a matter of convenience to said Thomas Early, and that they should be in fact his own checks, and paid by him as such, and that all such checks so drawn would be paid by the defendant M. D. Hill and the Exchange Bank of Earlham out of funds in said bank belonging to the said Thomas Early, and that when so paid they should be charged to the account of said Thomas Early with said Bank; that the said C. E. Sisson should have no interest in the purchase of said stock and in the drawing of said check, except as the agent of said Thomas Early." By an amendment it is further alleged as follows: "That by said verbal agreement it was agreed between the said Thomas Early and the said C. E. Sisson that the said Thomas Early should and would carry on said business in the name of C. E. Sisson; that in said name, C. E. Sisson, all purchases of said stock should be made, and all checks in payments for stock should be drawn; that said business of the said Thomas Early should be carried on in the name of C. E. Sisson for the convenience of the said Thomas Early and to enable the said Thomas Early to separate the part of his business which he should so carry on through the instrumentality of

said C. E. Sisson from other stock purchasing which
the said Thomas Early was then and there carrying on,
and for the purpose 'of concealing from the persons with
whom the said Thomas Early dealt in carrying on said business through the instrumentality of said C. E. Sisson the fact
that said business was the business of him, the said Thomas
Early." Judgment is asked in this count against Thomas
Early for one hundred and two dollars and forty-eight cents,
with interest. In the second count plaintiff, in addition to
the matters stated in the first, alleges, in substance, as follows:
That prior to November 19, 1892, plaintiff had general knowledge as to the manner in which checks were drawn in said
business by Sisson, and that said checks had been, and were
customarily, paid by the Bank of Earlham. That prior to
said date plaintiff had paid checks of said Sisson, drawn in
said manner, after inquiring as to each of M. D. Hill by
telephone. That on said nineteenth day of November, 1892,
certain checks so drawn by Sisson being presented to be
cashed, plaintiff made inquiry of M. D. Hill, by telephone,
through the agent of the telephone company at Adel, "whether
any and all checks thereafter drawn by the said C. E. Sisson
in said business of purchasing stock would be paid, and at the
same time in said manner informed said M. D. Hill that said
information was desired to avoid the necessity of calling him
up by telephone thereafter when each such check given in
said business should be presented." That in response thereto,
M. D. Hill authorized said telephone agent to deliver the following in writing to the plaintiff: "It will be all O. K. to
cash checks from C. E. Sisson to the amount of stock he gets.
[Signed] M. D. Hill." He alleges that, relying thereon,
plaintiff paid all checks made in said manner presented to it
without further inquiry, upon Sisson's statement that they
were given for stock, and that all of said checks were promptly
paid by M. D. Hill, as cashier, up to the date of the check to
J. C. Hill. In conclusion of this count plaintiff asks judgment against J. C. Hill, M. D. Hill, Exchange Bank of Earl-

ham, and Thomas Early for one hundred and two dollars and forty-eight cents. Thomas Early answered, admitting what we have stated as to undisputed facts, and denying every other allegation in the petition and amendment. M. D. Hill answered, admitting that said banks were banking institutions, and that he was proprietor of the Exchange Bank of Earlham; also admitting that Sisson gave J. C. Hill the check . set out, that Hill sold and indorsed it to the Adel Bank, and that the Bank of Earlham refused to pay the same, and that it was protested. He denies all other allegations in the first count. As to the second count he admits that he stated by telephone to the agent at Adel, on November 19, 1892, as set out in the petition, but alleges that it was in response to an inquiry asking him about certain checks named in the inquiry, and that said answer related to no other checks. He denies all other allegations in said second count. In an amendment filed to conform to the evidence, M. D. Hill and the Exchange Bank of Earlham say that the undertaking or promise sued on in the second count was not in writing signed by these defendants, or by their authority, and that they had no money of Sisson, when said check was made or presented. J. C. Hill answered, admitting the allegations of the petition, and alleging that, as between him and his co-defendants other than Sisson, he is liable only as surety; that by the indorsement of the check he intended to assign and transfer all causes of action in his favor growing out of the transaction to the plaintiff, "and consents that plaintiff may have judgment against his co-defendants therefor." - He asks that he be held liable as surety only. By way of cross petition against his co-defendants other than Sisson, he repeats the allegations of the petition, alleges knowledge of the insolvency of Sisson, and the solvency of the other defendants, and that he sold the stock and took the check in the belief that the defendants, or some other responsible party, were responsible for the payment of the check. He asks that, in case the plaintiff is not entitled to judgment, he have judgment against his co-defendants for the value of the stock sold and delivered. Judgment was rendered against J. C. Hill in favor of the plaintiff in a former trial as to him, and on the further trial the case was submitted on the issues joined between the plaintiff and Thomas Early, the Exchange Bank of Earlham, or M. D. Hill; and these are the only parties appearing to this appeal.

II. This case is presented with unusual elaboration on the part of the appellants. The questions discussed were raised in various ways during the progress of the trial, and each exception is separately urged. We will not follow the order of appellant's argument, but consider each contention upon all the exceptions by which it is raised. Section 2644 of subdivision 2 of the Code of 1873 required that the petition must contain "the names of the parties to the action, plaintiffs and defendants, followed by the word 'Petition.'" This petition is entitled "S. M. Leach, Cashier," as plaintiff. Section 2543 of said Code provided that "every action must be prosecuted in the name of the real party in interest, except as provided in the next section." The petition shows, and so does the proof, that this check was purchased by S. M. Leach, as cashier of the Adel Bank, with its funds, for that bank, and that whatever may be due on these causes of action is due to that bank. After the close of the evidence in chief, appellants moved for a verdict, "because the testimony shows without dispute that at the time the suit was brought, and now, the check upon which it is founded was owned by a corporation known as the Adel Bank, and, therefore, this plaintiff has no right, title, or interest in the alleged cause of action." Section 2544, Code 1873, provides that "an executor or administrator, a guardian, a trustee of an express trust, a party with whom, or in whose name, a contract is made for the benefit of another, or party expressly authorized by statute, may sue in his own name without joining with him the party for whose benefit the suit is prosecuted." In this, as in most of their contentions, appellants assume that the causes of action are based upon

the checks alone; and the authorities cited are only applicable
to such a case. As we view the petition, neither count asks to
recover upon the check alone, but upon the alleged agreements,
to which the check is but an incident. In the first count
plaintiff seeks to charge Early upon the alleged agreement
between him and Sisson, and in the second to charge the
appellants on that agreement and the further agreement,
alleged to have been made between Leach and Hill, cashiers,
by telephone. Without these alleged agreements there would
be no cause of action shown against either Early, M. D. Hill,
or the Bank of Earlham. It is by virtue of the contract with
J. C. Hill and with M. D. Hill that plaintiff is entitled to
recover, if at all; and, as these were made with S. M.
Leach, cashier, he may maintain an action thereon without
joining the bank. In *Rice v. Savery,* 22 Iowa, 477, wherein
sections 2757 and 2758 of the Revision, which were identical
with said sections 2543 and 2544, were under consideration,
it is said: "It is no longer absolutely necessary (sections
2757, 2758), that the party to whom a promise is made shall
be the plaintiff on the record, in an action to enforce it. That
is to say, if the promise is made for the benefit of another,
who is the real party in interest, the latter may sue, though
the contract or promise be made to an agent or trustee; or, in
the case last supposed, the agent, or trustee, or person in
whose name a contract is made for the benefit of another, may
sue without joining the party for whose benefit the suit is
prosecuted. This is well settled by the previous adjudica-
tions of this court. *Conyngham v. Smith,* 16 Iowa, 471;
Cottle v. Cole, 20 Iowa, 482; *Taylor v. Adair,* 22 Iowa, 279."
It cannot be questioned that payment to Leach, cashier, of
whatever liability appellants may be under to the Adel Bank,
would have been a full satisfaction as to that bank. His
authority as cashier is undisputed, and therefore he held this
claim as trustee of an express trust for the bank, and under
said section 2544 may sue in his own name. We conclude
that under the exceptions made in said section 2544 S. M.

Leach is entitled to prosecute this action in his representative capacity as cashier without joining the Adel Bank.

III. Appellants, again assuming that this action is upon the check alone, insist that the only right of action which passed to the plaintiff is that which arises upon the check, and that only those who appear thereby as parties thereto are chargeable thereunder, and therefore appellants, not appearing as parties to the check, are not liable in this action. *Watson v. Cheshire,* 18 Iowa, 209; *Ridgeway v. Raymond,* 82 Iowa, 592; and *First Nat. Bank of Canton v. Railway Co.,* 52 Iowa, 378, are cited. In the first case Cheshire, payee, indorsed the note of Moore "without recourse" to Griffith, who indorsed it "without recourse" to Watson. Held, that Watson could not sue Cheshire on the indorsement. It is said: "Under our statute it may be that Griffith might specially assign his cause of action against Cheshire to the plaintiff, but the mere indorsement of the note without recourse would not have this effect. Such an indorsement operates simply to transfer the title to the note, not an independent cause of action." The indorsement of this check is not without recourse. J. C. Hill is subject to recourse, and may well have intended, as he says he did, to transfer to plaintiff all his rights of action growing out of the sale of the stock. In *Ridgeway v. Raymond* a partnership had executed its note to a bank, and after a dissolution of the partnership one of the partners executed a renewal note in the name of the late firm, the bank having no knowledge of the dissolution, and not intending to release either partner. The bank transferred the second note to the plaintiff, who sought to recover on the first note. It was held that he could not treat the note assigned to him as a nullity and sue on the first, in the absence of a showing that the bank was without knowledge of the dissolution of the partnership. It is said: "There is no averment in the petition from which we may infer that the bank ever regarded the note as invalid, and, if it regarded it as valid, knowing the facts, its treatment of the note is conclusive upon its assignee, the plaintiff." In *First National Bank of Canton v. Railway Co.,* 52 Iowa, 378, it was held that a bill of exchange drawn upon a general fund, and not accepted, did not operate as an assignment of the fund, but was evidence to be considered in determining the intention of the parties, and that the evidence was not sufficient to show that the draft was intended as an assignment of a fund subsequently coming into the hands of the drawee. The case recognizes that there may be evidence other than the draft to show what was intended to be assigned. It is a well-established rule of law that where a contract is made for the benefit of a person not a party thereto such third party may bring action thereon. *Johnson v. Collins,* 14 Iowa, 64; *Knott v. Railway Co.,* 84 Iowa, 463; *Thomas v. Schee,* 80 Iowa, 237; *Becker v. Keokuk Water Works,* 79 Iowa, 419; *First M. E. Church v. Sweny,* 85 Iowa, 628. The alleged contract between Early and Sisson, if made, was manifestly for the benefit of those who might take Sisson's checks for stock purchased by him under that contract. The jury was warranted in finding that said contract was made, and it follows, under the rule first stated, that J. C. Hill had a right to charge Early under the contract with the price of the stock sold to Sisson. Now, it may be conceded that, if nothing further appeared than the check, and the action was thereon alone, appellants would not be liable, as they are not shown by the instrument to be parties to it. This action as to Early is not upon the check alone, but upon the contract under which he is liable, and which inured to the benefit of J. C. Hill. If nothing more appeared than the check and the indorsement thereof, it might be said that Early is not liable; but he is confronted by his contract with Sisson. This court has many times held that an assignment of a debt carries with it the security. It has been so held where promissory notes secured by mortgage were transferred, and we see no reason why the rule should not apply to the transfer of checks. Early's liability is in the nature of a security, and under this rule passed with the transfer of the check. J. C. Hill could transfer his right of action against Early by parol, and it is manifest that both he and Leach intended and understood that all rights which Hill had growing out of the transaction were to pass to the plaintiff. By his agreement Early promised acceptance and payment of the checks of Sisson given for stock purchased, and this obligation passed by the transfer of the check, and plaintiff is entitled to maintain an action thereon. See *Fairlee v. Herring,* 3 Bing, 625 ; *Spaulding v. Andrews,* 48 Pa. St. 411; *Barker v. Guilliam,* 5 Iowa, 511. Appellants, still assuming that this action is upon the check alone, contend that evidence of the alleged agreement is inadmissible. If the action was upon the check alone, the authorities cited would be in point; but, being upon the contract as well, plaintiff has the right to prove it.

4

IV. The jury was warranted in finding that the answer of M. D. Hill by telephone to the inquiry of S. M. Leach related to future checks given by Sisson "to the amount of stock he gets." Appellants contend that such acceptances must be on the instrument, or upon a separate paper after the instrument is drawn, or "by writing stating that a party may, in the future, draw a draft, and that the acceptor will honor it when presented." Counsel discuss the question whether the answer of M. D. Hill was in writing, the same having been taken down in writing by the telephone agent at Adel, and the writing delivered to the plaintiff. In the view we take of the case, it is not necessary to determine this question. In *Walton v. Mandeville,* 56 Iowa, 597, after a full review of the subject on a re-hearing, it was held that a verbal acceptance of an order is valid and enforceable only where the drawee has funds of the drawer in his hands, so that by payment of the order he satisfies his own debt. Now, it is true that M. D. Hill did not have any money of Sisson's in his hands, nor was it intended that he should; but he did have money of Early's. He was fully informed

5

as to the contract between Early and Sisson, and consented to pay and had paid the checks drawn by Sisson upon the creditor out of the funds of Early. When he gave that answer he knew that Sisson was acting for Early, and that the checks would be in effect the checks of Early. Under these circumstances we think it must be said that the acceptance is valid, even if it was verbal. A promise to accept future drafts is only binding for a reasonable time, but, in view of the nature of the business, this check was drawn within a reasonable time after the promise. There can be no doubt but that plaintiff paid the one hundred dollars for this claim of J. C. Hill relying upon the promise and assurance of M. D. Hill that Sisson's check would be honored. M. D. Hill did so because he had the credit and funds of Early to back him, and he should not now be excused from liability because Sisson had no funds in the Bank of Earlham.

V. Appellants discuss at length some thirty-five assignments of error based upon rulings on evidence and instructions. We have examined these assignments with care, and find that they are largely based upon the contentions already considered, and, for the reasons stated, are not well taken. The other rulings complained of, where at all questionable, were without prejudice to the appellants. Our conclusion upon the whole record is that the judgment of the district court should be AFFIRMED. -

---

H. D. FISCHER and J. P. KNORR, Appellants, v. JOHNSON LANE & Co., et al.

License: ABANDONMENT BY SALE. A sale of corn cribs constructed on land under a bare license or permission from the owner operates as a revocation of the license or tenancy at will and as a desertion or abandonment of the premises.

FIXTURES: *Personal property.* Corn cribs constructed upon the lands of another under his bare license of permission remains personal property and may be transferred as such.

TENANCY AT WILL: *Jury question.* Consent that corn cribs constructed on land under a bare license from the owner may remain thereon after their sale to a third person may be inferred from the fact that they remain on the land with the knowledge of the owner

8   and without objection on his part for such a length of time and under such circumstances that objection might have been expected if the owner of the land did not assent.

REMOVAL BY TENANT. An agreement that structures erected upon land by permission or license of the owner may be removed by the person making them will be implied in the absence of any

4   interest of the latter in enhancing the value of the land or of other facts or circumstances showing an intention that the structure should not be removed.

REMOVAL BY TRESPASSER. A trespasser who makes erections on the

8   land of another cannot remove the structures erected.

Evidence: BILL OF SALE. The bill of sale by which the personalty

2   is transferred is the best evidence of sale.

HARMLESS ADMISSION OF. The admission of evidence of conversations between the parties to a sale of corn cribs, at the time of the sale, in regard to the seller's statement as to the terms under which he had possession of the land on which the cribs were placed, in an action by a subsequent purchaser of the land against the buyer

6   for removing the cribs, was not prejudicial to plaintiff, where the court told the jury that the seller, as a tenant at will of the land, could not transfer the right of possession, and the sale amounted to an abandonment of the premises, and when this conversation was but a repetition of undisputed testimony.

Practice: ESTOPPEL: *Procedure.* A party is not estopped from asserting a claim on the trial by the fact that he made a different

5   representation in regard thereto to the adverse parties before the trial, where the latter was not misled thereby.

Appeal: OBJECTION BELOW. The objection to a motion to strike out

5   a motion to a pleading that the motion was not in writing, as required by Code, section 3551, cannot be first urged on appeal.

Vendor and Purchaser: NOTICE. A purchaser of land with notice

1   that corn cribs thereon were claimed by a third party, in possession acquires no better claim to the cribs than his vendor had.

Appeal from Hardin District Court.—HON. B. P. BIRDSALL, Judge.

FRIDAY, OCTOBER 7, 1898.

THE plaintiffs purchased eleven and two-tenths acres of land of the Western Town Lot Company, September 23,

1892, on which were standing five hundred and seventy-two feet of corn cribs and forty-two rods of fence, which the defendants removed in December of the same year. This is an action for the value of the cribs and fence. Trial to jury. Verdict and judgment for the defendants, and the plaintiffs appeal.—*Affirmed.*

Albrook & Lundy for appellants.

Wesley Martin and *Huff & Ward* for appellees.

LADD, J.—The corncribs in controversy were erected on what are called two inch by four or six inch stringers, resting on the earth, and on land belonging to Western Town Lot Company. All but five lengths were placed there by Nichols Bros., prior to 1886, by virtue of an oral understanding with the owner that they might remain on the land until sold, or the firm notified to remove them. In October, 1891, Nichols Bros. transferred these cribs by bill of sale to Johnson, Lane & Co., who constructed the five lengths mentioned. In September, 1892, the Western Town Lot Company contracted for the sale of this land to the plaintiffs, agreeing to execute a conveyance thereof, with usual covenants of warranty, upon the payment of the purchase price. These cribs were not mentioned, and in December of the same year were removed by the defendants, of whom compensation is claimed. It may be added that theretofore recovery for the value of the same property was denied plaintiffs in an action against the Western Town Lot Company. In that case it was alleged Johnson, Lane & Co. had the right to remove the cribs, while here it is asserted they have become a part of the realty. As the defendants do not appeal, however, we are not permitted to pass upon the ruling by which the plaintiffs were held not to be estopped from taking these contradictory positions. The evidence shows without dispute that neither Nichols Bros. nor Johnson, Lane & Co. intended these cribs as permanent improvements on the

land. They were placed near the railway to facilitate loading
corn for shipment over the line of the Chicago & Northwestern
Railway Company, which controlled the Western Town Lot
Company; and, if the defendants are deprived of their property or its value, this must be done because of the technical
rules of the law. The plaintiffs were fully advised, when
they purchased the land, of the occupancy for many years by
Nichols Bros., and that Johnson, Lane & Co. were then in
possession. The evidence also tends to show that they had
actual knowledge that the latter company claimed to own
the buildings. Whatever doubt, however, there may be on
the question of notice was resolved in favor of the defendants by the verdict. The plaintiffs, then, having notice,
acquired no better claim to the cribs than the Western Town
Lot Company had.

II.   Nichols Bros. had no interest in the land, and only
the bare license or permission to occupy it for a particular purpose. The cribs were then personal property, and
might be transferred as such. *Walton v. Wray,* 54
2   Iowa, 531; *Melhop v. Meinhart,* 70 Iowa, 685; *Mickle
v. Douglass,* 75 Iowa, 82; *Wilgus v. Gettings,* 21 Iowa,
178; *Bank v. Stanton,* 55 Minn. 211 (56 N. W. Rep. 821);
Carlin v. Ritter, 68 Md. 478 (13 Atl. Rep. 370; 16 Atl. Rep.
301). And of the sale the bill of sale was the best evidence.
But the sale or transfer of the right of occupancy operated
as a revocation of the license or tenancy at will, and must be
construed as a desertion or abandonment of the premises.
Cooper v. Adams, 6 Cush. 90; *King v. Lawson,* 98 Mass.
311; *Doak v. Donelson,* 2 Yerg. 249 (24 Am. Dec. 485).
This is because a mere tenant at will has no interest or estate
in the land. The important inquiry, then, was whether the
defendants were mere trespassers, or in possession with the
assent of the Western Town Lot Company. If as
3   trespassers, then they had no right to remove the
buildings; if in possession with the assent of the
owner, in the absence of other proof they were presumed to

be tenants at will. Code, section 2991. There is no direct testimony of consent on the part of the owner; but we think the circumstances were such that this might have been inferred, and was, therefore, a question of fact to be determined by the jury. The Western Town Lot Company was organized and existed for the purpose of promoting the business of the Chicago & Northwestern Railway Company. It was one of its agencies in carrying on its affairs, and was controlled and managed solely in its interest. Its land commissioner was that of the railroad company, whose division superintendents were authorized to exercise control over all its lands. It was customary to permit the erection of cribs and warehouses on these lands near the track, in order to promote the traffic over the railway. Leases were usually, though not always, made. Johnson, Lane & Co. had been in possession of the grain elevators and corncribs at Hubbard for nearly a year. The change in ownership had been brought to the attention of the railway company through its local agent. The grain had been shipped over its road, a part of the cribs constructed, and all of them filled with corn which was shipped during this time. Their possession was of such a character as to call the attention of the officers of the railway company as well as of the Town Lot Company to their occupancy of the land, and of their claims of the right to do so. No objection was made to such possession. It is true that the officers of the Town Lot Company deny knowledge of the location of the cribs. But this simply raises an issue, as there is no evidence denying such knowledge on the part of the division superintendents of the railway, who gave Nichols Bros. leave to construct the cribs, and who, under the evidence, were authorized to consent to the use of the premises by the defendants. We think, from these facts, in the absence of other evidence, knowledge on the part of the railroad officials, and their consent to such possession, may be inferred. The defendants had continued in possession for such a length of time and under such circumstances that objection might well have been expected had not the officials assented thereto.

That consent to occupancy may be inferred from actual possession with the knowledge of the owner, in the absence of objection, is settled in *Martin v. Knapp,* 57 Iowa, 342. It must be borne in mind we are not determining whether there was assent, but whether the circumstances were such that this issue was properly submitted for the determination of the jury.

III.   The question now arises whether, even though Johnson, Lane & Co. occupied the premises with their cribs, and erected others with the assent of the owner, they might remove them without any express agreement so to do.
4   We think that an agreement for the removal of the cribs may well be implied from a separate ownership of them and the real property. It is evident there was no intention by either party that they become a part of the land. The defendant had no estate in the realty, and for this reason no interest in enhancing its value. "Where the erections are made by one having no estate in the land, and hence no interest in enhancing it value, by the permission or license of the owner, an agreement that the structures shall remain the property of the person making them will be implied, in the absence of any other facts or circumstances tending to show a different intention." *Bank v. Stanton,* 55 Minn. 211 (56 N. W. Rep. 822).

IV.   The appellant pleaded in reply that the defendants were estopped from setting up occupancy as tenants at will, because Johnson, a member of the firm, had informed appellants that his firm held a lease of the premises from the Western Town Lot Company, which gave it ninety days within which to remove the cribs, and that on these statements they based their actions against the Western Land Company. This portion of the reply was stricken from the files on motion of the defendants, made orally during the course of the trial, but taken down by the official stenographer.
5   The appellants made no objection, at the time, to the manner of making the motion; and, having failed to do so, they will be deemed to have acquiesced therein, and to

have waived compliance with the statute which requires motions assailing pleadings to be in writing. Code, section 3551. Whether the ruling on this motion was correct, we need not determine, as the evidence shows conclusively that the plaintiffs were in no way misled by what Johnson is said to have stated. The action based upon this statement was dismissed, and another begun, after the plaintiffs were fully advised they could not rely on the alleged statement of Johnson.

V.   Nichols and Johnson were permitted to testify to a conversation had between them at the time of the sale of the cribs, in which Nichols related the terms under which he held possession. While this was in the nature of hearsay,

6   it was without prejudice, because (1) it was simply a repetition of what Nichols had testified to, and which was undisputed, and (2) the court advised the jury that Nichols Bros., as tenants at will, could not transfer right of possession, and the sale by them amounted to an abandonment of the premises.

What has been said disposes of the criticism of the instructions. Those requested, in so far as they announced correct rules of law, were included in those given by the court. The other errors assigned require no consideration. The judgment is AFFIRMED.

T. B. TURPIN, Appellant, v. JOHN F. GRESHAM, et al.

Reformation: EVIDENCE. A note contained a printed promise to pay the principal five years after date, with interest payable annually until paid; also a written recital that "this note is payable in installments of eight dollars or more per month, with interest on the amount paid." The two makers and the scrivener, who was the partner of the payee, testified that the agreement was that during the five years no payments were required other than the monthly installments, with interest thereon. Other witnesses testified to corroborative circumstances. The payee had accepted
1   monthly payments during the first year. The only evidence to support payee's contention that interest was payable annually was

that of himself, and the fact that the makers knew of the printed clause making it so payable. The makers claimed to have understood the written clause to prevail. *Held*, that the note should be reformed so as to make it conform to the makers' contention.

Notes and Bills: INCONSISTENT CONDITIONS. The fact that a note for six hundred and fifty dollars is payable in monthly installments of eight dollars or more is not inconsistent with a provision fixing its maturity at five years after its date for, while payments could not be less than eight dollars, any payment might be greater than that sum.

UNREASONABLENESS. An agent for the sale of land loaned six hundred and fifty dollars to another to effect a sale, on a note payable in five years in monthly installments, interest payable monthly on the amount of the installment then payable. *Held*, that, although the terms of payment were unusually liberal as to the borrower, they were not proven to be unreasonable as against the lender.

TENDER: *Costs*. After the commencement of an action by a payee claiming the entire note to be due, which was denied, the maker tendered an installment alleged by him to have become due on the note pending suit. On its rejection by the payee, the maker paid it into court, and set up the tender by supplemental pleading. *Held*, on a finding in favor of the maker as to the terms of payment, that the plea of tender, although needless, was not an admission of something due on the note when suit was brought, so as to entitle plaintiff to a judgment for the amount tendered with costs.

Appeal from Davis District Court.—Hon. W. S. Withrow, *Judge.*

Friday, October 7, 1898.

Action in equity upon a promissory note, and to foreclose a mortgage securing the same. From a decree in defendant's favor, the plaintiff appeals.—*Affirmed.*

H. C. Traverse for appellant.

Payne & Sowers for appellees.

Waterman, J.—The note in suit is in the following form: "$650.00   November 26th, 1895. Five years after date, for value received, we promise to pay to T. B. Turpin or order six hundred and fifty dollars, payable at Bloomfield, with interest payable annually at the rate of eight per cent. per annum, until paid. Interest when due to become principal, and draw eight per cent. interest. If this note is not paid when due, we agree to pay reasonable costs of collection, including attorney's fees, and also consent that judgment may be entered for the amount, by any justice of the peace. This note is payable in installments of eight dollars or more per month, with interest on the amount paid. John F. Gresham. Laura F. Gresham." The mortgage contained the usual condition for the payment of the note, and provided further: "If, however, any of these conditions are not complied with, said note shall become due and collectible at once," etc. This action is brought because of a failure to pay the first installment of interest on the face of the note. The defense set up is that the agreement between the parties was that the makers of the note were to pay the same in monthly installments, with interest on each of such amounts to the time of payment, and that no other payments were to be required of them until the maturity of the note, and that, by mistake, there was a failure to express this agreement clearly in the instruments as executed. The note and mortgage, as they stand, are certainly somewhat ambiguous in terms. The two defendants, Gresham and his wife, and the scrivener who drew the instruments, and who was the partner in business of plaintiff, all testify, in substance, that the agreement was that during the five years no payments were to be required of the makers other than the monthly installments, with the interest thereon. Other witnesses give evidence of corroborative circumstances, and the acts of the parties under the contract lend support to the claim to this extent, that these payments were so made and received during the period of one year. Against this we find only the testimony of the plaintiff, with the single incident that the maker.i of the note, at the time they executed the papers, knew of the printed clause, both in that instrument and in the mortgage relating to the payment of annual interest. This latter fact is met by the defendants with the assertion that the clause regarding the payments in installments was written in the note, and they were informed by the scrivener, and believed, that the written portion would control, and that the instrument as prepared would effect the purpose and intent of the parties.

In a case of this kind, where, either through mistake of law or fact, an instrument fails to express the contract of the parties, equity will interfere with appropriate relief. *Lee v. Percival,* 85 Iowa, 639; *Stafford v. Fetters,* 55 Iowa, 484; *Nowlin v. Pyne,* 47 Iowa, 293; 1 Story Equity 2   Jurisprudence, section 115. Appellant thinks that to give effect to defendant's claim will nullify the provision in the note which fixes the time of its maturity at five years after its date. It is said that no complaint is made of this portion of the instrument, and that it could not fall due at that time if the makers are allowed to pay at the rate of only eight dollars per month. It may be said in response to this that the makers are not limited to monthly payments of eight dollars. The provision in the note as reformed is that the payments shall not be in less amounts. They may, however, be of greater sums. This is in accordance with the weight of the testimony, and with the written clause in the original note. We do not see any want of consistency in the contract, as found by the trial court. Again, it is 3   said by appellant that the contract as claimed by defendant is unreasonable; that no man would loan money on such terms. That it is an unusual contract we readily concede; but it depends upon circumstances whether it was unreasonable, and the circumstances disclosed do not affirmatively show it to be so. We do not say that the evidence establishes it to be reasonable, but only that it does not establish the contrary. Plaintiff, as agent for the sale of a tract of real estate, loaned defendants the money in suit, with which to purchase it. He might have been willing to make more than usually favorable terms for the loan, in order to effect the sale. We cannot say from the evidence that the whole transaction was not to his advantage.

II. After this action was begun, a monthly installment fell due on the note. It was tendered by defendants, and, upon plaintiff's refusal to accept it, the amount was paid into court, and the fact of such tender was set up by a supplemental pleading in this case. Plaintiff contends that
4   this was an admission of something due him, and that he should at least have judgment for the amount tendered, with costs. This action was brought December 29, 1896. Plaintiff claimed the whole amount of the note to be then due and payable. The installment spoken of became due in January following, according to defendants' interpretation of the contract, and was promptly tendered. There was no occasion for setting up the transaction in this case, and the fact that it was pleaded by no means amounts to an admission that anything was due on the contract at the time plaintiff brought suit. Indeed, the contrary is clearly shown by the terms of the supplemental answer. It was defendants' duty to make the payment when due. The law would place them in a very awkward dilemma if, because of the performance of this duty, it entailed upon them the payment of costs, in an action unjustly brought against them. The trial court reformed the contract by leaving out of it the provision for the payment of annual interest. It found that plaintiff's action was prematurely brought, dismissed the same, and gave defendants judgment for costs. We see no cause to interfere with this holding.—AFFIRMED.

STATE OF IOWA v. C. C. HEACOCK, Appellant.

Libel: INDICTMENT. An indictment for libel, charging that the writing was printed and circulated to injure prosecutor "and others," and that it tended to provoke prosecutor "and others" to
1   wrath, etc., where it clearly shows that the alleged libel was directed against prosecutor and was designed to provoke him to
3   wrath, is not defective, since the words "and others" are surplusage.

COURT AND JURY. An instruction in a prosecution for libel that the
jury, in exercising the authority conferred upon them by Code,
1873, sections 4102, 4488, to determine the law as well as the facts,
10 should reflect whether from their habits of thought, their study
and experience they were better qualified than the court to judge
of the law, and that they should not reject the court's view of the
law, unless they have a deep and confident conviction that the
court is wrong and they are right, is proper.

SAME. It is the duty of the court to instruct the jury in a prosecution
11 for libel in regard to the law, notwithstanding the authority con.
ferred upon them by Code, 1873, sections 4102, 4488, to determine
the law as well as the facts.

SAME. The authority conferred upon the jury in prosecutions for
libel by Code, 1873, sections 4102, 4488, to determine the law as
well as the facts does not require them to determine all legal
11 questions which may arise on the trial, e. g , the sufficiency of the
indictment, the qualifications of jurors and the admissibility of
evidence, but only such matters as they may consider in deliberating upon a verdict.

EVIDENCE. It is competent in a prosecution for libel to introduce so
much of the copy of the paper in which the libel was published,
4 in addition to the portion showing the libelous article, as is necessary with other evidence to show that it was a paper published
by defendant.

SAME. It is not competent for defendant in a criminal case, whose
6 veracity has not been attacked, to show his reputation for truth
and veracity, but it is permissible to show his general good character or reputation as to the trait involved in the charge against
. him.

SAME. It is not competent for defendant charged with libel to testify
that the article in controversy "is true in every particular" where
8 from the nature and scope of the article such testimony would
necessarily be his conclusion and not a statement of facts within
his knowledge.

SAME. The testimony of defendant charged with libel as to what he
meant by the article in question is properly excluded where the
language of the article is not ambiguous.

HARMLESS ERROR. The exclusion of a question on the cross-examination of the prosecutor in a trial for libel tending to elicit a conversation between him and a third person showing bias against
5 the defendant, is not reversible error where the latter testified to
the conversation, since a denial by the prosecutor that he made
the statements showing bias would not have laid a foundation for
contradicting him on that point and thus impeaching him as a
witness.

IMPEACHMENT. The answer of a witness to questions asked on cross-
5 examination to show his bias cannot be contradicted by other
witnesses.

SUBSEQUENT LIBEL. Articles published by defendant charged with
4 libel, subsequent to that on which the indictment is based may be
competent for the purpose of showing the motive prompting the
article in question.

Instructions Construed Together. A charge that, "Before you will
be justified in convicting defendant. the state must have satisfied
9 you and from the evidence of the truthfulness," etc., without
mentioning reasonable doubt, is cured where the next paragraph
of the charge defines reasonable doubt, and states that the defendant must be acquitted if the jury are not satisfied of his guilt
beyond a reasonable doubt.

Misconduct of Judge. An editor charged with criminal libel defended
7 himself on the trial, though not a lawyer. He offered in evidence
the minutes of the testimony before the grand jury. The court
inquired if he intended to show that the evidence of the prosecutor was false, and that prosecutor knew it to be false when given,
which he answered in the affirmative, and the court said, "It is a
little dangerous, if you do not succeed," and admitted the papers.
After the evidence in the case was submitted, the minutes were
excluded on the ground that they had not been contradicted
according to the offer. *Held*, that the court's remark was not
prejudicial.

Appeal: CHANGE OF VENUE. An application for a transfer of a cause
to one or the other judges of the district for trial, on the ground
that the judge to whom the application is addressed is prejudiced
2 against the defendant to such an extent that he cannot obtain a
fair and impartial trial before him, is addressed to the sound des-
cretion of the judge and his decison will not be disturbed on
appeal in the absence of the abuse of such discretion.

OBJECTION BELOW. The objection that the introduction in evidence
of the entire copy of the newspaper in which the alleged libel
4 was printed was error cannot be urged on appeal, where the objection in the trial court to such evidence was based on an entirely
different ground.

Appeal from Washington District Court.—HON. A. R.
DEWEY, Judge.

FRIDAY, OCTOBER 7, 1898.

THE defendant was convicted of the crime of libel, and
from the judgment, which required that he pay a fine of six
VOL. 106 Ia—13

hundred dollars and costs, and that he stand committed to
the county jail until the fine should be paid, he appeals.—
Affirmed.

C. C. Heacock, M. W. Bailey and *H. & W. Scofield* for
appellant.

Milton Remley, Attorney General, *W. S. Brookhart,*
County Attorney, and *Jesse A. Miller* for the State.

ROBINSON, J.—The defendant publishes at Brighton a
newspaper known as the *"Brighton Enterprise."* The alleged
libel consists of an article prepared by the defendant, and
published by him in his paper, entitled "Impeached Impeach-
ers." The article purported to give an account of a trial in
justice's court, to which Heacock was a party, and which
involved the ownership of a harness and buggy. The defendant testified as a witness in his own behalf, and the article
states that one A. J. Johnson, commonly called "Doc" Johnson, and two others, who are referred to as Hen Jordan and
Tom Pierce, testified for the purpose of impeaching the
defendant as a witness. The article mentions Jordan and
Pierce in disparaging terms, and then refers to Johnson in
language which the jury was fully authorized to find
libelous. The indictment charges that the article was
maliciously and willfully inserted in the *Brighton
Enterprise* by the defendant, and that it was willfully and
maliciously circulated and distributed by him, "for the purpose of defaming, injuring and vilifying the person and
character of A. J. Johnson and others, and the same tended to
provoke the said A. J. Johnson and others to wrath, and to
expose them to public hatred, contempt, and ridicule, and to
deprive them of the benefits of public confidence and social
intercourse. * * *"

I. After the defendant was arraigned, he filed an application, verified by himself, for a transfer of the cause to one

of the other judges of the district for trial, on the ground that the judge to whom the application was addressed was "prejudiced against the defendant to such an extent that he cannot obtain a fair and impartial trial before him." An application of that character was to be granted or refused by the court, in the exercise of a sound discretion. We do not find anything in the record which shows an abuse of the discretion which was vested in the court.

II. It is claimed that the indictment is defective in not being direct and certain as to the offense charged and the particular circumstances of the offense. This claim is founded upon the fact that the indictment contains the words "and others," following the name of Johnson, in two instances, thus charging the defendant with the alleged libel, for the purpose of defaming, injuring, and vilifying "A. J. Johnson and others," and that it "tended to provoke the said A. J. Johnson and others to wrath," etc. Section 4306 of the Code of 1873, in force when this cause was tried, provided that no indictment was insufficient "for any surplusage or repugnant allegation, or for any repetition, when there is sufficient matter alleged to indicate clearly the offense and the person charged." The words "and others" were, at most, mere surplusage. The indictment showed clearly that the alleged libel was directed against Johnson, and was designed to provoke him to wrath, and to expose him to public hatred, contempt, and ridicule, and to deprive him of the benefits of public confidence and social intercourse. Prejudice could not have resulted to defendant from the improper use of the words in question. And that is true of the fifth paragraph of the charge, in which reference is made to the publication of the article in controversy "with the malicious intention of injuring the parties referred to" in the indictment. The subsequent portions of the paragraph required the jury, in order to convict, to find that the malicious intent of the defendant had especial reference to Johnson.

III. For the purpose of showing different articles pub-lished in the *Brighton Enterprise,* the state was permitted to introduce in evidence all of each copy of the paper which con-tained the article which was desired for use. The appel-
4   lant insists that only so much of each copy as showed the desired article contained therein should have been received. It was necessary to introduce so much of each copy as was necessary, with other evidence, to show that it was a paper published by the defendant. What, if anything, appeared in the copies in addition to the articles desired as evidence is not shown. Moreover, we are of the opinion that the appellant cannot rightfully complain of the admission of the copies in evidence, for the reason that his only objection thereto was stated in words as follows: "Defendant objects to any of the papers except the first one, the copy containing the libel; objects to all other papers published after." All of the copies were offered together, and it will be observed that the defendant failed to state any ground of objection to them. If it can be said that the objection was based upon the theory that publications made after the alleged libel appeared were immaterial, the answer is that the subsequent articles tended to show the motive with which the first one was published, and were competent evidence for that purpose.

IV. Johnson was a witness for the state, and on cross-examination was asked if he did not say to one La Mott, at a time and place specified, that if the defendant were lying in a ditch, drowning, and he could save him by reaching out his hand, he would not do so, but would let the defendant drown. An objection to the question was sustained, and of that ruling the appellant complains. The question was
       probably asked to show the bias of the witness. If it
5   was competent for that purpose, and an answer thereto
       should have been permitted, the error was without prejudice, for the reason that La Mott afterwards testified that Johnson did say to him what the question suggested, and his testimony was not contradicted. It is said, however,

that an answer should have been required of Johnson, in order that, if he had denied making the statement inquired for, he might have been contradicted by other witnesses; but that would not have been permissible practice. *State v. Townsend*, 66 Iowa, 741. Johnson was also asked on cross-examination in regard to a statement alleged to have been made by him to one White, respecting the testimony of one Buck in some proceedings had in Keokuk. The defendant stated that his purpose in asking the question was to show, if the witness denied the statement, that he had actually made it. Thereupon the court very properly sustained an objection to the question. White was offered by the defendant as a witness, and stated that Johnson had made to him the statement to which the question referred. His testimony upon that point was then stricken from the record. It was clearly irrelevant to any issue in the case, and immaterial, and the court did not err in striking it out.

V. The defendant attempted to show his reputation for truth and veracity in the neighborhood where he resided; his "character as to being malicious, vindictive, and very resentful;" whether he was a "square-dealing, honorable man;" his reputation as a "vindictive and fighting citizen;" his reputation, as editor of the *Enterprise*, "in exposing frauds, fraudulent fakes, or fakirs that may come into the community;" and similar matters. Objections to such questions were sustained. Nearly all of the questions were so manifestly improper as to form or subject-matter of the inquiry as to make any comment upon them unnecessary. The reputation of the defendant for truth and veracity had not been questioned, and was not in issue, and proof that his reputation was that of a truthful man would not have tended to show that he was guiltless of the offense charged. It is always permissible for a defendant in a criminal action to show his general good character or reputation as to the trait involved in the charge against him. *State v. Kinley*, 43 Iowa, 294. But character or reputation must be shown by competent evidence, and according to well-established rules of practice, which need not be repeated here. We do not find any error in the rulings respecting the introduction of evidence, of which the appellant can justly complain. It may be said in this connection that the appellant was not represented by an attorney in the district court, but conducted the defense in his own behalf. He is not an attorney, but that fact does not excuse his failure to observe the settled rules of procedure which govern the trial of causes.

VI. The defendant introduced in evidence the minutes of the testimony in this case taken by the grand jury. When they were offered, the court asked if the defendant expected to prove what Johnson testified to before the grand jury, and, being answered in the affirmative, the court then asked if the defendant intended to show that the testimony so given was not true, and that Johnson knew it was not true when he gave it, and, again being answered in the affirmative, the court said: "It is a little dangerous, if you do not succeed. You may produce the papers." The minutes were then offered and read. When the evidence in the case had been fully submitted, the state moved to exclude the minutes as evidence on the ground that no evidence had been given which tended to show that the testimony of Johnson before the grand jury was false, or that he knew it to be false when given, and the motion was sustained. The appellant complains of the remark of the court respecting the danger of introducing the minutes, if Johnson's testimony was not shown to be false, and states that, as the ruling on the motion to exclude the minutes showed that in the opinion of the court Johnson's testimony had not been shown to be false, the remark must have been prejudicial. The remark appears to have been made in the interest of the defendant, and may well have been prompted by his evident inexperience in the work he was attempting to do. There was nothing in the remark of the court which indicated its view of the value of the minutes as testimony. The minutes tended to show

the guilt of the defendant, and to offer them without showing
that the statements they contained were false would naturally
be prejudicial to the defendant by strengthening the case
against him. We do not think the remark of the court was
improper, in view of the circumstances under which it was
made, nor that it could have been prejudicial.

VII. The court excluded as evidence a statement of the
defendant that the article in controversy "is true in every
particular." Since, from the nature and scope of the article,
this answer was necessarily a conclusion of the witness,
8   and not a statement of facts within his knowledge, the
answer was properly excluded. The defendant was
then asked to explain the article,—to state what he meant
by it; but an objection to the question was sustained. The
guilt of the defendant was to be determined by the article
itself, and the meaning which would naturally be attributed
to the language used therein, and not be an unexpressed meaning, unknown to the readers of the article. The language of
the article was not ambiguous. We think the defendant's
explanation was properly excluded.

VIII. The court charged the jury that, "before you will
be justified in convicting the defendant, the state must have
satisfied you and from the evidence of the truthfulness" of all
the material allegations which had been recited. This,
9   taken alone, would have been erroneous, because it
omitted the element of reasonable doubt. But in the
next paragraph the jury was instructed as to what constitutes
a reasonable doubt, and told, in effect, that it must acquit the
defendant if not satisfied of his guilt beyond a reasonable
doubt. The term "reasonable doubt" was also used in another
paragraph of the charge, but the appellant complains that,
as it was not used in direct connection with the portion of the
charge quoted, nor in seven of the nine paragraphs into which
the charge was divided, the jury may not have understood
the proper application of what was said in regard to a reasonable doubt. But we think this criticism is not well founded.

The charge was to be taken as an entirety, and, when so considered, was not misleading.

IX. The court charged the jury as follows: "Our law provides that in all prosecutions for libel the jury, after receiving the direction of the court, shall have the right to determine, at their discretion, the law and the fact. In construing this law, you are instructed to review carefully the whole case, looking to these instructions for the law, and to the evidence for the facts, and after 10 * * * both and all, then with a rigid regard for the rights of the people and those claimed to be injured on the one hand, and as rigid and watchful care for the rights of the defendant on the other, seek to determine the truth of the issue. As to the right of the jury to determine the law and the fact, you are instructed that if the jury can say on their oaths that they know the law better than the court does, they have the right to do so, but before assuming so solemn a responsibility they should be sure that they are not acting from caprice and prejudice, that they are not controlled by their will or their wishes, but from a deep and confident conviction that the court is wrong, and that they are right. Before saying this on their oaths, it is their duty to reflect whether, from their habits of thought, their study and experience, they are better qualified to judge of the law than the court. If, under all these circumstances, they are prepared to say that the court is wrong in its exposition of the law, the statute has given them that right." Section 4102 of the Code of 1873 provided that "in all indictments or prosecutions for libel, the jury, after having received the direction of the court, shall have the right to determine at their discretion the law and the fact." Section 4438 provided that "on the trial of an indictment for a libel, the jury have the right to determine the law and the fact." The "direction of the court" referred to in section 4102 is the instruction or charge of the court to the jury. *Forshee v. Abrams,* 2 Iowa, 571, 580. And the jury will be so far presumed to have followed the charge of

the court that an erroneous instruction will be ground for a
new trial. *State v. Rice,* 56 Iowa, 431. The author-
11   ity conferred by the sections which we have cited, and
by similar statutes and constitutional provisions, does
not require that the jury determine all legal questions which
may arise on the trial, as the sufficiency of the indictment, the
qualification of jurors, and the admissibility of evidence; but
only such matters as it may consider in deliberating upon a
verdict. *Drake v. State,* 53 N. J. Law, 23 (20 Atl. Rep.
747); *Anderson v. State,* 104 Ind. 467 (4 N. E. Rep. 63,
and 5 N. E. Rep. 711); *Thibault v. Sessions,* 101 Mich. 279
(59 N. W. Rep. 624). And notwithstanding the fact that the
jury has the right to determine the law of the case within the
limit stated, it is the duty of the court to instruct the jury
in regard to the law. *State v. Syphrett,* 27 S. C. 29, (13
Am. St. Rep. 616, 2 S. E. Rep. 624); *State v. Armstrong,*
106 Mo. 395 (27 Am. St. Rep. 361, 16 S. W. Rep. 604);
Drake v. State, supra; Anderson v. State, supra; In re Lowe,
46 Kan. 255 (26 Pac. Rep. 749); *State v. Verry,* 36 Kan.
416 (13 Pac. Rep. 838); *People v. McDowell,* 71 Cal. 194
(11 Pac. Rep. 868); 2 McClain Criminal Law, section 1070.
The weight which the jury should give to the charge of the
court has been a subject of much discussion, many authorities
holding that the jury has no moral right to return a verdict
which is not sanctioned by the charge. See *Com. v. McManus,*
143 Pa. St 64 (21 Atl. Rep. 1018, and 22 Atl. Rep. 761);
State v. Tally, 23 La. Ann. 677. But the legal right of a
jury, in a criminal prosecution under the sections quoted, to
determine the law which should govern the verdict, even
though a decision in conflict with the charge of the court be
reached, cannot be doubted. The sections gave to the jury
in such cases not merely the power, but the right, to make such
a decision; and the jury was not required to follow the charge
of the court, which must be regarded as advisory, and not
conclusive as to the duty of the jury. *State v. Armstrong,*
supra; Kane v. Com. 89 Pa. St. 52; *State v. Zimmerman,*

31 Kan. 85 (1 Pac. Rep. 257); *In re Lowe,* 46 Kan. 255 (26 Pac. Rep. 749); *Hudleson v. State,* 94 Ind. 426. Did the portion of the charge under consideration correctly instruct the jury in regard to its right? The statute said that the jury had "the right to determine, at their discretion, the law and the fact." That gave to it freedom to act according to its own judgment as enlightened by the charge of the court. The jurors were charged, in effect, that before they could act upon their own judgment, in opposition to that of the court, they must say, under the sanction of their oath, that they knew the law better than did the court. It was certainly proper to caution the jurors against acting from caprice or prejudice, or from considerations personal to themselves, and to call their attention to their own habits of thought and study, and to their experience, as tending to show the probable accuracy and value of their judgment regarding the law, as compared with the probable accuracy of the opinion of the court and the weight which should be given to it. To require them to be able to say that they knew the law better than did the court, merely called their attention, in an impressive manner, to the decision which would necessarily be implied in thus reaching a conclusion in conflict with the opinion of the court, and tended to require of them greater care to reach a correct verdict. A similar instruction has been approved by the supreme court of Illinois under a statute which provides that "juries in all criminal cases shall be judges of the law and fact." See *Spies v. People,* 122 Ill. 1, 152 (12 N. E. Rep. 865, and 17 N. E. Rep. 898). Other portions of the charge are criticised, but, we think, without sufficient grounds.

X. It is urged that the fine imposed by the court is excessive. We do not think the record sustains that claim. The article in question was grossly libelous. That it was prepared and published maliciously is clearly shown, and nothing in mitigation of the offense appears in the record. It is true that the law of this state guarantees freedom of speech and liberty of the press, but that freedom and that liberty

must be exercised with due regard for the rights of all people.
The publication of the article in controversy was a willful
violation of the law, and we cannot say that the punishment
imposed is excessive.   The judgment of the district court is
AFFIRMED.

THOMAS MANATT *et al.*, Proponents, Appellant, v. W. F.
SCOTT, *et al.*, Contestants.

Will Contest: EVIDENCE.   Evidence as to the value of the estate of
a son of testatrix who died before either of his parents is admissible upon the question as to whether her will was reasonable or
11   natural,—especially where the proponents had introduced the will
of the husband of the testatrix, whom she survived, containing a
recital that he had made ample provision for such son during life.

SAME.   Where one of the grounds of objection to the probate of a will
was that decedent, by reason of old age and infirmity, had insuffi-
8   cient capacity to make a will, and it was claimed she was suffering
from *senile dementia*, testimony of a brother of decedent, with
whom she had been on friendly terms, but which friendship suddenly terminated, that the cessation of friendliness was all on
decedent's part, is admissible.

INCAPACITY.   An instruction on testamentary incapacity is proper
which states that it may exist although the person be not actually
13   insane or of unsound mind and may arise from weakness of intellect produced by extreme age, disease or bodily infirmities, providing such weakness really disqualifies the testatrix from knowing or appreciating the nature, effects or consequences of her act.

Evidence of.   An instruction in an action to set aside a will on the
ground of testamentary incapacity and undue influence is proper,
14   which authorizes the jury to take into consideration the provisions
of the will "Whether just or unjust, whether reasonable and
natural or unreasonable or unnatural as may be disclosed by the
evidence."

Rule applied.   Where testator left her property to well to-do relatives,
to the exclusion of her natural heirs, evidence that she overlooked
15   relatives of like relationship and a sister in abject poverty, is
admissible as a circumstance to be considered with other evidence
as showing a disordered mind or undue influence

SAME: *Declaration of Decedent.*   In contesting the validity of a will
on the ground of incapacity and undue influence, the admission
4   of declarations by decedent before the execution of the will as to
what devisees and proponents told her detrimental to contestants,

although erroneous, is cured by an instruction that the declarations could not be considered for the purpose of proving that devisees made such statements. And such declarations were admissible, however, as bearing on decedent's capacity to make the will.

RULE APPLIED TO. Declarations by a testatrix that her daughter-in-
4 law and children poisoned her husband and would poison her if she went to their homes, and that her brothers had so informed her.

SAME. Declarations of a testatrix that if it had not been for her daughter-in-law and children her husband would have been living
6 are admissible in an action to set aside a will because of *senile dementia* although made long after the execution of the will, as tending to show that the disease if it existed was of long standing and progressive.

EVIDENCE. An inventory and final report of a testatrix as executrix of her husband's estate, executed by her but prepared by her brother, which failed to refer to a large amount of personal prop-
5 erty included in the estate is admissible in evidence as tending to show that she was unaware of the extent of her property and to show that the brother concealed property from the court.

SAME. A sworn answer of testatrix to a suit brought against her on a contract, in which she alleged that she was very weak, unable
12 to read or write or to transact business intelligently, is admissible in an action to set aside her will on the ground of mental incapacity, as bearing upon the condition of her mind.

HARMLESS ERROR. Excluding evidence as to who were present at the
9 execution of certain receipts by a testatrix is not prejudicial error where there was no dispute as to the execution of the receipts.

Same. In contesting the validity of a will, where *senile dementia* is
10 charged, and proponents introduce evidence of commencement of a suit by contestants against decedent to explain her feelings against them, the admission of evidence of all the circumstances of the suit, the employment of the attorneys, and its dismissal as soon as all the facts were ascertained, although irrelevant, is harmless error.

HYPOTHETICAL QUESTIONS. A hypothetical question is proper where
8 the evidence tends to establish the material facts included in it although such facts are not proved to exist.

Same The question may cover several years before or after the
8 execution of a will, where long standing, progressive mental disease is involved.

NON-EXPERTS. Where testator's mental capacity to make a will was
7 in issue, a question put to a non-expert witness to state "any difference there was in decedent's actions or appearance, indicating

mental strength or weakness, at the time you last saw her, compared with the first time," does not call for witness' opinion, without detailing the facts to the jury.

Special Interrogatories. Submitting interrogatories to the jury asking for facts material to be determined, although some of them 16 were not ultimate, is not reversible error.

Appeal. The evidence rulings and exceptions will not be stricken from the abstract where the bill of exceptions contains the direc-
1 tion to the clerk to copy the shorthand reporter's report of the trial in full as extended, certified and signed by such reporter, because the clerk was not directed to copy the original notes.

ASSIGNMENT OF ERRORS. Under Code 1873. section 3207, providing that the assignment or error must, in a way as specific as the case
2 will allow. point out the error objected to, an assignment which states that the court erred in overruling the objection to the question propounded to a named witness "as shown in the 30th exception, at the bottom of page 47 and top of page 48 of the abstract, and also in overruling the objection to the further questions propounded to the same witness as shown in page 48 of the abstract, and in permitting the witness to answer the same " is sufficient where, on the page mentioned, the exception bears the corresponding number.

IDENTIFICATION. Instructions are sufficiently identified in the bill of exceptions by referring to them as filed in the case by their num-
1 bers and as duly indorsed by the presiding judge.

PRESUMPTIONS. It will be presumed that the reporter and clerk per-
1 formed their duty in preparing a record for appeal to the supreme court, in the absence of any showing to the contrary.

Appeal from Poweshiek District Court.—HON. BEN McCOY, Judge.

SATURDAY, OCTOBER 8, 1898.

ISSUES joined in the probate of will.   Verdict and judgment for contestants and proponents appeal.—*Affirmed.*

Haines & Lyman and *W. R. Lewis* for appellants.

John T. Scott and *H. S. Winslow* for appellees.

LADD, J.—Wiliam Scott and Eliza, his wife, settled in Poweshiek county in 1849, and resided there until death. William died in 1886, and Eliza ten years later.   They had but two children, one of whom, William, died, unmarried, soon after the father. The other son, Robert, died in 1885, leaving, him surviving, his widow and five children, viz. William F., Robert D., Ina Belle, Mary, and Elizabeth Ann Scott. Mary Scott intermarried with L. Reynolds, and upon her death left, surviving, her husband and two children, Robert L. and Scott S. Reynolds. Elizabeth Ann intermarried with Ed. McGinley, and upon her death left, surviving, her husband and two children, Edward Earl and William McGinley. These granchildren and great-grandchildren of Eliza Scott are the contestants to the probating of her will. It may be added that in 1870 William Scott conveyed to his son Robert three hundred and twenty acres of land, and, by his will, left the remainder of his estate to his wife and son William. This consisted of three hundred and eight-four acres of land and a large amount of personal property, which fell to Eliza under the will and as heir of the son. In 1892 she formally executed a will, bequeathing to her brothers, James, Thomas, and Irvin Manatt and her sister Susannah Gwin all her household goods, beds, bedding, and clothing, "to be divided equally between them, share and share alike," and devising the remainder of her property, real and personal, to the three brothers named. The will also contains this provision: "*Second.* I give and bequeath to my grandchildren Robert L. Scott, Reynolds Scott, Eliza Ann Reynolds, Wm. T. Scott, Robert D. Scott, and Belle Scott fifty dollars each, share and share alike." The objections interposed to the admission of this paper to probate are that the deceased, by reason of old age and mental infirmities, had not sufficient capacity to make a will; that she did not comprehend and understand the extent of her property, or those who had claims upon her bounty; that the will was procured by fraud and undue influence exercised by the proponents; and, further, that the fraud and undue influence consisted of poisoning the mind of testatrix, and inducing her to believe that her legal heirs were her enemies, and were plotting to do her bodily harm.

The jury found, by their general verdict, and in answer to the special interrogatories, for the contestants. There are sixty-eight assignments of error, and we can be expected to consider in detail those only which seem of the most importance.

I. The motion of the appellees to strike all the evidence, rulings, and exceptions from the abstract is overruled. The practice of incorporating the shorthand notes in the skeleton bill of exceptions has been fully approved by this court. *Hampton v. Moorhead,* 62 Iowa, 91; *Waller v. Waller,* 76 Iowa, 513; *Hill v. Halloway,* 52 Iowa, 678; *Gardner v. Railway Co.,* 68 Iowa, 590; *McCarthy v. Watrous,* 69 Iowa, 264. These are presumed to have been filed in the case, as it was the duty of the reporter to file them. The bill recites that they were filed, and that all the evidence, motions, objections, and exceptions, "having been extended * * * and transcribed into longhand, and certified and filed in due time after such trial by such shorthand reporter, are as follows, to-wit: (Clerk will here copy shorthand reporter's report of the trial in full, as extended, certified, and signed by Blue, shorthand reporter.)" The objection seems to be that the clerk was not directed to copy the original notes. For what conceivable purpose would such a copy be made? None. Whatever the direction, he is expected to copy the transcript made by the reporter. It is said that he might be unable to identify it as that of the particular trial. If it is filed in that case, properly entitled and duly certified, the identification is ample. The appellants seem to lose sight in their arguments of the fact that the reporter is an officer of the court, and will not be presumed to foist an unauthorized transcript on the record. The skeleton bill of exceptions is necessarily imperfect, and its expediency lies in saving the record until time or necessity requires its completion. A translation of the notes may not be required, and, in any event, need not be made, in a suit at law, until necessary for the preparation of the abstract. *Kassing v. Ordway,* 100

Iowa, 612; *Slone v. Berlin,* 88 Iowa, 205. The presumption
that the reporter and clerk performed their duties will prevail in the absence of any showing to the contrary, and the
record prepared as directed treated as genuine.

II. The point that the instructions are not identified
in the bill is not well taken. This was done by referring to
them as filed in this case by their numbers, and as duly
indorsed by the presiding judge. When so referred to, the
clerk will find no difficulty in making the selection.

III. The appellees insist that assignments of error
are not as specific as is required. The first fifty-two errors
relate to the introduction of evidence. The twenty-sixth
assignment is a fair illustration, of all, and is as
2   follows: "The court erred in overruling the proponents' objection to the question propounded to the
witness W. W. Woods, as shown in the thirtieth exception at
the bottom of page 47 and top of page 48 of the abstract, and
also erred in overruling the proponents' objection to the
further question propounded to the same witness, as shown on
page 48 of the abstract, and in permitting the witness to
answer the same." It will be noticed the particular ruling
is mentioned, as well as the witness, and the page of the
abstract; and it may be added that at the bottom of that page
the exception bears a corresponding number. The method
pursued is certainly a very convenient one, and enables the
court and counsel without loss of time to find, not only the
ruling, but the connection in which it is made. It clearly and
specifically indicates the very error complained of, and, in
so doing, complies with the statute. Code, section 4136. In
Wood v. Whitton, 66 Iowa, 297, the errors were not specifically mentioned or pointed out as found in any particular
part of the record, and it is there said: "An assignment
should plainly state the error complained of, and not refer
the opposite counsel and court to parts of the record wherein
the objection is said to appear." This language must be construed in connection with the alleged error in that case, and

which could only be discovered by the examination of the entire record. It has also been held that resort will not be had to the argument in order to determine the error assigned. *Calkins v. Railway Co.,* 92 Iowa, 715; *Smola v. McCaffrey,* 83 Iowa, 760. In *Stove Works v. Hammond,* 94 Iowa, 694, stating errors generally in ruling on the admissibility of the testimony of the witness named is held not sufficiently specific. In *Hamilton Buggy Co. v. Iowa Buggy Co.,* 88 Iowa, 367, it is said: "Each and all of these assignments relate to the admission of evidence against the objection of the intervener, and each assignment sufficiently points out the error, naming the witness, and specifying the evidence and rulings objected to. To require more would entail an unnecessary burden upon the appellants. While the law contemplates that such assignment shall clearly point out the error complained of, it is not necessary to incumber the record by setting out the whole examination in which the error is claimed to have occurred. *Union Bldg. Ass'n v. Rockford Ins. Co.,* 83 Iowa, 649." What is said in this case aptly applies to that at bar, and we not only hold the assignment sufficient, but approve the method of definitely pointing out the error and the part of the record where it may be found.

IV. William Manatt was asked this question: "You may state whether or not there was any cessation of friendliness on your part towards Mrs. Scott at that time, or was the ill-will all on her part,"—and over objection 3 answered: "All on her part. The ill-will was all on her part." The time referred to was when she left the farm, in 1886. It is conceded that the feeling of the witness might be shown, but it is said that the ill-will of the decedent ought not to be inquired into. It may be mentioned that the contestants claimed Mrs. Scott was suffering from *senile dementia,* and, according to the evidence of physicians, this disease is of slow development, and one of the symptoms is a sudden aversion or dislike conceived against those with whom the person afflicted has been on friendly terms. We

think it was admissible as bearing upon the condition of Mrs.
Scott's mind. She had been on friendly terms with this
brother for years, and, as soon as taken from the farm by
James and Thomas Manatt conceived a dislike for him. It
was part of the history of the case, and one of the circumstances to be considered with others in determining whether
she had testamentary capacity.

John Manatt testified that prior to the execution of the
will, Mrs. Scott had said to him that her daughter-in-law and
children gave her husband a dose, and helped him out of the
world; that, if she went to their homes, they
4   would treat her likewise; and that Thomas and James
Manatt had so informed her. The proponents moved
to strike out the statement that Thomas and James had told
her, as incompetent, hearsay, immaterial, and as declarations
made by the devisees under the will. This motion was overruled, and it is urged that the statement made by the deceased
testatrix of declarations by devisees cannot be received in
evidence against other devisees. The order of introduction of
evidence was within the discretion of the court. While the
statement that she based her belief on information derived
from James and Thomas could not be received as proving
that they in fact made such a report, it did have a tendency
to show that her mind was controlled by undue influence. Had
competent evidence been produced that James and Thomas had
in fact so advised her, the importance of this evidence would
be manifest. That is, not only the exertion of the influence,
but its direct effect upon the mind would have been established. *In re Hess' Will,* 48 Minn. 504 (31 Am. St. Rep.
665), and extended note (s. c. 51 N. W. Rep. 614). Such
evidence was, however, not adduced, and the court told the
jury that her statement could not be considered as tending
to show James and Thomas in fact so informed her. This
instruction obviates the exception urged. The authorities
relied upon by appellants are not in point. They simply
relate to declarations made by a devisee before or after the

execution of a will. *In re Ames,* 51 Iowa, 596; *Dye v. Young,* 55 Iowa, 433; *Parsons v. Parsons,* 66 Iowa, 754; *In re Goldthorp's Estate,* 94 Iowa, 336. That declarations made by the testatrix are admissible as bearing on capacity and undue influence, is well settled. \ *Waterman v. Whitney,* 11 N. Y. 157; *Bates v. Bates,* 27 Iowa, 112; *Stephenson v. Stephenson,* 62 Iowa, 165; *In re Goldthorp's Estate, supra; Lane v. Moore,* 151 Mass. 87 (21 Am. St. Rep. 430, 23 N. E. Rep. 828); Schouler Wills, sections 193, 243.] As said in *Bever v. Spangler,* 93 Iowa, 603: "Mental disturbance may be detected by declarations as surely as by conduct; hence the declarations of persons charged with insanity are admissible in a chain of logical connection, to show the mental condition existing when the will was executed." The evidence tended to show Mrs. Scott was then laboring under a delusion which of itself was a symptom of mental unsoundness.

V. The appellants complain of the ruling of the court in admitting in evidence the inventory and final report of Mrs. Scott, as executrix of her husband's estate, filed in 1886 and 1887. These were signed and sworn to by her, but prepared by or under the supervision of James Manatt. William
5   Scott left nearly six thousand dollars in cash, which was placed in the bank by James and Thomas Manatt. Soon after his death, a large amount of personal property was disposed of, and the proceeds handled by the same parties. Neither the report nor the inventory contained any reference to these amounts, and the omission tends to show that she did not know the extent of her property at that time; and, further, that James Manatt, knowing thereof, concealed these from the court in reports prepared by him or under his supervision. It may be said that this is remote in time, but the testatrix was then an aged woman, and the testimony tended to show that from that time on her property and business were managed and controlled by these proponents. We think it was also admissible as bearing upon her knowledge of her business and property. It is said that she may have given

away considerable amounts of money. This would not relieve her from making a truthful report and inventory. Besides, if this had been done, the knowledge of proponents of her affairs was such that they could readily have shown it.

VI. About three years after making the will, Mrs. Scott remarked to Eliza Breneman that, "if it had not been for that blackleg and them [referring to Dr. Reynolds, her daughter-in-law, and children] her husband would have been living this day." We have seen that declarations made by the deceased were admissible. But it is said that this was long after the execution of the will. The evidence tended to show, however, that the disease, if it existed, was of long standing and progressive; and, if so, the time was not too remote. *Bever v. Spangler, supra.*

. VII. It is asserted that nonexperts were allowed to give their opinion as to the sanity of the decedent without first detailing the facts to the jury. This criticism is not well founded. It is often difficult to draw the line between what is a fact and an opinion. *Yahn v. Ottumwa,* 60 Iowa, 429. A question to Woods will illustrate the exception taken. He was asked to state "any difference there was in Mr. Scott's actions or appearance, indicating mental strength or weakness, at the time you last saw her, compared with the first time that you saw her." Now, anything about the decedent indicating her strength or feebleness would be a fact, and this question calls, not for his opinion, but for the facts, as to her actions and appearance. *Severin v. Zack,* 55 Iowa, 28. In *Parsons v. Parsons,* 66 Iowa, 754, it is said: "We think evidence that a person acted strangely or in a childish manner are facts, and may be testified to by any one." *In re Goldthorp's Estate,* 94 Iowa, 343, it is said: "The witness might testify from what he saw that decedent was weak physically, and, in principle, we see no difference between such inquiry, whether it relates to the physical or mental organization, so long as it calls for facts ascertainable by observation alone." A careful examination of the evidence leads us to the conclusion that no nonexpert was permitted to give his opinion without first detailing to the jury the facts upon which it was based.

VIII. A hypothetical question was propounded to Dr. Vest, and it is urged that the facts stated have no support in the evidence. If there was no evidence tending to sustain some of the material facts included, then the exception is well founded. *In re Ames,* 51 Iowa, 596. But it is not essential that the facts be proven to exist. It is sufficient if the evidence tends to establish them. *Meeker v. Meeker,* 74 Iowa, 357; *Bever v. Spangler, supra.* Upon examination of the record, we find every fact stated, to have support in the evidence. For instance, it is said in the hypothetical question that the deceased was unable to read and write understandingly, and was wholly uneducated. It is admitted that she could not write, and several witnesses testify that, in reading she was required to spell out the simplest words. Some years before this, she is shown to have filed a sworn answer in a suit, alleging total want of education and inability to read. Again, the fact of her aversion to those who were near and dear to her is referred to, and exception is taken to this description. Her affection for her daughter-in-law and grandchildren at one time is fully established. But a detailed consideration of this evidence will serve no useful purpose. It is asserted that the time is not limited to the date of making the will. The age fixed indicated a period covering that time, and inquiry in a case like this may extend over several years, either before or after execution of the will.

IX. One Dorrance testified that he wrote certain receipts, and signed them as witness to the mark of Eliza Scott, and also her name, and that he believed that he had authority for doing so. One of the receipts is as follows:

"Brooklyn, Iowa, Jan. 18, 1889.

9   "Received of Thomas Manatt all moneys, papers, and property that he has had in his hand for my acct., in full to date.

her
"Eliza X Scott.
mark

"Witness: O. F. Dorrance."

The other, similar to this, was drawn to James Manatt. James testified to the execution of the receipt to Thomas, and Thomas to that to James. The record disclosed no objection to the evidence of these brothers. The court afterwards made this entry: "The motion of the contestant heretofore made to strike out from the record the evidence of James and Thomas Manatt relating to whether the persons were there at the time of signing the receipt [the Exhibits 11 and 12] is sustained, and the proponents except, and the jury is so instructed." The abstract does not contain the motion referred to. As the execution of the receipts was proved and undisputed, it was not important to know who were present when they were signed. If the ruling was erroneous, it was without the slightest prejudice.

X. The proponents introduced evidence showing the beginning of a suit in partition by the grandchildren against Mrs. Scott, and also pleadings therein. This was undoubtedly for the purpose of explaining any feeling testatrix

10   may have had against them. The contestants were permitted to show all the circumstances connected with the beginning of this action, and that it was dismissed as soon as the facts were learned. Some letters between the attorneys and one of the contestants were received in evidence. All this simply indicated the employment of an attorney in the usual way, a contract to pay him a part of the land recovered, and a dismissal of the suit. While it has no bearing whatever upon the issue the jury were required to determine, no prejudice could possibly have resulted.

XI.   Exception was taken because of the proof introduced showing the settlement of Robert Scott's estate, and the partition of two hundred and forty acres of land left the widow and heirs after the payment of his debts. This, we think, was admissible, as bearing upon the question whether the will of Eliza was reasonable and natural. The proponents had introduced the will of William Scott, reciting that he had made ample provision for Robert during life, and also a deed to him of three hundred and twenty acres of land, executed in 1870. As Robert died before his father, 11 this evidence showed how much he had at that time, and also the financial condition of the natural heirs of Eliza. And, if it was material to show the conveyance of the land, it was certainly important to understand its value. *Sim v. Russell,* 90 Iowa, 656.

XII.   A sworn answer of Mrs. Scott to a suit brought on a contract for the purchase of a monument was introduced in evidence, over the objection of the appellants. In it she alleged that she was very weak, unable to read or 12 write, or to transact business intelligently. This was filed when she was sixty-nine years of age, and we think it was admissible as an act of the deceased, and as bearing upon the condition of her mind. Indeed, the appellants insist that it shows her to have been a woman of remarkable memory. From this we understand them to object to the effect to be given to this answer, rather than its admission in evidence.

XIII.   Complaint is made of the fourth instruction, in which the court tells the jury that "testamentary incapacity does not necessarily require that a person shall actually be insane or of an unsound mind. Weakness of intel- 13 lect, whether it arises from extreme old age, from disease, or great bodily infirmities or suffering, or from all these combined, may render the testator incapable of making a valid will, providing such weakness really disqualifies her from knowing or appreciating the nature, effects, or consequences of the act she is engaged in. Eccentricity, peculiarities, oddities, or the like, or weakness of mind ordinarily attendant upon old age, do not of themselves necessarily establish a lack of testamentary capacity." In the previous paragraph the jurors were told that a sound mind was necessary to the execution of a valid will, and what was necessary to constitute a sound mind clearly defined, substantially as approved in *Bates v. Bates,* 27 Iowa, 110; *Re Convey,* 52 Iowa, 197; and *Meeker v. Meeker,* 74 Iowa, 357. We take it, the court intended to say that the mind need not necessarily be diseased, but weakness might incapacitate it; and that the instruction was so understood by the jury.

XIV. The jurors were also told that Eliza Scott had the right to dispose of her property as she desired, and, in the sixteenth instruction, that, in passing upon the issues, the provisions of the will might be considered, "whether just or unjust, whether reasonable and natural, or unreasonable and unnatural, as may be disclosed by the evidence." That 14 the inequities of a will may be taken into consideration in determining the mental capacity of the testator, or whether undue influence has been exercised, is too well settled to require an extended examination of the authorities. *Sim v. Russell, supra;* Schouler Wills, sections 78, 188; *Knox v. Knox,* 95 Ala. 495 (36 Am. St. Rep. 235, 11 South. Rep. 125); *Crandall's Appeal,* 63 Conn. 365 (28 Atl. Rep. 531, 38 Am. St. Rep. 375, and note); *Hammond v. Daike,* 42 Minn. 273 (18 Am. St. Rep. 503), 44 N. W. Rep. 61); *Davis v. Calvert,* 5 Gill & J. 269 (25 Am. Dec. 269); *Peck v. Cary,* 27 N. Y. 9 (84 Am. Dec. 226). But apparent inequality or inequity in the provisions of a will will not alone warrant the presumption of mental incapacity or undue influence. These may be only considered as circumstances in connection with other facts bearing on the condition of the testator's mind. *Turnure v. Turnure,* 35 N. J. Eq. 437; *In re Hess' Will,* 48 Minn. 504 (51 N. W. Rep. 614, 31 Am. St. Rep. 665, and note); *Maddox v. Maddox,* 114 Mo. 35 (35 Am. St. Rep. 734, 21 S.

W. Rep. 499) ; *Knox v. Knox, supra.* In a technical sense, a will cannot be said to be just or unjust, because the testator is under no obligation to leave his property to any particular person or institution, but the terms have been generally employed in this connection. What is meant by unjust, unreasonable. or unnatural provisions of a will is that they are not as a person in like situation and similar relationship would ordinarily and usually make them. · We think the instruction not subject to misinterpretation.

XV.   But inequality or inequity in the provisions of a will may not appear on its face, and, to show this, evidence is sometimes essential to establish relationship and conditions in life. Thus in *Sim v. Russell, supra*, it was held proper to show the financial condition of the son. The contestants were permitted to prove that a half-sister of Mrs. Scott, living just across the street, was so poor as to be an object of charity. It already appeared that proponents were well to do, and that Mrs. Gwin was of limited means. As the decedent preferred some of her brothers to her natural heirs, it was material, in looking into the equities of the will, to know that, in remembering proponents, she forgot several other brothers and this sister, in abject poverty. A will which bestows property on the wealthy, and overlooks the claims to bounty of those who are poor in like relationship, does not commend itself as reasonable or natural. It is a circumstance suggesting a disordered mind or the working of sinister influences. While it may not have a very strong bearing in this case, it was for the jury to take into consideration in connection with the other evidence introduced.

XVI.   The appellants insist that interrogatories not calling for ultimate facts were submitted to the jury. But every interrogatory asked for a fact material to be determined; and, while some of them may not have been ultimate, propounding the questions to the jury worked no prejudice. *British American Assurance Co. v. Neil*, 76 Iowa, 646. It is also said that the issue of undue influence ought not to have been submitted to the jury. This may be conceded. But there was a conflict in the evidence bearing upon the issue raised as to the mental capacity of Mrs. Scott to execute the will; and, whatever our views may be with reference to the full weight of the evidence, the determination by the jury is final. The jury especially found, in answer to the fifth interrogatory, that she did not have mental capacity to dispose of her property according to her desires. We shall not review the evidence in detail. It is enough to say that it tended to show the testatrix did not know the extent of her property, nor those who had claims upon her bounty; that she was possessed of a delusion that her daughter-in-law and her grandchildren and Dr. Reynolds were plotting to do her injury; and that her physical condition indicated that she was suffering from *senile dementia.* The sixty-eight errors assigned are argued. We have touched upon those the parties seem to consider of most importance. The other assignments appear to us to be without merit. The judgment is AFFIRMED.

THE HAWKEYE STATE SAVINGS AND LOAN ASSOCIATION v. O. P. JOHNSTON, *et al.,* Appellants.

Usury: BUILDING ASSOCIATION. A loan by a building and loan association to one of its members, made while Code, 1873, section 1185,
1 authorizing such associations to collect from their members such
2 premiums bid for the right of priority in taking loans as its by-laws might adopt was in force, is not usurious because the contract provides for the payment of premiums which were bid for the loan by the secretary under the authority of the borrower.

SAME. In the absence of evidence to the contrary, a stipulation in a mortgage to a building and loan association requiring the bor-
1 rower to pay a premium will be presumed to have been made under a bid to enable him to obtain a right of precedence in taking the loan as authorized by the Code, rather than a device to cover
2 up a usurious transaction, where the borrower in his application, authorized the secretary of the association to bid such a premium that he might have such precedence.

FORECLOSURE. A building and loan association may recover the interest, premium and dues maturing after the commencement of and before judgment in a suit to foreclose a mortgage and to
3 cancel shares of stock pledged as collateral security, under acts Twenty-sixth General Assembly, chapter 85, section 9. providing

that in cases of foreclosure the borrower member shall be charged
with the full amount of the loan made to him, together with the
dues, interest, premium and fines for which he is delinquent, and
shall be credited with the same value of his pledged shares
as if he had voluntarily withdrawn the same.

Appeal from Marion District Court.—HON. J. D. GAMBLE,
Judge.

SATURDAY, OCTOBER 8, 1898.

SUIT in equity to foreclose a mortgage and to cancel
certain shares of stock held by defendants in the plaintiff
association. Defense, usury and certain payments which were
not credited upon the notes. Decree for plaintiff, and defendants appeal.—*Affirmed.*

G. W. Crozier and *S. C. Johnston* for appellants.

J. E. Mershon and *L. N. Hays* for appellee.

DEEMER, C. J.—Appellee is a building and loan association, organized in the year 1894, under the then existing laws.
Appellant became a member of the association, and in the
year 1895 borrowed the sum of one thousand two hundred
dollars, agreeing to pay twenty dollars and forty cents per
month until the installments so paid, together with the profits
on twelve shares of stock, should equal the aggregate par value
of said stock. This monthly payment was made up of seven
dollars and twenty cents, the monthly installment on the
stock; six dollars, as interest; and seven dollars and twenty
cents, as premium bid for the loan. After making nine payments, appellant defaulted, and in November, 1896, this suit
was brought. Afterwards, and on the first day of March,
1897, appellee filed a supplemental petition, asking that it
recover three more of the monthly installments. Appellant
denies that he received the full sum of one thousand two hundred dollars, pleads usury, and, further, asks credit for the
sum of two hundred and twenty-five dollars paid by him.

While Johnston received but one thousand one hundred and sixty-two dollars and sixty cents at the time he made the loan, yet is clearly appears that the difference between this sum and the amount of his notes was applied upon the payment of an indebtedness he was then owing the association, and of expenses incurred in perfecting the papers incident to the loan. None of it was retained for use of the money borrowed, and it was not withheld for the purpose of avoiding the statute with reference to usury. Before securing the money,
1   appellant signed an application in which he stated that he agreed to pay a premium of sixty cents per share upon his twelve shares of stock, which premium he authorized the secretary of the association to bid in his name for priority of loan. Whether any bid was actually made does not appear, but it is conceded that he agreed to pay seven dollars and twenty cents per month as premium. This, it is contended, rendered the loan usurious, for it also appears that he agreed to pay six per cent. interest on the total amount received. When the loan was made, the law provided (Code 1873, section 1185) that such an association might levy, assess, and collect from its members such sums of money, in premiums bid by its members for the right of precedence in taking loans, as the corporation, by its by-laws, might adopt; and the premiums so paid by its members in addition to the legal rate of interest on loans so taken by them should not be construed to make the loans so taken usurious. The by-laws of this association provided for the payment of a premium bid for priority of loan not exceeding sixty cents per month on each share of stock borrowed upon, and obligated the borrower to pay six per cent. interest and the premium bid, in addition to the regular monthly payment of dues. As the associa-
2   tion was authorized by its by-laws, and by the statute before referred to, to receive premiums bid by its members for the right of precedence in taking loans, the contract was not usurious, unless it appears that there was in fact no bid, and that the premium paid was merely a device

to cover a usurious transaction. The burden is upon the appellant to establish the usurious character of the loan; that is to say, he must show that there was in fact no bidding for right of precedence, and that what was done was a scheme to disguise the real transaction. This he has failed to do. He authorized the secretary to make a certain bid for priority, and, in the absence of evidence to the contrary, it will be presumed that the bid was made and the money obtained thereby. If this be the true nature of the transaction, the contract is not usurious, for no interest was charged upon the premium. See *Association v. Heider,* 55 Iowa, 429.

Again, it is said the court was in error in allowing appellee to recover the interest, premium, and dues maturing after the commencement of the suit, and before judgment. Section 9, chapter 85, Acts Twenty-sixth General Assembly,
3   provides that in case of foreclosure the borrower shall be charged with the full amount of the loan made to him, together with the dues, interest, premium, and fines for which he is delinquent, and shall be credited with the same value of his pledged shares as if he had voluntarily withdrawn the same. The computation made by the trial court was in accord with the terms of this statute, and, while it may be true that appellant paid more than eight per cent. for the use of the money, it was exacted in strict accordance with the law. The legislature has in its wisdom given building and loan associations greater rights than those possessed by individuals, and its judgment and discretion in such matters cannot be questioned by the courts. Without reference to this statute, we think the computation was made in strict accord with the terms of the contract and of the law. Appellant does not claim that recovery should be limited by the last clause of section 1898 of the Code; hence that question is not considered.—AFFIRMED.

CHARLES KINKEAD v. McCORMACK HARVESTING MACHINE
COMPANY, Appellant.

Pleading: MATTER IN AVOIDANCE: *Reply.* Facts relied upon by
plaintiff in an action for the recovery of the price paid for a
1 machine, to avoid the effect of the plea of acceptance of the
machine after knowledge of its condition as a waiver of the warranty, must be set up in the reply by way of avoidance of the plea.

DENIAL BY LAW. The law operates as a denial of an affirmative
1 defense pleaded in the answer.

Appeal from Linn District Court.—HON. WILLIAM G.
THOMPSON, Judge. .

SATURDAY, OCTOBER 8, 1898.

In August, 1896, the plaintiff purchased of the defendant a corn binder, for which he gave his note for one hundred and thirty dollars, which note has been assigned by
defendant, and plaintiff is liable for the payment thereof.
From the petition it appears that the corn binder was warranted as follows: "These machines are all warranted to be
well made, of good material, and durable, with proper care.
If, upon one day's trial, the machine should not work well,
the purchaser shall give immediate notice to said McCormick
Harvesting Machine Company, or their agent, and allow time
to send a person to put it in order. If it cannot then be
made to work well, the purchaser shall at once return it to
the agent of whom he received it, and his payment (if any
has been made) will be refunded. Continuous use of the
machine, or use at intervals through harvest season, shall be
deemed an acceptance of the machine by the undersigned."
It also appears from the petition that plaintiff complied with
the conditions of the warranty by making the one day's trial
of the binder; that it would not work well; that he afterwards, on its failure to work well, notified defendant's agent,

who failed to make the same work as warranted, whereupon
he returned the machine to said agents of whom he received
it, and demanded a return of the note, which demand was
refused.   Judgment is asked for the purchase price of the
machine.   The answer admits the sale, the warranty, and
the return of·the machine, but denies the averments as to
dates.   As a separate defense it is pleaded that after the
delivery of the machine, and after plaintiff had tried the
same, and had full knowledge as to its compliance, or want
of compliance, with the warranty, he expressed himself as
satisfied with the machine and its workings, and gave his
note therefor, and that the transaction was a settlement of all
matters pertaining to the sale.   The cause went to trial to a
jury on the issues thus formed, that returned a verdict for
plaintiff, and from a judgment thereon the defendant
appealed.—*Reversed.*

Preston & Moffit for appellant.

Giffin & Voris for appellee.

GRANGER, J.—I.   There is a complaint that the court
presented to the jury an issue of fact not involved in the
pleadings.   The plaintiff pleaded as a basis of recovery his
purchase of the machine, the warranty thereof, a compliance
with the conditions on his part, a breach thereof by defend-
        ant, and his liability to pay the note.   The answer,
1   by denials, put in issue the allegations as to a breach
        of the warranty and full compliance with the condi-
tions of the warranty by plaintiff, and then, by way of
affirmative defense, pleaded a settlement by the giving of the
note after knowledge of the workings of the machine.   The
law operates as a denial of the averments as to settlement.   No
reply was filed.   The issues arising from the denials in the
answer were as to the breach of the warranty.   The law put
in issue the facts averred by defendant as to a settlement,
that is, it denied that there was such a settlement.   It appears

from the evidence that the machine was not returned, as alleged by plaintiff, or as required by the terms of the warranty, and there is evidence to show that it was retained beyond the time in which it should have been returned because of a request of defendant's agent that plaintiff should retain the machine to further test it. The court, after admitting such evidence, gave the following instruction: "You are instructed that the contract of warranty provides that continuous use of the machine, or use of the same through the harvest season, shall be deemed an acceptance of the machine by the party so using the same. Now, in this case, if you find from said evidence, the plaintiff, after trying and testing said machine, and he could not make it do the work, he at once notified the agents of defendant of that fact, and you also find that said agents attempted to make the machine do the work, and failed to do so, it was then the duty of plaintiff, under said contract, to return said machine to said agents at once; and you further find that plaintiff did not do so, or if you further find plaintiff used said machine during the harvest season of 1895,—he cannot recover in this action unless you find also from said evidence that the failure to return said machine when he knew that it would not do the work was because of the request of defendant or its agents that he should retain the same beyond said time, to further test said machine. And if you are satisfied from said evidence that defendant did so request plaintiff, then the failure to return the same within the time specified in said contract would not constitute an acceptance of the same by plaintiff." The complaint as to the instruction is of that part pleaded in avoidance of plaintiff's failure to return the machine as the contract required because of the agent's request to retain it longer, for the reason that the pleadings in no way present such an issue; and the complaint seems to be well founded. If the purpose was to avoid the matter pleaded in settlement by defendant, it was proper matter for a reply, by admitting the facts, and pleading in avoidance the request to hold the machine.

Such is the office of reply. Code 1873, section 2665. See, also, *Bank v. Wright,* 84 Iowa, 728; *Kervick v. Mitchell,* 68 Iowa, 273. The effect of the request not to return the machine, as the contract required, was to waive the provision; and a waiver, to make it available, must be pleaded. *Machine Co. v. Brower,* 88 Iowa, 607. Such a waiver is in the nature of an estoppel, which must always be pleaded. *Eikenberry v. Edwards,* 67 Iowa, 14. If the evidence as to the request to hold the machine for a longer time was not intended to avoid the plea of settlement, then the facts should have been pleaded in the petition to show that the contract was modified, and plaintiff then proven the contract as pleaded, and he should not plead it one way and prove it to be different. In any view of the case, the facts should have been pleaded to justify the evidence or the instruction as to the contract being changed. The judgment must be REVERSED.

ELLA M. SMITH v. THE ST. PAUL FIRE & MARINE INSUR-ANCE COMPANY, Appellant.

Mechanic's Lien: EQUITABLE INTERESTS. The interest of an equitable
1 owner of land may be subjected to a mechanic's lien.

OWNER OF BUILDING ALONE. Where one in possession of land to
1 which he has no title, erects a building thereon, it will be subject to mechanic's lien for material used in constructing it.

EVIDENCE. Insured testified that he purchased the materials for the insured building from certain mechanic's lien claimants whose
4 lien claim was introduced in evidence, and described the same land as that on which the insured testified that the insured building was located. *Held,* sufficient evidence to show that the lien was claimed on the insured building.

INSURANCE: *Forfeiture.* A provision for forfeiture of a policy of
1 insurance if the property shall be encumbered, or if any action or
2 proceeding shall be commenced affecting the title thereto is valid and enforceable, although the insured may not be responsible for the condition contemplated.

SAME. A mechanic's lien is an encumbrance within the provision of
1-3 a policy of insurance forfeiting the same if the property be encumbered.

SAME. The commencement of an action to foreclose a mechanic's
1 lien against the insured property operates as a forfeiture of the
policy, without reference to the validity of the liens claimed,
under a provision that the insurer shall not be liable if any action
5 or proceeding shall be commenced affecting the title to the property insured.

Appeal from Lyon District Court.—HON. WILLIAM HUTCH-
INSON, Judge.

SATURDAY, OCTOBER 8, 1898.

ACTION to recover upon a policy of fire insurance. There
was a jury trial; verdict and judgment for plaintiff. Defendant appeals.—*Reversed.*

McVey & McVey and *McMillan & Dunlap* for appellant.

C. B. Kennedy and *E. B. Roach* for appellee.

WATERMAN, J.—One of the questions in the case is
whether there were mechanics' liens against the insured property. Much attention is devoted by counsel to the matter of
the extent of the interest of J. E. Smith in the real estate on
which the building stood. Ella Smith originally
1   owned this real estate. She died, and her husband, J E.
Smith, took possession thereof under her will, which
gave him an interest or estate therein. While he was in
possession the building in question was erected. Inasmuch as
the mechanics' liens are but incidentally in issue, we are not
called upon to exactly determine or define the character or
extent of Smith's interest. It is enough to say that he had
such an equitable interest as could be made subject to a
mechanic's lien. Acts Sixteenth General Assembly, chapter
100, section 4; *Clark v. Parker,* 58 Iowa, 509. Even if he
had no title to the real estate, the building thereon might
have been made subject to such lien. *Lane v. Snow,* 66
Iowa, 544.

II.   The issue as to the mechanic's liens arises under a provision of the policy in suit, which reads as follows: "Loss or damage for which this company is not liable under this

2   policy: It is hereby declared and agreed that this company shall not be liable for loss * * * if the property, or any part thereof, shall be sold, transferred, or incumbered (by mortgage, judgment, or otherwise), or if any action or proceeding at law or otherwise shall be commenced affecting the title thereto, or if proceedings to foreclose any lien thereon shall be commenced in any way, or notice thereof shall be given, or if said property, or any part thereof, shall be levied upon, * * * without the consent of the company indorsed thereon." It may well be held, in construing this provision, that the consent of the company is to be obtained only for those acts included in its terms, which are voluntary on the part of the assured, such as the sale or mortgaging of the property.   But the condition of forfeiture relates also to the acts of third persons, for which, perhaps, in some instances, the assured may be in no wise responsible.   Nevertheless such condition is valid.   Litigation in respect to the title of insured property may be said to increase the risk of the insurer by adding to the moral hazard.   Whether the insured is responsible for it is not, in the first instance, material.   The company has the right to provide that the existence of such litigation shall relieve it from liability. *Meadows v. Insurance Co.,* 62 Iowa, 387; *Carey v. Insurance Co.,* 84 Wis. 80 (54 N. W. Rep. 18); *Burr v. Insurance Co.,* 84 Wis. 76 (54 N. W. Rep. 22).

III.   The next question is whether a mechanic's lien, or an action to enforce it, comes within the terms of the quoted

3   clause of the policy.   The incumbering of the property is forbidden.   There can be no doubt but that a mechanic's lien is an incumbrance. *Redmon v. Insurance Co.,* 51 Wis. 293.(8 N. W. Rep. 226).

IV.   The next matter for consideration is as to the claimed liens.   It is urged by appellee that it is not shown they were upon the building insured. We think the contention is not well founded. J. E. Smith testifies to

4   the location of the building, and to having purchased the material for its construction from the mechanic's lien claimants; and on the trial in the district court, when the evidence as to these liens was offered, no objection was made by plaintiff on the ground now urged. Besides this, the description of the real estate in the claim for a lien corresponds to the description given by Smith of the land upon which the building burned was located. Altogether, we think there can be no question but that the claims made are for the construction of the building covered by the policy in suit.

V. It is also said by appellee that it does not appear that the liens claimed are valid, and that no violation of the clause in question is shown unless defendant establishes this

5   fact. The testimony discloses that claims for liens on this building, properly verified, were filed by various material men, of whom Smith admits purchasing lumber and other material. Actions were begun in due season to enforce and foreclose these liens. No denial of the right to a lien seems to have been filed in any of the cases. Under the circumstances, it seems that we should accept the claims as valid. But there is still another answer to this argument. The clause of the policy which is under consideration avoids the risk, not only in case the property is incumbered, but also in event of an action being begun which affects the title thereto. It is idle to say that such a clause is not violated until the action is determined adversely to the insured. So soon as actions to foreclose these liens were begun, what we have called the moral hazard of the company was increased, and it was this added risk which this provision was intended to exempt the company from. It makes no difference that the insured was perhaps in no way responsible for the institution of such suits. *Carey v. Insurance Co.,* *supra.* He has made his contract, and we can neither annul nor change it at his request. For the breach of the condition

which we have been considering, the policy in suit was avoided, and the judgment of the district court must be REVERSED.

WILLIAM HEUSINKVELD for D. BRUINS v. THE ST. PAUL FIRE & MARINE INSURANCE COMPANY, Appellant.

Principal and Agent: EVIDENCE. Proof that a person who assumed to adjust a fire loss was the insurer's agent cannot be made by such person's declarations, and a local insurance agent having no autho.ity to adjust losses will not be presumed to have authority to bind the insurer by recognizing another as an agent authorized to adjust losses.

OBJECTION BELOW. Testimony that one person is the agent of another is admissible, though it is in the nature of a conclusion. Should cross-examination develop that the conclusion rests on hearsay, or the like, it may be stricken, on proper objection then made. But when no objection is made except at a time before cross-examination shows the testimony given in chief to be objectionable, it is proper to allow it to stand and be considered by the jury, though it is urged by a motion to direct, that conditions of the policy showed that said person lacked authority to make alleged waivers

Insurance: WAIVER. *Proof of loss.* A policy providing that only a specified agreement indorsed thereon shall be construed as a waiver of any condition, and that "the agent" of the insuring company has no authority to waive any condition does not preclude the company's adjuster from waiving a condition requiring insured to furnish proofs of loss.

Estoppel. After insurer's adjuster had investigated a loss, he told insured to send carpenter's estimate, as to what it would cost to replace the building. to insurer, "and it would be all right," and insured sent such estimates. *Held,* that insurer was estopped to claim that proofs of loss were insufficient.

FALSE REPRESENTATIONS. *Encumbrance.* Proof that plaintiff falsely told the agent after the policy was issued that a mortgage on the property was satisfied, then directing him to make the policy payable to insured, does not put the insurer in the same position as if the policy had been issued upon a false represent\ation that the property was unincumbered. (In this case there was an unsatisfied mortgage when the policy issued *originally,* of which fact the recording agent was advised.)

PLEA AND PROOF. *Harmless error.* Where an allegation that due notice of a loss was made is denied, the form and sufficiency of the notice is so in issue that plaintiff must prove the averment of his petition.

2 This, in the absence of objection below because there was no proof that the letter was received, is done by undisputed evidence that he mailed a letter to the insurer advising it that and when the building was destroyed by fire, and after testimony that a letter mailed so notified, it is harmless error to permit a statement of its contents to be given as primary evidence.

Appeal from Sioux District Court.—HON. SCOTT M. LADD, Judge.

SATURDAY, OCTOBER 8, 1898.

ACTION at law on a poliy of insurance issued by the defendant against loss or damage by fire on a store building in Maurice, Iowa. There was a trial by jury, and a verdict and judgment for the plaintiff. The defendant appeals.— *Affirmed.*

McVey & McVey for appellant.

G. T. Hatley and *C. A. Irwin* for appellee.

ROBINSON, J.—The building insured was destroyed by fire during the life of the policy, and was of greater value than the amount of the insurance.

I. The policy provides that "persons sustaining loss or damage by fire shall forthwith give notice of said loss to the company." It is claimed by the appellant that the notice thus required was not given. The appellee contends

1   that the question of such notice is not presented by the pleadings. The petition alleges that the building was destroyed by fire on the eleventh day of January, 1893, and that on the next day the plaintiff gave the defendant due notice of the fire and loss, by letter, directed to the defendant at St. Paul, Minn., duly stamped and deposited in the post office at Maurice. The answer contains a general denial, and the plaintiff offered evidence to show that notice had been given as pleaded. It is suggested by the plaintiff that the form and sufficiency of the notice was not in issue. The

defendant denied that any notice had been given, and thus placed upon the plaintiff the burden of proving the averment of his petition respecting notice. It is said that all of the evidence introduced in the district court is not before us; but that claim is denied, and the transcript shows that it is not well founded. The testimony in regard to the notice is, in substance, as follows: The plaintiff testified that "after the fire we sent letters to all the companies. We sent one to the St. Paul Fire & Marine Insurance Co. I have never seen that letter afterwards. * * * I think it was sent January 13th, after the fire." No objection was made to that testimony. The plaintiff further testified that he was present when Mr. Thompson wrote the notice, but that he did not see its contents; that he saw it mailed; and that it was addressed to the defendant at St. Paul, Minn., and stamped. Thompson testified as follows: "After the property was burned, Mr. Heusinkveld came to me to get me to prepare a paper. * * * I sent the St. Paul Fire & Marine Ins. Co. a notice of the fire. I wrote them a letter, and gave them the date of the fire. I put the notice in an envelope, and put it in the post office. The envelope was stamped and addressed to the St. Paul Fire & Marine Insurance Co., of St. Paul, Minn. I put it in the post office the day I wrote it, some time between one day and a week after the fire." He was then asked to state the contents of the notice, and notwithstanding an objection by the defendant that it was "incompetent, immaterial, and irrelevant, and not the best evidence," was permitted to answer that it told the defendant of the property which was burned, the date of the fire, the number of the policy, and its amount. The appellant contends that the court erred in permitting Thompson to answer the question objected to, for the reason that his statement respecting the letter was not the best evidence of its contents. Much is said in argument in regard to the necessity of producing the letter, or of giving notice to the defendant to produce it, and of the right of the plaintiff to give secondary evidence of its contents, without making a demand that it be produced, but we do not find it necessary to determine the question thus presented. The policy required the plaintiff, when the fire occurred, to "give notice," of the loss to the defendant; and we are of the opinion that the testimony of the plaintiff and Thompson to which there are no objections showed a sufficient compliance with the requirement of the policy. No evidence upon that issue was offered by the defendant. Therefore, the subsequent answer of Thompson, to which the objection was made, could not have been prejudicial. I, is suggested in argument that there is no proof that the notice was ever received by the defendant; but it does not appear that any objection of that kind was made in the district court, and it is not argued in this court.

II. The policy required, in addition to notice of loss, that the plaintiff, "within 60 days from the date of the fire, render a particular account of such loss, signed and sworn to by him," and setting out other matters which need not be specified. The compliance with that requirement which was attempted was to send to the defendant a plan of the building destroyed and estimates of its value and the cost of replacing it. Those papers were considered on a former appeal of this case, reported in 96 Iowa, 224, and held to be insufficient as proofs of loss. After the cause was remanded for further proceedings, the plaintiff filed an amendment to his petition in which he pleaded a waiver of all the requirements of the policy in regard to proofs of loss, and that such waiver was made orally by J. H. Hoffman, of Le Mars, Iowa, the recording agent who issued the policy, and by an adjusting agent of the defendant, whose name was unknown to the plaintiff. The evidence shows that the person described as an adjusting agent was a man named Maitland. The facts in regard to the alleged waiver are substantially as follows: The policy in suit was issued by Hoffman, as stated. Two weeks after the fire occurred, Hoffman and Maitland appeared in Maurice, and stated that they had come to adjust the loss. Adjusters for different companies, among whom was one Clark, were there, to adjust other losses under policies issued by their respective companies. Maitland looked for and found the plaintiff; told him to have two carpenters prepare a plan of the building, and an estimate showing its value when destroyed, and the cost of replacing it; and either he or Hoffman told the plaintiff to send the papers when completed, to the defendant, "and it would be all right"; or, as stated by another witness, Maitland said to the plaintiff, "that if he went and done as he had bargained, and sent it to the company, that it would be all right." The plaintiff did all he was directed to do by Maitland. It is insisted, however, that it is not shown by competent evidence that Maitland was the adjusting agent of the defendant. The evidence that he was such agent may be briefly stated as follows: Soon after the notice of loss was sent to the defendant, Maitland, with Hoffman, went to Maurice, and proceeded to adjust the loss as stated. He said repeatedly to Robey, an attorney who was acting for the plaintiff, that he was the general adjusting agent of the defendant. Campbell, an attorney for the defendant, was called as a witness for the plaintiff and testified that he did not know Maitland, but knew of him; that he traveled for the defendant at one time, but the witness did not know whether he did so in the year 1893, and did not know whether he was an adjuster of the defendant. Robey testified that he had met Maitland once, and when asked whether he knew his business in January, 1893, answered, "I think I do." He was then asked, "What was his business in January, 1893?" and answered, "He was the general adjusting agent for the St. Paul Fire & Marine Insurance Co." The witness then stated that Maitland visited Maurice January 25, 1893, with reference to the loss of the plaintiff; and, in answer to the question, "State, if you know, what he was there for," answered, "He was there looking after that loss." On cross-examination Robey was asked how he knew that Maitland was the general adjuster of the defendant, and answered: "I knew it from him telling me that he was; and Mr. Clark, of Des Moines, general adjusting agent for the Phœnix Insurance Co., was there, and another agent of the Aetna; and, in a general conversation between them and myself in regard to those losses, he repeatedly said that he was the general adjusting agent." Also: "Mr. Clark told me that Mr. Maitland was the adjusting agent for the St. Paul Company, and he told me two months ago, in Rock Valley, that he had known him [Maitland] to be the adjusting agent for the last seven or eight years. Mr. Maitland said he was the general adjusting agent. He used these terms when they were talking together, and how they had met together, and how nicely they had settled up the losses." That was the only time Robey ever met Maitland.

It is well settled that an agency cannot be proved by the declarations of the agent if objection be made. *Moffitt v. Cressler,* 8 Iowa, 122; *Graul v. Strutzel,* 53 Iowa, 712; *Renwick v. Bancroft,* 56 Iowa, 527; *Clanton v. Railway Co.,* 67 Iowa, 350; *Bigler v. Toy,* 68 Iowa, 687; *Drake v. Railway Co.,* 70 Iowa, 59. Therefore, proof of the declarations of Maitland was not competent to show the alleged 5   agency. The only evidence of the authority of Hoffman was the fact that he was the recording agent who issued the policy in suit. But the policy prescribed the proofs of loss required, and provided that "the agent of this company has no authority to waive, modify, or strike from this policy any of its printed conditions." That was sufficiently broad to include Hoffman, and the proof fails to show that he had any authority whatever respecting the adjustment of losses; and the mere fact that he acted with Maitland in adjusting the loss in question, and perhaps heard without objection the statements of the latter that he was the adjusting agent of the defendant, would not be competent proof of such agency. If Hoffman had no authority to bind the defendant by an adjustment of his own making, there is no presumption that he could bind the defendant in recognizing the agency of another. But the testimony of Campbell shows that Maitland had been an agent of the defendant, and it is not shown that the agency had terminated. For the reasons shown, we must indulge in the presumption that notice of the loss was received by the defendant in due time; and the arrival in Maurice of the agent who issued the policy, and of Maitland, to adjust the loss, was but a few days after the notice was so received. Robey stated without objection that Maitland was then the adjusting agent of the defendant. After the answer was given, the defendant moved to strike it out, "as incompetent, immaterial, and a conclusion of the witness," but the motion was overruled. The answer was certainly not immaterial, and, when the objection was made, did not appear to be incompetent. Although the relation of principal and agent is a legal one, depending upon the existence of certain facts, and the statement that it exists may be in the nature of a conclusion, yet the relation is also a condition of which any one having personal knowledge of it may testify, subject, however, to the test of cross-examination; and we are of the opinion that the court did not err in refusing to strike out the answer. The cross-examination of the witness showed that his knowledge of the alleged agency was based upon the statements of Maitland and Clark. No objection whatever was made to the testimony of Robey given on cross-examination, and no further attempt was made to exclude his answers on direct examination to which objection was made. As those objections were properly overruled when made, the ruling did not become erroneous when the cross-examination developed the basis of the answers. To be available, the objection should then have been renewed, or a further objection should then have been made. But nothing of that nature was done. When the evidence for the plaintiff was closed, the defendant asked the court to direct a verdict in its favor, and, as one of the grounds for that relief, stated that the authority of Hoffman or Maitland to waive proofs of loss had not been shown, because of a certain condition of the

policy, not because neither of them had been shown to be an
adjusting agent of the defendant.   That objection did not
raise the question we have been considering.   The case we
have appears to be this :   A witness gave to a question not
objected to an answer which was called for by the question,
and which appeared to be proper.   An objection to that answer
in view of the evidence at that time given was properly overruled.   On cross-examination the incompetency of the witness
was disclosed, but no further objection to the answer once
assailed was made.   Under these circumstances the court did
not err in permitting it to stand.   Robey's testimony respecting what Clark and Maitland said in regard to the agency of
the latter was hearsay; but, as no objection was made to it,
the jury was authorized to consider it.   Our conclusion, based
upon the facts enumerated is, that there was sufficient evidence to warrant the presumption that Maitland was the
adjusting agent of the defendant, with power to act for it in
adjusting the loss in question.   The defendant failed to offer
any evidence to rebut that presumption, and the finding of
the jury in regard to the authority of Maitland must stand.

III.   The policy provides that "the use of general terms,
or anything less than a distinct, specific agreement, clearly
expressed and indorsed in this policy, shall not be construed as
a waiver of any printed or writtten condition or restriction
therein ;" also, "that the agent of this company has no authority to waive, modify, or strike from this policy any of its
printed conditions."   It is insisted that the alleged
7   waiver of proofs of loss was prohibited by these provisions.   We have had occasion to consider the question
of the right of adjusting agents to waive formal proofs of
loss, under policies containing limitations as to waivers fully
as stringent as are those quoted, and have held that such proofs
may be waived.   *Ruthven v. Insurance Co.,* 102 Iowa, 550,
and cases therein cited ; *Brock v. Insurance Co.,* 106 Iowa,
30.   See, also, *Dyer v. Insurance Co.,* 103 Iowa, 524.   The
evidence authorized the jury to find that Maitland investi-

gated the loss, and agreed with the plaintiff as to what proofs would be required of him. He promptly furnished those proofs to the defendant; but with constructive, if not actual knowledge of the settlement Maitland had made, and that the estimates and plan of the carpenters were sent pursuant to that settlement, it made no objection to the proofs furnished, nor asked for anything in addition to them. The good faith of the loss, and the fact that it was much in excess of the amount of the policy, are established beyond question; and we do not think the defendant should now be heard to say that the proofs of loss were not sufficient.

IV. When the policy in suit was issued, there was an unsatisfied mortgage on the insured property, and the policy was made payable in case of loss to the mortgagee, as his interest might appear. Subsequently, the plaintiff contracted for the purchase of the mortgage which was executed by a former owner of the property, and claims that the contract price was fully paid before the loss occured. After the policy was issued, and before the fire, the plaintiff informed the agent, Hoffman, that the mortgage had been paid, and asked that the loss, if any, be made payable to the insured, which was done. It is shown that the mortgage was not
8   satisfied, and that one of the notes which it secured had not been taken up when the loss occurred; but the plaintiff insists that he had a claim against the party who contracted to sell him the mortgage for more than the remainder due thereon. It is contended by the appellant that the mortgage had not been paid, and that the case is the same as though the policy had been issued upon property which was falsely represented to the defendant to be free from incumbrance. The provision of the policy in regard to incumbrances is as follows: "Any false representation, omission to make known every incumbrance, whether a lien, mortgage, judgment, or otherwise, * * * then this policy shall be void; * * * or if the property or any part thereof shall be sold, transferred, or incumbered (by mortgage, judgment, or

otherwise), or if any action or proceeding at law or otherwise shall be commenced affecting the title thereto, or if proceedings to foreclose any lien thereon shall be commenced in any way, or notice thereof shall be given,   *   *   *   then, and in every such case, this policy shall be void." The answer, after setting out a part of these provisions and one or two others which are immaterial, states that, when the policy was issued, the insured property was incumbered by mortgage, which was still unsatisfied; that the plaintiff omitted to make known to the defendant the existence of the mortgage, and represented that the property was free from incumbrance, and thus violated the conditions of the policy. But it is clearly shown that the defendant, through its recording agent, was fully advised of the mortgage when the policy was issued. The question as to the effect of representing that the mortgage had been paid, and making the loss, if any, payable to the insured, which is discussed by the appellant, is not presented by the pleadings. It is said that the risk was increased by the change in the policy thus made, contrary to the provisions of the policy. That may be doubted in view of the evidence in the case; but, however that may be, we do not find any question in regard to it presented by the pleadings or assignments of error.

V.   An action to foreclose the mortgage was commenced, and it is said that notice of the suit was not given, as required by the policy. The evidence offered in regard to the action is too meager and uncertain to entitle the defendant to any relief on account of it, and the assignments of error do not present any question respecting it. The appellant has presented in argument numerous questions which are not of sufficient importance to merit separate mention. We have considered all question argued, without finding any ground upon which the judgment of the district court should be disturbed. The plaintiff has shown a meritorious cause of action. The defense has been made upon technical grounds, many of which were not presented to the district court. We are well satisfied that the plaintiff is entitled to recover of the defendant the amount for which judgment was rendered by the district court, and the judgment is therefore AFFIRMED.

BAKER WIRE COMPANY, Appellant, v. CHICAGO & NORTH-WESTERN RAILWAY COMPANY.

Limitation of actions: STATUTE PENALTY: *Carriers.* An action to recover damages for excessive freight charges under laws Twenty-second General Assembly, chapter 28, which permits such a recovery provided a demand in writing has been made upon the defendant for the money damages sustained for such excessive charges before suit is brought, is for a statutory penalty within Code, 1873, section 2529, subdivision 1, limiting actions for the recovery of statutory penalties to two years.

Appeal from Polk District Court.—HON. W. A. SPURRIER, Judge.

MONDAY, OCTOBER 10. 1898.

ACTION to recover treble damages for overcharges exacted on freight shipments over defendant railway. There was a demurrer to the petition, which was sustained. Plaintiff electing to stand on its petition, judgment was rendered in favor of defendant for costs. Plaintiff appeals.—*Affirmed.*

Dudley & Coffin for appellant.

Hubbard & Dawley for appellee.

WATERMAN, J.—This action was begun on December 24, 1891. On the ninth day of November, 1895, an amended and substituted petition was filed. It contains one hundred and fifty-nine separate counts, each count setting forth a particular shipment of freight, the amount of the overcharge, and a claim for treble the amount of such overcharge as damage. The total damages are laid at one thousand four hundred and nine dollars and twenty-two cents. There is also a claim in the petition for ten dollars attorney's fee on each count. The shipments mentioned began on July 11, 1888, and the last one was made on February 1, 1889. The demurrer is based on the ground that plaintiff's cause of action is barred, because it is for a statute penalty that accrued more than two years before suit begun. If this is an action to recover a statute penalty, it is conceded that the ruling below was correct. Subdivision 1 of section 2529 of the Code of 1873 fixes the period of two years after the cause of action accrues within which such action must be brought. The question we have to determine, then, is, what is the character of this action? Is it to recover a penalty, or merely to secure compensation for injuries suffered? The action is brought under chapter 28, Laws Twenty-second General Assembly. It is provided in this act that the board of railway commissioners shall fix reasonable and maximum rates for the transportation of freight. This, the petition alleges, was done; and the ground of complaint is that defendant exacted a greater amount than was so fixed on each of the shipments of which complaint is made. Section 9 of this act is as follows: "That in case any common carrier subject to the provision of this act shall do, cause to be done, or permit to be done, any act, matter or thing in this act prohibited, or declared to be unlawful, or shall omit to do any act, matter or thing, in this act required to be done, such common carrier shall be liable to the person or persons injured thereby, for three times the amount of damages sustained in consequence of any such violation of the provisions of this act, together with costs of suit and a reasonable counsel or attorney's fee to be fixed by the court in which the same is heard, on appeal or otherwise, which shall be taxed and collected as part of the costs in the case: provided that in all cases demand in writing on said common carrier shall be made, for the money damages sustained, before suit is brought for recovery under this section, and that no suit shall be brought until the expiration of fifteen days after such demand."

II. A question similar to that raised here has been twice before presented to and passed upon by this court. *Koons v. Railroad Co.*, 23 Iowa, 493; *Herriman v. Railway Co.*, 57 Iowa, 187. The first of these cases arose under section 6, chapter 169, Laws Ninth General Assembly, which was as follows: "Any railroad company hereafter running or operating its road in this state, and failing to fence such road on either or both sides thereof against live stock running at large at all points where said roads have the right to fence, shall be absolutely liable to the owner of any live stock injured, killed or destroyed, by reason of the want of such fence or fences as aforesaid, for the value of the property so injured, killed or destroyed, unless the injury complained of is occasioned by the willful act of the owner or his agent, and in the cases contemplated by this section, in order to recover, it shall only be necessary for the owner of the property to prove the injury or destruction complained of: provided, that in case the railroad company liable under the provisions of this section, shall neglect or refuse to pay the value of any property so injured or destroyed, after thirty days' notice in writing given, accompanied by an affidavit of the injury or destruction of said property to any officer of the company or any station or ticket agent employed in the management of its business in the county where such injury complained of shall have been committed, such company shall in any action brought to recover therefor, be held liable to pay double the value of the property injured, killed or destroyed as afore-. said." It was held that this statute did not impose a penalty, but simply fixed the measure of plaintiff's compensation in the event of his being compelled to bring suit. The *Herriman Case* involved the construction of a statute similar in purpose to the one that affords foundation for this action. Laws Fifteenth General Assembly chapter 68. This statute, among other things, fixed maximum rates for freight charges by railway companies. Section 11 thereof is in these words: "Any officer, agent, or employee of any railroad company, person, or corporation, operating a line of railroad within this state, who shall violate or be a party to the violation of any of the provisions of this act, or instrumental therein, shall be guilty of a misdemeanor, and shall, on conviction thereof, be punished for every such offense by fine not less than twenty dollars, nor more than one hundred dollars, or by imprisonment not less than five nor more than thirty days; or any such person, corporation, or railroad company as aforesaid, who shall authorize, direct, cause, permit, or allow any violation of the provisions of this act by any officer, agent, or employee, such railroad company, person or corporation shall forfeit and pay to the person injured five times the amount, compensation, or charge illegally taken or demanded, or five times the amount of damage caused, as the case may be, to be recovered with a reasonable attorney's fee by such person in a civil action in any court or before a justice of the peace, as the case may be, of this state; and if an appeal be taken from the judgment or any part thereof, it shall be the duty of the appellate court to include in the judgment an additional reasonable attorney's fee for services in the appellate court or courts; and for every such violation such railroad company, person, or corporation shall forfeit and pay to the state of Iowa, for the use of the school fund, the sum of five hundred dollars, to be recovered in any civil action in the name of the state; and it is hereby made the duty of the attorney-general of the state and of the several district-attorneys within their respective districts to sue for and recover all sums forfeited as aforesaid." The holding in the *Herriman Case* was that the amount allowed as recovery was in the nature of a penalty, and the *Koons Case* was distinguished. The fact that the act of the Fifteenth General Assembly provided in terms for a "forfeit" by the defendant of the amount fixed was allowed some significance in making the distinction and no little stress was laid upon the further fact that in the first statute a demand was required before suit brought and the railway company was thus given an opportunity to satisfy the claim; while the statute involved in the *Herriman Case* provided for the payment absolutely of five times the amount of the actual damage. It is said, in substance, by the court in this latter case, that the use of the word "forfeit" is not in itself controlling, and that the amount fixed as damages should not be conclusive, but that each of these matters should have some weight. The statute presented here resembles the act of the ninth general assembly in that it requires a demand upon the railway company before an action can be brought for the statutory damage, and it is dissimilar to the act of the fifteenth general assembly in respect to the fact that the amount allowed is not in terms styled a "forfeit." Both in the law of 1888 (Twenty-second General Assembly) and in the statute under consideration the act of exacting the overcharge is made a misdemeanor. See section 2 of latter statute. This feature was wholly lacking in the statute construed in the *Koons Case*. We have noted some verbal differences in the statutes construed in the two cases mentioned. Counsel for appellant think they are unlike in principle, but to this we cannot assent. We can perceive no substantial difference in character between them. Certainly the use of the word "forfeit" in one does not distinguish it in principle from the other. And we are not inclined to allow any force of the fact that a demand was required in the first statute, before an action could be maintained for the statutory damage. If it can be said that anything more than compensation is allowed, it is a penalty, whether given because of the refusal to comply with the demand or for the original exaction. There is no little conflict of authority on the question as to whether statutes like that involved here are remedial in character or of a penal nature. We find decisions which give support to the holding in the *Koons Case*. *Aylsworth v. Curtis,* 19 R. I. 517 (34 Atl. Rep. 1109); *Reed v. Northfield,* 13 Pick. 94; *Woodward v. Alston,* 12 Heisk. 581; *Frohock v. Pattee,* 38 Me. 103; *Huntington v. Attrill,* 146 U. S. 657 (13 Sup. Ct. Rep. 224). These cases hold, in substance, that a statute which

gives cumulative damages with the right of recovery in the
injured party is remedial only. It is manifest that this
principle is not in accord with the holding in the *Herriman
Case.* On the other hand, we find that this court has indirectly questioned the authority of the *Koons Case* by char-
acterizing the statute there construed as penal. *Miller v.
Railroad Co.,* 59 Iowa, 707; *Moriarity v. Railway Co.,* 64
Iowa, 696. These cases are in line with the *Herriman Case,*
and lend it support. So, too, does the case of *Taylor v. Telegraph Co.,* 95 Iowa, 740, in which we held a statute penal
which gave a plaintiff fifty dollars in addition to his actual
damages, for failure to transmit a telegram. The following
cases from other courts will also be found to uphold the rule
of the *Herriman Case.* *Barnett v. Railroad Co.,* 68 Mo. 56;
Missouri Pac. Ry. Co. v. Humes, 115 U. S. 512 (6 Sup. Ct.
Rep. 110); *Atchison T. & S. F. Ry. Co. v. Tanner,* 19 Colo.
Sup. 559 (36 Pac. Rep. 541); *Ashland Sav. Bank v. Bailey,*
66 N. H. 334 (21 Atl. Rep. 221); *Goodridge v. Railway Co.,*
35 Fed. Rep. 35. In the two first of these cases the question was discussed generally, and the statute involved was,
as in the *Koons Case,* one giving double damages for live
stock killed by a railway company through a failure to fence
its tracks. The issue in the other three cases arose, as here,
under a plea of the statute of limitations. In the *Goodrich
Case* the statute passed upon was similar to that in the case
at bar. It allowed treble damages for the exaction of unlawful freight charges by railway companies. The theory of the
cases is that a party civilly injured is entitled to full and
adequate compensation for all loss sustained, but to nothing
more; and that anything allowed in excess of this is in the
nature of punitive damages, which are always given by way
of punishment of the wrongdoer. Whatever we might think
if the question were an open one, we feel bound to accept the
opinion in the *Herriman Case,* re-inforced as it is by subsequent decisions of this court, to which we have called attention, as announcing the rule in this state. With the authori-

ties elsewhere in conflict there seems to be no controlling reason for our departing from the holding of that case.— AFFIRMED.

THE M. M. WALKER COMPANY, Appellant, v. THE DUBUQUE FRUIT AND PRODUCE COMPANY, JOHN CAR-TEGNEY and EDWARD MUNT.

Factors: LIEN. *Conversion.* A factor's lien for commission and advances is waived where, after having consented that the owner

2   might sell the goods himself, and after learning of a sale by the latter, the factor made a sale to a third person, it appearing that both the owner and the purchaser secured by him expressed their willingness to pay the factor's charges, since the sale by the factor, under such circumstances, amounted to a conversion of the goods.

RULE APPLIED. A fruit grower consigned to defendant four cars of apples The defendant agreed to sell them for ten per cent commission, paid the freight and advanced the shipper $100.00 thereon.

1   Defendant failed to sell the apples quickly, the shipper induced it to advance another $100.00, and it was agreed he might sell to some one else.   Acting upon the agreement the apples were sold to plaintiff, with whose agent the shipper went to the office of the

2   defendant, demanded the apples, and offered to pay all charges, advances and commission thereon.   Defendant's agent at first agreed to the arrangement, but subsequently refused to deliver the apples.   Subsequently, on the same day, defendant informed the shipper that the apples had been sold to a teamster in their employ, who gave his individual note for the purchase price   The teamster was joined as defendant in replevin, against defendant, to recover possession of the apples.   A verdict was directed for defendant.   *Held*, that defendant had no right to sell the property, after it was notified of the sale to plaintiff, and after the offer to pay all charges against the property, and a sale by it amounted to a conversion.

JURY QUESTION. The case should have gone to the jury on the ques-
2   tion of waiver of the lien and the sufficiency of the tender.

Appeal from Dubuque District Court.—HON. J. L. HUSTED, Judge.

MONDAY, OCTOBER 10. 1898.

ACTION of replevin to recover possession of seven hundred and sixty-seven barrels of apples.   The court directed a verdict for defendants, and plaintiff appeals. The facts will appear in the opinion.—*Reversed.*

Gibbs & Dohs and *D. E. Lyon* for appellant.

Matthews & Barnes for appellees.

DEEMER, C. J.—H. M. Scott is a fruit grower residing in the state of New York. In the year of 1896 he consigned to the Dubuque Fruit & Produce Company, which is a corporation engaged in the commission business in the city of Dubuque, four cars of apples to be sold on commission. The company advanced him one hundred dollars, paid the freight upon the apples and agreed to sell them for ten per cent. commission. For some reason, not material, however, to the issues presented, the defendant company did not sell the apples as rapidly as Scott anticipated; and he, becoming dissatisfied with the manner in which they were being handled, came to Iowa, and endeavored to sell them to the produce company. Failing in this, he induced the commission company to advance him another one hundred dollars; and the evidence tends to show that, after this advancement was made, the manager of the commission company gave Scott the names of various dealers in the city of Dubuque, and agreed that he might sell them to some one else. Acting upon this agreement, Scott went forth, and quickly sold the apples to the M. M. Walker Company. With an agent of this latter company, Scott went to the office of the produce company, and both he and an agent of the Walker Company demanded the apples, and agreed to pay all advancements, charges, and commissions. The agent of the produce company consented to this arrangement; but, as Scott and the representative of the Walker Company were leaving the store, the agent of the produce company changed his mind, and declared that he would not deliver them. Neither Scott nor the agent of the Walker Company knew the amount of the produce company's charges, but they offered and agreed to pay whatever sum was due, and the produce company made no objection to the offer.   This refusal on the part of the produce company to turn over the goods occurred some time in the morning of the eighteenth day of December, 1896.   In the afternoon of that day, Scott again visited the produce company, and was then informed that the apples had been sold by that company to a man by the name of Cartegney.   The evidence tends to show that this man was in the employ of the produce company as a teamster, and that he gave his individual note for the purchase price.   Cartegney is made a party to this suit, and it is claimed the sale to him was without authority, fraudulent, and void.   The trial court directed a verdict for the defendants, upon the theory that the produce company had a lien upon the property for advances made and charges paid, and that there was no evidence that such charges or advances had been paid or tendered before the commencement of the action.

That the produce company had a lien for all proper advancements, charges, and commissions is conceded; but it is claimed that it so conducted itself that it has waived its lien.   The rule seems to be that if a factor voluntarily parts with the possession of the goods, pledges them for his own debt, or suffers them to be attached, his lien is lost, and the owner may recover them notwithstanding the lien.   The lien is personal to the factor, and no one can assert it save the factor himself.   *Holly v. Huggeford,* 8 Pick 73.   This is upon the principle that one having a lien may waive it by claiming to own the property absolutely, or by doing any other act inconsistent with his right to a lien, and refusing to deliver the goods to the owner.   See *Andrews v. Wade* (Pa.) 6 Atl. Rep. 48.   Again, it has been held that if one having a right to a lien fails or refuses to disclose the full amount, and it cannot reasonably be presumed to be within the knowledge of the owner, so that he may make a tender of the true amount, the lien is deemed to have been waived.   *Thatcher v. Harlin,* 2 Houst. (Del.) 178;

Holbrook v. Wight, 24 Wend. 169; and other cases cited in *Munson v. Porter,* 63 Iowa, 456.

The produce company had no right to sell the property after it had been notified of the sale to Walker, unless such sale was necessary to the enforcement of its lien. And, as both appellant and Scott stood ready to pay the charges, the sale to Cartegney was without authority, and amounted to a conversion of the goods. The factor's lien was thereby extinguished, and plaintiff was entitled to recover. See *Holbrook v. Wight, supra; Kilpatrick v. Dean* (City Ct. N. Y.) 3 N. Y. Supp. 60; Id. (Com. Pl.) 4 N. Y. Supp. 708; *Davis v. Bigler,* 62 Pa. St. 242; *Andrews v. Wade, supra.* We have already discovered evidence tending to show that neither Scott nor appellant knew of the amount of the produce company's claims for charges and commissions; that they offered to pay what was due; and that the refusal of the defendant to deliver was not due to the insufficiency of the tender, or to the medium of payment, but to the claim that the produce company had sold the goods to one of its employes. This tends to show not only a waiver of the lien, but a waiver of the statutory tender as well. See *Auxier v. Taylor,* 102 Iowa, 673, and cases cited. *Judah v. Kemp,* 2 Johns. Cas. 411; Jones on Liens, section 1019, and cases cited; *Selby v. Hurd,* 51 Mich. 1 (16 N. W. Rep. 180).

The evidence adduced tended to show that the sale to Cartegney was without authority and fraudulent, and we think the case should have gone to the jury on the question of waiver of lien, and as to the sufficiency of the tender made by appellant.—REVERSED.

WILLIAM NEET, by his Guardian, America Mason v. THE
BURLINGTON, CEDAR RAPIDS & NORTHERN
RAILWAY COMPANY, Appellant.

Contributory Negligence: DUTY AFTER DISCOVERY OF. Contributory negligence will not preclude recovery for injuries which might have been prevented by the exercise of reasonable care by the defendant after learning of plaintiff's dangerous position.

RULE APPLIED: *Jury question.* A boy seventeen years old, not an employe, and having no right there, jumped on the rear platform of a moving freight train, and soon after, while the train was backing, was thrown upon the track in front of it, and was caught. and carried 254 feet, and both legs were crushed. He testified that he was caught in the back. through his clothing, by a rod, and that he paddled along on his hands, and was injured just before the train was stopped. A scar on his back and the condition of his clothing confirmed this. One witness saw him fall, and struggle to keep his legs from under the wheels. Another testified that he was run over immediately, and a third that he was run over before the cars had moved ten feet. The brakes had been set at once, and a small portion of his trousers on the leg was caught between the brakeshoe and the wheel. but this could have happened after the brakes were set. Both brakemen claimed that they knew nothing of the accident until the train had stopped, but a witness testified that one told the other that there was someone under the train, before it had moved a car length, and that neither made any effort to stop it. Another witness testified that he called to them that there was a man under the train (which they denied) and they signaled but made no effort to stop. The engineer could have stopped the train within a car length if he had received an emergency signal, but he received none; and by the application of brakes it could have been stopped within one hundred feet. *Held* that the question whether the injury might have been prevented by the exercise of reasonable care, after the discovery of the situation of the injured party, was for the jury.

Appeal from Grundy District Court.—HON. A. S. BLAIR, Judge.

MONDAY, OCTOBER 10. 1898.

ACTION for damages. Judgment for plaintiff, and defendant appeals.—*Affirmed.*

S. K. Tracy for appellant.

Williams & Kern and *Boies & Boies* for appellee.

LADD, J.—The only question presented is whether the verdict is sustained by the evidence. As a freight train, consisting of twenty-three loaded cars, one empty, and the caboose, was passing the depot at Rheinbeck, in a southeasterly direction, to a point beyond certain switches, William Neet jumped on the platform of the moving caboose. After passing the switches, the train stopped, and backed on the passing track in a northwesterly direction. The head brakeman, Jordan, signaled the engineer to stop, and undertook to pull a pin so as to uncouple the rear cars. This pin was wedged in by cinders so that it could not be readily pulled, and the train, in taking up a slack, caused the caboose to jerk, and threw Neet from the platform of the caboose back on the track. He was caught in some way and carried back two hundred and fifty-four feet before the train was stopped. The wheels of the truck ran over both legs, causing injuries which resulted in amputation. He was but seventeen years old, not in the employment of the defendant, and had no right to be on the train. It is not claimed that the defendant is responsible for injuries occasioned by the fall, or which resulted to him immediately afterwards. Indeed, recovery is based on injuries, if any, to him after the train had moved back, subsequent to his fall, one hundred and fifty feet. The charges of negligence are (1) that the brakeman failed to exercise ordinary diligence in stopping the train after being informed of Neet's perilous situation, and (2) that the head brakeman failed to give the engineer the emergency signal upon being so informed, and that, had such diligence been exercised, or signal been given, the train would have been stopped in time to have avoided the injury. Was there any evidence sufficient to go to the jury upon these two charges of negligence? The defendant insists that the evidence conclusively shows that the wheels ran over the legs immediately after Neet's fall. Neet testified that he fell inside of the rails, immediately turned over on his hands and knees, and was caught in the back through his clothing by a rod just back of the first brakebeam, from which he was torn loose when his legs were run over, and that he paddled along on his hands until the train was stopped. A scar on his back and the condition of his clothing, tended to confirm this story. He also said the wheels ran over his legs just before the train stopped. Davis saw the boy fall, and observed him struggle to keep his legs from under the wheels. Clifford was not positive, but thought his feet fell inside of the rails. On the other hand, Randall testified thàt the boy fell with his feet over the rails, and his legs were run over immediately. Gibson is unable to say whether his legs fell across the rails or whether he threw them there, but is positive that they were run over before the cars had moved ten feet. Barr, the conductor, felt the jar of the car wheels as though rising and going over something. All that can be said concerning this evidence is that it was in conflict. If the jurors believed Randall and Gibson, or relied upon the inference to be drawn from the statement of Barr, they might well have found that the injury occurred within the one hundred and fifty feet mentioned in the petition. But if they relied upon the testimony of the party injured, somewhat corroborated by other witnesses, then they might well have found that the injury occurred shortly before the train stopped. When Neet was taken from under the cars it was found that a small portion of his trousers on the right leg was caught between the brake shoe and the wheel,—enough to carry him along. It is said that, because the brake was set immediately after his fall, has pantaloons must have been caught at that time. If so, then this physical fact is conclusive that he was injured within the one hundred and fifty feet, as the conductor set this brake immediately after his fall. But it is shown that the brake-shoes raise and lower when set hard, if the train is in motion, so as to leave a little space between the shoe and the wheel. It is possible, then, that the clothing was caught after the brake was set. If before, owing to the loosening of the shoe, the cloth might have worked out. As, in backing, the wheel would naturally draw or carry everything next to it up to the end of the brake shoe, the cloth might have been caught after the brake was set. This would be more likely to occur after the wheel had passed over, as the jar would tend to raise the brake, and the mashing of the leg within the cloth would tend to hold that close to the wheel. We cannot say, from the record before us, whether the trousers were caught when the brake was set or at a time subsequent. It was a circumstance to go to the jury to aid in arriving at a just conclusion. But it is said that the brakemen knew nothing of the accident until the train had stopped. Both of them so testified. Mitchell testified that he heard Strong, one of the brakemen, tell Jordan not to pull the pin, as there was some one under the train; that then the train had moved but a car's length after Neet's fall, and that the brakemen made no effort to stop it, by setting brakes or otherwise. Davis testified that he saw the accident; called to the brakemen, who were up towards the engine; ran and told them that a man was under the train, when they gave signals, but made no other effort to stop it. The engineer said that he received no emergency signal, but, if he had, he could have stopped the train within a car's length. It was moving slowly when Davis went to where the brakemen were, and he says that between the time of the fall and when he informed them of Neet's peril it had moved about fifteen feet. As he was forty feet beyond the caboose, and the train about 900 feet long, we take it that his estimate of the distance the train had moved is not reliable. It is said that no man with feeling would have refused to stop the train, but such an omission may result from a mistaken conclusion that all possible injury has been done. It should be added that both brakeman deny receiving any information from Davis. No pressure was being applied by the engine, and by the application of brakes the train could have been stopped within one hundred feet. The mere statement of the evidence shows the issue was for the determination of the jury.

Again, it is argued that the injury to Neet was so immediately connected with his own negligence in jumping upon the train, and the fall therefrom, that he cannot recover. It

is settled in this state, that even though the plaintiff was
negligent, if the defendant, knowing this, might have avoided
injury by the exercise of reasonable care, and failed to do so,
recovery may be had. *Benton v. Railroad Co.,* 55 Iowa, 496;
Morris v. Railroad Co., 45 Iowa, 29; *Sutzin v. Railway Co.,*
95 Iowa, 304; *Orr v. Railway Co.,* 94 Iowa, 423; *Ford v.
Railway Co.,* 106 Iowa, 85. In *Ferguson v. Railway,* 100
Iowa, 733, it was held that the evidence did not warrant the
finding that the employes of the defendant had knowledge of
Ferguson's peril. We conclude that the evidence was such
as to warrant the submission of the issue to the jury, and the
judgment is AFFIRMED.

LEWIS J. KELSEY, Appellant, v. CHICAGO & NORTH WESTERN
RAILWAY COMPANY.

106
143

Railroad: NEGLIGENCE: *Signals to fireman.* A locomotive fireman,
while standing on the steam chest of the engine, saw a "quick
long" signal given, which indicated in a general way that the
engine was to back quite a distance, to couple to the rest of the
train. It started, and he stepped down to the pilot, to go around
to the cab; and, while moving to get hold of the flag staff to balance himself, the other cars were struck, and he was thrown off
and injured. The engine had gone but about one and one-half
car lengths. There was no evidence that the engine had been too
rapidly or unskillfully backed, nor that the standing cars were
negligently placed where they were. *Held,* that the giving of the
signal was not negligence of which the fireman might complain,
where the trainmen did not know and had no reason to think that
the fireman was in a place of danger.

CONTRIBUTORY NEGLIGENCE. A locomotive fireman, while standing
on the steam chest of the engine, adjusting one of its parts, saw
a signal to back eight or ten car lengths, which was obeyed,
and he started to step down to the pilot beam, intending to go
around into the cab as soon as the engine stopped. While stepping
forward to grasp the flagstaff, the cars which the engine was backing toward, to couple with, were struck, the engine having moved
but one or two car lengths; and he was thrown to the ground by
the shock, and injured. There was a handrail and foot board by
which he might have returned to the cab on the engineer's side,
and there was a brace from the pilot beam to the boiler front,

which was within reach, by which he could have steadied himself.
As an excuse for not going in on the engineer's side, it was stated
that the cab window was fastened inside, and the engineer was
busy. *Held*, that the fireman was guilty of contributory negligence.

Appeal from Clinton District Court.—HON. P. B. WOLFE,
·   Judge.

MONDAY, OCTOBER 10. 1898.

ACTION to recover damages for personal injuries sustained by the plaintiff while in the employment of the defendant as a locomotive fireman. He alleges that the engine upon
which he was employed, with several cars attached thereto,
"was suddenly, too rapidly, unskillfully, and negligently,
without proper warning or signal, backed against other cars
of said train, which had been negligently left standing by
defendant's employes upon the track," by reason of which he
was thrown from the engine and seriously injured, without
fault or negligence on his part. The defendant answered,
denying generally; and, at the close of the evidence on behalf
of the plaintiff, the court, on motion of the defendant, directed
a verdict for the defendant, and rendered judgment accordingly. Plaintiff appeals.—*Affirmed.*

Hayes & Schuyler and *Barker & McCoy* for Appellant.

Hubbard & Dawley for appellee.

GIVEN, J.—I. The grounds of defendant's motion for
a verdict were that there is not sufficient evidence to sustain a finding that the defendant was guilty of the negligence
alleged, and that the evidence shows without any dispute that
the plaintiff himself was guilty of negligence which directly
contributed to his injury. Plaintiff was, at the time he was
injured, and had been for over three years, in the employ of
the defendant as a locomotive fireman, and was familiar
with the duties of a fireman and the manner of making up

and moving trains of cars. On the night of June 24, 1893, the engine upon which he worked was engaged in making up a train of freight cars in the yards at Clinton, preparatory to running west. As was his duty, the plaintiff had lighted the headlight and sidelights on the front of the engine before it was brought from the roundhouse. After setting out some cars, the engine, with eight or ten cars, attached, was moving to a point west of Fifth street, where it stood for a time, headed west. The next thing to be done, upon signal, was to back the engine and eight or ten cars attached thereto eastward, and to couple to the other cars composing the train. While the engine was thus standing still, the plaintiff got down from the cab on the north or right-hand side, and passed around to the front of the engine, to see if the lights were burning properly, and, in doing so, discovered that the cap to what is called the "peep hole" was not in proper position. It appears that this cap is removed when the engines are being cleaned in the roundhouse, and that it is the duty of the fireman to see that it is in place when the engine is brought out, because, if not in place, it affects the draft, and impedes the generation of the steam. Seeing that the cap was not closed as it should be, the plaintiff went upon the front part of the engine, and, standing upon the steam chest, tightened the cap, and, while doing so, observed a signal given by some one in the rear of train, for the engine to back east, so that the coupling could be made. The engine and cars attached were promptly moved backward, and, while moving, the plaintiff stepped from the steam chest to the bulkhead of the engine, stooping down to get hold of the flagstaff to balance himself, with the view to getting off the engine at the front, and passing around to the entrance of the cab. While in that position, the standing cars were struck by the moving cars, and the plaintiff thereby thrown from his position on the bulkhead to the ground, and quite seriously injured. There was a footboard with a handrail extending from the cab to the front of the engine, by which the plaintiff could have, after adjusting the cap to the peep hole, returned to the cab in safety. He gives as a reason for not doing so that the cab window was closed, so that it could only be opened on the inside, and that the engineer was busy at the time. It also appears that there were two large iron braces in front of the engine, one of which was within easy reach of the plaintiff when on the bulkhead. The evidence shows that, in signaling for such movements, different signals are used, so as to indicate the distance to the point of coupling. Plaintiff describes the mode of signaling as follows: "If you want to move to a position, a swinging motion of the lantern means to back up. If it is quite a distance, they will give a quick signal, and sometimes a long signal. As a general thing they give a fast signal. If you get a fast signal, you have a good distance to go. In getting that, you expect to go eight or ten car lengths. If it is only one or two car lengths, you get a little jerk. If it is two little jerks, or three little jerks, you are to know that it is that number of cars, or the front of the train is to move that far." Witness Olny describes it as follows: "If the distance was short, they could give a slow easy signal, and, when they were about to strike, they would hold their lamps still, indicating they were pretty near there. In giving this round motion, there was a difference in the sweep of the signal to indicate a long distance or a short distance between the cars to be coupled. A quick motion, that there was quite a distance to go. The slow motion would indicate that you didn't have so far to go." Mr. O'Donald says: "If you want a train to back up, if they have a good distance to go, they give a big signal, the wide swing of the arm, a good, big swing, so they know there is quite a distance to go. And, if it is a short distance, they move the lamp slowly. These signals are given for the purpose of regulating the working of the engine and the working of steam upon the engine." Plaintiff says: "The man was on the side of the train, and gave the signal, swinging round with the full length of the arm. It was a quick long signal, and signified that we had quite a long distance to go before we came to the rest of the train." He further states : "At the time I saw the signal, we had gone back not over a car and a half. I stepped down onto the pilot, and stooped over, and, before I could get hold of the flag standard, they struck. I was going to sit down, instead of jumping off in the night-time, until it struck." Again he says: "It was while in the act of stooping over, and before I got down far enough to take hold of anything, that they struck and knocked me off. I did not take hold of this brace on the front end, that is down by the pilot beam. There was nothing between it and me. We never get hold of that, even when the engine is going, when we let go of the handrail."

II. There is no evidence whatever to support the charge that the engine and cars attached thereto were suddenly, too rapidly, or unskillfully moved against the standing cars, nor that there was any negligence in having the standing cars on the track where they were. The only indication of negligence upon the part of the defendant's employes was in the kind of signal given, or, in other words, that the signal given indicated a longer distance to the point of coupling than should have been indicated. The signals only indicate in a general way the distance to be passed, and the employe giving that signal did not know, and had no reason to expect that the plaintiff was in a place of danger, as he was. The signal was for the government of the movement of the engine and cars attached, and seems to have accomplished that purpose in a proper manner. We have not set out the evidence in full on this subject, but sufficiently so, we think, to show that there was no negligence in the giving of the signal of which plaintiff has a right to complain.

III. Knowing, as the plaintiff did, that the engine and eight or ten cars were being moved backward, and that in a very brief time they would come in contact with the standing cars, we think it was manifest negligence on his part not to have returned to the cab by way of the running board, where the handrail would have protected him from danger. It was not a sufficient excuse for going as he did that the engineer was busy at the time, and that the window would have to be opened from the inside. It was the way of safety, and he should have taken it. He testifies: "I knew what we were backing up for. I knew the cars were coming together afterwards. I knew that we would not expect to find them in less than eight or ten car lengths. I didn't know the exact distance. I expected them to back until they struck or reached the other cars. That is the reason that I started to sit down on the pilot beam, and got thrown off because they came together sooner than I thought they would." He failed to protect himself by taking hold of the brace or flag standard, as he could have done. The plaintiff has no reason whatever to assume that the impact of the cars would be a few seconds later than it was, and he was unquestionably guilty of great negligence in putting himself in that place of danger under the circumstances then known to him. We are in no doubt that the motion for verdict was properly sustained, and the judgment is therefore AFFIRMED.

STATE BANK OF OTTUMWA v. E. E. MCELROY, Receiver, Appellant.

Default: SETTING ASIDE: *Notice by publication.* It is not an abuse of discretion to overrule an application by the receiver of a non-resident association to set aside its default in attachment proceedings, under Code, 1873, section 2875, providing that a defendant served by publication alone may appear and defend, where its non-resident assignee appointed after the levy, as was also the receiver, had appeared and successfully moved to have the petition made more definite and thereafter made default, no excuse for which is shown by the receiver, who appeared as one of the attorneys for the assignee on such motion, and both the association and the assignee were as competent as the receiver to make the defense attempted by him, that the attaching creditor should not recover the full amount of his claim because the association was insolvent.

Appeal from Wapello District Court.—HON. T. M. FEE,
Judge.

MONDAY, OCTOBER 10, 1898.

ACTION at law, aided by attachment, to recover of the
Granite State Provident Association of Manchester, N. H.,
the par value of certain shares of fully-paid stock, with interest.   The association was adjudged to be in default.   Its
receiver, E. E. McElroy, filed an answer and an application to
set aside the default.   The application was denied, the
answer was stricken from the files, and judgment was rendered in favor of the plaintiff, and against the association,
for the amount claimed; and certain attached property was
subjected to the payment of the judgment.   The receiver
appeals.—*Affirmed.*

A. W. Enoch and *McElroy & Heindel* for appellant.

W. S. Cohen and *Jaques & Jaques* for appellee.

ROBINSON, J.—The original notice, directed to the
association, was served in May, 1896, by publication.   At
the next August term of the court, which closed on the tenth
day of October, David A. Taggart, as assignee of the association, appeared in the action, and filed a motion to have the
petition made more specific.   The motion was sustained, and
an amendment to the petition was filed on the nineteenth day
of September; but, nothing further having been done, a
default was entered against the association on the last day
of the August term.   On the first day of the next term, which
commenced October 26th, McElroy, as receiver, filed his
answer, in which he asked for permission to defend for the
association, and also filed his application to set aside its
default.   In January, 1897, exceptions to the application
were filed, and a motion to strike the answer, with the result
stated.

I.   The appellant complains of the refusal of the court to set aside the default of the association, and relies upon section 2875 of the Code of 1873, which is as follows: "A defendant served by publication alone, shall be allowed at any time before judgment to appear and defend the action, and upon a substantial defense being declared, time may be given on reasonable terms to prepare for trial." The answer filed by the receiver alleges that the association is insolvent, and that in March, 1896, the supreme court of New Hampshire adjudged it to be insolvent, and placed it in the hands of Taggart as assignee, who is now collecting the assets and determining the liabilities of the association; that not more than fifty per cent. of the par value of the stock, if so much, will be realized for the stockholders; and that Taggart is a resident of New Hampshire, and never qualified as, and is not, assignee in this state.   It is said that his appearance in this action was therefore without effect, and that, as the association was served by publication only, and had not entered an appearance, and judgment had not been entered when the appellant appeared and applied to have the default set aside, it was his right to defend for the association.   The receiver of the property of a party to litigation is not a necessary party to such litigation if no attempt is made thereby to interfere with the right of the receiver to the property intrusted to his care.   *Weigen v. Insurance Co.,* 104 Iowa, 410; *Allen v. Railroad Co.,* 42 Iowa, 683.   In this case the plaintiff seeks to subject the attached property of the association to the payment of its claim.   The action was commenced, and the attachment was issued and levied, on the ninth day of March, 1896.   The answer filed by the receiver alleges that the association was by the supreme court of New Hampshire adjudged to be insolvent, and placed in the hands of Taggart, as assignee, "in March, 1896."   The pleadings in this case do not show the day of the month named when that was done, but it appears to be admitted that it was on the sixteenth, or after the attachment in this case had been issued and levied. It is not shown what powers were conferred upon the assignee, and we will not presume that any attempt was made to give him the right of possession of the attached property, as against the plaintiff. By its prior attachment, the plaintiff had obtained a right to the property paramount to that of the assignee, which the courts will protect. That would have been true had the assignment been voluntary. See *Franzen v. Hutchinson,* 94 Iowa, 95. And involuntary assignments, like that in question, have less extra territorial effect. *Kelly v. Crapo,* 45 N. Y. 86; *Hutcheson v. Peshine,* 16 N. J. Eq. 167; 3 Am. & Eng. Enc. Law (2d ed.), 6, and notes.

It is urged that, as Taggart had not qualified as assignee in this state, he had no authority to appear for the association. It is clear that his appointment as assignee by the supreme court of New Hampshire, even if the duties of his office were those of a receiver under the laws of this state, did not alone give him the absolute right to appear for the association in the courts of this state. *Parker v. Lamb,* 99 Iowa, 265; *Ayres v. Siebel,* 82 Iowa, 347; High Receivers, section 239 *et seq.* We cannot say, however, that his appearance was wholly unauthorized. But, while the right of a receiver to appear in an action brought outside the state in which he was appointed is generally denied, yet he is frequently permitted to do so as a matter of comity. High Receivers, section 241; Beach Receivers (Alderson's ed.), 269. That this has been practiced was recognized in *Parker v. Lamb* and *Ayres v. Siebel, supra.*

In this case, Taggart appeared, and asked the court to permit him to defend, and moved that the plaintiff be required to make its petition more specific in certain particulars. No objection to his being permitted to defend was made; and, although the court did not give him permission to do so in express terms, yet it did so impliedly by not denying the permission, and by sustaining, in part, his motion. The association was, therefore, as fully represented in fact as it would have been had the appellant been permitted to defend. The application of the appellant does not in any manner attempt to excuse the default of Taggart, and is entitled to no greater consideration than it would have been had it been made by him. It must not be forgotten that a receiver does not have an unqualified right to appear and defend in an action to which he has not been made a party. He is subject to the control of the court. Code 1873, section 2905. In Beach Receivers, 758, it is said: "A receiver is a stranger to all proceedings which he finds in progress at the time of his appointment, until he is regularly brought into court. He cannot interfere in a pending suit, as by giving notice of a motion, or conducting an appeal in his own name, unless he has been made a party to the action by order of the court. Whether a receiver shall be permitted to defend an action already pending against his principal is wholly discretionary with the court." See, also, *Tracy v. Bank,* 37 N. Y. 523; *Patrick v. Eells,* 30 Kan. 680 (2 Pac. Rep. 116); 20 Am. & Eng. Enc. Law, 253. We cannot say that an abuse of the discretion lodged in the district court has been shown in this case. Taggart was represented in it by the same attorneys who appeared for the appellant. If there was any excuse for Taggart's default, they must have been advised in regard to it, but they fail to show what it was. The default was entered on the tenth day of October, 1896; and, five days later, the appellant, who is, we understand, one of the attorneys who appeared for Taggart, was appointed, by the court in which the action was pending, receiver of the association. The defense which he asked to make was, in substance, that the plaintiff should not be permitted to recover the full amount for which his contract with the association provides, because of the insolvency of the latter. As we have seen, the association had been made a party to the action, and, so far as the facts appear, was competent to make the defense attempted by the appellant; and the same is true of Taggart. Under these circumstances, we cannot say that the district court erred in refusing to set aside the default, and in refusing to permit the appellant to defend, and its judgment is there fore AFFIRMED.

J. A. VAN WAGENEN v. J. M. PARSONS, Appellant.

Appeal: REFEREE'S REPORT: *Review.* An order sustaining objections to a finding of fact by the referee has the effect of granting
2   a new trial, and the action of the district court in granting or refusing a new trial is largely one of discretion.

SAME. The action of the trial court in sustaining exceptions to the finding of fact of the referee will not be disturbed on appeal,
2   where the evidence was conflicting, although in the opinion of the appellate court the findings are supported by the evidence.

RULE APPLIED. Where the report of a referee was set aside, and a new trial granted, on a motion presenting several grounds, and it
2   did not appear on which one or more of such grounds the order was based, an abuse of discretion was not shown by assignments of error directed to the different grounds of such motion and to the exceptions to such report, when the arguments were not so directed, but only dealt generally with the merits of the case.

Appeal from Lyon District Court.—HON. F. R. GAYNOR, Judge.

MONDAY, OCTOBER 10, 1898.

THE parties to this suit are attorneys at law, and were, prior to May 29, 1895, partners in the practice of their profession. This action is on a promissory note made by defendant to plaintiff March 30, 1896, for six hundred and thirty-five dollars, due June 30th thereafter. The execution of the note is admitted, and, as a defense, it is made to appear in the answer that at the settlement of the partnership affairs defendant paid to plaintiff the sum of two thousand three hundred dollars, and plaintiff retired, leaving defendant successor to all the rights of the firm, including its business and accounts. The answer shows that plaintiff had previously collected accounts due the firm without making the proper credits therefor on the books of the firm; that he had made collections for different parties, and had not remitted the amounts, so that the firm was liable therefor; and that the defendant had been compelled to pay the same; and that plaintiff had placed on the books of the firm excessive charges for the purpose of swelling the accounts due the firm, with a view to defraud the defendant. The answer shows the aggregate of such items to be seven hundred and forty-seven dollars, and a judgment is asked for the excess over the amount of the note. A reply makes denials, and, with other facts, shows that after the settlement of partnership affairs the plaintiff brought a suit against defendant charging fraud in the settlement, and that "defendant in defense in that suit raised an issue in the testimony of the counterclaim in his answer here on file; and in the settlement of the original suit between these parties these items of counterclaim in this suit were all known to defendant, and taken into consideration, before and at the time of giving the note in suit." The reply further presents an additional claim for three thousand dollars because of accounts alleged to have been collected by defendant before the settlement, and not charged to him on the books of the firm. The case was given to a referee, who filed a report allowing a part of defendant's counterclaim, and finding a balance in favor of plaintiff for two hundred and ninety-two dollars and forty cents. On the coming in of the report the plaintiff filed four exceptions thereto, and then filed a motion to set the report aside, which the court sustained, and from such order the defendant appealed.— *Affirmed.*

J. M. Parsons pro se.

Geo. H. Stillman and *J. A. Van Wagenen* for appellee.

GRANGER, J.—We should not lose sight of the fact that this appeal is from an order in effect granting a new trial.

.The court did, in terms, set aside the report of the referee,
and grant a new trial.   The law authorizes a new trial
1   after a report of a referee.   Code 1873, section 2837.

This is a law action, to be considered here on assignments of error.   The only question for us to consider is, did
the court err in making the order for a new trial?   No judgment has been entered, and the order but subjects the issues
to a re-examination.   Section 2837, *supra*.   The action of
the district court in granting or refusing a new trial is
largely one of discretion.   *Donahue v. Lannan,* 70 Iowa, 73;
Pianoforte Co. v. Mueller, 38 Iowa, 552; *Kern v. May,* 92
Iowa, 674.   The holdings to the same effect are many.   In
the absence of an abuse of discretion, we do not interfere.

The motion upon which the ruling was made presents
several grounds, and it does not appear on what one or more
the ruling was based.   For us to interfere, it must appear
that there was an unjust exercise of discretion as to all of
them, for, if any one comes within the court's discretion, we
are concluded from interfering.   The assignments of error
are directed to the different grounds of the motion, and to the
exceptions, but the arguments are not so directed, but are general, dealing with the merits of the case before the referee and
the court.   Our position may be clearer by stating some of
the concluding language of appellant's argument: "The
honorable judge who set aside the report of the referee was
in a position analogous to that of an appellate court.   He did
not have the evidence.   He did not have the witnesses before
him.   The referee sat as a judge.   He heard the evidence.   He
observed the witnesses, and found the facts with defendant;
and there is no reason why the report should be set aside, for
it is amply supported by the evidence."   Omitting the final
statement, which is a mere conclusion, and conceding the other
statements to be true, there is no abuse of discretion shown
in awarding another hearing.   Even our concurrence in the
conclusion of appellant that the finding of the referee is
supported by the evidence would not show an abuse of discretion, for the trial court might have thought differently with

the condition of the record such that differences of opinion might exist. The arguments leave out of consideration this discretionary authority of the court in awarding new trials, which, in our judgment, controls the case on appeal; and we do not, nor should we, consider questions going to the merits of the case, if a new trial is to follow. The order is AFFIRMED.

C. C. CROWELL v. R. F. McGOON, Appellant.

Instructions. A requested instruction as to the wrongfulness of an
4 attachment which singles out some of the evidence and states that it would not justify the attachment, is properly refused.

HARMLESS ERROR. An order in the charge in reference to the dam-
1 ages to be assessed in the event an attachment was found to be wrongful is not prejudicial where it is found that the attachment was rightful.

Impeachment. An instruction that the jury has the right to disregard the testimony of a witness whose reputation for truth and verac-
8 ity, is bad, except where corroborated, is erroneous, since a partial corroboration is sufficient to justify the jury in believing him on points as to which he is not corroborated.

Misconduct of Judge. After counsel had taken much time in attempt-ing to introduce evidence which had been ruled out, and had been
2 cautioned against incumbering the record with irrelevant matter, the court stated that a question which he asked should not be taken down, and that no more questions on that point would be allowed, since the record on that issue was complete. *Held*, not prejudicial.

Appeal from Fayette District Court.—HON. L. E. FELLOWS, Judge.

TUESDAY, OCTOBER 11, 1898.

ACTION at law to recover damages of defendant for fail-ure to take and pay for certain corn sold him by the plain-tiff. The action was aided by an attachment. Defendant, in answer, claimed that he had purchased three thousand bushels of corn of plaintiff, which he (plaintiff) refused to deliver. He also pleaded a counterclaim for the wrongful suing out of the attachment; and asked damages for breach of contract and the wrongful suing out of the writ. The case was tried to a jury, resulting in a verdict and judgment for plaintiff, and defendant appeals.—*Affirmed.*

C. H. Quigley, Ainsworth & Ainsworth and *Hoyt & Hancock* for appellant.

Wm. E. Fuller and *D. W. Clements & Son* for appellee.

DEEMER, C. J.—After the attachment was levied, the plaintiff filed a motion, under section 4237 of McClain's Code, stating that the property levied upon, which was one thousand two hundred bushels of corn, was subject to decay and waste, and was likely to depreciate in value; and asking that the same be sold by the sheriff, and the proceeds held to await the determination of the suit. Defendant resisted this motion, and, after considering the affidavits filed, the court overruled it. In its instructions, the court charged that, as defendant resisted the motion to sell, he was not entitled to recover any damages, due to depreciation in the value of the corn since the resistance was filed, as the uncontradicted evidence showed that it was at that time of the same market value
1   as it was on the day it was attached. This instruction is complained of. Sufficient answer to this contention is found in the fact that the jury found specially that the attachment was not wrongfully sued out. If the attachment was properly issued, an error in the charge with reference to the damages to be assessed in the event the attachment was found to be wrongful was without prejudice. *Mayne v. Bank,* 80 Iowa, 710.

II. A number of unsatisfied mortgages executed by defendant upon certain personal property appeared upon the records of Fayette county; and these mortgages were introduced in evidence by plaintiff. Defendant offered to show that some of them had been paid, and that others did not in fact represent any indebtedness. This the court would not permit him to do, unless he would further show that plaintiff had knowledge of the facts at the time he sued out the attachment. The ruling is not seriously complained of, but it is said that the court made remarks in passing upon the objections interposed which were prejudicial to plaintiff's case. These remarks were generally made in answer to counsel's claim, and were in no sense erroneous or prejudicial.

2   After counsel had taken much time in an endeavor to introduce evidence which the court had held to be irrelevant, the court, after cautioning counsel against incumbering the record, finally said: "Do not take down that question in evidence. If it is in regard to getting the residence of these parties, I will make the order that no more questions in regard to the residence of these parties will be permitted to be asked. I will not permit the record to be incumbered further with that class of questions. There is not any question, and no lawyer would claim but what you have got a complete record, that will cover every question in regard to that, and you want to stop there. We cannot spend time here uselessly. The court has held that the plaintiff was not bound to make inquiries of these parties, and it does not make any difference where they live, and that makes your record." Viewing these remarks in the light of the previous record, we think there was no error.

III. Appellant asked an instruction in these words: "If you find from the evidence that the general reputation of any witness for truth and veracity is bad in the community in which he resides, you have the right to disregard his evidence, except where he is corroborated. The instruction was properly refused. *McMurrin v. Rigby*, 80 Iowa, 522; *State v. Larson*, 85 Iowa, 659.

IV. Another instruction asked by appellant was properly refused, for the reason that it singled out some of the evidence, and said that this evidence would not justify plaintiff in resorting to an attachment. The question as to the wrongfulness of the attachment was submitted under proper instructions.

V. Again, it is said the evidence shows without conflict that the writ was wrongfully sued out. We cannot agree to this proposition. The evidence was in conflict, and the jury was justified in finding that the writ was not wrongfully sued out. We discover no prejudicial error and the judgment is AFFIRMED.

MAY BLAIR v. WILLIAM BLAIR, Appellant.

Divorce: CRUEL AND INHUMAN TREATMENT. Plaintiff in divorce, an ordinarily strong and healthy woman, had lived with a married man as his wife before defendant married her. Frequent quarrels arose, for which both were at fault. The wife, though kind at times, was of hasty and violent temper, which caused her to use profane and abusive language towards her husband, and threaten and attempt bodily injury on him. At various times she took an ax, and threatened to break his head; threw a pan of lye water in his face, injuring his eyes; threatened to let his brains out with a smoothing iron; threw the lid of a butter dish at him; jumped for the butcher knife and threatened to cut his liver out, and used obscene language; threatened to open his head with a chair; and struck him with a buggy whip. The husband frequently came home under the influence of liquor, but only twice drunk. He did not use vulgar or profane language or seek the company of immoral women, but spent his evenings at home. When he had been drinking he was arrogant and boastful of his wealth, and was at times coarse in his language and provoking in his manner towards his wife. He spoke in coarse terms, to his brother-in-law, of her physical condition, secured a statement of a boy in his employ that she had hugged and kissed him, endeavored to induce him to be caught in an act of illicit intercourse with her, and made public on the trial her immoral conduct before marriage, which he had forgiven. On occasions he insinuated that she was too free with other men, and he used threats and violent language, but never attempted bodily harm, and the wife had no reason to fear personal violence. She was a strong and healthy woman, in as good health on separation as when she was married. *Held*, the husband's treatment was not such as to endanger the wife's life, and she was not entitled to a divorce on the ground of cruel and inhuman treatment.

Appeal from Webster District Court.—HON. B. P. BIRDSALL, Judge.

TUESDAY, OCTOBER 11, 1898.

ACTION for divorce and alimony upon the ground of "such cruel and inhuman conduct as to endanger the life of the plaintiff." Habitual drunkenness was also charged, but this charge was abandoned on the trial as a cause for divorce. Decree was rendered granting a divorce, and allowing the plaintiff three thousand dollars alimony. Defendant appeals. —*Reversed.*

J. A. O. Yeoman for appellant.

Botsford, Healy & Healy for appellee.

GIVEN, J.—I. Counsel cite may of the cases based upon cruel and inhuman treatment endangering life as a cause for divorce. We need not refer to them specifically, as the law is well settled that the divorce will only be granted on statutory grounds; that treatment as a cause must not only be cruel and inhuman, but also such as to endanger life. Whether a particular act or course of mistreatment is cruel and inhuman, and, if so, whether it is such as to endanger life, must be determined from the facts of each case. It may be said that vile, profane, or abusive language, threats or attempts of personal injury, and false accusations of infidelity from husband to wife or wife to husband, are acts of cruel or inhuman treatment, because of their relation and of the duties that each owes to the other. Whether such treatment endangers the life of the one so treated must be determined from the attending circumstances, such as temperment, disposition, and mental and physical condition of the one mistreated. Cruel and inhuman treatment towards one who was mentally or physically infirm might endanger life, when as to one who was in mental and physical health and vigor it would not have such an effect. As supporting these views, see footnotes to section 3174 of the Code, under "Inhuman Treatment."

II. These parties were married in December, 1888, the plaintiff then being twenty-three years of age, and the defendant fifty-three. Plaintiff, though in fact an unmarried woman, was known as Mrs. Marks, having previously lived with a married man of that name in Illinois as his wife. A former marriage of defendant had been dissolved by decree of divorce, and his divorced wife was then deceased. After a few months' acquaintance and a brief courtship, the defendant proposed marriage, whereupon the plaintiff informed him of her former relations with Marks, and referred him to her mother for facts. There is a dispute as to whether the defendant was informed that Marks was a married man, but, be this as it may, it could have had but little influence in bringing the defendant to the conclusion which he reached. With full information that plaintiff had previously sustained illicit relations with Marks, the defendant agreed to marry her, and that the fact of that relation should be buried and never referred to during their married life. Though it does not appear to have been referred to but once, his knowledge of the fact explains, in part, at least, the dissensions that soon followed their marriage. After their marriage, the plaintiff went to live with defendant at his home, on his farm, where he was largely engaged in farming and buying and selling stock. His business required him to keep hired help on the farm and in the house, and to be from home most of the time during the day. So far as appears, defendant provided well for his houshold, and the plaintiff was industrious and attentive to her household duties, and, in the absence of hired help, milked the cows and fed the calves. Plaintiff now makes complaint that she was required to do that kind of work; but it can be said to her credit that she did not seriously complain of it at the time, and that it was not the cause of the estrangement that arose between her and her husband. In 1892 they moved to the city of Fort Dodge, where they resided until their final separation, in August, 1895. Soon after their marriage, dissensions and disgraceful quarrels began, which grew in frequency and violence up to the time of their final separation. We are not required to consider these numerous

quarrels in detail, nor determine which party is to blame, or
most to blame, for any or all of them. It is sufficient to say
that the evidence shows beyond dispute that both were griev-
ously and inexcusably at fault.

If incompatibility were a ground for divorce, there could
be no doubt of the propriety of separating these parties; but
it is not a statutory ground for so doing, unless by reason of
the circumstances it endangers life. The characters and dis-
positions of these parties, as shown in the evidence, may be
briefly summed up: The plaintiff, though of kind disposition
at times, especially to persons in sickness or distress, was
possessed of a hasty and violent temper, which she did not
try to control when angered at her husband. Her temper
was so violent as to cause her, when angry, to use profane and
abusive language towards her husband; and to threaten and
attempt to inflict serious and bodily injury upon him. At one
time, when quarreling, she took an ax, and threatened to break
his head with it; and, when the defendant took the ax from
her, she threw a pan of lye water, with which she had been
washing milk cans, into his face, imperiling his eyes, and
injuring them to some extent. On another occasion she threatened to let his brains out with a smoothing iron; on another,
she threw the lid of a butter dish at him; and on another,
jumped for the butcher knife, and threatened to cut his liver
out, and to "gut the damned Swede bitch" (referring to their
hired woman). On another occasion, she threatened to open
the defendant's head with a chair, and on another struck him
a number of times with a buggy whip, until he drove out of
her reach. There was provocation for these attacks, but in no
instance was the violence threatened or attempted necessary
in her self-defense, or justified by the facts. The plaintiff
either denies or gives explanations for these transactions; but,
giving full credit to her denials and explanations, there can
be no doubt that she exercises a violent and dangerous temper
towards her husband, and sometimes on slight provocation.
Her conduct may be accounted for to some extent by the fact

that early in their married life she became jealous of her husband,—a jealousy that continued up to their separation. Much evidence was taken with respect to the defendant's habit of drinking, and, while it shows that he was not an habitual drunkard, it does show that he drank intoxicants socially with others when about the towns where he went on business, and, no doubt, frequently came home more or less stimulated by the liquor he had drunk. It does not appear that he was ever what the witnesses call drunk but twice after his marriage with the plaintiff. According to the evidence, he was not in the habit of using either profane or vulgar language, nor in seeking the company of lewd women, and, as a rule, spent his evenings at home. He was somewhat arrogant and boastful of his wealth when he had been drinking, and, though not cruel in disposition, he was not always kind and considerate, but at times coarse in his language and provoking in his manner towards the plaintiff. Within a month or so after their marriage, he began to insinuate to plaintiff that she was too intimate with other men,—a jealousy prompted, no doubt, by his knowledge of her former relations with Marks. His jealousy grew, and found expression in his suspicions of a young lad of sixteen, who was employed to do chores about the house while the defendant was sick. Plaintiff testified to several instances of threatened and of actual violence, and of the use of profane and abusive language towards her; but in this she stands contradicted by the defendant, and unsupported by any other witnesses. The evidence other than that of the parties as to their conduct, up to the time they left the farm, is largely from those employed as help; and, while this evidence shows threats and acts of violence on the part of the plaintiff, it does not show that in any instance the defendant threatened or attempted bodily harm to the plaintiff. We discover nothing either in the disposition or acts of the defendant to warrant the belief that the plaintiff had any reason to, or did, apprehend personal violence at his hands.

Counsel for plaintiff insists in argument that it was cruel and inhuman for the defendant to call out on the trial, and to thus make public, the fact of plaintiff's former relations with Marks. Let this be conceded; yet, happening when it did, it was not a cause for plaintiff's abandoning her husband. It was no more cruel than for plaintiff to claim, on the trial, that an ailment with which the defendant was afflicted was a loathsome disease, resulting from association with lewd women,—a claim which the plaintiff utterly failed to establish. While it would have been inexcusable in defendant to have made public plaintiff's relation to Marks under other circumstances, it was not so on the trial, as it was an important fact in the case, accounting, as we view it, for the defendant's unreasonable jealousy. If the defendant was cruel in thus making public this fact, yet, made public when and as it was, it does not sustain the grounds alleged for divorce.

One Hislop, whose wife is a sister of the plaintiff, testified to a conversation with the defendant about a sickness that plaintiff had had, and about her not having any children. According to this witness, defendant spoke of his wife and her physical condition in coarse and unbecoming terms, and this is urged as cruel treatment. From what is testified to by a large number of reputable persons as to defendant's habit of using language, it seems improbable that he would have used the language attributed to him by Hislop; and yet, if he did, it was in a private conversation with his brother-in-law, with whom he might properly talk on the subject of his wife's health and physical condition.

In 1892 the defendant visited Scotland, where he and the plaintiff were both born, without asking her to accompany him, and left her only forty or fifty dollars in cash to use during his absence of three months. This is claimed to have been cruel. We believe the defendant when he says that he went to Scotland to get away from his wife for a time, in the hope that matters might be better when he returned, and that it was for this reason that he did not ask her to go along. He brought her back some valuable presents, and they did live happily for a time after his return. In addition to the forty or fifty dollars cash, he left her his credit, which was good, upon which to buy what she needed; and it is not claimed that she lacked any needed comforts during his absence.

The most cruel and inhuman act of the defendant towards the plaintiff disclosed in this record was what he did and attempted with the sixteen-year-old boy shortly before their final separation. It is evident that the defendant had become so intensely jealous of the plaintiff by that time that he seized upon her every act of familiarity with others as confirmation of his jealous suspicions. The boy testifies, in effect, that defendant got him to sign a written statement that Mrs. Blair had hugged and kissed him, and that the defendant sought to engage the boy to get Mrs. Blair to go to the barn with him, so that the defendant might catch them in the act of illicit intercourse, and for this he would drop a sum of money where the boy could pick it up. Defendant denies that he so planned and promised, but admits that he was suspicious of the relations between the boy and his wife,—a suspicion for which he had no reasonable ground. In view of the defendant's intense jealousy, we are inclined to accept the statements of the boy as substantially true, and as disclosing most dastardly cruel and unreasonable conduct on the part of the defendant; but the question remains whether this, with his other acts, endangered the life of the plaintiff. So far as appears, plaintiff was an ordinarily strong and healthy woman, mentally and physically, and in the enjoyment of as good health at the time of the separation as at the marriage. There is certainly much to condemn in the conduct of both parties. Conceding that there is more than we have indicated upon the part of the defendant, yet, after a most careful consideration of the evidence, we are led to the conclusion that, however cruel and inhuman his treatment of the plaintiff was, it was not such as to have at any time endangered her life, nor to endanger it if they were compelled to still live together. When not in anger, they were kindly disposed towards each other, as is shown in the care which each took of the other in sickness, and by the fact that, though the plaintiff left her husband four or five times, she each time returned to him voluntarily, at his request. If this man and woman would bury and forget their groundless jealousies, control their tempers, and practice forbearance, each with the other, there would be nothing to prevent them from living peacefully and happily together. As we view the case, the plaintiff failed to establish the causes for divorce stated in her petition, and therefore her petition should be dismissed.—REVERSED.

PETER ELLER, Appellant, v. N. J. LOOMIS.

Master and Servant: NEGLIGENCE: *Jury question.* Plaintiff was injured by the falling of a scaffold on which he was working as a bricklayer, in pursuance of a contract of hiring made between his father and defendant. The father testified that, when the contract was made, defendant agreed to build the scaffold, which was corroborated by others, and denied by defendant, who claimed that he contracted with the father to furnish the man, and that the building of the scaffold was part of the employment. *Held,* that the question whether defendant agreed to build the scaffold was for the jury, since, in determining the sufficiency of the evidence to submit an issue to the jury, the test is whether plaintiff is entitled to the jury's judgment as to what it proves.

Plea and Proof: GENERAL DENIAL: *Custom.* Where an action is based on injuries caused by the falling of a scaffolding, the defense that there was a custom of bricklayers to build their own scaffolds is not available under general denial. Such must be specially pleaded, since section 2704, Code, 1873, limits evidence under such denial to a negation of what the other party is bound to prove.

PLEA AND CHARGE. The admission of immaterial evidence without objection does not justify an instruction raised only by such evidence.

Appeal from Dubuque District Court.—HON. J. L. HUSTED, Judge.

TUESDAY, OCTOBER 11, 1898.

ACTION for personal injuries. Judgment for defendant, and plaintiff appeals.—*Reversed.*

Dunham & Norris, Longueville & McCarthy, and *Utt & Michel* for appellant.

Lyon & Lenehan for appellee.

GRANGER, J.—I. Plaintiff is a brickmason by trade, and in November, 1893, he was employed to work on a building being erected by defendant at Farley, Iowa. While so engaged, he, with others, was on a scaffold that, because of the weight thereon, fell, and plaintiff was injured; and this action is for damages sustained by him, under a claim that defendant was required to and did erect the scaffold, and in so doing was negligent, because of which he (plaintiff) was injured. The answer put in issue the claim that defendant was required to make the scaffold, or that he did erect it, or was guilty of negligence. The issues were tried to a jury that returned a general verdict for defendant and special findings that Charles Anderson and George Loomis built the scaffolding on the north part of the building, including the part that fell, and that defendant did not do any of the work in building or directing the building of the scaffold which fell. A ground upon which rests the claim that

1   defendant was required to erect the scaffold is that he agreed so to do at the time of plaintiff's employment. The averment to that effect in the petition being denied, the court gave to the jury the following instruction: "There has also been testimony introduced before you bearing upon the question as to whether or not defendant entered into any contract by which he agreed to construct and furnish all the necessary scaffoldings for the brick and stone work upon the building in question. You are instructed that the testimony so introduced will not warrant you or justify you in finding that such contract was made, and you will therefore assume as a fact that no such contract was made." The effect

of the instruction was to settle the issue, as to an agreement by
defendant to construct the scaffolding, favorably to him, on
the ground that the evidence would not justify a finding
against him.   To sustain the instruction, the record must
show the evidence to be so in favor of defendant as to be without substantial conflict.   The record is clearly against such a
conclusion.   It appears from the evidence that plaintiff's
father is a brickmason and contractor, and that plaintiff and
others, who are bricklayers, came to work on the building
in pursuance of a talk between defendant and plaintiff's
father.   At the time of this talk, plaintiff, his two brothers,
and others were at work for plaintiff's father on another job,
and they came to defendant's job as a result of an understanding between the father and defendant.   If there was
ever an agreement that defendant should erect the scaffolding
himself, it was during the talk referred to.   The father is
a witness for plaintiff, and he states, in terms unmistakable,
that defendant preferred and agreed to make the scaffolds.
We give a part of the father's testimony, to show its char·
acter.   Referring to defendant, the witness said: "He says:
'We want to build every scaffold.   While the bricklayers are
building on the north side of the building, we will build the
scaffold on the other side,—me and my sons; and, if I need
any help, I can get the help down in Farley cheaper than I
can here,—if I need any more help.'   Says I: 'If you want
to build your own scaffolds, Mr. Loomis, you know what it is.
Scaffolding is the most particular business in that trade.'
'Well,' he says, 'hadn't I ought to know how to build a
scaffold,—a man that puts up so many building as I do?'
'Well,' says I, 'you ought to.'   'Well,' he says, 'if you will
let me have these men to work for me, I will give them a good
scaffold.'   'I will give them a good scaffold, and take care
of them,' he says.   Says I: 'That is all right, Mr. Loomis.
I trust to your word.'"   It appears from the testimony of
this witness that he, his two sons, and the defendant were all
that were present when the talk took place.   The two sons

were witnesses for plaintiff, and corroborated the testimony
of the father as to defendant's statements about building the
scaffolds. The defendant just as explicitly denies any such
talk or understanding. There is no basis for a reasonable
denial that the evidence on the question is in substantial conflict. It is defendant's theory that he did not employ the men,
but contracted with plaintiff's father to furnish the men to
do the work for specified daily wages, payment therefor to
be made to the father, and he to pay the men as his employes,
and that the building of the scaffolds was a part of the work
for which the men were employed. The law of this state as to
the obligation of a master to provide a safe place to work is
well settled. See *Fink v. Ice Co.,* 84 Iowa, 321; *Haworth v.
Manufacturing Co.,* 87 Iowa, 765; *Blazenic v. Coal Co.,*
102 Iowa, 706; *Corson v. Coal Co.,* 101 Iowa, 224; *Hump-
ton v. Unterkircher,* 97 Iowa, 509. In view of the well-
settled rule of these cases, the question of who was plaintiff's
employer was important, as was also the character of the
employment; that is, was the building of the scaffolds a part
of the work to be done by the masons, or was the place to work
to be provided by defendant? This question of fact was
plainly in issue. The instruction in question settled that
issue against plaintiff, to his prejudice, in view of the unmistakable conflict of evidence. The argument in support of
the action of the court goes to the question of what the evidence proves. We do not think that is the proper test. The
weight of the evidence settles that. The question we consider
is, had the plaintiff a right to the judgment of the jury as
to what was proven, in view of the evidence before it? We
are clearly of the opinion that he had, and that the court erred
in giving that instruction.

II.   The court gave the following instruction: "Under
the uncontradicted evidence in the case, according to the
custom of bricklayers, the duty of building the scaffold in
question, in the absence of a specific contract, was devolved
upon the plaintiff and his fellow bricklayers and helpers;

and, if you find from the testimony that they, or some of them, built the scaffold that fell down and caused the injury of which the plaintiff complains, then you are instructed that the plaintiff cannot recover against the defendant, even though you should find that the defendant's son, George Loomis, assisted said bricklayers, or their helpers, or some of them, in doing the work upon said scaffold, and your verdict should be for the defendant." The complaint is that no such custom was pleaded, and it is true that none was. Such a custom has not the force of law, so that the parties are presumed to have contracted with reference to it. That parties may con tract with reference to a custom known to them is well settled. *Hughes v. Stanley,* 45 Iowa, 622. The custom referred to in the instruction, to render it a part of the con tract, must have been considered in reaching the agreement. *Windland v. Deeds,* 44 Iowa, 98. Such a contract, if used to defeat a recovery, changes the issue from that presented by the petition and answer, and should be pleaded. In *Lindley v. Bank,* 76 Iowa, 629, it was sought to take advantage of a custom to change the effect of a contract as pleaded, and the right was denied because the custom was not pleaded.

2   So far as we know, the practice in this state, to make such a custom available, as affecting a contract, is to plead it. *Hughes v. Stanley, supra.* It would seem to be the reasonable rule, and in harmony with section 2704 of the Code of 1873, where the answer is a denial, as in this case: "Under a denial of an allegation, no evidence shall be intro duced which does not tend to negative some fact, the party making the controverted allegation is bound to prove." Proof of such a custom did not negative any fact plaintiff was bound to prove, and the statute seems clearly applicable.

3   It is said the evidence was admitted without objec tion. Such a fact would not justify the instruction, if otherwise erroneous. The most that could be said would be that the evidence could be considered under the issues formed. The admission of immaterial evidence will not justify the presentation of new issues in the instructions.

The case involves other errors that need not be separately noticed, as they seem to follow the conclusion of the court in holding the evidence insufficient to present a question of fact to the jury, as stated in the first division of the opinion. Complaint is made of a remark by the court, during the examination of a witness, that we need not set out or consider, as a repetition of it will not likely occur on another trial.— REVERSED.

LIZZIE A. CARNES v. IOWA STATE TRAVELING MEN'S ASSOCIATION, Appellant.

Insurance: CONTRACTS: *Amendment of Constitution.* An amendment of articles of incorporation and by-laws of an insurance association, limiting the indemnity to death effected through or by external, violent, or accidental means, does not affect existing
1   certificates issued while the constitution provided for indemnity whenever the death of a member occurred from an accidental cause with certain exceptions, where the constitution does not authorize an amendment binding a member to any change in the contract without his assent.

DEATH FROM ACCIDENT: *Poison.* When the death of an insured is caused by his taking more morphine than he intended, his beneficiary can recover on a policy of insurance against death "from an accidental cause;" but where the death is caused by his
2   taking morphine, knowing at the time how much he was taking, but not knowing that such an amount would cause death, his ben-
4   eficiary cannot recover on a policy of insurance against death "from an accidental cause."

EVIDENCE: *Presumptions.* In an action to recover indemnity under a certificate of insurance indemnifying against death from acci-
3   dental cause, the presumption is against suicide, in the absence of any evidence pointing to suicide.

BURDEN OF PROOF: *Suicide.* The burden resting on plaintiff in an action upon a certificate of insurance indemnifying against death
5   from accidental cause, is not met, where the evidence is equally as consistent with a cause not accidental as with an accidental cause.

Appeal from Polk District Court.—HON. W. A. SPURRIER, Judge.

TUESDAY, OCTOBER 11, 1898.

ACTION on accidental insurance policy. Judgment for plaintiff, and defendant appeals.—*Reversed.*

Cummins, Hewitt & Wright for appellant.

Baily & Ballreich for appellee.

LADD, J.—When the certificate of membership was issued to Oliver D. Carnes the constitution of the association provided for indemnity whenever the death of a member occurred "from an accidental cause, except while said member shall be under the influence of intoxicating liquors or narcotics." As afterwards amended, the articles of incorporation and by-laws, with the same exception, limited such indemnity to injuries "effected through or by external, violent, and accidental means." We may determine, then, at the outset, whether the liability of the association is fixed by the constitution and by-laws at the time the certificate was issued or those in force when Carnes died. The certificate entitled him to "all the benefits accruing from such membership, under the provisions of the constitution
1   and by-laws of the association. Now, the by-laws relate entirely to the manner of transacting the business, and the constitution contained all the provisions with respect to the terms and conditions of insurance. The power to amend the by-laws was limited to matters not provided for in the constitution, and that could be revised or amended only on a two-thirds vote of the members. Nothing in it authorized the association to amend, and thereby bind a member to any change in the contract without his assent, nor do the amended articles purport to change existing contracts or to authorize any such change by the adoption of by-laws. In the absence of such provisions, the articles and by-laws as amended cannot be treated as retroactive in their operation. Mere silence as to the effect of revision and amendment of the constitution and by-laws will not warrant the inference that any change wrought will limit

or extend the obligation theretofore created by the issuance of certificates of membership.   Statutes are construed so as to give them a prospective operation, unless the intention that they operate retrospectively is clear and undoubted, and it is not perceived why the same canon of construction should not be applied to the rules adopted by a mutual insurance association for the transaction of its business and the government of its members.   *Hobbs v. Association,* 82 Iowa, 107; *Sieverts v. Association,* 95 Iowa, 710; *Benton v. Brotherhood,* 146 Ill. 570 (34 N. E. Rep. 939).   Of the contention that, by changing from a voluntary to an incorporated association, the former ceased to exist, and recovery must be had, if at all, under the articles and by-laws of the latter, it is enough to say that such an issue is neither raised in the pleadings nor established by the proof.

II.   As no evidence indicated Carnes to have been under the influence of intoxicating liquors or narcotics, the important inquiry was whether his death occurred from an accidental cause.   The testimony is not in conflict.   On the sixteenth day of March, 1896, being Monday, he was suffering from neuralgia in the face, and remained at home during the afternoon and the following day.   He obtained morphine from some source, and during this time took it for the relief of the pain.   He went out for whisky Tuesday, but is not known to have obtained any.   The physician found him that day lying on a cot, with clothes on, complaining of pain and soreness in his face and the back of his neck, and was informed by Carnes that he had taken, during Monday night, two quarter-grain tablets of morphine. The doctor prescribed tablets with no morphine in them, and whisky, which was administered in the form of a hot punch. He undressed and went to bed downstairs, his clothes remaining in the room.   His wife left him at about 10 o'clock P. M., and found him unconscious at 6:30 the following morning. In the meantime he had taken none of the whisky or tablets prescribed, and no morphine was found in the room or about his clothes. He continued in a comatose condition for about four hours, when he died. That his death was caused by morphine taken between the time his wife left his bedside on Tuesday evening and when she found him dying the next morning is conceded. How much morphine he took is not known, but it was enough to cause death, and the physicians differ somewhat as to the amount necessary to do this. There are three possible ways to account for Carnes' death: (1) He may have taken the morphine with the purpose of committing suicide; (2) he may have taken more than he intended,—that is, several quarter-grain tablets instead of one or more; and (3) he may have intended to take the amount he did, and misjudged the effect it would produce. There is nothing in the evidence or surrounding circumstances pointing to suicide, and, as every one is supposed to be endowed with the instinct of self-preservation, he will be presumed not to have voluntarily ended his life. *Insurance Co. v. McConkey,* 127 U. S. 661 (8 Sup. Ct. Rep. 1360); *Cronkhite v. Insurance Co.,* 75 Wis. 116, 17 Am. St. Rep. 184, (43 N. W. Rep. 731); *Mallory v. Insurance Co.,* 47 N. Y. 52; *Freeman v. Insurance Co.,* 144 Mass. 572 (12 N. E. Rep. 372); *Insurance Co. v. Wiswell,* 56 Kan. Sup. 765 (44 Pac. Rep. 996). See 1 Am. & Eng. Enc. Law, 331. He must, then, have either taken more morphine than he intended, or taken what he intended and misjudged its effects. If he took more than he intended,—that is, intended to take one or two quarter grains, and, by mistake or inadvertence, took much more,—this was accidental, and, if death was so caused, the beneficiary is entitled to recover. But suppose he took just the amount of morphine he intended, and misjudged the effect it would produce; may death so occasioned be said to result from an accidental cause? Webster defines "accidental" as "happening by chance or unexpectedly; taking place not according to the usual course of things,"—and an "accident," as "an event that takes place without one's foresight or expectation; an undesigned, sudden and unexpected event; chance; contingency. Such unforeseen, extraordinary, extraneous interference as is out of the range of ordinary calculation." It is defined in *Paul v. Insurance Co.,* 112 N. Y. 472 (20 N. E. Rep. 347), as the "happening of an event without the aid and design of a person, and which is unforeseen." See valuable notes to this case in 8 Am. St. Rep. 763. In *McGlinchey v. Casualty Co.,* 80 Me. 251 (14 Atl. Rep. 13), it is said: "The definition of 'accident' generally assented to is an event happening without any human agency, or, if happening through human agency, an event which, under the circumstances, is unusual, and not expected, to the person to whom it happens." Bouvier thus defines "accident:" "An event which, under the circumstances, is unusual and unexpected by the person to whom it happens. The happening of an event without the concurrence of the will of the person by whose agency it was caused; or the happening of an event without any human agency." The courts have frequently defined accident, and an examination of the authorities indicates but little difference of opinion. See *Lovelace v. Association,* 126 Mo. Sup. 104 (28 S. W. Rep. 877); *Supreme Council v. Garrigus,* 104 Ind. 133 (3 N. E. Rep. 818); 1 Am. & Eng. Enc. Law, 291. It will be observed that this policy insures against death from an accidental cause, and not an accidental death. It is possible that under the definitions referred to the death of Carnes was accidental, but if he took the amount of morphine intended, and a result not anticipated occurred, then the cause of his death was not accidental, for he intended to do the very thing he did. The morphine was, under the circumstances, taken by design. The result only was unforeseen,—unintended. This distinction was recognized by Judge Dyer in *Barry v. Association,* 23 Fed. Rep. 712, who, in charging the jury said: "The term 'accident' is here used in its ordinary, popular sense, and in that sense it means happening by chance,—unexpectedly; taking place not according to the usual course of things, or not as

expected. In other words, if a result is such as follows from ordinary means voluntarily employed, in a not unusual or unexpected way, then, I suppose, it cannot be called a result affected by accidental means. But if, in the act which precedes the injury, something unforeseen, unexpected, unusual occurs, which produces the injury, then the injury has resulted from accident or through accidental means." See Id., 131 U. S. 100 (9 Sup. Ct. Rep. 755). In 3 Joyce Insurance, section 2863, quoting from *Clidero v. Insurance Co.,* 29 Scot. L. R. 303, it is said that "a person may do a certain act, the result of which act may produce unforeseen consequences, and may produce what is commonly called 'accidental' death, but the means are exactly what the man intended to use, and did use, and was prepared to use. The means were not accidental, but the result might be accidental." See, also, *American Accident Co. v. Carson,* 99 Ky. 441 (30 S. W. Rep. 879). Now, it is impossible to say, from the evidence, whether Carnes took more morphine tablets than he intended to take, or whether he took just what he did intend, and mis-
5   judged their effects. Death might have been occasioned in either way, and one is as likely as the other. Under such circumstances, can it be left to the jury to guess which? The burden of proof was upon the plaintiff to show that death resulted from an accidental cause, and, the evidence leaving this unestablished, she failed to make out a case. It is said, however, that death will be presumed to have resulted from accident, and that the burden of proof is upon the defendant to show the contrary. But an examination of the case does not sustain this contention. They go no further than to hold that, where the insured has introduced evidence tending to show an injury to be the result of an accident, the burden of proof is on the insurer to establish as a defense that the insured was within some exceptions of the policy. See *Hess v. Association,* 112 Mich. 196 (70 N. W. Rep. 460); *Bedenfeld v. Association,* 154 Mass. 77 (27 N. E. Rep. 769); *Association v. Wiswell,* 56 Kan. Sup. 765 (44

Pac. Rep. 996).   The plaintiff wholly failed to prove the cause to have been accidental, and this will not be presumed. It was necessary to do this in order to bring the case within the terms of the policy.—REVERSED.

CLARK VARNUM, Appellant, v. H. S. WINSLOW.

LIMITATION OF ACTIONS: *Dissolution of partnership.*   An action to recover *for a breach of the terms of an agreement for the dissolu-*
4 *tion of a partnership* is not barred because five years have elapsed from the date of the dissolution, although an accounting is asked.

Dissolution Contract Construed.   Under a dissolution agreement of a law firm, the partners were each to do his share of work on all unfinished business, one partner retaining the office with the firm papers. The other was not to be required to keep an office, but, for the purpose of finishing the business, was to be allowed to "use
6 such office and supplies and employes therein." The "expenses and earnings and profits and emoluments of all the business" were to be "equally divided between the parties hereto." *Held*, that the expenses referred to were court expenses and special expenses in the cases, and not ordinary office expenses, which were to be borne by the partner retaining the office.

Execution Sale: DEED: *Rents.*   The owners of real property sold
5 under a decree of foreclosure are entitled to the rent upon it up to the time of the execution of the sheriff's deed.

Appeal: HARMLESS ERROR: *Depositions.*   The overruling of a motion that a trial be had upon depositions is not prejudicial error where the complaining party had the right to take any deposition that he desired and did not avail himself of that right. It is a serious question whether the trial court does not have a discretion as to the granting of such motion.

CLERK'S FEES: *Securing of.*   A clerk who accepts service of a notice of appeal containing an admission that the provisions of McClain's
2 Code, section 4408, relating to security for his fees have been complied with, thereby waives a compliance with such statute.

TRIAL DE NOVO: *Assignments.*   Assignments of error relating to the
3 admission or exclusion of testimony are disregarded in a general appeal in equity, as such questions are necessarily passed upon in the hearing *de novo.*

Appeal from Jasper District Court.—HON. D. RYAN, Judge.

WEDNESDAY, OCTOBER 12, 1898.

THIS is an action in equity between partners for an accounting. Plaintiff and defendant are lawyers, and for a time were associated as co-partners in the practice of their profession. In the year 1889, the firm ceased doing business as such, and the following agreement was entered into in writing: "Agreement made this 30th day of September, A. D. 1889, between H. S. Winslow and Clark Varnum, sole members of the firm of Winslow & Varnum, witnesseth: That the partnership formed by said persons above named is, so far as now or future business is concerned, by the mutual agreement of both parties, terminated and ended, from and after this date, subject, however, to the following conditions relative to partnership business and property: *First.* All business now begun is to be finished by the said persons, each doing, so far as practical, his fair share of the labor of finishing such business, except that said Varnum shall not be required to remain in the office heretofore kept, or open and keep an office for such purposes; but, for the purpose of finishing such business, he may use such office and supplies and employes therein. But this does not relate to railroad cases now pending in the supreme court. As to those said Varnum shall have no interest. The expenses and earnings and profits and emoluments of all the business described in this paragraph shall be equally divided between the parties hereto. As fast as any particular item of business shall be finally closed, it shall cease to come under this clause, but shall not so cease until all connection of either partner therewith has completely and finally ended and terminated. *Second.* All property belonging to the firm of Winslow & Varnum, outside of the library and office furniture and fixtures, shall either be divided equally between such parties, or collected or sold or converted into money, and the money equally divided between them. No valuable property shall be disposed of, sold, or converted into money, except on concurrence of both parties. Either partner hereafter receiving any property or money for or on account of said firm shall account for same immediately, and pay over to the other partner his half after the debts of the firm shall have first been paid. *Third.* H. S. Winslow is to have the right to keep the office rooms now occupied by said firm, and is to be individually liable to pay the rent therefor from October 1, 1889, and also to pay all outstanding contracts for subscriptions to legal directories and other advertisements of the firm of Winslow & Varnum which may accrue after October 1, 1889. *Fourth.* Said Winslow shall have as his own individual property the whole of the office fixtures and furniture and library, save and except the following, and these said Varnum is to have, to wit: California Reports, Illinois Reports and Digests, and sundry other law books not necessary to be here described. *Fifth.* The books, records, papers, etc., accumulated by said firm shall be and remain in the possession of said Winslow, and be by him safely preserved; and either partner shall have the right of access to, and the use of, all such firm books, records, papers, etc., at all reasonable times, and for all reasonable purposes. H. S. Winslow, Clark Varnum." Under this agreement the parties proceeded to settle the firm business. On September 18, 1895, this action was brought, for an accounting and settlement. The petition also asks that a dissolution of the firm be decreed. There was a trial to the court, with the result that the partnership was dissolved, and defendant was given a judgment against plaintiff for the sum of two hundred and twenty dollars and ninety-seven cents. Plaintiff appeals.—*Modified* and *affirmed.*

Clark Varnum pro se.

W. R. Lewis and *C. O. McLain* for appellee.

WATERMAN, J.—Appellee moves to strike the evidence from the record, and dismiss the appeal "or affirm the decree below." This motion is based upon several grounds, and is quite elaborately argued by both parties. It is said, first, that the evidence is not properly certified. Some of the reasons given in support of this claim, we regard as captious.

2 None of them impress us as being sufficient to sustain such action as is asked. Again, it is urged that the clerk's fees for a transcript have not been paid or secured. In support of this branch of the case, there is filed an affidavit of the clerk, in which he says that his fees were not paid or secured. The clerk accepted service of the notice of appeal and this notice contained an admission that this requirement of law had been complied with. The provisions of McClain's Code, section 4408, relating to security for the clerk's fees, is, we think, for the benefit of that officer. He may waive a compliance with it if he sees fit to do so. His action in this case justifies us in holding that he made such waiver in plaintiff's behalf. *Hunt v. Johnston,* 105 Iowa, 311. Without going further into details on this motion, we will say that it appears to us without merit, and will therefore be overruled.

II. Proceeding now to the main case, we find that appellant has made certain assignments of error which he asks us to consider in connection with his "general appeal in

3 equity." With the exception of one matter, to which we devote some attention in the eighth division of this opinion, these errors relate entirely to the admission or exclusion of testimony. Questions of this kind are necessarily passed upon in the hearing *de novo,* so that we may with propriety disregard such assignments of error. See *Smith v. Wellslager,* 105 Iowa, 140.

III. The statute of limitations is interposed as a defense. It is said that an action for an accounting is barred in five years from the date of dissolution of the firm, and that the firm was dissolved in 1889, by the written agreement which is set out above. The trial court did not consider the co-partnership dissolved by this agreement, for it found that "each member is entitled to a full and final dissolution of the partnership," and then in formal terms decreed such dissolution. It seems to have been the thought of both parties, until this court was reached, that the written agreement, while it ended the business career of the firm, did not work a full dissolution; that it merely provided for bringing about such dissolution at some future time. But, however this may be, there is another and a conclusive answer to this plea. It is sought in this action to recover for a breach by defendant of the terms of the agreement. If the firm was fully dissolved in 1889, yet each member, under this contract, was to be liable to the other for such assets of the firm as he might reduce to possession. If defendant's theory is to prevail, plaintiff's right of action might be barred, before any liability accrued on the part of defendant. This position, we think, is not tenable.

IV. This brings us to a consideration of the various items of account between the parties. Before proceeding to discuss these matters, we wish to have understood the basis of our action. We have no way of ascertaining all the items taken into consideration by the trial court, in stating the account between the parties. All that is disclosed by the record is the result, viz. that a debit balance was found against plaintiff of two hundred and twenty dollars and ninety-seven cents. It does appear, however, that defendant admits having collected on firm account the sum of three thousand four hundred and fifty-one dollars and twenty-six cents, and claims to be entitled to credit in the amount of five thousand one hundred and twenty-four dollars and forty-eight cents. The various items going to make up these amounts are set out in the answer. The account as stated is attacked by plaintiff. He seeks both to surcharge and falsify it. We shall take up the specific matters presented by plaintiff ,and give each such attention as we think it deserves.

V. Sixty-five dollars is claimed by plaintiff as due the firm on a collection from one J. A. Young, and in the aggregate the sum of four hundred and fifty dollars and thirty-seven cents on account of certain litigation against the firm of

Flory & Newton. We are inclined to accept defendant's version of those matters, and also in relation to the shares of stock in the First National Bank of Newton. It would serve no good purpose to go into a detailed consideration of the testimony relating to these items. It is often conflicting, and not always definite or clear on either side. . The next item to be considered relates to the rent of what is called the "Means Farm," which was collected by defendant. One Chandler, as trustee, held a first mortgage on this land, which the firm of Winslow & Varnum had for collection.

5 Winslow and Varnum had a second mortgage. One John M. Day owned the fee. The second mortgage notes were assigned by Winslow & Varnum to Chandler, trustee; and a foreclosure proceeding was instituted in his name for the amount due on both mortgages. Day deeded the fee to Winslow & Varnum. A decree of foreclosure was obtained, and the land sold thereunder December 28, 1889, to Chandler. The certificate of sale was thereafter assigned to Winslow to facilitate a sale of the land. No deed was taken on said certificate until December 26, 1891. Winslow collected the rents for the years 1890 and 1891. We think he has accounted for the rent of 1890, but the rent of 1891 (three hundred and fifty dollars), he insists, the plaintiff has no interest in or right to. In this claim, we think, he is wrong. The fee owners, Winslow & Varnum were entitled to the rent up to the time of the execution of the sheriff's deed. Defendant should account to the firm for the sum of three hundred and fifty dollars. The title of the owner is not devested by the sale, but by the execution of the sheriff's deed. *Everingham v. Braden,* 58 Iowa, 133; *Curtis v. Millard,* 14 Iowa, 128.

VI. Taking up, now, the other side of the account, as rendered by defendant, and we find that he claims a credit for the firm of eight hundred dollars for fees received by Varnum in what are styled the *"Cerneau Cases."* We hold that plaintiff should account for seventy dollars, being the net amount of fees received in the first of these cases. The other case appears to have been begun after the separation and execution of the agreement for dissolution, and was therefore not firm business. Two other items of credit claimed by defendant are strenuously objected to by plaintiff. One is for the sum of one thousand dollars, claimed by defendant for extra services; and the other for four hundred dollars, for office rent, salary of stenographer, fuel, lights, stationery and postage. The amount asked for stationery and postage is twenty-five dollars. This, the plaintiff should be allowed. It seems plain, however, that he is not entitled to credit for the other amounts. It does not appear that the defendant did any more than plaintiff of the outside work in settling the firm matters. The office work he assumed to do, by keeping in his possession all papers of the firm. The office rent he distinctly undertook, in the agreement, to pay; and by fair implication, we think, he assumed to pay the ordinary office expenses. The expenses which, in the first clause of the agreement of separation, it is provided shall be divided, relate, as we believe, to the court expenses and moneys expended specially on account of the matters therein referred to. But as Winslow retained the office for his private use, and the stenographer to do his private business, it seems to us clear that the expenses made on these accounts must be borne by him alone.

VII. There are, in addition to the matters we have mentioned, some costs collected, which are in dispute. The amount is quite small, and the evidence relating thereto very indefinite. As the parties do not insist upon this branch of the case, we shall pass it without further notice. There is also a sum of twenty-five dollars which Varnum admits should be charged against him in favor of the firm, on account of a collection from one Snyder.

VIII. A proper statement of account between the parties is as follows:

Winslow's admitted debit to the firm...........$3,451 26
Add rent of Means' farm....................   350 00

    Total $3,801 26

Winslow claims credits, as shown on page 22 of
    appellant's abstract...................... $3,083 63
To this should be added:

    Item 1, as shown in said abstract.........   111 25
      " 2,   "   "   " 22 50
      " 3,   "   "   A abstract.....   67 10
      " 4, as shown in said abstract.........   5 00
      " 5,   "   "   " 10 00
    Error in check to Varnum..............   30 00
    Stationery and postage................   25 00

    Total $3,354 48

Winslow's debit $3,801 26
    "   credit 3,354 48

    Due the firm $446 78
There is due the firm from Varnum:
    On account of Cerneau case.... $ 70 00
    Snyder collection 25 00

                            95 00

    Total due from both partners............ $541 78

Of this amount, each partner is entitled to one-half, or two hundred and seventy dollars and eighty-nine cents. Deducting from this last-mentioned sum Varnum's debit of ninety-five dollars, and the remainder is one hundred and seventy-five dollars and eighty-nine cents, for which he is entitled to a judgment against defendant.

IX. One other matter remains to be noticed, in order that it may not be thought to have been overlooked. After the

issues were made up in the court below, plaintiff moved that
the trial be had upon depositions. The motion was
7   overruled. We are not prepared to say that section
2742 of the Code of 1873 leaves the court no discretion in passing upon such a request. We incline strongly to
the opposite view. But, in any event, plaintiff was not prejudiced by the ruling. He had a right to take any depositions
that he desired, and it does not appear that he availed himself
of it. The costs were taxed to plaintiff by the trial court.
All costs, including those made here, should be paid by defendant. As modified by what we have said, the decree below is.
AFFIRMED.

INDEPENDENT SCHOOL DISTRICT OF FOREST HOME v. J. C.
MARDIS, *et al.*, Appellants.   . $\begin{vmatrix} 106 \\ 130 \end{vmatrix}$

Building Contract: CONSTRUED: *Mechanic's lien.* A building con-
1   tract provided that in case of notice of any claim for mechanic's
liens or labor or material furnished by subcontractors, or if such
2   labor or material remain unpaid for, the right to withhold payment
was reserved until such liens, claims or demands were settled or
released. *Held,*

  a The right to reserve exists so long as such claims remain unpaid
3   and is not limited to demands for which a mechanic's lien might
be established.

  b Money borrowed by a contractor and used in payment of labor
4   and material furnished in the construction of a building is a debt
for such money and not for labor and material, within the meaning of the contract provision.

  c The owner may require claimants to interplead and establish
2   their demands against the fund although the contractor has.
assigned the amount due to some of them.

  d A material man who interpleads to establish his claim against
the fund due the contractor is not precluded from asserting his
5   rights under a provision of the building contract, by the fact
that he had taken an assignment from the contractor of any
balance due him.

Appeal from Polk District Court.—HON. C. P. HOLMES,.
Judge.

WEDNESDAY, OCTOBER 12, 1898.

OF the contract price for the construction of a high school building, three thousand six hundred and forty dollars was withheld by the plaintiff, and this action was brought to require the defendants, except the contractor, to interplead and establish their claims against said fund.   Decree was entered applying it *pro rata* on the claims of J. A. Garver & Co., J. K. & W. H. Gilcrest, Dunreath Quarry Company, Iowa Brick Company, and St. John & Barquist, and any balance remaining on that of the People's Savings Bank of Des Moines.   The People's Savings Bank and J. K. & W. H. Gilcrest appeal.—*Affirmed.*

Bailey & Ballreich and *Barcroft & McCaughan* for appellants.

Royal & Rawson, C. C. & C. L. Nourse, St. John & Stevenson, J. K. Macomber and *Hume & Bradshaw* for appellees.

LADD, J.—Eighty-five per centum of the cost of the construction of the high school building was paid on certificates of the superintendent as the work progressed.   The remaining fifteen per centum, or three thousand six hundred and forty dollars, was to be paid, under the contract, "in thirty days after the satisfactory completion and acceptance of the work herein named; provided, however, in case of any notice to the party of the second part of any claim for mechanics' liens for labor or material furnished by subcontractors or others, or in case any such labor or materials remain unpaid for by the party of the first part, the party of the second part reserves the right to withhold payments on this contract until said liens, claims or demands are settled or released."   The building was completed and accepted February 24, 1896, and for the labor and materials furnished by the subcontractors the contractor Mardis owed J. A. Garver & Co. eight hundred and eighteen dollars and eighty-two cents;

J. K. and W. H. Gilcrest, one thousand five hundred and
thirty-two dollars and forty-six cents; Dunreath Quarry Company, seventy-nine dollars and thirty-five cents; Iowa Brick
Company, one thousand two hundred and eight dollars and
eighteen cents; and St. John & Barquist, three hundred and
ninety-nine dollars.   The steps required were not taken to
establish these claims, under chapter 179, Acts Twentieth
General Assembly, and mechanics' liens could not be acquired.
Breneman v. Harvey, 70 Iowa, 479; *Charnock v. Colfax Dist.
Tp.,* 51 Iowa, 70.   Mardis gave J. K. & W. H. Gilcrest an
order on the district for the amount due them March 31,
1896, and assigned the balance owing by the district to the
People's Savings Bank of Des Moines in satisfaction of au
indebtedness due that bank.   On the same day he assigned
all interest he had in the fund, subject to the assignment to the
bank, to J. A. Garver & Co., to secure its claim.

From this statement it is apparent that, unless the district had the right to withhold the fund until all the subcontractors were paid such fund should be turned over to J. K.
and W. H. Gilcrest and the People's Savings Bank.   It is
conceded the district could provide in its agreement for the
payment of all debts for material and labor before the fifteen
per centum of the price should be available, and we think this
the evident purport of the contract.   In unmistakable terms
the district reserves the right to withhold payments in case
labor or materials remain unpaid for.   In other words, the
district is not required to pay Mardis until he has paid for
the labor and materials used in construction, and which furnish the basis of his compensation.   Satisfaction of these is
made a condition precedent to recovery by him, if the district
so elects.   Through their order and assignment, the appellants acquired only such interest in the fund as Mardis had,
and, as he could not enforce payment before the settlement or
release of the indebtedness for materials and labor,
they cannot.   But by bringing the action the plaintiff
waives its election to withhold the fund on condition
that it be applied *pro rata* in satisfaction of the debts pro-

tected by the contract. The clear implication is that it may thus insist on the application of the fund, for this could be its only interest in withholding it, unless it be the relief from passing on the validity of claims. Mardis or the appellants might have avoided this by complying with the contract, and neither, on failure to do so, is put in any worse position by such appropriation of the money. We think the district court rightly construed the provision quoted.

What has been said disposes of the contention that it is like the condition considered in *Weller v. Goble,* 66 Iowa, 113; and *Hunt v. King,* 97 Iowa, 88. Nor is it like the condition of the bond in *Jordan v. Kavanaugh,* 63 Iowa, 152; and *Baker v. Bryan,* 64 Iowa, 561. Whether the contract was purely for the benefit of the district or in part to protect subcontractors is not now involved. The labor and materials were to be paid for before liability for the remaining fifteen per cent. of the cost attached, and the district had the right, in the absence of such payment, to have such portion of the contract price so applied.

There is no merit in the contention of the appellants that the claims referred to in the contract are only such as might be established under chapter 179, Acts Twentieth General

3   Assembly, as the only condition is that they "remain unpaid for by the party of the first part," and that they be for labor and materials furnished. Nothing in the contract indicates that the word "claim" is used in such technical sense. But the contrary appears from reference to the clause, "claims or demands are settled or released."

II. ·While the testimony tends to show that Mardis used the money borrowed of the People's Savings Bank for the

4   payment of some portion of the labor and material furnished in the construction of the building, it is apparent the debt is for such money, and not for labor and material. See *Sherman v. King,* 51 Iowa, 182; *Davis v. Ritchey,* 55 Iowa, 719.

III.   It is said that J. A. Garyer & Co., by taking an assignment of any balance due subject to that of the bank, waived their right of asserting their claim under the contract.

It does not appear the firm had any knowledge of any other claim to the fund at that time, or that the People's Savings Bank was in any way misled. Indeed, there is no element of waiver shown. Garver & Co., in their cross petition, set up a claim under the assignment, but afterwards, by an amendment, in a separate count, claimed under the contract. Its action was for the same indebtedness, based somewhat on different instruments, and they had the right to assert their claim in separate counts on the assignment and under the contract. These were not necessarily inconsistent with either construction given the contract. The assignment carried any balance that might be found due to Mardis. The validity of the assignment is not involved, but the determination of the fund affected by it. Had the contention of the appellants prevailed, then Garver & Co. would have taken any balance left after satisfying the assignment of the People's Savings Bank, and possibly the order of the Gilcrests. But, as the contract is construed, the firm takes also subject to the payment of the other subcontractors. The court did not err in setting aside the default against the Iowa Brick Company, and its cross petition, in the absence of any answer, was rightly taken as true. The decree of the district court is AFFIRMED.

SARAH J. DENBY, Appellant, v. L. C. FIE, A. J. FIE and D. C. CAIN.

Demurrer: WAIVER: *Appeal.*   An order overruling a demurrer to a petition asking for the modification of an injunction because of a change in the law since the decree was entered will be reviewed on appeal although the party appearing made no further appearance after excepting to the ruling made on the demurrer. It being a case without a waiver by pleading over or securing time to plead and not one in which the law tenders an issue without further pleading, no formal election to stand on the demurrer was necessary.

Modification of Decree. A decree permanently enjoining defendant
from selling liquors will not be modified for the sole reason that
1   there has been a change in the liquor law since the decree was
rendered, which permits the sale of liquor under certain condi-
2   tions; since, if the law of itself modifies the decree, a decree of
court is not necessary, and, if it does not modify it, the court has
no power so to do under petition.

ATTORNEY'S FEES. Attorney's fees for defending a petition to modify
4   a decree cannot be taxed against a petitioner, in the absence of
statute.

Appeal from Sioux District Court.—HON. F. R. GAYNOR,
Judge.

WEDNESDAY, OCTOBER 12, 1898.

APPEAL from an order overruling a demurrer interposed
by plaintiff to a petition filed by defendants, asking the modification of a decree restraining defendants from selling intoxicating liquors in violation of law.—*Reversed.*

J. H. Powers for appellant.

Milt. H. Allen for appellees.

DEEMER, C. J.—The original decree was passed in the
year 1893, and it permanently enjoined the defendants from
selling or keeping for sale intoxicating liquors upon a certain
lot in the town of Hull, or elsewhere within the Fourth
judicial district. Thereafter, what is known as the "Mulct
Law" was enacted, authorizing the sale of liquors under certain conditions not necessary to be further mentioned.
1   Defendants filed their petition, asking for a modification of the original decree so that they might sell
intoxicating liquors under the provisions of that act. Plaintiff demurred to the petition, and the demurrer was overruled,
and exception taken. No further appearance was made on
behalf of plaintiff, and she was adjudged to be in default
for want of a pleading. The decree then recites that defendants introduced their evidence, and established all the allegations of the petition ; and a modification of the original decree

was granted as prayed. The appeal is from the ruling on the demurrer.

Defendants insist that the case cannot be considered, for the reason that plaintiff did not stand on her demurrer. The rule seems to be if one, after an adverse ruling on demurrer or motion, pleads over or secures time to plead,
2   he, by so doing, waives the error in the ruling. And it has likewise been held that, where the law tenders an issue without the filing of further pleadings, he who would take advantage of an order overruling a demurrer must stand upon the pleading in order to have his case reviewed. *Wilcox v. McCune,* 21 Iowa, 294. The case at bar does not fall under either of these rules. The plaintiff did not ask for further time to plead, nor did she in fact file any other paper. The record shows that she excepted to the ruling made on the demurrer, and made no further appearance. The petition, although denominated a petition for modification of an injunction, is really a bill of review, or in the nature of a bill of review, and does not stand denied by operation of law, as would a petition to reverse, vacate, or modify a judgment, under the provisions of Code 1873, sections 3154, 3155, *et seq.* In such case it is not necessary that the record show a formal election to stand on the demurrer. If it affirmatively appears that the defeated party did not waive the error in the ruling, it is sufficient. This is practically the holding in the *Wilcox Case,* and the rule there announced is not modified by the subsequent cases of *Standbrough v. Daniels,* 77 Iowa, 561, and *Hawkins v. Hawkins,* 82 Iowa, 718. · The demurrer in the *Standbrough Case* was to a reply which was denied by operation of law, and in the *Hawkins Case* the demurrer was to an answer, which was also denied by operation of law. Our conclusion finds support in the case of *Jaylor v. Langworthy,* 37 Iowa, 555.

II.   The action is to modify a decree which was properly granted; because of a change in the law long after the decree was entered. Claim is made that such relief may be granted, upon the theory that a court of equity may at any time modify,

amend, or vacate its decree. It is true that a court of
3   equity has such power; but, as a general rule, relief
         is granted because of fraud, mistake, or misconduct
in obtaining the original decree, as in the cases of
Partridge v. Harrow, 27 Iowa, 96; *Bowen v. Mill
Co.,* 31 Iowa, 460, and *Hoskins v. Hattenback,* 14 Iowa,
314. There is no such claim in this case. On the contrary,
it is conceded that the decree was properly granted, and relief
is sought against it for the sole reason that there has been a
modification of the law since the decree was passed. There
are cases where a proceeding in the nature of a bill of review
may be brought on account of new matter which has arisen
since the decree was entered, but we do not think this is one
of them. If defendants are entitled to a modification of the
decree, it is because of the enactment of what is known as the
"Mulct Law." And, if we should hold that this law did
modify the decree, we would simply be deciding an abstract
proposition, of which, as we shall see, defendants are not
entitled to avail themselves. In other words, if the law of
itself modifies the decree, no decree of court is necessary to
establish that fact. If it does not modify it, then the court
has no power to do so. These propositions are so self-evident
that we need not say more. Again, there is no allegation in
the petition that the Mulct law is in force in Sioux county or
the town of Hull, no statement that defendants have complied
with any of the conditions of that law if it is in force, and no
showing that they are in position to avail themselves of the
provisions suspending penalties for the illegal sale of liquors.
Courts are not given to deciding abstract questions in order
that parties may be advised as to their rights before an actual
controversy has arisen respecting such rights. We are of
opinion that the demurrer should have been sustained.

         Plaintiff asks us to tax attorney's fees for defending
         against the petition. There is no statute which author-
4   izes such an order, and, in the absence of statute,
         it is clear that she is not entitled to them. The judg-
ment is REVERSED.

RANDENI MEIER V. ELSA A. LEE and HELGE HOGFOSS, Appellants and PAUL H. PAULSON, *et al.*

Descent and Distribution. ALIENS: *Next of kin.* Code, 1873, section 2457, providing that, "if both parents be dead, the portion which would have fallen to their share by the above rules shall be disposed of in the same manner as if they had outlived the intestate,
1 and died in the possession and ownership of the portion thus falling to their shares," does not entitle claimants who are children of a sister of an intestate's father to inherit, when the mother through whom they claimed was disqualified because a non-resident alien, (Act April 9, 1888,) although such ancestor had died before claimant and before the intestate, and though said children are the nearest relatives of the intestate, all parties to this action being citizens of the United States.

TREATIES. A non-resident alien is not empowered to acquire or inherit an interest in lands in Iowa by virtue of the treaty of 1783 between
2 the king of Sweden and the United States providing that the subjects of the contracting parties in the respective states, although unnaturalized, may dispose of and inherit *goods and effects.*

Appeal from Mitchell District Court.—HON. J. C. SHERWIN, Judge.

WEDNESDAY, OCTOBER 12, 1898.

PLAINTIFF, widow of Paul E. Meier, who died a citizen of Mitchell county, Iowa, on the twenty-fourth day of May, 1892, intestate and without issue, brought this action to partition certain land in said county he owned at the time of his death, of which she claims one-half. Paul H. Paulson and the other defendant appellees answered, admitting that plaintiff was entitled to one-half of said land, and by cross bill alleged that they are the sole and only heirs at law of said deceased, other than the plaintiff, competent to inherit said real estate, and claiming the one-half thereof. The defendants Else A. Lee and Helge Hogfoss were served by publication, and, not appearing, decree was rendered giving to plaintiff one-half of

the land, and to said defendant appellees the other half.
Thereafter, and in due time, the appellants, Else A. Lee and
Helge Hogfoss, filed their motion to set aside the default and
decree, and their answer and cross petition, claiming that, as
heirs at law of said deceased, they are entitled to three-eighths
of said land. The defendants, appellees, demurred to said
answer and cross petition on the ground that the facts stated
do not entitle said cross petitioners, or any of them, to any
part of said land. This demurrer was sustained, and, said
cross petitioners electing to stand upon their petition, the
former judgment and decree were confirmed, and the defendants Else A. Lee and Helge Hogfoss appeal.—*Affirmed.*

W. L. Eaton for appellants.

Sweney & Lovejoy for appellees.

GIVEN, J.—I. The claim of the plaintiff to one-half of
the land is not disputed. The contention is between Paul H.
Paulson and the other defendant appellees on the one side,
and the defendant appellants on the other side. The facts as
shown in appellants' cross petition necessary to be noticed are
these: The deceased left neither parent, brother, sister,
grandparent, uncle, nor aunt surviving him, and the parties
to this appeal were his nearest living relatives. Appel-
1   lees were the decedent's cousins of half blood, having
with him a common grandfather, but a different grandmother. Appellants were decedent's cousins of full blood,
having with him a common grandfather and grandmother.
All parties to this action are citizens of the United States.
Prior to the death of Paul E. Meier, the common grandfather
and grandmother and the mother of appellants had died, non-
resident aliens; and the decedent's father and the father of
appellees, who were half-brother, had also died, both being
citizens of the United States at the time they died.

The following diagram presented by appellees' counsel
will better show the relation of the different persons, and the

lines of inheritable and non-inheritable blood, than can be
expressed in words:

EXHIBIT B.

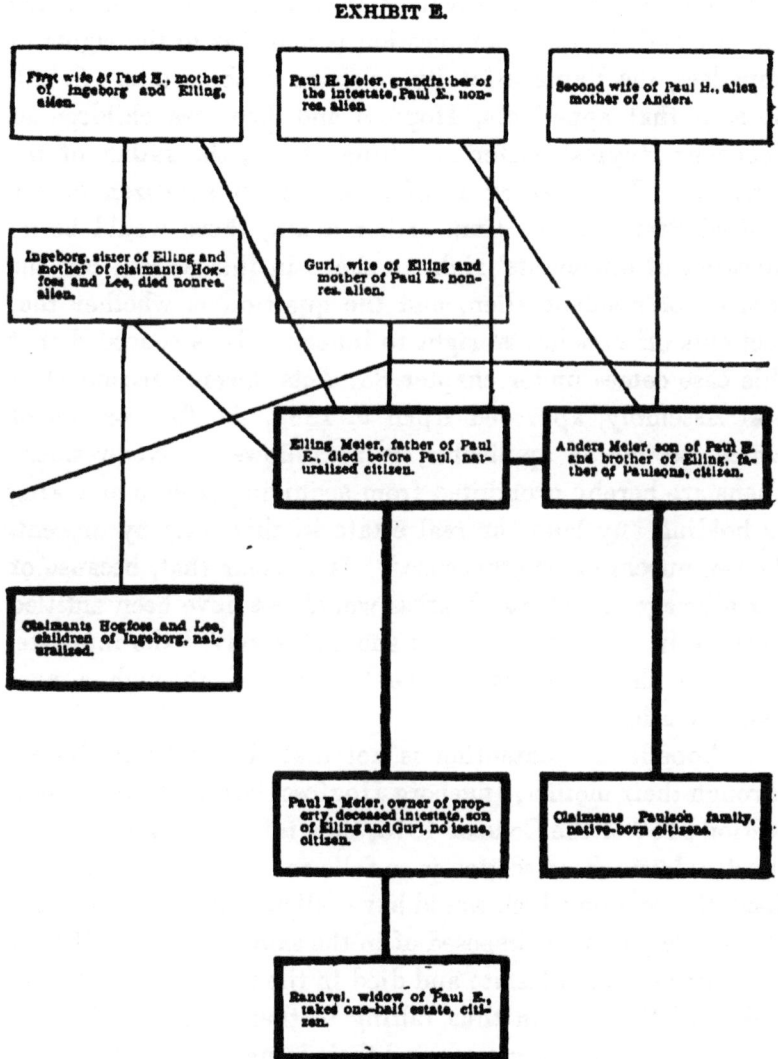

Heavy line is the line of inheritable blood.
Light line is the line of noninheritable blood.

From this it will be seen that appellees inherit through
their father, Anders Meier, brother of Elling Meier, father
of decedent, all citizens of the United States. Now, although

Elling and Anders died before the intestate, Paul E. Meier, yet, under section 2457 of the Code of 1873, the estate passes the same as if they had survived Paul E. Meier. Such being the law and the facts, no question is made as to the rights of appellees, the Paulson family, to share in the estate. It will be seen that appellants, Hogfoss and Lee, are children of Ingeborg Hogfoss, sister of Elling Meier, the father of the intestate. If Ingeborg Hogfoss had been a citizen of the United States at the time of her death, there would be no question of appellants' right to share in this estate; but she was a non-resident alien, and the question is whether that fact cuts off appellants' right to inherit. It is conceded that this case comes under chapter 85, Acts Twenty-second General Assembly, approved April 9, 1888, the first section of which, so far as applicable, is as follows: "Non-resident aliens are hereby prohibited from acquiring title to or taking or holding any lands or real estate in this state by descent, devise, purchase, or otherwise." It is clear that, because of her alienage, Ingeborg Hogfoss would not have been entitled to share in this estate, even if she had survived the intestate, and that the estate cannot be transmitted through a non-resident alien.

Appellants' contention is not that they take mediately through their mother, Ingeborg Hogfoss, but, that, under said section 2457 of the Code of 1873, they take immediately from the decedent. Said section is as follows: "If both parents be dead, the portion which would have fallen to their share by the above rules, shall be disposed of in the same manner as if they had outlived the intestate and died in the possession and ownership of the portion thus falling to their share, and so on through ascending ancestors and their issue." Appellants cite *Lash v. Lash*, 57 Iowa, 88, wherein it is said: "Whatever the plaintiff or any other heir of the intestate takes, he takes directly from the intestate, and not otherwise. Nothing, in fact, intervenes between the death of the intestate and the transmission of his estate to his heirs. The survivorship of

the parents is a fiction. We suppose it to determine the
descent." In that case there was no question of alienage to
intervene, the persons all being citizens. It was held that
the will of the intestate's father, who died before him, did
not convey property which belonged to his son, and that such
property constituted no part of the father's estate; therefore,
there was no fact in the case to intervene between the death
of the intestate and the transmission of his estate to his heirs.
Moore v. Weaver, 53 Iowa, 11, and *In re Parker's Estate,* 97
Iowa, 593, also cited, are not in point. The case of *Furenes
v. Mickelson,* 86 Iowa, 508, is so nearly like this in its facts,
and under the same statute, that we think it controlling in this
case. "Thor Olson, the decedent, was a brother of Steine
Olson, who is also deceased. Steine Olson was the grandfather of the plaintiff, but his son, the father of the plaintiff,
is living, and is, and always has been, a non-resident alien."
From this statement of the facts of that case it will be
observed that it only differs from this in that the father of
the plaintiff was living; while in this the mother of the appellants died before the intestate. This, however, cannot, under
said section 2457, make any difference. In that case, after
considering the distinction between mediate and immediate
descent, this court said: "The case of the plaintiff must be
determined according to his pedigree. The descent from
the decedent to him is not immediate, but mediate, through
his father. As the latter had no inheritable blood, the plaintiff
has acquired from him no right of inheritance. If chapter
85 of the Acts of the Twenty-Second General Assembly had
not been enacted, the father would have inherited the interest
now in controversy. That act took from him the right of
inheritance, but did not confer it upon the son." In *Burrow v.
Burrow,* 98 Iowa, 400, we said that in *Furenes v. Mickelson,
supra,* "we held that a resident whose father was a non-resident alien could not inherit through his father's brother, who
was a resident of the state, since he would derive his title
mediately, through his father, and not immediately, through

his uncle; and that, by reason of the provisions of the act of the Twenty-Second general assembly before quoted, the resident derived no title to the land in dispute." Counsel on both sides have argued this question with marked care and ability, and with many citations of authorities; but as the case rests upon our own statutes, which have been fully construed, we do not refer to other than Iowa cases. Following *Furenes v. Mickelson, supra,* we hold that the descent to appellants is mediate, and that they cannot take through their alien mother, as she could not have taken if alive, because of the provisions of said section 1, chapter 85, Acts Twenty-second General Assembly.

II. Appellants cite the treaty of 1783, between the king of Sweden and the United States (page 1042, Treaties and Conventions Between the United States and Other Powers), and insist that, under article 6 thereof, appellants' mother was not disqualified from inheriting an interest in this land. Article 6 contains the following: "The subjects of the contracting parties in the respective states may freely dispose of their goods and effects, either by testament, donation, or otherwise, in favor of such persons as they think proper; and their heirs, in whatever place they shall reside, shall receive the succession even *ab intestato,* either in person or by their attorney, without having occasion to take out letters of naturalization." Conceding that this treaty is still in force,—a matter we do not determine,— we are of the opinion that it does not apply to lands. "Goods: A valuable possession or piece of property; especially, and almost universally, in the plural, goods, wares, commodities, chattels." "Effects: Goods, movables, personal estate." Webster. "Goods and effects" have never been held to include real estate. The demurrer was properly sustained, and the decree is therefore AFFIRMED.

F. BRODY, Appellant, v. M. J. COHEN, as Constable, and
Another Case Between Same Parties,—the
two Being Consolidated.

Landlord and Mortgagee: LIEN AND POSSESSION. Where the mortgagee
of property on which there is a prior lien for rent, not yet enforce-
1 able, takes possession of the property, after which the lien becomes
enforceable, the landlord can, by virtue of his writ, take the property from the mortgagee.

REPLEVIN. A mortgagee took possession of certain property under
his mortgage, which belonged to a lessee, and removed it from the
leased premises. Before the expiration of the lease and after
2 the removal, rent became due, for which the landlord brought
action against the lessee, without making the mortgagee a party
and caused a landlord's attachment to be levied on the property.
Held, that the mortgagee could not, by replevin, recover possession
of such property from the officer levying the attachment, since
while the lien was being enforced, the right of possession for that
purpose became fixed in the landlord.

Appeal from Polk District Court.—HON. T. F. STEVENSON,
Judge.

WEDNESDAY, OCTOBER 12, 1898.

REPLEVIN for the possession of two safes, being a part
of a stock of goods. The basis of plaintiffs claim is two
chattel mortgages. The defendant's claim to the possession
is that, as constable, he took possession of the safes by virtue
of a landlord's attachment issued out of a justice's court in a
suit wherein William Johnson was plaintiff and C. W. Chittenden was defendant. The cases involve less than one hundred dollars, so that they come to us on certificates from the
trial judge. The certificate embraces two questions, but we
see no difference in the two, as legal propositions, and hence
we set out one, as follows: "(1) Where one leased certain
premises, under which the lessee took possession, with a stock
of goods and furniture not exempt from execution, and while

said stock of goods was on said premises in said lessee's possession, during the time of said lease, said lessee executed two chattel mortgages on said stock of goods, which are unsatisfied; and thereafter the mortgagees took possession of said stock of goods under and by virtue of said mortgages, and removed the same from said leased premises, with the knowledge of the lessor, and without objection on his part, and retained possession of the same until taken from him by said writ hereinafter mentioned; and before the expiration of said lease, and some time after said removal, rent became due under said lease, and the lessor brought an action by landlord's attachment against the lessee to recover the matured rent, without making the holder of the mortgages party to the action, and caused a writ of landlord's attachment to be levied on said property,—can the holder of said mortgages recover possession of said property as against the officer executing the said writ, by action of replevin, as provided for by statute to recover possession of specific personal property, and has he the right to recover in an action for possession of said property as against the officer holding the property under and by virtue of the writ of landlord's attachment?" There was a judgment for defendant, and the plaintiff appealed.— *Affirmed.*

Ayers, Woodin & Ayers for appellant.

Read & Read for appellee.

GRANGER, J.—I. It is the right of possession, not of ownership, that is involved in the inquiry. That right depends, not on ownership, but on liens, one being that of a landlord, and the other that of a mortgagee. The landlord's lien is prior in point of time, because the goods were on the leased premises before the mortgages were executed. *Gilbert v. Greenbaum,* 56 Iowa, 211. The landlord was not entitled to the possession of the property until his rent, or some part of it, became due. In other words, there must be rent due

before the action to enforce the lien can be brought. When rent is due, the property may be taken under the lien by attachment. In this case, when the mortgagee took possession of the property, no rent was due, and his mortgage gave him the right to possession; but, in taking such possession, he must do so subject to a lien that existed and might become
1　enforceable. That right of the landlord existed when he took his mortgages. The question, then, comes to this: A mortgagee of goods, on which there is a prior lien for rent, not yet enforceable, takes possession of the goods, and, while he holds them, the landlord's lien becomes enforceable. Can the landlord, by virtue of his writ, take the property from the mortgagee? The question, thus far, seems hardly doubtful. The superior right of the landlord settles the proposition in his favor. His lien is first, and the possession is neces-
2　sary for its enforcement. But the query goes one step further: Can the mortgagee come now, by replevin, and take the goods from the officer holding them by virtue of the landlord's writ? Such is the inquiry made by the question certified. As bearing on the question, appellant says the mortgagee had the legal title and right of possession, and had taken possession with the knowledge of the landlord, and without objection. We assume the statement to refer to the time when he took possession, and its correctness may be conceded. The landlord then had no right of possession, for no rent was due. To the mere fact of possession he had no right to object, for the mortgage contract fixed that right as between mortgagor and mortgagee. But the possession went from mortgagor to mortgagee, affected by the landlord's lien, which was prior, and might, by a default in payment, fix a right of possession for the purpose of enforcing the lien. It is said the landlord is not a party to this suit. That is true; but the appellant brings the suit, not against the landlord, but against the officer, to test his right of possession under the landlord's writ; so that the question is, what rights has the landlord enforceable under the writ that an officer may

justify under a writ by virtue of which he holds possession of property, see *Kingsbury v. Buchanan,* 11 Iowa, 387; *Parsons v. Hedges,* 15 Iowa, 119. It is a rule of universal recognition, we think. Indeed, it would be a strange doctrine that would deny to an officer, legally in the possession of property under legal process, the right to assert and prove that his possession was legal, as against one who might, by action, attempt to disposses him. It seems to be appellant's thought that, as the mortgagee was in lawful possession of the property, it took the judgment of a court, in a proceeding in which he was a party, to devest him of the possession. This can mean no more than that the mortgagee came legally into possession of the property. To admit that he was lawfully in possession, as against the landlord, when this suit was commenced, would, of course, end all controversy. The mortgagee did take the property lawfully, and so held it till other rights accrued; and when they accrued, so as to include a right of possession by the landlord, it did not need an adjudication to make it a right. An adjudication would only be to determine an existing right, and enforce it. Whenever the debt for rent matured, and the lien was being enforced, the right of possession for that purpose became fixed in the landlord, and the right of possession in the mortgagee, as against the landlord, was lost. Our conclusion leads to a negative answer to the question, and the judgment will stand AFFIRMED.

CORNELIUS RYAN, JR., v. CITY OF DUBUQUE, Appellant.

Public Improvement: GRADING: *Evidence.* One who has contracted with a municipal corporation to grade a street cannot recover therefor without showing the amount of grading he has done, under a contract which reserved to the city the right to change the grade and thus increase or diminish the amount of grading to be done and provided that if such amount was changed the compensation to be paid therefor should be increased or diminished in proportion to such change. Hence, it was error to deny defendant's motion for judgment where plaintiff introduced nothing in evidence except the contract, the ordinance showing that grades were required to be established and changed by resolution and that when streets are improved by contract the work is to be passed on by a committee which reports to the council, and a record of the council showing an acceptance of said street for the purposes of an assessment afterwards made for certain work done by plaintiff on the street, the grading in question being payable, however, from a general fund.

SAME. Evidence of the assistant of the engineer under whose supervision the grading was done, that a change in relation to the street was made after the contract was entered into, was admissible, notwithstanding a change in the grading of the street could be
2 legally made only by ordinance or resolution; since the specifications provide that the amount payable shall be increased or diminished if, from any change or grade or "other cause," the amount of grading shall be changed.

Appeal from Dubuque District Court.—HON. J. L. HUSTED, Judge.

WEDNESDAY, OCTOBER 12, 1898.

ACTION at law to recover an amount alleged to be due the plaintiff on a contract for grading. When the evidence had been fully submitted, a verdict was returned in favor of the plaintiff by direction of the court; and from the judgment rendered thereon, the defendant appeals.—*Reversed.*

Duffy & Maguire for appellant.

Longueville, McCarthy & Kenline for appellee.

ROBINSON, J.—On the twenty-first day of September, 1894, the plaintiff and the defendant entered into a contract in writing, by which the former agreed "to furnish all the materials, and do all the necessary work and labor, in grading
* * * Southern avenue, from Railroad avenue to Rowan street, * * * according to the plans and specifications prepared by the city engineer." The contract further
1 provided that, in consideration of the fulfillment of the contract, the city would pay to the plaintiff for "grading, in total, $2,679.60." The contract also provided

for curbing, guttering, and macadamizing the street, but
there is no controversy in regard to that work. The plaintiff,
acting under the contract, performed labor in grading the
street, and has received of the contract price for grading, the
sum of one thousand two hundred and one dollars and twenty
cents. He claims to be entitled to, and seeks to recover, the
remainder of the contract price, or one thousand four hundred and seventy-eight dollars and forty cents, with interest.
The answer of the defendant contains a general denial, and
avers that, after the contract was entered into, the amount of
grading which it required was diminished by the defendant,
as it was authorized to do, and that the grading done was by
virtue of that change, and that, although the original contract
required the grading of nineteen thousand one hundred and
forty-two cubic yards, the grading actually done amounted to
but eight thousand five hundred and eighty cubic yards, and
that the plaintiff had been fully paid for that amount. The
verdict returned and judgment rendered were for the full
amount of the grading fixed by the contract.

I. The plaintiff, to establish his claim, introduced in
evidence the contract and certain ordinances, and also records
of the city council, which showed that grades of the city were
required to be established and changed by resolution; that,
when streets are improved by contract, the work is to be
examined by a committee, and, if found completed in accordance with the contract, the committee is to accept the work,
and so report to the city council. A record of the city council
was also introduced, which showed that a committee reported
to the council in regard to the street in question, and others,
as follows: "Your committee report that the following streets
have been accepted for the purpose of special assessment."
It was further shown that the report was adopted, and that
the city council levied special assessments on the property
abutting on the part of Southern avenue included in the plaintiff's contract, to pay for the improvements made by him
exclusive of the grading, and that the grading was to be paid

for from the general fund of the city. When that showing had been made by the plaintiff, he rested; and the defendant thereupon moved for judgment in its favor, on various grounds, which were, in substance, that the evidence failed to show that the plaintiff was entitled to recover anything. The motion was overruled. We think it should have been sustained. The acceptance of the committee upon which the council acted, did not refer to the grading, and there was no evidence before the court that the amount specified in the contract had been done. The plans and specifications referred to in the contract were made a part of it, and the specifications contain the following: "The grading is estimated from an established grade of said street as shown by profile, cross section, and level notes on file in city engineer's office. * * * The city reserves the right to change the grade of said street, thereby increasing or diminishing the amount of grading as estimated; and if, from any change of grade or other cause, the amount of grading is changed, then the amount due and to be paid under this contract shall be increased or diminished in the same proportion." This recognized the fact that the amount of grading specified might not be done, and that, if but a part of it should be done, only a part of the contract price would be earned. It was necessary for the plaintiff to show that he had completed the contract according to its terms, or, if not, to show the amount of grading he had done under it, and that he wholly failed to do.

II.   The defendant, to establish its defense, attempted to show, by the testimony of its assistant city engineer, under whose supervision the work in question was done, that a change in relation to the street was made after the contract in suit was entered into; that the street was not brought to the established grade; and that the grading actually done was less in amount than that required by the contract when 2 made. All testimony of that character was excluded on the objection of the plaintiff. The theory upon which that ruling was based appears to be that the contract specified the amount of grading to be done, and the sum to be paid for it; that the work done was accepted by the city; and, therefore, that the sum specified in the contract must be paid, in the absence of proof that the city had changed the grade in the manner provided by ordinance, even though the amount of grading for which it provided was not done. In this connection attention is called to the answer, which avers that the city diminished the amount of grading to be done; and it is insisted that this averment would not be sustained by proof that the city engineer alone made the change. We do not think the theories suggested are sound. It is true that the contract reserved to the city only the right to change the grade of the street which was to be graded, and that such change could be made legally only by resolution or ordinance; but it is clear that the contract in suit did not contemplate payment for grading not actually done. It provides that "if, from any change of grade or other cause, the amount of grading should be changed, then the amount to be paid should be increased or diminished in the same proportion." If the amount was changed wrongfully, to the injury of the plaintiff, it may be that he would have a remedy against the wrongdoer, but he is not entitled to pay for work which he did not perform. See *Guthrie v. City of Dubuque*, 105 Iowa, 653. A record of formal action taken by the council to change the grade was not necessary to show that the plaintiff had not done the grading for which he sought to recover. Verbal evidence was competent to establish that fact, and the court erred in rejecting the testimony of the assistant city engineer. For the errors pointed out the judgment of the district court is REVERSED.

JOHN GRAPES and ELLEN GRAPES, Appellants v. THOMAS B. GRAPES and MONTICELLO BANK.

Incumbrance: HOW CREATED. A person who takes title to property as security for a loan made to one of its owners and executes to

2   the other owner a note showing her interest in the premises, thereby creates an incumbrance upon the property.

Cancellation: FRAUDULENT CONVEYANCE: *Defenses.* One to whom
real property was conveyed in fraud of creditors cannot in an
1   action for reconveyance avail himself of such fraud where he
claims the property under an alleged purchase made after the
original transactions were closed.

Costs: APPORTIONMENT: *Review.* A person deeded land to another as
security, and the grantee deeded the land to a bank as security
for a debt of his own. The grantor asked an accounting and a
reconveyance against the grantee and the bank. Plaintiff's deed
3   was found to be intended as security for a certain sum found
due thereon, and the grantee was decreed a lien for the amount
thereof, which judgment was to inure in favor of the bank as its
interest might appear, and both deeds were decreed to be can
celled, and it was ordered that the lien of the bank should be
inferior to the lien of the officers and others entitled to costs, except
the costs to which plaintiff and members of his family were
entitled. *Held,* that it was, in effect, an apportionment of costs,
which would not be disturbed.

SAME. The cost of making an abstract of evidence for use in the
4   trial court, in accordance with the provisions of section, 5, of the
rules of the district court, is not an item taxable as costs.

ATTORNEY FEE: *Deposition.* Plaintiff is not entitled to have the
4   expenses of his counsel incured in attending at three different
places in the state to take the deposition of a witness in an equity
cause, before it was finally secured, taxed as costs. If recoverable
at all, it must be in an independent suit.

Appeal. An appellant cannot complain of any matter which affects
3   the appellee alone.

Appeal from Woodbury District Court.—HON. A. VAN
WAGENEN, Judge.

THURSDAY, OCTOBER 13, 1898.

SUIT in equity for an accounting and for a re-conveyance of land, the title to which is in the defendant Thomas
B. Grapes, or the Monticello Bank. Defendants say that the
conveyance to Thomas B. Grapes was absolute, and that plaintiffs have no interest in the lands. Defendants further plead
that the deed under which Thomas Grapes claims was
delivered to him in the first instance as security for money

advanced, and that he afterwards acquired title by agreement between the parties. They ask that the title be quieted in them and for general relief. The trial court found that the deed to Thomas B. Grapes was intended as security; that there was due him the sum of five hundred and fifty dollars; that the Monticello Bank held title to the lands as security for an .indebtedness due it by Grapes; and decreed that defendant Thomas B. Grapes have judgment for the amount found due, which should be a lien upon the land, and that the conveyances to defendant Grapes and by him to the Monticello Bank be canceled; that a note executed by defendant Grapes to plaintiff Ellen Grapes be canceled, and that the judgment in favor of Thomas B. Grapes should inure to the benefit of the Monticello Bank, as its interest may appear. Both parties appeal, but, as plaintiffs have denominated themselves appellants, they will be so called in this court.— *Affirmed.*

J. S. Lothrop for appellants.

Thos. A. Cheshire for appellees.

DEEMER, C. J.—Plaintiffs entered into a contract for the purchase of the lands in controversy with one Ashby. A deed for the same was executed to Thomas B. Grapes, who was to hold the title as security for money advanced to plaintiffs. In January of the year 1891 defendant Grapes executed and delivered to John Grapes a deed for the land in dispute. This deed was never recorded, and thereafter it was handed back to defendant Thomas B. Grapes, who at the same time executed to Ellen Grapes a note for eight hundred dollars. Thereafter defendant destroyed this deed, which had been re-delivered to him, and the legal title then stood in the name of Thomas B. Grapes. Thereafter defendant Grapes executed a deed to the Monticello Bank for the real estate so held by him, which was intended as security for a loan made of the bank. Plaintiffs have held possession of the land ever since they made the contract of purchase with Ashby. The controversy is over the nature of these respective conveyances. Defendants say in argument that the reason why the title to the land was taken in the name of Thomas B. Grapes in the first instance was to hinder, delay, and defraud plaintiff's creditors in the collection of their claims; while, on the other hand, plaintiffs contend that defendant Grapes, who is the brother of plaintiff John Grapes, took title as security for money advanced and to be advanced by him to his brother John. While there is some evidence tending to show that the conveyance to Thomas Grapes was a cover to conceal the real ownership of the property, yet we are constrained to believe that it was made for the purpose of security, as alleged by plaintiffs; and as defendant Thomas Grapes re-conveyed the land to his brother, and is now insisting upon retaining the title because of an alleged purchase after the original transactions were closed, he is not in condition to avail himself of the fraud.

Again, it is said that when the deed was re-delivered to defendant Grapes, and when he executed the eight hundred dollar note to Ellen Grapes, he purchased all of plaintiffs' rights in and to the land, and that the re-delivery of the deed operated as a conveyance of the land to him. This raises an issue of fact which lies at the foundation of the case. An examination of the record leads us to believe that the re-delivery of the deed was not intended to operate as an absolute conveyance of the land, but was intended as a means by which defendant Grapes might be secured for the indebtedness then owing him by John Grapes. The eight
2   hundred dollar note was executed for the purpose of showing the interest that Ellen Grapes had in the land,—she having furnished a part of the consideration,—and was not given as a part of the purchase price. That an incumbrance may be so created seems to be well settled. *Blaney v. Hanks*, 14 Iowa, 400; Jones Real Property, section 1259.

As the deed was re-delivered for security, the question yet remains as to the state of the account between these parties. Each presents a long account against the other, and there is much dispute in the evidence regarding the several items. We need not set out the claims of the respective parties. It is sufficient to say that our examination leads to the conclusion that the account as stated by the trial court is as nearly correct as may be expected under the circumstances. Absolute precision cannot be expected in settling long accounts, every item of which is practically in dispute. Our figures are very close to those made by the trial court, and we are content to approve the conclusion reached.

Complaint is made by appellants of the decree in favor of the bank. As this is a matter affecting the appellees alone, we are not required to consider the point further. The trial court ordered the costs taxed against defendant Thomas B.

3   Grapes, and decreed that the lien of the bank "should be inferior to the lien of the officers and others entitled to costs, except the costs which John Grapes and the members of his family are entitled to draw." While this order is peculiar, it is, in effect, an apportionment of the costs, which we do not see fit to disturb.

II. Appellants ask us to sustain a motion to tax as costs certain expenses of counsel incurred in taking depositions. It is claimed that defendants gave notice of taking the deposition of a witness at three different places in the

4   state before it was finally secured by them, and that plaintiff and his attorney were compelled to attend and unnecessarily expend a large amount of money. We know of no authority for taxing such expenses as costs. If recoverable at all, it must be in an independent suit. Appellants also asked the trial court to tax the sum of sixty-five dollars and seventy cents for making an abstract of the evidence for use in the trial court, according to the provisions of section 5 of the rules adopted by the district judges of the state. See McClain's Code, page lviii. of preface. The motion was overruled. In this there was no error. The statute does not

authorize the taxing of such items. The several motions submitted with the case are each and all overruled. Our examination of the record leads us to the conclusion that the decree is right, and it is AFFIRMED.

F. HOOKER, Appellant, v. G. W. CHITTENDEN.

Attachment: DAMAGES. Evidence as to the relative condition of trade at the approach of holidays as compared with other seasons
4 of the year, in an action to recover damages for wrongful writ of attachment, is reversible error where the attachment debtor's trade was not interfered with by the levy of such writ.

Motion for New Trial: WHAT IS: *Review.* Plaintiff filed a motion to set aside a general verdict and certain special verdicts for defendant, and to have rendered a judgment for himself on a spe-
1 cial verdict in his favor, stating as reasons therefor certain grounds appropriate for a motion for new trial, none of which would authorize the court in sustaining this motion. *Held,* where plaintiff has not asked for a new trial, the record was in a condition which precluded a determination whether a new trial could have been granted.

SAME. The mere fact that such motion was designated in the judg-
1 ment as a motion for new trial does not authorize the conclusion that it was treated as a motion for new trial, in the lower court.

MOTION FOR JUDGMENT: *Waiver.* The failure to include errors
2 arising on the trial, which might be reviewed without motion for new trial, in a motion for a judgment on special findings, does not waive the right to have such errors reviewed on appeal. The motion for judgment cannot affect what is not involved in it.

Appeal: MISLEADING INSTRUCTION: *Curing.* The inadvertent use of the word "replevin" instead of "attachment" in an instruction authorizing the jury to award exemplary damages in case the
8 writ was sued out maliciously is reversible error, and is not cured by an additional instruction in which the correct word is used, where there was evidence of the issuing of a writ of replevin and it is clear from the verdict that the jury took into consideration the issuance of such writ, the damages sustained by which were not material to the issues in the case.

Appeal from Polk District Court.—HON. W. A. SPURRIER, Judge.

THURSDAY, OCTOBER 13, 1898.

ACTION to recover one thousand five hundred dollars, being the proceeds of goods sold by defendant at retail, for which he was to account to plaintiff at fixed prices. The defendant denied the indebtedness, and, by way of counterclaim, asked to be allowed damages for the wrongful and malicious suing out of a writ of attachment. Trial to jury. Verdict and judgment for defendant. Plaintiff appeals.— *Reversed.*

Ayers, Woodin & Ayers for appellant.

Read & Read for appellee.

LADD, J.—The general verdict was for the defendant and fixed the amount of his recovery at one hundred dollars. In the special verdicts, the jury found, by the fourth, that the plaintiff was entitled to recover one thousand five hundred dollars, as claimed in his petition; by the first, second, and third, that the writ of attachment was sued out wrongfully and maliciously; by the fifth, that the defendant suffered actual damages in the sum of two hundred dollars; and, by the sixth, that he was entitled to one thousand four hundred dollars as exemplary damages. It will be observed that these findings are not inconsistent with the general verdict.

1   Nevertheless, the plaintiff filed his motion, entitled "Motion in Arrest of Judgment," in words following: "Now comes the plaintiff, and moves the court to set aside the general verdict of the jury in this case, and to render a judgment for the plaintiff, and against the defendant, on the fourth special finding or verdict of the jury, and to set aside the first, second, third, fifth, and sixth findings and special verdicts of the jury, for the following reasons." Twenty-nine grounds appropriate for a motion of a new trial are then set out, none of which, if well founded, would authorize the court in sustaining this motion. No reasons are stated for rendering judgment, notwithstanding verdict, under sections 3757 and 3758 of the Code. It is somewhat difficult to determine

the purpose of appellant in presenting such a motion to the court. He urges that it complies with the requirements of section 3755, which is, in part: "A new trial is a re-examination in the same court of an issue of fact, or some part or portions thereof, after verdict by a jury, report of a referee, or a decision by the court. The former report, verdict, or descision, or some portion thereof, shall be vacated and a new trial granted, on the application of the party aggrieved, for the following causes affecting materially the substantial rights of such party." It is very evident, without setting out the causes enumerated, that, in order to obtain a new trial, the aggrieved party must apply therefor. While the title of this motion is a misnomer, the plaintiff may well be presumed to have asked the relief he desired. A new trial is not included in his request. Indeed, it is absolutely inconsistent with the judgment he prays. In asking that the general verdict be set aside, and also five of the special interrogatories, he sought only what was necessary to accomplish before the relief prayed could be granted. The appellant explains his motion by saying a new trial was only desired on the counterclaim. If so, he was unfortunate in not making his wishes known to the court. The record is in a condition which precludes determining whether a new trial could have been granted on a part of the issues. See *Bond v. Railway Co.,* 67 Iowa, 712; *Woodward v. Horst,* 10 Iowa, 120.

II. It is also urged that the motion was treated as a motion for a new trial in the lower court. The mere fact that it was so designated in the judgment does not authorize this conclusion, and we know of no rule requiring a party to point out the defects in such a motion made by his adversary.

III. The appellee insists that by filing this motion the plaintiff waived all errors not referred to therein, and which might have been considered without motion for new trial. We have held that filing of a motion for judgment does not waive the consideration of errors alleged in an application for new trial. *Pieart v. Railway Co.,* 82 Iowa, 148. And it is not perceived why a different rule should obtain as to errors which may be passed on without such an application. A motion for a new trial filed too late is not a waiver of errors proper to be determined without it. *Beems v. Railroad Co.,* 58 Iowa, 150; *Kaufman v. Manufacturing Co.,* 78 Iowa, 679. And, where such a motion is pending, an appeal from a judgment rendered on a verdict will be considered, and errors arising on the trial be passed on, although the motion is undetermined. *Hunt v. Railway Co.,* 86 Iowa, 15.

2   It fairly follows from these decisions that a motion for judgment which does not involve a consideration of errors arising during the course of a trial in no manner waives the right to have them reviewed. *Brown v. Rose,* 55 Iowa, 734.

IV. Before touching what we deem the important question in this case, it is well to know somewhat of the facts. The plaintiff began pressing Chittenden for security about December 18, 1895; and on the twenty-first the latter executed to Holland and McKinney two mortgages, covering his entire stock of goods, securing the payment of one thousand nine hundred and forty-five dollars. On the following day Hooker bought and took an assignment of these mortgages in the name of one Brody (whether at Chittenden's request need not now be determined) ; and as the latter still refused to give security, and also refused to surrender the stock of goods under the mortgage, proceedings in replevin were begun in the name of Brody, and the entire stock taken under the direction of Hooker and his attorney. Thereafter the writ of attachment was levied on a linoleum carpet and a show case; and one Welday, who held certain mortgages of Chittenden, amounting to six hundred dollars, was served with notice of garnishment. While there were other notices of garnishment, the claim for actual damage was based on the loss of use of the property referred to, and its depreciation in value. Chittenden was permitted to testify that these mortgages depreciated in value three or four hundred dollars, between the date of the levy and the trial, which could not have exceeded nine months, as judgment was rendered in September, 1896. The abstract does not disclose when the trial occurred. The cross-examination, however, shows this to have been a mere conjecture, and without any basis of fact whatever. No proof of depreciation in the other property is shown. Chittenden says the value of the use of the show case was the same as its value,—thirty dollars,—but that there was no rental value for it; and Hooker thinks its use might have been worth five dollars. The amount of actual damage, then, did not exceed thirty dollars. It is true, as the court did not have any opportunity to pass upon the insufficiency of the evidence to support the verdict, we cannot reverse the judgment on that ground. *Waterhouse v. Black,* 87 Iowa, 317. It is mentioned as bearing upon a portion of the eleventh instruction.

3   After correctly advising the jury under what circumstances to allow actual damages, and the measure thereof, this language is employed: "If, after considering the evidence under the instructions of the court, you find that the defendant had sustained actual damage, then you may inquire and determine whether or not the suing out of the writ of replevin was maliciously done by the plaintiff; that is, with the design to oppress, wrong, and injure the defendant. And if you find the writ so maliciously sued out by the plaintiff, and if you have found that the writ was wrongfully sued out, and that actual damage has thereby resulted to the defendant, then you may give the defendant, in addition to his other damages, such exemplary damages as you may deem proper, which damages are defined in the next instruction." In the next instruction, after defining exemplary damages, is found this sentence: "If you find that the defendant has sustained actual damages by reason of the wrongful suing out of said writ of attachment, and also that said writ of attachment was sued out for the purpose on the part of the plaintiff to injure the defendant, then you may allow, in

addition to the actual damages, such sum as you think should be allowed as exemplary damages, but in no case to exceed the sum sued for, to wit, $4,500." This does not cure the error. It permits the jury to allow exemplary damages also, in event the writ of attachment was sued out maliciously. Without doubt, the word "replevin" was used in the eleventh paragraph through inadvertence, and this would ordinarily be sufficiently explained in the context. But the trial in this case necessarily involved a review of the entire transaction and the dealings between the parties during the period of replevying the stock of goods and levying the writ of attachment. If the circumstances were as related by the defendant, and his entire stock of goods taken under the writ of replevin with a bad purpose just before the holiday trade, the jury might well feel that substantial punishment should be inflicted. But the levying of the writ of attachment on the show case and carpet, and the garnishment of Welday, did not interfere materially with his trade, nor interrupt his business. The actual damages caused thereby were inconsiderable, and the fact that exemplary damages were allowed in the sum of one thousand four hundred dollars,—out of all proportion to the actual damages suffered,—indicates that the jury was misled by this instruction, and took into consideration the fact that his trade was interrupted or destroyed, and his stock taken from him under the writ of replevin. In no other way can the finding of the jury be explained.

V. We think, also, that the court erred in permitting this question to be answered: "What, Mr. Chittenden, is the fact as to the relative condition of trade at the approach of the holidays, as compared with the other seasons of the year?"

4   As said, it does not appear that his trade was interfered with by the levy of the writ of attachment, and the answer would not aid the jury in passing upon any issue proper for their consideration. The fact that it was the most profitable season of the year was doubtless considered in determining the purpose of the plaintiff, as permitted, in

suing out the writ of replevin.   Many other errors are argued, but not of sufficient importance to require detailed consideration.   We discover none prejudicial except as indicated. Owing to those pointed out, the judgment is REVERSED.

JOHN A. BERRY v. JOHN W. WOOD & SONS. *et al.*, Appellants,

Execution: PARTIES: *Fraud.* Where interveners took judgment against an insolvent plaintiff, knowing that the action was brought in plaintiff's name without her knowledge, not as the real party in interest, but to prevent them from collecting any judgment they might secure, the fraud does not authorize an execution against the real party in interest. That one party practices a fraud upon another does not entitle the latter to sell the property of the former upon a judgment which they elected to take against a third.

Appeal from Harrison District Court.—HON. F. R. GAYNOR, Judge.

THURSDAY, OCTOBER 13, 1898.

ACTION to enjoin the sale of certain real estate belonging to the plaintiff under an execution in favor of the defendants J. L. Witt, J. W. Reed, and C. R. Bolter, against M. E. Berry, trustee.   Decree was rendered making the injunction perpetual.   Defendants appeal.—*Affirmed.*

L. R. Bolter & Sons for appellants.

John A. Berry, in pro per.

GIVEN, J.—I.   The following facts shown by the record will sufficiently indicate the points in dispute: In February, 1894, and for some time prior, plaintiff held money of Mrs. M. M. Seekell for investment.   Plaintiff purchased an open account for about two hundred dollars from Van Scoy Bros., against J. D. McKenney, and afterwards took the note of McKenney for the amount, payable to himself, which note he assigned to M. E. Berry, as trustee for Mrs. Seekell. This note was put into judgment, and in February, 1894, plaintiff purchased eighteen head of calves in payment from McKenney. Defendants John W. Woods & Sons took the calves, under a mortgage held by them from McKenney, from the possession of Berry, whereupon an action was commenced in the name of M. E. Berry, trustee, against John W. Woods & Sons and J. D. McKenney, to recover the calves, and possession taken thereunder. Defendants J. J. Witt, J. W. Reed, and C. R. Bolter intervened in that action, claiming the calves, and a verdict was rendered in their favor. They so electing, a money judgment was rendered in their favor for fifty dollars and forty-five cents, and for ninety-five dollars and seventy-five cents costs, against said plaintiff M. E. Berry, trustee. Said interveners caused execution to issue on said judgment, and to be levied upon the real estate of plaintiff, John A. Berry, and the decree in this case enjoins the sale of said land under said execution.

II.   It will be observed that plaintiff was not a party to the action of M. E. Berry, trustee, against Wood & Sons and McKenney; that the judgment rendered therein, and the execution issued thereon, are against M. E. Berry, trustee, and not against the plaintiff; and that the land sought to be sold under said execution is confessedly the land of the plaintiff. The defendants allege and contend that plaintiff brought said action of replevin for himself, but in the name of his wife, as trustee, for the purpose of hindering, delaying and preventing the interveners in said action from collecting any judgment they might obtain therein; that M. E. Berry is insolvent; and that she had no knowledge of said action. They ask that said judgment may be declared an equitable lien on the property levied upon. The evidence of the plaintiff that he held money of Mrs. Seekell for investment at his discretion, and that he transferred the note of McKenney to his wife, M. E. Berry, in trust for Mrs. Seekell, stands uncontradicted, and is open to no suspicion of unfairness, except what may be inferred from the relation of Mr. and Mrs. Berry, and the fact that Mrs. Berry was absent and knew nothing of the transactions. We fail to discover, and counsel fails to point out, how plaintiff could have intended to defraud appellants at the time he transferred the note, took judgment thereon, took the calves in payment, or brought the action of replevin. It does not appear that he then knew that said interveners had any claim. The trust being *bona fide,* so far as Mrs. Seekell is concerned, she will not be deprived of the benefit of it, even if the trustees did not know of the trust. We do not think the fraud charged against the plaintiff is established, but, conceding that it is, should appellants be allowed to sell his property on a judgment which they elected to take against another? May they sell his property without either judgment or execution against him? Surely not. If what they now claim is true, it was true and known to them at the time they elected to take, and took, their judgment against M. E. Berry. If this plaintiff was the real party in interest in that action, they should have made him a party, and taken their judgment against him. Appellants contend, on the authority of *Conger v. Chilcote,* 42 Iowa, 18, that as plaintiff was interested in the replevin action, and had actual knowledge of it, he is bound by the result, the same as if he had been a party to it. A comparison of the cases will show a wide difference in the facts, and that the holding in that case has no application to this. That case does not hold that you may sell the property of one person upon a judgment and execution against another, or that you may sell his property without judgment or execution against him. Plaintiff is not complaining of the result in the replevin suit. He is content to be bound by it. But that does not make him a party to the judgment, nor his property liable to execution under it.—AFFIRMED.

EMERSON & COMPANY, Appellant, v. G. E. CONVERSE.

Wrongful Attachment: DAMAGES: *Second attachment.* Defendant's property was attached, and placed in the custody of the sheriff. Plaintiff levied a subsequent attachment. A receiver was appointed in the suit of the first attaching creditor, and the prop-
2   erty sold for the benefit of both the attaching creditors. *Held,* that if plaintiff failed to recover, defendant was not entitled to recover on the attachment bond the difference between the sum realized from the sale of his interest in the property and the value of such interest at the time of the levy, since the measure of damages was only legal interest on the surplus, during the time it was wrongfully held by virtue of plaintiff's attachment.

Appeal: STRIKING AMENDMENT TO PLEADING. The discretion of the
1   trial court in granting a motion to strike an amendment to a petition in attachment proceedings which set up a new ground for attachment and was filed after the jury was impaneled will not be disturbed on appeal except for an abuse of such discretion.

Appeal from Polk District Court.—HON. THOMAS F. STEVENSON, Judge.

THURSDAY, OCTOBER 13, 1898.

ACTION, aided by attachment, upon two promissory notes. The defense was part payment, and there was a counterclaim for damages upon the attachment bond. Trial to jury. Verdict and judgment for defendant. Plaintiff appeals.—*Reversed.*

Bailey & Ballreich for appellant.

C. C. & C. L. Nourse for appellee.

WATERMAN, J.—The ground for attachment, as stated in the original petition, which was filed on the seventeenth day of February, 1894, was that "defendant is about to dispose of his property with intent to defraud his creditors." The answer and counterclaim were filed September 20, 1895.

On March 11, 1896, the cause was called for trial. After the jury was impaneled, plaintiff filed an amendment to his petition, in which, as an additional ground for attachment, he alleged "that the debt sued on herein is for property obtained under false pretenses." A motion to strike this amendment from the files was sustained, and this action of the court is the ground of the first assignment of error. It is urged in support of the court's ruling that section 3021 of the Code of 1873, which provides for the amendment of the petition, affidavit, or writ in attachment proceedings, does not authorize an amendment which sets up a new ground of attachment. We held otherwise in *Citizens Nat. Bank v. Converse,* 105 Iowa, 669. The amendment being proper in substance, we have only to consider whether the court abused its discretion in refusing to permit it to stand as a pleading in the case. Section 2689 of the Code of 1873 is as follows: "The court may on motion of either party at an time in furtherance of justice, and on such terms as may be proper, permit such party to amend any pleadings or proceedings by adding or striking out the name of a party or by correcting a mistake in the name of a party, or a mistake in any other respect, or by inserting other allegations material to the case, or when the amendment does not change substantially the claim or defense, by conforming the pleadings or proceedings to the facts proved." Under this section we have held that the rule is to permit amendments; to refuse them, the exception. *Hinkle v. Davenport,* 38 Iowa, 355; *Pride v. Wormwood,* 27 Iowa, 257. We have also held that the matter of allowing amendments is within the sound discretion of the trial court. *Brockman v. Berryhill,* 16 Iowa, 183; *Hays v. Turner,* 23 Iowa, 214; *Phillips v. Van Schaick,* 37 Iowa, 229. Coming, as this amendment did, after the trial had begun, we cannot say that it was any abuse of the court's discretion to disallow it. No good reason is given why this matter was not set up at an earlier date. While great liberality should be shown by the courts in the allowance of amendments that are in furtherance of justice, the right is not absolute, and attorneys should not be encouraged to wait until the last moment before presenting their cases. There was no error in sustaining the motion to strike. *Brewing Co. v. Armstrong*, 89 Iowa, 673.

II. It is next urged that the testimony does not show that the writ was wrongfully sued out. Upon this point, as may well be conceived, there is a conflict. We are not able to say that the finding of the jury is without substantial support.

III. The rule of damages, as given in the court's instructions, is next complained of by appellant. The particular instruction objected to is as follows: "If you find that the defendant is entitled to recover upon his counterclaim on the bond sued on, then your next inquiry should be as to the amount of his recovery. On this question you are instructed that under the undisputed evidence, at the time of the levy of the attachment of the plaintiffs on the said stock of goods, furniture, and fixtures, and leasehold interest in the storeroom No. 516 Walnut street, in the city of Des Moines, the Citizens' National Bank was in the possession of said property, and had the right to hold the same to the extent of nine thousand dollars in value, for the purpose of selling the same, and to sell the same, and to appropriate the proceeds of said sale, to the extent of six thousand dollars, to the payment of the debt owing it from the defendant; that the interest of the defendant in said stock, furniture, fixtures, and leasehold interests at the time of the levy of the attachment complained of in this case was that of absolute ownership, subject to the said rights of the Citizens' National Bank; and you may allow as actual damages whatever sum you may find, considering all the circumstances and facts shown in evidence, to be the difference in the value of the interest of the defendant in said property, as stated to you in this instruction, at the time of the levy of the attachment herein, and the sum realized from the sale thereof. In arriving at this sum you are to consider all the facts and circumstances shown in evidence tending to show the value of said property at the time of the levy of the attachment herein, and the value of the said interest of the defendant therein at the time last mentioned, and also the sum realized from the sale of said property, and defendant's said interest therein.

2   *   *   *" It will be observed from the conceded facts as stated in this paragraph that the whole of the property seized by plaintiff had been taken and was held by another creditor of defendant. The testimony shows beyond dispute that this was done under a prior writ of attachment; that a receiver was appointed, who sold the property for the benefit of the attaching creditors. Plaintiff, under his writ, did not deprive defendant of possession, for the latter was not in possession when this writ was levied. He did not force the sale of the attached property, for that was done by the first attaching creditor. All that plaintiff secured by this levy was a right, to the extent of his claim, to the surplus, if any, over and above the amount necessary to satisfy the first attachment. We do not think plaintiff's liability any greater, under the circumstances, than it would have been if he had garnished the sheriff while the latter was in possession under the first writ. In such case the measure of defendant's recovery would not ordinarily be more than interest on the surplus at six per cent. during the time it was wrongfully held. *Fourth Nat. Bank v. Mayer,* 96 Ga. 728 (24 S. E. Rep. 453); *Green Fruit Co. v. Pate,* 99 Ga. 60 (24 S. E. Rep. 455). As having a bearing, also, upon this question of damages, see *Schwartz v. Davis,* 90 Iowa, 324; *Porter v. Knight,* 63 Iowa, 365; Waples Attachment, page 448. The instruction announces an erroneous rule.

IV. Some other errors are discussed by counsel, but they are not matters which are likely to arise on another trial, and we need devote no attention to them.—REVERSED.

NETTIE BOTKIN v. P. M. CASSADY, Appellant.

Personal Injuries: INSTRUCTIONS. Refusal of an instruction in an
8 action for a miscarriage and other injuries alleged to have been
    induced by threats, that if the plaintiff was suffering from uremia
4 which might have brought on such injuries or if they might have
    occurred without the action complained of, she could not recover
    is reversible error, where she had previously had a miscarriage
    which might have caused the one in question and had been doing
    work which might have produced such a result.

SAME. An instruction "that it is a violation of law for any person to
    threaten with intent to compel another by threats to do an act
5 against his or her will" is reversible error in an action by a woman
    to recover for physical and other injuries alleged to have been
    induced by threats. Code, 1873, section 3871, making it a misde-
    meanor to maliciously threaten an accusation of crime, has no
    application to a civil action based on such injuries.

Impeachment. The mere fact that a witness has taken morphine
    (there being no evidence as to the frequency with which he took
1 it, or as to its effect upon his mind or memory) is immaterial as
    affecting his credibility, and his denial of the fact does not pre-
    sent a ground for impeachment.

SAME. Where a witness has given important testimony it is prejudi-
1 cial error to permit his impeachment based on his denial of an
    immaterial matter.

Trial: OPENING CLOSED CASE. It is within the discretion of the court
2 to permit plaintiff, at the close of the evidence on his behalf, and
    after defendant's motion for a verdict, to introduce further testi-
    mony.

Plea and Proof: MENTAL ANGUISH. Where allegations as to mental
    anguish caused by threats were coupled with allegations as to
6 physical injury, and damages were asked in a gross sum, the peti-
    tion did not present a case for a recovery for mental anguish
    alone.

Appeal from Lyon District Court.—HON. WILLIAM HUTCH-
INSON, Judge.

FRIDAY, OCTOBER 14, 1898.

PLAINTIFF states her cause of action in substance as
follows: That on and for several years prior to October 28,

1893, she was the wife of Robert Botkin, by whom she was, on that day in an advanced stage of pregnancy; that on that day the defendant, a stranger to her, knowing her condition, did, negligently, willfully, wrongfully, maliciously, and in an angry and violent manner, when alone with plaintiff, threaten her that if she did not tell him the whereabouts of her husband, who was then absent, or that if she did not write to him and tell him where her husband was, he would cause her husband to be accused of larceny and convicted thereof, and imprisoned in the penitentiary; that by reason thereof plaintiff was greatly scared, nervous, and depressed in body and mind, and so continued for a long time, and that because thereof she miscarried, on or about the fifteenth day of November, 1893, and was delivered of a still-born child, in about the eighth month of development; that because of said facts plaintiff suffered great pain of body and mental anguish, was greatly damaged in her health, and her ability to again bear children was impaired, and she was put to one hundred dollars expense for medicines, medical attendance, and nursing. In an amendment she alleges she has been rendered nervous, generally weaker physically and mentally, her memory injured, and her vision made poorer, as a result of said scare, fright, and miscarriage, wherefor she prays judgment for ten thousand dollars. The defendant answered, denying generally; and, upon a trial to a jury, verdict and judgment were rendered in favor of the plaintiff for one thousand dollars. Defendant appeals.—*Reversed.*

J. M. Parsons and *McMillan & Dunlap* for appellant.

E. Y. Greenleaf for appellee.

GIVEN, J.—I. The following facts appear without dispute: Prior to October 19, 1893, plaintiff and her husband resided at Little Rock, Iowa, where the defendant also resided, and was engaged in the banking business. Defendant held a chattel mortgage on certain property belonging to Robert

Botkin, plaintiff's husband. Robert left for parts unknown, leaving the plaintiff with but two dollars in money. Plaintiff went to the home of her sister, Mrs. Freet, near Lake Park, Iowa. Defendant, not finding the mortgaged property, sued out a warrant for the arrest of Botkin, and on said twenty-eighth day of October went to Mr. Freet's home, accompanied by a constable, in search of Botkin. While there, defendant asked for, and was granted, an interview with the plaintiff. They had a conversation in a room by themselves, other persons being in an adjoining room. It was in this interview that the alleged threats are claimed to have been made. Plaintiff was delivered of a stillborn child on November 15th following, in about the eighth month of development.

II. Appellant makes fifty-four assignments of error, most of which are not sufficiently specific to be entitled, under the rule, to consideration, and many of them are not argued. We will only notice such as, under the rule, we are required to consider.

Appellant argues a number of assignment on rulings in taking the testimony. We have examined these assignments with care, and reach the conclusion that, with one exception, they were either correct or without prejudice, and are not of sufficient importance to require notice. The exception is this: A Mrs. Adams was examined on behalf of the defendant, and gave important testimony as to statements made by the plaintiff. On cross-examination she was asked by plaintiff's counsel if she was addicted to the use of morphine, to which she answered, "I am not addicted to the use of morphine, and was not at that time." Plaintiff was called in rebuttal, and asked, "Do you know about Mrs. Adams using morphine or opium while you were there?" to which she answered, "Yes." She was then asked, "Did she use it regularly?" to which defendant objected as incompetent, immaterial, irrelevant, and not rebuttal. The objection was overruled, and the witness answered, "She took it every night while I was there." This evidence was manifestly called out

1

on behalf of the plaintiff on the assumption that the use of morphine impairs the intellect, and clouds the memory, and therefore rendered the testimony of Mrs. Adams less reliable. There was no evidence as to the frequency or amount of morphine taken by Mrs. Adams, nor whether taken on prescription of a physician or as a cure for some ailment; neither was there any evidence that the mind or memory of Mrs. Adams had been affected by the use of morphine. The fact alone that she had taken morphine was immaterial, and her denial did not present a ground for impeachment, as a witness cannot be impeached upon an immaterial matter. *State v. Maxwell,* 42 Iowa, 208. In view of the importance of the testimony of Mrs. Adams, and the claim made by the plaintiff as to the weight to be given thereto because of the evidence as to her use of morphine, we think it was error prejudicial to the defendant to permit the plaintiff to testify as she did in rebuttal.

III. At the close of the evidence on behalf of the plaintiff, the defendant moved for a verdict, and thereupon, by leave of the court, the plaintiff was re-called, and gave further testimony as to the threats made to her. Appellant

2   complains of this, but the matter was within the discretion of the court, and we do not think there was any abuse of that discretion. Appellant also complains in this connection of the overruling of his motion for a verdict, but, with this additional testimony given by the plaintiff, we think the motion was properly overruled.

IV. Dr. A. M. Vail called by the plaintiff, stated different causes that may produce miscarriage; among them, fright, fear, and uremia. He said: "It is often caused by a deteriorated condition of the kidneys. Uremia is a pre-

3   disposing condition. Uremia is a suppressing of the urine back into the system. It may come from the kidneys. Kidney troubles are liable to result from using the water here in Lyon county. Our surface waters are unfavorable to health. A dropsical condition would be caused by suppression of the circulation of the blood, either through the

liver or kidneys. Predisposing causes to kidney troubles are from bad water, colds, injuries, exposure. It is quite apt to be the case that, when a woman has once had a miscarriage, she will never have live infants after that; and there are many instances in which it is not traced to any active cause, though we are most watchful for a second miscarriage along about the same period of pregnancy where the first miscarriage occurred, though it is not a usual rule. Uremia would be cause enough to produce a miscarriage or cause the death of the child." He further said: "Uremia is frequently found with pregnant women, which shows in a kind of bloating of the face, swelling of the glands of the eyes." Dr. C. S. Schultz, who waited on the plaintiff during her confinement in November, 1893, testified as follows: "When I first saw the patient, she was in convulsions. After she came out of the spasm she was in when I saw her, then I began making some inquiries as to her condition and general health previously. The physical symptoms, such as could be seen by the eye, showed that she had a dropsical condition. Her face was bloated. There was a puffiness around the eyes. The limbs were swollen. Her tongue was very much swollen, from having been bitten during the convulsions previous to the time that I had seen her. Her lips were also swollen from the same cause. The opinion that I came to after examining her was that she had what was known as 'uremia.' Uremia is a retention in the blood of the constituents of urine that are eliminated from the blood by the kidneys. Those dropsical symptoms would arise from the kidneys being affected. At the time I saw her, I think she must have been in this condition at least six weeks. I hardly think the condition could arise in less time than that. I think it would take six weeks to bring the condition she was in. This condition could produce miscarriage. I think she must have been affected with uremia considerably, or she would not have had convulsions. That indicated a very serious derangement. The convulsions would tend to cause expulsion of the fetus when a woman was about eight months along."

Defendant asked an instruction as follows: "(1) If you find that the plaintiff was suffering from uremia at the time of her miscarriage in the fall of 1893, and you further find that such uremia brought on, occasioned, and was the cause of the plaintiff's miscarriage or other injuries complained of, and that such miscarriage and other injuries complained of would have happened had plaintiff not had the interview with defendant at the Freets' home, then you should find for the defendant." This instruction was refused, and no equivalent given to the jury. In view of the evidence, we think the defendant was entitled to this or a similar instruction upon that subject. There was evidence that plaintiff had had a previous miscarriage, and that that would predispose to, or might cause, the miscarriage in question; also, that she had said that she had been doing kinds of hard work that might produce such a result. These matters might well have been brought to the attention of the jury in the instructions.

V. The court instructed: "That it is a violation of law for any person to threaten with intent to compel another so threatened, by threats, to do an act against his or her will," —evidently referring to section 3871 of the Code of 1873. That section provides: "If any person * * * maliciously threaten to accuse another of a crime, * * * with intent thereby * * * to compel the person so threatened to do an act against his will, he shall be imprisoned," etc. This is not a proceeding to punish under that statute, and we fail to see its application to this case. The defendant's liability does not depend upon his having violated that statute, but upon whether or not he made the threats and produced the result alleged. The same is true as to negligence, and we do not think appellant's complaint that the court failed to instruct upon that subject is well founded. The court instructed to the effect that if, by reason of the making of the alleged threats, plaintiff was caused to suffer mental anguish, "then you will find for the plaintiff, though she suffered no physical injury, and though you do not find said miscarriage, if any she had, was the result of said threats, if any were made." This action was evidentlly not brought to recover for mental anguish alone. The allegations as to mental anguish are coupled with the allegations as to physical injury; and, whatever the right of the plaintiff might be to recover for mental anguish alone, such a case is not presented in the petition, and the instruction as given was erroneous. Other errors discussed and not noticed herein are not likely to arise on a re-trial. For the errors pointed out, the judgment of the district court is REVERSED.

LADD, J. took no part.

F. BRODY, Appellant, v. G. W. CHITTENDEN.

Replevin: INJUNCTION *pendente lite.* An answer in replevin denied plaintiff's right to possession in certain articles; alleged that the articles were not included in the mortgage under which plaintiff claimed possession, nor in the writ under which they were taken; that some of them were exempt, and that the balance were placed with him for repairs, his occupation being that of a jeweler; and asked for a return thereof, for damages for their detention,
1 and for an injunction restraining their sale. *Held*, since, under Code 1873, section 3226, prohibiting counterclaims in actions of replevin, defendant was entitled to recover the property and damages for its recovery, his answer was an "action by ordinary proceedings," within section 3386, providing that "in all cases of * * * injury, where the party injured is entitled to maintain and has brought an action by ordinary proceedings, he may in the same cause pray and have a writ of injunction * * * against * * * continuance of such * * * injury."

JURY QUESTION. What is "furniture in a store," or what articles are
2 legitimately a part of a stock of goods of a peculiar nature, or what tools a particular artisan uses, are questions of fact for the jury.

Injunction: MOTION TO DISSOLVE. A motion to dissolve an injunction
3 restraining the sale of property under a writ of replevin, directed to the injunction as a whole, will be denied if the injunction is good as to any part of the property.

TRIAL *de novo*. A motion to dissolve an injunction granted upon the answer, in an action of replevin to restrain the sale of property taken under the writ, is not an equitable proceeding, so as to authorize the supreme court to determine the facts anew upon an appeal from the denial of such motion.

Appeal from Polk District Court.—HON. W. F. CONRAD, Judge.

FRIDAY, OCTOBER 14, 1898.

THE defendant, Chittenden, gave to A. Holland and J. A. McKinney, each, a mortgage on his stock of goods, consisting of jewelry, silverware, glassware, and queensware, in a certain building in the city of Des Moines. The plaintiff became the owner of both mortgages, and under their terms he made a demand for the property, which was refused, and this action is replevin for its possession. The property was taken by virtue of the writ, and delivered to the plaintiff. The answer denies the right of plaintiff to the possession of the property, and shows that defendant is a jeweler and optician; that the stock of goods consists of watches, jewelry, rings, clocks and other articles; that in the stock taken under the writ were articles of the above description that were in the possession of defendant for the purpose of being altered, repaired, or changed in some form or another, and for the safety and return of which defendant was and is responsible. The answer further shows that the sheriff took, under the writ, three sets of jeweler scales, three bench stools, one Seth Thomas regulator, a bench lamp, and a Natshet trial case, not included in the mortgage or writ of replevin. The answer also shows that some of the articles so taken possessed peculiar value to the owners, being gifts; and that plaintiff is about to sell the property wrongfully taken; and asks an injunction to restrain the sale until the final hearing of the cause; and a temporary writ issued and was served. Plaintiff thereafter filed his reply, in which it appears that after the sheriff took possession of the goods the defendant, by agreement with plaintiff's attorney, went to the stock of goods, and identified and took all the articles belonging to other parties for repairs or storage, or afterwards sent orders for the same, so that but one watch remains which has not been called for. It further appears that some articles claimed to belong to others cannot be found in the stock, and that certain articles described in what appears in the records as Schedules A and B, being exhibits to the answer, have never been claimed as not being included in the mortgage, nor has demand been made therefor. It appears from the answer that defendant is the head of a family, and some of the articles claimed as not included in the mortgage are exempt from execution under the law. The reply admits that defendant is the head of a family, but denies that the articles are exempt from execution, and puts in issue the fact that such articles are not included in the mortgages, as well as others claimed not to be. Upon filing the reply the plaintiff moved the court to dissolve the temporary injunction. Affidavits were used on the hearing, and the court denied the motion, and from the ruling the plaintiff appealed. —*Affirmed.*

Ayers, Woodin & Ayers for appellant.

No appearance for appellee.

GRANGER, J.—I. The case is peculiar in some of its features. In such a case we should be favored with an argument from both parties. It is thought the injunction should have been dissolved on the face of the pleadings, because it should not have been granted; the reason being that defendant had a plain, speedy, and adequate remedy at law, there being a bond in the replevin suit giving ample security for any resulting damage. This is not an equity proceeding, in which that rule is so generally announced, but is a law action.

1   Conceding, for the purposes of the argument, that defendant is right in his claim that property has been taken and is being held by the plaintiff that is not included in

the mortgage, nor in the writ of replevin, and we meet one of
the peculiar features of the case, in this: that property is held
by plaintiff which he is about to sell, against which the writ
is not directed, and which plaintiff must hold as a trespasser.
Defendant asks for the return of such property and for damages. It is in the nature of a cross action. Section 3386,
Code 1873, provides that "in all cases of * * * injury,
where the party injured is entitled to maintain and has
brought an action by ordinary proceedings, he may in the
same cause pray and have a writ of injunction against the
repetition or continuance of such * * * injury," etc.
Aside from the above language, we know of no law to authorize the issuance of the injunction in this case. To authorize
the writ, the defendant must have been entitled to maintain,
and must have brought, an action by ordinary proceedings,
as a remedy for the injury in taking the property. Is what
defendant has pleaded, and in which he asks judgment, an
action by ordinary proceedings, within the meaning of the
statute? A counterclaim in an action of replevin is not
allowed. Code 1873, section 3226. But, in *McIntire v.
Eastman,* 76 Iowa, 455, we held in a replevin suit, and
when considering section 3226, that it did not prevent
defendant, from whom property had been taken on such a
writ, from asking for its return, and for damages for its
detention. After stating the provision of section 3226, it
is said, in that case: "But it is evident that it is not the
purpose of that section to prevent a recovery, by any party to
the action, of the property to which he is entitled, and damages for its detention." The case seems to recognize such
a proceeding as one for the recovery of property, and we think
it is so far an action as to come within the meaning of the
statute permitting an injunction in aid of the proceedings.
If such a ruling can be sustained, it would seem to be in
accord with the spirit of the statute. There is no attempt by
defendant to interfere with what is conceded to be property
mortgaged,—and what is not mortgaged plaintiff does not

claim,—but the issue is as to certain property being included in the mortgages. As a general rule, it would seem as if such a question ought to be settled in advance of a sale, and especially so where one is responsible for property of third parties, the sale of which might present difficult questions for adjustment. The reasoning in *McIntire v. Eastman, supra,* is that, in so far as it can well be done, one suit should determine the matter of title, right of possession, and matters that arise therefrom. Our view of the present question is in harmony with such a rule.

II. The issues of fact arising on the motion to dissolve the injunction were tried upon affidavits, and witnesses examined on the hearing. The mortgages describe the property pledged as follows: "All of my stock of goods, jewelry, silverware, glass, and queensware, of every kind and description, and all goods and merchandise now or hereafter in my store in the building and room known as '406 East Sixth (6th) Street,' in the city of Des Moines, Iowa, and all furniture and fixtures therein, including safes; said stock consisting of diamonds, watches, watch cases and movements, clocks, jewelry, optical goods, silverware, glass, and queensware, and decorated goods, and other articles of merchandise."

2   Much of the evidence taken is directed to questions of fact whether or not certain articles taken, such as jewelry scales, a regulator, bench stools, and bench lamp, come within the meaning of the words in the description, "all furniture and fixtures therein," or "other articles of merchandise," and whether certain articles in dispute are those with which a jeweler or optician habitually earns his living. The evidence includes that of experts, and it is much in conflict. Appellant thinks this proceeding

3   is an equitable one, so that we determine such facts anew; but we do not concur in that view. The hearing is upon a motion in a law action, and we know of no rule that changes the forum where such questions arise in a law action. There was no attempt to change the forum for the

purposes of the motion, but the hearing took place in the proceeding as it was instituted. The motion was to dissolve the injunction as a whole, and not as to any particular part of the property affected by it. We need not consider the case as to all the items of property involved, as, if the injunction should stand as to part, we cannot interfere, for no such question is presented, nor was it the duty of the court to sift out particular property to exempt it from the operation of the injunction when no such relief was asked. As we have said, the evidence as to whether certain articles of property constituted part of a stock of jewelry, etc., or was furniture or fixtures in a store like that conducted by defendant, and also whether certain articles were tools with which a jeweler or optician earned his living, is conflicting, and we do not disturb the finding of the court below under such circumstances. The law does not determine such questions, for, as appears in this case, experts differ as to the conclusion. The law makes no presumption as to what is proper furniture in a store, what is legitimately part of a stock of goods of a particular nature, nor what tools a particular artisan uses. Such questions are of fact when they arise. These conclusions are decisive of this case with us. The district court refused to disturb the injunction after a consideration of the facts. The order of the court is AFFIRMED.

GEORGE M. PARDOE, Appellant, v. THE IOWA STATE NATIONAL BANK.

Usury: NATIONAL BANKS. A trustee who gave his individual note
3   to a bank to obtain money to purchase a mortgage on trust property for its protection, which instrument he assigned to the bank as security, cannot maintain an action under United States Revised Statutes, section 5198, to recover back usurious interest exacted, since it was not paid by him within the meaning of the statute, although he advanced sums for that purpose for which the heirs repaid him.

SAME. A note, the amount of which is computed in the amount
1   loaned together with a sum illegally added thereto as usurious

2   interest and which bears interest at the highest lawful rate is
    usurious, and the interest wrongfully exacted may be recovered
    where the note was paid in full.

RENEWALS.   The payment of usurious interest upon a note taints all
1-2 the subsequent notes given in renewal of it with usury.

ASSIGNMENT.   The right conferred by the United States Revised
4   Statutes section 5198, upon a debtor from whom usurious interest
    has been exacted by a national bank, or his legal representatives,
    to recover back twice the amount is personal and cannot be trans-
    ferred by an ordinary sale or assignment.

Appeal from Woodbury District Court.—HON. SCOTT M.
LADD, Judge.

FRIDAY, OCTOBER 14, 1898.

ACTION at law to recover for money alleged to have been
paid as usurious interest. There was a trial by the court without a jury, and a judgment for the plaintiff, from which he
appeals.—*Affirmed.*

Geo. M. Pardoe, pro se.

Swan, Lawrence & Swan for appellee.

ROBINSON, J.—I.   The defendant is an association duly
organized and doing business under and by virtue of the laws
of the United States which relate to national banks.   On
the first day of August, 1892, it loaned to the plaintiff two
thousand nine hundred and twenty-two dollars and fifty cents,
and received therefor his promissory note for three thousand dollars, payable ninety days after its date, without interest before maturity.   The difference between the face of the
note and the amount of money paid to the plaintiff, or seventy-
seven dollars and fifty cents, was retained as interest on the
loan, making the rate charged a little more than ten per cent.
per annum.   At that time the laws of this state did not
authorize contracts for a higher rate of interest than eight
per cent. per annum.   Six days later a payment of five hundred dollars was made on the note.   On the second day of

November, 1892, the plaintiff renewed the note by giving a new one for two thousand five hundred dollars; payable ninety days after its date, without interest before maturity, and paid thereon as interest an allowance of seven dollars and sixty-nine cents for interest on the payment made on the first note before it became due, and in addition forty-two dollars and thirty-one cents in money. On the thirty-first day of January, 1893, the second note was renewed, as the first one had been, and on the same terms, including the payment of fifty dollars as interest. That note was not paid, and judgment has been rendered thereon against the plaintiff. The amount of the judgment is alleged by the defendant to be two thousand and thirty-nine dollars and thirty cents, with interest thereon from the nineteenth day of April, 1894, at the rate of eight per cent. per annum, but formal proof as to the amount has not been made. It is not disputed that the note first given was usurious, and the plaintiff contends that the renewal notes were tainted with usury, and that in consequence he is entitled to recover on account of interest paid on the first renewal note the sum of eighty-four dollars and sixty-two cents, and on account of the second renewal note the sum of one hundred dollars, or double the amount of usurious interest alleged to have been paid. That view seems to have been adopted by the trial court, as it rendered judgment in favor of the plaintiff for one hundred and eighty-four dollars and sixty-two cents, with interest thereon from the commencement of this action, although the judgment does not specify the notes on which it was rendered. As it appears to be conceded that the appellant's recovery was wholly on account of the notes we have described, and since he does not claim to be entitled to anything more than the court awarded him, this branch of the case will not be further considered.

II. On the twenty-ninth day of April, 1892, the plaintiff made to the defendant his promissory note for the sum of four thousand two hundred and seventy dollars, payable without interest ninety days after its date. He received for it four thousand one hundred and sixty-four dollars and six cents; the difference between that sum and the face of the note having been retained as discount or interest, at the rate of ten per cent. per annum. When the note became due, August 1, 1892, it was renewed by the giving of a new note for the same amount, and the payment of eighty-five dollars and forty cents as interest thereon. That note did not bear interest, and was payable ninety days after its date. A similar renewal note was given October 30, 1892, when one hundred and ten dollars were paid as interest; and another renewal note was given on the thirty-first day of January, 1893, at which time one hundred and ten dollars were paid as interest. Payments were made on that note as follows: On the fourth day of May, 1893, eighty dollars; on the thirty-first day of May, 1893, one thousand dollars, and interest thereon at the rate of ten per cent. per annum for ninety days; on the twenty-fifth day of August, 1893, eighty dollars; on the third day of November, 1893, three thousand two hundred and sixty dollars and thirty-four cents, as the remainder due on the note. The plaintiff claims that the payment 2   of usurious interest on the first note for four thousand two hundred and seventy dollars, tainted all the subsequent notes with usury, and that he is entitled to recover double the amount of usurious interest paid thereon, or the aggregate amount of one thousand three hundred and eight dollars and sixty cents, with interest thereon from the commencement of this action. Section 5197 of the Revised Statutes of the United States permits any national bank to charge and receive interest at the rate allowed by the laws of the state where it is located; and section 5198 provides that the charging and receiving of a rate "greater than that allowed by the preceding section, when knowingly done, shall be deemed a forfeiture of the entire interest which the note, bill, or other evidence of debt carries with it, or which has been agreed to be paid thereon." It further provides that, "in case the greater rate of interest has been paid, the person by whom it has been paid or his legal representatives, may recover back, in an action in the nature of an action of debt, twice the amount of interest thus paid, from the association taking or receiving the same; provided such action is commenced within two years from the time the usurious transactions occurred." The first note, for four thousand two hundred and seventy dollars, was usurious, and the usury was carried into the renewal note. *Brown v. Bank,* 18 Sup. Ct. Rep. 390. All of the payments made, excepting the one for one thousand dollars, and the one for three thousand two hundred and sixty dollars and thirty-four cents were, by the agreement of parties, applied to the payment of interest; and all were at usurious rates, excepting the one made August 1, 1892, and that was usurious, because it was nominally at the highest lawful rate, and was computed on the amount loaned, and also on one hundred and five dollars illegally added thereto as usurious interest. *Bank v. Eyre,* 52 Iowa, 114. This does not appear to be denied, but it is said that full payment of the note is not shown, and that until the full amount due is paid, or is placed in judgment, the right to recover usury paid does not exist. The claim that the last note has not been paid is, however, based upon a misapprehension of the record. That shows without dispute that the note is fully paid.

III. The further claim is made that the plaintiff is not entitled to recover because the notes he gave were not on his own account, and the payments he made thereon were not with his own money. It appears that on the fourteenth day of December, 1888, the plaintiff was appointed trustee for one Matthew Gaughran, and about that time all of the estate of said Gaughran, including both real and personal property, was transferred to the plaintiff, as trustee, to hold and manage so long as Gaughran should live. He died on the twenty-third day of April, 1892, leaving a son and a daughter as his only heirs; and the plaintiff became the administrator of his estate. He was discharged as administrator about the first day of January, 1894. The original note for four thousand two hundred and seventy dollars was given for the purpose of obtaining a mortgage which had been executed on the trust property by the plaintiff, as trustee, and by Gaughran. The mortgage,—and that term, as used in the record, we understand to include the mortgage debt as well as the security,—was assigned to an officer of the defendant to be held as collateral security for the payment of the note for four thousand two hundred and seventy dollars which the plaintiff then gave. The purpose of the transaction was to protect the Gaughran estate, and all that the plaintiff did was done to accomplish that end. The assignment of the mortgage not only secured the defendant, but doubtless was beneficial to the plaintiff also, in preserving a lien upon the estate to secure the debt which he assumed by giving his note. That note and the renewals thereof were signed by him individually, and not as trustee or administrator, but as between himself and the estate of Gaughran he was at all times a surety only. He made some of the payments of interest from his own funds, but the sums so paid were refunded to him from the estate, and the payments of one thousand dollars and three thousand two hundred and sixty dollars and thirty-four cents were with money furnished by the heirs of the decedent. As the plaintiff was not the principal debtor, and as the small amount of money he paid as interest was on account of the heirs, and was refunded to him, his acts were virtually those of an agent; and the interest in controversy was not paid by him, within the meaning of section 5198 of the Revised Statutes of the United States. That was designed for the benefit of the person who, being liable on the note or other obligation, pays the money for himself, and not for one who pays it merely as the agent of another. See *First Bank of Concorda v. Rawley*, 52 Kan. Sup. 394 (34 Pac. Rep. 1049). Had the plaintiff furnished the money which he paid, and had it not been refunded to him, a different question would have been presented, even though he was only surety; but the small amount he did furnish was merely advanced on account of the estate, and was refunded from it. We conclude that he is not entitled to recover in his own right.

IV.   It appears that, after the plaintiff was discharged as administrator, the heirs of Gaughran, as heirs, assigned him all right of action against the defendant to recover for usurious interest paid to it by the plaintiff, as trustee, 4 or by the heirs. It is claimed, although not with much apparent confidence, that the plaintiff is entitled to recover by reason of that assignment. In an action brought to enforce the penal provision of the statute, it must be construed strictly. *Tiffany v. Bank,* 18 Wall. 409. The statute authorizes a recovery of twice the amount of illegal interest paid by "the person by whom it has been paid, or his legal representatives," and that remedy is exclusive. *Barnet v. Bank,* 98 U. S. 555. The term "legal representative" ordinarily means executors and administrators, although it may be used in a different sense, and shown by the connection in which it is used to have a different meaning. *Lodge v. Weld,* 139 Mass. 504 (2 N. E. Rep. 95); *People v. Phelps,* 78 Ill. 149; *Bowman v. Long,* 89 Ill. 21; *Loos v. Insurance Co.,* 41 Mo. 538. In the case of *Osborn v. Bank,* 175 Pa. St. 494 (34 Atl. Rep. 858), it was held that the term, in the absence of anything to show that it is used in a different sense, means executors and administrators; and the right of an assignee, for the benefit of creditors to recover the statutory penalty was denied, although it has been held by some courts that an assignee in bankruptcy is a legal representative, within the meaning of the statute. It is well settled that a defense based upon usury is personal to the debtor, and cannot be maintained by a stranger to the contract. *Carmichael v. Bodfish,* 32 Iowa, 418; *Miller v. Clarke,* 37 Iowa, 325; *Insurance Co. v. Olmstead,* 52 Iowa, 354. In view of the language of the statute, and the general policy of the law to make personal to the debtor the right to take advantage of usury, we are of the opinion that the statute under consideration does not give to a debtor who had paid usurious interest the right to transfer his claim therefor by an ordinary sale or assignment of his right, and that the plaintiff did not acquire any right, as against the defendant, by the assignment which the heirs of Gaughran made to him. We conclude that, so far as the judgment of the district court is questioned on this appeal, it is right, and it is therefore AFFIRMED.

LADD, J., took no part.

S. D. PHILBRICK, *et al.*, Appellants, v. THE TOWN OF UNIVERSITY PLACE, *et al.*

Dedication: EVIDENCE. Though the board of supervisors has no jurisdiction to locate a street in an incorporated town, yet, in an action against the town for injury to land included in a highway
2 thus located, it may be shown, on the question of dedication, that plaintiff acquiesced in its being so used, that the highway was laid out at his instance and with his approval, and a record of the board showing that he filed a petition with it, asking for the location of a public highway on said land, is admissible on whether plaintiff intended to dedicate such land to the public use.

ABSENCE OF RULING. Where there is no ruling on objections to evi-
4 dence, errors relating thereto cannot be considered on appeal.

INSTRUCTIONS: *Presumptions.* An instruction will be presumed
3 proper where all the evidence is not preserved in the bill of exceptions, if the evidence might have been such as to warrant such an instruction.

Refusal of. Where instructions asked for are included in others
4 already given, it is not error to refuse them.

EVIDENCE: *Bill of exceptions.* Errors assigned may be considered on appeal although the bill of exceptions does not purport to con-
1 tain all of the evidence, where that included is identified by the judge as having been introduced at the trial.

Appeal: RECORD: *Judge and reporter.* Evidence taken down in
1 shorthand, after being transcribed, may, when duly certified by the trial judge, become a part of the record without the certificate of the official reporter.

Appeal from Polk District Court.—HON. C. P. HOLMES, Judge.

FRIDAY, OCTOBER 14, 1898.

ACTION for recovery of damages occasioned by the destruction of a hedge fence growing on land alleged to belong to the plaintiffs, but which, according to the answer of the defendants, had been dedicated to the public use as a highway. Trial to jury; verdict and judgment for the defendants; and plaintiffs appeal. The death of Mary A. Philbrick having been suggested, her administrators have been substituted as parties plaintiff in this court.—*Affirmed.*

Day & Corry for appellants.

J. K. Macomber for appellees.

LADD, J.—Our conclusion in *Deitz v. Capitol City B. & P. Co.,* 103 Iowa, 542, made a re-hearing in this case necessary, It was there held that evidence taken down in shorthand, after being transcribed, may, when duly certified by the trial
1   judge, become a part of the record without the certificate of the official reporter. While the bill of exceptions does not purport to contain all the evidence, that included is identified by the judge as having been introduced at the trial. The errors assigned, then, may be considered.

II.   The parcel of land, containing ten and five-tenths acres, belonging to the plaintiffs, is twenty-four rods wide on the south, and between it and the section line is a strip twenty-five feet wide, in the name of one Turner. North street is along the section line, includes this strip, and, as will be noticed, with the eight feet from the south end of the plaintiff's land, would be a highway of the usual width. The defense was that this strip of eight feet along the south end of plaintiff's land had been dedicated to the public use. A hedge which had been growing on it for twenty-five years was cut down and destroyed by the officers of the incorporated town of University Place. The right to recover damages, then, depends on whether this strip eight feet wide had been dedicated by plaintiffs and accepted by the public. In 1884, S. D. Philbrick, then owner, and others, petitioned the board of

supervisors for the location of a highway where North street
is, and which would include the land in controversy.

2   As this proposed street was situated in the limits of an
incorporated town, the board was without jurisdiction.
Gallaher v. Head, 72 Iowa, 173. We need not inquire, then,
whether the signature of Turner might have been dispensed
with because of an earlier dedication by him.

In the second instruction, after advising the jury concerning the law of dedication, the court told them that they
might consider the filing of this petition in connection with
the other evidence in determining whether Philbrick intended
to dedicate this land to the public use, and whether by signing
it he so intended. Exception is taken to this instruction, and
it is urged that he is presumed to have signed the petition
upon the consideration that all the other property owners
would do likewise, and because it permits the jury to construe the petition. But it is well settled that no particular
form is necessary for the dedication of land for a highway.
The vital question as against the owners is always whether
the *animus dedicandi* may be inferred from the facts proven.
Philbrick will be presumed to have acted for some purpose in
signing and presenting this petition to the board of supervisors. If that board had any jurisdiction over the street, it
might do to say that he signed in consideration of all other
property holders to be affected doing likewise. But, as appellants contend, he is presumed to know the law, and that whatever the board might do would be of no validity. What the
circumstances were in connection with the signing of the petition, its presentation, or the order by the board establishing
the road, is not disclosed by the record, as all the evidence is not
before us. If, immediately after the highway was petitioned
for and ordered, it was used by the public, and acquiesced in
by Philbrick and others, the natural inference to be drawn
would be that the parties had adopted their own method of
establishing the street; i. e. that of dedication. In other
words, the circumstances connected with the signing and presentation of this petition may have been such as to warrant

the conclusion that in doing so he intended to yield the eight-foot strip of land for the public use.

III.   In the fourth paragraph of the charge the jury are told the record of the board establishing the highway cannot be considered as showing a legal highway, but that "it was admitted in evidence as a matter of history, and as possibly throwing some light on the question whether or not S. D. Philbrick dedicated eight feet of the south side of his land to the public use as a street or highway." The consideration to be given this record necessarily depends upon the evidence adduced. If made at the instance and with the approval of Philbrick, it was not only important as a part of the history of the transaction, but might well be deemed to have some bearing on his purpose in signing and presenting the petition. In such event it became one of the circumstances to be considered in determining his intention in what he did.

3   Error must affirmatively appear; and, if the evidence might have been such as to warrant giving an instruction, the presumption will be indulged in favor of the action of the court.

IV.   The petition referred to was received in evidence without objection, and, though the record of the order establishing the road was objected to, there was no ruling. It is

4   needless to say that the errors relating to the introduction of this evidence, though earnestly argued, not being based on any ruling, require no attention. Other assignments relate to the refusal of instructions asked by appellants. These are stated rather than argued. The instructions asked, in so far as correct, are included in those given. The judgment will be AFFIRMED.

PETER WERNER, Appellant, v. MARY DOLAN, et al., Appellees.
HUGH REILLY, Appellant, v. Same Defendants.

Mortgages: LIFE ESTATE: *Remainders.* The interest of the remaindermen in real property, under a recorded conveyance, cannot be

defeated by the action of the life tenant in suffering a mortgage
upon the property to be foreclosed through her fault and conveying the property to third persons [after receiving a quitclaim
deed from the purchaser at the judicial sale.

RULE APPIED. Husband and wife executed a mortgage on his land
to secure a note executed by both. Afterwards the husband conveyed a life estate in the land to his wife, with the fee to his
children. Thereafter mortgagee foreclosed in an action to which
the children were not made parties, and the foreclosure purchaser
quitclaimed to the wife, who, together with the husband, conveyed to plaintiffs. *Held*, that since the wife, though a life tenant,
was charged by her execution of the note with the payment thereof, she simply became reinvested by the quitclaim deed with her
life estate with the fee in her children, devested of the incumbrance, and hence plaintiffs stand in her shoes as to the children.

Appeal from Dubuque District Court.—HON. J. L. HUSTED,
Judge.

FRIDAY, OCTOBER 14, 1898.

ACTIONS to quiet title. These two cases involve the
same question. They were tried together below, and are submitted here upon one record. The trial court entered a decree
for the defendants, and from this action plaintiffs appeal.—
Affirmed.

Longueville & McCarthy for appellants.

William Graham for appellees.

WATERMAN, J.—The facts are not in dispute. They consist entirely of matters of record. It appears that one John J.
Dolan, being the owner in fee of lots 1 and 2 of the northwest quarter of section 31, township 88 north, range 3, in
Dubuque county, together with his wife, executed a mortgage
thereon to one William G. Watters. This instrument bore
date May 29, 1888, and was properly recorded June 9, 1888.
Thereafter, on December 6, 1888, Dolan executed an instrument, which the parties hereto concede was a conveyance,
vesting a life estate in said property in his wife, and the fee

thereof in his children. This instrument was recorded on the day of its date. The Watters mortgage was assigned to one Le Clere, and at the September term, 1889, of the Dubuque district court, an action was begun to foreclose it. John J. and Mary Dolan, his wife, were the sole defendants in the proceeding. In due time a decree of foreclosure was entered, and the land sold. Under this sale a sheriff's deed was made to one T. O. Sullivan on December 23, 1890, and this was properly recorded three days later. December 27, 1890, Sullivan quitclaimed the land to Mary, the wife of John J. Dolan, and thereafter Mary Dolan and husband conveyed by warranty deed to one Kemler and one Hosford jointly. From these last-named grantees the plaintiffs acquired the respective titles which they assert in this action. The defendants here are the children of John J. and Mary Dolan. Their answer, in effect, denies plaintiff's title, and sets up a life estate in Mary Dolan, with the remainder in themselves. It is manifest that Mary Dolan, the mother, parted with any interest she had in the land by her conveyance to Kemler and Hosford. We have, then, to consider only whether plaintiffs are entitled to any relief as against the children, who held title in remainder. It appears that the Watters note was signed by both John J. and Mary Dolan. Each was equally bound for its payment. Ordinarily a life tenant is under no legal obligation to pay the principal of a prior incumbrance, but is charged only with keeping down interest. *Trego v. Studley,* 106 Iowa, post. But this case, by its facts, is taken out of that rule. The tenant for life, in this instance, is charged, by her contract, with the payment of both principal and interest. So far as disclosed by the record, the foreclosure of the Watters mortgage was caused by the default of the life tenant. It needs no citation of authorities to show that she could acquire no rights as against the remainder-men through her own breach of faith. It is a principle so well established as to have become crystallized into a maxim of the law that one can derive no advantage from his own wrong. When

Mary Dolan, by her purchase from Sullivan, acquired title, it inured to the benefit of those entitled in remainder. The plaintiffs, claiming, as they do, through Mary Dolan, have no greater right than she had. The decree of the district court is AFFIRMED.

Letitia Conway, Appellant v. J. Nichols, Atlantic National Bank, James E. Woodall, and H. A. Briggs.

Homesteads: ABANDONMENT. A homestead will be deemed abandoned where the owner removed therefrom with the intention of selling it, as he expected to do, although he intended to return to it if he could not make a sale.

Evidence: QUIETING TITLE. The burden is upon plaintiff in a suit to quiet title to land against the apparent lien of a judgment against his grantor, which the latter at one time occupied as a homestead to overcome the presumption of the latter's abandonment of the homestead arising from his removal therefrom before the sale and his making a new home and voting at a new place.

Appeal from Cass District Court.—Hon. W. R. Green, Judge.

Friday, October 14, 1898.

Suit in equity to quiet plaintiff's title to certain lands in Cass county against the apparent liens of four judgments rendered in favor of defendants and against one Davis, through whom plaintiff obtained title. It is claimed that at the time Davis conveyed the land it was his homestead, and not subject to the lien of the judgments. Defendants pleaded in defense that Davis abandoned the homestead before he sold the land, and that the lien of their judgments attached prior to the conveyance. The trial court dismissed the plaintiff's petition as to all defendants except Briggs, and plaintiff and defendant Briggs appeal. As Briggs has filed no argument, his appeal will not be considered.—*Affirmed.*

Delano & Meredith for appellant.

Curtis & Follett, H. M. Boorman, and *G. M. Lyon* for appellees.

DEEMER, C. J.—The real estate in question was used and occupied by Davis as a homestead until March 1, 1891. On this last-named date he leased the premises for the period of one year, and moved into the city of Atlantic. Appellees' judgments were obtained in the years 1889 and 1890. In October of the year 1891 Davis entered into a contract for the sale of the land to one Conrad, which was consummated in March of the year 1892. Thereafter Conrad sold the land to appellant, and she brought this suit to quiet her title thereto. It is conceded that the land was originally the homestead of Davis, and the only question in the case is whether or not he abandoned it before the sale to Conrad. The evidence shows that he rented the farm because his son was sick, and unable to look after the place upon which he (the son) was then living; and that after Davis' removal to Atlantic he assisted this son in the management and care of his (the son's) farm. He left a wagon upon the leased premises and did not sell it, or his farming implements and stock, until after the sale to Conrad. He saved grain grown upon his son's land with which to seed his own land the following spring, and did not dispose of it until after he made the contract for the sale of his farm; and he also arranged for timothy seed to sow upon his land in the spring of 1892. His contract with Conrad was made October 20, 1891, and Conrad at that time turned over a team of mules, a wagon, and harness to apply upon the purchase price. Davis registered as a voter in the city of Atlantic on the thirty-first day of October, 1891, and voted in said city at the following November election; and also voted in the same place at the next spring election. Shortly after renting his farm, he moved all his stock to the farm occupied by his son. As Davis removed from the homestead in March, 1891, and thereafter made his home in Atlantic, and voted in that place at the November election, the presumption arises that he intended to abandon his home-stead, and the burden is on plaintiff to show that, not-withstanding this apparent abandonment, he (Davis) left his farm temporarily, and with the definite and settled purpose of returning thereto and continuing it as his home. *Newman v. Franklin,* 69 Iowa, 244; *Maguire v. Hanson,* 105 Iowa, 215. Davis says: "I wanted to sell the place, and if I did not sell it, then I intended to go back there. * * * My intention all the time was to go back if I did not sell. I expected to sell it, but would go back if I did not sell it." "At the time of the sale to Conrad my family was living in town, and this was my home. I regarded this as my resi-dence and home then. * * * When I registered in October, 1891, I intended to go back on the place if I did not sell it, but I did not then claim my home on the farm, as I was out of my township then." The evidence further shows that Davis began his efforts to dispose of the farm within a few weeks after he moved to Atlantic, and finally made the contract with Conrad. It seems to us that these facts bring the case within the rule announced in *Kimball v. Wilson,* 59 Iowa, 638, wherein it is held that a removal from the homestead with the intention to return if the owner could not make a living at some other business, which contingency he intended to avoid, constitutes an abandonment. In that case the debtor said he intended to go back to the farm if he "could not make a living here" in the practice of his profession as a lawyer. In this case Davis says: "My intention was to go back if I did not sell. I expected to sell, but would go back if I did not sell." In each case there was an intention to abandon, qualified by a contingency. And the contingency was one which the debtor intended to avoid. See, also, *Cotton v. Hamil,* 58 Iowa, 594; *Maguire v. Hanson, supra.* We think Davis' removal constituted an abandonment of the homestead, and that the lien of appellant's judgments attached before the sale to Conrad.—AFFIRMED.

DANIEL H. TALBOT, Appellant, v. FIRST NATIONAL BANK OF
SIOUX CITY, IOWA.

Usury: NATIONAL BANKS: *Custom.* Under the laws of Iowa limiting
interest to six per cent. per annum in the absence of an agreement
for a higher rate, the charging of ten per cent. upon a depositor's
overdraft, arrived at by balancing the account monthly computed on the aggregate amount of the overdraft approximating
1 the nearest hundred for the month, on the basis of thirty days to
the month, is usury under the United States Revised statutes, 5197
which authorizes national banks to charge interest at the rate
allowed by the state in which such banks are located, and the said
charge of ten per cent. cannot be legalized by a custom of banks
which permits it.

RECOVERY BACK: *Limitation of statute.* A national bank charged
usurious interest. It was included in a note which was not otherwise tainted with usury. This note was secured by trust deed,
1 and on foreclosure of the deed the said excessive interest was
deducted by the decree. *Held,*

a The action provided by United States Revised Statute 5198,
2 allowing the recovery back of usurious interest applies only to
cases in which such interest has been actually paid. In this
case this was not done, for as said interest was left out of the
judgment, no property could have been sold under it to pay
what was not in the judgment.

b This action having been begun more than two years after said
8 note was given is barred by United States Revised Statute 5198
which allows it within two years "from the time the usurious
transaction occurred."

Appeal: RECORD BELOW. Only such matters as were presented on the
4 trial can be considered on appeal; and a motion, before submission, to have any other passed upon, will be denied.

Appeal from Woodbury District Court.—HON. SCOTT M.
LADD, Judge.

SATURDAY, OCTOBER 15, 1898.

PLAINTIFF brings this action under section 5198 of the
United States Revised Statutes to recover forty-seven thousand and twenty dollars and thirty-seven cents illegal

interest alleged to have been knowingly charged to him by the defendant, and to have been paid by him to the defendant without knowledge of such illegal charges. He also asks to recover the penalty provided in said section, demanding in all the sum of ninety-four thousand and forty dollars and seventy-four cents. The defendant answered, denying that it had charged, or that plaintiff paid, any illegal interest to the defendant, and alleging a -former adjudication, and that this action is barred by the statute under which it is brought. The case was referred to L. B. Green, Esq., who, after a full hearing, reported his findings of facts and conclusions of law. To these the plaintiff filed exceptions, and upon a hearing on the exceptions the report of the referee was approved, and judgment rendered dismissing plaintiff's petition, and for costs; from which judgment plaintiff appeals.—*Affirmed*.

D. H. Talbot in pro per.

Wright, Call & Hubbard for appellee.

GIVEN, J.—I.   Plaintiff presents this case in three hundred and fifty pages of abstract and an opening argument of one hundred and twenty-five pages, to which argument the defendant has responded in twelve pages. Plaintiff's substituted petition, as abstracted, covers one hundred and ninety-four pages, and the entire pleading one hundred and ten pages. We will not set out the details of this elaborate record, but proceed to consider questions raised by the exceptions to the report, namely, whether illegal interest was charged, and, if charged, whether it was paid, and the defenses of former adjudication, and bar of the statute.

II.   Section 5197 of the Revised Statutes of the United States authorizes national banks to charge "interest at the rate allowed by the laws of the state, territory or district where the bank is located." Section 5198 of said 1   statute provides as follows: "Sec. 5198. The taking, receiving, or charging a rate of interest greater than is allowed by the preceding section, when knowingly done, shall be deemed a forfeiture of the entire interest, which the note, bill, or other evidence of debt carries with it, or which has been agreed to be paid thereon.   In case the greater rate of interest has been paid, the person by whom it has been paid, or his legal representatives may recover back, in an action in the nature of an action of debt, twice the amount of the interest thus paid from the association taking or receiving the same: provided such action is commenced within two years from the time the usurious transaction occurred."   The evidence shows, and the referee found, that monthly during the period of these transactions plaintiff's account was balanced, and the interest computed on the overdraft at the rate of ten per cent. per annum, and the interest so charged added to the account.   Also that in computing said interest the defendant took the aggregate amount of overdraft approximating to the nearest hundred for the month on the basis of thirty days to the month, or three hundred and sixty days to the year.   Under the laws of Iowa, the plaintiff was only entitled, in the absence of contract, to charge interest at the rate of six per cent. per annum, and there is no evidence that these charges were made in pursuance of any contract. Defendant's counsel make some claim that the written contract of June 17, 1890, warranted this charge of interest; but we do not think so, nor do we think that the charge can be legalized by a custom of the banks as to the manner of computing interest, where the custom results in giving a higher rate of interest than is authorized by law.   The interest thus computed on the overdrafts was included in the notes given by the plaintiff from time to time, but the notes themselves did not otherwise draw illegal interest.   The referee correctly finds that the total interest on plaintiff's overdrafts amounts to two thousand and sixty-four dollars, that the average rate of interest charged was ten and twenty-two-hundredths per cent., and that the total amount of interest charged in excess of ten per cent. was seventy-two dollars.   We think it entirely

clear, under the evidence, that all interest charged on overdrafts in excess of six per cent. was a greater rate of interest
than was allowed by the laws of this state.

III. It will be observed that this is not an action to
forfeit the entire interest, under the first provision of said
section 5198, but an action to recover back said interest as
having been paid. In determining whether said interest has
been paid, and whether this matter has been formerly
adjudicated, the following facts appearing in the evidence must be considered: On the fifteenth day of
March, 1890, the plaintiff executed his one hundred negotiable
bonds, payable to the Union Loan & Trust Company, or bearer,
for one thousand dollars each, secured by a trust deed to said
company, as trustee, on lands in Woodbury and Plymouth
counties, Iowa. On June 17, 1890, he entered into a written
agreement with the defendant, reciting that the defendant
had that day canceled and surrendered to plaintiff the promissory notes enumerated, aggregating sixty-four thousand
and forty dollars and thirty-eight cents; also that the bank
had received· from plaintiff said one hundred bonds; and
that it was agreed that the bank and T. J. Stone should have
and own sixty-one of said bonds, to be applied on the indebtedness surrendered. It was further agreed that the balance
of said bonds should be sold by the defendant at not less than
the face, and the proceeds applied towards paying liens and
incumbrances upon the land prior to said trust deed. That
said instrument shows that: "To balance account to March
15, 1890, I have this day given the First National Bank
note six months after date, with option on or before, for the
sum of $3,040.30. June 17, 1890. [Signed] D. H. Talbot."
In March, 1892, the Union Loan & Trust Company, as
trustee, for this defendant and T. J. Stone, its president,
commenced an action against this plaintiff for judgment on
said sixty-one bonds, and to foreclose said trust deed. This
plaintiff answered in said action, setting up said illegal
charges of interest on overdrafts, and alleging that said

interest had been included in the notes afterwards given, and
that said notes were merged in the bonds in suit, and asking
that an accounting be had of the amount of excessive interest
charged, and that the amount so found be deducted from the
amount due on the bonds.   In support of this defense he
introduced evidence of the amount of interest charged on
overdrafts, and in the determination of the case the court
found that excessive interest on overdrafts to the amount
of two thousand and sixty-four dollars had been charged the
plaintiff, and ordered that that amount, with interest at the
rate named in the bonds, amounting in all to two thousand
and sixty-nine dollars and forty-six cents, be deducted from
the amount due on the bonds, and judgment and decree were
entered accordingly.   Thereafter the lands covered by the
trust deed were sold under said decree for eighty-seven thousand six hundred and ninety-nine dollars and fifteen cents,
leaving a balance of eleven thousand one hundred and forty-
one dollars and five cents unpaid on said judgment.   We have
seen that, unless the plaintiff has paid the illegal interest, he
is not entitled to recover it in this action.   If it may be said
that the delivery of the sixty-one bonds on June 17, 1890,
was a payment, this action is barred, as it was not commenced
"within two years from the time the usurious transactions
occurred," having been commenced March 8, 1895.   The
interest on overdrafts was surely not paid by the sale of the
land, for, as we have seen, it was not included in the decree.
As we view the case, we think the illegal charges of interest
have never been paid, and therefore the plaintiff is not
entitled to recover in this action.

   IV.   There is some dispute as to whether plaintiff set
up these charges of illegal interest in the action to foreclose
the trust deed, so as to constitute a former adjudication.
That he set it up, and that it was adjudicated, we have no
doubt.   True, it was not set up with the same fullness and
elaboration as in this case.   Unquestionably it is matter which
might have been pleaded in that case, and under a familiar

rule the plaintiff must be held to have asserted all available defenses to that action.

V.   Said section 5198 provides that actions to recover back illegal interest paid must be commenced "within two years from the time the usurious transaction occurred." Now, whether or not we call the delivery of the bonds a payment, it is evident that the usurious transaction occurred on and before June 17, 1890, and it follows that this action is barred.

3   These questions are so largely questions of fact, and rest upon familiar and undisputed principles of law, that we do not find it necessary to refer to any of the many authorities cited. The lower court was fully warranted in affirming the finding of fact as reported by the referee. While we do not concur in the conclusions of law that the interest on overdrafts was excessive, but not illegal or usurious, and that the custom of banks to compute interest on the commercial basis of thirty days to the month is legal, still it does not follow that the judgment of the district court is erroneous. It is correct, notwithstanding the charge of illegal interest, because the plaintiff has never paid that interest, but has been allowed the full benefit of the facts in the foreclosure case, and because this action was not brought within two years of the time the usurious transaction occurred.

VI.   A few days before the submission of this cause the plaintiff filed a motion to have certain matters not presented on the trial below considered. He presents the affidavit of L. F. Wakefield, showing his estimate of the value of the land covered by the trust deed, made at the instance of the defendant in February, 1894. He also presents his
4   own affidavit touching the disposition made by him of certain mineral specimens, bird skins, reptiles, mammals, skins, books in library, public letter correspondence, and all other natural history specimens in his possession, to the State University of Iowa. It is sufficient to say of this motion that only matters that were offered on the trial below can be considered on this appeal, and that the motion to have these matters considered must be overruled.—AFFIRMED.

LADD, J., took no part.

THOMPSON & SON v. W. H. BROWN and SUSANNAH BROWN, Appellants.

|105
,116
,116

]
1

Contract: BREACH: *Right of party not in fault.* One who hired another to drill a well in the vicinity of the house, which after being sunk to a considerable depth was of necessity abandoned by reason of a drill breaking in the well, after which he refused to
5　permit the contractor to begin a new well, cannot evade liability in an action for breach of the contract, on the ground that he offered to let a well be sunk upon a distant part of the farm; especially where a new agreement as well as a new site were demanded by defendant.

SAME. The contractor had the right to start a new well when so compelled without fault to abandon the first one, since ordinary risks
7　incidental to the work must be held to have been within the contemplation of the parties; and this though the landowner might under the contract, be compelled thus to board the workmen and teams, indefinitely.

SAME. A defendant who refused to permit the plaintiff to start a new well on his premises after a drill broke, which necessitated an
8　abandonment of the first location, cannot, in an action to recover
9　damages for breach of contract, deny the plaintiff's right to recover because he agreed to furnish a well and did not or because the work done was of no benefit to defendant.

JUSTIFICATION FOR. The use of profane and insulting language is no
6　excuse for a refusal to permit one to carry out a contract, where the conduct of the other party tended strongly to provoke an outburst of wrath.

DAMAGES. In an action to recover damages for defendant's refusal to permit the plaintiff to drill a new well on his premises, after the first location was necessarily abandoned on account of a broken
8　drill which could not be extracted, the plaintiff is entitled to recover such damages as would fully compensate him for labor done, and loss of time and material, where the contract price was to be computed by the depth of the well and was therefore uncertain.

ACTION: *Joint liability.* A wife who owned a farm and was present at the negotiations which led up to a contract with the plaintiffs
4　for the drilling of a well on the premises is a proper party defendant in an action for breach of the contract, where the agreement was drawn and signed in her presence and both she and her husband orally promised to give their joint note for the cost of the well.

CONTRACT AND QUANTUM MERUIT: *Pleading.* One prevented from the completing of a contract for the drilling of a well who sets
10   out his contract as a recital of fact and seeks to recover the reasonable value of work done and material furnished instead of the contract price, does not sue upon the contract but upon a *quantum meruit.*

Pleading: AMENDMENT: *Verification.* Under Code 1873, section 2680, authorizing courts to permit amendments without verification which do not inject a new and distinct cause of action, an unver-
2   ified amendment may be permitted, which alleges that a contract to drill a well was made for the benefit of one defendant, and that she knew 'it was being drilled on her land, where the petition alleged that she had agreed to pay for the work; and this, though both petition and answer are verified.

SURPRISE. A party cannot complain of surprise because the court
2   permitted an amendment to the petition to be filed on the day of trial, when it contained nothing of which evidence might not have been given under the original petition.

Appeal: SPECIAL INTERROGATORIES. An appellant cannot complain that special interrogatories presented by him were not submitted
12   to the jury where none of them called for ultimate facts, and where if answered in his favor they would have not controlled the general verdict.

ARGUMENT ON ASSIGNMENT. Errors not assigned will not be con-
8   sidered.

INSTRUCTIONS REFUSED. Error cannot be predicated upon the refusal
11   of instructions when the charge as given was full and accurate.

Appeal from Marshall District Court.—HON. OBED CAS-
WELL, Judge.

SATURDAY, OCTOBER 15, 1898.

ACTION to recover damages arising from a breach of contract. Trial to jury. Verdict and judgment for plaintiff, and defendants appeal.—*Affirmed.*

Boardman & Boardman for appellants.

Meeker & Meeker for appellee.

WATERMAN, J.—Plaintiff firm sues for breach of a contract partly written and partly oral, the written portion of which is as follows: "Bangor, Iowa, October 20, 1896. This

article of agreement, entered into between J. H. Thompson &
        Son, of the first part, and W. H. Brown, second part.
1   We, Thompson & Son, of the first part, agree to drill
        a well for W. H. Brown, second part, four-inch casing
galvanized as far down as possible. W. H. Brown, second
part, agrees to pay $1.00 per lineal foot, and furnish board for
men and team. Said J. H. Thompson & Son to furnish plenty
water, or no pay. Water to supply a $2\frac{1}{2}$ inch cylinder. W.
H. Brown." We shall refer to the oral terms of the agreement
hereafter. The petition alleges that the contract was that
plaintiff was to drill a well on the farm of. Susannah Brown,
the wife of W. H. Brown, at or near the dwelling house
thereon, for which defendants were to pay the sum of one
dollar per lineal foot; and each agreed to sign a bankable
promissory note for the full price, which note was to mature
January 10, 1897. It is further charged that plaintiff commenced drilling the well October 20, 1896; that it purchased
the required casing, especially ordered for said well, with the
knowledge of defendants, and continued drilling until about
November 20th of that year, and cased said well to the depth
of about eighty feet; that at the depth of about one hundred
and thirty feet plaintiff broke its drill in the well, and not
being able to extract it, was obliged to begin a new well;
that defendants refused to allow plaintiff to drill a new well,
but drove the members of the firm from the premises. Damages
are claimed in the reasonable value of the services of plaintiff
and team; for cost of casing repair of machinery, and the
wear and tear thereof. Susannah Brown answers for herself,
and denies having made any contract with plaintiff. W. H.
Brown, in his original answer, does not put in issue any
material fact alleged in the petition, but charges that plaintiff had been an unreasonable time at the work when he
refused to permit it to proceed with a new well. He sets up
also a counterclaim, in which he demands eight dollars and
seventy-five cents for keeping an extra horse during five

weeks; one dollar for caring for plaintiff's team on four different Sundays; forty-nine dollars for plaintiff's board, and the keep of animals; and fifty dollars for general damage caused by such failure. In an amendment to his answer, W. H. Brown alleges that he desired plaintiff to drill a new well at another place on the farm after the accident to its machinery, and the failure of its first attempt, and that said firm refused so to do. By way of amendment to the petition, it is averred that said contract was made for the benefit of

2　　　Susannah Brown, and that she knew said well was being drilled on her land. This amendment was filed on April 16, 1897, which was the day the cause came on for trial, and a motion to strike it was at once filed. As grounds for this motion, it is said that the amendment is not verified, although both petition and answer are sworn to; that it was filed too late, and takes defendants by surprise; and that the subject-matter thereof is immaterial. This motion was overruled and an exception duly taken. This exception affords basis for one of the numerous assignments of error. The court was justified in permitting the amendment to be filed without verification. Code 1873, section 2680. As to the matter of surprise, we have to say that the amendment contains nothing of which evidence might not have been given under the original petition. We might with propriety have

3　　　disposed of this matter on another ground. While this error is mentioned in appellants' brief, it is not argued. Under our well-known practice, errors not argued will not be considered. *Young v. Railway Co.,* 92 Iowa, 583, *Welch v. Spies,* 103 Iowa, 389. One of the chief grounds of the motion arises in another form, and as it is discussed by counsel, as thus presented, and is also a matter involved under the original pleadings, it will next be noticed.

II. It is contended that Susannah Brown, not being a party to the contract, cannot be held liable in this action. The assumption of counsel seems to be that the written instrument

signed by W. H. Brown constituted the whole agreement
between the parties. This is not in accord with the
4   case made by plaintiff. There is evidence tending to
show that the wife was present and took part in the
negotiations which led up to the agreement; that the writing
was drawn and signed in her presence, and after its execution
both she and her husband orally promised to give their joint
note for the cost of the well. We think there can be no question but that the wife is a proper defendant.

III. It is claimed by defendants that, after the first
well was abandoned, W. H. Brown pointed out a place upon
a distant part of the farm where he was willing plaintiff might
drill for a new well. Much is said by counsel for appellants
in support of Brown's right to select the spot where the work
should be done. It appears that the original contract was
for a well in the vicinity of the house and barn. The
5   place where Brown says he offered to permit plaintiff
to drill the new well was not less than eighty rods from
the buildings, and some of the witnesses say it was half a
mile. It is undisputed that plaintiff, after the accident to
its machinery, was willing to drill again in the vicinity of the
spot originally selected, and that Brown refused to permit it,
but, as defendants themselves claim, insisted that the work
be done at the distant location which he pointed out. On this
point the trial court instructed the jury, in substance, that,
if it was found the parties in the first instance agreed upon
the location where the well was to be drilled, then, when
the first well was abandoned, plaintiff could not be required
to move its machinery and drill a well in some distant place
on the farm, where the conditions and conveniences were
materially different from the original location. We regard
this instruction as correct. And we may add further, in this
connection, that, as we read the evidence, it shows beyond
dispute that Brown never consented to plaintiff continuing
work anywhere under the old contract, but insisted upon a
new agreement as well as a new site.

IV. Another defense urged is that one member of plaintiff firm used profane and insulting language towards Brown, and this, it is thought, justified the latter in refusing to permit plaintiff to continue the work. The use by the junior member of the firm of the language charged is 6 not denied. The circumstances under which he acted, as they appear in the evidence, lead us to think that Brown's conduct on this occasion tended most strongly to provoke an outburst of wrath. We need not go into details on this branch of the case. It is sufficient to say that after a careful reading of the whole record, we are convinced that this claim is more in the nature of a pretense than a reason.

V. From what has been said it is apparent that the trial court construed the contract as giving plaintiff a right to start a new well after having been compelled, without fault, to abandon the first one. This construction is complained of, and it is said to be unreasonable and unjust 7 to require defendants to board the members of plaintiff firm and keep their animals, indefinitely. There is evidence tending to show that the accident to the machinery that caused the abandonment of the first well was not unusual, but was an ordinary risk of the work; that plaintiff was in nowise to blame, and that the abandonment of the first work was necessary when it was unable to extract from the well the portion of the drill that broke off. Ordinary risks and incidents of the work must be held to have been within the contemplation of the parties when the contract was made. This was the holding of the trial court, and we think it affords no just ground of complaint.

VI. Next we come to the trial court's instructions as to the measure of damages. The jury was told that, if the finding was in favor of the plaintiff, such damages should be awarded as would fully recompense it for all loss of time, labor done, and loss of material used. It is said first 8 by appellants that plaintiff, having agreed to furnish a well, can recover nothing, because it failed to do so. Plaintiff's right to recover was properly based by the trial court upon the condition that plaintiff was prevented by the fault of defendants from fulfilling its contract. We hardly think in such a case a defendant can find very secure shelter behind his own wrong. Again, it is claimed that the proper measure of damage is the difference between the contract price and the cost of doing the work. This is a correct rule in some, and perhaps in most cases of this character. *Scale Co. v. Beed,* 52 Iowa, 307; *Feaster v. Cotton Mills,* 51 S. C. 143 (28 S. E. Rep. 301). It applies whenever the total contract price is fixed or ascertainable. In the case at bar, while the price per foot was specified, the total sum to be paid for the well could not be known until the work was completed. In such a case, it is manifest, the rule mentioned could not obtain. In *Barr v. Van Duyn,* 45 Iowa, 230,—a case similar in principle to the one at bar,—we approved the doctrine announced by the trial court here, and we have no disposition

9   to alter it or recede from it. An attempt is made to distinguish the *Barr Case* on the theory that the employer there received some value from the service rendered, while in the present case he does not. We think counsel, in their discussion of the matter, leave out of consideration some significant, and, indeed, controlling, facts. When a party renders some service under an entire contract, which is broken by his own fault, he may still recover, if he can show that his employer has been benefited thereby. *Crookshank v. Mallory* 2 G. Greene, 257; *Davis v. Fish,* 1 G. Greene, 406, *Eyser v. Weissgerber,* 2 Iowa 463; *Pixler v. Nichols,* 8 Iowa, 106; *Byerlee v. Mendel,* 39 Iowa, 382; *Wolf v. Gerr,* 43 Iowa, 339. But when the failure to fully perform the contract is owing, as in this case, to the fault of the employer, we know of no authority that requires the employe to show that the other party derived any benefit from what was done.

VII. Again, it is said that plaintiff, having sued upon the contract, cannot recover on a *quantum meruit.* This

10   action is not brought upon the contract. There is no claim made to recover the contract price. The agreement is set out in the petition merely as a part recital of the facts. The action is to recover the reasonable value of work done and material furnished.

VIII.   Twenty-nine instructions were asked by defendants and refused. There was no error in this action

11   of the trial court, for the charge as given was full and accurate.

IX.   A number of special interrogatories were also presented for submission to the jury. The court refused to submit them, and error is assigned on this action. None of these interrogatories called for ultimate facts; nor, if

12   answered favorably to defendants, would they necessarily have controlled the general verdict. Under the rule announced in *German Sav. Bank of Davenport v. Citizens' Nat. Bank,* 101 Iowa, 530, and cases therein cited, the action complained of must be approved.

These are the principal questions discussed by counsel. Of the many other errors assigned, we have only to say that they are without substantial merit.—AFFIRMED.

HENRY GEIERSHOFER & COMPANY, Trustees, Appellants, v. ISRAEL NUPUF, *et al.*

Attachment: MORTGAGED PROPERTY: *Priorities.* In an action to
2   foreclose a mortgage the decree is conclusive against the parties who fail to appeal.

Appeal: DECREE NOT APPEALED FROM. Act April 9, 1896, section 1 (Acts Twenty-first General Assembly, chapter 117), provides that mortgaged personal property may be attached, but before doing so plaintiff or the officer must pay or tender to the holder of the mortgage the amount due, or must deposit it in court. Section 4
1   provides that "nothing contained in the act shall in any way affect the right of any creditor to contest for any reason the validity of such mortgage." *Held,* that where an attachment of mortgaged property is made before the giving of a second mortgage, but the deposit to secure the prior mortgage is not made until

afterwards, the lien of the attachment is superior to that of the second mortgage. The attachment was always an apparent lien; and if it develops on such contest that the first mortgage is invalid, the lien of the attachment is prior to the second mortgage as to all the property covered by it, and not prior to the amount of the first mortgage, merely.

Appeal from Polk District Court.—HON. W. F. CONRAD, Judge.

SATURDAY, OCTOBER 15, 1898.

IN September, 1895, Nupuf commenced business in Des Moines as a clothing merchant. He was then indebted to Burgunder Bros. & Co. and to Mrs. Friedenberg, some clerks in his employ, and others. On September 9, 1895, he gave to Mrs. Friedenberg a chattel mortgage on his stock of goods, which was filed for record at 1:45 P. M. of that day. He also gave a mortgage to his clerks to secure the amounts due them, which was filed for record at 1:48 P. M. of that day. On the same day Burgunder Bros. & Co. commenced suit by attachment, and levied on the stock of goods at 3:45 P. M. of the same day, and took possession of it. It also attached the mortgagees as garnishees. September 13, 1895, Nupuf gave to the plaintiff firm, as trustee for certain of his creditors, a mortgage on the stock. The mortgages all provided that the mortgagees might take possession of the goods at their election, and sell the same for the payment of the debts secured. On September 14, 1895, Burgunder Bros. & Co. deposited money with the clerk to pay Mrs. Friedenberg and the clerks, who were mortgagees, and notified the clerk to hold the money, as it intended to contest the validity of the mortgages. Plaintiff Henry Geiershofer & Co., trustee, commenced this suit September 14, 1895, to foreclose its mortgage, making the mortgagees and Burgunder Bros. & Co. parties, and secured the appointment of a receiver, who is also a party. The goods, by due course of procedure, were converted into money, which is in the hands of the receiver. The issues are such that the mortgage to Mrs. Friedenberg was adjudged invalid, the mortgages to the clerks were adjudged valid, and a first lien on the money in the hands of the receiver. The attachment of Burgunder Bros. & Co. was sustained, and its claim is to be paid after the payment of the clerks and certain costs. The decree denied to plaintiff any claim on the money in the hands of the receiver, but gave judgment for the amounts due the respective parties represented. The plaintiff appealed.— *Affirmed.*

Dudley & Coffin and *Gatch, Connor & Weaver* for appellant.

Berryhill & Henry and *McVey & McVey* for appellee.

Granger, J.—A little sifting will bring more clearly to view the questions to be considered. The decree is not now questioned, in so far as it provides for the payment, first, of the clerks, as mortgagees. Mrs. Friedenberg does not appeal, and hence the judgment is conclusive as to her. The amounts due the clerks, who are to be paid first, added to the amount due Burgunder Bros. & Co., is more than the amount in the hands of the receiver, so that, under the decree, there could be nothing for plaintiff, which is likely the reason for denying to it any claim on the money. It will now be seen that the contentions arise between plaintiff and Burgunder Bros. over the money in the hands of the receiver in excess of the amount necessary to pay the clerks. To meet the contentions it is important to have some dates well in mind. The attachment proceedings of Burgunder Bros. & Co. was commenced September 9th, and the levy was made on that day. The mortgage to the plaintiff was made September 13th, and the deposit by Burgunder Bros. & Co., for the mortgagees, was made September 14th. Importance is attached to the fact that when the mortgage was given to plaintiff the deposit had not been made. Prior to the enactment of chapter 117 Acts Twenty-first General Assembly, which was approved April 9, 1886, no lien could be acquired on mortgaged personal property by levy of an attachment. That act changed the law in this respect, and we quote therefrom as follows: "Section 1. That personal property not exempt from execution hereafter mortgaged, or heretofore mortgaged when the debt secured thereby is due, may be taken on attachment or execution issued at the suit of a creditor of a mortgagor, but before the property is so taken the officer or plaintiff must pay or tender to the holder of the mortgage the amount of the mortgage debt and interest accrued, or must deposit the amount thereof with the clerk of the district court of the county wherein the mortgaged property is found payable to the order of the holder of the mortgage.   *   *   * Section 2. The holder of the mortgage shall state over his signature and under oath on the back of said mortgage, the amount due or to become due thereon, and deliver the same to the person paying him said amount, and if the said sum has been deposited with the clerk of the district court, the holder of the mortgage shall only receive the mortgage and other evidence of indebtedness, and the surplus, if any, shall be returned to the person who made the deposit: provided, however, that the execution or attaching creditor shall have the right to controvert, in the court from which the process issued, such statement of indebtedness in the manner provided in other garnishment proceedings, if he give notice in writing to the clerk at the time of the deposit; and the clerk shall hold the deposit until such matter is determined." It seems to be the thought of appellant that, as the deposit was not made until September 14th, the levy of the attachment was not complete till that date so as to be a lien; and, as its mortgage was made on the thirteenth, it is prior. That statute, in the respect suggested, has received quite careful consideration by this court. The case of *Clark v. Patton,* 92 Iowa, 247, is very similar, except that in that case there was no deposit, but an attachment issued, and property was taken under it. As indicating the question there determined, we quote from the opinion as follows: "The controlling question in this case is whether attaching creditors of a mortgagor of chattels acquire such an interest in the mortgaged property by levying their attachment thereon, under claim that the mortgage is void as to creditors, as entitles them to priority over a valid mortgage subsequently taken with knowledge of the levy." This further difference between the cases is claimed: That, in the *Clark-Patton Case* the attaching creditor secured only the amount of the invalid mortgages, while in this case the decree gives to Burgunder Bros. & Co. more than that, as, in fact, only the Friedenberg mortgage of about one thousand two hundred and fifty dollars, was adjudged invalid, and the amount in excess of what is to be paid to the clerks, and the costs, is more than the Friedenberg claim; the thought being that the attachment levy, without the deposit, could in no event secure to the attaching creditor more than the amount of the invalid mortgages. The application of such a rule would give to plaintiff a claim on a part of the money in the hands of the receiver. In the *Clark-Patton Case* is the following language: "Our conclusion is that, when a creditor of a mortgagor seeks to subject his interest in the mortgaged property to the payment of his debts, he may proceed by garnishment, or under said chapter 117, if the validity of the mortgage is not questioned; but, if the validity of the mortgage is questioned, he may make his levy or garnishment, and then proceed, by the mode recognized in the practice, to cancel the mortgage, and have his levy established as a lien upon the property, without complying with the requirements of chapter 117. It will be seen from what we have said that these attaching creditors, claiming that the prior mortgage was fraudulent, have a right to levy their attachments on the mortgaged property, and, having done so, to contest the validity of the prior mortgages, without complying with chapter 117; also that, while their levies did not create actual liens on the mortgaged property, they gave to the creditors such an apparent lien or interest as was necessary to and did entitle them to contest the validity of the mortgages, for the purpose of having their apparent liens fully established as against all or any part of the mortgages found to be fraudulent as to creditors." The concluding language of the quotation is thought to sustain appellant's view that the lien of an attachment is limited to what is proven to be fraudulent. Such was not the thought of the language. The court was not then considering the question we have in hand, but simply the right to contest fraudulent mortgages, and the methods of doing it, and simply expressed the thought indicated without an intent to determine the question whether the lien of such an attachment would reach further or not. We have repeatedly expressed the thought that language in an opinion must be limited by the subject to which it is applied. From the other parts of the language quoted it will be seen that, where the purpose is to contest the validity of a mortgage, the creditor may levy his attachment on the property, or garnish by attachment, without reference to chapter 117; and in so doing he has an apparent lien that protects the property until the issue is determined, and his lien, if he has one, is fully established. The thought as to an "apparent lien" was first expressed in *Thomas v. Manufacturing Co.,* 76 Iowa, 735, and its import is this: A levy is made with a view to contest the validity of a mortgage. If the mortgage is a valid one, as against the mortgage the attachment is really no lien. If valid, it is a lien. Pending the determination of the fact, the uncertainty makes the lien merely an apparent one. It does not mean that the lien of the attachment is limited to property sufficient in value to pay the mortgage, but it attaches upon all the property covered by the mortgage. The question presented by the proceeding is, is the mortgagee or the attaching creditor entitled to the property when the attachment is levied? The lien may be said to be apparent as to the mortgagee as well as the creditor. If the mortgage proves invalid, there was never more than what appeared to be a lien. It was not actual. Section 4 of chapter 117 is as follows: "But nothing contained in the act shall in any way affect the right of any creditor to contest for any reason the validity of such mortgage." It is this section,—being a part of chapter 117,—that has given rise to the holding that an attachment levy becomes a lien on mortgaged personal property without complying with other provisions of said chapter. It is said that to permit the attachment to become a lien on more property than is sufficient to pay the invalid mortgage is to overrule the former holdings of this court. Without concurring in that view, it is likely true that the holding effects a change in the law to some extent; but, if so, it is because of the change in the statute law. It is to be understood that the attachment does not cover property not covered by the mortgage, and as to which the mortgage was adjudged invalid; and we can see no reason why the attachment, from its levy, is not an apparent lien on all the property covered by the invalid mortgage, if levied upon all; and, if finally adjudged a lien, why it should not be on all such property. It matters not that some of the mortgages were adjudged invalid. As between Burgunder Bros. & Co. and plaintiff, the case is as if the Friedenberg mortgage had been the only one, and covered all the property. Our holding is that the lien of the attachment was operative as to all the property levied upon and covered by the mortgage, and when the mortgage was adjudged invalid the lien continued as to all the property, and that a junior mortgagee has no preference as to any part of it necessary to pay the attachment claim. These considerations are conclusive of the case, and the judgment is AFFIRMED.

WILLIAM KAHLER v. THE IOWA STATE INSURANCE COMPANY, Appellant.

Insurance: INDIVISIBLE CONTRACT: *Breach of conditions.* Defendant issued to plaintiff a policy for one thousand three hundred dollars, -one thousand dollars on the building, and three hundred dollars on machinery while contained therein. As premium,
1 plaintiff executed a note for one hundred and ninety-five dollars

"payable in portions and at such times as the directors of the company may require, * * * provided such assessment does not exceed fifteen per cent in any one year " The application
8   which was a part of the policy, contained a statement: "Amount $1,800, at 15 per cent; premium note $195; 5 per cent to be paid, $9." In fact, only a portion of such premium was to be paid and that portion was a gross assessment on the entire insurance. One of the conditions was that, in case of any change in the title in the property insured, in whole or in part, the policy was to be void. Plaintiff was not the real owner of the building, and, about ten days prior to the destruction of the whole property by fire, the owners obtained a decree against him quieting title. *Held*, that the contract was entire and indivisible, and the breach of the condition avoided the whole policy, on the machinery as well as the building.

WAIVER. Failure of an assessment fire insurance company, after knowledge of facts which rendered its policy invalid, to return
2   premiums which it had received in ignorance of such facts will not render the policy binding upon the company, in the absence of any acts upon its part since its knowledge of the policy's invalidity evincing its election to treat it as valid.

Pleading: ESTOPPEL: *Waiver.* A waiver of the conditions of a
2   policy, or an estoppel to claim the same void on a breach thereof, cannot be relied on unless pleaded.

Appeal from Clinton District Court.—HON. P. B. WOLFE,
Judge.

SATURDAY, OCTOBER 15, 1898.

ACTION at law upon a policy of insurance covering a frame building used as a grain elevator and certain elevator machinery. Defendant pleaded in defense that the building did not belong to the assured when the policy issued, failure to make proof of loss, and a breach of condition relating to change or transfer of title or interest in the property. Plaintiff, in reply, pleaded a waiver of proof of loss; that he had an insurable interest in the property at the time the policy issued ; and, although not the absolute owner, that defendant was aware of the fact, and is now estopped from relying upon defects in the title. The trial court found there was a waiver of proof of loss; that plaintiff did not have title to the elevator at the time he received the policy; but that defendant,

after knowledge of the fact, retained the premium paid, and
has not offered to repay or return the same; and that it is
estopped from pleading that the policy was void at its inception. The court further found that, after the issuance of the
policy, plaintiff's interest in and ownership of the building
was terminated by decree of court, and that, by reason of
such termination plaintiff could not recover for loss of the
building. It further found that plaintiff was entitled to
recover for loss of the personal property, and gave him judgment for the amount of the insurance thereon. Defendant
appeals.—*Reversed.*

McVey & McVey for appellant.

W. J. McCoy for appellee.

DEEMER, C. J.—The policy insured the plaintiff
against loss or damage by fire upon the following described
property, to wit: "$1,000 on his two-story frame building,
occupied by the assured as a grain elevator; * * *
$300 on his elevator machinery in said elevator,
including fanning mill,—all while contained in aforesaid building." As a part of the contract, plaintiff executed
a note to the insurer for the sum of one hundred and
ninety-five dollars, "payable in such portions and at such
times as the directors of the company may require,
* * * provided such assessment does not exceed 15
per cent. in any one year." The application, which
was made a part of the policy, asked for the insurance
as granted, and further contained these statements: "Amount,
$1,300, at 15 per cent.; premium note, $195; 5 per
cent. to be paid, $9." One of the conditions of the
policy was this: "And in case of any transfer or change
of title in the property insured, in whole or in part, or of any
interest therein, to any party or parties, such insurance shall
be void and cease." It appears from the evidence that the
plaintiff was in possession of the building at the time it was

insured, claiming and believing that he was the owner thereof by inheritance from his father, and through certain conveyances made to him by the other heirs. His father in fact had no title, and, some time after the policy issued, the real owners of the property obtained a decree against the plaintiff, quieting their title thereto, and ordering defendant therein to surrender possession thereof within thirty days from February 26, 1894. On March 7, 1894, the property was destroyed by fire. There is no evidence that any agent or employe of the insurance company knew of the condition of the title until after the fire. Plaintiff paid all assessments called for by his contract, and defendant has not returned or offered to repay any part thereof.

In support of the finding and judgment of the trial court, it is contended that, as defendant retained all the assessments paid, it is estopped from claiming that the policy is void because plaintiff did not own the property at the time the policy was issued. One all-sufficient answer to the contention is that plaintiff did not plead waiver or estoppel in his reply. His claim in this respect is that defendant's agents knew the true condition of the title, wrote the statements found in the application with reference thereto, and, as appellee had an insurable interest, the insurer is estopped from relying upon the defect. Aside from this, we do not think appellant has waived the breach of condition or warranty contained in the policy. Appellee paid his assessments as they came due, and appellant has done nothing since it learned of the failure of title to evince an election on its part to treat the policy as valid. The note was given simply as a basis for assessments which were to be made annually by the board of directors, and no asessments have been made since the defendant discovered the condition of the title. It is true, as held in the case of *Waller v. Insurance Co.,* 64 Iowa, 101, that where policies of insurance are viod *ab initio,* and there has been no fraud or deception on the part of the assured, he may recover back premiums paid as for money had and received for his use. But the mere retention of premiums paid, without knowledge of facts which avoid the policy, will not validate the instrument. *Houdeck v. Insurance Co.,* 102 Iowa, 303, and cases cited; May Insurance, sections 506, 567; *Harris v. Society,* 6 Thompson & C. 108. Appellant did no act after knowledge of facts avoiding the policy which would amount to a waiver of its conditions; and it was not required in this form of action to tender back the assessments paid.

II.   The trial court evidently proceeded upon the theory that the contract of insurance was divisible, and that recovery of indemnity for the personal property destroyed might be had, notwithstanding the forfeiture of the policy as to the building by reason of breach of condition or warranty as to transfer or change of title.   In the case of *Garver v. Insurance Co.,* 69 Iowa, 202, we held that, when the premium paid for a policy of fire insurance is in a gross sum, the contract is not divisible, although the amount of insurance on the different items of insured property is fixed in the policy, and that, where the policy is invalidated as to one item of property, it is avoided as to all; citing *Plath v. Insurance Co.,* 23 Minn. 479, and other cases. Counsel attempt to distinguish this case from that by reference to the application which says that the premium should be fifteen per cent. of the amount insured. It is clear, however, that the premium was not fifteen per cent. True, the note calls for one hundred and ninety-five dollars; yet it is evident that but ninety per cent. of it was to be paid, and that part of it which was to be paid was a gross assessment for the entire insurance. As said in the *Garver Case, supra:* "One party to such a contract cannot at his pleasure make it divisible or entire, as his interest may appear. When entered into, it was either one or the other." And we may add that in this case the parties saw fit to make it an entire and indivisible contract. The only effect of the apportionment of the amount of the insurance upon the separate items of property was to limit the extent of the insurer's risk on each item to the sum specified. Again, there is nothing to show that the rate of premium was the same upon each kind of property insured. The rate is fixed as a gross sum upon the total amount of insurance, and there is no evidence that it was the same upon the building as upon the machinery. Looking to the subject-matter of the contract, and to the evident purpose of the condition, we think it clearly appears that the contract is indivisible. Whatever affected the risk or hazard as to the building also affected the personal property, for it was located in the same building, and was insured only while it remained in that building. The policy provided that any transfer or change of title in the property insured in whole or in part, or of any interest therein to any party or parties, should avoid the policy. The condition is so broad that a violation thereof by a change of title to any part of the property avoids the entire policy; and, as a breach of the condition relating to the building affects the risk of the insurer upon the personal property, we are of opinion that the contract should be held to be entire and indivisible. See, as sustaining our conclusion, *Loomis v. Insurance Co.*, 77 Wis. 87 (8 L. R. A. 834, 45 N. W. Rep. 813); *McGowan v. Insurance Co.*, 54 Vt. 211, and cases cited; *Insurance Co. v. Pickel*, 119 Ind. 155 (21 N. E. Rep. 546); May Insurance, section 277. As the contract was indivisible, the breach of condition relating to the building avoided the policy, and there can be no recovery for loss of the machinery. —*Reversed.*

SARAH M. UPTAGRAFF, Appellant, v. R. H. SMITH, *et al.*

Dedication: REVOCATION: *Adverse possession.* Adverse possession under a claim of right for more than ten years, of a portion of a
2 plat of land designated thereon as a street, constitutes a revocation of the dedication as against the owner of lots situated on that plat.

SAME. A dedication of land for a public street is revoked where it was never accepted and the general public has acquiesced in the action of the grantor in using and occupying the alleged street as

2 lots for a period of more than ten years during most of which time taxes were levied upon the land and paid, and the town subsequently incorporated, including the land in question, has raised no objection to the action of the grantor.

Plats: VACATION. An addition cannot be replatted so as to vacate certain streets therein, where lots, though not abutting on the
1 streets attempted to be vacated, have been sold under the original plat, unless all the owners of the lots in the plat join in vacating the street, as required by Code, 1873, section 563.

Appeal from Dickinson District Court.—HON. W. B. QUARTON, Judge.

SATURDAY, OCTOBER 15, 1898.

ACTION in equity to quiet in the plaintiff the title to certain real estate which had once been platted as streets. There was a hearing on the merits, and a decree in favor of the defendants. The plaintiff appeals.—*Reversed.*

L. E. Francis for appellant.

No appearance for appellee.

ROBINSON, J.—In September, 1882, the plaintiff platted Uptagraff's addition to Minnewaukon Beach, and the plat was duly recorded. It included two streets, named, respectively, "Fourth Street" and "Fifth Street," which were dedicated to public use. These streets are alleged to have been unnecessary and useless. On the nineteenth day of August, 1885, the plaintiff filed for record a second plat, which she had executed, and which purported to vacate those streets, and they were re-platted and numbered as lots. The plaintiff asks to have the title to that property quieted in her because of the vacation, and for the further reason that she has occupied them adversely under a claim of title for more than ten years. The defendant, the town of Minnewaukon, was incorporated May 25, 1895, and includes the property in question. The interests of the defendants are not clearly shown, but some of them appear to own property in the addition. It is claimed in their behalf that the addition as originally platted contained but four streets, which led to the lake of Spirit Lake; and that, if those in question are closed, there will be but one street to the lake shore which can be used, for the reason that one of the two which will remain is obstructed by a high embankment, the removal of which will cause great expense; and that the vacation is illegal and void.

I. The evidence shows that when the second plat was recorded none of the lots abutting on the streets which the plaintiff attempted to vacate had been sold, and that but a few lots, at a considerable distance from Fourth and Fifth streets had been sold. Sections 562 to 567, inclusive, of the Code of 1873, provided for the vacation of town plats, or parts thereof, and of streets therein, and for the re-platting of what should be vacated. Section 563 provided for the vacation of a plat by the proprietor thereof, but required, in cases where lots had been sold, that all the owners of lots in that plat join in vacating it. Section 564 provided that any part of a plat might be vacated under the provisions and subject to the conditions of the chapter in which the sections referred to are found, if the rights and privileges of other proprietors in the plat were not thereby destroyed or abridged. It does not appear that any of the owners of lots in the addition joined in the vacation of the streets attempted by the plaintiff, and there is uncontradicted evidence to the effect that substantial rights and privileges of owners of lots in the addition will be abridged if the streets in question are permanently closed. We conclude, therefore, that the plaintiff has not shown that the vacation of the streets attempted by the second plat was authorized and effective.

II. We are next required to determine whether the plaintiff, by reason of adverse possession under claim of right, the failure of the public to use the streets, and the

acquiescence of the parties interested in the possession held
by her, is entitled to the relief she demands.   The
2   lots in question were never used or improved as streets.
Since the filing of the second plat, the plaintiff has
continuously, for more than ten years prior to the
commencement of this action, occupied them, and claimed and
treated them as her own.   Two-thirds of the lots were covered
with trees, and those she caused to be trimmed in the year
1885.   She also caused the portions of the lots not covered
with trees to be plowed, and used those portions for a garden.
She fenced the lots, and kept them inclosed for several years,
and used them for a pasture, and for several years she rented
them.   Taxes were levied on the lots for the year 1886, and for
subsequent years to and including the year 1894, and were
paid each year by the plaintiff.   During all of that time she
treated the lots as her own, and her title to them does not
appear to have been questioned by any one.   For nearly ten
years the lots were not within any incorporated town, but were
in the country.   There is no evidence whatever that the dedication of the lots and streets, tendered by the original plat, was
ever accepted, and for more than ten years the general public,
and, for the time during which it was incorporated, the town
of Minnewaukon, acquiesced in the occupation and use of
the lots by the plaintiff, and her claim of title, without objection.   That the dedication of a highway or street must be
accepted to be effectual is well settled.   *Incorporated Town
of Cambridge v. Cook,* 97 Iowa, 599, and cases therein cited;
Brown v. Taber, 103 Iowa, 1.   And that a city or town may
be estopped by its conduct to open a street or alley which has
been closed or occupied for many years by a private person
under a claim of right for many years, is also well settled.
*Incorporated Town of Cambridge v. Cook, supra; Johnson
v. City of Burlington,* 95 Iowa, 197; *Bell v. City of Burlington,* 68 Iowa, 296.   And the same rule has been applied to
public highways.   *Davis v. Huebner,* 45 Iowa, 574; *Orr v.
O'Brien,* 77 Iowa, 253; *Smith v. Gorrell,* 81 Iowa, 218.   The

cases of *Taraldson v. Town of Lime Springs,* 92 Iowa, 187, and *City of Waterloo v. Union Mill Co.,* 72 Iowa, 437, were governed by the rule that the statute of limitations will not run to defeat the exercise of the governmental functions of a city or town. Accordingly, it was held in the *Taraldson Case* that the failure of the town to keep open an alley, which had been accepted, for a term of ten years, did not deprive it of the right to open it thereafter; and in the *Waterloo Case* the same rule was applied to a street. In each case an estoppel was claimed and considered, but held not to be established. We conclude that the plaintiff is entitled to the relief she demands as against the defendant town, because an acceptance of the dedication of the streets is not shown, and for the further reason that she was permitted to claim, hold, and improve the alleged streets as lots, under a claim of absolute ownership, for more than ten years, for eight or nine of which they were taxed, and the taxes were paid by her. The plaintiff is entitled to the relief she demands as against the remaining defendants by virtue of her adverse possession under a claim of right for more than ten years. It follows from what we have said that the decree of the district court is erroneous.

III. A stipulation signed by the appellant and by appellee J. W. Cory in his own right has been filed. It provides that, in consideration of his refraining from making a defense in this court, the case as to him is settled, and no costs, whether incurred in the district court or in this court, shall be taxed to him. It is therefore adjudged that his share of all costs which have accrued in this case shall be taxed to the plaintiff. In all other respects the decree of the district court is REVERSED.

WILLIAM LEHMAN, Appellant, v. E. M. PRESS.

Bills and Notes: GOOD FAITH BUYER: *Evidence.* A negotiable note can be impeached in the hands of a holder for value before maturity only by direct or circumstantial evidence that he took the paper

2 with knowledge of its infirmities, or under circumstances indicative of such wilful neglect to inquire, or such gross carelessness in failing to do so when inquiry would have led to knowledge which would establish bad faith, but the fact that he was merely put on suspicion or was careless in not making inquiry is not sufficient.

INSTRUCTIONS: *Curing with.* An instruction which erroneously lays down a rule for finding the existence of bad faith on the part of a
8 purchaser of a note is not cured by other instructions informing the jury of the necessity of finding bad faith.

RULE APPLIED. Error in charging that facts which would merely put a reasonable man on inquiry will charge an indorsee with
2 notice of fraud in the inception of a note is not cured by a charge that something more than mere negligence in failing to discover fraud was necessary to defeat the holder's recovery, that bad faith
🔳 must be shown, and that if the holder had notice of the want of consideration, defendant might prove that there was none.

Indorsements: FOR COLLECTION: *Rights of indorsee.* A note was indorsed by the payee; also, "For collection, acct. G. D. & Co.;"
1 also, "For collection, and return to" a certain bank. Suit was brought thereon by a member of a firm individually; and defendant plead that the note was without consideration, had been transferred to plaintiff and by him sued, to cheat defendant. *Held,*
  a That the firm's indorsement did not tend to show that the firm had delivered the note to plaintiff for collection.
  b Defendant could not show that plaintiff had purchased the note as agent for a third person, who afterwards delivered it to him for collection.
  c One to whom a note is indorsed for collection may sue thereon.

Appeal from Lucas District Court.—HON. M. A. ROBERTS,
Judge.

SATURDAY, OCTOBER 15, 1898.

ACTION on six promissory notes. Trial to jury, verdict and judgment for defendant, and plaintiff appeals.— *Reversed.*

J. C. Mitchell and *G. G. Fancher* for appellant.

Stuart & Bartholomew for appellee.

LADD, J.—The six notes sued on were executed by the defendant to Mayer, Engle & Co., March 15, 1895, and are

for the payment of one thousand and fifty dollars. The
defense interposed was want of consideration, of which plaintiff had notice, and that he was not the real party in
interest. The first note became due April 29, 1895, and is
indorsed, "Without recourse. Meyer, Engle & Co." The
other five notes fell due a month apart, beginning with May
29, 1895, and upon each are the following indorsements:
"Without recourse. Mayer, Engle & Co. ;" "For collection,
acct. Gage, Downs & Co. ;" "For collection and return to
Nat'l Bank of Republic, Chicago. W. T. Fenton,
1   Cashier." The plaintiff testified that he purchased
these notes of Mayer, Engle & Co., April 30, 1895,
and paid therefor by check of one thousand dollars, afterwards cashed, signed Gage, Downs & Co., of which firm he was
a member. The eighth instruction is based on this evidence,
and is as follows: "If you find from the evidence that on the
30th day of April, 1895, the plaintiff, as the agent of Gage,
Downs&Co., purchased the notes in controversy for said Gage,
Downs & Co., and paid for them with the money and means
of said Gage, Downs & Co., and afterwards said Gage, Downs
& Co. indorsed said notes and delivered them to a bank, and
afterwards said Gage, Downs & Co. delivered said notes to
the plaintiff for collection for their benefit only, then you
are instructed that, under such findings and facts, the plaintiff
would not be a purchaser of said notes for value, and defendant would have the right to interpose any defense she had
thereto, the same as if suit had been brought thereon by
Mayer, Engle & Co., the original payees of said notes."
It will be observed that the evidence tended to show the
purchase of the notes the day after the first was due, but
before the expiration of the three days of grace, and therefore
before maturity. *Crosby v. Grant,* 36 N. H. 273. As to
this note, there was no evidence whatever of any transfer
except by Mayer, Engle & Co., and, as applied to it, the
instruction is unquestionably erroneous. As to the other
notes, it can rest on inference only, to be drawn from the

indorsements, that the notes were purchased by giving the check of Gage, Downs & Co., instead of his own. The indorsements were circumstances to be considered in determining whether the plaintiff was owner; but such indorsements had no tendency to show that Gage, Downs & Co. had delivered the notes to the plaintiff for collection or for any other purpose. Besides, there is no such issue in the pleadings. The defendant expressly alleges that they were transferred by Mayer, Engle & Co. to plaintiff, and that he instituted suit thereon at their request, to aid them in cheating the defendant. But suppose that the plaintiff was acting for Gage, Downs & Co., and that the notes were purchased by that firm, the rule announced cannot be sustained. One to whom a note is indorsed for collection may maintain an action thereon. *Bond Co. v. Hurd,* 85 Iowa, 559; *Cottle v. Cole,* 20 Iowa, 481. While the note is subject to defenses interposed by the payor against the principal, such defenses must be made in order to defeat recovery. If the plaintiff purchased the note for Gage, Downs & Co., and brought this action for their benefit, and value was paid without notice of the note's infirmities, and in good faith, the defense must fail. *Farwell v. Tyler,* 5 Iowa, 535. As affecting the rights of the payor, it is immaterial whether the principal or agent brings the action.

Exception was taken to the seventh instruction: "In order to sustain defendant's claim, it is not necessary that the evidence show that plaintiff had express, actual notice that said notes were without consideration. It will
2   be sufficient if the circumstances brought home to the
      plaintiff are of such a strong and pointed character as would necessarily cast a shade upon the transaction and put him upon inquiry. If the circumstances attending the transfer of the notes were such as to necessarily put the plaintiff on his guard, or if he must have known therefrom that Mayer, Engle & Co. had no right to transfer said notes, then he was bound to make inquiry, and, if he did not, he took them at his peril." This seems to have been

taken from the opinion in *Trustees v. Hill,* 12 Iowa, 462, with the important limitation contained in this sentence omitted: "They are not to be charged with notice because of any want of diligence on their part in making inquiry, or even if they took the note under suspicious circumstances, provided they had no notice, actual or constructive, of the alleged equities subsisting between Lambright and Hill." That case was referred to in *Lane v. Evans,* 49 Iowa, 156, and an instrection similar to that given condemned. It was there said: "Facts which would have put a reasonable man upon inquiry will not charge the indorsee with notice of fraud in inception of the note." As stated in *Lake v. Reed,* 29 Iowa, 258: "The distinction is this, to wit: The rule of law requires proof, direct or by circumstances, that the holder had notice of the defect or equities; whereas the rule as stated in the instruction only requires proof that the holder was in such a situation as that he might have had notice if he had been diligent in making inquiries which his situation offered and invited him to make." Because of the commercial character of negotiable paper, and the need of sustaining its negotiable quality, it cannot be impeached in the hands of a holder for value before maturity, unless acquired under circumstances such as indicate actual fraud by the party taking it. The fact that he was merely put on suspicion, or was careless in not making inquiry, is not sufficient. He must be shown, by direct or circumstantial evidence, to have taken the paper with knowledge or notice of its infirmities, or the circumstances must be such as indicate willful neglect to inquire, or such gross carelessness in failing to do so, when inquiry would have led to such knowledge, as shall establish bad faith. This rule has been adopted in this state, and is in harmony with that of England and the great weight of authority in this country. *Richards v. Monroe,* 85 Iowa, 359; *Cook v. Wierman,* 51 Iowa, 561; *Gage v. Sharp,* 24 Iowa, 15; *Davis v. Seely,* 71 Mich. 209 (38 N. W. Rep. 901); *Bank v. Young,* 41 N. J. Eq. 531 (7 Atl. Rep. 488); *Murray v. Lardner,* 2 Wall.

110; *Goodman v. Harvey,* 4 Adol. & E. 870; 4 Am. & Eng. Enc. Law, 299.

The appellant urges that the defect in this part of the court's charge was cured by paragraphs 5 and 9. The fifth instruction correctly advised the jury that something more than mere negligence in failing to discover fraud was necessary to defeat the holder's recovery,—that bad faith must be shown,—while the ninth instruction was to the effect that, if he had notice of the want of consideration, the defendant might prove that there was none. It will be readily seen that these instructions informed the jury of the necessity of finding bad faith, while No. 7 laid down a rule for finding its existence. The instructions would not be con· strued by the jury as essentially in conflict, but the conclusion reached that bad faith might be inferred as stated in the seventh paragraph of the charge. Because of the errors pointed out the judgment must be REVERSED.

ELIZABETH OWEN v. N. P. CHRISTENSEN, Executor of the Estate of Richard Owen, Deceased, Appellant.

Estoppel: ESTATES: *Widow.* Where, after a widow sued her husband's executor for the amount due on a certificate of deposit as her individual property, she applied for a year's support, stating that she was seventy-eight years of age, unable to work, and had to be cared for by a nurse, and that all she possessed in her own right was involved in the suit, and the allowance was made, and paid from the money due on the certificate, these facts did not amount to an election to treat the certificate as assets of the estate so as to estop her claim to it, where she did not ask that the allowance be paid out of the certificate and stated in the application that same was her property.

Evidence: DECLARATIONS: *Harmless error.* Where a widow sued her husband's executor for property she claimed in her own right, and a witness testified that at the time he drew the husband's will she declared in his presence that the property belonged to him, evidence of the husband's reply, was admissible, not as a declaration in his own interest, but to show, if he also stated it was his,

that she acquiesced, but the exclusion of such evidence was harmless, however, since it was merely cumulative, and added nothing
to the weight of evidence already given.

PLEA AND PROOF: *Fraud.* Where a widow sued her husband's
executor for property she claimed in her own right, the proceeds
5 of a farm he had conveyed to her, evidence that plaintiff did not
have the means to buy the farm from the husband was inadmissible, there being no charge of fraud.

Instructions. An instruction that if the evidence showed that plaintiff and her husband treated certain paper as their joint property,
1 and each permitted the other to exercise ownership over it, it
would authorize a finding that each had a half interest and that
2 any interest that either had inconsistent therewith was relinquished
to the other, did not tell the jury that proof of such facts was conclusive of joint ownership, but only that they might find it therefrom, and is not bad for assuming the establishment of a controverted fact.

Trial: QUOTIENT VERDICT. The action of the jury in aggregating
the several amounts which the different jurors are in favor of
awarding as their verdict and dividing their result by twelve will,
6 while not to be commended, not avoid a verdict thus obtained
where there was no previous agreement to abide by the result of
the computation and the amount was afterwards discussed, before
it was assented to as their verdict.

Appeal from Audubon District Court.—HON. W. R. GREEN,
Judge.

MONDAY, OCTOBER 17, 1898.

ACTION at law to recover the amount due on a certain
certificate of deposit, and for the possession or proceeds of
a certain promissory note, of which certificate and note the
plaintiff alleges that she is the owner, and that the defendant
has converted the same to his own use, as executor of said
estate. The defendant answered, claiming that said certificate and note are the property of said estate. Verdict and
judgment were rendered in favor of the plaintiff. Defendant
appeals.—*Affirmed.*

I. L. Statzel and *De Lano & Meredith* for appellant.

Nash, Phelps & Mosier and *Wonn & Noon* for appellee.

GIVEN, J.—I. Appellant's counsel state the facts as follows, which statement is sufficiently accurate for the purposes of the questions to be considered: "Richard Owen died on August 9, 1895, and the plaintiff is his widow. He left a will, and the defendant is the executor thereof. Prior to his death he had owned 160 acres of land, but he conveyed this to the plaintiff October 9, 1884, and the consideration expressed in the deed was one dollar and other valuable considerations. About the 1st of March, 1890, this land was sold and conveyed by them to one Emly, and the consideration of $4,290 was deposited in the bank and certificates of deposit issued to Richard Owen therefor. In October, 1890, Richard Owen and his wife went on a visit to England, and one of these certificates for $1,290, was cashed, and some money added to it, and a foreign draft issued to Richard Owen for $1,800. In December, 1891, the balance due on the other certificates of deposit was transferred to a bank in Exira, and certificates of deposit were issued therefor, made payable to Richard Owen and Elizabeth Owen. After their return from the trip to England, and on July 1, 1891, Richard Owen purchased a house and lot in Exira with the money he had taken when they went to England, and perhaps some portion of that left in the bank; and the title to this property was taken in the name of Richard Owen, and he still held this property at the time of his decease. On December 6, 1894, there had been loaned to Thos. F. Musson $500 of this money in the bank at Exira, and a note taken payable to Mr. and Mrs. Owen or order, and this note was unpaid at the time of the death of Richard Owen. At the date of the death of Richard Owen there was outstanding one certificate of deposit dated June 4, 1895, for $2,400, and on which there had been one payment made July 26, 1895, of $100. After his death, and prior to the appointment of the executor, the certificate was in the possession of the plaintiff; and there were three payments made to her during that time, aggregating $320. After the appointment of the executor, and on October 12, 1895, this certificate of deposit was surrendered to the executor by the plaintiff, but there is a wide discrepancy as to the object and purpose of this transaction. It appears that at the date of the surrender of the old certificate of deposit to the executor a new certificate was issued, and made payable to the executor; and the inventory of the executor shows that this last certificate of deposit, the Musson note, and a few items of personal property comprised the entire personal estate of Richard Owen, deceased. In November, 1895, the plaintiff filed her application with the court to have an allowance made for her support for one year out of the estate of her husband, and also an application to have the exempt property set off to her; and both of these applications were granted by the court, and $250 ordered paid by the executor for her support. The amount was paid out of the deposit represented by the certificate of the bank, and the personal property, outside of the certificate and Musson note, was set off to her as exempt property of her husband's estate. The plaintiff brought this suit to recover from the executor the balance of this certificate of deposit and the Musson note; claiming that they were her individual property, and not the property of her deceased husband, and that the executor had no right to them or their proceeds. The jury found that the plaintiff was entitled to $1,269 of the $1,775 due from the bank on the certificate, and that she was entitled to one-half of the Musson note. But on the ruling on the motion for a new trial the court required the plaintiff to remit all in excess of $878 due on the certificate of deposit, which was done, and the plaintiff had judgment for $878 and the costs. The jury found specially that the plaintiff was entitled to one-half of the Musson note, and, as it was then uncollected, judgment was suspended until it was paid in. From the judgment awarding the plaintiff $878 out of the certificate of deposit, the defendant appealed."

II.   Appellant's first complaint is of the following part
of the sixth instruction: "If it be shown by the evidence that
each of the parties treated the property in question as belonging to them jointly, and each permitted the other to
2   exercise ownership over the same, this would authorize
you to find that each had a one-half interest in the
property in controversy, and that any right or interest which
either had inconsistent-with such interest had been relinquished and given to the other." Appellant insists, as a
matter of law, "that the mere exercise of these acts of apparent joint ownership did not constitute a joint ownership in
fact, and the court was not warranted in assuming that they
did." It is argued that in this part of the instruction the
court usurped the province of the jury, and many authorities
are cited, from this and other states, holding that it is error
for the court to assume that any controverted fact is established. There is no controversy as to the law, but only as to
its application to this case. While acts of apparent joint
ownership are competent to be proven, and may be sufficient
to establish such ownership, they are not conclusive of it.
The part of the instruction objected to does not assume anything as to the disputed facts, but simply directs the jury
that if it is shown that each party treated the property as
belonging to them jointly, and permitted the other to exercise
ownership over it, this would authorize the jury to find a
joint ownership. The jury was not told that such act would
be conclusive as to the question of joint ownership, but only
that it might therefrom find such ownership. In other parts
of the same instruction, and in other instructions, it was made
plain to the jury that the acts of the parties with respect to the
ownership were not conclusive, yet proper to be considered in
determining the issue as to ownership. Attention was directed
in the seventh instruction to all the circumstances of
which there was evidence. As we view it, the instruction
complained of assumed nothing as to the facts in dispute,
and therefore the authorities cited by appellant are not
applicable.

III.   After the commencement of this action the plaintiff applied to the court in probate to be allowed two hundred and fifty dollars for her year's support as widow of Richard Owen, deceased.   As showing the necessity for an allowance, she said in her application that she was seventy-eight years of age, and unable to work, that she had to be cared 3   for by a nurse, and that all the property she possessed in her own right was involved in this suit.   The allowance was made, and the executor paid it out of the money represented by the certificate of deposit in controversy. Appellant insists that by asking and receiving this allowance the plaintiff is estopped from claiming owership of the certificate; that by so doing she elected to treat the certificate as assets of the estate, and should not now be heard to claim it as her own.   The fault of this contention is in assuming that the plaintiff conceded in that application that the certificate was an asset of the estate.   On the contrary, she showed, as a reason why she needed the allowance, that the certificate and note, her only property, were tied up in this litigation.   She did not ask to be paid an allowance out of the certificate or note, but out of the estate.   True, it appears by the inventory that there was no other personal property out of which to pay the allowance, but the deceased left a residence property that possibly might have been available. Surely it cannot be said that plaintiff admitted by her application that the estate owned this certificate and note, when in that application she states them to be her own property. There was no inconsistency in plaintiff's claiming the allowance to which she was entitled from the estate, and at the same time claiming ownership of this certificate and note.   If she had asked the allowance to be made out of this particular property, it might be otherwise, but her application negatives such a claim, and we fail to discover any inconsistency between her claim of ownership, as asserted in this action, and her application for an allowance for support as made to the probate court.   Defendant's counsel cite many authorities on

the subject of estoppel, each of which differs materially in its
facts from this case, and they are therefore not in point.
Under the facts of this case there is no estoppel, and there was
no election between inconsistent remedies.

IV. The defendant, Christensen, was examined on
behalf of the defendant, and testified that he was called upon
to prepare the will of Richard Owen, and that at that time
he asked the plaintiff who owned the property, and she said
it was her husband's property, and that she wanted him to
dispose of it as he saw fit. He further stated: "We
were talking about the Musson note, the money
deposited in the bank, the house and lot in Exira.
The plaintiff said it belonged to her husband, and she made
no claim to this money in the bank, the Musson note, or any
other property spoken of in that conversation." Witness
was then asked: "What did Richard Owen himself say when
you asked him the question as to who was the owner of the
property, and she made that kind of an answer?" This was
objected to as incompetent, immaterial, and calling for a
declaration of a party to prove his own interest, and the
objection was sustained. Ordinarily the declarations of a
party, made in his own interest, are not admissible to establish that interest; but, where the declaration is made in the
presence and hearing of his adversary, it is admissible, not
because of what is declared, but because of the manner in
which the declaration is treated by the adversary. If Mr.
Owen stated in the hearing of this witness that this property
was his, and she acquiesced in that statement, it would be evidence against her, because of her acquiescence. Under this
rule, the witness should have been permitted to answer the
question, but we think the ruling was without prejudice to
defendant. Let us assume that Richard Owen acquiesced in
the statement of the plaintiff that the property was his, or
that in her presence Richard Owen affirmed that the property
was his, and plaintiff acquiesced therein; we have only cumulative evidence to that already given, and of a character that

4

could add nothing to its weight. The defendant was seeking. to establish an admission by the plaintiff that the property belonged to her husband, and Mr. Christensen had testified that she so stated. Now, the defendant complains that at the same time he is not permitted to prove the same fact by showing that plaintiff acquiesced in Richard Owen's claim of ownership. While we think the court should have permitted the question to be answered, the refusal was without prejudice to the defendant. The defendant sought to show by Mrs. Baker that the plaintiff did not have the means with

5   which to buy the land conveyed to her by her husband, which evidence was excluded on plaintiff's objection.

There was no error in this ruling, as there was no charge of fraud in the conveyance of the farm, and no issue to which such evidence applied. It was undisputed that Mr. Owen conveyed the farm to his wife, as he had a right to do, without valuable consideration.

V. Defendant's remaining complaint is of the manner in which the verdict was arrived at. It appears by the affidavits of a number of jurors that after they had agreed to find for the plaintiff, and when considering as to the amount, it was agreed that each juror should mark the amount he was willing to allow on his ballot. This was done, and after the ballot was taken the several amounts were added, and the sum divided by twelve, which gave the quotient one thousand two hundred and sixty-nine dollars. It appears that after this was done this sum was not agreed to, but the jurors proceeded to consider further as to the amount, and after a half

6   hour's consideration, and efforts to agree upon an amount, it was then agreed that said sum of one thousand two hundred and sixty-nine dollars should be the amount of their verdict. As we have said the marking of the ballots and the adding and dividing of the aggregate amounts were without any previous agreement that the amount arrived at should be the verdict. In *Hamilton v. Railway Co.*, 36 Iowa, 31, this court said: "To render invalid a verdict

.arrived at by aggregating the several amounts which the different jurors are in favor of, and dividing the result by twelve,
there must have been an agreement on their part in advance
to be bound by the verdict thus obtained. If the verdict was
.arrived at in this way without any such agreement, and it was
.afterwards discussed and assented to as their verdict, it would
not be invalid." See, also, *Sullens v. Railway Co.*, 74 Iowa,
659. On passing upon defendant's motion for a new trial
the court required the plaintiff to remit three hundred and
ninety-one dollars from the amount of the verdict, or submit
to a new trial. The plaintiff elected to so remit, and to take
judgment for eight hundred and seventy-eight dollars. We
do not think that this action of the court is in confirmation of
the claim that this was a quotient verdict, and the defendant
(appellant) is not complaining that the *remittitur* was made.
While the course pursued by the jury is not to be commended,
it is not, in view of the cases cited, ground for reversing this
judgment. As we find no prejudicial error in the record, the
judgment of the district court is affirmed.

.J. H. PARKS, *et al.*, Trustees v. THE ANCHOR MUTUAL FIRE
INSURANCE COMPANY, Appellant.

Insurance: PROOF OF LOSS: *Sufficiency.* A written notice to an
insurance company of a loss under its policy accompanied by an
affidavit stating that the origin of the fire is unknown to the
insured, and that the loss is total, entire and complete satisfies the
1   provision in the policy requiring satisfactory proofs of loss as well
as the requirement of Code, section 1742, that notice in writing
must be given to the company of the loss accompanied by an affidavit stating how the loss occured so far as known and the extent
of the loss.

SAME. A proof of loss which complies with the statute and the
2   requirements of the policy is sufficient, although insured intended
it only as a notice.

Appeal from Union District Court.—HON. W. H. TEDFORD,
Judge.

MONDAY, OCTOBER 17, 1898.

ACTION on a policy of fire insurance.   Judgment for plaintiffs, and defendant appeals.—*Affirmed.*

Sullivan & Sullivan for appellant.

Milligan & Lee for appellees.

GRANGER, J.—I.   The plaintiffs, three in number, are the trustees of Dodge Center Methodist Episcopal Church. In June, 1893, the defendant company issued its policy of fire insurance to the plaintiffs, by which it insured, in the sum of one thousand dollars, the church building of said church and the furniture therein.   During the life of the policy, and on the eighth day of June, 1895, the insured property was totally destroyed by fire.   This action is to recover for the loss. The petition shows that notice and proofs of loss were furnished to defendant, and that the plaintiffs otherwise performed all the conditions of the policy on their part.   There was a demurrer to the petition, which the court overruled, and the defendant answered.   By both demurrer and answer a question is presented as to proofs of loss, and it is the only controverted question on the appeal.   It is admitted that plaintiffs furnished to defendant the following:

"To the Anchor Fire Insurance Co., Creston, Iowa— Gentlemen: You are hereby notified that the church building, located on section 10, township 73 north, range 29 west of the 5th P. M., Union county, Iowa, belonging to the Dodge Center M. E. Church, and insured in your company, under and by virtue of policy No. 6,238, dated June 15, 1893, expiring June 15, 1899, was destroyed by fire on the night of the 8th day of June, 1896; that said destruction was total, entire and complete.   The Dodge Center M. E. Church, by J. H. Parks, J. E. Turner, and C. A. Elliott, trustees."

"State of Iowa, Union County—ss.   We, J. H. Parks, J. E. Turner, and C. A. Elliott, trustees of the Dodge Center M. E. church, on oath, first being sworn, each for himself

depose and say : That we are the trustees of the Dodge Center
M. E. Church located at section 10, township 73 north, in
range No. 29 west of the 5th P. M., in Union county, Iowa;
that the church building located on said section 10-73-29,
belonging to said Dodge Center M. E. church, and insured in
the Anchor Fire Insurance Company, of Creston, Iowa, under
and by virtue of policy 6,238, was destroyed by fire on the
night of the 8th of June, 1895; that the destruction was
total, entire, and complete; that we have no knowledge as
to the origin of the fire or the cause thereof.   J. H. Parks.
J. E. Turner."

The policy provides that in case of loss it shall be paid in
"sixty days after satisfactory proofs are received at the
office" of the company.   After the company received the above
notice and affidavit, its secretary wrote the plaintiff the following letter: "Creston, Iowa, July 19th, 1895.   J. H.
Parks, J. E. Turner, and C. A. Elliott, Trustees Dodge Center
M. E. Church, Afton, Iowa.   Gentlemen: We are in receipt
of your notice of loss under policy No. 6,238.   We now await
your proof of loss made in conformity with the requirements
of the policy, you having refused to hold any conversation
with our adjuster who was sent to investigate the loss reported
by you.   Yours, truly, Geo. J. Delmege, Secretary."   By an
amendment to the petition, plaintiffs attempted to plead a
waiver of proof of loss, other than as above set out, and the
parties are in contention as to the sufficiency of such a plea,
which contention we do not find it necessary to settle, for we
think the notice and affidavit are a full compliance with the
requirements of the policy.   It will be seen that the policy
provides no details for the proofs of loss, but merely says the
loss shall be paid "sixty days after satisfactory proofs are
received."   The statutory requirement is that before an
assured can recover, he must show that "he has given the company or association notice in writing of such loss, accompanied
by an adffiavit stating the facts as to how the loss occurred, so
far as they are within his knowledge, and the extent of the

loss." It is conceded in argument that the statutory requir-
ment is the basis of the contract, and what must be
observed. It is quite apparent that the notice and affidavit
were made with the provisions of the statute in mind, for
they seem to be almost a literal compliance with its requirements. It is true, the words "proof of loss" are not used in
the paper furnished by plaintiffs, nor are such words used in
the law. Importance is attached to the fact that the paper
is not called by plaintiffs "proof of loss," but simply a notice.
That it contains a notice is true, and a notice is required. It
is further required that the notice shall be accompanied by
an affidavit, and this is done. Appellant, both in pleading
and argument, treats this statute as requiring proof of loss,
and, we think, correctly so. We also think the "satisfactory
proof" required by the policy means this statutory proof, for
we assume that, in the absence of particular specification, an
observance of the law would be satisfactory. We reach the
question, then, does the law require more than is stated in the
affidavit? The law requires that the affidavit shall show two
things: *First*, how the loss occurred, when known; and,
second, the extent of the loss. The affidavit in this case shows
that the plaintiffs do not know how the fire occurred, and
hence the statute does not require the fact to appear. It shows
that the loss was the entire property insured. It is thought
that such a statement does not show the extent of the loss
within the meaning of the law. The law requires that the
facts shall be stated showing the extent of the loss. It is
urged that the affidavit should show the actual cash value of
the church and of the personal property. We think not
necessarily so. The insurable value of the church, under the
terms of the policy, was eight hundred dollars, and that of
the furniture two hundred dollars. The affidavit shows that
all was destroyed. It seems to us that such a statement is one
of fact showing the extent of the loss within the meaning of
the law. Appellant thinks *Brock v. Insurance Co.*, 96 Iowa,
39, settles the point in its favor, but we do not so understand it.

It is true that in that case an affidavit is held insufficient as proof of loss, either under the law or the terms of the policy. The policy in that case was specific as to the facts to be shown in the proofs of loss, as to which there was not a compliance; and the statutory requirement was not met by stating the facts showing how the loss occurred, and it was not made to appear that such facts were not known. In this case it is made to appear that such facts were not known, and hence the requirement to show the facts is avoided.

Some importance is attached to the fact that one of the plaintiffs said in his testimony that the paper furnished defendant was only intended as a notice. That is said in one part of his testimony, but when all is considered a different meaning might be understood. But, with appellant's view, the legal effect is not different. The paper contains a notice and an affidavit as the law requires, and its sufficiency is not dependent on the intent of the trustees, but on the contents. If insufficient in statement, it would not amount to proof of loss, although so intended; nor, on the contrary, would mere intent take from a sufficient statement its legal effect.

Some question is made as to the admission of testimony by one of the trustees bearing on the question of waiver. With our view of the case, the question of waiver is not involved, and no prejudice could have resulted. The court could say, as a matter of law, that the proofs of loss were sufficient. The judgment is AFFIRMED.

STATE OF IOWA v. WILLIAM FIELDS, Appellant.

Demurrer to Indictment: FORMER ACQUITTAL. One whose demurrer to an indictment, on the ground that it contained matter which was a legal defense to the prosecution, was sustained by the district court and his discharge directed, may interpose a plea of former acquittal to a subsequent indictment setting out a little more fully the facts charged in the first where a resubmission of the cause was not ordered, and although the ruling of the district court was reversed on appeal.

SAME. A judgment sustaining a demurrer to an indictment is final
2 not only as to the indictment itself but as to all the issues presented by the demurrer.

SAME. Code, section 4366, provides that "the judgment for defendant on demurrer, except where it is otherwise provided, or for an objection to it in form or substance taken on the trial, or for var-
1 iance between the indictment and the proof, shall not bar another prosecution for the same offense." Section 4356 provides "if the demurrer is sustained because the indictment contains matter which is a legal defense or bar to the indictment, the judgment shall be final and the defendant must be discharged." *Held*, that a judgment sustaining a demurrer to an indictment because it presents a legal defense, is a bar to a second indictment.

DEMURRER AND MOTION. Code, section 4244, providing that "an order to set aside the indictment as provided in this chapter (relating to setting aside indictments on motion) shall be no bar to future prosecutions for the same offense," does not apply to an order holding an indictment insufficient on demurrer.

FINAL JUDGMENT. A ruling sustaining a demurrer to an indictment on the ground that it contained matter which was a legal defense
8 or bar to the prosecution and directing the discharge of the defendant and the release of his bondsmen is in legal effect a final judgment.

Same. The provision of Code, 1873, section 4364, that a conviction or acquittal by a judgment on a verdict shall bar another prosecution
2 for the same offense does not exclude a conviction or acquittal without a verdict from having the same effect.

Appeal from Buchanan District Court.—HON. A. S. BLAIR,
Judge.

MONDAY, OCTOBER 17, 1898.

THE defendant was convicted of the crime of fraudulent banking, and from the judgment rendered against him he appeals.—*Reversed.*

H. C. Hemenway, Powers, Lacy & Brown, Mullan & Pickett, Hemenway & Grundy, and *J. B. Powers* for appellant.

Milton Remley, Attorney General, for the State.

ROBINSON, J.—The indictment charges that the offense
of which the defendant was convicted was committed as follows: "The said William Fields on the 15th day of May
in the year of our Lord 1893, in the county [Blackhawk]
aforesaid, being then and there president of the First National
Bank of Cedar Falls, Iowa, a corporation duly organized
under the laws of the United States for the purpose of carrying on and transacting a banking business, and such First
National Bank being then and there insolvent, he, the said
William Fields, as such president, with knowledge of such
insolvency, did then and there, willfully, unlawfully, and
feloniously, permit to be received by the First National Bank
of Cedar Falls, Iowa, and did receive and accept for the First
National Bank of Cedar Falls, Iowa, from one Ben Hesser,
acting as clerk of Ed. Wilson, as a deposit, about one hundred
and ninety dollars in money, bank bills, treasury notes, and
currency of the United States, circulating as money or currency, and of the value of about one hundred and ninety dollars ($190.00), and the property of the said Ed. Wilson, con-
trary to the form of the statutes, and against the peace and
dignity of the state of Iowa." The defendant appeared to
the indictment, waived formal arraignment, and entered the
plea of not guilty; reserving the right, however, to withdraw
the plea for the purpose of filing a motion, or demurring to
the indictment, or entering a challenge to the grand jury.
Afterwards, on proper application, the place of trial was
changed from Blackhawk to Buchanan county, and the cause
was there tried.

The indictment on which the conviction of the defendant is based was returned by the grand jury of Blackhawk
county in September, 1895. It is the second one returned by
that body for the same act,—the receiving from Hesser, for
Ed. Wilson, of the sum specified, on the date stated.
1　　　The first indictment was returned in September,
　　　1893. The cause was transferred to Buchanan county.
A demurrer to the indictment was there sustained, and it

was ordered that the defendant be discharged. An appeal was taken by the state, and the judgment of the district court was reversed. See 98 Iowa, 748. It is insisted by the appellant that the judgment rendered by the district court on that demurrer was a final adjudication as to his guilt, and a bar to a second indictment for the same offense. The language of the two indictments is substantially the same, excepting the first indictment does not contain that portion of the second one which appears between the words "permit to be received," and "from Ben Hesser," which is as follows: "by the First National Bank of Cedar Falls, Iowa, and did receive and accept for the First National Bank of Cedar Falls, Iowa." The demurrer which was filed to the first indictment and sustained stated "*   *   * that the indictment contains matter which, if true, constitutes a legal defense and bar to the prosecution of this action, in this, to wit." Grounds of demurrer were then set out in seven distinct paragraphs. All but one of these were based upon the theory that as the bank of which the defendant was president, and for which the deposit in question was received, was a national bank, organized under and regulated by acts of congress which applied to national banks, the general assembly of this state lacked the power to prohibit or punish the act with which the defendant is charged; that the act of the general assembly under which the indictment was returned does not, for that reason, apply to national banks and their officers; that, so far as the act purports to apply to such banks and officers, it is unconstitutional; and that the state courts have no jurisdiction to try the defendant for the offense charged. The sixth ground of the demurrer was stated as follows: "The indictment does not substantially conform to the requirements of the Code of Iowa, and fails to state facts sufficient to constitute a crime under the laws of the state, in this: That said indictment fails to state that the money named in the indictment was deposited in or received by the First National Bank of Cedar Falls,

Iowa, as a deposit, and fails to state that the defendant knowingly received said money, or knowingly authorized or permitted said money to be received, as a deposit." The demurrer
was sustained upon all grounds but the sixth, and as to that
ground it was overruled, and it was ordered that the defendant be discharged, and that his bonds be released. The defendant pleaded to the second indictment the action thus had as
an acquittal, and that plea was withdrawn from the jury by
an instruction of the court.

The statutes which applied to this cause in the district
court are found in the Code of 1873. Section 4347 of that
Code provides that issues of law shall be tried by the court.
Section 4352 provides that "the defendant may demur to the
indictment when it appears upon its face either (1) that it
does not substantially conform to the requirements of the
Code, (2) that the indictment contains any matter which, if
true, would constitute a legal defense or bar to the prosecution." Section 4356 provides that, "if the demurrer is sustained because the indictment contains matter which is a
legal defense or bar to the indictment, the judgment shall
be final, and the defendant must be discharged." Section
4357 provides that if the demurrer is sustained on any other
ground than that the offense charged is within the exclusive
jurisdiction of another county of this state, or that the indictment contains matter which is a legal defense or bar to the
indictment, the defendant must be dealt with as provided in
section 4341 of the Code, unless the court, being of the opinion
that the objection can be remedied or avoided in another
indictment, orders the cause to be resubmitted, and when that
is done the defendant may be dealt with as provided by section 4342 of the Code. It may be that there are clerical errors
in the references to sections contained in section 4357, but we
have used the citations which it gives without, however,
determining that there are not errors, or the proper effect of
the section in cases to which it is applicable. It is enough
to say of it that it authorized the re-submission of a cause

to a grand jury where the indictment was found to be defective and the court believed the defect could be cured by another indictment, and where the court ordered the re-submission. This case does not come within that provision. The only ground of the demurrer which can be regarded as having been based upon a defect which could have been cured by a new indictment was the sixth, and the demurrer was overruled as to that ground, although the change in the new indictment was doubtless made to avoid it. The other grounds of the demurrer were, in effect, that the indictment contained matter which was a legal defense or bar to the indictment, and, as the demurrer was sustained on those grounds, the case was within the provisions of section 4356. The order made on the ruling was not in the form of a judgment, but, it, in terms, discharged the defendant and released his bonds, and was, in legal effect, a final judgment. *State v. Alverson,* 105 Iowa, 152. What is the effect of a final judgment for which section 4356 provides? It is said that the section does not state that the judgment and discharge of the defendant thereunder shall be a bar to further prosecution, and that they should not be given that effect; and section 4344 is cited as supporting this

2   theory. That section is as follows: "An order to set aside the indictment as provided in this chapter, shall be no bar to a future prosecution for the same offense." But the chapter in which that appears relates to the setting aside of indictments on motion, and not to indictments held to be insufficient on demurrer, and does not apply to this case. Section 4364 provides that "a conviction or acquittal by a judgment upon a verdict shall bar another prosecution for the same offense, notwithstanding a defect in form or substance in the indictment on which the conviction or acquittal took place," and section 4366 is as follows: "The judgment for the defendant on demurrer, except where it is otherwise provided, or for an objection to its form or substance taken on the trial, or for variance between the indictment and the proof, shall not bar another prosecution for the

same offense." The state relies on the first of these sections as tending strongly to show that a judgment of acquittal not based on a verdict will not bar another prosecution for the same offense, and it relies upon the second as conclusive that a judgment for the defendant on a demurrer does not bar another prosecution for the same offense, for it is contended that it is not "otherwise provided" by any statutory provision. We do not think the fact that section 4364 specifies only a conviction or acquittal by a judgment on a verdict tends to show that a conviction or acquittal without a verdict may not bar another prosecution for the same offense. The section refers to judgments rendered on verdicts in cases in which the indictments are defective in form or in substance, and not to judgments not rendered on verdicts. Section 4366 excepts from the general rule which it prescribes, that judgment for the defendant on a demurrer shall not bar another prosecution for the same offense, those cases "where it is otherwise provided." Sections 4355 and 4356 permit the district court to order a re-submission of the cause to the grand jury when a demurrer to the indictment has been sustained, if the demurrer was not sustained on the ground that the offense charged was within the exclusive jurisdiction of another county, or on the ground that the indictment contains matter which is a legal defense or bar to the indictment. In neither of those cases was a re-submission authorized, for the sufficient reason, no doubt, that the defect could not be cured or avoided by another indictment. When the defect was the jurisdictional one, there was provision for instituting proceedings in the proper county, and for securing the appearance thereto of the defendant; but, if the demurrer was sustained because the indictment showed facts which were a legal defense or bar to it, final judgment and the discharge of the defendant were required. It is suggested that the judgment was required to be final only as to the indictment to which the demurrer was sustained, but we are of the opinion that it is also final as to the issues presented by the demurrer. If the indictment shows that there cannot be a valid conviction for the offense charged, reason and sound public policy demand that the proceedings be terminated, and that neither the state nor the defendant be subject to the expense or annoyance of further prosecutions which cannot end in conviction. In such a case as much can be accomplished by one indictment as by many, and the judgment which the statute contemplates is as far-reaching and conclusive as to the defendant's liability for the crime charged as though.it had been rendered upon a verdict of not guilty.

3
See 1 Bushwell Criminal Procedure, 782; Wharton Criminal Practice, section 404. When the district court sustained the demurrer to the first indictment, it did not order a re-submission of the cause; and, although additional matter, which we have noted, was set out in the second indictment, it did not change the nature of the offense alleged, and was not made in consequence of any order of the court. The second indictment merely sets out a little more fully the facts charged in the first indictment, and is vulnerable to the objections which the district court held to be fatal to the first indictment. The fact that this court adjudged that the ruling of the district court on the demurrer and its judgment were erroneous did not affect the right of the defendant to insist that as to him the judgment was final. *State v. Kinney,* 44 Iowa, 444.

There is no controversy in regard to the facts of this case which we have been considering, and we conclude that the district court erred in withdrawing from the jury the plea of former acquittal. Since this conclusion is necessarily conclusive of the case, there is no necessity for determining numerous questions presented in argument, nor for approving or disapproving the opinion in *State v. Fields,* 98 Iowa, 748. For the error pointed out the judgment of the district court is REVERSED.

JAMES ROBERTSON, SR., Appellant v. THE MOLINE MILBURN
STODDARD COMPANY.

Deed as Mortgage: EVIDENCE. Agreement of grantee that if he does
not sell the property, and grantor pays a certain debt within a
year, he will convey the property back, does not make the deed a
mortgage.

REDEMPTION. A creditor to whom real estate has been conveyed by
an absolute deed for the purpose of securing a debt cannot redeem
the property from a sale on foreclosure after the nine months from
the date of sale.

Appeal from Cherokee District Court.—HON. SCOTT M.
LADD, Judge.

MONDAY, OCTOBER 17, 1898.

ACTION to have a deed, absolute upon its face, declared
a mortgage, and to quiet plaintiff's title against the mortgagee. Trial to court. Decree for defendant. Plaintiff
appeals.—*Affirmed.*

E. C. Herrick for appellant.

M. Wakefield and *J. D. F. Smith* for appellee.

WATERMAN, J.—The following statement discloses the
issues involved: In April, 1889, one W. W. Merideth was
engaged in business in Washta, Iowa. He failed about this
time, owing appellee the sum of one thousand six hundred dollars. Appellee commenced an action on its claim, and sued
out a writ of attachment, which was levied on Merideth's
property. Merideth was in possession of lot 7 in block 4 in
the town of Washta, the title being in the name of his wife.
Appellant has a mortgage on this lot to secure the sum of about
nine hundred dollars. The Des Moines Buggy Company also
has a mortgage thereon, securing a debt of two hundred and
fifty dollars. The property was worth less than the mortgage

debts.   After appellee's writ of attachment was sued out,
Merideth and wife gave to Smith, appellee's attorney, and
who acted for it in the attachment proceeding, a warranty
deed of said lot.   This deed contained full covenants of warranty, except as against the mortgages mentioned.   Appellant
foreclosed his mortgage on the lot, sold the same on execution,
and bid it in for about four hundred and fifty dollars.   The
Des Moines Buggy Company, appellee, and Smith, were
parties defendant in the foreclosure proceeding.   Smith conveyed the property to appellee, who redeemed from the foreclosure sale within one year, but after nine months from the
date of the sale.

The appellant now claims that the deed from Merideth to
Smith was a mortgage only; that redemption should have been
made by appellee as creditor, and, not having been made
within nine months from date of sale, such right is barred;
and that appellant is now the owner and entitled to a deed.
On a former appeal of this case (88 Iowa, 463), it was
held that a creditor, to whom the real estate has been conveyed
by an absolute deed for the purpose of securing a debt, is not
a vendee of the debtor, in such sense as to allow of his making
redemption during the last three months of the year succeeding the sale.   This holding is the law of this case.   *Rice v.
Grand Lodge*, 103 Iowa, 643.   In order to have an absolute
conveyance declared a mortgage, the proof should be clear
and satisfactory.   *Langer v. Meservey*, 80 Iowa, 158, and
cases cited.   In *Kibby v. Harsh*, 61 Iowa, 196, it is said
such proof must be conclusive.   There was testimony on the
part of plaintiff tending to show that the deed was given as
security only.   But there was evidence on behalf of defendant
which was directly in conflict with this claim.   It was the
contention of defendant, and it offered evidence in support
of it, that Smith took an absolute title under the deed, but
that, by oral agreement, he was to sell the property and make
a certain application of the proceeds.   Appellant claims that

this agreement created an express trust, and that oral evidence was not competent to establish it. This may be conceded, but we cannot perceive that it in any wise strengthens plaintiff's case. The denial that the conveyance was taken as security still stands. If all testimony relating to the so-called "trust" is stricken out, it in no manner detracts from the evidence offered in defendant's behalf, to the effect that there was no agreement or understanding that Merideth was to retain a right of redemption.

It is argued by appellant that Smith, who was the principal witness for the defense, admits that the Merideths retained a right of redemption. We do not so understand his testimony. He does say it was agreed that if he did not sell the property, and if Merideth paid a certain debt within one year, he (Smith) was to deed the property back. While it is not clear, there is some evidence tending to show that this agreement to re-convey was made after the delivery of the deed, and was purely voluntary on Smith's part. However this may be, such an arrangement is far from giving or reserving a right of redemption. It in no way fettered Smith's right to sell at any time. Smith testified that this agreement was in writing, and counsel for appellant argues earnestly and at some length that, under the issues, his evidence on this point should not have been admitted. The claim is that an oral trust agreement was pleaded, and no other could properly be proved. Since we allow no weight to the trust agreement in our consideration of the case, this matter is wholly immaterial. But we think counsel is in error on this point. The oral agreement pleaded was that creating the trust; the written agreement testified to did not relate to the application Smith was to make of the proceeds of the property when sold, but only to a right given the Merideths to re-purchase within a fixed period if he did not dispose of the land. The testimony is not of such a convincing character as to warrant us holding the conveyance to be a mortgage. The decree of the district court is therefore AFFIRMED.

LADD, J., took no part.

L. L. BENJAMIN, Appellant, v. W. J. FLITTON and H. W. SQUIRES.

Evidence: RELIANCE. Evidence as to whether the holder of a note which was given in part payment of a piano sold by her would
1 have accepted it if the indorser had not agreed to guarantee the payment thereof is inadmissible in an action upon the note, where the negotiations for the sale were conducted entirely by the husband of the holder of the note.

Pleading: INSTRUCTIONS. An instruction in an action on a promissory note that if an indorser agreed to waive demand and protest
2 and guaranteed the note he could not set up his own default in failing to comply with his promise, is properly refused where the holder of the note did not plead waiver or estoppel.

SAME. An instruction in an action upon a promissory note that if the indorser authorized or consented to a waiver of demand and protest and guaranteed the note he is estopped from denying liability
3 thereon, is properly refused where the plaintiff did not plead waiver or estoppel and did not rely upon an oral waiver of demand and protest, instead, declaring on a written waiver.

NEW TRIAL. A new trial on the ground of newly discovered evidence is properly refused where the witness who is to give such evidence
4 was so connected with the transaction in regard to which he would testify that ordinary diligence would have suggested inquiries of him before the trial but no such inquiries were made, and no excuse is given for not making them.

Appeal from Marshall District Court.—HON. OBED CASWELL, Judge.

MONDAY, OCTOBER 17, 1898.

ACTION at law upon a promissory note made by W. J. Flitton to H. W. Squires, and by Squires indorsed to plaintiff. On the back of the note is the following indorsement and contract of guaranty: "For value received, I hereby guaranty payment of the within note, and waive demand and notice of protest on the same when due." "Pay to L. L. Benjamin. [Signed] H. W. Squires." Plaintiff seeks to recover the amount of the note from Squires upon the contract of guaranty. Squires denies that he signed the guaranty, and alleges that all that part of it preceding the word "pay" was written upon the note without his assent or authority. On the issues thus joined the case was submitted to a jury, resulting in a verdict and judgment for defendant Squires, and plaintiff appeals.—*Affirmed.*

A. F. & F. M. Haradon for appellant.

J. M. Parker for appellees.

DEEMER, C. J.—It is conceded that that part of appellee's contract constituting the guaranty was made with a rubber stamp after he had signed an ordinary contract of indorsement; and the main contention in the case is whether or not it was placed thereon with authority. This was a question of fact, which was fairly submitted to the jury upon conflicting evidence, and with its findings we cannot interfere.

II. Appellant was asked whether or not she would have accepted the note, which was given in part payment of a piano sold by her to Squires, if he (Squires) had not agreed to guaranty the payment thereof. Objection to the question was sustained, and error is assigned upon the ruling. As the negotiations for the sale were conducted entirely by appellant's husband, the testimony was immaterial and irrelevant. The husband was a witness for plaintiff and testified to the terms of sale, and to the agreement of Squires to guaranty the note.

III. Plaintiff asked an instruction to the effect that, if Squires agreed to waive demand and protest, and guaranty the note, he then could not be heard to plead his own default in failing to comply with his promise, and the jury should find for plaintiff. This instruction was refused, and, we think, properly so, for the reason that appellant did not plead waiver or estoppel. The argument in support of the instruction proceeds upon the theory that an indorser or guarantor may orally waive demand and notice of protest. If it be conceded that this is the law, still it does not aid appellant, for the reason that she declares upon a written waiver.

IV. Another instruction asked by appellant, to the effect that if Squires at any time authorized or consented to the contract, he would thereafter be estopped from denying liability thereon, was refused, and error is assigned upon this ruling. The ruling was correct. Plaintiff did not plead waiver or estoppel, nor did she rely upon an oral waiver of demand and protest. Moreover, the court instructed the jury, in the fourth paragraph of its charge, that if Squires agreed to guaranty the note in form substantially as now appears, that the contract was placed over his signature in compliance with this agreement, and that this indorsement was seen, known of, or assented to by Squires as part of the consideration of the original contract of sale, then they should find for plaintiff. This embodied the thought contained in the instruction which was refused, and the jury evidently found with defendant on the facts.

V. One of the grounds of the motion for a new trial was newly-discovered evidence. The greater part of this evidence was cumulative, and some of it was impeaching in character. A part of it did not belong to either class, and would have justified a new trial, had proper diligence been exercised to obtain it. The witness who it is said would deliver this evidence was so connected with the transactions of which it is claimed he would testify that ordinary diligence would have suggested inquiries be made of him before the trial, in order to discover what he knew of the case. No such inquiries were made, and no excuse is given for not making them. Inquiry seems to have been made the next day after the verdict was returned, and the discovery is said to have then been made. Exercise of the same amount of diligence before as after verdict would no doubt have led to knowledge of this evidence. Diligence to obtain evidence

should begin before the verdict is returned.   Appellee has
filed an amended abstract purporting to supply omissions in
the original abstract.   We do not find any such omission, and
the cost of preparing the same will be taxed to appellee.
Upon the filing of this abstract appellant secured an order for
a transcript from one of the judges of this court.   This transcript was also unnecessary, and the cost of procuring the
same will also be taxed to the appellee.—AFFIRMED.

GREEN BAY LUMBER COMPANY, Appellant, v. EDWIN
THOMAS, *et al.*

Mechanic's Lien: CLAIMS AGAINST COUNTY: *Filing.* Under Acts
Twentieth General Assembly, chapter 179, section 2, providing for
payment of sub-contractors of public building by the municipality
on the filing of verified claims with the officer on whose order
payment for such building is to be made, and the Code, section 482,
requiring payment by county treasurers to be made only on warrants of the county auditor, a claim for material furnished for a
1 county building must be filed with the county auditor, even where
the board of supervisors appoint one member of the board a superintendent for the building, and direct the auditor to draw warrants for work on the building on his order. While the supervisor
is a public officer, the law does not authorize him by virtue of his
office to issue an order for payment of public money.

FRAUD IN STATEMENT: *Rights of sub-contractors.* A contractor who
erected one building for a private person and also a jail with
material furnished by a sub-contractor, made the latter a pay-
3 ment half of which was credited on the jail account. This application was, later, so changed as to make it, instead, a credit on the
private building. The contractor insists that the change was
made simply because he did not desire that a lien should exist
against the private house. The weight of the evidence, however,
shows that such change was made because the contractor represented that the original application was due to mistake. *Held,*
a   Under such circumstances, the change of account on the part of
the sub-contractor, though it increased its claim against the jail
by $200, which if allowed, would diminish the fund for the pay-
ment of the other sub-contractors, by that sum, did not amount
to a fraud which would destroy its mechanic's lien.
b   But while this evidence negatives such fraud it does not establish that a mistake was in fact made in the application of the
payment

c   So, while a judgment for the sum due after such change was
    made, might properly be rendered against the contractor, for the
    reason that debtor and creditor may change the application of
4   a payment at will, as between themselves, such change will not
    be allowed to deprive other sub-contractors of any portion of
    the fund subject to their liens, and as to them, the representa-
    tion by which the contractor obtained the change, are mere
    hearsay.

PAYMENT: *Variation of books of account.*   A sub-contractor received
    a warrant for $400, from the contractor, paid him $100 in cash,
2   credited him on its books with $400 and charged him with said
    $100.   *Held,* it might be shown by parol that nothing more than
    reducing the sub-contractor's lien claim, by $300 was intended by
    the transaction.

Appeal from Jackson District Court.—HON. A. J. HOUSE,
Judge.

MONDAY, OCTOBER 17, 1898.

ACTION to establish a claim against Jackson county for
materials furnished in the erection of a jail. Six other sub-
contractors filed cross petitions. The claim of plaintiff was
not allowed, but judgment was rendered against the contractor, Edwin Thomas, for two hundred dollars less than the
amount claimed. The claims of cross petitioners were
allowed. The plaintiff appeals.—*Reversed.*

C. C. & C. L. Nourse, D. A. Fletcher, and *G. L. Johnson* for appellant.

*D. A. Wynkoop, W. C. Gregory, Levi Keck, Murray &
Farr, D. T. Bauman,* and *R. W. Henry* for appellees.

LADD, J.—When the jail of Jackson county was completed, in 1896, there remained a balance unpaid to the
contractor, Edwin Thomas, of one thousand one hundred and
eighty dollars. The plaintiffs and defendants, except
Thomas, are subcontractors, seeking to have their various
claims allowed and paid out of this fund under the provisions
of Chapter 179 of the Acts of the Twentieth General Assembly. Sworn and itemized accounts were filed with the

county auditor within the time limited,—that of plaintiff first,—but the other claimants also filed their accounts with one George Cooper, a member of the board of supervisors, who had been appointed by that body to superintend the construction of the building. This resolution had been adopted by the board: "The auditor is hereby authorized to draw warrants in favor of Edwin Thomas for building a jail in accordance with the contract on file upon certificate of Supervisor Cooper." In making payments the auditor had Cooper direct him on a piece of paper to issue a warrant for a particular amount, whereupon he would comply therewith. The defendant urges that under this state of facts, as plaintiff's claim was not filed with Cooper, no relief can be had; in other words, that as the auditor was directed by the board to issue warrants on the certificate of Cooper, claims must be filed with the latter, rather than with the county auditor. Section 2 of the chapter referred to is as follows: "Such claims shall be made by filing with the public officer through whose order the payment is to be made an itemized and sworn statement of the demand within 30 days after the performance of the last labor, or the furnishing of the last portion of the material, and claims shall have priority in the order in which they shall be filed." That George Cooper, as supervisor, was a public officer, is not questioned, but the law nowhere authorizes him, by virtue of that office, to issue an order for the payment of money. If he acquired such authority, it was by virtue of the resolution of the board. But that simply authorized the auditor to act under the direction of Cooper. The latter might audit the bill as just and true, and so certify it. This amounted to no more than a recommendation on which the auditor was directed by the board to act. The statute very evidently contemplates an officer authorized by law to issue warrants on the public treasury. If it were otherwise, then there would be no certainty as to the proper official with whom to file a claim, as this would depend upon the facts of each particular case. As the auditor is the only officer "through whose order payment may be made" by the county treasurer (section 482, Code), we conclude that claims of this character must be filed with the auditor.

II.   The plaintiff's account, after rejecting some minor matters, concerning which there is no dispute, amounted to six hundred dollars and fifty-nine cents. Two items only are questioned. On October 2, 1896, Thomas, wishing to pay the company three hundred dollars and his employes one hundred dollars, procured a warrant of four hundred dollars from the county, transferred it to the plaintiff, and received one hundred dollars back. Instead of crediting him with the amount actually paid, the company credited him on the book with the amount of the warrant, and charged him one hundred dollars cash. It is insisted this cash item must be deducted from the account, because no lien may be established for money had and received. This would be giving more importance to the shadow than the real thing. Bookkeeping has not arrived at that state of perfection which precludes all oral explanation. *Christman v. Pearson,* 100 Iowa, 634. The entries as made indicated the right net credit, and oral evidence was admissible to show that both items were a part of the same transaction, and, rightly understood, showed the payment of three hundred dollars on the account.

III.   The contractors paid the plaintiff $400 on the thirtieth day of October, 1890, and this was acknowledged in a receipt in the words: "Received of Ed. Thomas $400; $200 on Dunham and $200 on jail." This two hundred dollars appeared on the books also credited on the materials furnished for the construction of the jail. Thomas called on Busby, the company's agent, December 23, 1896, and requested that this credit be transferred from the jail account, so as to apply on material furnished for the building

of a house for one Grant, against which the plaintiff had
filed a mechanic's lien.   There is a dispute as to
3   what was said at that time.   Thomas insists he gave
as the only reason for asking a change his desire that
a lien should not be placed on Grant's house, and that Busby
declined to make the change, saying: "It might be, if we
could put it with the jail bill, and that was allowed, then it
could be credited on the Grant occount."   The agent denies
positively having made this statement, and both he and his
brother, the company's bookkeeper, testify in the most positive way that Thomas insisted the two hundred dollars
should have been credited on materials furnished for Grant's
house; that Grant had paid the money, and that he (Thomas)
had so directed Busby, and that the latter had misunderstood him; and further charged him with misapplying it pur-
posely because of being on Thomas' bond for building the
jail, and declared that the credit must be changed, and the
mistakes corrected.   They further testify that the items of
credit were erased from the account of material furnished
for the jail and the footings changed accordingly, and, as
so changed, the account, when verified, was filed with the
auditor.   The evidence also shows that a single account was
kept with Thomas, but the materials going into different
buildings distinguished.   Thus, on the book this two hundred
dollars credit was followed by the word "Jail."   Through this
a pencil mark was drawn, and "Grant" written instead.   No
change was made in the account filed with the lien against
Grant's house.   We think this evidence fails to establish the
fraud alleged by Suthers and Thomas, subcontractors.
Thomas would hardly ask such a correction without stating
a substantial reason for doing so.   His version of the transaction is borne down by the testimony of two equally cred-
itable witnesses and the attending circumstances.   Neither
Busby nor the company had the slightest interest in changing
the item.   Much stress is laid on the meager changes on the
book of accounts.   That book, as to these jobs, had been made

up, and alterations made at that time would not have helped matters, but they rather subjected the transaction to suspicion. The reasons suggested by Thomas as proving the mistake are such as might well have convinced Busby, and in making the correction the evidence fails to show that he acted in bad faith, or attempted double dealing. That an honest mistake in making up an account will not deprive the claimant of a lien is well established by the authorities. *Chase v. Mining Co.,* 90 Iowa, 25; *Lumber Co. v. Miller,* 98 Iowa, 468; *McMonagle v. Wilson,* 103 Mich, 264 (61 N. W. Rep. 495). We have found it unnecessary to determine whether the same rule applies against public corporations as in the case of a mechanic's lien, as, so conceding, the evidence fails to establish fraud on the part of the plaintiff.

IV.   But no mistake in fact has been shown as against the subcontractors. The receipt was drawn in accordance with the understanding of Busby and the representations of Thomas, which, while they establish the good faith of Busby, do not establish a mistake against the subcontractors.

4   Thomas denies having made them, and, as against defendants other than him, they are not admissible in evidence as tending to prove a mistake, being in the nature of hearsay. As a general rule, a change in the application of payment may be made by the mutual consent of the parties. But this is subject of the just limitation that it cannot be done when third parties will be injuriously affected thereby. See *Hargroves v. Cooke,* 15 Ga. 321; *Thayer v. Denton,* 4 Mich. 192; *Smith v. Wood,* 1 N. J. Eq. 74; *Terhune v. Colton,* 12 N. J. Eq. 232; *Berghaus v. Alter,* 9 Watts, 396; *Chancellor v. Schott,* 23 Pa. St. 68. To permit the change here would deprive the subcontractors of that portion of their fund, as the entire amount will not satisfy their claims. That, under such circumstances, change in the application of payment may not be made, is determined in *Chicago Lumber Co. v. Woods,* 53 Iowa 552. That was a mechanics' lien case, but the principle is the same whether the claim is charged

against a building or a particular fund. As no mistake was
made in the application of the two hundred dollars, the
parties had no authority to change it in a manner to injure
the subcontractors.

V. As between the plaintiff and Thomas, however, the
change was binding. They could have payments applied and
changed at will between themselves. It follows that the
plaintiff is entitled to judgment against Thomas for the
sum of six hundred dollars and fifty-nine cents, with
interest, and to have four hundred dollars and fifty-nine cents
of this established as a claim against the fund due from the
county.—REVERSED.

JULIA BARCE v. THE CITY OF SHENANDOAH, Appellant.

Negligence: CONTRIBUTION: *Jury question.* One is, as matter of
law, guilty of contributory negligence precluding recovery for a
1   fall caused by the uneven condition of the sidewalk, where she
knew the exact condition of the walk, having passed over it frequently and having previously fallen at the very same place, and,
though walking rapidly, nothing had occurred to distract her attention.

SAME. An instruction that if a municipal corporation negligently
2   constructed a sidewalk, one who sustained injuries from a fall
caused by its unevenness may recover if free from contributory
negligence, is erroneous where there is no evidence that the city
was negligent in constructing the sidewalk.

Appeal from Page District Court.—HON. A. B. THORNELL,
Judge.

TUESDAY, OCTOBER 18, 1898.

ACTION by Julia Barce against the city of Shenandoah to recover damages for injuries sustained by her
upon one of the sidewalks of the defendant city. The
case was tried to a jury, resulting in a verdict and
judgment for plaintiff in the sum of five hundred and eighty-
eight dollars, and defendant appeals.—*Reversed.*

G. B. Jennings for appellant.

S. C. Keenan for appellee.

DEEMER, C. J.—Plaintiff claims that on the fifth day of November, 1895, she tripped and fell on a street in the defendant city, and, in consequence, received serious injuries, for which she seeks compensation. Defendant denies liability for the accident, and pleads a settlement.

I. No formal answer was made to an amendment to the petition filed during the progress of the trial, but, as the averments were treated as denied, they will be so considered in this court. Appellee contends that the allegations of the petition were admitted, and that defendant's only defense was a settlement. We have already seen that the answer was a denial, as well as a plea of settlement. There was no admission of liability.

II. That plaintiff fell upon one of the sidewalks in the defendant city, and received injuries in consequence thereof, is well established. It is claimed, however, that the defendant is not responsible for the fall. Plaintiff's evidence in her own behalf is somewhat confused, and it is with difficulty that we give her version of the affair. As we under-

1   stand it, she was hurriedly passing over one of defendant's sidewalks, attempting to reach home before a rainstorm should overtake her. While passing along the walk, she tripped upon one of the boards, and fell upon the sidewalk, receiving the injuries of which she complains. The boards of the walk were laid upon three 2x4 or 2x6 stringers, and, at the place where the accident occurred, there was a thick board and a thin one. The thin one was about seven-eighths of an inch thick, and the thick one was what is called two inches thick; probably it was one and three-fourths or one and seven-eighths inches. Plaintiff says she stepped upon the thin board, and it sprung down, and she stubbed

her foot, and fell. She also said, in answer to a leading question, that her son-in-law called the attention of some members of the city council to the fact that the walk was "wiggly," and that she told these officers how the board gave down. Other witnesses for the plaintiff testified that the stringers were old and shaky, and that the whole walk at the place of accident sprung down when they walked over it. The witnesses all say that one board was about an inch thicker than the other; and the plaintiff says she stubbed her toe against the thicker board, and fell to the walk. While she says the board upon which she stepped sprung down, yet it does not appear that this was the cause of her fall. The unevenness of the walk was undoubtedly the proximate cause. The evidence further shows that some of the stringers were a little rotten, and that the walk as a whole shook a little when pedestrians passed over it. It appears without dispute that the boards were nailed firmly to the stringers, and that the alleged rotten condition of the walk had nothing to do with the accident. After plaintiff received her injuries she stated that she struck her foot against the thicker board, and that her fall was due to the unevenness of the walk.

Appellant contends that these facts do not make such a showing of negligence as justified the court in submitting the case to the jury. In view of our holding on the issue of contributory negligence, it is not necessary to determine that question. The evidence shows without dispute that plaintiff knew the exact condition of the walk. She had passed over it frequently, and had, at least once before, stumbled and fallen at the very same place, and against the identical board. At the time of the accident she was walking rapidly towards her home, but there was nothing whatever to distract her attention. She says that she was "noticing the walk, just as any person would, walking along," and that she could readily detect a thick board from a thin one in passing along the walk. It seems to us that, by the exercise of ordinary care, plaintiff might have avoided the injury. Had there been anything to divert her attention, the case might be different; but, as we have said, there was nothing of that kind. She knew of the defect, if there was one, and knew of the danger, because she had once before, at least, stumbled at the same place. Moreover, there was no evidence that she was obliged to take this walk. That she was guilty of such negligence as bars her of recovery seems to be settled by the following, among other, authorities: *Raymond v. Lowell,* 6 Cush. 524; *Dale v. Webster County,* 76 Iowa, 370; *McLaury v. City of McGregor,* 54 Iowa, 717; *Tuffree v. State Center,* 57 Iowa, 538; *Cosner v. City of Centerville,* 90 Iowa, 33; *Achtenbagen v. City of Watertown,* 18 Wis. 331; *Gribble v. City of Sioux City,* 38 Iowa, 390; *Marshall v. City of Belle Plaine,* 106 Iowa, *post.*

III. There was no evidence that the city was guilty of any fault in the original construction of the walk; yet the court instructed that, if the city was guilty of negligence in erecting the same, then plaintiff, if free from negligence, might recover. That it is error to instruct upon a matter of which there is no evidence, is familiar doctrine, and no authorities need be cited to sustain it. As sustaining our conclusion on this branch of the case, however, see *Barnes v. Newton,* 46 Iowa, 567. For the errors pointed out, the judgment is REVERSED.

The Finance Company of Iowa, Appellant v. Frank Anderson & Company, *et al.*

Landlord and Tenant: LEASE. A clause in a lease providing that live stock and growing crops on the premises shall be security for the sums due or to become due from the lessees to the lessor arising out of the lease "as evidenced by book account or note held by the lessor," secures only such claims as are evidenced by such book account or note.

Appeal from Woodbury District Court.—Hon. Scott M. Ladd, Judge.

Tuesday, October 18, 1898.

THE firm of Frank Anderson & Co. is composed of Frank Anderson, A. H. Parsons, and George O. West. Frank Anderson & Co. made its note to the plaintiff, and this action is to recover thereon, aided by an attachment. A. H. Parsons and George O. West, of the firm of Anderson & Co., constitute the firm of Parsons & West, and were lessees of a farm, known as the "Barlow Hall Farm," with the intervener A. K. Barlow as lessor. The lease expired March 25, 1894. The firm of Parsons & West was succeeded by Parsons & West Company, a corporation, after March 25, 1894, and became lessee of the Barlow Hall farm, under a new lease, for one year. On the farm, at the commencement of this suit, was hay, raised in the years 1892 and 1893, known in the record as the "old hay," on which the writ of attachment was levied. A. K. Barlow intervenes, claiming a lien on said hay superior to the lien of the attachment, because of a provision of the lease to that effect. The district court sustained the lien of intervener Barlow as prior to the attachment, and, from such holding, the plaintiff appealed.—*Reversed.*

The attachment was also levied on hay and corn raised on the farm in 1894, and Parsons & West Company intervened, claiming the ownership thereof freed from the lien of the attachment. The answer of plaintiff to such intervention petition, among other matters, denied its corporate capacity. The district court held the company not to be a corporation, that defendants Parsons & West owned the property, and denied intervener's right to it. From such a holding, the intervener appealed.—*Affirmed.*

William Milchrist for plaintiff.

Geo. Conway for intervener A. K. Barlow.

J. P. Blood & Co. and *Lynn & Foley* for intervener Parsons & West Co.

GRANGER, J.—I. We first notice plaintiff's appeal, which alone concerns the claims of plaintiff and intervener

Barlow to the old hay.   The intervener's only right to the hay is by virtue of what is called a "mortgage clause" in the lease, as follows: "All live stock and crops growing or in stack, crib, or granary, on said premises, shall be security for the sums due or to become due, from the parties of the second part to the party of the first part, arising out of this agreement, as evidenced by book account or note held by party of the first part."   A contention arises over the words "as evidenced by book account or note held by party of the first part."   Appellee insists that the only claims secured by the clause quoted from the lease are such as are evidenced by book account or note; while appellant contends that such a construction is narrow, and that the proper construction is that the provision secures all "claims arising out of the agreement."   If the words on which appellant relies as a limitation should be stricken from the lease, it would read and mean just what appellee claims; so that, if we adopt his construction, we must treat the words "as evidenced by book account or note" as without meaning.   The word "as" is sometimes used for "when."   See Standard Dictionary.   Substitute the word "when" for "as," and the meaning would be clear that the lien would only attach to claims arising out of the agreement evidenced in a particular manner.   Appellee's thought is that the words "as evidenced by book account or note" were used only "to show that, even if a note were taken for the rent, that would make no difference in the obligation created."   The words are not apt, or even proper, to express such a thought.   They are rather against it, and especially so when that would be the meaning without their use; for, omitting the words as to book account and note, and we have a lease with precisely appellee's meaning, and so plainly so as not to be open to construction.   We know of no rule or theory on which the words can be disregarded, and, if a meaning is given them, it must be that claimed by appellant. We conclude that appellee is not entitled to a lien by virtue of the lease.

II. We next consider the appeal of Parsons & West Company, intervener. The district court held the company not to be a corporation, and that defendants A. H. Parsons and George O. West owned the property attached. An issue on this branch of the case is that the property attached is owned by A. H. Parsons and George O. West, or by the firm of Parsons & West, composed of said persons, and that any transfer of said property to Parsons & West Company was without consideration, and for the purpose of defrauding the creditors of said A. H. Parsons and George O. West. Parsons & West, as a firm, and the individual members, are parties defendant; and the finding by the court that the defendants own the property means that Parsons & West owns it. The finding has such support in the evidence that, in a law action, we should not interfere. In fact, the conclusion seems entirely just.

On plaintiff's appeal the judgment is REVERSED. On intervener's it is AFFIRMED.

ROBINSON and LADD, JJ., took no part.

VICTORIA BRUGUIER V. ALFRED PEPIN, Appellant.

Cancellation: FRAUD: *Evidence.* Plaintiff was seventy years of age, the owner in her own right of a farm worth about twenty thousand dollars, upon which there was an incumbrance of four thousand dollars and corn worth about one thousand three hundred dollars. Plaintiff was greatly affected by the death of her husband, her actions at times indicating much mental distress. After the filing of her husband's will she received notice from defendant that a daughter of decedent by an Indian wife intended to contest it. Two days thereafter she met the defendant, in whom she placed great confidence, who told her the children would give her trouble, and proposed that he purchase the farm in order to avoid it, and plaintiff executed a deed of the farm and a bill of sale of the corn to defendant, and he executed an undertaking to pay her six hundred dollars a year during her life, a note for five thousand dollars payable five years after date without interest, a note for six hundred dollars and a mortgage on part of the farm to secure the payments. On the day the papers were executed plaintiff

threatened to commit suicide, and stated to a friend that defendant had taken the corn from her, and was anxious to know if the
papers were all right.   She did not sleep that night and was so ill
the next day that a physician and priest were called to attend her,
and for some days she remained in an unnatural condition.
Defendant claimed that the transaction was *bona fide*, and that
the papers were read over and explained to her and that he
informed plaintiff that the will contest would not affect her farm.
He also claimed that the corn was purchased in consideration of
the six hundred dollar note and a claim for services rendered
plaintiff amounting to nine hundred and twenty five dollars.
Defendant's claim for services was largely ficticious.   Plaintiff
offered to return a certificate of deposit for six hundred dollars
which defendant delivered to her in payment of his note, a day or
two after it was given.   *Held*, that a decree cancelling the deed
of the farm and the bill of sale of the corn, and requiring defendant to execute a reconveyance of the land, would not be disturbed.

Appeal from Woodbury District Court.—HON. GEORGE W.
WAKEFIELD, Judge.

TUESDAY, OCTOBER 18, 1898.

ACTION in equity for the cancellation of certain instruments in writing which purport to convey real and personal property to the defendant, to enjoin him from exercising acts of ownership over the property, and for general
equitable relief.   There was a hearing on the merits, and a
decree for the plaintiff.   The defendant appeals.—*Affirmed.*

C. A. Irwin for appellant.

O. C. Treadway for appellee.

ROBINSON, J.—The plaintiff is the widow of Theophile
Bruguier, who died testate on the eighteenth day of February,
1896.   His will gave to the plaintiff all of the property of the
decedent, and that included a quantity of corn which is in
controversy.   For many years the plaintiff had owned a farm
of four hundred and thirty-eight acres in Woodbury county,
but it had been managed by her husband, and upon him she
had relied for counsel and assistance.   The defendant was

-engaged in the real estate and loan business in Salix, a town
near the farm, and had frequently assisted Bruguier in his
business transactions, and was esteemed by him. After his
death, the plaintiff, having confidence in the defendant, asked
him to assist her in the business of her late husband's estate.
A few days after his death his will was filed for probate.
At that time the plaintiff was seventy years of age. Her
educational advantages had been few. She spoke the French
language, and was able to read English print, but was not able
to write or read writing in that language. She married Rou-
ville Brunnette when quite young, and spent several years on
the plains and at western army posts. In the year 1857 she
went to Sioux City, and since that time has resided near that
place. About the year 1860 she married Bruguier, and lived
with him as his wife until his death, but had no children.
Before he met her he had married two or more Indian women,
by whom he had had several children. After the will was
filed as stated, a daughter of the decedent by an Indian wife
gave notice of an intention to contest the will, and the plaintiff was informed of that fact by the defendant on or about
the twenty-eighth day of March, 1896. On the thirtieth day
of that month she started from her home on the farm to go
to Sioux City, and stopped at the defendant's house in Salix,
to await the train, and there met the defendant. Her testimony of what occurred is substantially as follows: The
defendant had a copy of the notice that the will would be
contested, and read it to her twice. He told her that the
children of the decedent would give her trouble, and proposed
to purchase the farm of her. In payment, he offered to
assume a mortgage of four thousand dollars, with which it
was incumbered, pay her five thousand dollars, and six hundred dollars annually during her lifetime. He told her that
by selling the farm she would avoid the trouble which was
threatened, but she did not say much in response to his offer.
However, they went to Sioux City together, and visited the
office of an attorney, to whom the defendant gave directions

respecting the drawing of papers. In the afternoon they
again visited the attorney, and the papers he had drawn were
signed. They included a deed from the plaintiff to the
defendant for her farm, and a bill of sale for the corn; an
undertaking of the defendant to pay to the plaintiff during
the remainder of her natural life the sum of six hundred dollars a year; a promissory note for the sum of five thousand
dollars, payable five years after its date, without interest; a
promissory note for six hundred dollars, and a mortgage on
a part of the farm to secure the payments to be made to the
plaintiff during the term of her natural life and the five
thousand dollar note. The plaintiff claims that she did not
know until that time that the corn was to be included in the
transaction, but that the defendant said, in effect, that he
must have it "to fight the Indians with,"—meaning the children of the decedent. The plaintiff also claims that she did
not comprehend that transaction, but, on returning with the
defendant to his home that evening, she heard him say to
his wife: "Old woman, I made a good day. I made a clean
sweep out of everything,—the land, the corn, the notes, and
horse and buggy, and even the featherbed." The plaintiff
states that the defendant did not know she heard the remark;
that she was "nearly confounded" by it, and did not know
what she was doing. It appears that the defendant had, prior
to that time, managed a sale of personal property which
belonged to the estate of the decedent, and held the notes and
other proceeds therefrom to the amount of about one thousand two hundred and forty dollars, and that proceedings in
court were afterwards required to compel him to surrender
them to the representatives of the estate.

The defendant contends that the transaction was in good
faith on his part; that it was first proposed by the plaintiff; that
he told her repeatedly that the contesting of the will would not
affect her right to the farm; that before the papers were signed
they were fully explained to her, and that she understood
them; that there were but eight thousand six hundred and

eighty-six bushels of corn, which were worth but thirteen cents
per bushel, or one thousand one hundred and twenty-nine
dollars and eighteen cents in all; and that he paid for it by
giving his note for six hundred dollars, as stated, and by
satisfying claims he held against the plaintiff to the amount
of nine hundred and twenty-five dollars. The district court
canceled the deed for the farm, and the bill of sale of the
corn, and required the defendant to execute to the plaintiff
a re-conveyance of the land.

There is much in the record which tends to sustain the
claims of the defendant, and so much conflict in the evidence
respecting essential facts that a conclusion entirely free from
doubt cannot be reached. But we are of the opinion that
the preponderance of the evidence establishes the following:
The plaintiff was warmly attached to her late husband, and
was greatly affected by his death, at times wandering from her
home, and into the fields, at such times and in such manner
as to indicate much mental distress. She was unable to sleep
well after his death, and sometimes did not retire to bed at
night, but walked the floor. She manifested excessive grief,
talking much of her deceased husband, and weeping, at times
expressing a wish to die, and even threatening to take her own
life. She was also much troubled about her business affairs.
Her farm was worth not less than twenty thousand dollars,
and its annual rental value was not less than one thousand
five hundred dollars. There were not less than ten thousand
bushels of corn, worth not less than one thousand three hundred dollars. The total value of the property which she conveyed to the defendant, after deducting therefrom the
incumbrance of four thousand dollars on the farm, which the
writings did not require him to pay, was more than seventeen thousand dollars. The expectancy of life of a person of
her age was eight and a half years, and the cash value of the
annuity which the defendant agreed to pay her was but three
thousand five hundred and thirty-seven dollars and sixty

cents. His claims for services rendered were largely fictitious, and it is at least doubtful if he was entitled to one hundred dollars therefor. The present worth of the five thousand dollar note was less than four thousand dollars. Hence it appears that for property worth more than seventeen thousand dollars the defendant was to give but about eight thousand dollars in value. On the day the papers were drawn the plaintiff was weak, nervous, and excitable, and her conduct was such as to alarm an old friend, with whom she stopped for an hour or more. At that time she spoke about the corn, said the defendant had taken it from her, and was anxious to know that the papers were right. She was despondent, and threatened to commit suicide. She returned to her home, but did not sleep that night, and the next day was so ill that a physician and a priest were called to attend her, and for some days thereafter she was in an unnatural condition. We are satisfied that when the papers in question were executed she did not comprehend what was done nor understand fully her rights; that she was not competent to act for herself in so important a transaction; and that the defendant knew that fact, and took advantage of her condition and her confidence in him to induce her to make the conveyances in question. That the transaction was contrary to her interests and prejudicial to her is clear, and that the defendant's part in it was wrongful is shown by the evidence, including his own declarations to disinterested persons. The plaintiff offers to return to him a certificate of deposit for six hundred dollars which he delivered to her in payment of his note a day or two after it was given, and that is all she has received from him. We are satisfied that the decree of the district court does substantial justice, and it is AFFIRMED.

G. N. LEACH, Appellant, v. S. E. MINICK, *et al.*

Mechanic's Lien: MORTGAGE AND LIEN: *Priority and Distribution.* McClain's Code, section 3317, subdivision 4, provides that, where

a mechanic's lien for buildings erected on land incumbered with
prior liens has attached, the court may order such building to be
separately sold to satisfy the mechanic's lien, and the purchaser
may remove same; but that if. in the discretion of the court, the
building should not be separately sold, the proceeds of the sale of
the whole premises shall be rateably ditributed between the prior
lien holders and the holder of the mechanic's lien according to the
respective values of the land and the building; and that, "in case
the premises do not sell for more than sufficient to pay off the
prior mortgage or other liens, the proceeds shall be applied on the
prior mortgage or other liens." *Held*, that where the building is a
part of the realty, so that it cannot be removed and separately
sold, and the proceeds of the sale of the entire property are more
than sufficient to satisfy the prior lien, but are insufficient to satisfy such liens and the subsequent mechanic's lien the proceeds
must be applied in full payment of the prior liens; the holder of
the subsequent lien not being entitled to a priority to the amount
of the value of the building.

Appeal from Buchanan District Court.—HON. A. S. BLAIR,.
Judge.

TUESDAY, OCTOBER 18, 1898.

IN this case several actions were submitted upon the same
evidence for the purpose of determining the order of priority
of several liens upon certain real estate in Independence,
Iowa, and the manner in which the proceeds that might arise
from the sale of the property should be applied. From the
decree rendered, the plaintiff, G. N. Leach, appeals, and the
defendants Price & Smith appeal from so much thereof as is
adverse to them. The only contentions presented on this
appeal are between the plaintiff and the defendants Price &
Smith.—*Modified* and *affirmed*.

Cook & Leach for plaintiff.

E. E. Hasner for defendants Price & Smith; *H. W. Hol-
man* for defendant Jacobs; *F. J. O'Brien* for defendant
Burke; *Ransier & Everett* for defendan Hussey.

No appearance for J. E. Moore, Betsy Ann Moore, and
John Wengert.

GIVEN, J.—I.   It is shown by the record that on November 2, 1891, the defendant J. E. Moore, the then owner of the lot in question, his wife joining therein, executed a mortgage thereon to defendant John Wengert, to secure the payment of one thousand two hundred and fifty dollars, with seven per cent. interest. Afterwards Moore deeded the lot to the defendant John Hussey, who assumed to pay said mortgage indebtedness, and on February 29, 1896, Hussey conveyed the lot to the defendant Minick, who assumed to pay said mortgage indebtedness. Minick erected a barn on the lot, the defendants Price & Smith furnishing material therefor to the amount of three hundred and ninety-nine dollars and eight cents. On October 5, 1896, said barn was destroyed by fire, only a small part of the lumber and foundation walls being saved. On the next day Price & Smith filed their duly verified statement for a mechanic's lien in said sum of three hundred and ninety-nine dollars and eight cents. Minick, having decided to erect another and larger barn on the same lot, did, about November 20, 1896, contract with the plaintiff, Leach, to furnish materials therefor, which he did, to the amount of one thousand eight hundred and eighty-five dollars and sixty-five cents, and for which he filed his duly verified statement for a mechanic's lien. The defendant Thomas Burke furnished material for the new barn to the amount of twenty-seven dollars and twenty cents, for which a statement for a lien was filed prior to that of the plaintiff. Defendant Randall Jacobs furnished material to the amount of sixty-eight dollars and eighty-seven cents, and defendant Clark-Woodward Company to the amount of forty-two dollars, for each of which a statement for a lien was filed. March 30, 1894, plaintiff commenced this action against Minick to foreclose his mechanic's lien. May 6, 1897, Wengert commenced an action to foreclose his mortgage, and May 13th Price & Smith commenced an action to foreclose their mechanic's lien. On May 25, 1897, judgment for one thousand two hundred and ninety-nine dollars and thirty-three cents and seventy dollars and

thirty-nine cents costs and decree of foreclosure of said mortgage was rendered in favor of Wengert, the decree providing
that the real estate described in the mortgage, and the property of S. E. Minick, should be first exhausted before resorting
to the property of John Hussey. The record shows that the
remainder of said cause was consolidated with this case by
agreement of parties and order of court entered of record.
On June 1, 1897, this cause came on for trial, and the following stipulation and agreement was made and entered of
record: "It is stipulated and agreed that the testimony
taken in this case shall be used and received by the court in
the trial and disposition of cases No. 9,830 and 9,797, equity,
the same as though the evidence had been separately taken in
each of said cases, and all of said causes are submitted for
trial and decision upon the evidence taken in this case." There
is no dispute as to the amount due to either lienholder, except
to Price & Smith. Their statement for lien, as made and verified, was for three hundred and ninety-nine dollars and eight
cents, but by mistake the clerk indorsed and entered it as for
three hundred and twenty-nine dollars and eight cents. As no
one has been misled by this error, Price & Smith are entitled
to be allowed in this adjustment the correct amount, namely,
three hundred and ninety-nine dollars and eight cents. The
court admitted evidence upon which it found that the value
of the lot was one thousand five hundred dollars; the value
of the new barn, two thousand five hundred; the lot and new
barn, four thousand dollars; and that the value of the materials saved from the burnt barn that went into the new barn was
one hundred and seventy-five dollars. Judgment was entered
in favor of Price & Smith for four hundred and ten dollars
and eighty-two cents with interest, and twenty-one dollars
and ninety-five cents costs, which was decreed to be a second
lien, and superior to those of Leach, Minick, Burke, Jacobs,
and Clark-Woodward Company to the extent of three hundred and five dollars and twenty-eight cents and twenty-one
dollars and ninety-five cents costs, and that the balance of

their judgment is junior to the lien of Leach, Burke, Jacobs, and Clark-Woodward Company. The claim of Burke was established as a third lien, and prior to Leach, Jacobs, Clark-Woodward Company, and junior to Price & Smith and Wengert. Judgment was rendered in favor of plaintiff, G. N. Leach, for one thousand nine hundred and forty-seven dollars and eighty-two cents, with interest, and eighty-nine dollars and forty-eight cents costs, and his lien established and decreed to be junior to the liens of Wengert and Burke, "and the lien of Price & Smith to the extent of three hundred and five dollars and twenty-eight cents, and the same is superior to the rights, interests, and claims of S. E. Minick, Randall Jacobs, and Clark-Woodward Company in said premises." It was decreed that the proceeds arising from the sale of said premises be appropriated as follows: "First, to the payment of John Wengert's claim and costs in full; second, to the payment of Price & Smith's claim to the extent of three hundred and five dollars and twenty-eight cents and costs; third, to the payment of Thomas Burke's to the extent of twenty-nine dollars and four cents; fourth, in satisfaction of his own claim and costs,"—meaning the claim of plaintiff. Judgments were rendered in favor of Jacobs and Clark-Woodward Company, and their liens established as junior to the liens of Wengert, Leach, Burke, and of Price & Smith to the extent of three hundred and five dollars and twenty-eight cents. It was decreed "that the lien of Price & Smith, over and above the sum of $305.28, is junior and inferior to that of G. L. Leach, John Wengert, Thomas Burke, Randall Jacobs, and Clark-Woodward Company."

• II. John Hussey, though claiming not to be a party to this action, has filed an additional abstract, in which he shows the decree in the foreclosure case of Wengert against Moore et al. on the mortgage. He also presents an argument in which he claims he is entitled to the benefit accorded to him in that decree. It is provided in that decree that the mortgaged property and the property of Minick shall be first exhausted before pursuing the property of Hussey. This decree fully recognizes and follows that decree; therefore Mr. Hussey has no cause for complaint.

III. As already stated, the contentions which we are called upon to consider are solely between the plaintiff, Leach, and the defendants Price & Smith, and are as to which of their liens is entitled to priority. Plaintiff concedes that Wengert and Price & Smith have the first liens on the lot, and claims that he has the first lien on the new building, subject only to the lien of Burke for twenty-seven dollars and twenty cents, which was filed before his. He contends that, as the building cannot be removed, the lot and building should be sold together, their separate values ascertained, and the proceeds of the sale distributed so as to secure to Wengert and to Price & Smith priority on the lot, and to plaintiff priority upon the barn; "provided, always, that, in case the premises do not sell for more than sufficient to pay off the Wengert mortgage and Price & Smith lien, with interest and costs, then the proceeds shall be applied on said mortgage, and lien, interest, and costs." Section 3311, McClain's Ann. Code, provides for a lien in favor of every person who does labor upon, or furnishes materials, machinery, or fixtures for, any building, erection, or other improvement upon land. The fourth subdivision of section 3317, McClain's Ann. Code, is as follows: "Fourth. The liens for the things aforesaid or the work including those for additions, repairs and betterments, shall attach to the building, erections or improvements for which they were furnished or done, in preference to any prior lien, or incumbrance, or mortgage, upon the land upon which such erection, building or improvement belongs, or is erected or put. If such material was furnished or labor performed in the erection or construction of an original independent building, erection or other improvement commenced since the attaching or execution of such prior lien, incumbrance, or mortgage, the court may, in its discretion, order and direct such building, erection or improvement to be separately sold under execution, and the purchaser may remove the same within such reasonable time as the court may fix. But, if, in the discretion of the court, such building should not be separately sold, the court shall take an account and ascertain the separate value of the land, and the erection, building, or other improvement, and distribute the proceeds of sale so as to secure to the prior mortgage or other lien priority upon the land, and to the mechanic's lien priority upon the building, erection or other improvement. If the material furnished or labor performed was for addition to, repairs of, or betterments upon, buildings, erections or other improvements, the court shall take an account of the values before such material was furnished or labor performed, and the enhanced value caused by such additions, repairs or betterments, and upon the sale of the premises, distribute the proceeds of the sale so as to secure to the prior mortgage or lien priority upon the land and improvements as they existed prior to the attaching of the mechanic's lien, and to the mechanic's lien priority upon the enhanced value caused by such additions, repairs or betterments. In case the premises do not sell for more than sufficient to pay off the prior mortgage or other lien, the proceeds shall be applied on the prior mortgage or other liens."

The materials which plaintiff furnished were for the erection of an original, independent building, which the court found, and the parties concede, should not be separately sold. If it were not for the concluding sentence of said fourth paragraph, there would be no question but that plaintiff is entitled to a lien upon the building prior to the mortgage of Wengert and to the lien of Price & Smith, and that in that case the court should take an account, ascertain the separate values, "and distribute the proceeds of sale so as to secure to the prior mortgage, or other lien, priority upon the land, and to the mechanic's lien priority upon the building." This part of said section 3317 was construed in *Bank v. Schloth,* 59 Iowa, 316, an action to enforce a mechanic's lien: "The machinery

and material for which the lien is claimed were put up and
used in a building before erected, and, as we have seen, it is
conceded they became a part of the realty." After quoting
said last sentence of section 3317, and referring to the argument of counsel, the court says as follows: "The plain
language we have quoted must be regarded as a limitation
upon the language preceding it in the same section, to the
effect that, if the premises do not sell for more than enough
to pay off the prior mortgage or other lien, the accounting
and distribution of proceeds of sale shall not be required. In
this view, it is not in conflict with any other words of the
statute. We must enforce the provision as it reads, and cannot wrest its meaning on the ground that another construction would be more equitable, and would not be in conflict
with other provisions of the same statute. It must be admitted
that paragraph 4, section 2135, is obscure and capable of
adverse construction. The interpretation we adopt gives
more nearly full effect to all its language,—'*Ut res magis
valeat quam pereat.*' It also gives the language quoted the
force of a proviso which has the effect, without being directly
contrary to the purview of the statute, of limiting its
application. This is the office of a proviso. A different
interpretation would wholly nullify the language under consideration." In *Curtis v. Broadwell,* 66 Iowa, 662,—an
action to enforce a mechanic's lien,—the facts were as follows: October 20, 1882, Broadwell executed to defendant C.
Wright, trustee, a deed to secure an indebtedness then existing. Thereafter, on November 9, 1882, plaintiff commenced
furnishing Broadwell materials used in the erection of a
building, the last being furnished on April 3, 1883. The
district court found the value of the land to be two thousand
five hundred dollars, and the value of the building to be three
thousand dollars, and decreed that both be sold together, and
that of the proceeds two dollars of each five dollars be paid
to C. Wright, and three dollars of each five dollars to the
plaintiffs; thus holding that the trust deed did not attach

to and bind the building, and that the sum realized from the sale of the building should be applied to the plaintiff's claim. This court referred to *Bank v. Schloth, supra,* and said: "We held in that case that additions to a building which became a part of the realty are subject to a mortgage as against a subsequent mechanic's lien." The holding that the last sentence of said section had the force of a proviso limiting the application of the provision, without being directly contrary to its purview, was adhered to. It was further said: "It cannot be doubted that, if this section does not stand in the way, a prior mortgage will prevail against a subsequent mechanic's lien for buildings or improvements which become a part of the realty. Under the plain language of the section, it is obvious that the same rule applies alike to improvements, betterments, or additions to buildings and to new and inde-
. pendent structures. It cannot be questioned that the building for which materials were furnished by plaintiffs did become a part of the real estate. The case was remanded for decree "providing that C. Wright's deed of trust is superior to plaintiff's lien, and Palmer's judgment inferior thereto." Palmer was an attaching creditor. These cases clearly held that where the building or other improvement becomes a part of the real estate, so that it may not be separately sold and removed, prior mortgagees or lienholders are entitled to priority over subsequent lienholders for improvements or independent structures to the extent of such prior liens. In the recent case of *Tower v. Moore,* 104 Iowa, 345, it was held otherwise; the court finding that the building could be removed without material injury to the security of the earlier lienholders. That was an action to foreclose a mortgage given in 1892, and appellee filed a cross bill asking to have a mechanic's lien established upon the building for material furnished for its erection, and subsequent to said mortgage, and that his lien be decreed superior to the mortgage. The court below found in appellee's favor, although it was shown that the value of the premises, including the improvements, did not exceed the amount of the mortgage indebtedness. It was claimed by appellant that

under no circumstances can the holder of a mechanc's lien be given a preference, as against an independent building, over a prior mortgage of the land, unless the value of the lien, with such improvement, exceeds the mortgage debt. The court says: "A proper construction of this statute, we think, must give to the holder of a mechanic's lien against an independent building the priority of right in every case where the court shall find as a fact that such building can be removed without material injury to the security of the earlier lienholder; but, where no such finding is made, the land must be sold, and the purchase price applied first in payment of the prior incumbrances." This decision is based upon, and in harmony with the provision of said fourth subdivision, in cases where the court finds that the building, erection, or improvement should be separately sold. In this case, and in the case of *Bank v. Schloth,* and also that of *Curtis v. Broadwell, supra,* it was found that the building, erection, or improvement should be separately sold. *Eagle Iron Works v. Des Moines S. Ry. Co.,* 101 Iowa, 290, is cited, but we do not find that this question was considered in that case. Adhering to the law as announced in *Bank v. Schloth* and *Curtis v. Broadwell, supra,* we hold that as the new barn has become a part of the realty, and cannot be separately sold and removed, the property must be sold as an entirety, and that the defendants Wengert and Price & Smith are entitled to be first paid out of the proceeds of the sale, and that the other lienholders are entitled to be paid, in the order decreed by the district court, out of any balance that may remain after satisfying said liens of Wengert and of Price & Smith.

IV. It will be observed that the judgment in favor of Price & Smith is for four hundred and ten dollars and eighty-two cents, and that the court decreed three hundred and five dollars and twenty-eight cents thereof as a prior lien to the lien of the plaintiff, Leach, and of this Price & Smith complain on their appeal. It follows from what we have said that Price & Smith are entitled to priority over the plaintiff to the full amount of their claim. The decree of the district court is modified on the appeal of Price & Smith, and affirmed on the appeal of G. N. Leach, and the case is remanded for decree in harmony with this opinion.—MODIFIED in part, and AFFIRMED in part.

JAMES C. YOUNG, S. M. GOODHUE v. IOWA TOILERS PROTECTIVE ASSOCIATION, *et al.*, Appellants.

Tax Title: PURCHASER: *Agency.* An agent who has in his possession money of his principal wherewith to pay taxes on property
1 owned by the former cannot through his neglect to do so obtain a valid tax title as against the principal, neither can such title be acquired by a purchaser who buys at a tax sale, through such agent.

SAME. Where a purchaser at foreclosure sale gives an agent money to pay the taxes on the premises, which he neglects to do, a valid
1 tax title against said principal cannot rest on the facts, that a creditor of the agent furnished him money to bid in the land at tax sale, that he did so, that he assigned the certificate to his creditor as security and that said creditor quit-claimed to an association of which said agent was an officer, taking back a mortgage which was simply a change of security.

Tax Deed: PRESUMPTIONS. The fact that a tax deed was issued is *prima facie* evidence that notice of the expiration of the period of
2 redemption was given and the presumption is not overcome although the notice of service by publication is defective when it is not shown that the owner was a non-resident or that no other notice was served.

Appeal: COSTS: *Re-taxation below.* A party failing to move for a re-
2 taxation of costs in the trial court cannot complain of the taxation of costs, on appeal

Appeal from Linn District Court.—HON. GEORGE W. BURNHAM, Judge.

WEDNESDAY, OCTOBER 19, 1898.

SUIT in equity to set aside a tax deed held by defendant Goodhue to a certain lot in the city of Cedar Rapids; to recover possession of the property; and the rent received for the use thereof. Decree for plaintiff, and defendants appeal.— *Affirmed.*

J. W. Jamison for appellants.

Rickel & Crocker for appellee.

DEEMER, C. J.—On and prior to May 14, 1883, Agnes Field held the legal title to the property in dispute. On the twenty-second day of May, 1888, she executed a mortgage on the same to the Western Mortgage Company. This mortgage was assigned to Clara A. McCooke on June 6, 1888. Thereafter the mortgage was foreclosed, and plaintiff obtained a sheriff's deed to the property under this foreclosure on the twenty-eighth day of November, 1892. The property was sold for taxes in October of the year 1888, and we find the following indorsement on the back of the certificate: "This property was bid off by the Union Investment Company, and the certificate made out on the bid, and the said company failed to pay the money and take the same from treasurer; whereupon S. N. Goodhue paid the money, and took up the same as his own, and since that time has been the owner and lawful holder of this certificate. Union Invest. Company, by Geo. W. Wilson, Secretary." On the eighteenth day of December, 1891, a tax deed issued to S. N. Goodhue for the property in controversy. George W. Wilson, who was manager of the Union Investment Company, a corporation doing business in the city of Cedar Rapids, conducted all the business relating to the tax sale and deed. On March 14, 1892, Goodhue quitclaimed the property to the Iowa Toilers' Protective Association, another corporation of which Wilson was the manager. This corporation at the same time made a mortgage back to Goodhue for a part or all of what was called the purchase price. Plaintiff claims that the tax deed was issued upon an insufficient notice of the time of redemption; that Wilson was at the time of the tax sale the agent of the Western Mortgage Company, mortgagee, and of the Union Investment Company, the original purchaser at tax sale; and that he had in his possession the money with which to pay the taxes

upon the property; that, instead of paying the taxes, he fraudulently procured the issuance of the certificate to Goodhue,
and finally secured the title to the property by quitclaim
deed.   Plaintiff further alleges that Wilson was the agent of
McCooke, the assignee of the mortgage, and as such could not
procure a title to the property; that Goodhue had knowledge of
this agency at the time he took the certificate; and that the
sale and deed are void.   He further claims that Wilson had
no authority from the Union Investment Company to assign
the tax-sale certificate.   Certain claims for rents and profits
are also made. Defendants deny all allegations of fraud and
want of notice, plead a counterclaim for repairs and taxes
paid, and the defendant Goodhue asks the foreclosure of his
mortgage against the Iowa Toilers' Protective Association.
The trial court found that the tax deed and all conveyances
and incumbrances subsequent thereto were void, quieted the
title to the property in plaintiff, and ordered that a writ of
possession issue against defendants.   The appeal is from this
decree.

While there is a decided conflict in the evidence, we are
satisfied that J. C. Young, who was president of the Western
Mortgage Company, had an arrangement with Wilson, as
manager of the Union Investment Company, by which Wilson
was to pay the taxes upon all property on which the Western
Mortgage Company had taken mortgages, and that Wilson
or the investment company had money in their possession,
belonging to the mortgage company, with which to pay the
taxes upon the lot in question, at the time it was sold.   This
being true, neither Wilson nor his company could procure a
tax title which would be of any validity as against Young.
Ellsworth v. Cordrey, 63 Iowa, 675.   It is said, however, that
Goodhue furnished the money and took the certificate in his
own name, and that, whatever the arrangement between
Young and Wilson, he is not bound by it, and the tax
deed should be sustained.   While it is no doubt true
that Goodhue furnished the money with which to purchase the lot at tax sale, yet we are satisfied it was

a loan to Wilson, and that the tax certificate was assigned, as we have heretofore stated, as collateral security for the loan so made, as well as for other money theretofore advanced to Wilson. In these transactions Goodhue was acting for the First National Bank, of which he was cashier, and there is no evidence from which it can be ascertained whether or not these loans have been paid. Goodhue indorsed the notes, and he says the bank has never come back on him for the amount. Again, he says: "I think these are either paid or renewed within a year." If it be true, however, as defendants claim, that Goodhue was the purchaser of the property at tax sale, they are in no better position, for the reason that Wilson acted as Goodhue's agent in the purchase of property, and his knowledge of the situation should be imputed to Goodhue. Having knowledge of the arrangement between Young and Wilson, and the fact that Wilson had the money with which to pay the taxes, Goodhue could not take title to the premises through a tax sale, and thus defeat Young, who was Wilson's principal. In neither event could Goodhue procure such a title as would defeat Young. If Goodhue received the certificate as collateral security for a loan made to Wilson, he is to be charged with notice of all infirmities existing therein. *Light v. West,* 42 Iowa. 138; *Watson v. Phelps,* 40 Iowa, 482. And as Goodhue had notice, through Wilson, of the agreement to pay the taxes, he cannot take a title which will be free from equities. The Iowa Toilers' Protective Association acquired its title by a quitclaim deed, and it also appears that Wilson is the manager of this corporation, and it is not entitled to protection as an innocent purchaser from Goodhue. We are constrained to believe that Goodhue held the certificate and the title acquired thereunder as collateral security; that the making of the quitclaim deed to the Iowa Toilers' Protective Association, and the taking of the mortgage back, was simply a change of security, and that Wilson, as manager of the investment company and of the protective association, has at all times been the real claimant of the property. If this be true, then it is clear that the tax deed should be canceled, and plaintiff given possession of the property. The protective association has had possession of the land since it received its deed, in March, 1892, and has received the rents and profits thereof, amounting to at least one hundred and twenty-five dollars. It has also made some repairs upon the property, and has paid subsequent taxes thereon. The exact cost of these repairs we are unable to estimate, but are of opinion that the correct amount, added to the taxes paid, will not overbalance the rent account, and that the trial court was right in offsetting one account against the other.

II.   It is not important that we pass upon the sufficiency of the notice of expiration of the period of redemption. The fact that a deed was issued is *prima facie* evidence that notice was given. The notice which appears in the record as having been served upon the owner of the land was 2 served by publication. This notice is defective in several particulars, but there is no showing that the owner was a non-resident, that she was not personally served with notice, or that the notice by publication is the only one of record in the treasurer's office. It would seem that the presumption of due notice has not been overcome.

The defendants other than Goodhue and the Iowa Toilers' Protective Association complain of the taxation of costs against them. As they made no motion to re-tax in the trial court, they are not entitled to relief here. *Snell v. Railway Co.*, 88 Iowa, 442, and cases cited. The decree is right and it is AFFIRMED.

WILLIAM LIEFHEIT, Appellant, v. JOS. SCHLITZ BREWING COMPANY.

Appeal: INSTRUCTIONS: *Objections b low.* Where instructions were 1 not excepted to when given, they will not be reviewed on appeal.

REVIEW: *Abstract.* Excluding evidence as to whether a copy of an exhibit was served on one of the parties is not error although the abstract of the party complaining of the ruling contains an alleged 2 copy of the exhibit, where the transcript discloses no such paper

as offered in evidence and the abstract of the other party to the
appeal denies that any such exhibit was identified or introduced.

HARMLESS ERROR   Striking out evidence as to the particular matters
    for which a debtor paid money to other parties at his creditor's
8   request is not prejudicial error in an action to recover the money
    so paid on the ground that the debt due from the debtor to the
    creditor was incurred on an illegal contract, where the amount.
    and nature of payment is not disputed.

Appeal from Linn District Court.—HON. WILLIAM G.
THOMPSON, Judge.

WEDNESDAY, OCTOBER 19, 1898.

ONE Jurries purchased ii. toxicating liquors of defendant
company, and paid therefor, and this action by his assignee
is to recover the amount so paid, together with a smaller sum
which, it is claimed, was advanced and paid by Jurries for
different purposes, at defendant's request.   There was a jury
trial which resulted in a verdict for defendant, upon which
judgment was duly entered.   Plaintiff appeals.—*Affirmed.*

Timothy Brown, E. C. Preston, Jamison & Smyth, and
McVey & McVey for appellant.

Preston, Wheeler & Moffet, Rickel & Crocker, and
George H. Wahl for appellee.

WATERMAN, J.—Counsel for appellant devote a very
considerable portion of their argument to a discussion of
matters which we may accept as established in accordance with
their claims.   We start, then, with the assumption that the
sales in question were made in Iowa; that they were illegal;
and that the money so paid may, under our law, upon a proper
showing, be recovered back.   The court, in the third paragraph of its charge to the jury, said, in substance, that, to
entitle plaintiff to recover, he must prove that he made demand
upon defendant for the money claimed, before suit brought.
No complaint is made of this rule of law.   But it is argued
at great length that the evidence shows that no demand was in

fact made. The testimony is conflicting on this point, and, if the jury found, as we think it must, that no demand was made, the finding cannot be said to be without reasonable support. The petition is in two counts. In the first, claim is made for ten thousand seven hundred and three dollars and thirty-three cents, money paid defendant for beer purchased; and, in the second count, seven hundred and seventy-eight dollars and forty-five cents is claimed as having been paid to different parties at defendant's request. The court applied the doctrine of demand to the whole amount sued for. No exception is taken to this, however.

II.   Complaint is made of the court's refusal to give the ninth instruction asked by plaintiff. We think the subject-matter of this instruction is fully covered by the fourth paragraph of the charge as given.

III.   Errors are also assigned on the giving of the second and fifth paragraphs of the charge. As to the second instruction, it does not profess to announce a rule of law governing the case, but is merely the statement of an issue tendered by defendant in its answer. It does not say, as counsel seem to think, that the liquors were purchased in the state of Wisconsin, and the sale was therefore lawful. It says only that defendant asserts this in its answer, and so, in fact, it does. Among other criticisms of this instruction, it is said it assumes that the sale of intoxicating liquor is lawful in the state of Wisconsin, when the presumption is that the law of that state is the same as our own. Unfortunately for this presumption, we find in the transcript to which we have been frequently driven by the confused state of the record, an agreement of counsel to the effect that the traffic in intoxicating liquors is lawful in the state of Wisconsin.

The objection to the fifth instruction we cannot consider. In the abstract of appellant it is stated generally that all of the instructions were excepted to when given. This is denied by appellee, and it is expressly charged that 1   no objection was made to paragraph 5. The record, including the original instructions, has been certified to this court, and, after a careful examination, we find that

appellee is correct. Under the circumstances, we must decline
to review the legal proposition contained in this paragraph.
Stove Works v. Hammond, 94 Iowa, 694; *Norris v. Kipp,* 74
Iowa, 444; *Kirk v. Litterst,* 71 Iowa, 71.

IV.   Jurries, while upon the witness stand, was asked,
on behalf of plaintiff, this question: "State whether or not
a copy of Exhibit Q2, and of the account thereto attached,
was served upon the defendant company; if so, upon what
officer of the company and when and where?" Defendant's
objection, that it was incompetent and immaterial, was sustained, and error is predicated upon the ruling. An
2   exhibit marked "Q2" appears in the abstract of appellant, but appellee denies, in an additional abstract, that
any such exhibit was ever identified or introduced. The
transcript discloses no such paper as having been offered by
counsel or identified by the reporter. With the record in this
condition, we cannot say there was any error in the ruling,
for, without the paper referred to, the question is not
intelligible.

V.   The witness Jurries gave testimony with relation to
the particular matters for which he paid the money that is
claimed in the second count of his petition. On defendant's
motion this evidence was stricken out. It might have been
permitted to stand, but the ruling was not and could not have
been prejudicial. The amount he paid was not dis-
3   puted. The immediate purpose of the payment was
not in itself material, foi the money so paid was with
his consent, in all cases, and, in some, at his express request,
applied on his account for the purchase of beer; that is, he
paid in these instances for the beer, not directly to defendant,
but to other persons, who were appointed by defendant to
receive the money. Some other issues are discussed relating
to matters of evidence, but, as the testimony is in conflict, we
shall not review them. No reason appears to warrant us in
interfering with the judgment. It is therefore AFFIRMED.

SAMUEL A. TOLMAN, Appellant, v. G. O. JANSON.

Bills and Notes: NEGOTIABILITY. A note otherwise negotiable is not rendered non-negotiable in Iowa by a provision in it authorizing 2 an attorney to appear at any time and confess judgment thereon, on the ground that the time of payment is thereby rendered uncertain, since such a provision is illegal and no part of the note.

PRESUMPTIONS AS TO HOLDER. The holder of a note is presumed to be 1 a *bona fide* holder.

LAW OF SISTER STATE. In an action on a note made in a foreign state, the laws of such state concerning provision for power of attorney 8 to confess judgment will be presumed to be the same as those of Iowa, in the absence of pleading and proof to the contrary.

Appeal from Des Moines District Court.—HON. JAMES D. SMYTH, Judge.

WEDNESDAY, OCTOBER 19, 1898.

THE plaintiff is the holder of four promissory notes, on which recovery is sought in this action. The following is a copy of one of the notes, the others being the same except as to dates of payment: "$43.75. Chicago, April 1st, 1892. Thirty months after date, without grace, for value received, I promise of pay to the order of Jernberg & Rylander, forty-three 75-100 dollars in gold coin of the United States, with interest at six per cent. per annum, payable —— annually, interest at seven per cent. after maturity, at the banking office of Jernberg, Griffin & Co., Chicago, Illinois. This note is secured by a trust deed of even date herewith to ——. And to further secure the payment of said amount —— hereby authorize irrevocably any attorney of any court of record to appear for —— in such court, in term time or vacation, at any time hereafter, and confess a judgment, without process, in favor of the holder of this note, for such amount as may appear to be unpaid thereon, together with costs and twenty-five dollars attorney's fees, and to waive and release all errors which may intervene in any such proceeding, and consent to immediate execution upon such judgment, hereby ratifying and confirming all that ——— said attorney may do by virtue hereof. G. O. Janson." The notes are indorsed in blank by the payees, and the plaintiff claims to be a *bona fide* holder thereof. From the answer it appears that the consideration for the notes was a certain lot, to which the payees in the notes agreed to give a clear title, which has not been done, and cannot be, because of which there is an entire failure of the consideration. The cause was tried to the court without a jury, who gave judgment for the defendant, and the plaintiff appealed.—*Reversed.*

Dodge & Dodge and *Ashcroft, Gordon & Cox* for appellant.

Charles Willner and *Hedge & Blythe* for appellee.

GRANGER, J.—The plaintiff put in evidence the notes sued on, and rested his case. Defendant then introduced evidence directed to his defense of a failure of consideration, and upon the submission of the case judgment was entered for defendant. The conclusion of the court could have been based on no other finding than that the notes were nonnegotiable, because of which the plaintiff is not protected as an innocent holder of value. Being the holder of the notes, he has in his favor such a presumption, which must be overcome by proof, before the defense pleaded is available as against him. *Manufacturing Co. v. Thomas,* 53 Iowa, 558; *Trustees v. Hill,* 12 Iowa, 462; *Richards v. Monroe,* 85 Iowa, 359. Authorities to the same effect are numerous. That the court below based its conclusion on a finding that the defense could be urged against plaintiff on the ground of the non-negotiability of the notes is conceded by appellee in argument, for he says, "The only legal question relevant or pertinent is the negotiability of the notes." It is then said

that the district court held that they were not negotiable, and
that the defense was good. The only ground on which
2   the notes are said to be non-negotiable is the provision
authorizing any attorney to appear and confess judgment, because it makes uncertain the time of payment. The
conclusion is, likely, correct under our holding in *Culbertson
v. Nelson,* 93 Iowa, 187. But, unfortunately for appellee,
we meet another question not presented in argument. The
notes were made in Illinois. The pleadings contain no averment that the law of Illinois differs from ours on the subject
of provisions in a note for the confession of judgment by an
attorney. In *Hamilton v. Schoenberger,* 47 Iowa, 385, it is
expressly held that such a provision in a note cannot be
enforced in the courts of this state, and is not authorized nor
contemplated by our laws. For the purposes of this
3   case we must regard the law of Illinois the same as
ours, unless pleaded and proven to be otherwise. *Bean
v. Briggs,* 4 Iowa, 464; *Crafts v. Clark,* 31 Iowa, 77; *Webster
v. Hunter,* 50 Iowa, 215; *Hadley v. Gregory,* 57 Iowa, 157.
From this the unmistakable conclusion is that the provision of
the notes as to confession of judgment was never of any validity, and hence no part of the notes. The argument of appellee
practically concedes that the notes, without the provision as
to confession of judgment, are negotiable, as they surely are.
Such a conclusion, under the conditions of the record, entitles
the plaintiff to judgment. This conclusion is not on the line
of the arguments presented, but, nevertheless, it seems conclusive, and the judgment must stand REVERSED.

WILLIAM FITZGERALD v. THE METROPOLITAN ACCIDENT
ASSOCIATION OF CHICAGO, ILLINOIS, Appellant.

Accident Insurance. In an action by an assignee upon a certificate
of membership for the payment of a weekly indemnity in case of
accidental injury to the insured, the by-laws of the defendant
association are admissible in evidence to show that the plaintiff's
assignor was suspended and not entitled to benefits and that the
action was not brought within the time limited by the by-laws,

which are stated to be a part of the certificate, although not indorsed thereon or attached thereto and the plaintiff's assignor had no actual knowledge of their contents.

Appeal from Linn District Court.—HON. WILLIAM G. THOMPSON, Judge.

WEDNESDAY, OCTOBER 19, 1898.

THIS action is to recover upon a certificate of membership issued by the defendant to plaintiff's assignor for the payment of certain weekly indemnity in case of accidental injuries sustained by the assured. The defendant set up as a defense that the assured had forfeited his membership by failure to pay the expenses on his certificate which were due September 9, 1894, at the time they were due and payable, and that the action is barred by the limitation contained in its by-laws. At the close of the testimony the court instructed the jury to find for the plaintiff in the sum of seventy dollars, and entered judgment on the verdict. The amount in controversy being less than one hundred dollars, the court granted a certificate as authorized by section 4402 of McClain's Code, upon which the defendant appeals.—*Reversed.*

Rothrock & Grimm for appellant.

John M. Redmond for appellee.

GIVEN, J.—I. The questions certified are stated as follows: *First.* Whether the provisions of the certificate of membership, stating that the by-laws of the association are made a part thereof, is sufficient to authorize the introduction of said by-laws in evidence in behalf of the defendant and on the trial for the purpose of showing the plaintiff's assignor had been suspended from membership at the time he received his injury, and that, under said by-laws, he was therefore not entitled to any benefits under his said certificate of membership, a copy of said by-laws not being attached to or indorsed on said certificate; the evidence failing to show any knowledge or notice to plaintiff of the plan of insurance or of any of the defendant company's by-laws prior to the time of filing its said answer, except such knowledge or notice as was given him by the certificate itself. *Second.* Whether the provisions of said by-laws with reference to the time within which action for the recovery of indemnity or benefits shall be commenced were admissible in evidence for the purpose of showing that the suit was not commenced within the time provided and limited by the said by-laws, a copy of the said by-laws not being attached to or indorsed on said certificate of membership; the evidence failing to show any knowledge or notice to said plaintiff of the plan of insurance or any of the defendant company's by-laws prior to the time of filing its said answer, except such knowledge or notice as was given him by the certificate itself.

It is the law that members of mutual associations are bound to take notice of, and be governed by, its by-laws. See *Simeral v. Insurance Co.,* 18 Iowa, 319; *Coles v. Insurance Co.,* 18 Iowa, 425; *Walsh v. Insurance Co.,* 30 Iowa, 133. It is also the law that, where the contract of insurance makes by-laws adopted after the making of the contract a part of the contract, the insured is bound to take notice of them and be governed thereby. *Hobbs v. Association,* 82 Iowa, 107.

Appellee's objection to appellant's offer of an authenticated copy of its by-laws in evidence seems to have been sustained for two reasons: *First,* because no copy of the by-laws was attached to or indorsed on the certificate; and, *second,* because the evidence failed to show knowledge on the part of the assured of the plan of insurance or of the by-laws prior to the filing of the answer herein.

Section 2, chapter 211, Acts Eighteenth General Assembly, provided that all insurance companies should, upon the issuing of the policy, "attach to such policy, or indorse thereon, a true copy of any application or representations of the assured, which, by the terms of such policy, are made a part thereof, or, of the contract of insurance, or referred to therein, or which may in any manner affect the validity of such policy." It was further provided that an omission so to do should preclude the company or association "from pleading, alleging or proving such application or representations, or any part thereof, or falsity thereof, or any part thereof, in any action upon such policy." It is the application or representations of the assured only that are required to be attached to, or indorsed upon, the policy. This is made plain by the restriction placed upon the company or association as to its allegations and proofs. If it omits to attach or indorse the application or representations of the assured on the policy, it is precluded from alleging or proving such application or representations.

We are not referred to any authority which required the appellant to attach or indorse its by-laws upon this certificate. The assured must be held to have had whatever knowledge this certificate imparted. The first paragraph thereof recites "that Marion Snyder is entitled to a benefit in the event of personal bodily injuries effected, while a member of this association, through external, violent, and purely accidental causes;" and he is spoken of throughout the certificate as a member of the association. This, and the provisions of the certificate generally, are such as to show that the certificate was upon the mutual plan, and the appellant a mutual association.

The certificate of membership contains the following: "The consideration of this insurance is, and shall be, the warranties and agreements contained in the application therefor, which, with the by-laws of this association now in force or hereafter enacted by the members of this association, are made a part thereof, and the payment, when due, of the various calls which may have been made thereon." By this the assured was not only informed that there were by-laws, but also that they were made a part of the contract. He was not only bound by the law, as a member of this mutual association, to take notice of its by-laws, and be governed thereby, but he was also bound by his contract; and, being thus bound, it cannot be said that the evidence fails to show any knowledge or notice to the assured of the plan of insurance or of the by-laws. We think the provisions of the certificate are sufficient to authorize the introduction of the by-laws in evidence. The defendant was entitled to have in evidence the provisions of the by-laws as to the time that payments were required to be made upon this certificate, and the time within which action could be brought thereon. What we have said as to the first question certified fully answers the second, and leads to the conclusion that both must be answered in the affirmative. REVERSED.

HIRAM ALDRICH v. D. D. PAINE, J. R. ROBSON, J. S. PRITCH-ARD, H. PINKHAM, H. H. KINGBORN, Members of the Board of Supervisors of Wright County, and A. A. TAFT, County Auditor, Appellants, and ANNA MORRISON, Intervener.

Drains: COUNTY BOARD: *Towns and cities.* Under Code, 1873, section 1207. authorizing the board of supervisors of counties having a population of five thousand inhabitants to construct "ditches or drains * * * in such county whenever the same will be conducive to the public health, convenience or welfare," the power of the board is not territorially restricted to portions of a county outside of the limits of incorporated towns, in as much as no such authority has been conferred on such towns, and its exercise is not inimical or repugnant to their powers.
ROBINSON and WATERMAN, JJ., dissenting.

Appeal: REVIEW FOR APPELLEE. In a proceeding for the construction of a ditch, appellees, in whose favor it was decided that a majority of the resident owners have signed a petition for the improvement, cannot question on appeal the correctness of the special findings of fact in the decree filed on the same day as the findings of fact in their favor, when no exception was reserved to them.

Appeal from Wright District Court.—HON. D. R. HINDMAN, Judge.

WEDNESDAY, OCTOBER 19, 1898.

A PETITION having been previously filed with the county auditor, the board of supervisors of Wright county ordered the construction of a ditch commencing in the northwest

quarter of southwest quarter of section 31, township 92, range
24 west of the fifth principal meridian, and running
thence to a point on the west line of section 14, township 91, range 25,—a distance of six miles, and all within
the limits of the incorporated town of Clarion, except
that part in said section 14. The ditch was constructed
in the manner provided by law; that part passing through
the two blocks of the platted portion of the town, and
as far as the Burlington, Cedar Rapids & Northern Railway,
—a distance of eighty rods,—being a tile drain, with tiling two
feet in diameter, securely covered. The total cost of eight
thousand seven hundred and thirty-three dollars and three
cents was apportioned and assessed against lands according to
the benefits. A writ of *certiorari* was issued by the district
court, and on hearing the petition was found to be signed by the
requisite number of adjacent owners, but the board of supervisors was held to have acted without jurisdiction in ordering
the construction of the ditch within the limits of the incorporated town of Clarion. The only difference between the petition of the plaintiff and that of intervention of Anna Morrison arises from the situation of their land,—that of Aldrich
lying within and that of Morrison without the corporate
limits. The defendants appeal—*Reversed.*

McGrath, Peterson & Humphrey and *Bottsford, Healy
& Healy* for appellants.

Nagle & Nagle and *Ladd & Rogers* for appellees.

LADD, J.—I. The trial court found that a majority of
the resident owners of land adjacent signed the petition setting forth the necessity, starting point, terminal, and route of
the ditch. The record, which must be regarded as conclusive,
shows this finding of fact to have been filed on the same day,
and presumably at the same time, the decree was entered.
It is doubtless true the appellees had no occasion to object to
a judgment in their favor. This, however, did not
1   relieve them from excepting to those special findings
with which they were not content, and, having failed
to do so, they will be deemed to have acquiesced in the con-

clusions reached. *Assurance Co. v. Neil,* 76 Iowa, 648; 8 Enc. Pl. & Prac. 275, and cases collected. As no exception was saved, they cannot be heard to question the correctness of the findings, and their appeal will be dismissed.

II. The question raised by the defendants' appeal is whether the board of supervisors had authority to order the construction of that portion of the ditch within the limits of the incorporated town of Clarion. Section 1207 of the Code of 1873 is as follows: "The board of supervisors of any county having a population of five thousand inhabitants, as shown by the last preceding census, may locate and cause to be constructed levees, ditches or drains, or change the direction of any watercourse in such county, whenever the same will be conducive to the public health, convenience or welfare." This language is general, and the authority of the board is not restricted in terms or by necessary inference to territory outside of towns and cities. Nor is there any such limitation in any of the sections of this chapter, or amendments thereto, or of chapter 186 of the Acts of the Twentieth General Assembly. The situation may sometimes be such that the ditch must pass through corporate limits in order to carry off the water from lands drained to a stream, and large areas of land requiring proper drainage may lie within such limits. The authority apparently granted to the board of supervisors must be held to extend to all parts of the county, unless so repugnant to the powers granted to cities and towns as to indicate a contrary legislative intention. The decision of this question involves a somewhat detailed consideration of the drainage laws of this state, and of those powers exercised by cities and towns said to be antagonistic to the construction and maintenance of ditches and drains within their limits under the authority of the county. Section 1208 of the Code of 1873 requires that a "petition signed by a majority of persons, resident in the county, owning land adjacent to such improvement shall be first filed in the office of the county auditor, setting forth the necessity of

the same, the starting point, route and termini." In addition to this the basis of the proceeding may be a "petition of
one hundred legal voters of the county setting forth that any
body or district of land in said county, described by metes and
bounds, or otherwise, is subject to overflow or too wet for cultivation ; and that in the opinion of petitioners the public health,
convenience, or welfare, will be promoted by draining or level-
ing the same." Acts Twentieth General Assembly, chapter
186, section 2. The satisfactory and economical construction of the ditch is assured by preliminary provisions
requiring a survey and report with plat and profile, notice to
the owners of the land to be affected, the filing of claims for
damages, the hearing by the board of supervisors, and, if
ordered, then the division of the ditch into sections, and the
letting the work to the lowest bidder. Payment is made "out
of the county treasury, from the fund to be collected for that
purpose, on the order of the county auditor." Section 1214
is as follows: "There shall be made an equitable apportionment of the cost, expenses, costs of construction, fees, and
compensation for property appropriated, or damages sustained by the construction of any such ditch, drain, change
of direction of such water course or repairing and reopening
the same * * * which apportionment shall accrue and
be assessed among the owners of the land benefited by
the location, construction or the reopening and repairing
of such ditch, drain or water course, in proportion to
the benefit to each of them, through, along the line, or
in the vicinity of whose lands the same may be located,
constructed or reopened or repaired respectively, and the same
may be levied upon the land of the owners so benefited in said
proportions, and collected in the same manner that other taxes
are levied and collected for county purposes. And the amount
so collected shall be paid out of the county treasury from the
fund collected for that purpose on the order of the county
auditor * * * and the diverting, obstructing, impeding
or filling up of such drains, ditches or watercourses in any
manner by any person without legal authority, is hereby

declared a nuisance, and any person convicted of such crime, shall be punished as provided in title 24, chapter 15 of the Code for the punishment of nuisances." And said supervisors shall, when necessary, cause said ditches, drains or watercourses to be reopened or repaired, and the costs thereof shall be apportioned, assessed, levied and collected as hereinbefore provided for the costs of the construction of such ditches or drains. It will be observed that any abuse of power by the board of supervisors is carefully guarded against by the requirement of petitions, and the opportunity of being heard afforded every owner of land to be affected; also that, although the necessity for the ditch lies in the public health, convenience, or welfare, those whose lands are beneficially affected must pay for the improvement.

No authority is conferred on incorporated towns to construct ditches or drains in the manner or for the purposes here contemplated. Section 480 of the Code of 1873 authorizes municipal corporations "to cause any lot of land within their limits on which water at any time becomes stagnant to be filled up or drained in such manner as may be directed by a resolution of the council or trustees." But this very evidently relates to water standing in depressions or pools, and not to large areas of low, wet, or swampy land which absorb the water, and on which it seldom stands, and never becomes stagnant. Besides, the authority of the council is limited to ordering such drainage only, or the lot to be so filled, as to obviate the nuisance occasioned by the standing of stagnant water. *Bush v. City of Dubuque*, 69 Iowa, 236.

Again, under section 18 of chapter 116 of the Acts of the Sixteenth General Assembly (now section 699 of the Code) the owner or lessee of land, who, by grading or filling it, obstructs the flow of water through a water course of any kind, may be required to construct a sufficient drain or passageway. This amounts to no more than the restoration of the natural course for surface or other water. Cities are authorized "to deepen, widen, cover, wall, alter or change the channel of water courses within their corporate limits," by section 3 of

VOL. 106 Ia—30

·chapter 89 of the Acts of the Nineteenth General Assembly,
·and, in addition to this, any city of the first class may "build
and construct artificial channels, covered drains or sewers
sufficient to carry the water theretofore flowing in any such
water courses," divert it thereto, and fill up the old channel.
Acts Twenty-third General Assembly, chapter 6, section 1.
These enactments were long subsequent to the statutes giving
authority to the board of supervisors, and, as they relate to
cities only, do not aid in determining the point to be settled.
They make clear, however, that the legislature was of the
opinion the particular powers granted were not previously
possessed by cities.   The power to change any water course
has never been conferred on the incorporated town, and does
not exist, unless as possibly incidental to the care of the
streets.   See *Freburg v. City of Davenport,* 63 Iowa, 110;
Knostman v. City of Davenport, 99 Iowa, 589; *Morris v. City
of Council Bluffs,* 67 Iowa, 343.   Our attention is called to
the statute giving the town authority to grade and repair
streets and alleys and to construct sewers, and requiring that
it shall defray the expenses of the same out of the general
·funds of such city or town.   Code of 1873, section 465.   This
refers to the building of sewers along the public streets and
alleys for the purpose of carrying off the surface water and
filth.   The right to so construct sewers is usually regarded as
incident to the power of maintaining the streets. *Cone v. City
of Hartford,* 28 Conn., 363; *Leeds v. City of Richmond,* 102
Ind., 372 (1 N. E. Rep. 711); *Griswold v. Bay City,* 35
Mich., 452; *Stoudinger v. Newark,* 28 N. J. Eq., 187;
Codman v. Evans, 5 Allen, 309; *In re Fowler,* 53 N. Y. 60;
City of St. Louis v. Oeters, 36 Mo., 456.   See 6 Am. & Eng.
Enc. Law, 19.   The word "sewer" does not seem to have a
meaning essentially differing from "ditch" or "drain."   Webster defines it as "a drain or passage to carry off water and
filth underground; the subterraneous channels, particularly
in cities."   It has also been applied to an underground structure for conducting the water of a natural stream. *Bennett
v. City of New Bedford,* 110 Mass., 433.   In *Clay v. City*

of Grand Rapids, 60 Mich., 451 (27 N. W. Rep. 596), it is said: "Neither is sewerage necessarily, if it is generally, intended as the escape of filthy water. It includes all kinds of drainage or water discharge." The sewer is usually closed, but not necessarily so, and is ordinarily applied to drains in the city, whether of water or filth, or both. The difference seems to be largely a matter of location. What is a ditch or drain in the country is called a sewer in the city, and *vice versa.* But there is no provision for this construction of sewers through private property within incorporated towns, though the power to condemn for this purpose is conferred on cities. Acts Twenty-fourth General Assembly, chapter 8. That a ditch or drain cannot be so constructed without compensation has been recognized by this court. *Fleming v. Hull,* 73 Iowa, 598; *Hatch v. Pottawattamie County,* 43 Iowa, 442. Sewers or gutters along the street or highway would prove utterly inadequate to the drainage of large areas of land, and would involve much expense with little or no corresponding advantages to the incorporation aside from that to the general public. The main benefit is to the owner, and he, and not the public, should bear the burden. It is argued that these drains might be made in order to promote the public health. That this may be done in a locality controlled by the town may be conceded. *State v. City Council of Charleston,* 12 Rich. Law, 702. But permanent appropriation of land for its use for that purpose, without compensation, cannot be made, even though for the public good, and no general powers to condemn appertain to the duties of corporation officers. See *Bryant v. Robbins,* 70 Wis., 258 (35 N. W. Rep. 546); *Martin v. Tyler,* 4 N. D., 278 (60 N. W. Rep. 392). It must be borne in mind that municipal corporations have and can exercise such powers only as are expressly granted by their charters or legislative acts, or are necessarily implied therefrom, or are necessarily incidental thereto. *Brockman v. City of Creston,* 79 Iowa, 589; *Becker v. Waterworks,* 79 Iowa, 422; *Clark v. City of Des Moines,* 19 Iowa, 212; *McPherson v. Foster,* 43 Iowa, 57; *Keokuk v. Scroggs,* 39 Iowa, 447; *Clark v. City of Davenport,* 14 Iowa, 494.

It appearing, then, that the power is not conferred on the
incorporated town, we may consider the objections urged
against the possession thereof by the board of supervisors.
The board may locate a highway along the ditch "in the same
manner as on the report of a highway commissioner."
Undoubtedly, its authority in this respect is limited to territory outside of the cities and towns. *Gallaher v. Head,* 72
Iowa, 173. In that case it was held that the general authority
of the board of supervisors to establish highways was
restricted to territory outside of cities and towns by section
464 of the Code of 1873, conferring on these the power
to "lay off, widen, straighten, narrow, vacate, extend, and
establish streets." This conclusion appears to be based on
these grounds: (1) under the authority of the board the
highway must be opened and worked by the highway supervisor, who is not authorized to do so within a town or city,
and the land within the incorporation is taxed by it for such
purposes; (2) cities and towns have control of certain purposes (such as abating nuisances, regulating travel, prohibiting the laying of tracks, etc.) of all territory within their
limits; and, (3) the jurisdiction and liability of the county
would cease with its establishment, and the burden of maintaining it be cast on the city or town, which might immediately vacate it. If this case is decisive, as asserted by
appellees, it must be because of the reasons on which the
decision is based, rather than the language of the statute; for
here the same power is not conferred on the county and the
incorporated town, and the jurisdiction is not concurrent.
The situation is rather that of no power to act on the part of
the incorporated town and plenary power on the part of the
county. But the reasoning is not applicable. The town,
as owner of the fee of the street, may, if the street is
damaged by appropriation of its use in part for the construction of a drain or ditch, file its claim for damages under
section 1210, which provides that "any person claiming compensation for land required for the purpose of constructing

any levee, ditch, drain or water-course * * * shall make his application in writing therefor to the county supervisors on or before the first day of the session at which the petition is set for hearing." From the determination of the board an appeal may be taken to the courts. The term "person," as here used, must be extended to bodies corporate. Section 45, subd. 13. If injury will be done the streets, or an additional burden of expense cast upon the corporation, we discover no reason why damages may not be claimed by it as well as by the individual owners through whose land the improvement extends. See *Railway Co. v. Starkweather*, 97 Iowa, 159. The objection that the responsibility of the county would end with the completion of the ditch is not well founded. It is given authority to reopen and repair. Section 1210; *Yeoman v. Riddle,* 84 Iowa, 147. Besides, it has been held that, though the county may construct bridges, or aid therein, the city may be held responsible for their care and control. *Bell v. Foutch,* 21 Iowa, 129; *Oskaloosa Steam Engine Works v. Pottawattamie County,* 72 Iowa, 135; *McCullom v. Blackhawk County,* 21 Iowa, 413; *Railway Co. v. Murphy,* 106 Iowa, *post.* See *Clark v. Town of Epworth,* 56 Iowa, 462. The contingency suggested, that the council, in its discretion, might conclude the ditch ought to be filled, and fill it, is guarded against by section 1214, declaring one so doing guilty of causing a nuisance, and punishable accordingly. The control of the corporation, like that of the owner of the land through which the ditch passes, must be consistent with its continuted existence and the purpose of its construction. The appellees assert that, if the supervisors have authority to construct a drain within corporate limits, an open ditch might be made through the populous portion of a city, and left in such a condition as to be a menace to health, and a dangerous obstruction to travel. The same objection can as well be made in behalf of a thickly-settled portion of an unincorporated town or village. It must not be forgotten that drainage is undertaken for the public good, and not for the private advantage or disadvantage of the owners of the land affected.

Patterson v. Baumer, 43 Iowa, 477. The cost of the improvement is paid by the assessement of benefits, and these would not be such in the settled portion of a town or city as to make possible the contingency supposed. Nor would it be possible to secure the petition required. Besides, the supervisors act for the people of the cities and towns as well as for those of others portions of the county, and in the discharge of their responsible duties will not work a great injury to these communities while attempting to promote their health, convenience, or welfare. Some discretion must always be lodged with officers authorized to act for the public in making improvements of this character, and the presumption in favor of their fidelity was vindicated in this case. The town of Clarion includes fourteen and one-half sections of land, much of which is wet and marshy. The ditch extending through the suburbs of the platted portion and in the streets was securely covered. The very possibilities suggested by the appellees were carefully guarded against. The character of the ditch is one of the matters to be considered at the hearing before the board of supervisors, and, if a covered ditch is necessary, it may well be presumed that it will be so constructed. It is urged, however, that if this were not done, or if the ditch should get out of repair, the city or town would be liable for any injury occasioned by its unsafe condition, owing to its ownership and control of the streets. If this be true, it is not inconsistent with any power granted, as the responsibility for the care of the streets remains unchanged, except that another burden is added. No injustice is involved because this may be taken into consideration in fixing compensation for damages. We think the objections urged by the appellees go to the possibilities of abuse of power, rather than want thereof, by the board of supervisors. These were doubtless given due weight by the legislature, and, as it saw fit not to confine the exercise of authority by the board to territory outside of cities and towns, we are not inclined to ingraft such a limitation. The necessity of ditches and drains within the limits of such municipalities will seldom arise, and the board of supervisors, when called upon to order their construction, may well be intrusted to act with due regard for all the interests involved.   We conclude that, as the authority to construct drains and ditches or change water courses, as possessed by the board of supervisors, has not been conferred on incorporated towns, and as its exercise is not inimical or repugnant to any of the powers granted to such corporations, it was not the purpose of the legislature to restrict such authority, by implication or otherwise, to that portion of the county outside of their limits.   Judgment may be entered in this court dismissing the plaintiff's petition and that of the intervener.—*Reversed*.

ROBINSON, J. (dissenting).—The statute under which the proceedings in controversy were had was first enacted in the year 1872 (Acts Fourteenth General Assembly, chapter 220), and was incorporated in title 10 of the Code of 1873, which related to internal improvements.   There is nothing in the language of the statute which indicates specifically that it was designed to apply to territory within incorporated cities and towns.   It does not refer to them, nor does it contain any of the terms ordinarily used to designate real estate within such corporations, as, "lots."   That fact, considered alone, would be of little, if any, importance in view of the general power given by the statute to boards of supervisors to cause to be constructed ditches and drains whenever it would "be conducive to the public health, convenience, or welfare."   But the statute does not state that the board of supervisors may cause a ditch or drain to be constructed *wherever* it would be conducive to the public health, convenience, or welfare.   A petition signed by persons owning "land" adjacent to the improvement is required, and the statute provides for the assessment of all "land" benefited by the ditch or drain, for the cost of constructing, repairing, or opening it.   The terms "land" and "real estate," it is true, are interchangeable, and town lots are land; but it is true, as a general rule, when real estate in a city or town is intended to be included within the purview of a legislative act of this state, that the terms "lots and lands," or "lots and parcels of land," or similar designations, are most commonly used. Thus the general assembly which first enacted the statute in question also enacted a statute which referred to the platting of "any town lot or parcel of ground within any incorporated city or town, or any tract of land containing forty acres or less," which had been divided for the purposes of sale, when the subdivisions could not be accurately described without noting the metes and bounds. Chapter 94, Acts Fourteenth General Assembly (sections 478 and 479, Code of 1873), related to assessments by municipal corporations for street improvements, and used the terms "lots or lands," "lots or parcels of land," and "lot or land," in designating real estate subject to such assessments. The fact that these and similar terms are most commonly used to designate real estate within cities and towns, although not in any sense controlling, may properly be considered with other relevant facts to ascertain the legislative intent in enacting the statute in question. From a time before that was enacted, incorporated cities and towns have had the power to lay off, open, establish, and extend streets, alleys, and public grounds (Code of 1873, section 464); to provide for the grading and repair of streets, avenues, and alleys, and the construction of sewers (section 465); to construct sidewalks, and to curb, pave, gravel, macadamize, and gutter any highway or alley therein (section 466); to procure and control public squares, streets, parks, commons, cemeteries, and hospital grounds (section 470); to erect waterworks (section 471); and, by a later statute, to establish and maintain gas works or electric light plants (Acts Twenty-second General Assembly, chapter 11). Such corporations also have power "to prevent injury or annoyance from anything dangerous, offensive or unhealthy, and to cause any nuisance to be abated" (Code of 1873, section 456), and to do many other things which need not be enumerated. Section 920 of the Code of 1873 gave to each board of supervisors "general supervision over the highways in the county, with power to establish and change them," as provided by the Code. The language of the Code did not limit the power of such boards to territory outside incorporated cities and towns, but was broad enough to include territory within them.   This court held, however, in *Gallaher v. Head*, 72 Iowa, 173, that the jurisdiction and power of such corporations over territory within their limits was exclusive for the purpose of establishing highways or streets on or through such territory. ˙ Section 969 of the Code of 1873, authorized township trustees to "divide their respective townships into such number of highway districts as they may deem necessary for the public good."   That provision was considered in *Clark v. Town of Epworth*, 56 Iowa, 462, and said to be broad enough to confer upon the trustees unrestricted control over the establishment of highway districts in their townships; but it was held, in effect, that such power would be inconsistent with that conferred upon cities and towns within the townships.   See, also, *Railway Co. v. Murphy*, 106 Iowa, *post.* I am of the opinion that the rule of the cases cited is applicable in this case, and should be controlling. The streets, alleys, and other public grounds of incorporated cities and towns, their sewers and drains, are usually established and improved according to well-defined plans, and grades duly fixed, with the design of perfecting a system of improvements which shall be efficient, and harmonious in all its parts.   But if boards of supervisors may invade such cities and towns, cut ditches therein, and construct drains, without reference to the powers of the municipalities invaded, or the system of improvements they have established, it is evident that serious conflict of authority may arise.   The board of supervisors might conclude to establish an open ditch where the interests of the people of the city or town demanded a closed sewer, or to so locate and construct the ditch as to greatly impair or destroy the sewerage system of the city or town, or injure its public parks or other grounds, or to require the construction of bridges where, under the plan of the municipality, none would have been required, or to interfere in numerous other ways with the proper exercise of municipal functions.   To say that the boards of supervisors act for the people of cities and towns as well as for other

people of their counties, and for the benefit of all, does not
answer the objections suggested.   Experience shows that it is
not often, if ever, in the interest of the public, to vest in two
separate and independent bodies concurrent but independent
jurisdiction of the same subject-matter, and that, where it is
done, unseemly conflict in the exercise of authority, greatly to
the injury of the public, is apt to ensue.   For that reason, as
well as others, concurrent power is rarely vested by legislative
acts in separate and independent bodies or agencies.

It is said, however, that incorporated cities and towns did
not have power to drain such land as that in question, but only
to drain water standing in depressions or pools.   Even if that
were true, it would not follow that the board of supervisors
could have drained such lands by constructing ditches or
drains within incorporated cities and towns.   But, in my opinion, it is not true that such corporations lacked the power to
drain wet land which was a menace to public health. They had
power "to prevent injury or annoyance from anything dangerous, offensive or unhealthy, and to cause any nuisance to be
abated."   Code of 1873, section 456.   The manner in which
the power thus conferred should be exercised was not pointed
out, but of necessity it authorized the doing of whatever was
reasonably necessary and lawful to accomplish the end authorized; and, if a ditch or drain were necessary to accomplish it,
then the power to construct the ditch or drain was included in
that given.   The fact that the cost of such ditch or drain could
not have been assessed upon the real property which was
benefited by it, in the manner provided by the general drainage
act, does not seem to me to be important to ascertain the power
given.   The purpose of the drain would not be to reclaim land
for the purposes of cultivation, but to preserve the public
health.   I do not assent, however, to the conclusion of the
majority that the land in question was not within the scope of
section 480 of the Code of 1873. That provided that "municipal corporations shall have power to cause any lot or land
within their limits on which water at any time becomes
stagnant, to be filled up or drained in such manner as may be

directed by a resolution of the council or trustees," and to do
the work required at the expense of the corporation in the first
instance, in case the owner of the land neglected or refused to
do the work.   But the cost of the work in such a case was a
debt collectible of the landowner, and a lien upon the property
drained was given.   The petition on which the board of supervisors ordered the construction of the ditch stated, in substance, that upon the land to be drained were "large collections of standing water, * * * endangering the public
health, convenience, and welfare."   The report of the county
surveyor shows that the land to be drained was low and
swampy, "which, of an ordinary year, would contain stagnant
water."   That this is true is not denied, but is affirmed by the
appellants, who state in argument that "it clearly appears
from the abstracts on file in this case that a large area of farm
lands lying to the east, south, and southwest of the incorporated town of Clarion, in Wright county, to the extent of
several miles, is low, wet, marshy, and covered with stagnant
water in ordinary years; that these stagnant waters were a
continual menace to the health of the inhabitants of the surrounding country ; * * * that due regard for the public
health, convenience, and welfare of the inhabitants of the surrounding country imperatively required the draining or ditching of these lands."   The location of the land is evidently thus
fixed by reference to the platted portion of the town of Clarion.
It is shown that nearly all of the land to be drained is within
the territorial limits of the town, and it is admitted that in
ordinary seasons water becomes stagnant on the land.   It thus
appears beyond question that it is within both the letter and
spirit of section 480, and that the town had ample authority
to cause it to be drained.   It appears to me clear that it could
not have been the legislative intent to give to the board of
supervisors also the power to do the same.   That would be
repugnant to the power expressly conferred upon the town, and
contrary to the general policy which is followed in the enactment of statutes.   The probable fact that a large area of wet,

swampy land was included within the corporate limits of Clarion, which was not needed for dwelling houses or other ordinary purposes of a town, and which could, if drained, be used most profitably for agricultural purposes, and the fact that the cost of draining might be more equitably assessed and promptly collected under the statute in question, if applicable, than under the provisions of section 480, do not authorize the conclusion that the statute in question applies. It was within the legislative power to prescribe one method for draining land outside incorporated cities and towns, and another for draining lots and lands within their limits; and that appears to me to be what was done. If a mistake in that respect was made by the general assembly, it may give the remedy. For reasons indicated I am of the opinion that sections 1207 to 1216, inclusive, of the Code of 1873, did not authorize boards of supervisors to construct ditches or drains within municipal corporations. The fact that the ditch in question may have been for the public benefit, and that it was so constructed as not to injure property owners, did not authorize the assessments in controversy. If the board lacked the power to construct the ditch, it could not make the property affected liable for its cost. The opinion of the majority discusses various matters which do not appear to me to be involved in a determination of this case, and I do not express any opinion in regard to them, but on grounds set out I think the judgment of the district court should be AFFIRMED.

WATERMAN, J., concurs in this dissent.

The Cedar Rapids & Marion City Railway Company, Appellant, v. The City of Cedar Rapids, et al.

Street Railway Defined: TAXATION. A railway was constructed within a city, and also along a highway to a neighboring town. It was operated at first by steam, but afterwards by overhead trolly. It was built and operated under Acts Eighteenth General Assembly, chapter 32, relating expressly to street railways, and authorizing their extension beyond the limits of the city. It carried a small amount of freight and some express matter between the towns. *Held*, that it was a street railway, and therefore not within Code, 1873, section 1317, providing for the assessment of railways for taxation by the state executive council, but subject to taxation by the local assessors.

Taxation: APPEAL TO DISTRICT COURT. On appeal from the decision of the board of equalization upon an assessment, the district court has jurisdiction to strike from the assessment three lots described **2** by the assessor which were not the property of the corporation assessed and to include two parts of lots which were its property, where the board of equalization failed to act upon the corporation's request to make such correction and such parts of lots were in fact included in the valuation but were by mistake described as the three lots.

SAME. The board of equalization assessed only that portion of a street railroad which lay within the city. The company applied to the board to have a misdescription of part of such property corrected, **2** and, on refusal, appealed to the district court. On the appeal the city sought to have the property outside the city added to the assessment. *Held*, that, as the district court had no power to make an original assessment, it could not make such addition, as that issue was not raised by the appeal.

TO SUPREME COURT. The supreme court will change an assessment, **3** on appeal, to the amount which the weight of evidence shows most nearly represents the actual value of the property assessed.

Appeal from Linn District Court.—HON. WILLIAM G. THOMPSON, Judge.

THURSDAY, OCTOBER 20, 1898.

THIS action is before us on an appeal by the plaintiff from a judgment rendered by the district court on an assessment for taxation made against the plaintiff, for the year 1895. The issues and facts appear in the opinion.—*Modified* and *Affirmed*.

Charles A. Clark for appellant.

Warren Harmon for appellees.

GIVEN, J.—I. On the first day of January, 1895, the plaintiff owned and was operating a line of railway from a

point within the limits of Cedar Rapids, through the incorporated town of Kenwood, and over certain unincorporated
territory, into the incorporated city of Marion. It also
owned and operated in connection therewith certain other
lines or branches entirely within the limits of the city of
Cedar Rapids. These tracks were laid upon and at the grade
of the streets of these municipalities, and upon and at the
grade of the public highway connecting said cities, over the
unincorporated territory, including certain county bridges
in said highway. Originally, the line to Marion
started at Fifteenth street, in Cedar Rapids, then a
boundary street of said city, and was operated by
steam engines, under chapter 32, Acts Eighteenth General
Assembly, authorizing any street railway company extending
its lines beyond the limits of the city to build and operate
its road over and along any portion of a highway of a width
of one hundred feet or more. On and for some time prior
to January, 1895, the tracks within the city of Cedar Rapids
and that to Marion were operated together; electricity,
applied by the overhead or trolly system, being used as the
motive power. One or more of the steam engines formerly
used were kept in a motor house near Indian creek, for use
in case of deep snows or other emergency rendering their use
desirable. Cars were operated on these tracks mainly for
the carriage of passengers in the manner practiced by street
railways. Plaintiff had four cars which it used in carrying
freight between said cities, and it also carried such express
matter as was offered at either end of the line or at any point
between. The power house and principal car sheds were in
Cedar Rapids, and most of the rolling stock was kept therein
when not in use, the other cars being kept in Marion for convenience in starting from that end of the line in the mornings.
Plaintiff did not have freight nor passenger depots and agents
along the line, as commercial railroads have, but took up and
discharged passengers and express matter at cross streets and
other convenient points. In short, it was operated in all its
branches as street railways are operated, except that it

received and carried freight and express matter, to a limited extent, between the two cities. The assessor of the defendant city assessed the plaintiff's property within that city, for the year 1895, at one hundred and fifty thousand dollars, including therein three certain lots that did not belong to the plaintiff, and omitting therefrom parts of two other lots that did belong to the plaintiff, and were used in the operation of the road. On application to the board of equalization, said assessment was reduced to one hundred thousand dollars; and, on appeal to the district court, said three lots were stricken from the assessment, and the parts of said two lots owned by the plaintiff added thereto, and the assessment sustained at one hundred thousand dollars.

II.   The Code of 1873 provides as follows: "Section 1317.   On the first Monday of March in each year, the executive council shall assess all the property of each railway corporation in this state, excepting lands, lots, and other real estate belonging thereto not used in the operation of any railway." Plaintiff's first contention is that it is a "railway corporation," within the meaning of said section, and subject only to assessment by the executive council. So maintaining, it made returns to, and asked to be assessed by, that body; but the council held, on advice of the attorney general, that it had no power to assess the plaintiff's said property. Plaintiff's counsel state the question thus: "Whether appellant's main line, with or without the lines in the streets of Cedar Rapids, is subject to assessment and valuation by the local authorities, or whether such assessment must be made by the executive council of the state of Iowa." That plaintiff is a "railway corporation," in the broadest signification of that term, may be conceded, but our inquiry is as to the sense in which those words are used in said section 1317. We need not quote the many provisions of the statute with respect to railroads which show that a distinction is recognized between what we may call "commercial railroad corporations" and "street railroad corporations." That there is a distinction is not questioned, but the dispute is as to which class the plaintiff corporation belongs. See *Fidelity Loan & Trust Co. v. Douglas,* 104 Iowa, 532. The development of railways in and about towns and cities has brought the question before the courts whether a particular railway was a street or commercial railway, and the question has always been determined in the light of the statute and the facts of the particular case. The part of this road extending from Cedar Rapids to Marion was constructed and operated by the plaintiff corporation, under authority of chapter 32, Acts Eighteenth General Assembly. See *Linn County v. Hewitt,* 55 Iowa, 507. The act relates expressly to street railways, and authorizes the extension of such railways beyond the limits of the city or town, the location thereof along any portion of a highway which is of a width of one hundred feet or more, and the operation of the railway by either animal or motor power. The fact that the line between Cedar Rapids and Marion was laid and operated along the highway as authorized by said act, relating exclusively to street railways, seems to us conclusive that the plaintiff is a street railway corporation and not a railway corporation, within the meaning of said section 1317, Code 1873. The fact that plaintiff's street railway was authorized to be extended and laid and operated along a highway, precludes the conclusion that it was intended to be other than a street railway. Street railways constructed and operated as they are in streets and highways do not exclude other travel therefrom; but not so as to other railways constructed and operated along a street or highway. Plaintiff's railway is identical in its construction and operation with other street railways, except in that it carries freight and express, to a limited extent, as well as passengers, while most others carry passengers only. It is unlike other than street railways in almost every other particular. It is insisted that this alone distinguishes it from street railways, and authorities are cited wherein it is said that a "distinctive and essential feature of a street railway in relation to other railroads is that it 'a exclusively for the transportation of passengers, and not for goods." Ordinarily that is true, but in this case we have a street railway corporation organized to operate a street railway in the city of Cedar Rapids, extending its railway beyond the limits of said city, under authority of said chapter 32, Acts Eighteenth General Assembly, expressly relating to street railway companies. Surely the mere fact that plaintiff carries goods and express matter does not take it out of the class of railways where this statute puts it. It is not a "railway corporation," as contemplated in said section 1317, but a street railway, and is therefore subject to assessment by the local assessors.

III. We have seen that the district court struck from the assessment the three lots described by the assesor that did not belong to the plaintiff, and inserted the two parts of lots that did belong to plaintiff. Plaintiff denies that the

2   court had jurisdiction so to do. It is insisted that the district court had no power to make an original assessment, and that there was no evidence to show at what valuation the assessor included the three lots, nor what the value of the two parts of lots was. The fact is that plaintiff's power house and principal car sheds were situated on said parts of two lots, and that it was said lots that were in fact included in the valuation, and by mistake described as the three lots. Plaintiff asked the equalization board to make this correction, but it failed to do so, and on the plaintiff's appeal the district court had jurisdiction to do it. It was not an original assessment, as in *Brown v. Town of Grand Junction,* 75 Iowa, 488. In that case Brown had been assessed ten thousand dollars upon goods and merchandise when he did not own any, but it appeared that he had moneys and credits upon which he might properly have been assessed that amount. It was held error to allow defendants to amend, and ask an assessment on moneys and credits, because no such issue was presented by the appeal. By plaintiff's application the issue was presented as to its right to have the error in the description of the lots corrected. The lots that plaintiff did own were

the ones included in the valuation, and the court had jurisdiction to correct the assessment in that particular.

IV.   Plaintiff contends that the assessment in question,
in so far as it exceeds seventy thousand dollars, is excessive.
Defendants' counsel cite *Capital City Gas Light Co. v.
Charter Oak Ins. Co.*, 51 Iowa, 31. *In re Des Moines Water
Works Co.*, 48 Iowa, 324, and *Oskaloosa Water Co. v. Board
of Equalization of City of Oskaloosa*, 84 Iowa, 407, and
insist, upon the authority of those cases, that plaintiff's
property lying without the defendant city should be included
in the assessment as appurtenant to the real estate in said
city.   In *Brown v. Town of Grand Junction, supra*, it is
said: "We think the court could not try any other issue than
that presented by the appeal." It is further said: "It never
has been held by this court that the district court has power
to make an original assessment of property for taxation."
Turning to this record, we see that the assessment made by
the assessor, and revised by the board and by the district
court, was of the plaintiff's property within the city of Cedar
Rapids only.   The defendants have never assumed to include
any of the property outside of said city in the assessment
under consideration, and the plaintiff is not asking that it be
included.   In taking the testimony, both parties proceeded
upon the theory that, if the property was not subject to
assessment by the executive council, then only that part lying
within the defendant city could be assessed by it.   True,
there is some reference to the value of outlying property, but
it is merely incidental to the inquiries as to the value of that
within the city.   We are not called upon to determine whether
that part of the property lying without the defendant city
might have been included in this assessment, nor to consider
its value, as no such issues are presented by this appeal.   To
add this property to the assessment would be quite different
from correcting a misdescription of property that was valued
and included.

V.   We now inquire as to the value of plaintiff's property included in this assessment.   Estimating values is often

so largely a matter of judgment that such estimates cannot always. be said to bo perfectly accurate. The testimony on this subject is somewhat voluminous, and we will not notice it in detail. Mr. Hall, president, Mr. Disrens, superintendent, and Mr. Elsom, former superintendent, testify on behalf of the plaintiff. These gentlemen testify from an intimate knowledge of the cost and present condition of the property, and their testimony may be summed up as placing the value of the property in Cedar Rapids, including all the cars run in that city and half those run to Marion, at seventy-two thousand seven hundred and seventy-eight dollars. Mr. Bliss, called by the defendant, testifies from a large experience and knowledge of the cost of constructing and equipping such railroads; and, after a careful examination of this property,

3   Mr. Bliss' valuation is upon a somewhat different basis and higher than that of the other witnesses.

We think his estimates in several particulars, especially as to the cost of rail in 1895, are excessive. The weight of the evidence is in favor of the conclusion that the value of plaintiff's property included in the assessment in question was seventy-two thousand seven hundred and seventy-eight dollars, and the assessment is modified accordingly.—MODIFIED and AFFIRMED.

STATE OF IOWA v. CHARLES CARNAGY, Appellant.

Rape: ASSAULT TO: *Elements.* It is not an essential element of the crime of assault with intent to commit rape that the defendant
8 intended to accomplish his purpose in spite of any resistance, where the prosecutrix is a child under the age of consent. And it does not matter that he expected no opposition.

PENETRATION: *Evidence.* In a trial for rape the evidence of penetration is sufficient to warrant a submission of the cause to the
2 jury where it is shown in addition to the injured condition of the genital organs that the defendant did his utmost to accomplish his purpose and if he failed it was because of the tender years of his victim.

INSTRUCTIONS: *Failure of accused to testify.* Code, section 5484, provides that, should a defendant elect not to become a witness, that fact shall not have any weight against him on the trial, nor shall the state's attorney refer to such fact during the trial. *Held*, that irrespective of whether anything has occurred during the trial to direct the attention of the jury to defendant's failure to testify, it is error to refuse to instruct the jury thereon.

CORROBORATION: *Failure to instruct on.* Failure to instruct that defendant in a prosecution for rape or assault with intent to commit rape cannot be convicted on the uncorroborated evidence of the prosecutrix (Code, section 5488) is prejudicial error, though no request to so instruct was made, and though there was, in fact, corroborating evidence.

Indictment: VARIANCE: *Name of prosecutrix.* An indictment charged a rape on "Anna Brown " The evidence showed that her name was "Anna Grubb," but that she had always been known by the former name, taking it from her stepfather. *Held*, that the erroneous allegation was immaterial, within Code, section 5286, the offense being otherwise described with sufficient certainty, and since defendant was not prejudiced in any way by the erroneous allegation.

Presence of Judge. The absence of the judge from the court during the opening address to the jury in a criminal case, as shown by an entry wherein he refuses to rule on an objection to the line of argument pursued by the state's attorney, for such reason, where not affirmatively shown to have been without prejudice, is prejudicial error.

GIVEN, J., dissenting.

Appeal from Linn District Court.—HON. WILLIAM G. THOMPSON, Judge.

THURSDAY, OCTOBER 20, 1898.

THE defendant, having been accused of the crime of rape, and convicted of an assault with intent to commit rape, appeals.—*Reversed.*

Giffen & Voris for appellant.

Milton Remley, Attorney General, and *Jesse A. Miller* for the State.

LADD, J.—The name of the child of eleven years upon whom the assault is claimed to have been made was, in fact,

"Anna Grubb," though alleged in the indictment as "Anna Brown." She has always been known by the latter name, taking it from her stepfather. When these facts
1   appeared in evidence, the defendant asked that, because of the variance between the names alleged and proven, her testimony be stricken from the record. This motion was properly overruled, as the defendant was in no way prejudiced by the defect in naming the person injured. Code, section 5286; *State v. Carr,* 43 Iowa, 418; *State v. Cunningham,* 21 Iowa, 433; *State v. Emeigh,* 18 Iowa, 122; *State v. Flynn,* 42 Iowa, 164; *State v. Crawford,* 66 Iowa, 318; *State v. Fogarty,* 105 Iowa, 32; *State v. Bell,* 65 N. C. 313; *State v. Windahl,* 95 Iowa. 470.

II.   If there was no evidence of penetration, it may be conceded that the issue as to whether the defendant was guilty of rape ought not to have been submitted to the jury. See *State v. Kyne,* 86 Iowa, 616. The prosecution, however, was not bound to rely upon the testimony of the injured party alone, as penetration, like any other element of crime, may be established by circumstantial evidence. *State*
2   *v. Tarr,* 28 Iowa, 397; *State v. Watson,* 81 Iowa, 389; *Brauer v. State,* 25 Wis. 413; *Taylor v. State,* 111 Ind. 279 (12 N. E. Rep. 400); *State v. Depoister,* 21 Nev. 107 (25 Pac. Rep. 1000). Proof of the slightest penetration is sufficient to sustain the charge of rape. See cases above cited, and also *State v. Hargrave,* 65 N. C. 466; *People v. Crowley,* 102 N. Y. 234 (6 N. E. Rep. 384); *Rodgers v. State,* 30 Tex. App. 510 (17 S. W. Rep. 1077); *Reg. v. Allen,* 9 Car. & P. 31. The evidence in this case tends to show that the defendant did his utmost to accomplish his wicked purpose, and, if he failed, it was because of the tender years of his victim. This, together with evidence concerning the injured condition of her genital organs, was sufficient to warrant the submission of the issue to the jury.

III.   It is insisted the jury ought to have been told, as requested by the defendant, that, in order to warrant his

conviction, it must appear he intended to have the intercourse in spite of any resistance.   In an instruction given,
the jury was substantially so directed.   Our statute makes it
rape to carnally know and abuse any female child under the
age of fifteen years, without reference to whether she
3   consent or refuse.   Under that age she is incapable of
giving her consent to such an act.   If the defendant
attempted to have sexual intercourse with this child, and
failed, he was guilty of an assault with intent to commit rape,
even though she made no resistance whatever, and he expected
to accomplish his purpose without opposition. *State v. Grossheim,* 79 Iowa, 75; *State v. Newton,* 44 Iowa, 45.   See, also,
State v. Ruhl 8 Iowa, 447; *Fizell v. State,* 25 Wis. 365;
Com. v. Roosnell, 143 Mass. 32 (8 N. E. Rep. 747); *People
v. McDonald,* 9 Mich. 150; *State v. Johnston,* 76 N. C.
209; *Stephen v. State,* 11 Ga. 226; *People v. Gordon,* 70
Cal. 467 (11 Pac. Rep. 762); *Hays v. People,* 1 Hill
(N. Y.) 351; *Territory v. Keyes,* 5 Dak. 244 (38 N.
W. Rep. 440); *Davis v. State,* 31 Neb. 247 (47 N. W. Rep.
854); *State v. Wheat,* 63 Vt. 673 (22 Atl. Rep. 720); *Murphy
v. State,* 120 Ind. 115 (22 N. E. Rep. 106); *Glover v. Com.,*
86 Va. 382 (10 S. E. Rep. 420); *McKinny v. State,* 29
Fla. 565 (10 South Rep. 732); *State v. West,* 39 Minn.
321 (40 N. W. Rep. 249); *State v. Meinhart,* 73 Mo.
562; *In re Loyd,* 51 Kan. Sup. 501 (33 Pac. Rep. 307);
McClain Criminal Law, section 464; Wharton Criminal
Law, section 577.   *Contra,* see *Hardin v. State* (Tex. Cr.
App.) 46 S. W. Rep. 803; *Smith v. State,* 12 Ohio, St.
466; *State v. Pickett,* 11 Nev. 255; *Whitcher v. State,* 2
Wash. St. 286 (26 Pac. Rep. 268); *Reg. v. Read,* 2 Car. & K.
957; *Hardwick v. State,* 6 Lea. 103.

IV.   During the opening address to the jury by the
county attorney, counsel for the defendant interposed objections to the line of argument pursued.   What this was does
not appear, except from the objection, which indicated that
he was stating what he conceived to be the law applicable to
the case.   The judge was absent, and, upon his return, caused

the following entry to be made: "The court, not being present, but out of the court room, could not hear the argument; and the court says he cannot pass on the objection, and will not do so, because the court did not hear a word of the objection or the argument, as he was absent from the court house." There is no affirmative showing of prejudice, unless it be in the omission to rule on the objection made.

4   But we think the absence of the judge from the court room, beyond the hearing of the proceedings, when not shown affirmatively to have been without prejudice, is in itself error, alone sufficient to warrant the reversal of a judgment. There can be no court without a judge, and his presence, as the presiding genius of the trial, is as essential at one time as another. The argument is an important part of the proceedings, during which the judge cannot properly absent himself. He should remain within hearing, that he may not even temporarily relinquish control of the proceedings and the conduct of the trial. This is necessary to enable him to intelligently review the proceedings on motion for new trial. So doing will not prevent him from changing his seat, or even being in an adjoining room, if not out of hearing of the proceedings, or from reading or writing or temporarily engaging in conversation, for he is not bound to listen to every word of the argument. But he at all times must be in readiness to assert authority in keeping the argument within legitimate limits, and to interpose whenever the conduct of officers of the court, jurors, or spectators may require. In all criminal prosecutions the law exacts a speedy and public trial, and all formalities should be scrupulously observed, that the public may know the majesty of the law is being upheld, and the accused accord that fair and impartial hearing guaranteed by the constitution. The accused is entitled to a trial in a court duly constituted, and, if the presiding judge abandons the trial or relinquishes control of the proceedings, he has ground for complaint. *Turbeyville v. State,* 56 Miss. 793; *O'Brien v. People,* 17 Colo. 561 (31 Pac. Rep. 230); *Palin v. State,* 38 Neb. 862 (57 N. W. Rep.

743); *State v. Smith,* 49 Conn. 376); *Thompson v. People,* 144 Ill. 378 (32 N. E. Rep. 968); *State v. Beuerman* (Kan.) 53 Pac. Rep. 874; *Hayes v. State,* 58 Ga. 35; *Meredith v. People,* 84 Ill. 479.

Our attention has not been called to any authority to the contrary. In *State v. Porter,* 105 Iowa, 677, neither party claimed any prejudice because of the absence of the judge, who, in fact, heard all that was said. In *Baxter v. Ray.* 62 Iowa, 336, there was no claim of prejudice, and none appeared. The reversal of *Hall v. Wolff,* 61 Iowa, 562, was because of misconduct of counsel in argument. The withdrawal of the judge there approved is by consent of parties in a civil case. In *State v. Griffin,* 79 Iowa, 570, misconduct of the counsel, not absence of the judge, was held to be without prejudice. Undoubtedly, error of the judge in temporarily relinquishing control of the proceedings in the trial of a civil cause may be cured by an affirmative showing that no prejudice resulted. Whether this may be done in a criminal action, the record in this case does not permit us to determine, as no showing whatever was-attempted. See, however, the authorities cited. In any event, the better practice requires the visible presence of the presiding judge, and that he be within hearing every moment during the actual progress of trials involving the life or the liberty of those accused of crime.

V. The defendant requested the court to give the jury this instruction, and complains of the refusal to do so: "You are instructed that the fact that the defendant has not been called as a witness to testify in this case cannot be considered by you for any purpose, and you are instructed that you will not, in your deliberation, consider the fact of his not so testifying for any purpose in arriving at your verdict." Section 5484 of the Code provides that, "should a defendant not elect to become a witness, that fact shall not have any weight against him on the trial, nor shall the attorney or attorneys for the state, during the trial, refer to the fact that the defendant did not testify in his own behalf; and should they do so, such attorney or attorneys will be guilty of a misdemeanor, and

defendant, for that cause alone, be entitled to a new trial."
Whether giving such an instruction would have been beneficial to the defendant, we shall not undertake to
5   determine. It is urged that, where nothing has
occurred during the trial to direct the attention of
the jury to the defendant's failure to testify, such an instruction might emphasize that fact, and be treated as an intimation of the effect on the court's mind of an omission to explain
any criminating circumstances. See *Ruloff v. People,* 45 N.
Y. 213; *Baker v. People,* 105 Ill. 452. But the jurors may
have noted such an omission without suggestion from the
court, and given it weight. It was said in *State v. Weems,*
96 Iowa, 426, where a similar instruction was given without
request: "The instruction was in the interest of defendant,
and was induced, likely, by an apprehension that the jury
might of its own motion consider the fact that the defendant
did not take the witness stand to testify, and draw improper
inferences therefrom. Certainly, the instruction could have
done no harm." To the same effect, see *Fulcher v. State,* 28
Tex. App. 465 (13 S. W. Rep. 750); *Metz v. State,* 46 Neb.
547 (65 N. W. Rep. 190); *Ruloff v. People, supra.* It seems
that in Vermont and Washington the jury must be directed
not to take into consideration the defendant's omission to testify. *State v. Cameron,* 40 Vt. 556; *Linbeck v. State,* 1 Wash.
336 (25 Pac. Rep. 452.) In the absence of a request such an
instruction is not required in this state. *State v. Stevens,* 67 Iowa, 557. In that case it was said: "Had such
instruction been requested, it, doubtless, would have been
given." A similar intimation is found in *Metz v. State,
supra.* In *State v. Pearce,* 56 Minn. 226 (57 N. W. Rep.
654), a refusal to so instruct is upheld on the ground that
the statute of Minnesota prohibits any allusion or comment
on defendant's neglect to testify by the prosecuting attorney,
or by the court. See, also, *State v. Robinson,* 117 Mo. 663
(23 S. W. Rep. 1066). The supreme court of Illinois, in
Farrell v. People, 133 Ill. 244 (24 N. E. Rep. 423), held the
refusal to so instruct, when requested, reversible error. The

same rule obtains in Maine. *State v. Landry,* 85 Me. 95 (26 Atl. Rep. 998). The statutes of these states are like ours. This statute was enacted for the protection of those accused of crime, and to enable them to insist upon the establishment of their guilt by the state, without inferences to be drawn from their silence when they might speak. The state may be put to its proof. The natural inclinations of the jurors would lead them to adopt the very presumption from which the statute was intended to shield the accused. The instruction requested contained a correct statement of the law, and the defendant had the right to have it given. It related to a special feature of the case, upon which the giving of instructions was discretionary if not demanded, but upon which the law should have been stated when requested by the accused, who had brought himself within its provisions.

VI. No instruction was given upon the necessity of corroborating the testimony of the injured party. Exception to this omission is met by the assertion that there was, in

6   fact, corroborating evidence, and the omission to so instruct, in the absence of a request, was not error.

The Code provides that the defendant in a prosecution for rape or assault with intent to commit rape cannot be convicted upon the testimony of the person injured, unless she be corroborated by other evidence tending to connect the defendant with the commission of the offense. Code, section 5488. Undoubtedly, the court must determine whether there is any such evidence, but the jury is to pass upon its weight and sufficiency. *State v. McLaughlin,* 44 Iowa, 82; *State v. Bell,* 49 Iowa, 440. The evident purpose of the statute was to guard against convictions based alone on the testimony of an injured party in a class of cases where the interest and feeling are so apt to control, and the motives of revenge or sinister design so frequently exist. Corroboration is one of the essentials of conviction, without which the accused is entitled to an acquittal. We have held it to be the duty of the court to instruct the jury on the material questions of law involved in the case, whether requested or not. *State v.*

Helm, 97 Iowa, 378; *State v. Donahoe,* 78 Iowa, 490; *State v. Brainard,* 25 Iowa, 578; *State v. O'Hagan,* 38 Iowa, 506. The defendant was on trial for the commission of one of the gravest offenses known to the law, involving his liberty for life or a term of years; and we think the law relating thereto, and the issues, should have been fully stated to the jurors, for their guidance in the performance of their responsible duties. Other errors assigned will not be likely to arise on another trial. Because of those pointed out, the judgment is REVERSED.

GIVEN J. (dissenting).—While I concur in the result reached in this case, and in the conclusion that a trial judge should not even temporarily relinquish control of the proceedings, I do not agree that it is in itself error, or that prejudice should be inferred from the fact of the judge's withdrawing beyond hearing during arguments to the jury. Under our practice, the judge is required to instruct the jury in writing,—a duty that is always important, often difficult, and requiring careful reflection and an examination of authorities. If the judge may not retire to his room, within easy call, to prepare his instructions during arguments to the jury, he must adjourn the trial, dismiss or lock up the jury, or prepare them when his attention is divided between the trial and the preparation of the instructions. I am convinced that, if judges were afforded better opportunity for preparing their instructions, they would be less voluminous, more easily understood, more applicable to the case, and freer from errors. If the practice of preparing instructions in important cases during the trial, or during the hours of rest at noon and night, were abandoned, we would have better instructions. I think it should be left to the discretion of the trial judge whether he may withdraw from the court room to a place within easy call, to prepare his instructions during the argument on the issues of facts to the jury. It is only in exceptional instances that prejudice will result from his so doing, and in such cases give the prejudiced party the benefit of the fact when shown, but do not presume prejudice when its occurrence is the exception and not the rule. The presence of the bailiff is usually sufficient to preserve order, and, when counsel appreciate and observe the privileges of argument, there is no necessity for the constant presence of the judge. If counsel abuse their privilege, let discipline be administered to them, not to the judge. Disturbances or disputes during arguments to the jury, such as require the presence of the judge, are very exceptional; and, if he is within easy call, he may readily restore order or ascertain and decide the dispute. The error in this case is that the judge did not ascertain and decide the matter in dispute. My observation leads me to believe that the cause of justice and the interest of litigants require that encouragement be given to the exercise of the utmost care in the preparation of instructions, and that thereby errors therein will be greatly lessened. It is a marvel to me that instructions prepared amid the surroundings of a trial are as free from prejudicial errors as they are, but I believe they may be made more so by better opportunity for their preparation.

H. E. SCHAFFER v. EMMA W. SCHAFFER, Appellant.

Divorce: EVIDENCE. A wife was somewhat ill-tempered. was not a good housekeeper, spent considerable time away from home while engaged in public enterprises, and made some debts. Several witnesses testified that she had wilfully abused and beaten her husband. and had used abusive language to him in the presence of their children. Prior to the advent in their home of a domestic, their relations were reasonably harmonious. When trouble arose between the wife and the domestic, the husband refused to have her discharged, and he afterwards occupied a bed apart from his wife in a room that was separated by a closet only from the room occupied by the domestic. He frequently went to places of amusement with the domestic, leaving his wife at home. *Held*, that the husband was not entitled to a divorce.

Appeal from Mills District Court.—HON. W. R. GREEN, Judge.

THURSDAY, OCTOBER 20, 1898.

ACTION in equity for a divorce, and for the custody of minor children. There was a hearing on the merits, and a decree of divorce in favor of the plaintiff. The defendant appeals.—*Reversed.*

Stone & Dawson for appellant.

No appearance for appellee.

ROBINSON, J.—The parties to this action were married to each other in October, 1867. Nine children have been born to them, of whom six are living and four are grown. They have resided in Malvern for ten years. As grounds for divorce the plaintiff alleges that the defendant has willfully abused and beaten him, and has become angry, and used vulgar and indecent language to him in the presence of their children; that she cannot control her temper, and has made violent threats against members of the family, and has annoyed and harassed the plaintiff; that she has neglected her household duties and her duties as a wife, has absented herself from home the larger part of the time, and has so conducted herself as to impair his health; and for ten months preceding the commencement of this action the plaintiff had felt that his life was actually endangered by her. The defendant denies all allegation of improper conduct on her part. The district court granted to the plaintiff a divorce, but did not make any provisions for the custody of the minor children. The testimony of the plaintiff and of his daughter Maggie, who is twenty-six years of age, and of his son De, who is seventeen years of age, and of a Mrs. Crow, who lived in the family as a domestic, tends to sustain the claims of the plaintiff. But the evidence shows the following facts: The defendant has for a number of years been engaged in numerous enterprises of a public nature; has been active in the church, Sunday school, and temperance work; has been interested in the science of healing; has written essays; and has canvassed for the sale of different articles. She spent considerable time in preparing a chart on a roll of cloth seventy feet in length;

designed to illustrate a "plan of redemption." She spent considerable time away from home, was not a superior housekeeper, and contracted some debts. The plaintiff was in sympathy with the larger part of the work in which the defendant was engaged, and claims to have said to her: "I don't object to your attending to temperance work, church, woman suffrage, or mental science, anything of the kind, if you do it outside of your household duties; but I would like to have them attended to first." Maggie states that three-fourths of her mother's time was spent away from home, and of that spent at home one-half at least was spent "with books on questions of temperance, or letters on temperance, essays on temperance, and receiving calls outside of family affairs." The plaintiff claims that the defendant was away from home one-fourth of the time, excepting the year preceding the trial, during which, he states, she was away three-fourths of the time. He claims, also, that there have been dissensions between himself and his wife at intervals throughout their married life. We are satisfied, however, that there was no serious trouble between them, and that their life together was reasonably harmonious until Mrs. Crow was taken into the family. Neighbors who visited the family frequently for many years, and who had opportunities for knowing the actual relations which existed between the plaintiff and the defendant, testified that they appeared to live together pleasantly until some time after Mrs. Crow was employed, and that the defendant did not neglect her household duties to the extent claimed by the plaintiff. A son and a daughter testify to the same effect. We are satisfied that, although the defendant might well have devoted more of her time and thought to her family, and less to matters of a public nature, yet that the plaintiff did not regard her course as especially reprehensible, nor as affecting his health, until after the arrival of Mrs. Crow. On the contrary, he sympathized with and approved what his wife did, although he occasionally complained that she was required by others to do too much church and other work. On the nineteenth day of January, 1893, the plaintiff

wrote to his daughter Maggie a letter, which was devoted
largely to his family affairs. In that letter he spoke of some
of his children as disobedient and ungrateful. Among other
things, he said : "I know both ma and myself made mistakes,
and many of them, but it was not because we wish to do so.
We both wish to do what is right, and to be impartial to all
you children, but you will not give us credit for it. It is
a terrible way the boys treat and talk to their mother. The
raising of six children and the care of three others will try
the patience of a Job, or the goodness of an angel, and I don't
think there is a woman living who could maintain a good
temper under all circumstances, and be, as De said to her the
other day, 'If you was the right kind of a mother we could
do better.' " Although the letter did not say the conduct of
the defendant had not been reprehensible in any respect, it
made no complaint respecting her, but was such a letter as a
husband who had a proper regard for his wife might have
written under the same circumstances, even though she had
been at fault in some respects. The evidence satisfies us, however, that it fairly represented the feeling of the plaintiff for
his wife at the time it was written. Mrs. Schaffer incurred a
few debts, but provided for the payment of nearly all of them.
In November, 1892, Mary Crow, a woman about twenty-three
years of age, expecting a divorce from her husband, was
employed as a domestic in the plaintiff's family. She had been
known to the defendant, and was probably employed by her.
Mrs. Crow brought with her a child less than one year old.
She appears to have done satisfactory work, and there was no
trouble until the twelfth day of March, 1894, when there was
some disagreement between Mrs. Crow and Susie Schaffer,
a daughter of the parties to this action, then about twenty
years of age. Mrs. Schaffer defended her daughter, and warm
words followed. Mrs Schaffer reported the matter to her
husband. A question of veracity between herself and Mrs.
Crow arose, and her husband declared his belief that Mrs.
Crow was right. That made the defendant angry, and she
started to enter the room in which Mrs. Crow was lying in

bed, declaring that she would make Mrs. Crow tell the truth, or "mash her teeth down her throat." The plaintiff interfered to prevent a collision, and states that his wife then struck him. He is corroborated in that by Mrs. Crow, and contradicted by his wife and his daughter Alice, who was then in the room. It is at least doubtful if the plaintiff received any blow from the defendant at that time, but, if he did, it can be said that it was given under great excitement, and with some provocation. From that time the defendant insisted that Mrs. Crow should leave the house, accused her of being a woman of bad character, and spoke of her as a prostitute, a harlot, a hell cat, and a woman of hell. The plaintiff refused to discharge Mrs. Crow, saying that she should not go until the charges against her character were withdrawn. Mrs. Crow treated the defendant with contempt, refused to obey her directions, and illtreated the children. The defendant complained to the plaintiff of Mrs. Crow continually, and he finally said if the complaints were not stopped he would occupy a bed apart from his wife, and about the first of April he left his wife's bed, and occupied one in a room in the northwest corner of the house. Mrs. Crow occupied a room in the northeast corner of the house, and between the two rooms was a closet which opened into both rooms, so that when the closet doors were unlocked persons could readily pass from one room to the other through the closet. There were two doors which opened into Mrs. Crow's room exclusive of the closet entrance, both of which were kept locked at night. In addition to the closet door, there was one door which opened into the room of the plaintiff, and that door he kept locked at night, but both closet doors were kept unlocked. The defendant and others, including her son Dell, remonstrated with the plaintiff on account of the course he was pursuing, but without avail. When the plaintiff left the defendant's bed, she asked that she and her children might be permitted to occupy the room in which Mrs. Crow slept, but the request was refused. The plaintiff and Mrs. Crow went to church and to places of amusement together, leaving the defendant at home, and Mrs.

Crow sought the presence and society of the plaintiff, to the great annoyance of the defendant. The plaintiff, the defendant, and Mrs. Crow were members of the same church. An elder of the church was called in, and attempted to effect a settlement which should include the withdrawal of Mrs. Crow from the house, but the settlement was defeated by the plaintiff. The elder sent to the plaintiff a notice in terms requiring him to make choice between his wife and children and the church on one hand and Mrs. Crow on the other, but the plaintiff denied that he had done any wrong. The defendant did not accuse him of criminal intercourse with Mrs. Crow, but charges were preferred against him and he was expelled from the church for "disorderly walk." Threats of treating him to a coat of tar and feathers were made in anonymous letters which he received. Mrs. Crow received what she terms "white cap letters," and, finally, on the advice of friends, she left the house about the first of August, 1894. Some months after Mrs. Crow left, the plaintiff divided the house, and one of the two parts thus made was occupied by himself, Maggie, and De, with Mrs. Crow's child, and the other part was occupied by the defendant and two of her daughters. She resisted this separation, but without avail. Maggie corresponded with Mrs. Crow, and the plaintiff sent with Maggie's communications letters which he wrote to Mrs. Crow. A few days before the trial in the district court was commenced, Mrs. Crow visited the part of the house occupied by the plaintiff, and the defendant thereupon went into it, and, as she admits, "pounded Mrs. Crow." There is no doubt that Mrs. Schaffer is high tempered, and that, when angry on account of Mrs. Crow, she has used improper language, and has attempted violence, with some success in one instance. But she had been subjected to great provocation. The course the plaintiff has pursued respecting Mrs. Crow cannot be justified on any ground. He defended and exalted her, at the same time offending and humiliating his wife. His course was of a nature to cause the troubles of which he complains, and that it was the cause of the larger part of them we have no doubt.

The health of the plaintiff is not good. He has suffered for
many years from a disease contracted in the army, and ·for
which he draws a pension. He is naturally nervous, and
claims that his wife's conduct so excites his nervous system
that he cannot sleep. He states that when he is excited
"his heart commences to thump so he can hear it," and that
it is caused and made worse by the treatment he has received
from his wife. As we have said, we do not find that his wife's
conduct caused him any serious trouble before the advent of
Mrs. Crow, and his troubles since that time have been largely
of his own making. We are satisfied that when he gives to his
wife the treatment to which she is entitled, he has nothing to
fear from her. We conclude that he has failed to establish a
sufficient ground for divorce, and the decree of the district
court is REVERSED.

HIRSCH, ELSON & COMPANY and KAHN BROTHERS & COM-
PANY v. M. B. ISRAEL, MAURICE DES PRES, *et al.*,
Appellants.

Creditors' Suit: FRAUDULENT CONVEYANCE: *Possession of debtor.*
Code, 1873, sections 3150-3152, authorizing a judgment creditor to
bring equitable proceedings to subject property of the debtor to
payment of the judgment, and providing that persons holding
1 property in which the judgment debtor has any interest may be
2 made defendants and that a lien shall thereby be created on the
property of the judgment debtor in the hands of any defendant
or under his control, applies to cases where the judgment debtor
has possession of the property himself.

RECEIVER. A suit in equity by judgment creditors for the purpose of
subjecting personalty in the possession of the debtor, and claimed
2 to have been fraudulenily mortgaged, to the payment of the plaintiff's judgment, affords a sufficient basis for the appointment of a
receiver.

SAME. The appointment of a receiver in an action by judgment
creditors to subject to the lien of their judgments personalty in
2 the possession of the debtor and claimed to have been fraudulently mortgaged will not, independent of statute, be denied on
the ground that the plaintiffs had an adequate remedy at law by
levy and sale under execution, since such remedy is not exclusive.

EVIDENCE. A mortgagor of a stock of goods retained possession and
control of them, and the mortgage gave him the right [to sell
them, and replenish the stock and retain from the sale sufficient
money to pay current expenses, and to pay for his own time and
family living expenses. *Held,* that a petition by a judgment
creditor of the mortgagor to set aside the mortgage, alleging
3 fraud and the insolvency of the mortgagor, is, under such facts, a
sufficient showing, on the giving of security, for the appointment
of a receiver, under Code, 1873, section 2903, providing for such
appointment where the party shows a probable right or interest in
the property, and that such property is, or its rents or profits are, in
danger of being lost or injured, and when the interest of one or
both parties will be promoted thereby, and the substantial rights
of neither unduly infringed.

Appeal from Cass District Court.—HON. N. W. MACY,
Judge.

THURSDAY, OCTOBER 20, 1898.

SUIT in equity by two judgment creditors of M. B. Israel
to subject certain personal property in his possession to the
payment of their judgments, and for the appointment of a
receiver. The other defendants, aside from Israel, are mortgagees of the property. It is alleged in the petition that these
mortgages are fraudulent; that Israel is insolvent; and that
he retains possession and control of the mortgaged property,
the proceeds of which he is applying to his own use. The petition further recites that plaintiffs caused execution to issue
upon their judgments, and to be levied upon the property,
and that defendants thereupon served written notice upon
the sheriff requiring him to release the same; that they thereupon caused an original notice and copy of the petition to be
served upon M. B. Israel, the party in possession of the property. Defendants filed a resistance to the application for a
receiver, in which they denied the alleged fraud, and further
stated that plaintiffs had no lien upon the property; that the
property was not of sufficient value to pay all mortgages in
full except by the most judicious management; that they
will suffer irreparable injury if the goods are placed
in the hands of a receiver; that plaintiffs have a plain,

speedy, and adequate remedy at law; that Israel was in possession of the goods as agent of the mortgagees, and was selling the same, and with the proceeds satisfying the mortgage indebtedness; that plaintiffs have no interest in the goods except as there may be a surplus over and above the mortgage indebtedness; and that there will be no surplus. Upon the issues thus tendered, the application was submitted to the court, resulting in an order appointing a receiver for the mortgaged property. Defendants appeal.—*Affirmed.*

Curtis, Follett & Curtis and *J. B. Rockafellow* for appellants.

Phelps & Temple for appellees.

DEEMER, C. J.—The first point made by appellants is that appellees have no lien upon the property, and are therefore not entitled to the appointment of a receiver. The pro-
1   ceeding was commenced for the purpose of canceling the mortgages, and subjecting the property to the payment of appellees' judgments. Such proceedings seem to be authorized by section 3150 and 3151 of the Code of 1873; and section 3152 of the same Code provides that a lien is created upon the property of a judgment debtor, or his interest therein, in the hands of the defendant or under his control, which is sufficiently described in the petition, from the time of service of notice and copy of petition on the defendant holding or controlling such property. Appellants contend that these sections of the Code do not apply to a case where the defendant has possession of the property. We are inclined to think they do. See *Ware v. Delahaye,* 95 Iowa, 667. But, if they do not, then it is clear that plaintiffs had the right to bring a suit in equity, independent of statute, for the purpose of subjecting the property to the payment of their judgments; and such suit would be a sufficient basis for the appointment of a receiver. *Falker v. Linehan,* 88 Iowa, 641; *O'Brien v. Stambach,* 101 Iowa, 40; Beach Modern Equity Jurisprudence, sections 883, 885, 887, 925; Wait

Fraudulent Conveyances, sections 61, 68, and cases cited in notes.

Again, it is insisted that plaintiffs had a plain, speedy, and adequate remedy at law, by levy and sale under execution. It has frequently been decided that a mortgagor of personal property has no such interest in it as that it
2   may be seized and sold under execution. The Twenty-first General Assembly passed an act relating to levies upon mortgaged personal property which allows such property to be seized and sold under certain conditions not necessary to be more particularly mentioned. But we have already held that such proceeding is not exclusive. *Buck-Reiner Co. v. Beatty,* 82 Iowa, 353; *Hibbard v. Zenor,* 75 Iowa, 479; *Clark v. Patton,* 92 Iowa, 247, and cases cited; *Geirshofer v. Nupuf,* 105 Iowa, 374; *Thomas v. Farley,* 76 Iowa, 735. We are well satisfied that when, as in this case, it is claimed the mortgages are fraudulent, a judgment creditor is not compelled to make his levy under the provisions of chapter 117 of the Acts of the Twenty-first General Assembly, but may proceed by garnishment when the property is in the hands of a third person, or by creditors' bill or other equitable proceedings when the property is in the possession of the judgment defendant; and that, when he does proceed by creditors' bill or other action in equity, he acquires such a right to or apparent lien upon the property as will support an application for the appointment of a receiver.

Appellants further contend that no such showing was made as entitled appellees to the appointment. Section 2903 of the Code of 1873 provides for the appointment of a
3   receiver in a civil action upon petition wherein the party shows that he has a probable right to or interest in any property which is the subject of controversy, and that such property or its rents or profits are in danger of being lost or materially injured or destroyed, and the court is satisfied that the interests of one or both parties will be thereby promoted, and the substantial rights of neither unduly infringed, and upon the whole case may make such order as

will be for the best interest of all parties concerned. By the
terms of the mortgage, Israel was given the right to remain in
possession of the mortgaged goods, and he expressly reserved
from the sale sufficient to pay current expenses of the store,
rent, insurance, clerk hire, fuel, light, etc., to purchase
necessary goods for replenishing stock, and for his own time
and living expenses for himself and family, and actual attorney's fees necessary for his protection. While this reservation probably did not of itself render the mortgage fraudulent,
yet it is a crcumstance to be considered in connection with the
other evidence in the case tending to show fraud. And as the
mortgagor is insolvent, and has complete control of the goods
and of the proceeds arising therefrom, we think the court
was justified in appointing the receiver, especially in view of
the fact that plaintiffs were required to file bond in the sum
of eight hundred dollars to protect defendants from loss
or damage growing out of the order of appointment. The
general rule seems to be that a receiver will be appointed in
creditors' suits when the property is in danger of waste,
almost as a matter of course. Wait Fraudulent Conveyances, section 184; *Farnham v. Campbell,* 10 Paige, 601;
Lent v. McQueen, 15 How. Prac. 313; *Minkler v. Sheep Co.,*
4 N. D. 507; 33 L. R. A. 546 (62 N. W. Rep. 594) and
cases cited; 5 Enc. Pl. & Prac. p. 593, and cases cited; *Blood-
good v. Clark,* 4 Paige, 574. In view of the allegations of
fraud and insolvency, we think the trial court was right in
appointing the receiver, and its order is AFFIRMED.

JAMES F. TAYLOR v. WOODBURY COUNTY, Appellant.

Counties: PAUPERS: *Physicians.* A county is liable for medical
   services rendered a pauper patient at the request of township
2 trustees although it had a regularly employed physician to attend
   the poor, when his contract did not extend to the township in
   question, even though the patient was afterwards removed to
   another township covered by the contract.

SAME. A physician, summoned to attend a pauper, called in another
2 to assist in the performance of a surgical operation, but no claim

8 was made against the county except by the former. *Held*, that, such employment not being a delegation of authority, the county was liable.

RATIFICATION. A county cannot defend an action to recover for med-
1 ical services rendered a pauper patient, on the ground that the plaintiff's services were not authorized by the township trustees when they thereafter sanctioned them by written certificate.

CERTIFICATE OF TRUSTEES. A certificate by township trustees that
4 medical services to a specified value were rendered a pauper patient at their request is binding on the county, in the absence of fraud.

SAME. A physician was summoned unofficially by the trustees of a
8 township to attend a pauper, and after the services were rendered the trustees officially signed a certificate that the physician acted on their official request. *Held*, that such certificate was, in the absence of fraud, binding on the county.

Appeal from Woodbury District Court.—HON. G. W. WAKEFIELD, Judge.

THURSDAY, OCTOBER 20, 1898.

ACTION to recover for medical and surgical services rendered a pauper patient at the request of township trustees. There was a judgment for plaintiff, and defendant appeals.— *Affirmed.*

Hallam & Stevenson for appellant.

Jepson & Jepson for appellee.

WATERMAN, J.—No question is made but the services were rendered, and the evidence, we think, shows that the amount allowed therefor is reasonable.

I. The first point made by appellant that deserves notice is that plaintiff was never authorized to render service to the patient, one Anderson, by the township trustees. Anderson was a resident of Liberty township, in
1 defendant county. It appears without dispute that, at different times, two of the trustees requested plaintiff to attend him. It is claimed, however, that what was said by them was in their personal capacity, and not as officers of

the township.   The thought seems to be that they could take
no action which would be binding on the municipality except
in a formal board meeting.   This claim might be conceded
without availing plaintiff.   It appears that after the services
were rendered, the township trustees united in giving a
written certificate to plaintiff, stating the services rendered
and their value, and also the fact that plaintiff acted on their
official request.   This is a ratification of what had been done.
Even if plaintiff performed the service originally without
proper legal sanction, the giving of this certificate cured any
such defect.   *Mussel v. Tama County,* 73 Iowa, 101.

II.   It is said that the defendant had a regularly
employed physician to look after and attend the poor; and the
cases of *Mansfield v. Sac County,* 59 Iowa, 694, and *Gawley v.
Jones County,* 60 Iowa, 159, are cited as opposed to a recovery
here.   To like effect is the recent case of *Lacy v. Kossuth
County,* 106 Iowa, 16.   These cases hold that, when
2   the board of supervisors employs a competent
physician to attend all the poor of the county,
the township trustees cannot disregard such employment,
and engage other physicians to render such services at
the expense of the county.   The case at bar, however, is by
its facts taken out of the rule thus established, because the
record here does not show that the physician employed by the
board of supervisors was under any obligation to attend the
poor of Liberty township.   The contract of employment with
him seems to have been for a limited service on his part.   It
was as a resident of that township that Anderson was treated;
and although he was afterwards moved to another township,
which was covered by the contract of the physician employed
by the board, in order to secure facilities for better care and
nursing, yet this was but an incident of the service rendered.
When plaintiff was requested to give attention to, and first
took charge of, the case, Anderson was not within the territory
throughout which the physician employed by the county
authorities was obliged to attend.

III. Another defense is that plaintiff did not personally perform all the services for which he claims.   The fact is, that the patient's condition required the performance of a somewhat difficult surgical operation, and that plain-

3   tiff procured another to do this work, he assisting. No claim is made against the county except by plaintiff. He is responsible to his fellow surgeon.   We cannot understand just how these facts lend support to defendant's refusal to pay.   If the treatment was necessary, and was given by authority, and the amount claimed therefor is reasonable, we do not see what more defendant can require as a condition precedent to paying therefor.   It was not, as urged by appellant, a delegation of authority.   Plaintiff performed the services required of him in part through another.   Of this defendant has no reason to complain.   In *Scott v. Winneshiek County,* 52 Iowa, 579, the plaintiff was allowed a recovery for services rendered by others who assisted him.

IV. Our conclusion is that the certificate signed by the trustees was binding on the county, in the absence of fraud, and no charge of fraud is made.   *Mussel v. Tama*

4   *County, supra; Hardin County v. Wright County,* 67 Iowa, 127.   The judgment of the district court will be AFFIRMED.

SECOND NATIONAL BANK OF DUBUQUE, IOWA, Appellant, v. G. HAERLING, *et al.*

Judgments: ATTACHMENT: *Conclusiveness.* Code, 1873, section 3011, provides that, when judgment is rendered for the plaintiff in attachment, the court shall apply to the judgment the proceeds of perishable property attached, or shall order a sale of attached property not yet sold. Plaintiff recovered judgment in an action where attached property was sold as perishable, and the judgment contained no reference to the proceeds, and plaintiff thereafter moved for an order applying the proceeds to his judgment, which motion was denied. No appeal was taken, and the sheriff paid over the proceeds to the judgment debtor. *Held,* in an action by the judgment creditors against the sheriff and sureties for conversion, that the motion was a part of the former judgment, which had become final by failure to appeal, and hence determined plaintiff's rights in the attached property.

Appeal From Plymouth District Court.—Hon. Scott M. Ladd, Judge.

Friday, October 21, 1898.

The defendant Haerling is sheriff of Plymouth county, and the other defendants are sureties on his official bond. In July, 1884, the plaintiff's assignor brought suit against Frahm & Mitchell and Ida Frahm in the district court of Ida county, asking judgment for three thousand dollars, and sued out a writ of attachment, which was levied upon personal property of the defendants. The levy of the writ was made July 17, 1884, and the property was afterwards sold, as perishable, on the fourteenth of October, 1884, the amount realized therefrom being one thousand, nine hundred and thirty-nine dollars and fifty-seven cents. Prior to the levy of the writ of attachment, all the property seized by virtue of it, had been sold to Ida Frahm, and at the time of the levy she was the sole owner thereof. On the trial of said cause, and on November 28, 1890, judgment was entered for plaintiff against Ida Frahm for $4,173, with interest and costs. The judgment was personal, and contained no order or direction as to the attached property; and after the rendition of said judgment, and before the commencement of this suit, the sheriff, without the consent of plaintiff, paid the proceeds of said property to Ida Frahm. In May, 1891, a motion was filed for an order correcting the judgment entry so as to require the money to be paid on the judgement, which motion was overruled. Thereafter, in February, 1893 this suit in equity was commenced against the sheriff and the sureties on his bond, asking judgment for the amount of the judgment in the other suit, on the ground that the sheriff had wrongfully converted the property levied upon. The district court dismissed the petition, and the plaintiff appealed.—*Affirmed.*

Wright, Call & Hubbard for appellant.

T. P. Murphy for appellees.

GRANGER, J.—The legal proposition first considered in argument is the effect of no order being included in the judgment as to the attaching property.   We are cited to several cases in this state by appellant, and they are thought to be controlling, and to fix the liability of the sheriff, because without the judgment entry, the lien of the attachment continued.   The statute applicable to this case, governing the disposition of attached property after the judgment is rendered for plaintiff, is section 3011, Code of 1873, as follows: "If judgment is rendered for the plaintiff in any case in which an attachment has been issued, the court shall apply in satisfaction thereof, the money arising from the sales of perishable property, and if the same is not sufficient to satisfy the plaintiff's claim, the court shall order a sale by the sheriff of any other attached property which may be under his control."   We do not find it necessary to consider the question as to the effect of not sustaining the attachment or ordering special execution in the judgment in the attachment suit at the time it was entered.   The judgment was entered in November, 1890.   In May thereafter, the motion was made to correct the judgment so as to order a sale of the property, or for disposition of the proceeds of the same, which was refused.   The motion is in the following words: "Plaintiff moves the court for an order in the above-entitled cause for sale of attached property, or for the disposition of the proceeds of the same, and to correct the record so as to include said order."   This motion was a direct application for the court to apply, in satisfaction of the judgment, the money arising from the sale of the attached property, under the provisions of section 3011, above quoted.   The denial of the motion was a judicial determination in that proceeding that plaintiff was not entitled to such an order.   The grounds of the holding do not appear, and we do not inquire for them; nor do we inquire as to the correctness of the holding. The ruling on the motion was a part of the record and judgment entry in that case, and the judgment, by lapse of time, has become final, there having been no appeal. Such a judgment operates to discharge the attached property, and concludes the rights of the parties thereto under the attachment. If the judgment, as finally made, was erroneous, the remedy was by appeal. This action is by equitable proceedings, and a defense, pleaded and relied on is that no grounds for equitable relief are shown. This seems to be true, and, as the district court so held, its judgment must stand AFFIRMED.

LADD, J., took no part.

THOMAS E. MARSHALL, Appellant, v. THE CITY OF BELLE PLAINE, IOWA.

Highway: CONTRIBUTORY NEGLIGENCE. A pedestrian who knows that a part of a street crossing is sloping, slippery with ice and snow and dangerous, but who uses no care to avoid the peril although he might easily have done so, cannot recover for injuries sustained by a fall.

Appeal from Benton District Court.—HON. G. W. BURNHAM, Judge.

FRIDAY, OCTOBER 21, 1898.

ACTION at law to recover for personal injuries alleged to have been caused by negligence on the part of the defendant. After the plaintiff had submitted his evidence, the district court sustained a motion to direct a verdict for the defendant, a verdict was directed and returned accordingly, and judgment was rendered in favor of the defendant for costs. The plaintiff appeals.—*Affirmed.*

Tom H. Milner for appellant.

J. J. Mosnat and *L. E. Cox* for appellee.

Robinson, J.—The defendant is a city of the second class. On the fourteenth day of January, 1895, at about 9 o'clock in the evening, the plaintiff fell in a street of the defendant, and received injuries which prevented him from following his vocation, that of a barber, for several weeks. The accident occurred on an apron which led from a sidewalk to a street crossing in a part of the city which was devoted to business and much frequented. The apron was four feet in width, and seven feet three inches in length, with a fall of fourteen inches. It was made of four boards, each of which was twelve inches wide, placed lengthwise, without cross cleats on the upper surface to keep pedestrians from slipping. At the time of the accident the apron was covered with a coating of snow and ice, and was slippery, and the plaintiff fell in consequence of slipping on it. The plaintiff claims that the defendant was negligent in permitting snow and ice to accumulate and remain upon the apron, and that the accident was caused by that negligence and negligence in the construction of the apron. The answer of the defendant contains a general denial.

At the time of the accident the plaintiff was sixty years of age. He wore boots without rubbers. He was familiar with the street crossing, including the apron, and used it frequently, although he does not recollect whether he had passed over it before on the day of the accident. There had been some ice and snow on the apron for several days, and in the morning of the day on which the accident occurred, or the night before, rain and sleet had fallen, and the sidewalks were slippery. The plaintiff knew that fact, and states that he knew that the crossing where he fell was in bad condition and slippery. He knew it was sloping, and that it was not supplied with cleats, and consequently he must have known that it would be dangerous for him to attempt to pass over it. He could have passed around it easily, and thus have avoided the danger, but it did not occur to him to do so, and he did not give the apron any thought, but fell the moment he stepped upon it. He does not claim to have used any care to avoid the danger, and it is clear that he did not do so. He was carrying a pail and conversing with a companion when he stepped upon the apron but there was nothing in the conditions then existing which would naturally and properly so absorb his attention as to withdraw it wholly from the dangers to which he was exposed. The conclusion which must inevitably be drawn from the undisputed facts is that the accident was due, in part, at least, to negligence of the plaintiff. He should have exercised the care to avoid danger which an ordinarily careful and prudent man would have used under the same circumstances, and, had he done so, the accident would not have occurred. It was said in *Hartman v. City of Muscatine,* 70 Iowa, 511, of a person who had been injured in crossing a street and was seeking to recover for the injuries received, that "if, knowing it was dangerous, he knew, or ought to have known, that it was not prudent to walk over the crossing and down the slope, and there was another way he could have taken without material inconvenience, then he cannot recover." That rule was applied and followed in *Cosner v. City of Centerville,* 90 Iowa, 33. See, also, *Barnes v. Town of Marcus,* 96 Iowa, 675; *Parkhill v. Town of Brighton,* 61 Iowa, 108; *McGinty v. City of Keokuk,* 66 Iowa, 726; *Waterbury v. Railroad Co.,* 104 Iowa, 32; *Beem v. Light Co.,* 104 Iowa, 563; *Koch v. City of Ashland,* 88 Wis., 603 (60 N. W. Rep. 990); *City of Erie v. Magill,* 101 Pa. St. 616 (47 Am. Rep. 739).

It is true that a person who knows that a way is dangerous is not necessarily negligent in attempting to use it, even though there be another safe and convenient way. The cases of *Nichols v. Incorporated Town of Laurens,* 96 Iowa, 388, and *Graham v. Town of Oxford,* 105 Iowa, 705, illustrate that rule. But in each of those cases there was evidence which authorized the jury to find that, although the person injured knew of the defect which caused the injury in time to have avoided it by going another way, yet he acted as a person of ordinary care and prudence to avoid the injury while using the defective way, and therefore could recover.   But we have seen that in this case the plaintiff did not so act, and since there is no serious conflict in the evidence as to what he did, his own testimony showing negligence on his part, there was no question in regard to that to submit to the jury.

Complaint is made of certain rulings on the admission and exclusion of evidence, but, as none of them could have affected the determination of the case, they need not be further considered.

It was also unnecessary to decide whether there was evidence sufficient to show negligence on the part of the defendant.   We do not find any reason for disturbing the judgment of the district court, and it is AFFIRMED.

CHARLES B. LOGAN, Appellant, v. W. W. MILLER.

106 5
113

106
f133

Deed in Blank: GRANTEE: *Contracts.* A deed executed in blank as
1   to the grantee confers authority on the real grantee to contract
2   for the sale of lands, and to fill in his own grantee's name.

Assumption of Mortgage: PAROL VARIANCE. While a *party* to a
deed may not contradict its recitals as to consideration by parol
evidence, no-one but a party is under such disability. Hence,
1   where a deed was left blank as to grantee, one whose name was
3   inserted as grantee by him to whom the blank deed was made,
may show, in a suit to charge him with a mortgage assumed by
recital in the deed, that, under an agreement with the first grantee,
the person whose name was inserted was not to assume said
mortgage; and his acceptance of the deed does not estop him to
urge said agreement.

Equity Jurisdiction. A grantee of lands need not go into equity to
avail himself of a defense against personal liability for a mortgage
4   which his deed recites he assumes, where the deed had been executed in blank to a preceding grantee, and by him filled in with
the present owner's name, on a sale made for a different consideration.

Appeal from Marshall District Court.—HON. G. W. BURN-
HAM, Judge.

FRIDAY, OCTOBER 21, 1898.

ACTION to charge the defendant with a certain indebtedness secured by mortgage on lands which were conveyed to the defendant upon an alleged agreement expressed in the deed whereby defendant assumed and agreed to pay said mortgage indebtedness. Defendant answered, as will hereafter appear, and the plaintiff demurred to the answer. The demurrer being overruled, and plaintiff electing to stand thereon and refusing to further plead, judgment was entered dismissing his petition, from which he appeals.—*Affirmed.*

Sutton & Marsh for appellant.

B. F. Cummings for appellee.

GIVEN, J.—I. The petition alleges, in substance, as follows: That William and Adeline Barnard were indebted to plaintiff in the sum of one thousand dollars, for which they gave their promissory note and mortgage on certain land in Nebraska; that thereafter defendant purchased said land from said Barnards, and received a warranty deed therefor, "by the terms of which he covenanted and agreed to pay the aforesaid indebtedness of the Barnards to this plaintiff as a part of the purchase money for the said premises, and made said indebtedness, and all of it, his own." The deed set out is dated April 12, 1888, and is from William and Adeline Barnard to W. W. Miller, and recites the consideration as two thousand, five hundred dollars, and said mortgage for one thousand dollars, and says: "Which amount the second party hereto hereby assumes as part of said purchase money." The petition shows that the mortgaged property has been exhausted, and that but six hundred and seventy-four dollars have been paid on said indebtedness thereby, and asks judgment against the defendant for the balance. Defendant answered, admitting the mortgage, the foreclosure thereof, the sale of the land, and the application of the proceeds to the judgment. For a further answer, he alleges that in the spring of 1888 he entered into a written contract with one R. A. Salisbury, which contract he alleges has been lost and destroyed, by the terms of which he agreed with Salisbury to exchange certain real estate in Marshalltown, Iowa, for the equity of redemption in said mortgaged real estate, which equity was then owned by Salisbury; "that said contract provided only for an exchange of the properties above described, and expressly provided that defendant should take a conveyance of said property, subject only to said mortgage of one thousand dollars thereon, but not that he should assume, or agree to pay, or in any manner become personally liable therefor." The answer further states that Salisbury had taken a conveyance from the former owners of the land, in which the name of the grantee was left blank, and after the sale of said property to the defendant, in place of making a new conveyance, Salisbury wrote in the name of this defendant as grantee in the original conveyance, and delivered the same to the defendant, who in turn delivered to him a deed for the property in Marsalltown. Defendant further says that

1　　said deed does not state the true consideration that was agreed upon in said written contract to be paid for said equity of redemption, but that in truth the true consideration, as determined by defendant and Salisbury, and as set forth in the written contract, was only the conveyance of said Marshalltown property, and that defendant should take a conveyance of said land subject to said mortgage thereon only, and did not provide that defendant should assume or in any manner become personally liable therefor. The plaintiff demurred to said answer upon the following grounds: *"First,* because the answer admits facts which avoid the defenses pleaded; *second,* because the facts stated in the answer are not sufficient to constitute a defense to plaintiff's cause of action, for the following reasons." The ·reasons given are, in substance, that the answer attempts to vary the terms of the written conveyance by parol testimony, and by pleading terms and conditions of a prior contract, in pursuance of which the conveyance was executed; that defendant attempts to plead and prove by parol a contract relating to real estate; that he refers to the alleged contract without presenting a copy or

showing diligence to obtain it; that he attempts to deny and
vary the recitals of the deed absolute, which he accepted and
under which he held title; that he attempts to vary the effect
of a deed absolute by showing a consideration different from
that expressed; and because he seeks to subject the terms of
a deed absolute to a prior contract between him and Salisbury,
who is not a party to this action, and not shown to have ever
had any title to the lands.

II.   Appellant states, as his first contention, that "the
alleged contract with Salisbury cannot constitute a defense,
because Salisbury is a third party, who never owned the land
          in question, and could not legally contract in regard to
2   it; the deed in blank which he held never being filled
          out with his name."   In *McClain v. McClain,* 52
Iowa, 272, it is held that such a deed is valid when delivered
with authority to fill the blank, and the blank is filled with
the name of a grantee.   While such a deed, before being filled
out and filed for record, may be void as to purchasers without
notice, it certainly conferred authority on Salisbury to contract for the sale of the land, and to fill in his own or
another's name as grantee.   If Salisbury did not have
authority to contract in regard to the land, plaintiff has no
cause of action against the defendant, as he and the defendant
had no contract whatever.   Plaintiff is seeking to recover
solely upon the alleged assumption by the defendant of the
mortgage debt, upon the ground that that assumption inures
to his benefit.   According to the petition, defendant agreed
with the Barnards to assume and pay that debt, but, according
to the answer, his agreement, whatever it was, was with Salisbury, and not with the Barnards.   Plaintiff insists that,
though the agreement was with Salisbury, he has a right to
recover upon that agreement as expressed in the deed; while
defendant insists that he has not a right to recover, because
of the terms of said alleged written contract.   Both parties
recognized the right of Salisbury to contract with respect to
that land.   If he had no such right, the defendant made no
contract that has inured to the benefit of the plaintiff.

III. Appellant contends that the terms of the alleged contract were merged in the deed, and that the defendant cannot change the face of his deed by showing a consideration different from that expressed therein, and adverse thereto. In the recitals of this deed the consideration is not only the two thousand five hundred dollars, but two thousand five hundred dollars, one thousand dollars of which were to be paid in a particular manner. It recites the existence of the one thousand dollar mortgage, "which amount the second party hereto hereby assumes as a part of said puchase money." This assumption as to the manner of paying the one thousand dollars of the purchase money is a part of the consideration for the deed, and the contention is whether, as against this recitation of the consideration, the defendant may show what the true consideration was, as provided in the alleged contract. In *De Goey v. Van Wyk,* 97 Iowa, 491, this court said as follows: "There is much conflict in the authorities as to what may be shown regarding the consideration of a written instrument. Many authorities hold that the consideration may be shown by parol to be greater or less, other or different from, or something additional to, that stated in the writing." After citing authorities, it is further said: "Other authorities seem to go so far as to permit a consideration to be shown which is inconsistent with, or contrary to, that stated in the instrument. In our state, and in cases where the facts involved make the holdings applicable to the facts of the case at bar, the rule has been adhered to that, when the considerations are expressed and fully stated in unmistakable language in the written instrument, it is not competent or admissible to change or vary them by parol evidence." After again citing authorities, it is further said: "If, then, the defendant Uithoven had been a party to the mortgage, this evidence would not have been admissible. While, under our statute, Uithoven, if a party for whose benefit the mortgage was made, might have availed himself of it (Code 1873, section 2552), still he is in no legal sense a party to it, so as to bring him within the rule which excludes the parties to such instruments from adding to or varying them by parol evidence. The rule excluding such parol evidence applies only to those who are parties to the instrument, the effect of which may be sought to be changed. It cannot affect third persons, who, were it otherwise, might thereby be precluded from establishing the truth as to matters with regard to which they had nothing to do. Inasmuch as the defendant was not a party to the mortgage, there was no error in permitting him to show that in fact there was a consideration other than that stated therein."

The instrument the consideration of which is sought to be proven to have been different from that recited is the deed to the defendant. The plaintiff, Logan, is not a party to that instrument, and therefore, under the rule just quoted, the true consideration may, as between him and the defendant, be shown. The question whether the true consideration might be shown as between parties to the instrument was not involved in that case, nor is it in this. Therefore we are not called upon to affirm what is said in that opinion argumentatively on that subject. We think the terms of the written contract, as set up in the answer, relate to the consideration, and that the defendant may be allowed to prove the same. To prove the true consideration as to amount and manner of payment does not in any way affect the title conveyed by the deed, for, with these made according to the truth, the deed still stands as a valid conveyance. It 4   is insisted that, to avail himself of this defense, the defendant should go into equity to have the alleged mistake in the deed corrected; but in *Lawton v. Buckingham,* 15 Iowa, 22, the court says: "If the amount was inserted by mistake an averment to that effect is not necessary to let in the proposed testimony."

IV. Appellant's further contention is that "defendant, having accepted a deed by the terms of which he assumed payment of plaintiff's mortgage, is now estopped from denying liability thereon." While this may be true as to covenants in the deed, it cannot, in view of what we have said, be true as to the consideration. As we view it, the defendant has the right to show what the real consideration was, both as to amount and manner of payment, for the deed under which plaintiff seeks to charge him.   Therefore the demurrer was properly overruled, and judgment rendered.—Affirmed.

John McDonald, Appellant, v. The Second National Bank of Nashua, N. H., and C. W. Hoitt, Assignee of Mechanics Savings Bank, Nashua, N. H.

Mortgage Foreclosure: jurisdiction: *Redemption.* Plaintiff's grantor conveyed to him certain land, subject to two mortgages. The first mortgage was foreclosed and the land sold to the mortgagees. The debt secured by the second mortgage was also secured
1 by a mortgage on real estate in another county, on which the mortgagor resided, and made his home, and also by a mortgage on personal property. The assignee of such second mortgage,
3 having subjected the mortgaged chattels to the debt, obtained a personal judgment against the mortgagor, in the county of his residence, and a decree directing a sale of all the mortgaged real estate, which was subsequently conveyed by the sheriff to an assignee of the certificate of sale, who thereupon redeemed from the sale under the first mortgage. Plaintiff, who was not a party to either action, though he had actual notice thereof and of such mortgages when he received his deed, sued to foreclose such deed as a mortgage, and to redeem from such prior mortgages, claiming that the court had acquired no jurisdiction to foreclose the second mortgage on the land in question, as it was situated in another county, and that, as the purchaser had made redemption from the first sale more than nine months after such sale, he had no remedy against such land. *Held,* that there was no equity in such claim. In this case it was proper and necessary to sell the land in the county of the suit, first, because of the homestead character of the lots in the other county, and by such sale to make the amount to come from the homestead, definite.

Separate mortgage: *Construction.* Separate mortgages on lands in different counties, executed at the same time, by and to the
2 same parties, and to secure the same indebtedness, cannot be construed as constituting a single instrument, though a note and mortgage will be read together and construed, only with respect to debt, as parts of one contract.

Suit on note and foreclosure. Under Code, section 3493, providing that an action to foreclose shall be brought in the county in which the property to be affected, or some part thereof, is situated,

and section 4288, providing that, if separate actions are brought
8 in the same county on the note and on the mortgage, the plaintiff
must elect which to prosecute, and that, "the other will be discontinued at his cost," a suit may be maintained in one county on the
note, and, in a proper case, an action for the foreclosure of the
mortgage to secure it in another.

Misjoinder. Misjoinder of causes of action exists under Code, section 3493, providing that an action to foreclose a mortgage on real
property shall be brought in the county in which the property to
be affected or some part thereof is situated, where suit is brought
4 to foreclose two mortgages on real property executed by and to
the same parties at the same time and to secure the same debt and
the property covered by one of the mortgages is not situated in
the county where the venue is laid.

Waiver: *Motion to transfer.* Where an action to foreclose several
mortgages on real estate situated in different counties, was brought
5 in one of such counties, all objections on the ground of such misjoinder of actions were waived by failure of the mortgagors to
appear and move therein.

Same. Under Code, section 3504, providing that, if an action is brought
in the wrong county, it may there be prosecuted to a termination, unless the defendant, before answer, demands a change of
venue, a decree of foreclosure was not invalid for want of juris-
5 diction where a portion of the mortgaged property was situated
in a different county from that in which the action was brought,
and such action was *in personam* as well as *in rem*, and the mortgagors entered no appearance therein, as their right to insist on a
trial in the other county was waived by their default.

Right of possession: *Injunction.* One in possession of land under
6 a deed effective only as a mortgage, and having a plain remedy at
law, if entitled to protection, was not entitled to an injunction
restraining the purchasei of such property at a sale on foreclosure
of a prior mortgage, from interfering with such possession.

Appeal from Plymouth District Court.—Hon. F. R. Gaynor,
Judge.

Friday, October 21, 1898.

Action to foreclose a deed executed as a mortgage, and
to redeem. From the decree entered, plaintiff appeals.—
Affirmed.

J. S. Lothrop for appellant.

Joy, Call & Joy for appellees.

LADD, J.—The plaintiff, only, appeals, and the decree, in so far as favorable to him, requires no consideration. *McWhirter v. Crawford,* 104 Iowa, 555. We shall assume, then, that Donald McDonald and wife, on the eighteenth day of January, 1893, conveyed the farm, of about one thousand four hundred acres, in Plymouth county, to the plaintiff, as security for the indebtedness then due him, and that his acts of possession were such as to put everyone on inquiry with reference to his interest therein. This farm was incumbered at that time by two mortgages,—one dated May 1, 1889, for sixteen thousand dollars, to Beyer & Co., and another dated

1   October 18, 1890, for eighteen thousand dollars, to A. S. Garretson. At the same time, and to secure the same debt a mortgage was executed by the same parties to Garretson on certain lots situated in Sioux City, Woodbury county, and also a chattel mortgage on a large amount of personal property. Garretson assigned these three mortgages to the Second National Bank of Nashua, N. H. The mortgage to Beyer & Co. was foreclosed, and the land sold to the mortgagees at the sheriff's sale, December 16, 1893. The proceeds of the property covered by the chattel mortgage were applied on the debt secured. It will be observed that the mortgages securing the notes assigned by Garretson to the bank covered real estate in two counties,—one, lots in Woodbury county, where the mortgagors resided, and the other, land in Plymouth county. The bank began an action in Woodbury county on both mortgages, obtained personal judgment against Donald McDonald, and a decree directing the sale of all the property. Special execution was issued to the sheriff of Plymouth county, the land sold thereunder, and a sheriff's deed executed to C. W. Hoitt, assignee, who held the certificate of sale, October 30, 1894, and he redeemed from the sale to Beyer & Co., a few days later. The appellant asserts that the court sitting in Woodbury county acquired no jurisdiction to enter a decree foreclosing the mortgage on the Plymouth county land, and, as redemption from the sale to Beyer & Co. was made more than nine months after the sale, the bank or Hoitt

has no remedy against the land. The plaintiff was not made party to any of these actions, though he had actual notice of their pendency, and had both actual and constructive notice of the mortgages when he received the deed. It thus appears there is no equity in his claim, and that, if his contention is allowed, it must be because of the technical construction of the statute.

Section 3493 of the Code is as follows: "An action for the foreclosure of a mortgage of real property, or for the sale thereof under an incumbrance or charge, or to enforce a mechanic's lien thereon, shall be brought in the county in which the property to be affected, or some part thereof, is situated."

II. The appellee insists that the two mortgages should be construed as one instrument. As already mentioned, these were executed at the same time, by and to the same parties, and to secure the same indebtedness. These circum-
2   stances show them to have been a part of the same transaction, but not the same instrument. If security was taken in two mortgages instead of one, for convenience in recording, this confirms the thought that separate mortgages were intended. The note and mortgages will be read together and construed only with respect to the debt as parts of one contract. *Fetes v. O'Laughlin,* 62 Iowa, 532, and cases cited; *Kennion v. Kelsey,* 10 Iowa, 443; 1 Jones Mortgages, section 71. The fact that several mortgages may be considered in connection with the same note will not affect their identity as separate instruments. It is said that because the conditions of defeasance are identical (*i. e.* the payment of the debt) the case falls within the rule announced in *Lomax v. Smyth,* 50 Iowa, 232. This distinction is ignored; here the mortgages are complete within themselves, while there the deeds were executed conveying land in different counties, but the condition of defeasance with respect to all such land was contained in a single instrument. While a mortgage need not necessarily consist of one paper, to hold that such an instrument, complete in itself, without evidence to the con-

trary, is not a distinct mortgage, would be ignoring the technical as well as common meaning of the word.

III.   The words "shall be" in the section of the Code quoted were substituted for "may be" by chapter 126 of the Acts of the Twentieth General Assembly. This section, before this amendment, was construed as permissive only. *Insurance Co. v. Gleason,* 56 Iowa, 47; *Trust Co. v. Day,* 63 Iowa, 459. And under a similar provision of the Code of 1851 it was held that an action might be maintained in the county where the defendant resided, though the land was situated elsewhere in the state. *Finnigan v. Manchester,* 12 Iowa, 521; *Cole v. Conner,* 10 Iowa, 299. Under section 2795 of the Revision, which provided that the action "must be brought in the county in which the subject of the action, or some part thereof is situated," the court, in *Chadbourne v. Gilman,* 29 Iowa, 181, had occasion to pass upon a motion to strike out of a petition so much as related to five separate mortgages on land outside of Dubuque county, where the suit was pending. It appeared that six mortgages covered land in six counties, and each secured a distinct portion of the debt; and it was held that, as the mortgage on the land in Dubuque county was not part of the subject of the action on the other mortgages, and because of a misjoinder of actions, the motion should have been sustained. The difference between that case and the one at bar is apparent. There a distinct portion of the debt was secured by each mortgage. Here both mortgages secured the same debt. We think this not very material, however, because foreclosure proceedings might have been maintained in Plymouth county after judgment was obtained in Woodbury. *Banta v. Wood,* 32 Iowa, 469; *Brown v. Cascaden,* 43 Iowa, 103; *Morrison v. Morrison,* 38 Iowa, 73. Indeed, there appears to be no good reason why appropriate actions might not have been maintained in both counties at the same time. Section 4288 provides that "if separate actions are brought in the same county on the bond or note and on the mortgage given to secure it, the plaintiff must elect which to prosecute. The other will be discontinued at his cost." By fair implication, a suit may be maintained on the note in one county, and, in a proper case, an action for the foreclosure of the mortgage in another. Difficulty in fixing the portion of the debt secured by each mortgage is obviated by the sale of the different parcels. In this case the lots constituted the homestead of Donald McDonald, and the security on the farm was necessarily first exhausted. Code, section 2976. The sale of the farm made definite the amount secured by the mortgage on the lots.

IV.   In bringing suit on both mortgages in Woodbury county, there was then a misjoinder of actions, and so much as related to that on the farm in Plymouth county might have been stricken on motion, under the ruling in *Chad-*

4   *bourne's Case.* Code, section 3547. But, by failing to appear, all objections on this ground were waived. Code, section 3548. Where the motion is made, however, the plaintiff may, on application, separate his actions, and file a petition for each. Code, section 3549.

V.   But the mere fact that an action is prosecuted in the wrong county does not deprive the court of jurisdiction. This happens when the action is purely *in rem,* and not *in personam* as well. *Orcutt v. Hanson,* 71 Iowa, 514. But if the action is personal, and also pertains to the *res,* and is brought in the wrong county, the only remedy is that provided by section 3504 of the Code, which is, in part: "If an action is brought in a wrong county, it may there be prosecuted to a termination, unless the defendant, before answer, demands a change of place of trial to the proper county." *Lyon v. Cloud,* 7 Iowa, 1; *Cole v. Conner,* 10 Iowa, 299; *Goldsmith v. Wilson,* 67 Iowa, 662. Thus jurisdiction is acquired of a non-resident in a county other than that wherein served with the original notice. *Marquardt v. Thompson,* 78 Iowa, 158. The only remedy in a replevin suit brought in the wrong county is that of the above statute. *Goldsmith v. Willson, supra.* Though the statute restricts the issuance of a writ of attachment to the county of defendant's residence, or where the written contract is made payable, the writ issued in another county is voidable only. *Payne v. Dicus,* 88 Iowa, 423. The action to foreclose a mortgage is not purely *in rem,* but *in personam* as well. Originally it was regarded as transitory. In so far as local, it is so made by statute. The action, in seeking to cut off the equity of redemption of the mortgagors, and to obtain judgment for the debt, is personal; but that part of the procedure which is directed against the hypothecated property for the purpose of subjecting it to the payment of the debt is *in rem*, and may be said to be local. In other words, the action is dual in form, but partakes so much of a personal suit that the statute with reference to change of venue must be held applicable. This appears from *Cole v. Conner, supra*, where it is said: "It is believed, however, that the jurisdiction is local, and can obtain only in the county where the land lies, and where the object of the proceeding is only to sell and foreclose the equity of redemption. Still, in such an event, the suit should not be dismissed, but should be sent to the proper county, under section 1702 of the Code." *Chadbourne v. Gilman, supra*, does not announce a different rule; and it is supported by the reasoning 5 in *Orcutt v. Hanson, supra*. Whether section 3504, relating to changes of venue when the action is brought in the wrong county, applies to purely local action, we shall not now determine. But see *Barnes v. Davis*, 2 Iowa, 160; *Decatur County v. Maxwell*, 26 Iowa, 398; *College of Physicians and Surgeons v. Guilbert*, 100 Iowa, 213. The statute conferred on the defendants the right to insist upon the foreclosure suit being tried in the county in which the subject-matter was situated, but this right was waived by their default. The conclusion we have reached finds support in the following authorities: *Lane v. Burdick*, 17 Wis. 95; *Gill v. Bradley*, 21 Minn. 15; *O'Neil v. O'Neil*, 54 Cal. 187; *Territory v. Judge*, 5 Dak. 275 (38 N. W. Rep. 439); *Tucker v. Lake*, — N. H. — (29 Atl. Rep. 406); *Fletcher v. Stowell*, 17 Colo. Sup. 94 (28 Pac. Rep. 326); *Chouteau v. Allen*, 70 Mo. 353. See, also, 9 Enc. Pl. & Prac. 256. The mortgagors, having been made parties defendant, had the undoubted right to have the cause of action relating to the land in Plymouth county stricken on motion because of misjoinder, and, in event of filing a separate petition under section 3549 of the Code, might have had it transferred to the proper county. But by failing to appear or move they waived all objections to the place of bringing either cause of action, and the decree entered must be adjudged valid.

VI. The plaintiff insists the court erred in dissolving the writ of injunction by which defendants were enjoined from interferring with his possession. But according to his own allegations the deed under which he claims must 6   be construed as a mortgage. The possession of a mere mortgagee is not entitled to protection as against the owner of the fee obtained under a sale made in pursuance of the foreclosure of a prior mortgage. Besides, if entitled to possession, he has a plain remedy at law. The plaintiff will be permitted to make redemption on the terms fixed in the decree of the district court at any time prior to February 1, 1899.—AFFIRMED.

F. BRODY, Appellant, v. G. W. CHITTENDEN.

Mortgages: "FURNITURE" DEFINED. On an issue whether certain
1   articles kept in a place of business were covered by a mortgage of
2   "furniture," an instruction that the appliances, implements, instruments, and like articles used in carrying on the business conducted at the place would not be furniture was error.

Evidence: COMPETENCY OF WITNESS: *Cross-examination.* A banker who had no particular knowledge of the jewelry business testified
8   that he sold defendant a part of defendant's stock and that he took a mortgage upon it. *Held,*
   a It was improper to ask him *on cross-examination* as to defendant's using certain tools in his business and the use made therein of regulators.
   b The witness was incompetent.

SAME. In replevin for articles claimed under a mortgage covering a jeweler's stock of goods by a general description, including merchandise, furniture and fixtures, where the defense is that the arti-
5   cles named were not included therein, evidence of jewelers and dealers in jewelry, watches, etc., as to how these articles are regarded by the trade in relation to being part of a jewelry stock, is admissible.

INTENT. In replevin for goods claimed under a mortgage given for the price of the goods, which were sold to the defendant by the mortgagee, it was competent to ask defendant whether a clock
4 claimed to be included in the mortgage was not listed at the time of the sale with the show case and other fixtures included in the mortgage, which described in general terms a stock of goods, furniture, fixtures, etc., since it was material to show how the clock was treated by the parties at the time of the sale.

Appeal: WAIVER. When plaintiffs ask an instruction that the jury
6 has nothing to do with the stock involved in a replevin suit, they cannot complain because the court charged that the stock had a certain value.

Appeal from Polk District Court.—HON. T. F. STEVENSON, Judge.

SATURDAY, OCTOBER 22, 1898.

ACTION of replevin, involving the right to the possession of the following goods: One Seth Thomas regulator, one Swiss regulator, one jardiniere, one jeweler's scales, one Natchet trial case, one diamond scale, one pair of sleeve buttons, two pairs of eardrops, one watch movement, one pair glasses, one watch, one gold pin, one chain, one garnet pin and one chain. Plaintiff claims he is entitled to the possession thereof as assignee of two chattel mortgages executed by defendant,—one to Holland and the other to J. A. McKinney. Defendant denies that the property was included in either of these mortgages, and further pleads that he did not own the last nine items of property, but held the same as bailee for the true owners thereof. The case was tried to a jury, resulting in a verdict for defendant. Plaintiff filed a motion for a new trial, and the court ordered that the verdict, in so far as it related to the Swiss clock, the jardiniere, and the three bench stools, which were included therein, be set aside. The motion was otherwise overruled, and judgment was rendered on the verdict. Plaintiff appeals.—*Reversed.*

Ayers, Woodin & Ayers for appellant.

Read & Read for appellee.

DEEMER, C. J.—On and prior to the twenty-first day of December, 1895, defendant was engaged in the jewelry business in the city of Des Moines. He also handled glass, queen's and decorated ware, and optical goods. On the last-named date he executed the mortgages upon which this action is bottomed. The description of the property is practically the same in each, and reads as follows: "All of my

1   stock of goods, jewelry, silverware, glass and queens-ware, of every kind and description, and all goods and merchandise now or hereafter in my store in the building and room known as 406 East Sixth (6th) street, in the city of Des Moines, Iowa, and all furniture and fixtures therein, including safes; said stock consisting principally of diamonds, watches, watch cases and movements, clocks, jewelry, optical goods, silverware, glass and queensware, and decorated goods, and other articles of merchandise." It is conceded that no one of the first six items of property named in the preceding statement was a part of defendant's stock of goods, and it is practically conceded that none of them may properly be said to be fixtures. The sole question in the case seemed to be whether or not they, or any of them, were intended to be included in the mortgage under the designation of "furniture." That question was submitted to the jury, and it found for the defendant. As the court set aside the verdict in so far as it related to the Swiss clock, the jardiniere, and three bench stools, we have only to inquire as to the other items of

2   property. The court instructed, in the fourth paragraph of its charge, as follows: "Generally, furniture consists of those articles which are used and prepared to be used in fitting up the place in question to adapt it as a place for the purpose for which it is intended to be used. The machinery, tools, apparatus, appliances, implements, instruments, and such like articles that are used in carrying on the business conducted at the place would not be furniture." This instruction is complained of, and we think the error assigned must be sustained. The word "furniture" ordinarily

means that with which anything is supplied; the equipment or outfit of a trade or business; whatever may be supplied to a stock of goods or to a business, to make it convenient, useful, or gainful. As said in the case of *Fore v. Hibbard,* 63 Ala. 412, in construing a mortgage of a drug-store furniture and fixtures, "the articles, utensils, and implements used in a drug store, or other store, as the furniture thereof, differ in kind according to the purpose which they are intended to subserve; yet, being put and employed in the several purposes, as the equipment thereof, for ornament, or to promote comfort, or to facilitate the business therein done, and being kept or intended to be kept for those or some other purpose, they pertain to such places, respectively, and constitute the furniture thereof." See, also, *Bell v. Golding,* 27 Ind. 173. The instruction says that appliances, implements, instruments, and such like articles used in carrying on the business would not be furniture. Herein lies the error of the instruction. Certainly the implements and instruments used in carrying on the business may be a part of the furnishings of the business.

II.   One J. A. McKinney, the cashier of a bank to which one of the mortgages was given, was a witness for the plaintiff, and testified to selling the defendant a part of the mortgaged goods, including the Seth Thomas regulator, and also to the taking of the mortgage upon the stock. On cross-examination he was asked, over plaintiff's objection, as to defendant's using certain instruments and tools in his business as a jewelryman, and as to the use made by jewelers of regulators. This was clearly not cross-examination; and it was also incompetent, for the witness said he was a banker and had no particular knowledge of the jewelry business.

III.   It was for the jury to determine, under proper instructions from the court, whether the property in controversy, or any part of it, was covered by the mortgage. This was largely a question of intent. In arriving at this intent, the situation of the parties and all the surrounding circum-

stances were proper to be considered. *Myers v. Snyder,* 96
Iowa, 107. Plaintiff asked the defendant when on
4   the witness stand, if the Seth Thomas regulator was not
listed with the show case and other fixtures when he
bought the stock of McKinney. Objection to the question on
the ground of immateriality was sustained. As McKinney
sold the stock to Chittenden and took a mortgage back for the
purchase price,—this mortgage being one under which
plaintiff claims,—it seems to us that it was quite material to
show how this regulator was treated by the parties at the
time of the sale.

IV. Certain jewelers, and dealers in jewelry, watches,
etc., were placed on the witness stand by the plaintiff,
and asked as to how regulators were regarded by the
trade,—whether as part of the stock, as fixtures, or as
tools. Some of them were also asked as to how diamond
scales were treated and regarded. Objections to
5   these questions were sustained. We think the evidence
should have been admitted. When a word is used
in a technical or peculiar sense, as applicable to any trade or
business, it is proper to receive testimony of witnesses having
special knowledge of such words as to the meaning attached
to it. *Brown v. Brown,* 8 Metc. (Mass.) 573; *Miller v.
Stevens,* 100 Mass. 518; *Downs v. Sprague,* 1 Abb. Dec.
550; *Eaton v. Smith,* 20 Pick. 156; *Collender v. Dunsmore,*
55 N. Y. 200; *Newhall v. Appleton,* 114 N. Y. 140 (21 N.
E. Rep. 105); Greenleaf Evidence, sections 292, 294; *Schaub
v. Brewing Co.,* 80 Tex. 634 (16 S. W. Rep. 429). Evidence
as to the meaning attributed to these words, or as to how regulators and scales are regarded by the trade, was proper to be
considered in arriving at the identity of the goods intended to
be covered by the mortgage.

V. Complaint is made of the first instruction, wherein
the jury is told that the goods had a certain value. As the
plaintiff asked an instruction to the effect that the jury
6   had nothing to do with the question of value, and
should disregard all the evidence on the subject, he
is not in position to complain.

VI.   Some other questions are discussed by counsel, but, as they are not likely to arise upon a re-trial, we do not consider them.   For the errors pointed out, the judgment is REVERSED.

_____

L. C. HENDERSHOT v. THE WESTERN UNION TELEGRAPH COMPANY, *Appellant.*

Telegram Delivery: NEGLIGENCE: *Jury question.* In an action against a telegraph company for damages for failure to promptly
1 deliver a message, the evidence showed that the message reached
2 its destination at eight o'clock A. M., and was delivered on the same
3 day at one thirty P. M.; that the message was urgent; that the company's messenger made several attempts to find the addressee down town, and went to his office twice for that purpose but did not leave a notice under the door or visit his residence, which was within the company's free delivery limits, where the addressee was all the forenoon. *Held,* sufficient to sustain a finding of negligence.

PROXIMATE DAMAGES: *Jury question.* A telegraph message reading "Bravo is sick; come and fetch Miller at once," was sent to plaintiff. There was a delay of about five hours in its delivery.
4 Bravo was a valuable horse of plaintiff, at a training stable about twelve miles from plaintiff's home. Miller was a veterinary surgeon. The evidence shows that the horse was taken sick about seven A. M.; that, if Miller had reached the horse about five or six hours earlier, his chances for recovery would have been greater; and that in all reasonable possibility the horse would have been saved, had it been treated five or six hours earlier. *Held,* sufficient to sustain a finding that the delay in the delivery of the message was the proximate cause of the death of the horse.

DAMAGES: *Proximateness.* Damages sought against a telegraph company for the death of a valuable horse, alleged to be due to the
6 defendant's delay in the delivery of a message are within the contemplation of the contract and not too remote where both the receiving and sending parties knew from the nature of the dispatch that promptness was required.

RULE APPLIED. A telegraphic message reading "Bravo is sick; come and fetch Miller at once;" Bravo being a valuable horse of the
5 addressee and Miller a veterinary surgeon, is sufficient notice to
6 the company of the damages that might result from the failure to promptly deliver the message; especially when the receiving agent was asked to hurry.

Evidence: INSTRUCTIONS: *Issue.* In an action to recover damages for the death of a valuable horse alleged to have been due to the defendant's delay in delivering a telegram the burden of proof is on the plaintiff to show by a preponderance of the evidence that in all reasonable possibility the cause of the death of the horse was the failure to deliver the message in due time, and the sole issue is whether the death is attributable to delay in treatment
6 caused by the failure to deliver the message. Hence, an instruction that negligence in the surgeon's treatment of the animal after the dispatch was received is imputable to the plaintiff, is erroneous. The only complaint is, that the surgeon did not visit the horse enough after reaching him. If this tends to account for the death, it is immaterial whether or not the failure to visit was negligence.

DEEMER, C. J.—Concurring specially.

PRIVILEGED COMMUNICATION: *Veterinaries.* Statements made by the owner of a horse to a veterinary surgeon called to treat the animal are not protected by Code, 1873, section 3643, prohibiting a dis-
7 closure of a professional communication, and their exclusion will be presumed to have been prejudicial when they might have had an important bearing on the cause of the horse's death, which was in issue.

Appeal from Wapello District Court.—HON. M. A. ROBERTS, Judge.

SATURDAY, OCTOBER 22, 1898.

ACTION at law to recover damages for delay in transmitting and delivering a telegram sent to the plaintiff. Verdict and judgment for the plaintiff for one thousand two hundred and thirty-four dollars and thirty-five cents. Defendant appeals.—*Reversed.*

Geo. H. Fearsons and *McNett & Tisdale* for appellant.

W. W. Cory and *Jacques & Jacques* for appellee.

GIVEN, J.—I. The following facts are undisputed, and a statement thereof will sufficiently show the issues: Plaintiff, for a long time a well-known resident and practicing attorney of Ottumwa, Iowa, was the owner of a valuable stallion and speed horse, called "Bravo." which he had in charge of one E. Daggett, for care and training, at the track and training stable at Hedrick, Iowa, about twelve miles distant from Ottumwa. On June 28, 1893, at about 7 A. M., Daggett discovered that the horse was ailing, and at 7:30 o'clock A. M., delivered to the defendant's agent at Hedrick for transmission, with the request that it be promptly forwarded, a dispatch, as follows: "6-28, 1893. To C. Hendershot, Ottumwa, Iowa: Bravo is sick; come and fetch Miller at once. [Signed] E. Daggett. "The message was received by defendant's agent at Ottumwa between 8 and 8:30 the same morning, and was delivered to the plaintiff between 1 and 2 o'clock that afternoon. There being then no railway train by which Hedrick could be sooner reached, the plaintiff and Dr. Miller, a skillful and competent veterinary surgeon, proceeded by train to Hedrick, where they arrived between 3 and 4:30 o'clock that evening, when Dr. Miller found that the horse had pneumonia, or lung fever, and proceeded to treat it for that disease. The horse continued sick until the seventh day thereafter, when it died. There is dispute as to whether the defendant was negligent in not sooner delivering the dispatch to the plaintiff, whether the delay was the proximate cause of the death of the horse, whether plaintiff was negligent in the care of the horse, and as to its value. The facts as to these disputed questions will be noticed further on.

II. Appellant moved for a verdict at the close of the plaintiff's evidence, and again at the close of all the evidence, upon the grounds that the evidence failed to make out a case for the plaintiff, for that the damages claimed are too remote, for that it fails to show that the death of the horse was the proximate result of any act or omission of defendant, and for that there is not sufficient proof of negligence on the part of the defendant; also, that the evidence shows that plaintiff was guilty of contributory negligence. Appellant also included these grounds in its motion for a new trial, and, these several motions being overruled, the rulings are assigned as error. The state of the evidence was not so materially changed, following the first motion, as to require a separate consideration of these rulings. They may be considered under the general inquiry as to the sufficiency of the evidence.

III.   We first inquire as to the sufficiency of the evidence to sustain the charge of negligence in failing to deliver the dispatch.   The jury returned twenty-four special findings, of which the following is the substance of those relating to the alleged negligence.   These findings, we think, are warranted by the evidence.   The jury found that the message was delivered at Hedrick for transmission at 7:30 o'clock A. M.; that it was received at Ottumwa at 8 o'clock, and delivered to the plaintiff at 1:30 P. M.; that the messenger went to plaintiff's office twice,—the first time at about 8:15 A. M.; that he left no notice of the message under the door; and that there was a negligent delay of five hours in delivering the message.   They also found that the plaintiff's residence was within a radius of one mile from defendant's Ottumwa office.   One mile was the radius of free delivery.   The defendant's agent at Ottumwa who received the dispatch says he knew Dr. Miller, and implied from the message that some one was sick and that a physician was wanted.   While this message was not sent as an emergency message, there was surely reason to understand from its language that promptness should be exercised in its delivery.   The messenger made several efforts to find Mr. Hendershott down town, but did not go to his residence, which the jury found was within the radius of free delivery.   Plaintiff remained at his residence until after dinner that day, but, as his residence was within the limits of free delivery, the message should have been taken there,—especially so in view of what its words disclosed.   There is a conflict in the evidence as to whether the residence was within a radius of one mile, but, if it was not, it was at most but a few feet beyond; and, in view of the character of the message, promptness, and good faith required that it should have been taken to the residence, even though it was a few feet beyond the limits of free delivery.   We think, however, the finding of the jury as to the distance is warranted.   We are in no doubt that the plaintiff's evidence in chief and the entire evidence were such as to warrant the court in submitting the issue of negligence to the jury, and to warrant the jury in finding that the defendant was negligent in not sooner delivering the message to plaintiff.

IV.   Appellant contends that "the negligent delay, if any there was, in the delivery of the message, and the consequent failure of the veterinary surgeon to reach the horse as soon as he otherwise would, by the space of five hours, as found by the jury, was not the proximate cause of the death of the horse," and the law applied to the facts did not warrant the court in submitting to the jury the question whether the delay in the delivery of the message was the proximate cause of the death of the horse. To determine these contentions, we must first ascertain the rule as to the degree of evidence which plaintiff must present to entitle him to recover. The court instructed that, to recover, the plaintiff must establish that the defendant was negligent in not sooner delivering the message, that plaintiff was not guilty of negligence contributing to the death of the horse, and "that the death of the horse was directly and proximately caused by the delay in delivering the dispatch, or that but for such delay the horse would not, in all reasonable probability, have died." The instructions throughout direct the jury that the burden was on the plaintiff to prove that, "in all reasonable probability," the death of the horse was caused by reason of Dr. Miller's not reaching it as soon as he would had the message beeen delivered when it should have been, and that it did not rest upon the defendant to prove that the horse would have died even if Dr. Miller had reached it as much ___ ___ the delivery of the dispatch was delayed.   In ___ ___ ___orks Co., 95 Iowa, 514, this court quoted ___ ___ Gores v. Graff, 77 Wis. 174 (46 N ___ ___ gainst a surgeon for negli ___ ___ atient), as follows ___ ___ reason-abl ___ ___ d had ___ ___ ___ce of such ___ ___at is, facts and cir-___ ___tly to bring conviction to resorting to mere conjecture or uncertainty, and inconclusive inference or bare possibilities that the surgeon's neglect of duty was the proximate cause of the death of his patient." In *Taylor v. Telegraph Co.*, 95 Iowa, 744, wherein the question was whether the death of a horse had been caused by exposure, it is said: "The evidence as to the death of the animal from exposure on that night is not as definite and certain as if the death had been caused by accident or violent means, such as a collision of trains, or the like, but we think it was a fair question for the jury." In the nature of things, reasonable probability as to the cause of the death of the horse is the most that can be proven in a case like this; and, if the evidence discloses facts which show such reasonable probability as convinces the jurors as to the cause of death, they may surely act upon it, though, as they were told, they must not indulge in conjecture, speculation, or guesswork. Absolute certainty is not required to entitle a party to recover, but only a preponderance of the evidence. Holding the plaintiff to the burden of proving that in all reasonable probability the cause of the death of the horse was the failure to deliver the message in due time, we inquire as to the sufficiency of the evidence to warrant the court in submitting the issue to the jury, and in overruling the motion for new trial.

V. There is much evidence as to the nature of the disease, the best time for its treatment, and the condition of the horse from day to day during its sickness. This evidence is so minute and lengthy that we will not do more than refer to it in a general way. Dr. Miller states condition of the horse at the time he saw it (June 28th) to be as follows: "The horse had pneumonia, commonly called 'lung fever.' He was breathing rapidly. His pulse was increased, his temperature raised. His nostrils were somewhat dilated. His mucous membranes were heightened in color, and he looked depressed,—held his head lower than usual. He was breathing about 18 per minute. Normal would be about 10 or 12 times a minute. His pulse was 64 to the minute; normal, 40, though it varies with the change of temperature some. Temperature, 103½; normal, 100. The color of his nose is usually a pale red, while it became a brighter red. His breathing was shorter, quicker than natural, and more labored. His lungs were in a congested condition,—the right one,—while the left one was in also a congested condition, except the lower part of it, which had passed into what we call the 'second stage,'—consolidated stage. I would have to consider that the horse had passed into the second stage of the disease. When I got there I considered the horse to be in rather a critical condition." He further stated the fact that both lungs being involved added very greatly to the danger of the disease, and that there is much more mortality when both lungs are involved; that, if he had reached the horse five or six hours earlier, the chances of recovery would have been greater; that the best time to commence treatment is in the earlier stages of the disease; and that, when taken in its incipient stages, the per cent. of loss is one in ten to thirteen. The evidence of other experts and of standard authors tends to show that in all reasonable probability the life of the horse would have been saved had it been treated four or five hours sooner than it was. There is also evidence showing that the horse was first observed to be ailing about 7 o'clock in the morning, and continued to grow worse up to the time that Dr. Miller came, and that during the four hours he remained it did not seem to change for either better or worse. The jury found specially that the horse remained in the same condition up to July 3d, when it became worse. We will not discuss this evidence further, but content ourselves with saying that it discloses facts which tend to show that in all reasonable probability the life of the horse would have been saved, had Dr. Miller reached and treated it four hours sooner than he did. Appellant cites a number of cases in which it was held that there was no evidence or not sufficient evidence upon which to submit the question of probable cause to the jury. *Kerr v. Waterworks Co., supra,* is cited. In that case there was not a fact testified to showing that the death resulted from the trip to the waterworks. There was nothing upon which to find for the plaintiffs, but conjecture and inconclusive inferences; but in this we have evidence of facts tending to show that treatment four or five hours earlier would, in all reasonable probability, have saved the horse. The same want of evidence is true of *Trapnell v. City of Red Oak Junction,* 76 Iowa, 745, also cited. In that case there was no evidence of facts which tended to prove that the diseased condition of plaintiff's breast was caused by the fall, and, on the contrary, the physicians testified, without conflict, that the disease was hereditary. There was no evidence in that case tending to connect the disease with the fall, and such connection was left merely to conjecture. *Telegraph Co. v. Swoveland,* 14 Ind. App. 341 (42 N. E. Rep. 1035), is also cited. In that opinion many cases are referred to. That action was to recover for defendant's negligent failure to put the plaintiff in communication with a veterinary surgeon whom he desired to consult and call to see a sick horse, and in consequence of which it was alleged the horse died. It was held that the value of the horse could not be considered as an element of damages, the question whether the horse would have been saved had the messenger taken the call at once being entirely a matter of speculation. The only evidence in that case was the opinion of the veterinary surgeon, who did not arrive until after the horse had died, which opinion was based upon supposed conditions. The court, after citing cases wherein there was a like failure of evidence to connect the effect with the cause, concluded as follows: "We do not wish to be understood as holding that cases may not arise in which, under similar circumstances, it would be proper to submit the question as to whether the death of the animal may be traced to the negligence of the company, but we do not think there is any proper evidence in this case upon which the jury could base a verdict for damages by reason of the death of the horse." The cases cited in that opinion and referred to by appellant were lacking in evidence tending to connect the alleged fact as a proximate cause of the negligence charged.

Brown v. Telegraph Co., 6 Utah, 219 (21 Pac. Rep. 988), was an action to recover damages for failure to deliver a message saying: "Send doctor on first train. Katy has broken her finger." Because of a failure to deliver the dispatch a doctor was not sent, and on the next day plaintiff took Katy to a doctor by whom the finger was amputated. The contention was whether amputation was rendered necessary by the delay, and there being evidence to the effect that the broken part had become dead, and the circulation strangled so that the parts would not unite, the court held that it was a question for the jury. While we are of the opinion that courts should carefully guard against verdicts based upon mere conjecture, we think that under the evidence in this case there was no error in overruling the appellant's motions for a verdict, nor the motion for a new trial upon the grounds under consideration.

VI. Appellant states as a further contention as follows: "Not only were the claimed damages too remote, but in view of the obscure language of the dispatch, were not within the contemplation of the parties, or within the contract involved in the dispatch." This refers to the damage claimed for the loss of the horse. *Hadley v. Baxendale,* 9 Exch. 341, cited and approved in *Manufacturing Co. v. Day,* 50 Iowa, 250, cited by appellant, states the rule as follows: "Where two parties have made a contract which one of them has broken, the damages which the other party ought to receive in respect of such breach of contract should be such as may fairly and reasonably be considered either arising naturally (*i. e.* according to the usual course of things) from such breach of contract itself, or such as may reasonably be supposed to have been in contemplation of both parties, at the time they made the contract, as the probable result of the breach of it. Now, if the special circumstances under which the contract was actually made were communicated by the plaintiffs to the defendants, and thus known to both parties, the damages resulting from the breach of such a contract, which they would reasonably contemplate, would be the

amount of injury which would ordinarily follow from a
breach of contract under these special circumstances so
known and communicated. But, on the other hand, if these
special circumstances were wholly unknown to the party
breaking the contract, he, at the most, could only be supposed
to have had in his contemplation the amount which would
arise generally, and in the great multitude of cases not affected
by any special circumstances, from such a breach." Defendant's agent at Hedrick, who received the dispatch for transmission, did not know Bravo, nor the persons named in the
dispatch, but he did know, from the dispatch itself,
5   that Bravo was sick; that Hendershott and Miller
were wanted to come at once; and, as he expresses it,
that it was a "hurry dispatch." He was also asked to send it
promptly. Defendant's manager at Ottumwa did not know
Bravo, nor whether Bravo was man or animal, but he says:
"I knew Dr. Miller. I implied from the message some one
was sick. When I saw it addressed to Hendershott, and it
said, 'bring Miller,' it occurred to me that it meant 'send
physician.' " With this knowledge of the special circumstances, surely these parties must have understood that it was
their duty to make prompt delivery of the dispatch, to avoid
injury to the sick Bravo. They must have foreseen from the
dispatch itself that delay in delivering it might result in
injury or death or both because of the sickness, and that the
purpose of the dispatch was to avoid such consequences. The
case is, we think, clearly within the rule above quoted. Appellant cites *Telegraph Co. v. Kirkpatrick*, 76 Tex. 217 (13 S.
W. Rep. 70); *Same v. Smith,* 76 Tex. Sup. 253 (13 S. W.
Rep. 169); and *Same v. Bryant,* 17 Ind. App. 70 (46 N.
E. Rep. 358), where it was held that the damages claimed
were too remote. The damages claimed in those cases were
so different from that under consideration that the cases are
not in point. Our conclusion finds support in *Brown v. Telegraph Co., supra; Garrett v. Telegraph Co.,* 83 Iowa, 257;
Herron v. Telegraph Co., 90 Iowa, 129; *Mentzer v. Telegraph*

Co., 93 Iowa, 752; *Taylor v. Telegraph Co., supra;* and
Evans v. Telegraph Co., 102 Iowa, 219.

VII.   Appellant's next contention is that "plaintiff was
guilty of contributory negligence in not seeing that the horse
received more frequent attention during his sickness."   As
we view the case, there is no question of negligence on the
part of the plaintiff or the surgeon involved in this case.   The
question is whether it is shown that in all reasonable probability the horse died because of the delay in being treated in
consequence of the failure to deliver the dispatch in time.
Any evidence tending to rebut the conclusion that the death
resulted from that delay is certainly competent, regardless of
whether or not negligence is shown.   The only complaint is
that the surgeon failed to visit the horse as often as he should
have done.   Now, if such failure tends to account for the
death of the horse, it is immaterial whether or not the failure
was negligence on the part of the surgeon or of the plaintiff.
Collins v. Council Bluffs, 32 Iowa, 324, and *Rice v. City of
Des Moines,* 40 Iowa, 638, are cited, but are not in point, as
in those cases the question of negligence was involved.

6   Counsel discuss, with numerous citations, the question
whether the plaintiff is responsible for the failure of
the surgeon to visit the horse with sufficient frequency, but we
think that is immaterial, inasmuch as the failure bears with
like force upon the question of the cause of the death, whether
or not the failure was negligent.   The court instructed upon
the theory that the question of contributory negligence was
involved, and that "the negligence of Dr. Miller would, so far
as the defendant is concerned, be the negligence of the plaintiff, and would have the same effect."   We think the court
erred in so instructing, and that the inquiry should have
been submitted simply as to the cause of death, regardless of
negligence in the treatment of the horse after the dispatch
was received.

VIII.   In the course of the cross-examination of Dr.
Miller, and of his examination in chief on behalf of the
defendant, he was asked what the plaintiff said as to the

doctor's visiting the horse, and the report that had been
received from the keeper as to the condition of the
7.   horse. To these questions the plaintiff objected, as
calling for privileged communications, and the objections were sustained as being in conflict with section 3643
of the Code of 1873, prohibiting a disclosure of professional
communications. Plaintiff's counsel say in argument: "We
have no case exactly in point to cite." We think that none
can be found to sustain the ruling. The reasons upon which
said section is based have no application whatever to a case
like this. Communications are privileged in certain cases
for the reason that full and free communication in those cases
is necessary and to be encouraged, but these reasons do not
apply to veterinary surgeons called to treat animals. The
ruling must be presumed to have been prejudicial, as the
evidence sought might have had an important bearing upon
the cause of death.

Other questions are argued, but they are not such as are
likely to arise upon a re-trial. Our conclusion is that for the
errors pointed out the judgment of the district court must be
REVERSED.

DEEMER, C. J. (Concurring.)—I agree to the conclusion,
but do not wish to be bound by what is said in the seventh
division of the opinion with reference to the instruction relating to contributory negligence.

THE KEOKUK COUNTY STATE BANK v. EUNICE HALL,
Appellant.

Principal and Agent: INFANTS. A surety upon the promissory note
2 of a minor is not liable thereon where the minor upon attaining
majority disaffirmed the contract and returned the property for
the purchase price of which the note was given.

Bills and Notes: BONA FIDE HOLDER. A bank is not a *bona fide*
1 holder of a note which it received as further security for a pre-
existing debt without giving any new consideration or incurring
any additional responsibility.

Appeal from Keokuk District Court.—HON. D. RYAN, Judge.

SATURDAY, OCTOBER 22, 1898.

THIS action is founded upon a promissory note. The answer, with its several amendments, sets up defenses, the substance of which may be thus stated: Defendant signed the note in suit, together with one A. L. Hill, who was at the time a minor. Defendant was a surety only, although her name appears as a joint maker. The note was given to the firm of Skinner Bros., as part of the price of a livery stock purchased from said firm by Hill. It is further averred that Hill was induced to make such purchase by the fraudulent representations and concealments of said Skinner Bros.; that there was a failure of consideration; that, upon attaining his majority, Hill disaffirmed the contract; and that plaintiff is not a *bona fide* holder of said note. After the testimony was all in, under the direction of the court, the jury returned a verdict for plaintiff. From the judgment rendered thereon defendant appeals.—*Reversed.*

C. M. Brown and *Woodin & Son* for appellant.

A. G. Schulte and *J. P. Talley* for appellee.

WATERMAN, J.—The note was transferred to the plaintiff by the following endorsement: "This note is hereby assigned to S. W. Brunt, cashier, as collateral security on our note or notes, and we hereby waive demand, notice, protest, and all legal formalities of every kind. Skinner Bros." Brunt was cashier of plaintiff bank, and it claims to own the note under this indorsement, and the claim is not disputed.

1   It does not appear that any new consideration was given by the bank or any additional responsibility incurred. So far as shown, it took the note as further security only, for a pre-existing debt of Skinner Bros. Under these circumstances, it is not a *bona fide* holder. *Trustees v. Hill*, 12 Iowa, 462; *Ryan v. Chew*, 13 Iowa, 589; *Ruddick*

v. Lloyd, 15 Iowa, 441; *Bank v. Barber,* 56 Iowa, 559; *Bone v. Tharp,* 63 Iowa, 223.

II.   On the trial Hill was a witness for defendant, and was asked this question: "State whether or not, upon your arriving at majority, about the 1st of February, 1896, you rescinded the contract entered into on the 9th day of September, 1895, and delivered back to Skinner Bros. all the property that you received or had in your possession when you arrived at the age of majority." This was objected to by plaintiff as immaterial, and the objection was sustained. Two other questions, relating to the disaffirmance of the contract by Hill, were objected to on like grounds, and the objections sustained.   These rulings were duly excepted to, and error is assigned on the court's refusal to admit the evidence, which the questions indicate was called for.   It is alleged in the answer, as we have already said, that Hill, on attaining his majority, disaffirmed the contract, and returned the property purchased to Skinner Bros., who received and kept the same.   The general rule is that where a party becomes surety for an infant he is bound, though his principal is not.   *Jones v. Crossthwaite,* 17 Iowa, 393; *Allen v. Berryhill,* 27 Iowa, 534; 1 Brandt Suretyship, section 153.   But to this as to most other rules there are exceptions.   When the principal disaffirms the contract, and returns the consideration received under it, the surety is thereby discharged.   1 Brandt Suretyship, section 153; *Baker v. Kennett,* 54 Mo., 82; *Patterson v. Cave,* 61 Mo. 439.   In the first of these cases an infant purchased real estate, and gave his promissory note, with sureties thereon, for the price.   On reaching his majority, the infant disaffirmed the contract, and restored the real estate to the vendor.   The court says: "It would be a strange doctrine which would give him [the creditor] back his land, and permit him to recover from the sureties the purchase money also."   If Hill did in fact disaffirm the contract, and return the property received thereunder to Skinner Bros., it would be a complete defense for the surety, and we think the court erred in refusing to receive the offered evidence.

III.   Another question that seems, at first sight, to be in issue under the pleadings, is as to the right of a surety to plead that the contract of his principal was procured by fraud. The authorities are in conflict on this subject.   Many courts hold that such a plea is personal to the principal, while others sustain the right of the surety to maintain such defense.   See 1 Brandt Suretyship, section 12, and *Griffith v. Sitgreaves,* 90 Pa. St. 161, where the cases are collected and criticised. Upon a careful examination, the matter suggested will appear to be not involved here.   If this were a case where the infant retained the property purchased, and the plea of fraud was set up in abatement of the price, such question would have to be passed upon.   That, however, is not the situation presented in the controversy before us.   The fraud is alleged here only as a ground warranting the disaffirmance of the contract by the principal.   An infant needs no such reason to sustain a disaffirmance by him of his contract and the infancy of Hill is not questioned.

IV.   Some other matters are discussed by counsel for appellant, but they are not of such a character as to lead us to believe they will again arise.   For the errors mentioned the judgment will be reversed.

Joseph Podhaisky v. City of Cedar Rapids, Appellant.

Instructions: measure of damages.   In an action against a city to recover for the removal of ground protecting the plaintiff's property and the diversion of water so that it washed away his
1   land, an instruction which authorizes the jury to allow as damages the difference between the value of the premises prior to such wrongful acts and their value afterwards is erroneous where such acts occurred four years before the trial, since the depreciation might have been due in part to other causes than the defendant's acts.

Charge and evidence: *Presumption on appeal.*   An instruction that the measure of damages for injury to land was the difference
2   in value before and after such injury is erroneous, where there is no evidence as to the value and unless an erroneous instruction is shown to be harmless, it will be presumed to be prejudicial.

SAME. Plaintiff sought to recover damages for the reduction in the
rental value of his property resulting from odors caused from
stagnant waters, but made no complaint of certain bridges. He
testified, without objection, as to its rental value, and that the
8 rent would amount to a certain sum "if those bridges were removed
and the smell were taken away." Another testified that the rental
value would be increased one-half "if the nuisance were removed."
His other testimony showed that by "nuisance," he meant the
odors and gases, and not the bridges. *Held*, that there was sufficient evidence of value to justify an instruction that the measure
of damages would be the difference between the rental value as i
was and as it would be free from the odors and gases.

Appeal from Linn District Court.—HON. H. M. REMLEY,
Judge.

SATURDAY, OCTOBER 22, 1898.

ACTION at law to recover for injuries alleged to have
been caused by negligence and wrongful acts on the part of the
defendant in connection with one of its streets. There was
a trial by jury, and a verdict and judgment for the plaintiff.
The defendant appeals.—*Reversed.*

Warren Harman and *J. J. Powell,* for appellant.

. . *Bingham & Mekota,* for appellee.

ROBINSON, J.—The evidence tends to establish the following facts: The plaintiff is the owner of one entire lot and
parts of four other lots, which are situated about 1,200 feet
west of the Cedar river. They are between Third and Fourth
streets, and front southward on E avenue, which extends from
the river westward, and is commonly known as the "Vinton
Ditch." It was, at one time, a part of the Vinton road, but
about the year 1864 it commenced to wash out from a point
a considerable distance west of the river, and in the spring
of the year 1868 the ditch thus made reached the river. Since
that time it has been the outlet for a large quantity of surface
water, and in front of the property of the plaintiff it is a little more than sixty feet in width, occupying nearly the entire
street at that point, and is there about seven feet in depth.

When the plaintiff acquired title to the lot and parts of lots
in controversy, some twelve years before the trial was had in
the district court, the street was in much the same condition
that it is now, excepting that in it, in front of the lots, was an
island about twenty-five feet in length, twenty feet in width,
and seven feet in height.   That has been removed by the
defendant.   The premises in controversy have been included
within the territorial limits of the defendant since the year
1879.   The defendant has commenced to build a large sewer
in the center of the street, but it has not yet reached the property of the plaintiff.   The plaintiff has three dwelling houses
on the lot and parts of lots described, two of which front on
E avenue, and all of which are within fifteen feet of the
ditch.

The petition contains two counts. In the first the plaintiff
states that the defendant has negligently caused and permitted large volumes of surface water to be diverted from
their natural course and drained into E avenue, causing the
part of the avenue next to the plaintiff's property to be
washed away until the avenue has become impassable, and
causing a portion of his property to be undermined and
carried away, to his damage in the sum of one thousand dollars.   The second count includes the averments of the first
count, and states, in addition, that the defendant has permitted the accumulation of stagnant water, garbage, the car-
casses of animals, and other filth by the side of and near to
the property described, until the accumulations have become
green and putrid, emitting odors and poisonous gases, which
have endangered the health and life of the plaintiff and his
family, deprived him of the free, quiet, and peaceable possession of the property, and greatly injured and depreciated
its rental value, and that plaintiff has been compelled to fill
his lots where they were washed out at a great expense, to his
damage in the sum of one thousand dollar.

I.   It was the theory of the plaintiff that the defendant
had diverted to the ditch water which would naturally have
flowed elsewhere and that the removal of the island caused the

water in the ditch to be directed against his lots in such
manner as to wash portions of them away, thus making it
necessary to fill in and protect them, at considerable expense.

      The district court charged the jury in regard to it as
1   follows: "If you find, under the evidence, that the
      plaintiff is entitled to recover anything on the first
count of his petition, you are instructed that the measure of
his damages would be the difference in the value of his said
premises as they were just before defendant did remove said
dirt and make said additional ditches, if you so find,
and what they were worth after any of said lots was washed
away which would not have been washed away had the defendant not performed said acts." The defendant justly complains of that paragraph of the charge. The island was
removed about four years before the trial in the district court
was had, and within five years preceding that time the defendant made the changes which it is claimed diverted water from
other outlets to the ditch. This action was commenced on the
fourteenth day of March, 1896. The plaintiff states that he
was obliged to fill in his lots and protect them against the
water every year; that he drove piling and put in plank and
filling in the spring of each of the years 1892, 1893, 1894, and
1895. Under the charge given, the jury was authorized to
allow as damages the difference between the value of the premises just before the island was removed and the new ditches
were made and their value at any time afterwards, during the
entire term of four or more years, even though the depreciation might have been due in part to other causes. The charge
should have limited plaintiff's recovery to the damages caused
by the wrongful acts or negligence of the defendant.

      A further objection to the portion of the charge quoted
is that there was no evidence from which the jury could have
determined the difference in value to which the charge refers.

      Nothing in the record shows the value of the lots at any
2   time, and the difference in value, if any, which the
      jury was instructed to find, could only have been deter-
mined by conjecture. That it is erroneous to submit to a jury

a material issue of fact, concerning which there is no evidence is well settled. *Trapnell v. City of Red Oak Junction,* 76 Iowa, 744; *Stein v. City of Council Bluffs,* 72 Iowa, 180; *Reed v. Railroad Co.,* 57 Iowa, 23; *Moffitt v. Cressler,* 8 Iowa, 122. We do not think it is shown that the error was harmless, and we must presume that it was prejudicial.

II. The court charged the jury that, if the plaintiff was entitled to recovery on the second count of his petition, the measure of his recovery would be the difference between the rental value of the premises if they had been free from odor and noxious gases arising from the garbage and other filth in E avenue and as they were with such odors and gases present. The defendant complains of this on the ground that the evidence did not show what such difference 3 was. It appears that E avenue had been bridged at Third and also at Fourth street, although no complaint of the bridges is made in the petition. The plaintiff testified that he could rent his houses for but ten dollars per month, but that they would have brought eighteen to twenty dollars per month during the preceding five years "if those bridges were removed and the smell taken away." He did not give any other testimony in regard to the rental value of the property had the odors and gases from the ditch been prevented, and, so far as the portion of the charge relates to his testimony, the objection urged is well founded. But no objection was made to the testimony so given, and another witness stated that the rental value of the property would be increased one-half "if the nuisance were abated." His testimony shows that by "nuisance" he referred to the condition caused by the accumulation of rubbish and filth of various kinds in the ditch near the premises of the plaintiff, and the odors and gases therefrom, and not to the bridges. That testimony is not disputed. Therefore the claim that there was no evidence upon which to base the portion of the charge under consideration is not well founded. The conclusions we have expressed dispose of all questions presented in argument which are likely to arise during another trial. For the errors pointed out the judgment of the district court is REVERSED.

MRS. AGNES WHALEN v. THE LEISY BREWING COMPANY, et
al., Appellants.

Landlord and Tenant: LIQUOR SELLING: *Public policy.* In an action
to recover rent reserved in a lease it cannot be contended in defense
1 that the lease is void because the premises were let for traffic in
intoxicating liquors or that the business was unlawfully carried
on, when the lease expressly provided that the traffic should be
conducted in a legal manner.

EVIDENCE. It will be presumed in an action to recover rent reserved
in a lease by which the lessees covenanted to conduct the sale of
1 intoxicating liquors upon the premises in a lawful manner that
they had in mind sales as pharmacists which they might legally
make.

RENEWAL OF LEASE. On expiration of a written lease, a written
renewal was executed, but afterwards the lessor refused to allow
2 the lessee to use the premises until the mulct law, regulating the
sale of intoxicating liquors, had been complied with. After compliance therewith, the lessor verbally agreed that the lessee could
occupy the premises. *Held,* that the verbal agreement carried with
it all the terms and conditions of the prior written lease, so far as
applicable.

Appeal from Polk District Court.

MONDAY, OCTOBER 24, 1898.

ACTION at law to recover the rent reserved in a lease
made by plaintiff to defendants. Defendants pleaded that the
lease was made to enable them to violate the intoxicating
liquor laws of the state, and was and is void. The trial court
sustained plaintiff's demurrer to certain parts of the answer,
and rendered judgment for plaintiff for the full amount of
her claim. Defendant's appeal.—*Affirmed.*

J. F. Conrad and *T. L. Sellers* for appellants.

Nugent & Connolly for appellee.

DEEMER, C. J.—The lease was made upon condition that the second party should "(2) use said premises, viz. store room No. 216 and basement thereof, for the traffic in intoxicating liquors, and for no other purpose, and only in manner and form as provided by law. This lease to terminate at the option of the first party, in the event that the said second party violates the laws of Iowa in the use of said premises. (3) Not permit any unlawful business to be conducted thereon, and deliver the same free and clear of any tax, lien, claim or demand under the law taxing the traffic in intoxicating liquors." "(11) That any failure on the part of the party of the second part to comply with any of the terms and conditions of this lease shall make the whole amount of the rent, for the said term due, and the party of the first part may proceed to collect the same." This lease expired on the first day of June, 1895. On the sixth of June, 1895, a written renewal was executed by the parties, by the terms of which the lease was extended upon the same conditions as the original lease. Defendants pleaded in answer that at the time the renewal lease was executed the provisions of the mulct law had not been complied with in Polk county, for that the requisite petition of consent had not beeen filed with the county auditor, and that plaintiff refused to let defendants occupy or use said premises under the renewal. They also pleaded that thereafter, and on the fifth day of July, 1895, the petition was secured, and that plaintiff then verbally agreed that defendants might use and occupy the premises for the purpose of trafficking in intoxicating liquors; that they are willing to pay the reasonable rental value, and consent to judgment against them for about half of plaintiff's claim. They also further pleaded that the lease was made for the purpose of allowing them to traffic in intoxicating liquors, and was therefore void. The trial court sustained a demurrer to this answer, and rendered judgment for the amount due under the written lease.

In the case of *McKeever v. Beacom*, 101 Iowa, 173, we held that a landlord may recover his rent for a building used

for the purpose of carrying on the liquor business under the
provisions of the mulct law. Appellants contend, how-
1   ever, that they leased the building for an unlawful purpose, and that they did in fact do an unlawful business
therein. References to the lease will show that, while the
premises were leased to appellants in order that they might
traffic in intoxicating liquors, it was distinctly agreed that
that traffic should be lawful. The purpose was not to aid
defendants in the violation of law, but to enable them to conduct the traffic in a legal manner. As we have said, if they
complied with the provisions of the mulct law, the traffic was
not illegal in such sense as that the lease should be avoided. It
was evidently intended that defendants should do those things
which would enable them to sell under the provisions of chapter 62, Acts Twenty-fifth General Assembly, and if they failed
to do so they cannot be heard to say that by reason of their
failure the lease should be avoided. Again, the defendants might
have made lawful sales as pharmacists, and, as they covenanted to conduct a lawful business, it may well be presumed
that they had in mind such sales. The verbal lease of
2   date July 5, 1895, pleaded by defendants, was, in
effect, a renewal of the prior lease, and carried with
it all the terms and conditions of that lease so far as applicable. *Newell v. Sanford,* 13 Iowa, 191. If not a renewal, it
was an agreement that the written renewal should apply to
the changed conditions, and, in either event, the defendants
should pay the rent reserved. The matters pleaded in answer
do not constitute a defense to plaintiff's cause of action, and
the demurrer was properly sustained. AFFIRMED.

W. C. and ELIZA COOPER, Executors, v. PARK DISBROW,
et al., Appellants.

Judgment: SETTING DEFAULT ASIDE. The district court may vacate
a default judgment entered against certain creditors of a bank
where on the face of the record the parties seeking to set aside .
2   the judgment were not in default at the time it was entered but

were entitled to judgment on an allegation in a cross petition
brought by a creditor in behalf of herself and all the other creditors of the bank.

LACHES. The fact that certain creditors of an insolvent had neglected
    for years, while litigation concerning creditors' rights was pend-
4 ing, to actively participate therein, does not estop them from
    asserting rights which they had been deprived of by a judgment
    entered by default, when in fact they were not in default.

APPEAL: *Review.* In a proceeding for the appointment of a receiver
    for an insolvent bank, a cross petition by several stockholders was
    filed for the adjustment of all creditors' claims against the stock-
1 holders, making the bank and all the creditors parties thereto, and
    notice was given to all except three. An order was made therein,
    allowing cross petitioners to prosecute the petition as a separate
    suit, and ordering all the creditors to plead by a day certain.
    Judgment was entered against petitioners for the amount of stock
    held by them, and against certain creditors by reason of their
    alleged default, barring them from relief against petitioners.
    Held, that on appeal from an order setting aside the judgment
    against the defaulting creditors no specific order can be made as
    to the judgment against the stockholders.

JUDGMENT BY CONSENT. The fact that the record contains no evi-
    dence does not justify an assumption that the judgment therein
3 was entered by consent, since Code, 1873, section 2361, allowing
    the entry of judgments by consent and providing that, if not
    entered in open court, the judgment agreed to shall be in writing,
    signed and filed by the clerk, contemplates that the agreement
    shall appear in the record.

Appeal from Cass District Court.—HON. N. W. MACY,
Judge.

MONDAY, OCTOBER 24, 1898.

IN DECEMBER, 1893, Isaac Dickerson, as a stockholder,
brought a suit in equity to wind up the affairs of the Cass
County Bank, it being insolvent, and procured the appointment of a receiver,—Theodore G. Steinke. Thereafter suits
were commenced against the bank and its stockholders by creditors of the bank. One ground of recovery against the stockholders was a provision in the articles of incorporation for
double liability. The appellants in this case are Park Disbrow
and some twenty-eight others, who were creditors of the bank,

and are defendants, and known in its proceedings as cross petitioners. In May, 1894, T. N. Heselgrave, in his own behalf
and that of sixteen others, being creditors of the bank, commenced a suit by attachment against the bank and its stockholders, among which were W. C. and Eliza Cooper, as
executors and trustees under the will of one John W. Russell,
deceased. Throughout the case the Coopers are parties only in
their representative capacity, and may be referred to by their
own name. They were the owners of twelve thousand dollars
of the stock of the bank, and were also creditors of the bank.
Cornelia K. Winslow was the owner of six thousand dollars of
the stock of the bank, a creditor, and a defendant in the attachment proceeding. The case of Dickerson against Cass County
Bank is designated in the record as number 4069. In September, 1894, the Coopers filed their cross petition in the original
case,—that of Dickerson against Cass County Bank, No.
4069,—making Dickerson, the Cass County Bank, and all the
creditors of the bank—more than six hundred in all—parties
thereto, and gave notice to all except three, they being Ernestine Cotton, Susan Osgood, and Michael McEniry. The cross
petition asked, upon an averment of facts, relief as follows:
"That all matters and claims of individual liability against
the several stockholders to the various creditors of said Cass
County Bank be fully adjusted, ascertained, settled and determined, and that all parties therein be compelled to set forth
their respective claims against the stockholders of said Cass
County Bank and said cross petitioners, and that the court
grant full, complete, equitable relief in the premises." To
that petition the appellants in this case, Disbrow and others,
and Cornelia K. Winslow appeared, but none of the other
creditors. On motion of the appellants, the cross petition was
stricken from the files "so far as to strike therefrom all that
part thereof in relation to the double liability of the stockholders of the said Cass County Bank, and in relation to the attachment of the private property of the stockholders, and the
enjoining of suits against the stockholders on account of the
misjoinder of actions." To the above is added the following

order: "Leave is, however, given the cross petitioners to docket said matter so stricken from their cross petition as a separate suit, and the clerk of said court is so ordered to docket said matters, and the cause, when docketed, shall be entitled in the name of these cross petitioners as plaintiffs, and against all the defendants named in said cross petition, and the said cross petitioners are hereby allowed to prosecute said cause as a separate action; and it is ordered that all defendants to said petition, served with notice, shall plead to the said cause when so docketed, on or before noon of the second day of the November term, 1894, of this court,—to all of which finding both of said parties at the time except." On the twenty-third of November, 1894, the Coopers caused to be docketed what is known as "Equity Case No. 4411," being, in substance, the cross action in case No. 4069, with W. C. and Eliza Cooper, executors and trustees, plaintiffs. This case—No. 4411—is the one now on appeal in this court, and will be the one hereafter referred to, unless otherwise expressed. To the petition in this case appellants and Cornelia K. Winslow answered, but none of the other creditors of the bank, notwithstanding the order of the court above set out, except C. R. Winslow, a creditor, who presented an answer and cross petition. Appellants filed answers to plaintiffs' petition, and each filed his cross petition against plaintiffs, and also against Cornelia K. Winslow and other stockholders, based substantially on the grounds set forth in their several actions at law then pending against plaintiffs and other stockholders; and their several actions at law were, by agreement of parties, and order of the court, transferred to the equity docket, and consolidated with this case. Cornelia K. Winslow also answered the petition in this case, admitting that she owned six thousand dollars of the stock of the bank, and alleging that in the summer of 1893 she signed notes with the Cass County Bank, on which she became liable, and which she has paid, and will be compelled to pay thirty thousand dollars; and she asks for a full accounting and adjustment of the claim. It is also to be said that plaintiffs were depositors in the Cass County Bank in the sum of some sixteen or seventeen thousand dollars, which they ask to have considered in the adjustment. Denials were filed so as to put in issue all counterclaims or cross demands, and thereafter the court gave judgment for appellants, on their cross petitions, against Cornelia K. Winslow for six thousand dollars and denied to her any offset because of her claim against the bank. The court also gave to appellants, as cross petitioners, a judgment against plaintiffs, as representatives of the estate of John W. Russell, for twelve thousand dollars, and denied to the estate any relief on account of their claim as depositors. The court also entered the default of the defendants served, but not answering, and estopped them from making any claim as to matters involved in the issues presented by plaintiffs and cross petitioners. These judgments were entered May 21, 1896. On the second of June following, Theodore G. Steinke and some twenty-one others, including Cotton, Osgood, and McEniry—creditors not served—filed a motion to set aside the default and decree entered May 21, 1896. The motion makes it appear that the movers had never been served with notice in the proceedings in which the Coopers are plaintiffs; that they filed their claims under orders of the court, in the suit of Dickerson against Cass County Bank, and that in said suit an order was entered establishing their respective claims; that none of the movers were, by original notice or otherwise, notified of the kind of proceedings adopted in this case, by which they were adjudged not to be entitled to share with all other creditors of the bank in what might be adjudged to be due from stockholders on account of their statutory liability; that they believed that the filing and allowance of their claims was all that was necessary to entitle them to share in a distribution of money so received, and they did not believe such a decree would be entered. A motion to strike part of this motion was filed, and evidence taken, and upon the submission the court denied the motion to strike, and sustained the motion to set aside the default and decree. From this order Park Disbrow and twenty-one others appealed.—*Affirmed.*

Willard & Willard and *De Lano & Meredith* for appellants.

H. S. Winslow, J. D. Critchfield, Phelps & Temple, and *John W. Scott* for appellees, W. C. and Eliza Cooper and Cornelia K. Winslow.

J. B. Rockafellow for Theo. G. Steinke and others.

GRANGER, J.—I. We may first notice the attitude of plaintiffs and Mrs. Cornelia K. Winslow on the appeal. It will be remembered that, as to plaintiffs, there is a judgment against them in favor of the appellants for twelve thousand dollars, and as to Mrs. Winslow there is a judgment in favor of appellants for six thousand dollars. These judgments are evidently based on the statutory liability of stockholders for an amount equal to the amount of stock held by them.

1   From these judgments there is no appeal, and no question is made here as to their validity. Their contention in this court is that the judgments so entered are the full measure of their liability to any and all creditors of the bank, and that, in no event, should there be such a change in the proceedings as to increase their liability over the amount of the judgments entered against them. It is their express claim that they shall be so protected as that they shall not pay these judgments, and then be liable to other creditors of the bank for a like amount, so as to bear a double burden. This appeal brings in question alone the validity of the order of the court in setting aside the default and decree so as to permit a new trial. If we reverse the order, the effect will be to restore and perpetuate the judgments as they were entered. If we affirm the order the effect will be to leave the case without judgment for the parties to proceed as advised. As we view the record, we cannot make any specific order as to the plaintiffs and Mrs. Winslow, but can only affirm or reverse the order, as our conclusion may require, and leave it to the law, or to further procedure under it, to fix the rights of the parties.

II. The articles of incorporation of the Cass County Bank contain a provision for liability of stockholders much to the same effect as our statute, since enacted, by which stockholders are made liable for an additional amount equal to the stock owned by them. The act creating this liability was considered in the somewhat late case of *State v. Bank,* 103 Iowa, 549. Our reference to that case is only to call attention to the application to be made of the fund derived from stockholders by virtue of such a liability. It is there said that the fund is to be distributed equally among all the creditors of the corporation in proportion to the amount due each. Such is the language of the statute creating the liability. See section 2 of the act (Acts of the Eighteenth General Assembly chapter 208.). We have called attention to this provision of the law in view of some points urged in argument. The judgments entered by the district court gave to a part of the creditors of the corporation eighteen thousand dollars of such a fund, and in terms estopped the other creditors from making any claim, in the following language: "It is further ordered, adjudged, and decreed by the court that the other defendants, being those in default, having failed to appear and set up their claims, be, and they are hereby, forever barred and estopped from setting up and making any claim arising out of the matters set out in plaintiffs' petition and set out in defendant's cross petition." The order of the court in setting aside the default and decree is, in so far as it is important, as follows: "And the said motions being duly submitted to the court on this fourteenth day of July, 1896, the court overrules the said motion filed by the said Park Disbrow et al., to which ruling they at the time except; and the said default heretofore entered against the other creditors of the Cass County Bank, and the judgments rendered against the said Coopers and the said C. K. Winslow are set aside, and held for naught, upon the grounds that the creditors of the Cass County Bank served with notice of the cross petition of W. C. and Ann Eliza Cooper, executor and executrix, etc., were not in default at the time the same were taken and entered, but had an answer and cross petition on file in the third count of the answer and cross petition of C. R. Winslow, filed February 10, 1896, made for and on behalf of all of the creditors of the Cass County Bank, and were entitled to have the issues as tendered on their behalf determined, and their rights preserved; and it is found that no original notice was served upon the defendants Michael McEniry, Ernestine Cotton, and Susan Osgood, and the same entry and judgment made as to them." It should be borne in mind that the decree was based on the default of these defendants and creditors. The answer and cross petition of C. R. Winslow entitled her to, and in fact gave her, equal rights in the judgment with the other appellants. In the third count of her cross petition she alleges that the action is brought on behalf of herself and all the other creditors, depositors of the Cass County Bank, and the count is based on the double liability of the stockholders under the law. The averments of that part of the cross petition entitled the other creditors in whose behalf she pleaded to the same measure of relief she was entitled to, unless it should be denied them because of a difference in facts when the proofs were submitted. It is said the judgments, as entered, were by consent. This can mean only that appellants and plaintiffs so consented. There is no pretense of a consent by those moving to set aside the decree. The record, however, does not show a judgment by consent. In so far as it shows how the issues were submitted, it was upon evidence taken. The record shows that a trial was had upon the claims made against plaintiffs and C. K. Winslow and "such evidence as was offered by the parties." The record, however contains no evidence. If we may assume that there was no evidence, still it does not follow, as a legal conclusion, that the judgments were by consent. This fact is important, because appellants, in argument, place great stress upon it, and claim for the judgments, because by consent, peculiar legal attributes, in that they may not be as readily disturbed or set aside as other judgments. In fact, it is urged that they are practically invulnerable to an attack

3

like the one in this case. To make a judgment by consent or
agreement, we think the fact must appear of record. Our
law provides for a judgment by agreement, and that it may
be entered at any time, and, if not done in open court, the
judgment agreed to shall be in writing, signed and filed with
the clerk, who shall enter the same accordingly. Code 1873,
section 2861. The law evidently contemplates that, to constitute a judgment by agreement, the fact that it is such a
judgment shall appear in the proceedings. In *Hershee v. Her-
shey,* 15 Iowa, 185, it is not held that it must so appear,
but the court refused to consider a judgment (one by
argument) because the record failed to show the fact.
That it is competent for the court to vacate and set
aside its judgments is conceded. See *Taylor v. Lusk,* 9
Iowa, 444; *Boals v. Shules,* 29 Iowa, 507. It is said
that the right of the court to set aside a judgment is not an
arbitrary one, but is a discretionary one, controlled by fixed
legal principles. The proposition is, no doubt, a correct one.
We can hardly conceive of a stronger reason for setting aside
a judgment than that it has been erroneously entered to the
prejudice of parties. By the judgments in this case the parties asking their vacation were adjudged in default when they
were not. As a result of such a judgment, they were denied
a recovery which, assuming a statutory liability of plaintiffs
and C. K. Winslow, they were absolutely entitled to, and what
belonged to them is given to appellants. If the judgments are
to stand, the result is a forfeiture, by these movers, of what
belonged to them, and the appellants are to take it because of
what is charged as neglect, during this proceeding, to protect
their rights. Of course, rights are thus lost and gained, but

4
such results can only be justified under the plain
requirements of the law. It is urged that these parties had neglected for years, while the litigation was
going on, to come in, and take part in securing the rights of
the creditors, while appellants had been active in the prosecution of suits. This is likely true, but it does not reach the
merits of the question before us. One of these appellants had
thought it advisable to bring them in, and prosecute for them;

and being thus in the case, and on the face of the record, entitled to judgment for just what the appellants were, and being erroneously adjudged in default, and, as a consequence, denied a recovery, and when the court below has discovered this, and set aside the default and decree, to correct the error, ought its ruling to be disturbed? We do not regard what occurred during the years of litigation as controlling. What we do regard as controlling is that on the twenty-first day of May, 1896, when the judgments were entered, on the face of the record, these parties, seeking to set aside the judgments, were not in default, and, with the exception of the three not in court, were entitled to judgment. It is said in argument that the decrees were prepared and agreed to by the plaintiffs and appellants, and signed by the court. If so, the appellants, barring C. K. Winslow, secured judgments unwarranted by the record, because of which result the court set them aside. The error was not the result of *laches* or neglect. It was not because, as the case stood, the parties were not entitled to relief, but because the court signed an erroneous decree, both as to the facts and the law, as the case was presented. Nothing more need be said than that none of the considerations urged ought to disturb the order of the court in setting aside the decrees. AFFIRMED.

UPTON E. TRAER, Appellant, v. THE STATE BOARD OF MEDICAL EXAMINERS, *et al.*

106
140
140

Certiorari: REVIEW. The action of the state board of medical exam-
1 iners in revoking the certificate of a practicing physician cannot be cured by *certiorari* proceedings, where it did not proceed arbi-
6 trarily or unreasonably, but considered evidence and afforded the accused opportunity to defend himself against the charges made of the nature of which he was notified. *Certiorari* is not available to review the sufficiency and competency of testimony.

Evidence: BEST: *Transcript.* A certified transcript of documents
1-2 filed in the office of the clerk of the district court is under Code,
3-4 1873, section 3702, evidence of equal credibility with the original so filed.

SAME. Under Code, 1873, section 3702, making a certified transcript
of equal credit with an original, a certified transcript of a coro-
1   ner's return containing the written evidence and the names of
2   witnesses before an inquisition, as required by Code, 1873, section
3   865, though such evidence was adduced by means of affidavits, is
proper evidence before the state board of medical examiners in a
proceeding to revoke a certificate to practice medicine, where it
was not objected to.

Oaths: CONSTRUCTION OF STATUTE: *Board of medical examiners.* The
provision of Acts Twenty-first General Assembly, chapter 104, that
the president or any member of the board of state medical exam-
5   iners may administer oaths and take testimony in relation to matters pertaining to their official duties is not exclusive and does
not prevent consideration by the board of evidence not so taken.

Appeal from Polk District.—HON. C. P. HOLMES, Judge.

MONDAY, OCTOBER 24, 1898.

ACTION of *certiorari* to review the proceedings of the
State Board of Medical Examiners which terminated in the
revocation of the certificate previously issued to the plaintiff
which authorized him to practice as a physician and surgeon
within this state. A writ of *certiorari* was, by authority of
the district court of Polk county, issued on the petition of
the plaintiff, and a return made thereto. A hearing was had
in that court, and judgment was rendered in favor of the
defendants, the board and its members and officers, for costs.
The plaintiff appeals.—*Affirmed.*

J. D. & C. Nichols and *Nichols & Kirkland* for appellant.

Milton Remley, Attorney General, for appellees.

ROBINSON, J.—The petition states that the plaintiff is a
physician and surgeon and a resident of this state; that on the
twenty-fourth day of January, 1887, the State Board of Medical Examiners issued to him a certificate authorizing him to
practice his profession in this state; that about the thirty-
first day of October, 1894, the board undertook to revoke the
certificate, and, in so doing, exceeded its jurisdiction, and

acted illegally, in that no information or charge was ever preferred against the plaintiff, and no evidence was offered or produced before the board against the plaintiff, and the order of revocation was not based upon any charge or evidence. The return to the writ made by the defendants shows the following facts: On a date not given, a petition purporting to be signed by five physicians of O'Brien county and two physicians of neighboring counties was presented to the board.

1   The petition asked that the certificate of the plaintiff be revoked for incompetency, and was accompanied by a certified transcript of all the evidence submitted to the coroner of O'Brien county, at an inquest held in April, 1894, upon the dead body of Mrs. Carrie B. Hitchings, and the findings of the jurors. The evidence consisted of an affidavit made by Mrs. Hitchings the day before she died, and in the belief, as stated in the affidavit, that she could live but a short time; the testimony of several witnesses which appears to have been given in the presence of the coroner and jurors, and then taken down in writing, and signed by the witnesses; the affidavits of several persons who do not seem to have been otherwise examined; and minutes of an autopsy made for the purpose of ascertaining the cause of the death of Mrs. Hitchings, and verified by a physician who acted as clerk during the autopsy. The minutes of the proceedings of the board show that at its meeting for May, 1894, the secretary read the petition; that it was received, and the secretary was directed to inform Dr. Traer of the charges, and to furnish him with a copy of them, and to notify him to be present at the next meeting of the board, and show cause why his certificate should not be revoked because of incompetency; that afterwards, pursuant to the direction so given, the secretary furnished Dr. Traer with a copy of the charges against him, and informed him that the case would come on for hearing at the August meeting of the board; that, at the August meeting Dr. Traer was represented by an attorney upon whose application the case was continued until the next meeting of the board; that at that meeting, which commenced on the first day of the next

November, the case was called, but Dr. Traer did not appear
in person nor by any representative; that the secretary
informed the board that he had notified Dr. Traer and his
attorneys of the time and place of the meeting, and that he
should be present and show cause why his certificate should
not be revoked for palpable evidence of incompetency as
charged. Thereupon the charges were read, togther with the
evidence submitted to the coroner to which we have already
referred. No other evidence was considered by the board. The
question of revoking the certificate of the plaintiff was then
submitted, and a unanimous vote of the members of the board
in favor of such revocation was given. The secretary
announced the vote, and the president declared that the certificate was revoked. The cause was submitted in the district
court, on the petition of the plaintiff and the answer of the
defendants and their return to the writ of *certiorari,* including
the evidence upon which the board acted.

The only contention made by the appellant in this court
is that "no evidence was ever offered or produced before the
board against the appellant." This claim involves a consideration of the character of the evidence upon which, in
2   the absence of objection made at the time, the board
may act. Chapter 104 of the Acts of the Twenty-first
General Assembly was designed to regulate the practice of
medicine and surgery in this state. It provided for the issuing by the State Board of Examiners of certificates which
would entitle the holders thereof to practice medicine, surgery, and obstetrics within the state, and authorized the board
to revoke a certificate whose holder should have been convicted of a felony committed in the practice of his profession
or in connection therewith, or "for palpable evidence of incompetency." The statute does not prescribe the practice to be
followed in cases instituted for the revocation of certificates;
and although it may, when practicable, follow somewhat the
methods of the courts, yet, from the nature of the board and
the character of the duties it is required to perform, a more
flexible practice than that allowable in the courts must, of

necessity, be followed in many cases. The person whose right
it is to hold a certificate which has been issued to him should
be given a fair opportunity to meet the charges and evidence
against him. What would be "palpable evidence of incom-
tency," within the meaning of the statute is not easy to define,
although it must be sufficient to make plain and obvious the
incompetency of the accused to practice as a physician and
surgeon ; and we are of the opinion that, in the absence of
objection, evidence which tends to prove or disprove the competency of the accused my be considered, even though it is
not the best evidence which could be produced for that purpose. As a general rule, affidavits are not admitted as evidence
upon the trial of an issue of fact, unless as admissions against
the person who made or used them. 1 Enc. Pl. & Prac, 334.
See, also, *Ashbach v. Railway Co.,* 86 Iowa, 101. But the
use of affidavits as presumptive evidence of material facts is
authorized by statute in many instances in proceedings in
court, as well as in other cases. The use of affidavits is so
common and well known that it is not necessary to refer to
particular cases. It was said in *Geyer v. Douglass,* 85 Iowa,
99, that "affidavits are recognized as competent evidence on
the hearing of applications for temporary injunction and for
other purposes, and, by agreement, they are frequently treated
as·competent evidence on the final hearing of a cause. There
can be no objection to their being so used when all par-
3   ties in interest assent to it." It is true that in this
·   case the original affidavits, records of the oral testimony taken in writing, of the autopsy, the findings of the
jurors, and the coroner's report, were not before the board;
that its action in revoking the certificate was based upon a
transcript of the documents and record specified; and that
the plaintiff was not actually before the board when it considered the transcript, and did not formally assent to its use
as evidence. But he had been duly served with notice to
appear, and had done so, and obtained a continuance, at a
previous meeting of the board; and it was as fully authorized

to act as though he had been before it in person or by a duly-authorized representative. The coroner who held the inquest over the dead body of Mrs. Hitchings was required to return to the district court the inquisition, the written evidence, and a list of the witnesses who testified to material matter. Code 1873, section 365. He did so. His return with the accompanying documents, was filed in the office of the clerk of the district court, and that officer certified the transcript which was used by the board. The transcript so certified was evidence of equal credibility with the originals so filed. Code 1873, section 3702. It thus appears that the transcript considered by the board was entitled to the credit which should have been given to the original document and records had they been presented to the board. We do not overlook the fact that the originals would not have been evidence in a court of law, which could have been introduced over the objection of the plaintiff; but they constituted evidence competent for some purposes, and tended to show that the certificate of the plaintiff should be revoked. Although, in law, he had the opportunity to object to their use, he did not do so. The board did not act without evidence, but, taking the view most favorable to the plaintiff, acted upon evidence which should have been excluded had objections been duly made. The provision of the statute which gave to the president or any member of the board authority to administer oaths and take testimony in matters relating to their duties as examiners, if it applied to the revocation of certificates, was not exclusive, and did not prevent the consideration by the board of evidence not so taken.

It was within the jurisdiction of the board to determine the competency and sufficiency of the evidence submitted to it, and, if it erred in admitting evidence or in giving to it undue weight, the error cannot be corrected by *certiorari* proceedings. *Hildreth v. Crawford,* 65 Iowa, 339, 345; *Association v. Schrader,* 87 Iowa, 659, and cases therein cited. The action of the board is not shown to have been arbitrary or unreasonable. On the contrary, it was

taken only after the plaintiff had been given due notice and
sufficient opportunity to defend himself against the charges
and the showing made; and, if an error was committed, it
cannot be corrected in this action. We do not find any ground
for disturbing the judgment of the district court, and it is
AFFIRMED.

Lois STOLTENBERG, Appellant, v. THE CONTINENTAL INSUR-
ANCE COMPANY.

Insurance: VACANCY. A policy of fire insurance conditioned that it
shall be void if the building covered by it "be or become vacant
1 or unoccupied" is invalidated where at the time loss occurred the
premises had been vacated by a tenant and were not occupied by
a subsequent lessee.

SAME. Farm buildings are not "occupied" within the meaning of an
insurance policy stipulating that it shall be void if the insured
5 property becomes vacant or unoccupied, when the premises were
rented and cultivated by one who lived near by but made no use
of the farm dwelling house.

Evidence: HEARSAY. Testimony that witness heard another tell
2 insurer's agent that he was occupying the insured premises is
hearsay as against the insurer.

ADMISSION. A letter written by an insurance agent to its general
4 adjuster, that the premises had been let and sublet, and the subtenant had left them about three hours before the fire, is not an
admission of their occupancy.

PRESUMPTIONS. A building proved to have been vacated by a tenant
3 will be presumed to have been unoccupied at the time of a fire
which occurred shortly thereafter unless it is shown that a subsequent lessee had taken possession.

Appeal from Dickinson District Court.—HON. W. B. QUAR-
TON, Judge.

MONDAY, OCTOBER 24, 1898.

ACTION on fire insurance policy. Judgment for defendant on verdict directed by the court, and plaintiff appeals.—
Affirmed.

J. W. Cory for appellant.

McVey & McVey for appellee.

LADD, J.—The policy of the defendant, dated September 30, 1892, covered the dwelling house and barn situated on plaintiff's farm, in Osceola county, consumed by fire May 20, 1893. On May 25th of the same year its agent at Lake Park mailed to the general western agent of the defendant particulars of the loss, as required, on one of its blanks. This was not accompanied by any affidavits or proofs of loss, and none were ever furnished. The plaintiff alleged waiver of such proofs, and the defendant pleaded forfeiture of the policy by reason of the transfer of title, and vacancy of the building. At the conclusion of the plaintiff's evidence, the jury, under the instructions of the court, returned a verdict for the defendant. Conceding that the company's adjuster, Henry Paine, had authority to deny liability, and that such denial dispensed with proofs of loss, as a useless ceremony,—*Boyd v. Insurance Co.,* 70 Iowa, 325; *Carson v. Insurance Co.,* 62 Iowa, 440; *Tayloe v. Insurance Co.,* 9 How. 390; *Western Home Ins. Co. v. Richardson,* 40 Neb. 1 (58 N. W. Rep. 597),—the

1   ruling of the district court must be sustained because of the vacancy of the building. The policy contains a condition that it shall be null and void if the building insured "be or become vacant or unoccupied," and to this especial attention is directed in another portion of the contract. The vacancy of the buildings at the time of the fire is established by the undisputed evidence. The plaintiff was about to leave Lake Park in the spring of 1893, and directed M. D. Green to rent the farm on which these buildings were located, to another, in event the tenant concluded to move away. Upon being informed the tenant had left, Green leased the premises to one Smith, living south of the land. Green testified: "I cannot give you the name of the man who occupied the premises when plaintiff left. I didn't know him. It was a man with his family, living on the land. I do not know how long he had

been living there. When I went down to rent the farm, the plaintiff's man who had been living on it had just moved out. Mr. Smith, to whom I rented this farm, lived south of this land. I do not think Mr. Smith lived on the land, or moved onto it. The contract between Mr. Smith and me was verbal. He was to pay grain rent. I don't think Mr. Smith was actually living on the land when the fire occurred." From this it clearly appears that the tenant in possession when the policy was issued had vacated the buildings a short time before the fire, and that they were not occupied by the subsequent

2   lessee. On cross-examination, Green stated that he heard one Bowden tell Paine that he was occupying the buildings when the fire occurred, and this was stricken out because incompetent and hearsay. That it was hearsay admits of no doubt. If plaintiff claimed such occupancy, Bowden or others who knew the facts should have been

3   called to so testify. The buildings, appearing to have been recently vacated by the tenant, are presumed to continue in that condition, unless shown to have been subsequently occupied. A letter by Paine to the general adjuster, dated June 20, 1893, was received in evidence, and it contained this statement: "The farm has been rented to

4   a Mr. Smith, living near, and he had sublet the buildings to a single man, who was running a breaking outfit. He left the place about 7 A. M., and fire was discovered between 10 and 11 A. M.; all the farm buildings being destroyed." But this does not admit the occupancy of the buildings. It goes no further than stating they had been sublet. Whether the man had moved into the house, or was living there, is not disclosed by the record.

The appellant insists that change of possession is not pleaded. While the policy prohibits any such change, the defendant does not urge forfeiture on that ground. But that

5   the policy was suspended because the buildings were vacant and occupied is expressly averred in the answer.

We understand the appellant to say that the control and use of the premises by Smith as tenant, without living in the house, would obviate this condition of the policy. To this we cannot assent. Occupancy of a house implies its actual use as a dwelling house; and that of the barn, its use as is ordinarily incident to a barn belonging to an occupied house. The insurer has a right to the care involved in such an occupancy. *Ashworth v. Insurance Co.*, 112 Mass., 422. A house is unoccupied when no one is living in it. *Cook v. Insurance Co.*, 70 Mo. 612; *Insurance Co. v. Padfield,* 78 Ill. 169; *Feshe v. Insurance Co.*, 74 Iowa, 677; *Dennison v. Insurance Co.*, 52 Iowa, 457; *Sexton v. Insurance Co.*, 69 Iowa, 99; *Herman v. Insurance Co.*, 85 N. Y. 163; *Weidert v. Insurance Co.*, 19 Or. 261 (24 Pac. Rep. 242).

As the undisputed evidence showed the policy void because of the buildings being unoccupied at the time of the fire, the ruling of the district court in directing a verdict must be approved. Our conclusion renders unnecessary any ruling on the motions filed. AFFIRMED.

DES MOINES SAVINGS BANK v. E. J. GOODE and SARAH D. GOODE, Appellants.

Fraudulent Conveyance: EVIDENCE. By quitclaim, reciting only a nominal consideration a son, engaged in the real estate business, and insolvent, conveyed a house to his father, and then contracted for repairs thereon, with persons knowing of the transfer. The father and son testified that the repairs were contracted for at the son's expense, as part of the contract of sale, and that the 3 true consideration was the assumption of a mortgage on the premises, and a credit on a debt due the father from the son; there being a discrepancy as to the amount of such credit. The son testified that he kept deeds executed in blank by his wife, in his office, and the quitclaim, with the nominal consideration written in, was the only one on hand at the time. *Held*, insufficient to establish fraud on the part of the son in contracting for the improvements.

SAME. A conveyance by a son to his father is not shown to have been fraudulent because the grantee states that the consideration was 3 eight thousand dollars, while the grantor testified that it was nine thousand, when the former's evidence was taken by deposition in the absence of his books of accounts.

Liens: CONTRACTS. A plumbing company, which, after request of one engaged in the business of buying, improving and selling real estate, did work for him on credit on property which it knew he had sold, cannot, upon discovery of his insolvency, enforce a
1 mechanic's lien against the grantee or owner, with neither of whom it sustained contract relations, and for whom the debtor did not act as agent.

INSOLVENCY. It is not a sufficient reason for establishing a lien against property owned by a third person, for plumbing work done at the request and upon the credit of one engaged in the improvement and sale of real estate, that such person is insolvent
2 and therefore indifferent as to whether personal judgment is obtained against him.

Contracts: PERSONAL LIABILITY: *Sale.* The grantee is not person-
1-2 ally liable for repairs on the premises made under a contract with
4 the grantor, even where he stipulated for such repairs in the contract of purchase.

SAME. Where the grantor, as part of the contract of sale, undertakes
2 to repair the premises, and after the conveyance contracts there-
4 for with a third person having knowledge of the conveyance, and who does the work on the grantor's personal credit, the property
1 is not subject to a mechanic's lien for such repairs.

Appeal from Polk District Court.—HON. W. F. CONRAD, Judge.

MONDAY, OCTOBER 24, 1898.

PLAINTIFF, as assignee, of the Scoville Plumbing Company, brings this action in equity to recover judgment against E. J. Goode for nine hundred and six dollars and fifty cents and interest, and for the establishment and foreclosure of a mechanic's lien on real estate described. Defendants answer, joining issues as will appear in the opinion. Decree was rendered in favor of the plaintiff as prayed. Defendants appealed. —*Reversed.*

Bishop, Bowen & Fleming and *W. G. Harvison* for appellant.

Berryhill & Henry for appellee.

GIVEN, J.—I. In the spring of 1893, and for several years prior thereto, L. W. Goode, son of the defendants, was engaged in buying, selling and improving real estate in the city of Des Moines. The firm of Laing & Scoville, predecessors to the Scoville Plumbing Company, did the plumbing work for L. W. Goode in the buildings built and remodeled by him up to the time said firm was dissolved, and thereafter such plumbing was done by the Scoville Plumbing Company.

1   The account with Laing & Scoville was fully settled, and does not enter into this controversy. In April, 1892, L. W. Goode acquired title, by purchase, to the property in question,—a residence property, then having an old house thereon. November 8, 1892, L. W. Goode conveyed said property, by quitclaim deed, for the recited consideration of one dollar, to the defendant E. J. Goode. This deed was filed for record November 10, 1892, and thereafter, on October 21, 1893, E. J. Goode conveyed said property to the defendant Sarah D. Goode for the consideration of eight thousand dollars. After the conveyance to E. J. Goode, L. W. Goode proceeded to remodel the old house according to plans prepared by him and his mother, and contracted with the Scoville Plumbing Company to furnish the materials and do the plumbing in said house according to said plans. As soon as the house was completed, the defendants took possession thereof as their residence. The account of the Scoville Plumbing Company for this labor and materials was kept against L. W. Goode, and on August 31, 1893, a verified statement thereof as against him was filed for a mechanic's lien against said real estate. On May 1, 1895, another verified statement of the same account, as against E. J. Goode and Sarah D. Goode, was filed for a mechanic's lien against the same property. The statement for the lien first filed was assigned to the plaintiff by the Scoville Plumbing Company on the first day of February, 1895, and the second statement was also so assigned on May 1, 1895. The account shows the first item to be of date December 20, 1892, and the last June 2, 1893.

II. We may first notice the contention whether the evidence shows any liability on the part of E. J. Goode. The claim of the defendants is that E. J. Goode, being at that

time without a residence property, and desiring to purchase
one, purchased the property in question from L. W. Goode,
under an agreement that L. W. Goode would remodel the
house according to said plans, as was afterwards done. E. J.
Goode states in his deposition that the consideration was eight
thousand dollars, and L. W. Goode testified on the trial that
it was nine thousand dollars. They both say that the consideration was paid by E. J. Goode assuming a mortgage indebtedness on the property of four thousand dollars, and crediting
L. W. Goode, on his indebtedness to him, for the balance. The
plaintiff insists that the sale and conveyance to E. J. Goode
was a scheme on the part of L. W. Goode to defraud the Scoville Plumbing Company; also, that L. W. Goode was the
agent of E. J. Goode in contracting for this plumbing. Counsel say in argument: "We desire at the outset to acquit the
venerable father and mother of Lowry W. Goode of any
responsibility in devising this ingenious scheme for defrauding the Scoville Plumbing Company." Under the evidence,
this concession as to the defendants may well be made, as there
is nothing to indicate that the defendants are other than innocent, good-faith purchasers of the property. As we view the
testimony, we think it fails to support the claim of fraudulent
intention on the part of L. W. Goode. So far as appears, he
was then carrying on his business of buying, improving, and
selling real estate and had this property for sale. E. J. Goode
being at that time without a home, and desirious of securing
one, and this property being such as he desired, it was certainly reasonable that L. W. Goode should make the sale that
he did, as by it he not only relieved himself from the mortgage indebtedness of four thousand dollars, but received credit
   for the balance of the consideration on his indebted-
2   ness to his father. The Scoville Plumbing Company,
   with knowledge of the sale and conveyance, contracted
with L. W. Goode alone to do this work, as they had done similar work for him theretofore. L. W. Goode may have been
insolvent at the time, but, be that as it may, there can be no

doubt that in contracting to do this work the Scoville Plumbing Company did so on the credit of L. W. Goode alone. The facts relied upon as showing a fraudulent purpose upon the part of L. W. Goode are the discrepancy as to the amount of the consideration, the consideration stated in the quitclaim deed, the fact that it was a quit claim deed, and the present insolvency of L. W. Goode. E. J. Goode gave his deposition in the state of New York, and, as he said, in the absence of his books of account. L. W. Goode stated on the trial, with the matter specially called to his attention, that his father was mistaken in stating that the consideration was eight thousand dollars, and that in fact it was nine thousand dollars.

8   We are inclined to believe that on account of the absence of his books, and because of the amount of the consideration not being specially brought to his attention, E. J. Goode was mistaken in stating that it was eight thousand dollars; but, whether or not this is true, it is undisputed that the actual consideration was either eight thousand dollars or nine thousand dollars. Therefore this discrepancy does not show the fraudulent purpose claimed. The consideration named in the deed to E. J. Goode is one dollar, and the deed is in form an ordinary quitclaim deed. L. W. Goode testifies that it was his custom to keep deeds signed by his wife in his office, for convenience of delivery, and that when he came to make out the deed to his father the only form in the office signed by his wife was this quitclaim deed, and, being the only one, he used it. It is argued that it was as easy to write the true consideration in the quitclaim deed as in any other, or to have written one dollar therein. We understand that the one dollar had been previously written in that blank, but, if not, the fact remains undisputed that the real consideration was eight thousand dollars or nine thousand dollars. The giving of such a deed, under the circumstances, was somewhat unusual; but L. W. Goode stands undisputed in his explanation as to why it was done and we see no reason to disbelieve his statements. It is argued that L. W. Goode is at present insolvent, and therefore indifferent as to whether personal

judgment is obtained against him for this work. If this be true, it can only go to the weight of his evidence. It is not a sufficient reason for charging the defendants, or their property, with his debts. As to the claim that L. W. Goode acted as the agent of E. J. Goode, or of Mrs. Goode, in contracting for this plumbing, there is no testimony whatever to support it, while the testimony of the defendants and of L. W. Goode is positive that he was not such agent.

We have examined the evidence as presented in the record with much care, and reach the conclusion that plaintiff's assignor contracted to, and did, furnish the materials and labor charged for on the personal credit of L. W. Goode alone, and with knowledge that this property had been sold and conveyed to E. J. Goode. We are also of the opinion that the contract by which L. W. Goode was to remodel the house at his
4   own expense was a valid and *bona fide* contract. Plaintiff's assignor having not contracted directly or indirectly with E. J. Goode, the owner of the property, for these repairs, it is not, therefore, entitled to charge him or his property therewith. This conclusion finds support in *Mallory v. Waterworks Co.,* 77 Iowa, 715 ; and *Templin v. Railway Co.,* 73 Iowa, 548.

Other questions are discussed, but as it follows from the conclusions already stated that the decree of the district court must be reversed, and the plaintiff's petition dismissed, they need not be considered. REVERSED.

THE SIOUX CITY ELECTRICAL SUPPLY COMPANY v. THE SIOUX CITY AND LEEDS ELECTRIC RAILWAY COMPANY, *et al.,* Appellants.

Liens: PRIORITIES. A mortgage executed on corporate property prior to the time a contractor furnished labor and material, and which was thereafter discharged of record, is not entitled to priority as a continuing lien by reason of an unrecorded written agreement that the corporate bonds secured by a trust deed should be sold and creditors including the mortgagee paid with the proceeds and the rule that the lien of the mortgage is presumed to continue until the debt is paid notwithstanding any change in the evidence of the debt, has no application.

SAME. The lien for labor and material furnished for "improvements and repairs" is superior to a deed of trust on the property executed after the work and materials were furnished.

Appeal from Woodbury District Court.—HON. SCOTT M. LADD, Judge.

TUESDAY, OCTOBER 25, 1898.

ACTION for judgment and for decree establishing and foreclosing a mechanic's lien for four hundred and eighty-eight dollars and eighty-eight cents and interest, on the defendant's property. The Guarantee Trust Company and W. E. Higman were made defendants, as claiming a lien or interest in the property. The defendant railway company alone answered, joining a number of issues, only one of which is discussed on this appeal, namely, the right of the plaintiff to priority over certain other liens. Judgment and decree were rendered in favor of the plaintiff as prayed. The defendant railway company appeals.—*Affirmed.*

Swan, Lawrence & Swan for appellant.

Roberts & Roberts and *J. M. Cleland* for appellee.

GIVEN, J.—Plaintiff's claim is for labor and material, the first item of which was furnished November 10, 1892, and the last February 27, 1893. The statement for a lien was filed June 27, 1893. The evidence leaves no doubt but the items charged were furnished in pursuance of a contract with the defendant appellant, and that plaintiff is entitled to a lien therefor. On August 10, 1892, the defendant company executed to the Guarantee Trust Company a mortgage on all its property to secure the payment of its promissory notes aggregating thirty thousand dollars. As of date January 1, 1892, appellant executed a deed of trust to Gilman, Son & Co., trustees, to secure the payment of its bonds to the amount of two hundred thousand dolllars, of which one hundred and twenty-five thousand dollars were to be issued at once, and the remainder on future contingencies. The evidence shows beyond question that this deed of trust was in fact executed January 1, 1893, instead of 1892, and that the same was unintentionally erroneously dated as January 1, 1892. There is a dispute as to whether the labor and material furnished by the plaintiff were for the original construction and equipment of the railway, or for improvements thereon. We are inclined to think that part was for construction, and part for improvements; but, as we view the case, the contention is immaterial. Let it be conceded that the labor and material were all for improvements and repairs, and that, therefore, the lien did not attach from the commencement of the construction; yet, being furnished before the execution of the deed of trust, it is entitled to priority over the deed.

The mortgage to the Guarantee Trust Company is prior in point of date to the furnishing of the labor and materials; but it appears that on April 8, 1893, the company executed a release of its mortgage, which was filed for record April 17, 1893, reciting that said mortgage "is redeemed, paid off, satisfied, and discharged in full." It appears that on the third day of April, 1893, an agreement in writing was entered into between appellant and certain of its creditors, including the Guarantee Trust Company, by which certain of its bonds secured by said trust deed were to be placed in the hands of E. W. Skury, as trustee, to sell the same, and to pay said creditors with the proceeds in the order named. It does not apppear that said agreement was placed on record. Appellant's counsel contend that, notwithstanding the satisfaction of said mortgage, the security of the Guarantee Trust Company continued, by virtue of said agreement and the trust deed. Many authorities are cited to the effect that the lien of a mortgage is presumed to continue until the debt is paid, and that a change in the form of the evidence of the debt, such as substituting new notes or bonds, does not extinguish the lien. Among those cited, we mention Jones, Corporation Bonds, 318; *Sloan v. Rice,* 41 Iowa, 465; *Swan v.*

Yaple, 35 Iowa, 248; *Thorp v. Durbon,* 45 Iowa, 192.   The cases cited are not in point.   This is not a case where the evidence of the indebtedness was changed, and the security left open upon the record.   Unlike any of those cases, this security was canceled, and all presumptions as to its continuance ended.   It was therefore, as to third persons, as if no such mortgage had ever been given.   The judgment and decree is manifestly correct, and it is AFFIRMED.

LADD, J., took no part.

FRANK WATSON v. NOAH BARTHOLOMEW and IDA BARTHOLOMEW, Appellants.

Action: ELECTION. In an action where the plaintiff alleges that he purchased a lot of the defendants which they falsely represented to be a certain number and that he took a conveyance from them by that description, which does not cover the land contracted for,
2 by reason of which he seek a rescission of the sale and a recovery of damages, he will not be required to elect between a claim on the covenants of the deed or for damages because of fraud and misrepresentation, though Code of 1873, section 2646, provided that a petition which alleged more than one cause of action might be separated into counts.

Transfer to Equity. Where plaintiff in an action for damages, on
1 reseinding a contract for alleged false representations on the part of the defendants, asks only a money judgment, such action can only be at law.

SAME. In an action for damages on rescinding a. contract for the
1 purchase of real estate, the question as to the forum in which such cause should proceed was not affected by a prayer that a certain portion of plaintiff's recovery be ordered paid to one who was not a party to such action, and that plaintiff be required to reconvey to defendants.

SAME. Where plaintiff alleged, as ground for recovery in an action for damages on rescinding a contract for the purchase of a certain lot, that defendants falsely represented such lot as described by a certain number, and that the lot was described by such number in
1 the conveyance which he received from them, but that such description did not cover the lot purchased, the court erred in transferring the cause to the equity docket, and thus depriving defendants of their right to a trial by jury.

Appeal from Polk District Court.—Hon. W. F. CONRAD, Judge.

TUESDAY, OCTOBER 25, 1898.

PLAINTIFF began proceedings in this case by filing a petition at law, asking damages. Thereafter he filed a substituted petition, which, though quite lengthy, we are compelled to set out in full, in order that the issues may be fully understood. It is in these words: "(1) That on or about May 1, 1890, defendants represented to plaintiff that they were the owners of a certain lot, which plaintiff then desired to buy, and which defendants claimed was platted and described as lot 19 in Gaston's subdivision of lot 37, etc. (2) That on May 26, 1890, plaintiff bought of defendants said lot for two hundred dollars, and on the same day defendants conveyed said lot to plaintiff as lot 19 aforesaid; said conveyance being in the form of an ordinary warranty deed. (3) Prior to making improvements upon said lot by plaintiff as hereinafter stated, and about October 1, 1890, defendants, at the request of plaintiff, measured off to plaintiff said lot, and then stated that said lot was No. 19 in said addition, and was the property of defendants. (4) Immediately after the happening of the matters above stated, plaintiff proceeded to improve said lot by grading same, setting out trees, digging well, and building a residence thereon, at an expense of about twelve hundred dollars. (5) That about December 1, 1891, plaintiff discovered that the lot selected and bought by him was not lot 19, and thereupon communicated said fact to defendants; whereupon defendants stated to plaintiff that said lot was No. 20 of said addition, and thereupon defendants deeded to plaintiff lot 20 of said addition; the deed therefor being an ordinary warranty deed, containing the additional provisions: 'This deed is made to correct a deed in which the wrong lot was conveyed, dated, May 26, 1890.' That thereupon plaintiff deeded lot 19 back to defendants. (6) That about January 1, 1894, plaintiff discovered that the lot so selected and bought by him of defendants was neither lot 19 nor lot 20 of said addition, but was lot 21 thereof, and was the property of one W. H. Clifford. (7) That immediately thereafter plaintiff communicated such fact to defendants, and demanded of them that they protect his title to said lot, and make good their covenants in said deed, but that defendants refused and still refuse so to do, or to make any other reparation to this plaintiff. (8) That since the beginning of this suit, and December 20, 1894, said W. H. Clifford began a suit at law in this court against this plaintiff to recover possession of said lot, and for damages. The files of said action are hereby made a part hereof, as fully as if set out at length. (9) That since the bringing of said suit by said Clifford this plaintiff, acting in good faith, and for the best interests of all parties concerned, has settled with said Clifford, and has bought said lot 21 in said addition, and paid him therefor the sum of three hundred dollars, which amount plaintiff says said lot was reasonably and fairly worth at the time of said settlement. (10) That plaintiff is a poor man, and all the property he has is invested in said lot and improvements thereon, and that when making said improvements he was compelled to borrow money on said lot, and did borrow of the Iowa Loan & Trust Company, on said lot, the sum of three hundred dollars, and mortgaged said lot to said company; describing the same in said mortgage as the same was described by defendants in said deed of December 5, 1891. (11) In making said settlement with said Clifford, plaintiff was compelled to borrow money with which to pay for said lot, and that plaintiff did borrow of the Iowa Loan & Trust Company the further sum of three hundred dollars, and gave to said Iowa Loan & Trust Company a mortgage on both of said lots 20 and 21 for the sum of six hundred dollars; said amount being the sum of both said loans, and the last loan being procured on ——, and the note and mortgage representing the same being dated, April 30, 1895. (12) That defendants carelessly, negligently, and fraudulently made to plaintiff the statements and representations alleged concerning their ownership of said lot, and their right to convey the same, and to plaintiff's damage as hereinafter shown. (13) That defendants have failed and refused, and now fail and refuse, to defend said premises against the lawful claims of all persons whomsoever, and principally against the claims of said Clifford, to plaintiff's damage as hereinafter shown. (14) That said lot so selected by plaintiff and bought of defendants was not the property of defendants, and defendants never had any title or right to sell and convey the same, and that the statements and representations made by defendants as aforesaid were false and fraudulent, and known to be so by defendants when made. (15). That said statements of defendants to plaintiff were made with intent to mislead and defraud plaintiff, and for the purpose of causing plaintiff to part with his money without consideration. (16) That the statements and representations so made by the defendants were relied upon by the plaintiff and believed by him to be true when made, and that so relying and believing said statements, plaintiff was induced to buy said property of defendants, to his damage as hereinafter shown. (17) That by reason of the foregoing plaintiff has been damaged in the manner and amounts following:

To amount paid defendant for said lot........... $200 00
To interest on same at 8 per cent., May 26, '90, to
    Dec. 26, '95............................. 85 35
To 5 days' time changing deeds of lots 19, 20...... 10 00
To recording deeds of lots 19, 20..............   1 50
Taxes paid on lots 19, 20, and interest.......... 20 00
To 3 days trying to induce defendants to correct
    error and protect title to lot 21..............   6 00
To amount paid attorney conducting suit Clifford
    vs. Watson 100 00
To time lost attending suit of Clifford vs. Watson.. 10 00
To abstract of lot 21, and recording fees in making
    loan on said lot 4 65

To amount paid Clifford in excess of agreed price
    on lot 21 ....   100 00
To interest on said $100 from April 30, 1895, to
    Sept. 28, 1895 ....   3 35
To amount for attorney's fees in prosecuting this
    suit 150 00
                                              _____
    Total $690 85

—Wherefore plaintiff prays judgment against defendants for
the sum of six hundred and ninety dollars and eighty-five
cents, with interest and costs; and the sum of three hundred
dollars of said judgment be ordered paid to the Iowa Loan
& Trust Company, so as to reduce plaintiff's mortgage upon
said lot 21 to the original sum by plaintiff borrowed from
said company upon said lot, and that upon the payment of
said sum of three hundred dollars to said company by said
defendants the said company be ordered and required to
release its said mortgage upon said lot 20; and that this plaintiff be then ordered and required to transfer said lot 20 back
to defendants, or that the said deed thereto from defendants to plaintiff be cancelled; and for such other and
further relief as may be equitable in the premises."
Thereafter plaintiff filed a motion to transfer the cause
to the equity docket. This motion was sustained, defendants duly excepting. Plaintiff then filed this amendment to the petition: "(1) That plaintiff has procured
from the Iowa Loan & Trust Company a release of said
mortgage on lot 20, and hereby tenders the same to defendants; a copy of said release being hereto attached, marked
'Exhibit C.' (2) Plaintiff has executed, and hereby tenders
to defendants, a special warranty deed of said lot 20; a copy
of said deed being hereto attached, marked 'Exhibit D.' (3)
Plaintiff further says that in borrowing the further sum of
three hundred dollars of the Iowa Loan & Trust Company,
and in executing the mortgage for six hundred dollars on
lots 20 and 21, on April 20, 1895, as set out in paragraph 11
of the amended and substituted petition, plaintiff had no
thought or intention of ratifying the deed made and so given

by defendants to plaintiffs for said lot 20, but said mortgage
so given by plaintiff upon both of said lots 20 and 21 was
demanded to be so done by said company, and that said plaintiff being without any money with which to pay said
Clifford and settle with him, and being unable to procure said money from any other party or in any other
way than the same was procured, and acting in good
faith, and only with the intention and purpose of protecting
himself, and also for the purpose herein stated, and by reason of defendants' failure and refusal to make good their
covenants in said deed, this plaintiff was forced and obliged
to make and execute said mortgage upon said lots. Wherefore plaintiff prays judgment against defendants for the
damages shown in his amended and substituted petition, in
the sum of six hundred and ninety dollars and eighty-five
cents; that whatever contract may have existed between plaintiff and defendants in reference to said lot 20 by reason of
the matters and things stated herein and in the amended and
substituted petition be rescinded; and for such other relief
as may be equitable." The next action taken was by defendants, who moved the court to compel plaintiff to elect on
which cause of action he relied,—whether he claimed on the
covenants of the deed, or for damages because of fraud and
misrepresentation,—and also moved to strike from the petition paragraphs 4, 8, 9, 10, 11, and 13, and from the amendment paragraphs 1, 2, and 3, and all of paragraph 17 of the
original petition, except the first two items. This motion
was overruled, and the ruling excepted to in proper form. A
demurrer was then interposed by defendants, and overruled
by the court. Defendants answered, putting in issue the allegations of the petition. There was a trial to the court, and
a decree canceling the deed to plaintiff of lot 20, and awarding judgment against defendants for the sum of three hundred and thirty-five dollars and fifty cents, with interest
thereon at eight per cent. from June 6, 1896, and making
the sum a special lien on said lot 20. Defendants appeal.—
Reversed.

Bishop, Bowen & Fleming for appellants.

Joseph H. Jones for appelle.

WATERMAN, J.—The first claim urged is that the case made by plaintiff is a strictly legal one, and that the court erred in transferring it to the equity docket, thus depriving defendants of a jury trial. The gist of plaintiff's action is that he purchased of defendants a certain lot, which they
1   falsely represented to be lot No. 20, and that he took a conveyance from them by that description; that the description does not cover the land contracted for, and he desires to rescind the sale. Stripped of much verbiage and many immaterial allegations, this is the case. If plaintiff had given some specific property for the lot, and, on a rescission, desired to have it reconveyed to him, equity would have been the proper forum; but that is not this case. If plaintiff desires to rescind, and has grounds for so doing, he needs only to tender back a deed for the lot, and he then has a right of action at law. And where, as in this case, he asks only a money judgment against defendants, his action can be at law only. The prayer that three hundred dollars of the amount of the recovery be ordered paid to the Iowa Loan & Trust Company, and that he (plaintiff) be required to reconvey lot 20 to defendants, involves somewhat peculiar requests, but they are not of a character to affect the question of what forum the action should proceed in. The trust company is not a party to this suit. If it is entitled to any part of the judgment plaintiff may recover, he does not need the aid of any court to enable him to pay it. Nor does he need the court's decree against himself before tendering the deed to defendants. No court could prevent him from taking steps to rescind the sale, if he sees fit to do so. We cannot discern any matter of equitable cognizance in the case. In any possible view, it seems but an action for damages. We think the court erred in transferring the cause to the equity docket, and thus depriving defendants of their right to a trial by jury.

II.   What we have said disposes of the case, so far as this court is concerned; and inasmuch as there must be another trial, and before a jury, if defendants demand it, we shall express no opinion upon the merits of the case.   On

2   the motion to compel plaintiff to elect as to his cause of action, and also on that to strike, it may be for the interest of the parties that we say something.   While plaintiff might well have been required to separate his petition into counts (Code 1873, section 2646, subd. 5), we can see no reason for putting him to an election.   On this ground the motion should have been overruled.   On all other grounds it should have been sustained.   The case will be remanded for proceedings at law.   That such is the proper order here, see *Kershman v. Swehla,* 62 Iowa, 654; *Jordan v. Winser,* 48 Iowa, 180.   Under this order, there is no other question in the case that requires notice at this time. REVERSED.

GEORGE W. WILSON, Plaintiff, v. H. M. REMLEY, *one of the Judges of the Eighteenth Judicial District of Iowa,* Defendant.

Certiorari.   A disbarred attorney, whose right to appear in and prosecute an action brought by him as trustee is denied, cannot maintain certiorari proceedings to review the decision, since he has no interest save as an attorney at law, and as such is not entitled to prosecute the action.

TUESDAY, OCTOBER 25, 1898.

Certiorari proceedings commenced in this court to review the proceedings of H. M. Remley, one of the judges of the Eighteenth Judicial District, while sitting as a court in Linn county, Iowa, in refusing to allow plaintiff to appear in and prosecute a cause in which he, as trustee, was a party plaintiff.—*Dismissed.*

Jamison & Smyth for plaintiff.

Milo P. Smith, J. H. Preston, and *Henry Rickel* for defendant.

DEEMER, C. J.—Plaintiff is an attorney at law who was disbarred from practice in the courts of this state by the district court of Linn county, Iowa, prior to the happening of the matters complained of. On the twenty-third day of July, 1895, one J. W. Scott assigned to plaintiff, as trustee, a judgment rendered in his favor by a justice of the peace. Wilson, as trustee, brought suit on this judgment before a justice of the peace, and recovered a judgment thereon. The defendants in that judgment appealed to the district court. When the case came on to be heard in that court, objection was made to plaintiff's appearing, for the reason that he had been disbarred. This objection was sustained, the court holding that plaintiff had no right to appear save in cases where he was personally a party. The court also found that Wilson had appeared as trustee in a number of cases in that court, and was demanding the right to appear for himself, or to appear as attorney for himself. Plaintiff neglected to obtain counsel, and his cause was dismissed. This proceeding is to review the aforesaid action of the court.

An insuperable objection to the proceeding is that plaintiff in his individual capacity has no interest in the proceedings save as an attorney at law, and as such he is not entitled to prosecute the action, for the reason that he has been disbarred. In the year 1853 it was held that a stranger to the record, who is noway affected by the proceedings, has no right to the writ. *Davis County v. Horn,* 4 G. Greene, 94. As Wilson in his individual capacity was not a party to the record before the district court, he cannot prosecute this action. *Iske v. City of Newton,* 54 Iowa, 586. Aside from this consideration, which we regard as conclusive, we may say that we think plaintiff's right to appear as trustee is extremely doubtful. See *Cobb v. Judge,* 43 Mich. 289 (5 N. W. Rep.

809); *Paul v. Purcell,* 1 Browne, 348. The writ is DISMISSED.

THRESA DETTMER v. FRITZ BEHRENS, and FRITZ BEHRENS as Administrator of the Estate of PHILIPHINE BEHRENS, Deceased, Appellants.

Estates: HOMESTEADS: *Creditors.* Creditors cannot complain that
1 a testatrix sold her homestead for a certain sum, to be paid her
2 during life, and left a deed thereof with the depositary of her will to be turned over to the purchaser upon the payment of a
3 specified additional sum, whether the deed be regarded as testa-
4 mentary in character or as deposited in escrow.

EXEMPTIONS. The homestead of a testatrix who leaves neither hus-
2 band or children surviving her, is subject to the payment of any claims established against her estate under Code, section 2986.

Deeds: DELIVERY. The delivery of a deed after the grantor's death
1 to a purchaser in possession of the premises by one with whom
2 the grantor has deposited it with directions to make such delivery upon payment of the balance of the purchase price, is, upon ful-
4 fillment of the condition, valid and effectual and relates back to the first delivery.

Witnesses. A wife who was present at a conversation between her
3 husband and a deceased person but did not participate therein is competent as a witness although her husband is prohibited from testifying under Code, section 4604.

Appeal from Lee District Court.—HON. HENRY BANK, JR., Judge.

TUESDAY, OCTOBER 25, 1898.

ACTION to subject certain land to the payment of the claims established against the estate of Philiphine Behrens. Decree as prayed, and defendants appeal.—*Reversed.*

J. D. M. Hamilton and *J. L. Benbow* for appellants.

Herminghausen & Herminghausen for appellee.

LADD, J.—Philiphine Behrens died May 26, 1893; and on September 11th, of the same year, her will, made July 27,

1892, was admitted to probate. With it was a warranty deed, signed and acknowledged by her, conveying the house and
      lot in controversy to Fritz Behrens, and to which the
1   third clause of the will evidently related: "The war-
      ranty deed inclosed herewith shall be held by my exec-
utor until the grantee, Fritz Behrens, shall pay over to the executor the sum of one hundred dollars, which shall be done within one year after my death; then the deed shall be given him." The deed and will were drawn by one Stoevener at the same time, and placed in one envelope, which was sealed. It was her direction and intention that he hold both, and deliver the deed when the one hundred dollars was paid; but, advising her the proper place was with the clerk, he left it there, inclosed as stated. As Stoevener failed to qualify as executor, though so nominated in the will, Fritz Behrens was appointed administrator with the will annexed. On his application, showing the payment of the one hundred dollars, the
      court ordered the clerk to deliver the deed to him,
2   which was accordingly done. The testatrix left
      neither husband nor children surviving her, and the
real estate in controversy, though her homestead, unless disposed of to Behrens, is subject to the payment of any claims established against her estate. Code, section 2986. The plaintiff procured the establishment of her claim against the estate of the deceased in the sum of one hundred and sixty-nine dollars and five cents, with interest, as of the third class, and others aggregating about two hundred dollars were allowed. This action is brought to have the land mentioned sold, and the proceeds applied in payment of these claims. Behrens sets up in his answer that he purchased the property of the testatrix in 1890, for the agreed consideration of five hundred dollars, of which four hundred dollars was paid during the life of Mrs. Behrens in board and nursing, at the agreed price of three dollars per week, and that the remaining one hundred dollars was to be paid after her death, in order to provide for necessary funeral expenses, and upon this payment the deed which she was to leave fully prepared

with Stoevener should be delivered. The facts thus pleaded are fully established by the evidence.

Even though it be conceded that Behrens was prohibited from testifying by section 4604 of the Code, his wife, who claimed to have been present, and not to have participated in the conversation, is competent as a witness. *Aucham-paugh v. Schmidt,* 77 Iowa, 17; *Lines v. Lines,* 54 Iowa, 600; *Johnson v. Johnson,* 52 Iowa, 586. She testified to the facts alleged in the answer, is uncontradicted, and we must regard them as established. From her evidence it also appears that the testatrix told Behrens, who had been a tenant, that the lease was at an end, and he should take possession at once. He continued in occupancy of the premises, and made some improvements. The testatrix boarded with him from June 6, 1890, till November 6, 1892, after which she occupied rooms until her death, though taking her meals with others. We have, then, an agreement for the sale of the house and lot at a fair valuation, with the greater part of the consideration paid during life, according to the contract, and the deed to be delivered to the grantee after the death of the grantor upon the payment of the remainder of the purchase price to the executor of the grantor's estate. In our view of the case, it is not very material whether the deed be regarded as testamentary in character, as contended by appellee, or the deposit with the will under the control of the executor named in the nature of an escrow, as urged by the appellant. In either event Behrens had the right to have the deed turned over to him upon the performance of the condition. If the deed had not been made or incorporated with the terms of the will, the executor would have been required, under the law, to complete the sale by executing a conveyance on the payment of the balance of the purchase price. Possession had been given, and a part of the purchase price paid, and surely the courts will order the completion of such a contract. The creditors were in no manner prejudiced. As it was her homestead, she might dispose of it during her life, regardless of their claims. Code, section 2973. *Delashmut v.*

Trau, 44 Iowa, 613; *Officer v. Evans,* 48 Iowa, 557; *Griffin v. Sheley,* 55 Iowa, 513; *Addicken v. Humphal,* 56 Iowa, 365; *Aultman v. Héiney,* 59 Iowa, 654; *Butler v. Nelson,* 72 Iowa, 732; *Manufacturing Co. v. Bjelland,* 97 Iowa, 637. And, in the absence of prejudice to the creditors, she might lawfully prescribe the entire manner in which her estate shall be administered. Code, section 3336. So, it is quite immaterial whether she direct the executor to execute the deed upon the payment of the balance of the purchase price, or leave the deed for him to deliver upon the happening of the contingency. See *Robinson v. Schly,* 6 Ga. 526.

If, however, we agree with the appellant, and say that this deed shall not be construed as a part of the will, we must regard Behrens as having acquired the title by its delivery. The rule is well settled that the death of a grantor

4   will not prevent the delivery of a deed if the condition under which it is held by a third person is complied with. *Lindley v. Groff,* 37 Minn. 338 (34 N. W. Rep. 28); *Ruggles v. Lawson,* 13 Johns. 285, (7 Am. Dec. 375); *Stone v. Duvall,* 77 Ill. 480; *Davis v. Clark,* 58 Kan. 100 (48 Pac. Rep. 563). Here all conditions are met; *i. e.,* the death of the grantor and the payment of one hundred dollars to her executor. True, there are cases holding that if a grantor places a conveyance in the hands of a third party, to be delivered to the grantee after the grantor's death, a delivery under such circumstances is inoperative, as the agency created ends with the death of the principal. See *Wellborn v. Weaver,* 17 Ga. 267 (63 Am. Dec. 235). It has been said that a deed may not be delivered by a dead hand. But delivery may be incomplete in life to become absolute after death. *Stone v. Duvall, supra; Foster v. Mansfield,* 3 Metc. (Mass.) 412. And where the grantor places the deed in the hands of a third person, to be delivered to the grantee named therein after the grantor's death, without reservation to recall, and it is not recalled, but remains in the hands of the depositary till the happening of that event, and is then turned over to the grantee, there appears to be no good reason

why the delivery shall not be regarded as valid and effectual, and relate back to the first delivery. *Wheelwright v. Wheelwright,* 2 Mass. 447 (3 Am. Dec. 66); *Belden v. Carter,* 4 Day, 66; *Belden v. Carter,* 4 Am. Dec. 185, and note; *Shed v. Shed,* 3 N. H. 432; *Morse v. Slason,* 13 Vt. 296; *Hatch v. Hatch,* 9 Mass. 307 (6 Am. Dec. 67); *Howard v. Patrick,* 38 Mich. 805; *Phillips v. Housten,* 50 N. C. 302; *Hocket v. Jones,* 70 Ind. 227; *Stevens v. Huss,* 54 Pa.St. 20; *Garnons v. Knight,* 5 Barn. & C. 689; *Mather v. Corliss,* 103 Mass. 568; *Hathaway v. Payne,* 34 N. Y. 92. Appellee asserts the deed never passed beyond the control of the grantor. The facts that it was left with the depositary with her last testament, and in accordance with her agreement, that she repeatedly remarked that it would be delivered to Behrens upon payment of the balance of the consideration, and that she yielded possession, and accepted the part of the consideration, fully established her determination never to recall it. As said in *Newton v. Bealer,* 41 Iowa, 339: "Where one who has the mental power to alter his intention, and the physical power to destroy a deed in his possession, dies without doing either, there is, it seems to us, but little reason for saying that his deed shall be inoperative simply because during life he might have done that which he did not do. It is much more consonant with reason to determine the effect of the deed by the intention existing up to the time of death than to refuse to give it that effect because the intention might have been changed." In *Trask v. Trask,* 90 Iowa, 318, this language is used: "The facts attending the delivery to a third person which may pass the title to the grantee are not required to be such as that it is beyond the mental power of the grantor to alter his intention, or that he has not the physical power to regain possession of the deed. *Newton v. Bealer,* 41 Iowa, 334. As we have seen, the intention of the grantor is the polar star by which courts must be guided in determining the question." The rights of the creditors are in no way involved, because in no event would Behrens be held liable for more than the balance of the purchase price. We discover no reason

for interfering with the consummation of this agreement in
the manner agreed upon by the parties. The deed, when
given, related back to the time it was deposited with Stoevener and the title became perfect in Behrens. The motion to
strike requires no consideration, and is overruled. The decree
of the district court is REVERSED.

L. W. Smith, et al., Appellants, v. The City of Des Moines,
et al.

Public Improvements: ASSESSMENT. Under Acts Twenty-fifth General Assembly, chapter 7, section 12, providing that an assessment
for a street improvement, "shall be a lien upon the property abutting the street" on which the improvement is made and that it
1 "shall be limited to the lot or lands bounding or abutting on such
street," where a tract has been platted into lots the platted bound-
2 ary lines must control, and the assessment must be limited to the
lot or parcel of ground which actually abuts on the street, and
cannot be extended to a contiguous point though the latter, with
the abutting lot constitute a single tract, and is used jointly for a
single purpose, as a residence, and fronts on the street to be
improved.

SAME. A special assessment for street improvements is not void
3-4 because erroneously made against the owner as well as against
the property.

ROBINSON, J., dissenting.

FRAUDULENT CONVEYANCE. The levy of an assessment for street
2 improvements cannot be defeated by a conveyance of the property
liable therefor, made with the intent to evade it.

ASSESSMENT CERTIFICATES: *Rights of holders.* The holder of a special assessment certificate canot be prevented from intervening in
4 an action to enjoin the collection of the assessment, and asking
for the enforcement of his lien, on the ground that the city has
elected to have the property sold by the county treasurer and that
such election was final.

Appeal from Polk District Court.—Hon. C. P. Holmes,
Judge.

Tuesday, October 25, 1898.

ACTION in equity to enjoin the collection of special assessments for grading and paving a street, and for the cancellation of the assessments. There was a hearing on the merits, and a decree in favor of the defendant, the city of Des Moines, and the intervener, the Flint Brick Company. The plaintiffs appeal.—*Reversed.*

Charles Mackenzie for appellants.

J. E. Mershon for appellee city of Des Moines; *J. K. Macomber* for appellee Flint Brick Company.

ROBINSON, J.—Lots numbered 19, 20, and 21 of Wilson T. Smith's subdivision of part of lots 10 and 11 of Dean's outlots, in the city of Des Moines, extend lengthwise from north to south, are one hundred and forty-six feet in length, and are numbered from west to east. Each lot, as platted, was fifty feet in width; but, when platted, Pennsylvania avenue, which extends from north to south, and bounded lot 21 on its east side, was not of full width, and the east part of lot 21, constituting a strip forty feet wide, and extending the entire length of the lot, was added to the avenue, to widen it. That left a strip of the western part of the lot ten feet wide and one hundred and forty-six feet long, and that and lot numbered 20 were, at the time the assessments in question were levied, owned by Mary T. Smith, now deceased, and lot numbered 20 is now owned by the plaintiff L. W. Smith. Lots 19 and 20 and the remaining part of lot 21 are used together as one tract, which is occupied by L. W. Smith as a place of residence. The dwelling house rests in part upon lot 19 and in part upon lot 20, and fronts eastward upon Pennsylvania avenue and southward upon Walker street, which forms the south boundary of the lots, and was erected before the avenue was widened. The east front of the house is the principal one, and is reached from the avenue by means of a board walk, which is parallel to, and about forty feet north of Walker street. There have not been any improvements upon the remaining part of lot 21 since the avenue was widened. It is

covered with grass, and constitutes a part of the lawn, which
is uninclosed, and is used in connection with the dwelling
house. The plaintiffs seek to have the assessments canceled
as to lot 20, and to have the sale thereof for the assessments
enjoined.

I. On the eighth day of April, 1895, the city of Des
Moines entered into an agreement in writing with M. H. King
for excavating and paving portions of three streets, including
that part of Pennsylvania avenue in front of lot 21. The
work was to be completed between the fifteenth day of August
and the first day of November, 1895. King transferred his
interest in the contract to the Flint Brick Company, by which
          the material and labor required by the contract were
1   furnished. On the ninth day of September, 1895, the
          contract having been performed, the city of Des
Moines, by its proper officers, assessed upon the remaining
part of lot 21 and upon lot 20, and against Mary T. Smith,
the sum of three hundred and seventy dollars and four cents,
as the pro rata share of that property of the cost of the
improvements made. A similar assessment for curbing was
made in July, and relief on account of it is asked in the petition, but nothing is claimed in this court on account of it. On
the thirty-first day of July, 1895, Mrs. Smith conveyed the
remaining part of lot 21 to H. W. Smith. He resided in
California at the time the conveyance was made, is a brother
of L. W. Smith, is without property, and does not appear to
have asked for the conveyance, nor to have given any attention to the property since the conveyance was made. It is
admitted that the object of the conveyance was to defeat the
levy of the assessment upon lot 20. Some attention is given
          in argument to the time when a lien for the improve-
2   ment attached, but we do not regard that as important.
     If lot 20 would have been subject to the assessment
had the conveyance not been made, then the latter was fraudulent and of no effect as against the assessment, under the rule
announced in *Eagle Mfg. Co. v. City of Davenport,* 101 Iowa,
493. The question of chief importance which we are required

to determine is, was lot 20 so located and used that it was subject to the assessment in question? It is nòt, at any point, within ten feet of the street which was improved; and the appellant contends that it cannot be subjected to the assessment, because it did not abut on that street. The improvement in question was made under the provisions of chapter 7 of the Acts of the Twenty-fifth General Assembly. Section 12 of that act provides that an assessment for improving a street, with interest accruing thereon, "shall be a lien upon the property abutting upon the street or streets" on which the improvement is made, and that such lien "shall be limited to the lots or lands bounding or abutting on such street or streets, or on such improvements, and not exceeding in depth therefrom 150 feet, except in the case of sewer improvements. * * *" Does this mean that the lien of the assessment is limited to lots which actually abut on the street, or may it extend to all lots used together as one tract, one or more of which abut on the street? The adjudicated cases called to our attention give but little aid in determining which is the correct theory. In *Amery v. City of Keokuk,* 72 Iowa, 701, it was held, in effect, that, where parts of a lot which abutted on a street were owned by different persons, that part only which was adjacent to the street was liable for an assessment made for improving the street. That case arose under chapter 45 of the General and Public Acts of the Fourteenth General Assembly, which authorized assessments for street improvements "upon the lots or parcels of ground, or any part of either of the same, fronting upon or lying along the street, avenue or alley" which was improved. That statute, in terms, authorized the levy of assessments upon parts of lots fronting upon the street improved; and the case cited construed that provision, and does not support the theory that a lot which does not front upon the street improved may not be subjected to assessments for the improvement. The statute under consideration differs from that construed in the *Amery Case,* and we shall be aided in reaching a correct conclusion by considering various provisions of the act which controls

this case. Section 10 of that act provides for the assessment
of the cost of a street improvement "upon the property fronting or abutting on, or adjacent to, said improvement." Section
11 provides for the making of plats of places where improvements are made, "showing the separate lots or parcels of
ground subject to assessment for such improvement, or a specified portion thereof." Section 12, as already noticed, authorizes a lien "upon the property abutting upon the street" on
which the improvement is made, and limits the lien "to the
lots or land bounded or abutting on such street. * * *"
Section 13 provides for the discharge of a part of property
subject to assessment which shall have been divided, by a
pro rata payment for the part discharged, "calculated by the
ratio of front feet, or square feet in area of such lot or lots,
or parcel or parcels to the feet front or the area of the whole
lot." And section 19 provides that the city council shall not
have the right to authorize any improvement of a street, unless
the owners of a majority of the feet front, or square feet in
area, of the property abutting upon or adjacent to the street
or streets to be improved, shall petition therefor, unless three-
fourths of the members of the council shall vote for it. It is
the opinion of the majority of the members of this court that
the act in question must be strictly construed; that, under the
various provisions to which reference has been made, where
a tract of land has been platted into lots the platted boundary
lines must control; that an assessment must be limited to the
lot or parcel of ground which abuts on the street, however
small, without regard to the use made of it, and that no subdivision which does not actually abut on the street improved, can
rightfully be assessed for the improvement; and, therefore, that
the assessment made upon lot 20 in controversy was unauthorized and illegal. In that view, as applied to the facts in this
and similar cases, the writer does not concur. Undoubtedly
it was the legislative intent to subject property abutting on a
street which is improved to the payment of a proportional
share of the cost of the improvement, which in most, if not
all, cases will be fixed by the frontage of the property on the

street. If that property is used as an entirety for a single purpose, there is no good reason, aside from the statute, for holding that only a part of the property, to be determined by artificial lines, shall be subject to the cost. The statute limits the lien or liability for the cost of paving a street to property within one hundred and fifty feet of it, but there is no language in the statute which limits the lien to such lots as separately abut on the street, unless it be this: "That such lien shall be limited to the lots or lands bounding or abutting on such street or streets. * * *" But that does not seem to the writer to require that each one of several lots or parts of lots, which together constitute but a single tract, used for a single purpose, shall bound or abut on a street, in order to make it liable on account of the improvement. If the language is to be construed to mean that only those lots which, considered separately, abut on the street improved, are subject to a lien for the improvement, then it appears to me that the same literalness of interpretation would lead to the conclusion that the entire lot or parcel of ground, as platted, which so abuts, would be subject to the lien, even though it were divided into two parts, one of which is not adjacent to the street, and which are owned by different persons and devoted to separate and distinct uses. That a parcel of ground which is adjacent to a street which has been improved may be divided, and a part of it be sold in good faith, and be thus relieved from liability to a lien for the street improvement, although within one hundred and fifty feet of the street, was held in *Eagle Mfg. Co. v. City of Davenport, supra,* under a statute which contained a proviso indentical in language with that under consideration. I am of the opinion, founded upon the general provisions of the statute which refer to the "property" abutting on the street improved, and the spirit and evident purpose of the statute, that mere platted boundary lines, although within one hundred and fifty feet of the street improved, do not necessarily limit the liens for the cost of the improvement, and that all of several lots within the limited distance, which together constitute a single tract of land,

may be regarded as abutting on a street, for the purpose of
an assessment, if a part of them so abut. It appears in this
case that the portion of lot 21 which has not been taken for
the avenue is worthless, excepting for use with lot 20; and I
am of the opinion that, for the reasons stated, both were properly
treated as a single lot or tract of land abutting on the
avenue, and were rightly assessed for their share of the cost
of improving it.

II.   Before the special assessment was levied, Mrs.
Smith died. The appellants contend that the assessment is
void because made against Mrs. Smith as well as against the
property. The statute provides that the assessment
3   shall be made upon the property which is liable for its
payment; and although the statute also requires that
the plat of the place or places to be improved shall show the
separate lots or parcels of ground subject to assessment, and
the names of the several owners, it also provides that any mistake
in the name of the owner shall not vitiate the lien of the
assessment. The property assessed is liable for it, and the
error in also making the assessment as against Mrs. Smith is
immaterial and without legal effect.

III.   The intervener asked for judgment for the amount
due on the assessment certificate which had been issued against
the west part of lot 21 and all of lot 20, and for general equitable
relief. The district court determined the amount due on
the certificate, established a lien therefor on the property specified,
and directed that a special execution issue for the sale
of the property. Of that the appellants complain, on
4   the ground that the city had elected to have the property
sold by the county treasurer, and that the election
thus made was final. The argument for the appellants in support
of this claim is brief. It is not noticed in the argument
of the appellees, and we shall not, therefore, discuss it at
length. We content ourselves with saying that the intervener
is the rightful holder and owner of the certificate, that section
15 of chapter 7 of the Acts of the Twenty-fifth General
Assembly authorizes the owner of such certificates to collect

them by any of the methods provided by law for the collection
of assessments for local improvements, and that section 478
of the Code of 1873, as amended, authorizes the collection of
the assessment, and the enforcement of the lien therefor, by
the owner thereof, by a proceeding in equity. It does not
appear that the intervener has made any election, or done
anything which precludes it from recovering in this action.
But the opinion of the majority decides that the plaintiffs were
entitled to have the assessment canceled as to lot 20, and to
have the sale thereof enjoined, and that the intervener is not
entitled to any relief as to said lot. The decree of the district
court is therefore REVERSED.

ROBINSON, J., dissenting, as shown in the opinon.

SALLY A. STILLMAN, Appellant, v. JAMES WICKHAM and O. [106]
P. MCKESSON.

Builders' Contract: ALTERATION: *Sureties.* A surety on a bond, con-
1 ditioned for the performance of a builders' written contract accord
ing to specifications, may insist on the strict terms of his obligation,
3 and claim a discharge for a material alteration of the contract,
though made for his benefit.

SAME. The action of one for whom a house is being built, in directing the workmen, rejecting materials conforming to the specifica-
2 tions and buying others without consulting the contractors is
such an alteration of the contract for its construction, requiring
3 the contractors to furnish materials called for in the plans and
specifications, as relieves the sureties from liability on the latter's
bond conditioned for his compliance with all the conditions of the
contract, although the contract permitted the owner to change the
plans or designs and provided that the character of the materials
furnished by the contractor was to be submitted to the judgment
of the owner's superintendent.

RULE APPLIED. Where one signed as surety a bond conditioned for
the performance of a builders' written contract, and the owner
2 changed the plans, and extra work was done as she requested, on
her oral promise to pay, without a special agreement minuted on
the original contract as therein required, and she took the erection
of the building from the contractor's control, directed the workmen, and rejected material duly furnished by the contractor and

bought other, without consulting him, the surety is discharged, notwithstanding the contractor's acquiescence in all that was done.

WAIVER. Where a surety on a bond conditioned for the performance of a builder's contract according to specifications, signed orders
4 for the payment of certain work, including extras, it does not constitute a waiver of objections to alterations in the contract, where it is not shown that he knew of the omission to comply with the terms.

Plea and Issue. An issue not tendered in the pleadings cannot be
4 considered.

Appeal from Pottawattamie District Court.—HON. WALTER I. SMITH, Judge.

WEDNESDAY, OCTOBER 26, 1898.

BY the terms of a written contract, G. S. Monroe agreed to construct a tenement house for the plaintiff according to specifications, and save her harmless of all liens and incumbrances. Mechanics' liens were established, however, amounting to three thousand, seven hundred and sixty-one dollars and fourteen cents, which the plaintiff was compelled to pay. With sums already paid, this was one thousand, nine hundred and ninety-two dollars and thirty-three cents more than the contract price. And this amount, with interest, the plaintiff seeks to recover from the sureties on Monroe's bond, conditioned for the performance of his contract. The defense interposed was that defendants were relieved from liability by alteration of the contract. Trial to court, judgment for defendants, and plaintiff appeals. AFFIRMED.

Stone & Tinley and *Stillman & Stillman* for appellant.

Harl & McCabe for appellees.

LADD, J.—The liability of the defendants, as sureties on the contractor's bond, for the amount paid to satisfy the mechanics' liens in excess of the contract price, is conceded, unless avoided by some change in the contract. Owing to the situation of the surety, he must be treated with the utmost good faith, and may insist on the strict terms of his obligation. *School Dist. v. Reichard,* 50 Iowa, 98; *Starr v. Blatner,* 76 Iowa, 358; *Brigham v. Wentworth,* 11 Cush. 123; *Plow Co. v. Walmsley,* 110 Ind. 242 (11 N. E. Rep. 232); *Erickson v. Brandt,* 53 Minn. 10 (55 N.W. Rep. 62); *Bragg v. Shain,* 49 Cal. 131; *Mayhew v. Boyd,* 5 Md. 102; *Miller v. Stewart,* 9 Wheat. 680. If a material alteration

1

is made in the contract without the surety's consent, he is discharged, even though the alteration may be for his benefit. Brandt Suretyship, section 338. We inquire, then, whether the contract between plaintiff and Monroe was altered or any of its conditions waived by the parties. In

2

establishing the mechanic's lien the court found that the contractor had done extra work, valued at five hundred and seventy-four dollars. This was without special bargain evidenced in writing, as required by the contract, a portion of which we set out: "Extra work: In case it is deemed necessary during the construction of the building to have more or extra work done than is specified or shown in the plans, such work is to be done by the contractor, but he is required not to proceed to make such work without a special bargain or contract for the same, and minuted on the back of the original contract; otherwise it is not binding upon either of the parties." The evident object of this clause was to prevent changes or alterations on mere suggestion, without fixing their extent, and to avoid controversy and litigation as to what were extras and their value. But the extra work was done at the request of the plaintiff, and upon her oral promise to pay, without special bargain or agreement minuted on the original contract, as therein required. To our inquiry it is quite immaterial whether the parties might waive this condition, and substitute the method pursued. But see *Smith v. Gugerty,* 4 Barb. 614; *Bartlett v. Stanchfield,* 148 Mass. 394 (19 N. E. Rep. 549); *Osborne & Co. v. Backer,* 81 Iowa, 379; *Viele v. Insurance Co.,* 26 Iowa, 53; *King v. Insurance Co.,* 72 Iowa, 315.

By the terms of the original contract, each party was relieved from liability unless the extra work was done in pursuance of a special bargain in writing. It was not on the original contract that plaintiff was held for the extra work in the action referred to, but because of the separate oral agreement made with Monroe, substituted therefor. The obligations of the sureties was that the contractor "comply with all the conditions of said contract, and faithfully perform all the undertakings therein stipulated by him to be performed." Monroe was not bound to do the extra work save on the conditions stipulated, and, if plaintiff suffered loss by reason of the adoption of another method, the sureties are under no obligation to recoup it. Nor does this change affect other portions of the contract, as it expressly provides for such a contingency. This alteration was such as the parties were permitted to make, on the condition that liability should not attach.

II. The contract provided that Monroe "furnish all materials such as are called for in the plans, detail drawings, and specifications," and that he use "such materials as hereinafter described." There is also a provision that "he 8   will be further held to submit, as to the character of the materials to be used and work done, to the judgment of the superintendent, and to secure from him all necessary interpretations of the designs and plans, and all necessary certificates regarding his payments on the contract; also for all additions to, or deductions from, the same, which may result from extra work or changes of designs or plans." The owner was permitted to change the plans or designs, and, in so far as necessary to meet such change, material differing from that specified might be required. This much must necessarily be inferred from the right to make such alterations. Further than this, and in no other way, the right to require material of a quality or character other than described in the specifications is not reserved to the owner. True, the character of the materials was to be submitted to the judgment of the superintendent, but only for his determination whether these were as required by the contract. This condition does not allow the superintendent to reject material furnished in strict accordance with the specifications, and arbitrarily substitute that of different quality or construction to suit his whim or fancy. No one could safely contract for the erection of a building, and give another such an option. And the contractor was to furnish the materials, and not the owner, at his expense. But the evidence in this case clearly shows that the plaintiff virtually took the erection of the building from the control of the contractor. She directed the workmen, rejected material which conformed to the specifications, and bought other, without consulting Monroe. Lumber bought, after advertisement, of the lowest bidder, was rejected, and that of a different quality, at an increased price, procured of another firm. The hardware was changed, at an additional expense of eighty-three dollars. The millwork, after delivery, was refused, and ordered of another. Indeed, the contractor was not permitted to choose from whom he would purchase materials. Doubtless the plaintiff has a better house because of these changes, but by ignoring and altering the conditions of her contract the sureties were relieved from liability. They contracted for compliance with the terms of the contract, that Monroe furnish materials, and that these be of the character fixed by the specifications. The importance of the alterations is apparent. The contractor was deprived of the advantage of competition in purchasing, and obliged to pay much more than he would for that specified. It is no answer to say Monroe acquiesced in all this. The parties had the right to waive conditions, but in doing so disregarded those on which the indemnity rested. The extent of these alterations we need not determine. They were material, and there the inquiry must end. *Bethune v. Dozier,* 10 Ga. 235; *Simonson v. Grant,* 36 Minn. 439 (31 N. W. Rep. 861); *Paine v. Jones,* 76 N. Y. 274; *Brennan v. Clark,* 29 Neb. 385 (45 N. W. Rep. 472); 24 Am. & Eng. Enc. Law, 837.

III.   The plaintiff urged that by signing orders for the payment of certain work, including extras, the defendants

have waived objections to alterations in the contract. But it
is not shown that they had any knowledge of the omis-
4   sion to comply with its terms. There can be no waiver
without knowledge of the facts upon which it is based.
But, aside from this reason, such an issue was not tendered
in the pleadings, and therefore cannot be considered. The
decree of the district court is AFFIRMED.

DAVID ALLEN, Minor, by WILLIAM ALLEN, His Next Friend,
   v. THE AMES COLLEGE RAILWAY COMPANY, Appellant.

Contributory Negligence: INFANTS: *Jury question.* Whether a boy
   six years old was guilty of contributory negligence in going in
2 front of a moving train at or near a street crossing was properly
   submitted to the jury, under an instruction holding him to such
   care as might reasonably be expected, under the circumstance
   from a child of his age.

SAME. Whether a railway company was negligent in backing a coach
1 across a street without giving a signal or alarm and without having a lookout on the coach is a question of fact for the jury.

HARMLESS ERROR. Admission of evidence that parents of plaintiff, a
   six-year-old boy, carefully endeavored to guard against his having
   to cross by himself a railroad track where he was injured, on the
5 way from school, is harmless error, where the jury was charged
   that it was plaintiff's want of care contributing to the injury
   which would bar recovery, and thus, inferentially, that the parents'
   care was immaterial.

Evidence: CARLISLE TABLES. The Carlisle tables are admissible in
4 evidence where the plaintiff's injury is permanent and his expectancy of life is a material inquiry.

Appeal: ABSENCE OF TRIAL JUDGE. The absence of the trial judge
6 during the argument of the cause, although improper, is not
   ground for reversal unless it affirmatively appears that the appellant was prejudiced thereby.

EXCESSIVE VERDICT. A verdict of seven thousand dollars awarded a
   child injured by a passenger coach which was backed across the
7 street will not be disturbed where pain and suffering was an ele
   ment of damages in addition to the actual disfigurement and loss
   of actual earning capacity.

REVIEW OF CONFLICT. A verdict based on conflicting evidence will
1 not be disturbed on appeal.

REFUSAL OF INSTRUCTIONS.   Refusal to give requested instructions is
8   not error, where they are substantially and clearly embodied in
those given.

Appeal from Story District Court.—HON. S. M. WEAVER,
Judge.

WEDNESDAY, OCTOBER 26, 1898.

ACTION at law to recover damages for injuries sustained
by plaintiff growing out of the alleged negligence of the
defendant in backing its train upon him without warning or
signals, and without having a lookout at the rear end of the
train.   Trial to a jury, resulting in a verdict and judgment
for plaintiff in the sum of seven thousand dollars.   Defendant
appeals.—*Affirmed.*

McCarthy & Lee and *J. L. Carney* for appellant.

G. A. Underwood and *J. F. Martin* for appellee.

DEEMER, C. J.—Defendant is a railway corporation
operating a line of road about two miles long between the city
of Ames, in Story county, and the State Agricultural College.
Its motive power is steam, and it not only transports passengers, but is a carrier of freight as well.   One of its terminals
and its depot and train shed is adjacent to what is known as
"Onondaga Street," in the city of Ames.   This street runs
nearly east and west, and is intersected just west of the depot
by what is known as "Duff Street."   David Allen, the plaintiff, a boy of about six years of age, was passing west along
or near Onondaga street, going from school to his home, when
he was struck by a coach which was being backed from the
train shed out onto the main line of the defendant's road.
Prior to the time the car was set in motion it had been stand·
ing partially in the street, with the engine so attached as to
push it out onto the main line.   It is claimed that the
1   engineer gave no signal or alarm before starting, and
the company was negligent in not having a lookout
upon the coach.   This question of negligence was properly

submitted to the jury, and with its findings we cannot interfere.

Appellant contends that plaintiff was a trespasser at the time he was struck by the train, and that it owed him no duty except the negative one of not injuring him willfully and maliciously. There is much conflict in the evidence regarding the place where the boy was when injured, and it was a fair question for the jury to determine whether he was within the lines of the street, or so close to it as that the company owed him the duty of watchfulness. The jury evidently found that he was within the boundaries of the street, and, as the verdict has substantial support in the evidence, we should not interfere.

Again, it is said that the evidence shows without dispute that plaintiff was a trespasser, and therefore cannot recover. As we have said, there was a conflict in the evidence upon this point, and we do not interfere with the verdict in such cases.

Claim is made that plaintiff was guilty of contributory negligence in going in front of a moving train. As the boy was a mere child, it was a question for the jury to determine
2   whether he exercised such care as might reasonably be expected from a child of his age, under the circumstances disclosed in evidence. This question was properly submitted to the jury, and it evidently found against appellant's contention.

Complaint is made of the court's refusal to give certain instructions asked by appellant, and also of certain instructions given. We need not set them out. The requests, in so
3   far as they contained correct rules of law, were embodied in the charge, and those given enunciated the rules applicable to such cases in a clear and comprehensive manner.

Error is predicated upon the admission of the Carlisle tables in evidence. We think they were properly received. The injury was permanent, and plaintiff's expectancy of life
4   was a material inquiry. *Knapp v. Railroad Co.,* 71 Iowa, 41. The case of *Nelson v. Railroad Co.,* 38 Iowa, 564, relied upon by appellant, was overruled by the *Knapp Case.*

Mrs. William Allen, the plaintiff's mother, was allowed to testify, over defendant's objections, that she had tried to arrange to have David kept at school with the other children, so that he would not have to come home alone. We then find this in the record: "Q. What had you done in that regard? A. I had sent with the children, and asked Miss Watts to have him go in some other room, and wait, so our children could accompany him. She said that it was against the rules. (The defendant objects as incompetent and immaterial, and moves to strike out the answer for the same reason. Motion denied, and defendant excepts.)" This also appears in the record in connection with Lizzie Allen's evidence: "Q. What was the practice of your people about letting David go up town alone? (Objected to as incompetent, immaterial, and rebuttal. Overruled, and defendant excepts.) A. Well, we did not let him go up town alone. On the way to school he went with the other children. Q. How did he happen to come home from school alone? (Same objection. Overruled, and defendant excepts.) A. Because the other children were kept in an hour or so later than he was. Q. Is it the custom there at this school to dismiss the little ones earlier than the others? (Objected to as incompetent, immaterial, irrelevant, and there is no custom pleaded. Overruled, and defendant excepts.) A. Yes, sir." It is manifest that each and all of these rulings were erroneous. The evidence was offered in rebuttal, but we find nothing which it rebuts. Again, the care exercised by the parents or relatives of plaintiff was wholly immaterial to any issue in the case. We are of opinion, however, that the error was without prejudice, for the reason that the court instructed the jury that it was plainiff's want of care contributing to his injury which would bar him of recovery. True, nothing was said in the charge about his parents' duty. But the necessary inference to be drawn from the charge was that it was plaintiff's want of care alone which would constitute contributory negligence, and that the care exercised by his parents, or the want of it, was an immaterial matter.

II.   Appellee's counsel in his closing argument referred to a number of cases decided by this court in which verdicts for large amounts have been permitted to stand.   Objection was made to this line of argument, but, as the presiding judge was absent from the room, he had to be called, that the matter might be considered.   After due deliberation, the court held that the argument was improper, and directed the jury not to consider it.   As we understand it, a further colloquy was had

6   between counsel, after the judge had returned to the room, over what had been done in some other cases.   It is insisted that the case should be reversed because of the absence of the judge during the argument of the case.   We have already condemned such practice.   *State v. Carnagy,* 106 Iowa, 483.   But we further said in that case that, if it is satisfactorily appears that no prejudice resulted, the case will not be reversed for this ground alone.   It affirmatively appears that no prejudice resulted in this case; indeed, counsel for appellant does not contend that there was any.

III.   We are asked to reduce the verdict.   While it is quite large, yet we are not justified in disturbing it.   Pain and suffering was an element of damage in addition to the

7   actual physical disfigurement and loss of earning capacity, and we cannot interfere.   There are no prejudicial errors, and the judgment is AFFIRMED.

THE BENTON COUNTY SAVINGS BANK, Appellant, v. THOMAS T. STRAND, Executor.

Alteration of Note: JURY QUESTION.   The executor of the indorsee of a note defended an action thereon against him in his representative capacity on the ground that when his testator indorsed the note the words "demand, notice, and protest waived," stamped in red ink between the order to pay, written with a pen, and the indorsee's signature underneath, were not on the note.   The executor who was a witness of the indorsement, testified that the
1   words were not there when the indorsement was made, but his conclusion was reached under circumstances that made its correctness doubtful.   *Held,* that it was error to refuse to admit the

note itself as evidence, since the indorsement thereon being a considerable space below the order to pay, raised a question for the jury as to the correctness of the executor's statement.

PERSONAL TRANSACTION WITH DECEDENT. In an action by the holder of a note, his immediate indorser is incompetent to testify, as against the estate of the deceased payee, that, before the name of a witness to payee's indorsement was placed on the paper, the

3 words, "demand, notice, and protest waived," were on the back of the note, since the evidence is, in effect, that the words were there when the payee's name was indorsed, which would be testifying to a personal transaction between himself and his deceased indorser as to the circumstances under which she indorsed the note.

Witnesses: CONTRADICTION BY ONE CALLING. A party is not bound
2 by statements of his own witness, if shown to be untrue by other evidence.

Probate Law: PLEA AND PROOF. Code, 1873, section 2410, provides that all claims filed against an estate, not expressly admitted in writing and signed by the executor with the approbation of the court, shall be considered as denied without any pleading on behalf of the estate. Acts Twenty-sixth General Assembly, chap-
4 ter 25, amending the section reads "provided that the burden of proving that a claim is unpaid shall not be placed on the party filing the claim against the estate; but that the executor or administrator may, on the trial of said cause, subject the claimant to an examination on the question of payment, but the estate shall not be concluded or bound thereby." *Held,* that under such law an executor in a probate proceeding need not plead a special defense to a note executed by testator in order to permit such defense to be proven.

Appeal from Benton District Court.—HON. G. W. BURNHAM, Judge.

THURSDAY, OCTOBER 27, 1898.

G. A. MILLER & SONS and V. A. Thomas executed their joint note to the plaintiff bank for one thousand dollars April 28, 1892. E. E. Hartung is the cashier of the plaintiff bank. On the back of the note are the following indorsements:

"Pay E. E. Hartung or order. Demand, notice, and protest waived.   her

                                                  "Sophia X Johnson.
        "Witness: Axel Mehlberg.   mark.
        "Pay to Benton County Savings Bank.
                                                  "E. E. Hartung."

Sophia Johnson has since died, and this is a proceeding to have the note established as a claim against her estate, because of the indorsement. The claim was filed in due form, and the issue thereon is such as arises by operation of law, no answer being filed. A jury was impaneled to try the issues, and at the close of the evidence the court, on motion of the administrator, instructed for a verdict in his favor, and the plaintiff appealed.—*Reversed.*

Tom H. Milner for appellant.

Gilchrist & Whipple and *B. L. Wick* for appellee.

Granger, J.—I.　Axel Mehlberg is the present executor of the estate, and is substituted as defendant in lieu of Thomas T. Strand, now deceased. Mehlberg is the witness to the signature of Sophia Johnson on the back of the note. The executor denies liability on the note, on a claim that when Mrs. Johnson indorsed the note the words, "Demand,

1　notice, and protest waived," were not on the note. We have the original note for inspection, and the words, "Pay to the order of E. E. Hartung," are written in ink with a pen. Just below these words, in red ink, as made by a stamp, are the words, "Demand, notice, and protest waived," followed by the signatures. At the trial, Mehlberg was the witness for plaintiff, and testified that he was a son-in-law of Mrs. Johnson, knew her in her lifetime, and was present when the indorsement was made. He also testified that when the indorsement was made he did not see the words, "Demand, notice, and protest waived;" and later in his testimony he said that, when the signature of Mrs. Johnson was placed on the note, only the words written in ink were above the signature. This means that the words, "Demand, notice, and protest waived," were not there. The plaintiff offered the note in evidence, which the court, on objection by defendant refused, and the ruling is assigned as error. To a proper consideration of the question, it should be borne in mind that the signature of Mrs. Johnson on the note is not questioned. It conclusively appears. The issue of fact in the case is, ·was the stamp impression of the words, "Demand, notice, and protest waived," placed on the note after the signature was made ? It is not easy to give the true state of Mehlberg's testimony as it appears in the record. It is not too much to say that his conclusion that the words were not there when the signature was made is reached under circumstances that make the conclusion doubtful. There is in his testimony, taken as a whole, an element of uncertainty. As we have said, the note is before us for inspection, and it is not to be said that the note, as evidence, would not aid to a conclusion of the fact at issue. The manner in which the writing in ink first appears, then the stamp impression followed by the signature, showing the spaces with the indorsements as they new are, and as they would be with the words in dispute omitted, would certainly aid in determining the question of fact. It is to be borne in mind that to admit the note in evidence is not to concede a liability thereon, but to merely make it evidence, so that the manner and appearance of the indorsement may be considerd with other evidence to know whether it has been changed or not. In case of a disputed signature, when the issue is made, the signature in question is proper in evidence on the question of its genuineness. We do not see why the same rule ·does not obtain here, where the genuineness of an indorsement is involved. By the ruling the issue of fact was taken from the jury; the court saying, in effect, that the indorsement itself could not be considered to discredit the testimony of Mehlberg, if, as evidence, it would have that effect. And we may properly say that, with the note in evidence, we think there would have been a question for the jury. That Mehlberg was plaintiff's witness makes no difference. Plaintiff was not bound by his statements, if shown untrue by other evidence.

II. In view of a new trial, it is probably well that we should settle a dispute as to the competency of E. E. Hartung as a witness for plaintiff. It will be remembered that he is the indorsee in the indorsement in question, so that it was a

personal transaction between him and Mrs. Johnson. He was
present when the indorsement was made, and was a witness
for plaintiff, and testified to the time when he first saw the
words, "Demand, notice, and protest waived," on the back of
the note. He testified to the fact in different ways, as that he
saw the words there before the name of Axel Mehlberg
3   was written there. The purpose of the evidence was to
show that he saw the words there before the name of
Mrs. Johnson was placed to the indorsement. The court
struck out such evidence as being incompetent under section
3639 of the Code of 1873. The ruling was right. For the
witness to say that he saw the words on the note before Mehlberg's name was there was to say, in effect, that the words
were there when Mrs. Johnson's name was placed there, which
he would not be permitted to do, because it would be testifying
as to a personal transaction between himself and Mrs. Johnson, by stating the circumstances under which she signed the
note. It is said that, if she were alive, she could not contradict
the statement of the witness that he did see the words there
before Mehlberg's name was there, but we think she could.
Mehlberg's name was placed on the note to witness her signature, which she knew; and, if she knew that the words were not
there when she signed, she could say that they were not there
when Mehlberg signed. It is to be said that the indorsement,
including the witnessing, was a transaction between Mrs.
Johnson and Hartung, at which both were present; and any
testimony by Hartung that would disclose the transaction as
then seen by him would be within the provisions of the section,
and prohibited. It is thought that some language in *McElhen-
ney v. Hendricks,* 82 Iowa, 657, authorizes such testimony,
wherein it is said that "the statute does not exclude the proof
of facts from which by inference other facts may be found."
The language is applied to a different state of facts from those
in this case, and as applied is correct.

III.   It is probably well that we should settle the question of the necessity to plead the special defense before it could

be proven. It will be remembered that a denial of the claim was
the statutory one only, and it is thought that, as the
4   claim of an alteration of the indorsement is a special
defense, it should have been pleaded as such, even in a
probate proceeding. A statute in force when the cause was tried
is as follows: "All claims filed and not expressly admitted in
writing, signed by the executor with the approbation of the
court, shall be considered as denied without any pleading on
behalf of the estate." Code 1873, section 2410. The section
was amended by chapter 75, Acts Twenty-sixth General
Assembly, as follows: " 'Provided that the burden of proving
that a claim is unpaid shall not be placed upon the party filing
a claim against the estate;' but that the executor or administrator may, on the trial of said cause, subject the claimant to
an examination on the question of payment, but the estate shall
not be concluded or bound thereby." The law as amended
does not make it necessary to plead special defenses, as in other
cases. The present law provides that special defenses must
be pleaded. Code, section 3340. The question must be determined under the law as it was when determined below. Under
the law as it then stood, the claimant was required to show that
he had a valid claim, even to the extent of showing that the
signature was genuine, without a compliance with our general statutory provision as to how the genuineness of a signature can be put in issue. Code 1873, section 2730. We think
in this case the issue is such that the question of the liability
of the estate for the payment of the note is presented. When
the signature to the note is so established as to admit the note
in evidence with the indorsements, it may be sufficient, *prima
facie,* to show a right of recovery. If so, it would be a compliance with the rule that the law puts in issue the truth of every
allegation and claim which is essential to the plaintiff's recovery. If afterwards the integrity of the claim is assailed, the
right of recovery must depend on the weight of the evidence.
For the error in excluding the note when offered in evidence,
the judgment must be REVERSED.

612
388

CONRAD SCHOPP *v.* C. C. TAFT AND COMPANY, *et al.,*
Appellants.

Sale: ACCEPTANCE: *Warranty.* A purchaser is liable for the agreed
1 price of goods accepted by him without objections after oppor-
nity of inspection, in the absence of a warranty intended to survive acceptance.

Evidence. In an action to recover the purchase price of strawberries,
defended on the ground that the goods were not of a character
and quality ordered, a receipt given by the defendant to the rail-
8 way company for the car and its contents after partial inspection
which stated "received above O. K." is admissible in evidence.

Appeal: OBJECTION BELOW. The failure of a party to plead waiver
2 cannot be taken advantage of on appeal where the cause is tried
as if such plea had been filed, and the attention of the trial court
was not called to the defect.

Appeal from Polk District Court.—HON. W. A. SPURRIER,
Judge.

THURSDAY, OCTOBER 27, 1898.

ACTION at law to recover the purchase price of certain
strawberries sold and delivered to the defendants. Defendants admit the purchase, but plead that the berries were not
of the character and quality ordered. They say that when
delivered the berries were badly decayed, and were not worth
to exceed the sum of one hundred and sixty dollars, which
amount they tendered to the plaintiff, with costs of suit.
Defendants further aver that the plaintiff negligently and
carelessly shipped the berries in a car partially filled with
cabbage; that the cabbage caused the car to become heated,
that the berries were injured thereby; and that defendants have been damaged in the sum of two hundred and eighty
dollars. The case was submitted to a jury, resulting in a verdict and judgment for the plaintiff, and defendants appeal.—
Affirmed.

Berryhill & Henry for appellants.

Cummins, Hewitt & Wright for appellee.

DEEMER, C. J.—The trial court submitted the case to the jury on the issue of negligence, and refused an instruction asked by the defendants in the following words: "If the contract was for a certain quality of berries, and you find that the berries were not of that quality when loaded in St. Louis, then defendants are not prevented, by reason of taking the berries from the car, from recovering such damages as resulted to the defendants from the fact that the berries were not of the quality ordered, or from the fact, if you find it to be a fact, that the berries were shipped with cabbage, and that the presence of such cabbages brought about the injury or damage to the berries. If you find that such damages resulted to the defendants, then you are to allow such damages as a credit upon the contract price for the berries." Error is assigned upon this refusal. It will be noticed that defendants do not plead breach of warranty in the sale of the property. Their defense is that the berries were not of the kind and quality ordered, and were not worth to exceed the sum of one hundred and sixty dollars.

1   The evidence shows that they accepted the fruit without objection, and refused to pay because it was not what they ordered. We understand the law to be well settled that when goods are tendered by the seller in performance of an executory contract of sale, and accepted by the buyer after opportunity of inspection, without objection, the purchaser is liable for the price agreed upon, unless there be a warranty intended to survive the acceptance. *Allison v. Vaughan,* 40 Iowa, 421; *Hirshhorn v. Stewart,* 49 Iowa, 418; *Mackey v. Swartz,* 60 Iowa, 710.

Defendants insist, however, that this rule of law is based upon waiver, and that, as plaintiff did not plead waiver, he cannot rely upon it. For the purposes of the case, we may concede that plaintiff should have pleaded waiver in

2   his reply in order to properly present the issue; but we find, upon examining the record, that the case was tried upon the theory that such a pleading was not necessary

to present the question. Evidence to sustain the waiver was introduced without objection, and the case was tried as if such issue was tendered. Moreover, the instructions given by the court were not excepted to. The sole complaint with reference thereto is that the court failed to give the instruction asked. That, as we have seen, related to breach of warranty or of contract, and to the damages resulting therefrom, and, as we have seen, was properly refused. Again, by the terms of the contract between the parties, the fruit was to be delivered to the purchasers at St. Louis, Mo., and there is no evidence as to the actual value of the goods in St. Louis at the time they were delivered. As counsel were content to try the case in the trial court as if a reply pleading waiver had been filed, and as they did not properly call the attention of the trial court to the defect, requests for instructions or otherwise, they are in no position to take advantage of the omission. See *Beach v. Wakefield*, 107 Iowa, — (76 N. W. Rep. 688), and cases cited.

II. After partially inspecting the goods, defendants gave a receipt to the railroad company for the car and its contents, which contained this statement, "Received above O. K."

3   This receipt was offered in evidence by the plaintiff, and admitted over defendants' objection. There was no error in this. The condition of the goods when received was a material inquiry, and defendants' written admission that they were "O· K." was relevant and competent evidence. We discover no prejudicial error, and the judgment is AFFIRMED.

CHARLES EHRCK v. IDA A. EHRCK, Appellant.

Homesteads: SELECTION. Where a wife living apart from her hus-
1   band selects a homestead in lands owned by her, her selection will
not, in the absence of evidence of bad faith on her part in making
2   it, be set aside, and the selection of the husband adopted, though
the wife's selection is from the roughest and most unproductive
portion of the tract and cut off from convenient access to a highway.

DESERTING WIFE: *Occupancy by husband.* A wife who chooses to
8 live apart from her husband is not entitled to any benefit from
the homestead property set off in land owned by her, but the husband has full right during his occupancy to cultivate it.

Appeal from Plymouth District Court.—HON. J. F. OLIVER,
Judge.

THURSDAY, OCTOBER 27, 1898.

ACTION in equity, wherein the plaintiff and defendant,
husband and wife, living apart from each other, each ask that
the selection of a homestead made by them severally in a certain eighty-acre tract of land owned by the defendant be confirmed. Plaintiff prays that he may be allowed the full use of
the homestead, and that the defendant be restrained from
taking possession of the house, and from removing the property therefrom, and that the selection of a homestead made by
the defendant be set aside. Defendant prays in her cross
petition that she be granted the exclusive right to cultivate
the homestead selected by her, and that plaintiff's selection
of a homestead be set aside. Decree was rendered confirm-
ing the selection of a homestead as made by plaintiff, and
enjoining the defendant from interfering with or preventing
the plaintiff from enjoying said homestead as prayed by him
"during the time she shall fail to live on the same ——, but
defendant may equally occupy, use, and enjoy such homestead jointly with the plaintiff whenever she may desire to
return and live upon the same as a homestead." It was further decreed that, during the time defendant remains absent
from said homestead as selected by the plaintiff, plaintiff shall
have the full right to farm and cultivate the same for homestead purposes during the time he may continue to live upon
and occupy the same, and to use the crops raised thereon by
him during the time she does not live upon the same. From
this decree the defendant appeals.—*Reversed.*

Zink & Rosberry for appellant.

I. S. Struble for appellee.

GIVEN, J.—I.   Plaintiff and defendant were married in Iowa in 1880, and soon thereafter removed to Oregon, where they lived together for a time, after which the defendant returned to Plymouth county, Iowa; the plaintiff remaining in Oregon.   After about eleven years' separation, the defendant returned to Oregon, and there lived with her husband until 1893, when they returned to Plymouth county, and went to live together on a certain eighty-acre tract ·
1   of land owned by the defendant.   They lived together thereon until October 20, 1896, when the defendant left the plaintiff, and has ever since lived apart from him; he continuing to live upon and cultivate said land.   Defendant brought an action for divorce on the ground of cruel and inhuman treatment, and in November, 1896, after a hearing on the merits, her petition was dismissed.   Soon thereafter the defendant, without the plaintiff's knowledge, caused a survey and plat of a homestead in said land to be made and recorded, which she now asks to have confirmed.   Thereafter plaintiff commenced this action to set aside said selection, and to restrain the defendant, as already stated.   Pending this action the plaintiff caused the west forty of said eighty acres to be surveyed, platted, and recorded as a homestead, and it is this selection which he asks to have confirmed.

II.   Appellant's counsel state the questions to be considered as follows: "(1)   Which of the homesteads selected, platted and recorded (the one by the appellant, or the one by her husband) shall be preferred, and allowed to stand as the homestead of the family?   (2)   Who is entitled to cultivate the homestead, whichever it may be, and to enjoy the crops, the rents and profits therefrom?"   They say: "As to which one of the two selections of homestead shall be allowed to stand depends upon the rights of the respective parties, at the times they made their respective selections, to select, plat, and record a homestead from the eighty-acre tract

owned by the appellant, and occupied by them as a homestead,
and not upon the form, the fairness, or the convenience
2   of such selections." Appellee does not question that
the right to select the homestead was primarily in the
owner, nor that her selection, if fairly made, with due regard
to his rights, should control. He insists that her selection
was made in bad faith, and with intent to deprive him of
his homestead rights; that she selected the poorest, roughest,
and most unproductive part of the land; and that her selection is cut off from convenient access to the highway. Appellant's selection is out of the southeast corner of the eighty;·
the lines being at right angles, and so as to include the buildings, and ready access to a highway. If it be true that the
land selected by appellant is not the most productive part of
the eighty, yet we know of no law that would compel the
appellant to select the most productive part. There are many
reasons that might control in making such a selection,—as,
for instance, that the most productive part should be reserved
for the purpose of renting. If it may be said that appellant
was bound to make her selection with regard to the rights of
appellee, we think the evidence fails to show that her selection
was not so made. The right to select being primarily, if not
exclusively, in the appellant, and she having made the selection that she did, we conclude that that selection must control.
Having reached this conclusion, we are not required to
determine whether the right of selection was exclusively with
the appellant, nor whether appellee had any right to select.

III. The further contention as to which of these parties is entitled to enjoy the homestead is easily answered.
They are both entitled to live upon and enjoy it, but, so long
as appellant chooses to live elsewhere, she is not
3   entitled to any benefit from the homestead, and
appellee is entitled to have the full right to farm and
cultivate the same so long as he continues to live upon and
occupy it as a homestead. The decree of the district court is
reversed, and the case remanded for a decree in conformity
with this opinion. REVERSED.

F. M. HUBBELL v. POLK COUNTY, *et al.*, Appellants.

Intoxicating Liquors: LEVY OF TAX. The requirement of Acts
1 Twenty fifth General Assembly, chapter 62, section 9, that the
2 board of supervisors at the regular meeting in September shall
8 levy an annual tax upon premises used for the sale of liquors is
   directory, and the fact that levy was not made until December
   will not invalidate it when the delay did not prejudice the person
   assessed.

EVIDENCE: *Presumptions.* It will be presumed in support of the
   validity of a tax that it was levied at a regular meeting of the
4 board of supervisors where that is an essential requirement and
   the contrary is not shown.

DEEMER, C. J. and GRANGER, J., dissenting.

REBATE. One against whose property used for the sale of intoxicating
   liquors the annual tax of six hundred dollars provided for by Acts
   Twenty fifth General Assembly, chapter 62, section 9, has been
2 levied is not entitled to a remission of the tax for the balance of
   the year where the sales were suspended after continuing about
   nine months.

Appeal from Polk District Court.—HON. T. F. STEVENSON,
Judge.

THURSDAY, OCTOBER 27, 1898.

ACTION at law to recover an amount alleged to have been
paid as a liquor tax, under protest. There was a trial by the
court without a jury, and a judgment in favor of the plaintiff
for the amount claimed. The defendants appeal.—*Reversed.*

W. G. Harvison for appellants.

St. John & Stevenson for appellee.

ROBINSON, J.—On the thirtieth day of May, 1894, the
plaintiff, being the owner of lot 5 in block 25 of the original
town of Ft. Des Moines, now a part of the city of Des Moines,
leased it to F. V. Newman, who took possession of the leased

premises, and commenced therein the business of keeping for sale and selling intoxicating liquors, under the provisions of chapter 62, Acts Twenty-fifth General Assembly. Before Newman commenced the business, he reported the property to the county auditor for taxation, under the act specified. At a session of the board of supervisors of Polk county held on the twentieth day of June, 1894, a tax was levied on the property for the period commencing June 8, and ending December 31, 1894, which was paid by Newman. The board of supervisors did not levy any liquor tax on the property at the regular September meeting, but on the twenty-eight day of December, 1894, the board levied a liquor tax on the property, and against the plaintiff and Newman, in the sum of six hundred dollars, for the year 1895. The tax thus levied was entered upon the tax list, which was delivered to the county treasurer for collection. Newman paid the portions of the tax which fell due on the first days of January, April, and July; and on the thirtieth day of September, 1895, he discontinued business, and no intoxicating liquors were kept for sale or sold on the premises during the remainder of the year. The plaintiff appeared before the board of supervisors at its October, 1895, meeting, and asked that the portion of the tax then unpaid be remitted, on the ground that the business for which it was levied had been discontinued; but the request was denied. The property was advertised by the county treasurer for sale for the unpaid portions of the tax; and on the sixteenth day of December, 1895, the plaintiff, to prevent the sale of his property, paid, under protest, the amount for which the sale was advertised. This action is brought against the county and its treasurer, to recover the amount thus paid, with interest.

Section 9, chapter 62, Acts Twenty-fifth General Assembly, which governs this case, contains the following: "At the regular meeting of the board of supervisors in September, they shall levy an annual tax of six hundred dollars   *   *   * against each person carrying on or conducting a place for the sale of intoxicating liquors, and also against the real property, and the owner thereof, in which or upon which said place is located . * * * At all regular meetings, the board of supervisors shall examine the assessment book of liquor dealers, and levy taxes against such persons as shall have become liable thereto under the provisions of this act, who have not already been taxed as herein provided for the same year, but only a pro rata amount of the tax for the remainder of the year, dependent upon the time of assessment." It was determined in *David v. Hardin County,* 104 Iowa, 204, that the year contemplated in that section is a calendar year; and in *Engelthaler v. Linn County,* 104 Iowa, 293, it was decided that there cannot be a rebate of any part of the tax levied where the sales are continued more than six months of 2   the year. The sales involved in this case were continued nine months of the year 1895. Therefore the relief demanded should be denied if there was a valid levy of the tax for that year. It is claimed that the levy was without effect, because made in December, instead of in September of the year 1894. Is the statute directory or mandatory? It was said in *French v. Edwards,* 13 Wall. 506, that "there are undoubtedly many statutory requirements intended for the guide of officers in the conduct of business devolved upon them, which do not limit their power or render its exercise in disregard of the requisitions ineffectual. Such, generally, are regulations designed to secure order, system, and dispatch in proceedings, and by a disregard of which the rights of parties cannot be injuriously affected. Provisions of this character are not usually regarded as mandatory, unless accompanied by negative words importing that the acts required shall not be done in any other manner or time than that designated. But when the requisitions prescribed are intended for the protection of the citizen, and to prevent a sacrifice of his property, and by a disregard of which his rights might be and generally would be injuriously affected, they are not directory, but mandatory. They must be followed, or the acts done will be invalid. The power of the officer in all such cases is limited by the measure and conditions prescribed for its exercise." In Cooley Constitutional Limitations (5th ed.), 92, after a review of authorities, the rule is stated as follows: "Those directions which are not of the essence of the thing to be done, but which are given with a view merely to a proper, orderly, and prompt conduct of business, and by a failure to obey which the rights of those interested will not be prejudiced, are not commonly to be regarded as mandatory; and if the act is performed, but not in the time or in the precise mode indicated, it may still be sufficient if that which is done accomplishes the substantial purpose of the statute. But this rule presupposes that no negative words are employed in the statute which expressly or by necessary implication forbid the doing of the act at any other time or in any other manner than as directed." In Sutherland Statutory Construction, sections 446-448, rules are stated as follows: "The consequential distinction between directory and mandatory statutes is that the violation of the former is attended with no consequences, while a failure to comply with the requirements of the other is productive of serious results. This distinction grows out of a fundamental difference in the nature, importance, and relation to the legislative purpose of the statute so classified." And "where the provision is in affirmative words, and there are no negative words, and it relates to the time or manner of doing the acts which constitute the chief purpose of the law, or those incidental or subsidiary thereto, by an official person, the provision has been usually treated as directory. Generally it is so, but it is a question of intent." Also, "provisions regulating the duties of public officers, and specifying the time for their performance, are in that regard generally directory. Though a statute directs a thing to be done at a particular time, it does not necessarily follow that it may not be done afterwards. In other words, as the cases universally hold, a statute specifying a time within which a public officer is to perform an official act regarding the rights and duties of others is directory, unless the nature of the act to be performed, or the phraseology of the statute, is such that the designation of time must be considered as a limitation of the power of the officer." In 23 Am. & Eng. Enc. Law, 455, it is said: "It is, in general, true, that negative terms in a statute show a legislative intent to make the provision imperative, requiring a strict performance in respect of both time and manner. Yet, as a rule of universal application, this cannot be relied upon, as provisions framed in negative language have been adjudged to be directory merely. Nevertheless, it is undoubtedly true that a design to make a provision merely directory is more rarely to be found under negative words. On the other hand, the absence of negative words from a statute is not always conclusive of an intention that the provision is to be regarded as directory simply, as affirmative words, if absolute, explicit, and peremptory, showing that no discretion was intended to be given, may, and often have been, held to render the statute mandatory." On page 458 of the same work the rule is stated as follows: "Statutory prescriptions in regard to the time, form, and mode of proceeding by public functionaries are generally directory, as they are not of the essence of the thing to be done, but are given simply with a view to secure system, uniformity, and dispatch in the conduct of public business."

These rules have abundant support in adjudicated cases, and apply to statutes which prescribe methods of levying taxes. It is said in Cooley on Taxation (page 284) that "all legislation must be supposed to take into account the possible, if not the probable, mistakes and irregularities of officers in executing the provisions of the law; and it is hardly reasonable to infer an intent on the part of a legislative body that a failure of administrative officers to comply with any provision made for the benefit of the state exclusively, or merely as a guide in orderly proceedings, should deprive the state of all benefit to be derived from a compliance with other provisions that embody the main purpose and object of the law. Nor, on the other hand, is it to be supposed the legislature intended its own securities for the protection of individual rights and property should be disregarded with impunity." The decisions of this court are in accord with the authorities cited. Section 746 of the Revision of 1860 provided that "at the regular meeting in June in each and every year the board of supervisors shall levy the requisite taxes for the current year, in accordance with law." Section 2, chapter 24, of the Acts of the Extra Session of the Eighth General Assembly, which took effect in June, 1861, provided that "the board of supervisors of each county shall hold a session on the first Monday of September, in the year 1861, and each year, thereafter, at which session they shall levy the several taxes as required by sections 710 and 746" of the Revision. Yet it was held in *Easton v. Savery*, 44 Iowa, 654, that the statute last mentioned was directory, and that taxes levied at the June meeting of the board were valid. It was said: "No one should be at liberty to plant himself upon the nonfeasance or misfeasance of officers under the revenue law, which in no way concern himself, and make them the excuse for a failure on his part to perform his own duty. It was the duty of the defendants to pay their taxes, and it is no excuse that the officers did not strictly perform their duty unless, as we have said, defendants were prejudiced thereby." In *Perrin v. Benson*, 49 Iowa, 325, it was held that "where a levy is not made at a proper time, through negligence or mistake, it may be made at the time fixed by law for making the succeeding tax levy." It appeared in that case that a school-house tax, which was voted, and should have been levied in the year 1875, was levied in the year 1876, and the legality of the tax was affirmed. See, also, *Hill v. Wolfe*, 28 Iowa, 577; *Prouty v. Tallman*, 65 Iowa, 354; *Burlington Gas Light Co. v. City of Burlington*, 101 Iowa, 458.

The levying of the tax in controversy did not in any manner prejudice the plaintiff. He did not lose any right by the delay from September to December in making the levy. The undisputed fact is that the tax in question ought to have been levied in September, 1894, and the plaintiff should not be permitted to profit by the mistake or negligence of the board of supervisors in not making

3

the levy until December. The only part of the section fixing
the time for making the levy which can be regarded as negative in character is this: "But only a pro rata amount of the
tax for the remainder of the year, dependent upon the time of
the assessment." It seems to be clear, however, that the negative or limiting effect of that clause relates to the amount, and
not to the time of the assessment. The preceding words, "for
the same year," refer not to the year in which the meeting of
the board of supervisors at which the tax is levied is held, but
to the year for which a tax has already been levied. That the
tax for an entire year may be legally levied at a meeting other
than the one for September is, we think, evident. If Newman
had commenced the sale of intoxicating liquors in December,
1894, and the place in which the business was carried on had
been listed for taxation in that month, the board of supervisors would have had the power at the meeting of January,
1895, to levy a tax for the part of the month of
December, during which the business was carried on, and also
for all of the year 1895, notwithstanding the provision that
"only a pro rata amount of the tax for the remainder of the
year" should be levied; and we are of the opinion that there
is no well-grounded reason for denying to the board the power
to levy the 1895 tax in the year 1894, after the September
meeting.

Whether the levy in question was made at a regular meeting is not shown. The law in force at that time provided that
the members of the board should meet on the first Mondays
of January, April, June, September, and the first
4   Monday after the general election in each year. The
record does not show affirmatively that the tax in question was levied at a regular meeting of the board, but the appellant states in argument that it was levied during the "November meeting, and on December 28, 1894." This is not denied by
the plaintiff; but he states that "counsel for the county says
that this meeting in December was an adjourned session of
the regular November meeting of the board, * * * but
he is not borne out by the record." Still, conceding this to

be so, we have the question yet to determine: "For what period may the board of supervisors, at any regular session in a given year, other than the September meeting, levy a liquor tax?" The presumption is that the tax was levied at a proper time, and the burden was on the plaintiff to show that the presumption is not well founded. Having failed to do so, we must presume that the tax was levied at a regular meeting, if that was essential to its validity. Since it is clear that the plaintiff was not prejudiced by the levying of the tax in December instead of in September, there does not seem to be any sufficient reason, in view of the language of the statute and the authorities cited, for depriving the county and city of the benefit of the tax. We conclude that judgment should have been rendered in favor of the defendant for costs, and the judgment of the district court is therefore REVERSED.

GRANGER, J. (dissenting).—The pivotal question is as to the authority of the board of supervisors to levy the annual tax at another meeting of the board than the regular one in September. The holding of the majority is that it may be done at a regular meeting not in September, and it is left in doubt if even a levy at a regular meeting would be essential to its validity. From such a holding I dissent, because I think it violates the letter and spirit of the statute, is opposed to a former construction of the law by this court on the same subject, and it is inequitable. I make no contention as to the general rules announced in the opinion, and I favor a liberal construction of the law, to the end that the general revenues for the conduct of the government may be secured; and I may add that I favor a liberal construction of the law in question to the end that the legislative purpose may be as fully attained as possible. That the principal object of the law was the attainment of revenue I do not think; but, on the contrary, I regard its provisions as to assessments as but incidental, and designed, mainly as a burden upon the liquor traffic, with a view to discourage it; so that the reasons for treating the general law as to public revenues as directory are without special, if any, force in its construction. These reasons, however, might not lead me to treat the provisions of the law in question, as to the levy of the annual tax, otherwise than as directory, were it not for the conclusive terms of the law against such a construction. Section 9 of the act is the one giving authority to levy the annual tax, and it also makes provision for the levy of a pro rata tax. The section is so much of an argument in itself that I quote it in this connection: "Sec. 9. At the regular meeting of the board of supervisors in September, they shall levy an annual tax of six hundred dollars, payable semi-annually at the time and place as hereinafter provided against each person carrying on or conducting a place for the sale of intoxicating liquors, and also against the real property, and the owner thereof, in which or upon which said place is located: provided, that if the application is made to cancel the tax as hereinbefore provided, and the trial of the cause should be delayed for any reason, then the levy, if any be made, shall be made at the next regular meeting of the board. At all regular meetings, the board of supervisors shall examine the assessment book of liquor dealers, and levy taxes against such persons as shall have become liable thereto under the terms of this act, who have not already been taxed as herein provided for the same year, but only a pro rata amount of the tax for the remainder of the year, dependent upon the time of assessment." Prior sections of the act provided for an application to rebate or cancel the tax after it has been listed by the assessor. To meet conditions under which the levy might not be made at the prescribed session, because of delays occasioned by such applications, the section authorizes such a tax to be levied at the next regular meeting of the board. In both cases there is a limitation, by the language of the law, to a particular session. These might not be conclusive against construing the statute as directory; but, having prescribed the time for the levy of the annual tax, the section proceeds to provide what the board may do at all regular meetings, which is that, as to taxes not already levied as therein provided for the same year, the board may levy taxes, but with this limitation: "But only a pro rata amount of the tax for the remainder of the year, dependent on the time of the assessment." Thus, we see that the legislature has, in terms, prescribed what may be done by the board at each of its regular meetings, and, as to such meetings, other than the levy of the annual tax, "as herein provided," there is the plain limitation upon the authority of the board to levy other than a pro rata tax. The statute seems to me hardly open to construction. I feel confident no case can be found where a court has held such a statute directory. As I view the statute, it is as if there was a provision that the annual tax should not be levied at a time other than as specified. The provisions for the levy of the pro rata tax make the public absolutely secure against loss of revenue because of a failure to levy the annual tax; so that the reasons fail under which statutes providing for general revenues are held directory.

This court has once expressed itself on this subject in what seems to me to be plain and conclusive terms. In *David v. Hardin County,* 104 Iowa, 204, we had under consideration the authority of the board, at its January meeting, to levy taxes for a part of the preceding year. The authority of the board to levy such taxes at a January meeting was so far involved that we stated the substance of section 9 of the act, as to the levy of the annual tax at the September meeting; and then, touching its authority at other meetings, we also stated the substance of the law showing such authority, and then quoted the limitations thereon as follows: "But only a pro rata tax for the remainder of the year depending upon the time of the assessment." In the opinion it is further said: "The assessment in this case was not made in time so that the board could make the levy at its September meeting. Not having been made until December 26th, the board could not make the levy until the January meeting, and the statute says that, when so levied, it shall be but a pro rata amount of the tax for the remainder of the year, dependent upon the time of the assessment." My view of the law could not well have a more direct recognition by this court. I should say that the

question of the authority of the board to levy the annual tax
was not involved in that case directly, but that of authority to
levy the pro rata tax was, which, incidentally, includes the
other.

I have said that the conclusion of the majority is inequitable. My reason for the statement is this: The careful reader
of the act authorizing the levy of the tax will see that the purpose was to impose such taxes for the period in which the business was carried on, except in cases of the annual levy, when
it is carried on more than six months of the year, but not the
full year. In cases where the business is not carried on to
exceed six months, the law provides for a rebate of the tax
pro rata. The seller in this case was not standing on techni-
calities, but paid the taxes quarterly, as if legally levied, for
three-fourths of the year, and as long as the business was conducted. The payment of the tax in question for which recovery is sought was demanded after the business was closed, and
paid under protest. In my judgment, it ought to be refunded,
and the judgment below AFFIRMED.

DEEMER, C. J.—I concur in the conclusion reached by
GRANGER, J., in his dissenting opinion.

HENRY BENNETT and ELLA BENNETT, Appellants, v. THE
CITY OF MARION.

Eminent Domain. The determination of the city council as to the
3 amount of land necessary to be taken for a proposed sewer outlet
is not final but subject to review by the courts.

SAME. The decision of a city council as to the amount of land necessary to be taken for a proposed sewer outlet will not be interfered
3 with on appeal if the land sought to be taken will to some extent
conduce to the public use, but any abuse of power will be
restrained.

SAME. A city, while allowed to determine for itself whether a sewer
outlet shall be constructed in a certain locality, should not be permitted to fix arbitrarily on *ex parte* consideration the amount of
2 land to be taken therefor but the land owner shall be allowed to

controvert allegations of the application by answer or other pleadings.

DAMAGES.   The jury in assessing damages for land condemned by the municipality for a sewer outlet may consider the effect upon the value of the remainder of the landowner's property or to what extent he will be inconvenienced in the use of it.

SAME.   The measure of damages for property condemned by a city for a sewer outlet is the difference between the fair market value of the whole tract immediately before the taking of the part condemned and the fair market value of the remainder immediately after the taking, less any advantage to the owner on account of the improvements.

INSTRUCTIONS.   An instruction not to allow damages for a possible misuse of land condemned for a sewer outlet, nor to assume that it will be made a nuisance, "or otherwise inconvenience plaintiff or lessen the value of his premises, except as hereinbefore explained," is too restrictive, where no explanation precedes

SAME.   An instruction that the material question in fixing the value of land condemned is its fair market value at the time of the appropriation, and another that the measure of damages is the difference between the market value of the whole tract immediately before taking and that of the remainder immediately afterwards, are erroneous, as conflicting.

Municipal Corporation: RESOLUTIONS.   A resolution of the council of a city of the second class having less than eight thousand inhabitants directing the mayor to institute proceedings to condemn property declared necessary for a sewer outlet need not be signed by the mayor, since by Acts Twentieth General Assembly, chapter 192, such requirement is limited to cities of the first class and those of the second class having over eight thousand inhabitants.

Evidence: JUDICIAL NOTICE.   The court will take judicial notice of the population of a city as determined by the last census.

Appeal from Linn District Court.—HON. WILLIAM G. THOMPSON, Judge.

THURSDAY, OCTOBER 27, 1898.

PROCEEDINGS to condemn a portion of the plaintiffs' farm for sewer purposes. The damages were fixed at three thousand two hundred dollars, and plaintiffs appeal.— *Reversed.*

Rickel & Crocker for appellants.

Charles J. Haas and *Jamison & Smyth* for appellees.

LADD, J.—The city council of Marion adopted a resolution on the fourteenth day of October, 1896, that about eighty-six acres of the plaintiffs' farm of one hundred and forty acres, adjoining the corporate limits, were necessary for a sewer outlet, and directed the mayor to institute proceedings necessary for condemnation. This resolution was not invalid because not signed by the mayor. The city, as appears by the last census, has a population of less than eight thousand inhabitants. This is a matter of which the courts will take judicial notice. *Kalbrien v. Leonard*, 34 Ind. 497; *People v. Page*, 6 Utah, 353 (23 Pac. Rep. 761); *Mertz v. City of Brooklyn*, 128 N. Y. 617 (28 N. E. Rep. 253); *City of Savannah v. Dickey*, 33 Mo. App. 522; Bradner Evidence, 98. Chapter 192 of the Acts of the Twentieth General Assembly, requiring the mayor to sign resolutions, is limited in its operation to cities of the first class, and those of the second class having over eight thousand inhabitants. *Heins v. Lincoln*, 102 Iowa, 69, relied on by appellants, involved a resolution by the council of a city of the first class.

II. The necessity for condemning private property for a public use is not of judicial cognizance, but lies exclusively within the province of the legislature. The power to condemn may, as in this case, be delegated to municipalities or agencies, and when this is done they have the same powers as the state acting through any regularly constituted authority. *Hanson v. Vernon*, 27 Iowa, 33; *Bankhead v. Brown*, 25 Iowa, 544; *Barrett v. Kemp*, 91 Iowa, 296; *Smith v. Hall*, 103 Iowa, 95; *State v. Rapp*, 39 Minn. 65 (38 N. W. Rep. 926); *Aldridge v. Spears*, 101 Mo. 400 (14 S. W. Rep. 118); *Tait's Ex'r v. Asylum*, 84 Va. 271 (4 S. E. Rep. 697); *Lumbering Co. v. Urquhart*, 16 Or. 67 (19 Pac. Rep. 78); *In re Poughkeepsie Bridge Co.*, 108 N. Y. 483 (15 N. E. Rep. 601); *Boom Co. v. Patterson*, 98 U. S. 406; Lewis Eminent Domain, section 238; Cooley Constitutional Limitations, section 538; *Lynch v. Forbes*, 161 Mass. 302 (42 Am. St. Rep. 402, 37 N. E. Rep. 437); 6 Am. & Eng. Enc. Law, 517. See *Town of Cherokee v. Sioux City & I. F. Town Lot & Land Co.*, 52

Iowa, 279; *Dewey v. City of Des Moines,* 101 Iowa, 416.
"Power to acquire real estate within and without their territorial limits, necessary for the purpose of outlets for their
sewers," is given cities of the second class by chapter 8 of the
Acts of Twenty-sixth General Assembly. See Code, section
881. A distinction is sought to be made between the necessity
for some land, and fixing the amount of the area necessary. The city may well be allowed to determine for
itself whether a particular improvement shall be made
(*e. g.* that a sewer outlet shall be constructed in a certain locality), but will it be permitted to say arbitrarily, and on *ex
parte* consideration, the amount of land it will have for that
purpose? This question was made by written objection filed,
and also by answer. These objections and the answer were
stricken, on motion of the city. The Code makes no provision
for raising jurisdictional issues in condemnation proceedings.
Where the averments of the application to condemn are not
traversed in any way, the court may well treat them as
admitted, and proceed to assess the damages under the statute. See *South Carolina Railroad Co. v. Blake,* 9 Rich. Law,
228. But suppose the owner insists he has not refused to
convey, or that he and the corporation have not failed to agree
on the compensation, or that all or a portion of the land is not
required or being appropriated for the public use; shall he
not be permitted to raise these issues in some appropriate manner? It is not so material how this is done, as it is that the
landowner be permitted to have them presented to the court in
some way and determined. We discover no reason for denying him the right to controvert the allegations of the application by answer or other pleading. While this is not authorized, by the statute, it is not prohibited, and is more definite
and convenient than resort to oral objections. *Rockwell v.
Bowers,* 88 Iowa, 88. See *Keokuk & N. W. Railway Co. v.
Donnell,* 77 Iowa, 221; *Hartley v. Railway Co.,* 85 Iowa,
458; *O'Hare v. Railroad Co.,* 139 Ill. Sup. 151 (28 N. E.
Rep. 924); *Corbin v. Railway Co.,* 66 Iowa, 269.

III. Is the determination of the city council of the amount of land necessary for use as a sewer outlet final, or may the question be reviewed by the courts? If the amount sought to be condemned is in excess of that necessary for the improvement, the appropriation of such excess is not for the public use. It will be noticed that the precise property, or the amount thereof, is not fixed by the legislature, but authority is conferred upon the city council to take for the public use only that real estate necessary therefor. If the use be not public, or the necessity does not exist, the owner ought not to be deprived of his property, notwithstanding compensation. With the policy or expediency of condemnation the courts have nothing to do. The necessity and the extent of the exercise of the power of eminent domain belong exclusively to the legislature,—the use being public,— provided such compensation is made, and the property sought to be taken will conduce to some extent to the accomplishment of the object to which it is devoted. Thus the mere public convenience will not justify the appropriation of property. *Memphis Freight Co. v. Mayor, etc., of Memphis,* 4 Cold. 425. *Prather v. Railroad Co.,* 52 Ind. 36: "Necessity is not made out by proof of great convenience, nor the enhancement of values, nor of the accumulation of property of the same kind for the same use." In other words, the appropriation may not be made for collateral purposes. *Spring Valley Waterworks v. San Mateo Waterworks,* 64 Cal. 133 (28 Pac. Rep. 447); *Jefferson v. Hazeur,* 7 La. Ann. 182; *Railroad Co. v. Davis,* 43 N. Y. 137. The city council had the power to finally determine the necessity of the improvement and its location, but its determination of the amount of land necessary therefor is subject to review by the courts. In many cases it may be difficult for the court to determine whether all the property sought by the corporation will be necessary, and it may be well to say that the opportunities of the latter to judge of its needs must be taken into consideration. The danger always to be guarded against is the abuse of power, in taking more from the citizen than is reasonably required for the improvement contemplated. The rule adopted in New York is that the property sought to be acquired must be for the purposes of the corporation, and reasonably necessary for the use for which it is condemned. *In re New York Cent. & H. R. Ry. Co.*, 77 N. Y. 248; *Railroad Co. v. Davis, supra.* The same rule obtains in other states. *Tracy v. Railroad Co.*, 80 Ky. 266; *Spring Valley Waterworks v. San Mateo Waterworks, supra; Railroad Co. v. Wiltse*, 116 Ill. 454 (6 N. E. Rep. 49); *O'Hare v. Railroad Co.*, 139 Ill. Sup. 151 (28 N. E. Rep. 925). A large discretion is lodged with the city council in fixing the amount of land necessary for the particular improvement, and its detemination should only be interfered with to prevent the abuse of power. If the land sought to be taken will to some extent conduce to the public use for which it is to be devoted, the decision of the municipality that it is necessary therefor should not be interfered with; otherwise it should be set aside. As supporting these views, see Lewis Eminent Domain, section 393; *O'Hare v. Railroad Co.*, 139 Ill. 151 (28 N. E. Rep. 293); *In re St. Paul & N. P. Ry. Co.*, 34 Minn. 227 (25 N. W. Rep. 345); *Wisconsin Cent. R. Co. v. Cornell University*, 52 Wis. 537 (8 N. W. Rep. 491); *Olmstead v. Proprietors*, 46 N. J. Law, 495; *Railroad Co. v. Davis*, 43 N. Y. 137; *Spring Valley Waterworks v. San Mateo Waterworks*, 64 Cal. 123 (28 Pac. Rep. 447); *Baltimore & O. R. Co. v. Pittsburg, W. & Ky. R. Co.*, 17 W. Va. 812; *Railway Co. v. Blake*, 9 Rich. Law, 228; *Railway Co. v. Love*, 81 N. C. 434; *McWhirter v. Cockrell*, 2 Head, 9; *Railway Co. v. Gay*, 32 La. Ann. 472. *Lynch v. Forbes*, 161 Mass. 302 (42 Am. St. Rep. 406, 37 N. E. Rep. 437) on which appellees rely, goes no further than to hold that the necessity for an improvement, and its location, are for the selectmen of the town to determine. The appropriation of land in excess or at variance with their powers was not involved. In *Stark v. Railroad Co.*, 43 Iowa, 502, it was held that land within the limit fixed by the legislature for a right of way is conclusively presumed to be necessary. *Barrett v.*

Kemp, supra, construed a statute essentially differing from that under consideration.

III.   At the request of the defendant the court gave the following instruction: "You are not to assume or consider that the land proposed to be appropriated will not be used in a lawful and proper manner for the purpose proposed by the defendant city, and you will not consider or allow any damages based upon the claim that said land proposed to be condemned will be used in such a manner as to constitute a nuisance or otherwise inconvenience the plaintiff or lessen the

4   value of his premises, except as hereinbefore explained." The portion of this instruction directing the jury that they cannot consider any possible unlawful or improper use of the premises is undoubtedly correct. If the sewer should so be used as to constitute a nuisance, it may be abated. Until the contrary is shown, it will be presumed that the city will construct and maintain it in a lawful manner. *King v. Railroad Co.,* 34 Iowa, 459; *Miller v. Railway Co.,* 63 Iowa, 685. The error in the instruction, however, lies in the prohibition from allowing any damages based on the use of the land so as to "otherwise inconvenience the plaintiff or lessen the value of the premises, except as hereinbefore explained." The exception amounts to nothing, as there is no explanation preceding it. This not only excludes the consideration of the improper use of the land, but also the natural and probable effect of the use for which it is condemned. We think it was proper for the jury to consider in what way the taking of land for the purpose would inconvenience the plaintiff in the use of the remainder of his farm, or lessen its value. If sewers properly constructed would affect the atmosphere, or otherwise interfere with the use and enjoyment of the premises, the jury should take this into consideration in making up their verdict. Such is the rule applicable to the condemnation of land for railroad purposes. *Smalley v. Railroad Co.,* 36 Iowa, 573; *Bell v. Railway Co.,* 74 Iowa, 345; *Ellsworth v. Railway Co.,* 91 Iowa, 391; *Dudley v. Railway Co.,*

77 Iowa, 408; *Dreher v. Railroad Co.,* 59 Iowa, 599; *Kuche-man v. Railway Co.,* 46 Iowa, 376. And we discover no reason why the same rule should not govern in the taking by a city.

IV. In the second paragraph of the instructions the jury are told the material question for their determination is "what was the fair market value of the said land at the time it was taken, to-wit, October 23, 1896"; and in the fifth paragraph the jury are required to use this form of verdict: "We, the jury, find the fair value of the land in controversy was on the 23d day of October, 1896, to be $——." The error of these instructions is manifest. They ignore any possible depreciation in the value of the remainder of the premises resulting from the appropriation of the eighty-six acres by the city. But for an omission, the correct rule was given, in an instruction asked by the defendant, as "the difference between the fair market value of the whole 140 acres immediately before the taking and appropriation of the 86 acres, and the fair market value of the remaining portion of 54 acres immediately after the taking and appropriation of the 86 acres." This should have been qualified so as to exclude any advantages to the owner on account of the improvement. Constitution, article 1, section 18; *Sater v. Plank-Road Co.,* 1 Iowa, 392; *Smalley v. Railroad Co.,* 36 Iowa, 571; *Gear v. Railroad Co.,* 39 Iowa, 23; *Renwick v. Railway Co.,* 49 Iowa, 664;*Hartshorn v. Railroad Co.,* 52 Iowa, 613; *Ham v. Railway Co.,* 61 Iowa, 716; *Ellsworth v. Railway Co.,* 91 Iowa, 386. And, too, these instructions are conflicting, as they furnish the jury different measures of damage. In one, and the form of verdict, the measure is fixed as the value of the land taken; and in the other, the loss occasioned by the taking, made up of its value and the injury to the remainder of the farm. That the jury was in doubt as to which rule must be followed is made apparent by the verdict returned in form as set out, with these words added: "$3,200 for the condemned part." Evidently the second paragraph was followed, rather than the correct rule. REVERSED.

STATE OF IOWA v. WILLIAM F. GOERING, Appellant.

Self Defense: INSTRUCTIONS. Where on a trial for assault, there was
1   evidence justifying a charge as to self defense, a charge convey-
2   ing the idea that one assaulted cannot defend himself unless it
3   reasonably appears that his life is in danger, or that he is likely to
4   suffer great bodily harm, is erroneous, since one assaulted may
5   repel force with force.

Appeal: REVIEW OF INSTRUCTIONS. Where affirmative error appears
6   in a charge, accused is not estopped to urge the objection on appeal
   by failure to ask a different charge.

Appeal from Marion District Court.—HON. J. D. GAMBLE,
Judge.

WEDNESDAY, DECEMBER 14, 1898.

DEFENDANT was charged by indictment with the crime
of assault with intent to inflict a great bodily injury. From
a judgment of conviction, he prosecutes this appeal.—
Reversed.

Crozier & McCormack for appellant.

Milton Remley, Attorney General, and *W. C. Kinkead*
for the State.

WATERMAN, J.—The assault is charged to have been
made upon one Lewis Leits. The evidence is not before us.
The record we have, sets out the indictment and the instructions given the jury, and this statement of facts: "There was
evidence on the part of the state tending to prove that the
defendant struck and beat one Lewis Leits with a club and
whip, the said Lewis Leits being at the time unarmed. On
the part of defendant, there was evidence tending to show that
the said Lewis Leits assaulted the defendant with a knife in
his hand, and that, when said assault was made, the defendant
struck him several blows, but with his fists only, and that he

did not at any time strike him with anything but his fists."
The sole complaint is of the tenth paragraph of the court's
charge to the jury, which is as follows: "The defendant
pleads not guilty, which plea puts in issue every material fact
necessary to support the indictment, and which must be established by the evidence beyond a reasonable doubt.

1   And, for further and additional defense, the defendant
claims that, at the time of the altercation with the said
Lewis Leits, he was acting in self-defense. It is incumbent
upon the state to prove beyond a reasonable doubt that the
defendant at the time did not act in self-defense. *It is the
law that a person may resist force with force in the defense
of his person against one who manifestly intends or endeavors
by violence to kill him or inflict upon him great bodily injury,*
and if a conflict ensues in such a case, and injury follows, such
resistance is justifiable. To justify the defendant, however,
in thus resisting and inflicting such injuries in self-defense,
he is authorized to use such force, and such force only, as
may be necessary, or appear to him, as a reasonably careful,
prudent and cautious man, to be necessary, to protect himself from injury. While the danger must be imminent and
perilous, yet it is not necessary that the danger should be
actual, but it must appear to him as a reasonably
careful, prudent, and cautious man, to be actual, and
such as that a reasonably careful, prudent, and cau-
2   tious man *would have good reason to believe that his
life was in danger, or that he was about to suffer great
bodily injury. And, if such be the fact, he would then be
authorized under the law, to make resistance thereto,* even
though such resistance might result in the death of his assailant, or in his suffering great bodily injury. Where an assault
is made, and there is a reasonable opportunity for the assailed
party to withdraw and avoid the conflict and the threatened
or feared injury, it is his duty to withdraw and avoid the
conflict or injury. If he has such reasonable opportunity to
withdraw, and fails to do so, then he would not be justified in
self-defense in inflicting painful or hurtful wounds upon his

assailant. An assailed party is not required to run away or withdraw when an assault is made with such a violence that he cannot safely withdraw, or if it appear to him, as a reasonably careful, prudent, and cautious man, that he could not safely withdraw and avoid the conflict and the injury threatened; but under such circumstances he would be authorized to stand and resist the assault with such force, and only such force, and with such weapons or means, as were necessary therefor, or such as would appear to him as a reasonably careful, prudent, and cautious man, under like circumstances necessary therefor. And in this case, if you find from the evidence that Lewis Leits assaulted the defendant *in such a manner and under such circumstances as that the defendant did believe, or as a reasonably careful, prudent, and cautious man had reason to believe, that he was about to be killed, or to suffer some great bodily injury,* and that he could not reasonably withdraw and avoid the assault and encounter, *then he would be justified in using such force, and such force only, as would enable him to resist the assault,* and protect his life, or protect himself from such great bodily injury, and would be authorized, if it were necessary, as hereinbefore defined, to inflict upon the said Lewis Leits such injury as was reasonably necessary for his protection. But if he could have withdrawn from the conflict, and avoided the same, or if it were not necessary, *or if it did not appear to him, as a reasonably careful, prudent, and cautious man, necessary to protect his life, or to protect himself from great bodily injury or harm,* to inflict painful or hurtful wounds or other injury upon the said Lewis Leits, *then he would not be authorized under the law, in self-defense, to have inflicted such painful or hurtful wounds or other injury upon the said Lewis Leits.* In determining whether an assault, if any, was made in such a manner by Lewis Leits as would authorize the defendant in self-defense, as hereinbefore defined, to inflict upon the said Lewis Leits painful or hurtful wounds, if any, or to inflict upon him any injury, you should take into

3

4

consideration the relative strength of the two contending parties; the nature and character of the assault, if any, made by Lewis Leits upon the defendant; whether made with arms or weapons of some kind, or whether made simply with the hands or fists; the feeling existing between the parties at the time of and prior to the assault; the character and number of blows given by the defendant, if any; and all the other surrounding facts and circumstances disclosed and shown by the evidence in this case."

The complaint made of this instruction is that it limits the right of defendant to act in self-defense to cases where he is in reasonable fear of losing his life or of suffering great bodily harm, at the hands of his adversary. We have
5　　italicized the portions of the instruction to which appellant excepts. A very cursory reading will show that there is good ground for the criticism made. Four times in this single paragraph is the thought repeated that, if Leits assaulted defendant, the latter had no right to defend himself unless it reasonably appeared to him that his life was in danger, or that he was likely to suffer great bodily harm from such assault. As an abstract proposition of law, this statement is incorrect. The rule is elementary that one unlawfully assailed may, in self-protection, repel force with force. The extent to which he may go is to be measured by the character of the assault; but the right as we have stated it, exists under any and all circumstances. Counsel for the state insist that the instruction may have been correct under the evidence in this case, and that, as the evidence is not before us, we should presume a state of facts justifying the rule given. It does, however, appear in the record, that there was evidence on the part of defendant tending to prove that Leits, armed with a knife, assaulted him, and that defendant, in resistance, struck his assailant with his fists, and with those only. It is manifest that the rule announced is erroneous when applied to any such state of facts.

II.　　But counsel for the state say that the defendant cannot be heard now to urge an objection to this instruction,

because he did not ask that any different rule be given. Where
the court undertakes to give the law to the jury, it is
6   its duty to do so correctly; and a failure in this respect
can be taken advantage of by defendant. The rule
that counsel have in mind, doubtless, is that where the instructions given are correct, so far as they go, but objection is made
that they are not sufficiently specific, such complaint will not
be heard, if no more specific requests are submitted. *State
v. Viers,* 82 Iowa, 397, and cases cited. We know of no rule
that requires a party to do more than except to an instruction
containing affirmative error, in order to secure its review by
this court. For the error complained of in this instruction,
the judgment is REVERSED.

STATE OF IOWA v. J. A. DYER, Appellant.

Oil Inspectors: SALARY. Under Acts Twenty-fourth General Assembly, chapter 52, section 8, authorizing a deputy oil inspector to
retain for service fees earned by him, up to fifty dollars per month,
and twenty-five per cent. thereafter, not to exceed one hundred
dollars per month, where one inspector died in the middle of the
month, and his successor filled out the time, two salaries of one
hundred dollars each are not authorized, and this, though the fees
for each month were sufficient to warrant them.

Appeal from Polk District Court.—HON. THOMAS F. STEV-
ENSON, Judge.

WEDNESDAY, DECEMBER 14, 1898.

JOHN MORRIS died December 15, 1893, and during that
month, as deputy inspector of oil, had tested three thousand,
three hundred and seventy-six barrels of oil, entitling him
to charge as fees the sum of three hundred and thirty-seven
dollars and sixty-one cents. The defendant was appointed
deputy inspector to succeed Morris, and during the remainder
of the month tested three thousand, five hundred and sixty-one
barrels of oil, entitling him to charge fees amounting to three

hundred and fifty-one dollars and sixty cents. He reported to the inspector of oils the total work of himself and Morris, and retained from the moneys received one hundred dollars as compensation for his services, and the same amount for the estate of Morris. As the executive council decided only one hundred dollars could be allowed for the services of both during December, he paid the inspector another one hundred dollars, but at the time of settling with him in May, 1893, again retained the one hundred dollars from the fees collected by him during that month and April; and this action was brought to recover that amount, with interest. Judgment was entered as prayed, and defendant appeals.—*Affirmed.*

J. A. Dyer and *Dale, Kinkead & Bissell* for appellant.

Milton Remley, Attorney General, and *Jesse A. Miller* for the State.

LADD, J.—The very point in controversy is whether an officer who is paid, in fees collected, a salary not exceeding a fixed sum, and whose entire time belongs to the state, in event there is work to do, shall receive a month's salary for a half month's service. The number of deputy oil inspectors must be approved by the board of health, and their compensation is fixed for each calendar month. The deputy is allowed certain expenses, and must report under oath to the state inspector "at the beginning of each month for the calendar month preceding." Acts Twenty-fourth General Assembly, chapter 52. Section 3 of that chapter is in part as follows: "Each deputy inspector shall collect all fees and commissions, now or hereafter provided by law for inspecting products of petroleum, earned by him, and each deputy inspector may retain for his services actually rendered, all fees and commissions earned by him until the same amount to fifty dollars per month; also twenty-five per cent. thereafter: provided, that no deputy inspector shall be allowed to receive as salary, fees or commissions exceeding one hundred dollars per month." It is plain that the legislature intended the maximum salary for a full month's labor. But Morris was prevented by death from working longer than one-half month. He was entitled, then, at the most, to no more than one-half a month's salary. The same rule applies to defendant. The intention was that all fees received during the month in excess of the maximum salary fixed should go to the state. And the fact that the fees collected during the half month would warrant the full salary would not relieve the officers from giving the entire month to the inspection of oils. If two performing services during part of the same month may each receive the entire salary for that month, then any number may accomplish the same end. The number of these officers is limited, and one simply succeeds his predecessor in the work. Men change, but the office continues. And to this office is attached a defined compensation for a calendar month. Each was only entitled to the pro rata share of the maximum salary. See *State v. Frizzell,* 31 Minn. 460 (18 N. W. Rep. 316), and *Ex parte Lawrence,* 1 Ohio St. 431. We do not find it necessary to determine whether, after payment under protest, the defendant could insist upon his right to retain this money.— AFFIRMED.

STATE OF IOWA v. JAMES MINOR, CHARLES FARLOW, and FRANK FARLOW, Appellants.

Larceny: EVIDENCE. Soon after an owner missed a steer, one similarly marked, appeared in a certain pasture, where it remained until a certain day, during which it was seen to stand near a spot where the entrails of a steer were afterwards found. A gun shot was heard on that day, and fresh wagon tracks and mule tracks passed by the entrails, and led to and from the home of one of the

1 defendants, and defendants were about the pasture about the same time. The tracks showed that one of the mules had a broken hoof, similar to a hoof of one of defendant's mules. Next day fresh steer meat was found in defendant's smoke house. *Held,* sufficient to sustain a conviction for larceny.

SAME. There was evidence that defendants killed another's steer, and fresh meat was found in defendant's smoke house. Defend-

4 ant testified that the meat came from a steer of his own. *Held,*

proper to refuse to charge to acquit if the jury found that the meat came from his steer, as such fact was not necessarily inconsistent with his guilt

CORPUS DELICTI.   The *corpus delicti* of larceny may be established by
2 circumstantial evidence.

INSTRUCTIONS.   A charge that an intent to appropriate another's prop-
3 erty is an ingredient of larceny is not erroneous, as failing to state
that the intent must be "felonious "

SAME.   Where defendant, accused of larceny, denies taking the prop-
4 erty, a failure to define the intent of taking more fully than to
state that accused must have intended to appropriate the property
to his own use is harmless.

SAME: *Imp·achment,*   An instruction to reject the evidence of wit-
4 nesses if their testimony is not believed, is proper.

MISCONDUCT OF JUROR.   The mere fact that a material prosecuting
witness treated two of the jurors to beer, in a saloon, before any
5 deliberation on the verdict was commenced, is not sufficient to
show that the jurors were guilty of misconduct.

Talesman: OBJECTION BELOW.   An accused's objection that the first
appearing talesman, drawn under Code, section 349, was called to
6 the jury box, without reference to the order in which names were
drawn from the talesmen box, is waived, if not made before the
jury is accepted.

Appeal from Harrison District Court.—HON. GEORGE W.
WAKEFIELD, Judge.

WEDNESDAY, DECEMBER 14, 1898.

THE defendants were indicted and convicted of stealing
a steer, and appeal.—*Affirmed.*

S. H. Cochran for appellants.

Milton Remley, Attorney General, and *W. H. Redman*
for the State.

LADD, J.—Falk purchased forty-six steers at Nickerson,
Neb., and brought them past the Dray pasture to his farm, in
Harrison county, in April, 1896.   One of these (a white-
faced, red, two year old steer, with right horn lopping to the

right eye, and brands not especially noticed at the time) disappeared about June 15th of the same year. At about
1   the same time a stray steer, of like description, with
brands identified as a "pick" and a "U," appeared in
the Dray pasture, and continued there till Sunday, October
4th. It was last seen between 4 and 5 o'clock P. M. of
that day, within 300 feet of where the entrails of a steer were
discovered the next day. One Granger was through the pasture near this locality earlier Sunday afternoon, and did not
notice entrails at that time. A gunshot was heard by King
from that direction at about 5 o'clock. The tracks of a wagon
and team of mules standing were observed near by. These
indicated that a piece of the right forefoot of the near mule,
about one and one-half inches long, was broken from the outside and front quarter. The tracks of this team and wagon
were traced one and one-half miles to the gate of the pasture
at the Blair bridge, and from there more than that distance
past the house of Jeff Minor, to and from the locality of the
entrails. Rain fell shortly after 5 o'clock Sunday, and the difference in these tracks indicated that those leading to the
entrails were made before the rain, and those therefrom afterwards. Other mule teams had been in the pasture that day,—
one with a defective foot,—but had left through the east gate,
near Dray's house. Several witnesses testify to the tracks;
and whether, owing to the character of the soil, they could be
observed, was a question for the jury. The defendant James
Minor had three colts and a mule in this pasture, and had been
there to see them on each of the three Sundays previous. He
and the other defendants started there, by way of the house of
Jeff Minor, on the fourth of October, and left the latter's
place, in the direction of the Blair bridge, for that purpose,
about 4 o'clock in the afternoon. They testify that, owing to the
appearance of a dark cloud in the west, they were apprehen-
sive of a storm, and drove on without entering the pasture.
The evidence tended to show that on Tuesday the feet of the
mules then driven by Minor were measured, that a piece was
gone from the right forefoot of the near mule, and that these

corresponded with the tracks. At the same time one hundred and thirty-two pounds of fresh meat were found in his smoke-house, one hundred and seventy-five pounds in a tub in the second story of Frank Farlow's house, and eight or ten pounds at Chance Farlow's home. All this meat had been recently salted down, and was shown by a butcher to be from a steer. On the part of the defense it was claimed: That James Minor killed a two year old crippled steer, belonging to himself and mother, October 2d, and sold the one hundred and seventy-five pounds of meat to Frank Farlow in payment of a debt, and that at the home of Chance was purchased by his brother. That delivered to Frank was not weighed, nor was the price agreed. Dogs had carried away the head and hoofs of the steer, and a Jew peddler received its hide in payment for trousers. Whether the mother and James had such a steer in 1896 is put in issue by the evidence. One witness testified that she saw defendants near home between 5 and 6 o'clock P. M. Sunday, but the impeaching evidence was such that the jury might have rejected her story. It may also be added that the traditional tall and short man were seen along the river in this pasture, with a Winchester rifle, and a dead red steer on the sand bar. We have found it necessary to set out the evidence somewhat in detail, in order to pass upon the points raised by the appellants.

I.   The circumstances all point to the killing of the stray steer October 4, 1896, at about 5 o'clock in the afternoon. It was last seen after 4 o'clock, near where the entrails of a steer were found the next day. The sound of a gunshot was heard from there within an hour. The team and wagon were there at about that time. The mark of the broken hoof of the mule, similar to that of Minor's, going before the rain and returning afterwards; the fall of the rain shortly after 5 o'clock; the defendants' purpose of going to the pasture at that time; and all confirmed by their possession of the meat of a steer,—warranted the jury, if believed, not only in finding the particular steer was killed, but that these defendants did the killing, and appropriated the meat to their own use.

II.   The steer was peculiarly marked by the drooping horn and white face. Falk and his employes noticed brands, but not their character, while Dray observed that of a "pick," and also "U." It disappeared from Falk's farm at about the time it appeared in Dray's pasture, which was near the road it had been driven when brought from Nebraska. The positive identification of animals is always a matter of some difficulty, but we are of the opinion that the similarity in the description and size, when considered in connection with the other circumstances, was such that the identity of the steer killed as that of Falk might well be left to the judgment of the jury.

III.   Whether the *corpus delicti* may be established by circumstantial evidence is not an open question in this state. *State v. Keeler,* 28 Iowa, 551 ; *State v. Millmeier,* 102 Iowa, 692. Counsel seem to have confused this with the mooted question mentioned in *State v. Clemons,* 51 Iowa, 277, which is whether, "where a party is sought to be convicted upon circumstantial evidence alone, the evidence of the circumstance relied upon must be direct, and not circumstantial."

IV.   "Larceny" is thus defined in paragraph 4 of the court's charge: " 'Larceny' is the felonious taking of the property of another without the knowledge or consent of that other, and with the intent of the party taking, at the time of the taking, to permanently deprive the owner thereof, and with the further intent at said times to wholly and permanently appropriate it to the use of the party taking." It is said the word "felonious" should have been used in describing the intent. The virtue of this instruction is in explaining to the jury just what constitutes the felonious intent in taking, without employing that word in doing so. See *Georgia v. Kepford,* 45 Iowa, 51. In paragraph 5 the elements of the crime are set out, and the third part, relating to the intent, was as follows: "That said defendants took said property with intent at the time of taking

to wholly and permanently deprive the owner of it, and to permanently appropriate it to the use of defendants, or some of them." It will be noticed that the word "felonious" was not used as describing the intent, nor is the taking required to be without the knowledge or consent of the owner. But the court, as seen, had so indicated in the instruction quoted. We have often held that all instructions must be considered together. In this case the defendants denied all taking or knowledge of the steer alleged to have been stolen, and we think that the omission to more fully define the intent of the taking required was wholly without prejudice to the defend-
4   ants. The criticism of the sixth instruction is without any foundation whatever. The court did not instruct the jury to reject the evidence of witnesses, if found to be impeached, but simply that, if the jury believed their testimony untrue, they might reject it. Again, complaint is made because the court refused to instruct the jury that, if the meat found was from a steer belonging to James Minor, the defendants were entitled to an acquittal. The fact, if so found, would have been a strong circumstance in favor of the defendants, but not inconsistent with their guilt.

V.   Complaint is made of misconduct on the part of some of the jurors and the officers in charge. One Wilson was a material witness for the state, and it is shown by affidavit that on the evening of November 10, 1897, he treated
5   two of the jurors to beer at a saloon in Logan. Whether this was during the progress of the trial, or after its conclusion, we have no means of knowing. We are satisfied, however, that it was not while the jurors were deliberating on their verdict. No other intimacy between Wilson and these jurors is shown. While we are not prepared to say that, under some circumstances, the taking of intoxicating liquors by jurors from a witness might not be such misconduct as to render a new trial necessary, the mere indulgence in this social custom, without anything more, will not warrant the inference of any wrong-doing. See *State v. Bruce,* 48 Iowa, 530; *State v. Livingston,* 64 Iowa, 560. The conclusion of the lower court that

the jurors were properly cared for by the officers when deliberating upon their verdict is fully substantiated by the affidavits filed.

VI.   The regular panel of jurors having been exhausted, talesmen were drawn, as provided in section 349 of the Code. The one first appearing in court was called to the jury box, and this without reference to the order in which names were drawn from the talesmen box.   No objection was made by the defendants, and it is now argued that talesmen should be called to the jury only in the order drawn from that box.   The section referred to is in part as follows: "In drawing such names, the clerk, when the court directs, shall reject those known to be unable to serve or absent from the territory from which drawn, and proceed until the required number is secured.   The persons whose names are so drawn, or as many thereof as may be found within the territory, from which talesmen are selected, shall be immediately summoned by the sheriff to appear forthwith, and the jury shall be completed from the persons so summoned and appearing.   The names of jurors so drawn, and who serve, shall be placed in a safe receptacle from time to time until all the ballots are drawn from the talesmen's box, when such ballots shall be returned to the said box, to be drawn in like manner as before."   It will be observed that the statute does not in direct terms require talesmen to be called to the box in the order drawn.   Usually a sufficient number are drawn and summoned to meet the requirements of the particular case.   To procure one at a time would occasion inexcusable delay.   The statute relating to the manner of procedure by public officers, where no negative words are used, are generally construed as directory. *Dishon v. Smith,* 10 Iowa, 212; *Parish v. Elwell,* 46 Iowa, 162.   A challenge to the panel must be exercised before a juror is sworn.   Code, section 3680.   The drawing of talesmen is in open court, and subject to the inspection of all parties.   The defendants were as well advised (or, by giving attention, might have been) as the court of the method pursued.   It was their duty to urge any objection to the drawing or summoning of talesmen before the jury was accepted, and, having failed to do so, they will be deemed to have acquiesced in the method pursued. See *State v. Pickett,* 103 Iowa, 714.

AFFIRMED.

HENRY W. KING & COMPANY, Appellant, v. AMANDA E. WELLS.

Fraudulent Conveyanc : SUBSEQUENT CREDITORS. Where a conveyance from a husband to a wife is not made to hinder or defraud subsequent creditors, it will not be set aside in favor of such a
1 creditor, although made without adequate consideration, and where a wife paid for property largely with her own labor, the fact that her husband contributed his labor towards the purchase will not give his subsequent creditors a claim against the property.

SAME. The fact that notes transferred by a wife as her separate property in payment of land had been made payable to her husband for convenience will not give the husband's creditors a claim
2 against the land, where they were not misled by the fact.

Appeal: OBJECTION BELOW. The claim that a conveyance should be set aside because the property conveyed is the proceeds of partnership property and could not be used to pay the debt of one
4 partner without the consent of the other, cannot first be urged on appeal.

ARGUMENT. Matter not urged in appellant's argument in chief will
8 not receive special consideration, though it is referred to in the reply.

Appeal from Decatur District Court.—HON. W. H. TEDFORD, Judge.

WEDNESDAY, DECEMBER 14, 1898.

ACTION in equity to subject property claimed by the defendant to a judgment in favor of the plaintiff, and against the firm of J. W. Wells & Co. There was a hearing on the merits, and a judgment in favor of the defendants for costs. The plaintiff appeals.—*Affirmed.*

Stookey & Brooks for appellants.

Harvey & Parrish and *C. W. Hoffman* for appellee.

ROBINSON, J.—The co-partnership of J. W. Wells & Co., consisting of J. W. Wells and N. Wells, commenced doing a general mercantile business at Decatur City, Iowa, in the year 1894. The business was continued until July, 1895, when J. W. Wells disposed of the stock of merchandise to one E. W. Townsend. In February, 1895, the plaintiff sold and delivered to J. W. Wells & Co. merchandise to the amount of six hundred and eighty-four dollars. Judgment for that amount and costs was rendered in favor of the plaintiff, and against J. W. Wells & Co. and the members of that firm, in November, 1895, and is wholly unpaid. The firm and its members are now, and were when they closed business insolvent. In exchange for the merchandise, Townsend executed to the defendant, who is the wife of J. W. Wells, a deed for one hundred and ninety acres of land, subject to mortgages thereon to the amount of one thousand and three hundred dollars. At the same time, the defendant received from her husband a certificate of deposit for nine hundred and seventy-one dollars. The plaintiff claims that the conveyance of the land and the delivery of the certificate of deposit to Mrs. Wells were fraudulent, and by this action seeks to subject the land and the money represented by the certificate to the payment of the judgment. Mrs. Wells claims they were transferred to her without fraud, in payment of a debt which her husband was owing to her.

I. The evidence establishes facts as follows: In the first part of the year 1895, Mrs. Wells sold to one L. M. Smith; and, by some arrangement with him, she and her husband conveyed to E. W. Townsend two hundred acres of land which she claimed to own, and forty-eight acres of land owned by her husband and one Pray. She received for the land one thousand dollars in money, one thousand eight hundred dollars in notes, and, in addition, six hundred dollars in notes,

secured by mortgages on a lot in Omaha, and one hundred and
sixty acres of land in Nebraska, subject to a mortgage. Nothing was realized on the notes and the land last described. She
loaned the one thousand dollars in money and the one thous-
and and eight hundred dollars in notes to her husband, and
he made to her his promissory note for two thousand and eight
hundred dollars. The land and certificate of deposit
1   in controversy were transferred to her in payment of
that note. The two hundred acres of land sold by the
defendant in the year 1895 were acquired by her as follows:
Her husband conveyed to her, in the year 1888, eighty acres
of land, subject to mortgages thereon .to the amount of one
thousand dollars. At that time, her husband agreed to take
care of and support his mother, and received from her forty
acres of land, subject to a claim of four hundred and fifty
dollars. The defendant was averse to the arrangement, for
the reason that the mother "was hard to get along with," but
finally consented, on condition that the land be conveyed to
her, because of the fact that he was extravagant, and at that
time somewhat dissipated, and the burden of supporting the
mother and caring for the family would be upon her. She
has since supported the mother. The remainder of the two
hundred acres was purchased by the defendant at various
times. It is claimed that the consideration for the conveyance by her husband was insufficient, and that his earnings
contributed to the purchase of the remainder. If these claims
are well founded, it would not follow that the wife did not
acquire a title to the land, valid as against the plaintiff. When
the conveyance of 1888 was made, the husband was not in
debt, and there is nothing in the record which authorizes the
presumption that it was designed to hinder, delay, or in any
manner defraud subsequent creditors. The same is true of
the labor of the husband, which may have contributed to the
purchase of the remainder of the two hundred acres of land.
The defendant, in addition to doing her housework, labored in
the fields for fifteen years; and it was through her labors and
prudent management that the land which she sold was

obtained. The fact that her husband worked with her, and aided with his labor in purchasing it, did not affect her title to it, nor give his subsequent creditors any right to subject it to their claims. *Hoag v. Martin,* 80 Iowa, 714; *Jamison v. Weaver,* 87 Iowa, 72; *Brundage v. Cheneworth,* 101 Iowa, 256; and cases therein cited. The cases of *Hamill v. Augustine,* 81 Iowa, 302; *Hamilton v. Lightner,* 53 Iowa, 470; *Bank v. Harvey,* 16 Iowa, 141, and *Harrison v. Kramer,* 3 Iowa, 543, involved controlling facts which were not subject to the rule applicable in this case, and are not in point. That is also true of *Romans v. Maddux,* 77 Iowa, 203, especially relied upon by the appellant.

The notes for one thousand and eight hundred dollars, which formed a part of the consideration for the sale of the land in 1894, were taken in the name of J. W. Wells, for con-

2   venience in disposing of them; but the plaintiff was not in any manner misled by that fact. Other facts are relied upon as tending to show that the land sold really belonged to the husband, but the evidence satisfies us that the two hundred acres in question were owned by the wife, and that his creditors had no rights which they could have enforced against it.

Nothing is claimed in appellant's argument in chief on account of the forty-eight-acre tract conveyed, which was owned by her husband and Pray; and, although it is referred

3   to in the reply, the plaintiff is not entitled to have any special consideration given it. The evidence does not show, and we do not understand the plaintiff to contend, that the interest claimed by the defendant in the two hundred acres was not worth what she received for it. It is insisted, however, that the land conveyed to her by Townsend in July, 1895, and the certificate of deposit, were worth more than the amount of the note made to her by her husband. The certificate of deposit was used in paying the debts of her husband. The testimony as to the value of the land is conflicting; but we are satisfied that its value, after deducting therefrom the mortgages upon it, was much less than two

thousand and eight hundred dollars, and that the aggregate
value of the interest the defendant acquired therein, and of
the certificate, did not exceed the amount of the note in payment of which they were received.

II.   The claim of the plaintiff is based upon a debt contracted by the firm of J. W. Wells & Co., and it is claimed
that the note of Wells to his wife was paid with the proceeds
of partnership property, upon which the creditors of the partnership had claims paramount to the right of the wife to
receive the proceeds in payment of the note, and that the consent of the retiring partner to the payment of the note with
the proceeds of the sale has not been shown.   It appears from
the evidence that, before the stock of merchandise was traded
to Townsend, the partnership was dissolved, and thereafter
the stock was owned, and the business was conducted, by J. W.
Wells.   He had the right to prefer his wife to other creditors,
and therefore the transfer of the land and certificate to her
in payment of the note was in fact valid.   But it is insisted
that the petition alleges, and the answer admits, that the firm
of J. W. Wells & Co. continued in business until July, 1895,
and traded the stock to Townsend.   That is true, but
4   the answer also alleges that the stock was sold by J. W.
Wells.   Under ordinary circumstances, this conflict in
the averments of the answer would be resolved in favor of the
plaintiff; but a careful examination of the entire record satisfies us that the plaintiff did not in any manner assail in the
district court the transfer of the property in question, on the
ground that it was the proceeds of partnership property, and
could not be used to pay the debt of one of the partners without the consent of the other.   There is not the slightest indication that any claim of that kind was made in the district
court.   On the contrary, the plaintiff presented its case upon
the theory that the transaction was fraudulent, because made
without a legal consideration, and to defraud the creditors of
J. W. Wells & Co.   That a ground for relief cannot be urged
for the first time in this court is well settled.   It is also settled
in this state that partnership property may be used, with the

assent of all the partners, in the payment of individual debts of the partners. *Smith v. Smith,* 87 Iowa, 93; *Sylvester v. Henrich,* 93 Iowa, 489. See, also, *City of Maquoketa v. Willey,* 35 Iowa, 323; *Johnston v. Robuck,* 104 Iowa, 523. The evidence fails to show that the plaintiff has any right to the property in question. The judgment of the district court effectuates justice, and it is AFFIRMED.

F. W. SHUPE v. ELIZA J. BARTLETT, *et al.,* Appellants.

Trusts: EVIDENCE. Where a wife allowed her husband to use her property in his business, expecting that she would be compensated
1 therefor, and he invested it in real estate in his own name, -there
2 being no understanding that the title should be taken in her name,—and no claim that her property was used to pay for property taken in his name without her knowledge or consent, there is no constructive trust, nor a resulting trust.

Partition: PREMATURE SUIT. Where a decree in a suit to partition realty belonging to a testator's unsettled estate provided that par-
3 tition should not be ordered until settlement of the estate, and until the widow, who refused to take under the will, would elect whether she would take a homestead right or a distributive share, she cannot complain that the suit was prematurely brought.

Appeal from Warren District Court.—HON. J. H. APPLE-GATE, Judge.

WEDNESDAY, DECEMBER 14, 1898.

ACTION in equity for the partition of real estate. Eliza J. Bartlett claims to be the owner of the real estate, and both she and her co-defendant, Eulah H. Bartlett, contend that, if the plaintiff has an interest in the property, this action was prematurely brought. There was a hearing on the merits, and a decree from which the defendants named appeal.—*Affirmed.*

H. McNeil for appellants.

Henderson & Berry for appellee.

ROBINSON, J.—Eliza J. Bartlett is the widow of E. G. Bartlett, deceased. He died testate in February, 1895, and at that time held the legal title to the real estate in controversy, consisting of a farm of about one hundred and ten acres of land in Warren county, and parts of certain lots·in the town of Lacona, and provided in his will that his wife should have all of his property, both real and personal, during her lifetime, and that "at her death she shall have, by will or otherwise, the disposing of one-third of said farm,—never before." The remainder of the property of the testator was to revert at the death of his widow "to body heirs, including Frank W. Shupe." Mrs. Bartlett filed in the proper court a writing by which she declined to accept under the will, and refused to be bound by it. She denies that the decedent owned the real property in question, and insists that it belongs to her, and was held by the decedent in trust for her benefit, but asks, in case that is not found to be true, that her refusal to take under the will be set aside, on the ground that it was made by her attorney without her knowledge or consent, and before she was fully advised as to her rights under the will. She also alleges that the estate of the decedent is not settled, and that partition of the real estate cannot be made.   The defendant Eulah H. Bartlett, a daughter of the decedent, resists this proceeding on the ground that the estate is unsettled. The plaintiff is a grandson of the decedent, and claims to have inherited from him an undivided one-fifth of the estate. The district court adjudged that the decedent was the owner of the property in question, and did not hold it as trustee; that Mrs. Bartlett was bound by her refusal to take under the will, and that her only interest in the property was a homestead right, or the right to a distributive share thereof; that within sixty days after the debts of the estate and the expenses of the administration should be settled and paid, she be required to elect which right she will take; and, after that is done, that a decree ordering the partition of the lands be entered.

Mrs. Bartlett married the decedent in May, 1872. At that time she had some property, the larger part of which appears to have been obtained through a former husband. The decedent had also been married before, and each had

1   several children. The amount of property owned by the decedent at that time is not clearly shown, but he then owned property in Lacona which was occupied as a homestead after the marriage, and perhaps other town property in controversy, and was carrying on an hotel and a store. There is evidence which shows that on several occasions he stated to different persons that he would not have had any property when he married in 1872, had his debts been paid, that he had used money and other property which belonged to his wife, that the farm now in controversy belonged to her, and that he intended to protect her against loss on account of the property which she had owned and he had used. She claims that she let him have money, a note, horses and cattle and hogs, of the value of about one thousand dollars, and a house and two lots. Much of her testimony is incompetent, and was taken under objection. The competent evidence does not show that the husband received property of the value claimed. A considerable amount of it was loaned to the decedent before the marriage. Of the property of the wife used by the husband after the marriage, only the house and two lots are traced into the property in controversy. They were conveyed to one Joe Pressley, at a valuation of $300, in part payment for a forty-acre tract of land which was conveyed to the decedent for the agreed price of $800, all of which was paid by him, excepting that portion paid by the conveyance of the house and lots. All of the remainder of the property in con-

2   troversy was purchased and paid for by the decedent. There is no competent evidence which shows that there was any understanding or agreement that the title of any of the property so acquired should be taken in the name of Mrs. Bartlett. It is probable that the money and the proceeds of the note and stock which she furnished to her husband were used in his business, and that he became indebted to her for

the property so received, and intended that she should be compensated for it. No fraud, actual or constructive, is shown on the part of the decedent, and there is no ground for claim· ing that a constructive trust has been established. *Acker v. Priest,* 92 Iowa, 610; 1 Pomeroy Equity Jurisprudence, section 155; 2 Pomeroy Equity Jurisprudence, sections 1044-1046; 1 Perry Trusts, section 166. The only part of the real estate in controversy into which the property of Mrs. Bartlett has been traced is the Pressley forty, but even as to that the evidence fails to show a resulting trust with that clearness and certainty which is essential. *Murphy v. Hanscome,* 76 Iowa, 192; *Richardson v. Haney,* 76 Iowa, 101; *Trout v. Trout,* 44 Iowa, 471; 1 Perry Trusts, section 133; 2 Pomeroy Equity Jurisprudence, section 1031; 10 Am. & Eng. Enc. Law, 29. We conclude that the evidence fails to show that Mrs. Bartlett is the owner of the property in controversy, and that it fails to establish a trust of any character. Had the decedent used property of his wife for the purchase of land, the title of which he took in his own name without her knowledge or consent, a different question would have been presented.

II. The evidence shows that the instrument executed in the name of Mrs. Bartlett, which purported to be a refusal on her part to take under the will, was filed with her knowledge, and, no doubt, with her consent. She testifies that her attorney did not fully explain her rights under the will, but no sufficient reason for setting aside the instrument filed is shown, and no claim that it should be set aside is urged in this court. Therefore it must remain in force.

III. The appellants insist that the suit was prematurely brought. The district court found that the estate of the decedent had not been settled, and provided that a partition should not be decreed until the settlement should be completed, and until Mrs. Bartlett had been given an opportunity to elect, of the rights of which she was entitled, which one she would take. The interests of the appellants were thus fully protected, and there is nothing in the

decree of which they can justly complain. It is therefore
AFFIRMED.

State of Iowa v. John Fisher, Thomas Fisher and
George Meyers, John Fisher, Appellant.

Larceny: EVIDENCE. In a prosecution for larceny, where defendant
1   was allowed to show all that took place in the room where he ob-
     tained the money, and the manner in which he obtained possession
2   of it, he cannot complain of the exclusion of evidence of matters
     occurring after the alleged larceny which was immaterial or im-
     proper cross-examination.

Same. Prosecutor, a country boy, met defendant casually on the
     train. Both got off at the same place, and defendant promised to
     take prosecutor to a ticket broker, where he could purchase a
1   cheap ticket to continue his journey They went first to a saloon,
     then to the broker's office, which was not open, and then to a gam-
     bling house. Defendant had been engaged in working around
     saloons and gambling houses. While in the gambling house
     defendant asked prosecutor to loan him a quarter, and then
     snatched his pocketbook. Prosecutor protested, but defendant
     told him not to make a fool of himself, that he would get his
     money back. *Held*, sufficient to sustain a conviction for larceny
     from the person.

INSTRUCTIONS. In a prosecution for larceny where defendant claimed
     he obtained the money in question from prosecutor with his con-
8   sent, defendant cannot complain that no instructions were given
     along his line of defense, where the court instructed that, to con-
     vict, the jury must find that defendant took the money unlawfully
     and feloniously, with intent to convert it to his own use, and per-
     manently deprive prosecutor of his money without his consent.

INDICTMENT: *Money.* An indictment charging defendant with the
     larceny of "$22.50 in lawful money of the United States, of the
     value of $22.50," sufficiently describes the money alleged to have
     been stolen, without an averment that a more particular descrip-
     tion was to the grand jurors unknown, under Code, sections 5280,
     5289, providing that an indictment must contain a statement of
     the facts constituting the offense in ordinary and concise lan-
     guage; and section 5282, directing the indictment to be direct and
4   certain as regards the offense charged and the circumstances con-
     stituting it; and section 5287, providing that words used in an
     indictment must be construed in their common acceptation; and
     section 5290, providing that no indictment is insufficient, nor can
     the judgment thereon be affected, by reason of any "other matter

which was formerly admitted a defect or imperfection, but which does not tend to prejudice the substantial rights of the defendant upon the merits;" and section 5462, providing that on appeals in criminal cases "the supreme court must examine the record without regard to technical errors or defects which do not affect the substantial rights of the parties."

Appeal from Woodbury District Court.—HON. F. R. GAYNOR, Judge.

WEDNESDAY, DECEMBER 14, 1898.

THE defendants were jointly indicted for the crime of larceny of twenty-two dollars and fifty cents in money from the person of John Cullinan. The defendant John Fisher pleaded not guilty, and was separately tried, convicted, and judgment of imprisonment in the penitentiary for two years and for costs rendered against him, from which he appeals.— *Affirmed.*

T. F. Bevington for appellant.

Milton Remley, Attorney General, *Jesse A. Miller* and *J. W. Hallam* for the State.

GIVEN, J.—I. The testimony on behalf of the state tends to show that John Cullinan, aged 21 years, and with little experience in the ways of city life, left his home on a farm near Independence, Iowa, for Cripple Creek, Colo., where he had brothers in business, having a passage ticket as far as Sioux City. At Ft. Dodge, defendant, a stranger to Cullinan, came on the train, and approached Cullinan.
1   They became acquainted, and rode together to Sioux City, where they arrived early in the morning. During the ride, defendant learned by inquiries where Cullinan was going, and that he was only ticketed to Sioux City, whereupon he informed Cullinan that he could take him to a broker in the city, where he could buy a ticket at a discount of twenty cents on the dollar. On arriving at Sioux City, where Cullinan was a stranger, defendant took him to a saloon,

then to the broker's office, which was not open, and then to a
gambling house. Cullinan testifies that, while in the gambling
room, defendant introduced him to his brother, Tom Fisher.
"Then he asked me if I had change for a quarter, or if I
would loan him a quarter. I put my hand in my pocketbook,
and, as I did so, he snatched it. I did not give him the pocketbook with the money in it. He walked over to the table,
turned the pocketbook upside down, and stuck the twenty
dollar bill in his pocket. Two dollars and fifty cents dropped
out. I think it was twenty-two dollars and fifty cents altogether,—a twenty dollar bill and two dollars and fifty cents
in silver. He put the twenty dollar bill in his pants pocket.
I told him to give me back my money. He said not to make
a damn fool of myself, and I would get my money all right.
He put the two dollars and fifty cents on the 36, I think. I
don't know whether he won or lost. I don't know whether
the money changed hands. Then he went into the back room,
and these other fellows, Tom Fisher and George Meyers, followed him. They were there when he went up. I followed
them back, and told them I wanted my money. He said, 'We
will go and see about that ticket right away.' He came out,
and went down the street. I did not do any playing up there.
He said, when we got to this saloon, he would pay me that
money. When we got down there, I asked him for it, and he
said: 'Don't make such a fool of yourself. Come and have
a drink with me.' I told him all I wanted was my money, and
I said, 'If you don't give it to me, there will be some fun.' Just
then Tom Fisher and Meyers came in. Tom put his hand in
his pocket, pulled out his knife, and said, 'I will cut your
damn throat.' The knife was open. I stepped around the
stove, and, as I did so, they came at me. John Fisher hit me
over the eye, and Myers hit me on the breast. Tom hit me
on the nose. There is a scar there now. Then John Fisher
and Meyers went out. I followed them. They went into an
alley, and said, if I would come back, they would give me the
money. I went back, and they went up to this back room
again, in the same building. I followed them. They tried

to bolt the door. I shoved it in. Just then Policeman Olson came. He arrested Tom Fisher. John Fisher and Myers went out. I guess Myers was arrested in a gambling house. The total amount the defendant took from me was twenty-two dollars and seventy-five cents. They never paid me back, nor offered to. This money was taken from me here in Sioux City." The testimony of the defendant shows that he was a young man of twenty-one, engaged in working around saloons and gambling houses, and is substantially the same as that of Cullinan as to what was said and done prior to going into the gambling house, except as to Cullinan's drinking. Tom Fisher, George Meyers, and Harry Baker were present when Cullinan and defendant came into the gambling room. Defendant says he got to playing, and lost what money he had; that Meyers handed him some money to play; that he won, and gave Meyers his half. "Next, I got some money from John Cullinan, and played the wheel. I got twenty-two dollars and fifty cents from him. He said he would divide the money he won. The table played on was about the same size as the table here. The dealer was standing behind the table, right in the middle. I was standing at the south end of the table, and Cullinan at the corner. We were standing at each corner at the end of the table when he took out his pocketbook. The table is about two and a half or three feet wide. When he handed me his pocketbook, I emptied the money out on the table in front of me, and handed the pocketbook back to him. He put it back in his pocket. I played roulette with the money. Cullinan stood all of this time at the end of the table. The proprietor of the gambling house was there, and four or five others. Cullinan made no objection to my playing this money, not a word. I won sixteen dollars there. Then we had a few drinks, and then went down to the ticket man,—to Hattenbach's. Cullinan did not go into the back room where I was, and ask for the money, as he testified. I had no conversation with him back there. When we went down to Hattenbach's to get the ticket, they were not open. Then we went down to Orton's saloon. We

had some drinks in there, and I offered him half of this
money, and he would not take it. He wanted it all. He
offered me five dollars for winning. We were all drinking
whisky there,—Cullinan with us. We were all somewhat
intoxicated there at that time. I noticed Cullinan in a sort
of drunken stupor. I offered him his money there at that
time, and part of the winnings." Defendant testifies that,
"after the row came up I left the money there for Cullinan
with Ed Burk. It was afterwards turned over to Billy Nead,
and then I turned it over to Mr. Foley." Harry Burk testified that he was an employe at the gambling room. "I seen
him [defendant] put his hand out, and get some money from
this gentleman [Cullinan]. I am pretty sure it was a pocketbook. He then put some silver in the center column. No, sir;
I am positive there was no grabbing or snatching of the
pocketbook from any one in my presence. There was no complaint there before me. If any was made, I would have heard
it." He further says: "Didn't see any twenty dollar bill.
He didn't change any twenty dollar bill with me. Yes; Fisher
won some money there. I thought it was in the neighborhood
of fifteen dollars to eighteen dollars." E. L. Burk, bartender
at Orton's saloon, testifies that defendant left money with him
in a sealed envelope for Cullinan; that he offered it to Cullinan, and he refused to accept it. There is a conflict in the
evidence as to whether Cullinan was drinking and drunk.
Defendant says: "He drank nine or ten glasses of whisky and
one glass of beer;" while Cullinan says he did not drink any,
and several disinterested persons say that Cullinan was not
intoxicated. We have stated sufficient of the testimony to
show what the claims of the parties are, and somewhat as to
the merits of those claims.

II. Of the nineteen assignments of error, all except
four relate to rulings on evidence. The contention is that
defendant was entitled to introduce evidence in support of
his theory of defense, and it is complained that he was prevented from going into a full explanation in reference thereto.
The defense is that defendant did not snatch the money from

Cullinan; that he did not take it feloniously, but with Cullinan's consent. We have read the evidence with care, and do not find a single instance wherein the defendant was denied

2   the right to evidence that tended to support his defense. He and his witnesses were permitted to testify, without objection, to all that took place in the gambling room, and as to the manner in which the money came into the possession of the defendant. The rulings objected to relate to matters occurring after the alleged larceny, that were immaterial or not proper cross-examination.

III. Defendant's next complaint is that "there is not an instruction along the line of the defendant's theory of defense." The court plainly instructed that, to convict, the jury must find beyond a reasonable doubt, that defendant did

3   take the money of John Cullinan unlawfully and feloniously, with the intent then and there to convert the same to his own use, and permanently deprive the said John Cullinan of said money without the consent and against the will of the said John Cullinan. There was no error in the instructions in the respect complained of.

IV. Among the grounds for a new trial it is alleged that the indictment does not plainly conform to the requirements of the Code, "because the offense charged is not stated in ordinary, concise language, and in such manner as to enable a person of common understanding to know what is intended, and the court to pronounce judgment upon the indictment according to the law of the case." It is contended in support of this allegation that there is not a sufficient description in the indictment of the money alleged to have been stolen, nor

4   an averment that a more particular description was to the grand jurors unknown. The indictment charges the stealing of "twenty-two dollars and fifty cents in lawful money of the United States, of the value of twenty-two dollars and fifty cents." Defendant's counsel cite a large number of authorities to show what the common-law rule is as to the description that must be given of the money stolen, and the states in which this rule is applied. Some of these hold

that the particular kind of money must be stated,—that is,
whether coin or paper, and the kind of coin and paper, but
not a description of each particular coin or bill; while others
hold that the coins or bills should be individualized by the
number of pieces or bills, and their respective denominations
and kinds.   The authorities generally agree that the more
general description may be excused by an averment that a
more particular description is to the grand jurors unknown.
Among the citations are Clark Criminal Procedure, 221 ; Bish.
Criminal Procedure, section 702, and following; Wharton
Criminal Pleadings and Practice, 134, and following; 1
McClain Criminal Law, section 592; *Merwin v. People,* 26
Mich. 298.   There is no dispute but that, if the rule of the
common law is to be applied, this indictment is defective.
Therefore we need not further notice the authorities cited in
support of the rule, but proceed to inquire whether that rule
applies in this state.

In Michigan, Missouri, Indiana, and possibly other
states, there are statutes providing, in effect, that it is sufficient to describe the money simply as money, without specifying any particular coin, note, bill, or currency.   We have no
statute identical with these, but it is urged on behalf of the
state that, under the construction given to our statute by this
court, the rule of the common law in this respect has been
held not to apply in this state.   "If any person steal, take and
carry away of the property of another any money, goods or
chattels,   *   *   *   he is guilty of larceny."   Code, section
4831.   Larceny from the person is punishable by imprisonment in the penitentiary, not exceeding ten nor less than two
years.   Code, section 4755.   We now turn to the provisions of
our Code with respect to the indictment.   The indictment
must contain "(2) a statement of the facts constituting the
offense in ordinary and concise language without repetition,
and in such manner as to enable a person of common understanding to know what is intended."   Section 5280.   "The
indictment must be direct and certain as regards   *   *   *
(2) the offense charged; (3) the particular circumstances of

the offense charged, when they are necessary to constitute a complete offense." Section 5282. "The words used in an indictment must be construed in their usual acceptation in common language, except words and phrases defined by law, which are to be construed according to their legal meaning." Section 5287. "The indictment is sufficient if it can be understood therefrom *   *   * (5) that the act or omission charged as the offense is stated in ordinary and concise language, with such certainty and in such manner as to enable a person of common understanding to know what is intended, and the court to pronounce judgment according to law upon a conviction." Section 5289. "No indictment is insufficient, nor can the trial, judgment or other proceeding thereon be affected, by reason of any of the following matters: *   *   * (5) For any other matter which was formerly admitted a defect or imperfection, but which does not tend to prejudice the substantial rights of the defendant upon the merits." Section 5290. Section 5462 provides that, on appeal by the defendant in a criminal case, "the supreme court must examine the record, without regard to technical errors or defects which do not affect the substantial rights of the parties, and render such judgment on the record as the law demands." It cannot be doubted that the purpose of these statutes is to dispense with those technical rules of the common law that sometimes prevent a disposition of cases upon their merits, whenever the same can be done without prejudice to the rights of parties. Such is undoubtedly the tendency of modern legislation and decisions.

In the early case of *Munson v. State,* 4 G. Greene, 483, it was charged that the defendant "did feloniously steal, take, and carry away twenty-four dollars of Clark's Exchange Bank bills, of the value of twenty-four dollars, and seven dollars of other bank bills, the names of the banks to the grand jurors unknown, of the value of seven dollars, and one hundred and nine dollars of gold and silver coin, of the value of one hundred and nine dollars, the whole being of the value of one hundred and forty dollars." That indictment was found under a section of the Code identical with section 4831, quoted above. The court says: "The description of the money and bank notes alleged to have been stolen comes fully up to the requirements of the Code. Money is sufficiently designated by the words 'gold and silver coin.' Bank notes are sufficiently designated by the words 'Clark's Exchange Bank bills, of the value of twenty-four dollars,' and also the words 'seven dollars of other bank bills, the names of the banks to the jurors unknown.' This court has repeatedly decided that an offense is sufficiently charged in an indictment if it is substantially in the language of the statute. * * * In *People v. Kent,* 1 Doug, (Mich.) 42, it was held that a description of the property stolen as 'bank notes' or 'bank bills,' merely following the language of the statute, is sufficient. It will be observed that the allegation that the names of the banks were to the grand jurors unknown refers to the seven dollars of other bank bills." In *State v. Hockenberry,* 30 Iowa, 504, it was charged that the defendant stole "one hundred and eighty dollars in bank notes, usually known and described as 'greenbacks.'" The court says: "Without doubt it was practicable to have described the property stolen with more clearness and exactness, but we are of opinion that the language is such as to 'enable a person of common understanding to know what was intended.' * * * The crime being charged in such a manner as to enable a person of common understanding to know what is intended, and the court to pronounce judgment, etc., the indictment under the statute is sufficient." In *State v. Hoppe,* 39 Iowa, 468, it was charged that the defendant stole "divers bank bills, commonly known and denominated 'national currency,' of divers denominations, the number and denominations of which are to the grand jurors unknown, of the amount and value of six hundred and fifty dollars." The court says: "If a more full description should be required, it would in many cases afford the thief entire immunity. No one from whose safe five hundred dollars of the usual denominations received in ordinary business should be stolen could testify as to date, num-

ber, and denomination of the bills taken. It would be a mere
chance if he would be able to identify certainly a single bill.
The law should not, and does not, require unreasonable
things. The indictment, we think, is sufficient." In that
case it was averred that the number and denomination of the
bills were to the grand jury unknown. In *State v. Graham,*
65 Iowa, 617, it was charged that the defendants stole "seven
one hundred dollar notes, of the value and denomination of
one hundred dollars each, consisting of national bank notes
and national currency notes, called 'greenbacks,' and all of
the aggregate value of seven hundred dollars." The demurrer
to this indictment was overruled, and this court said: "We
have set out the indictment as the very best argument that
could be made in support of the decision of the court in overruling the demurrer. If we were to hold that this indictment
is demurrable, we should very greatly astonish the legal profession. The only respect in which it could well be made more
specific is that it might have stated how many of the one
hundred dollar notes were national bank notes, and how many
were national currency notes. But this was wholly unnecessary, because, if there was one of each, or of either, of
the value of one hundred dollars, the indictment was sufficient." In *State v. Pierson,* 59 Iowa, 271, the defendant
was charged with stealing "a bill of exchange, to-wit, an order
for the payment of money, purporting to be signed by C. S.
Bartlett, and payable at the Union National Bank, Chicago,
Ill., and of date of the sixth day of June, 1881, and of the
value of twenty dollars and ninety-seven cents." The court
says: "There is no requirement that, in an indictment for
the larceny of an instrument in writing, the property shall
be any more particularly described than any other stolen
property. We have in this indictment a charge that the
defendant stole an order or bank check for the payment of
money, naming its date, owner, and place of payment, and
an allegation of its value. There is no more reason for requiring any more particular description of the stolen property
than there would be to require that an indictment for the

larceny of a horse could describe the animal by color, age, and marks and brands." In *State v. Alverson*, 105 Iowa, 152, the indictment charged the embezzlement of four hundred dollars of moneys. Section 4317 of the Code of 1873 provides that in such cases it was sufficient to allege the embezzlement of money generally, without designating its particular species. The indictment was held sufficient. In *People v. Reavey*, 38 Hun. 419, the defendant was charged with larceny by false pretenses. The averment was that he obtained from her "the sum of two hundred and seventy-five dollars in money, lawful money of the United States, and of the value of two hundred and seventy-five dollars." It was contended that this was not a sufficient description of the money. The court says: "But the sufficiency of the indictment is not to be determined by these authorities conceding and applying the technical principles of the common law; for they have been in a great measure superseded by the enactment of the Code of Criminal Procedure; and the question, accordingly, to be considered, is not whether the indictment might in this respect be held to be defective under the preceding practice, but whether it is sufficient under the provisions of the Code of Criminal Procedure." The opinion shows that the Code of Criminal Procedure of New York contained provisions quite similar to those of our Code quoted above. For instance, no more was required in the indictment than a plain and concise statement of the act constituting the crime; a brief description of it as it is given in the statute; and that the indictment is sufficient in the description of the crime if it can be understood from it that the crime charged was committed within the jurisdiction prior to the finding of the indictment, and that the act or omission charged as the crime is plainly and concisely set forth, and that it is stated with such a degree of certainty as to enable the court to pronounce judgment upon the conviction according to the right of the case. It was further provided that "no indictment is insufficient, nor can the trial, judgment or other proceedings thereon be affected, by reason of any imperfection in matter of form, which does not tend to the prejudice of the substantial rights of the defendant upon the merits." The court said: "This indictment was clearly sufficient, within these sections of the Code of Criminal Procedure, for it distinctly charged the defendant with unlawfully, by means of false pretenses and representations, known to him to be false, obtained this sum of money from the complaining witness. It was framed in such a manner as clearly and distinctly to charge this offense, and to be incapable of being misunderstood by the defendant when he was arraigned and tried upon it. That it was not misunderstood appears by his own testimony, in which he acknowledged the receipt of this sum of one hundred and sixty-five dollars, as well as the other smaller amounts mentioned by the witness in the course of her evidence." See, also, *Com. v. Stebbins,* 8 Gray, 492; *Com. v. O'Connell,* 12 Allen, 451; *State v. Hurst,* 11 W. Va. 54; *State v. Ziord,* 30 La. Ann. 867; *State v. Green,* 27 La. Ann. 598; *Goldstein v. State* (Tex. Cr. App.) 23 S. W. Rep. 686. The purpose of the description of the stolen property is to identify the particular transaction so that the accused may not be put upon trial for a different offense from that charged; and the conviction or acquittal may bar further prosecution; that the accused may be informed of the particular transaction constituting the offense, so that he may prepare his defense; and that the court may pronounce judgment according to law. Bishop Criminal Procedure, section 702; *Merwin v. People, supra.*

We think it cannot be said, in the light of our statutes and decisions, that the rule of the common law as to the description, in an indictment, of money alleged to have been stolen obtains in all its requirements in this state. This indictment is direct and certain as regards the offense charged, namely, the larceny "from the person and pocket of one John Cullinan twenty-two dollars and fifty cents, in lawful money of the United States, of the value of twenty-two dollars and fifty cents," in Woodbury county, Iowa, on or about the fifteenth day of December, 1896. It is hardly possible that the transaction charged could have been taken for any other, either in preparing the defense, in the trial, or in pronouncing judgment. To have added to the charge the kinds of money and a number or denomination of the several pieces, or that a more particular description than that given was to the grand jurors unknown, would not have rendered it any more a charge of a crime, nor aided the defendant in making his defense. Many authorities, recognizing the difficulty of describing stolen money, hold that less particularity should be required than in describing other kinds of stolen property. We conclude that this indictment is sufficiently definite as to the description of the property stolen, under the rule of our statutes and decisions.

V. The sufficiency of the evidence to sustain the verdict is presented by the assignments of error, but not argued. Counsel for defendant have urged with zeal and ability every point that could properly be raised upon the record, and they are excusable for not arguing this assignment, as the evidence leaves no reasonable ground to doubt the guilt of the defendant. AFFIRMED.

J. W. EDGERLY & COMPANY, Appellant, v. AARON COVER and CHARLES SEATON and L. W. HATTER, Administrator of the Estate of J. V. HATTER, Deceased.

A merchant's son-in-law, who managed the business as agent, and bought and paid for stock, and who, on the principal's becoming sick, was told to do the best he could, and to make collections and take notes for outstanding accounts. and apply them on a certain claim and "to work things to the best advantage and to do anything he (the agent) could to keep the business going," had no authority to execute a chattel mortgage on the stock; that not being effective to keep the business going, though the principal was too sick for consultation and the mortgage made to avoid an attachment of the stock.

Appeal from Iowa District Court.—HON. M. J. WADE, Judge.

THURSDAY, DECEMBER 15, 1898.

ACTION to foreclose a chattel mortgage covering a stock of goods owned by J. V. Hatter in his lifetime, alleged to have been executed February 6, 1896, by John L. Miller, as his agent. The defendant Aaron Cover has two mortgages, each covering the same stock of goods, executed by Hatter on the twenty-eighth day of February and the twenty-third day of April, 1896. The defendants Seaton and Hatter are administrators of the estate of J. V. Hatter, deceased. The sole question is whether John L. Miller had authority from J. V. Hatter to execute the mortgage to plaintiff. The district court found he had not, and dismissed the petition. The plaintiff appeals.—*Affirmed.*

Thomas Stapleton, McNett & Tisdale, and *W. A. Work* for appellant.

Hedges & Rumple for appellees.

LADD, J.—That J. V. Hatter was indebted to the plaintiff on the sixth day of February, 1896, as alleged, is not questioned. At that time he was very sick, and, because of the advice of his physician, could not be consulted. His son-in-law, John L. Miller, had been in his employment as clerk in the drug store for seven years, and for two or three years bought the goods, kept the books, made collections, paid the bills, and waited on the trade. In addition to this, during the last six months of Hatter's life, he conducted the correspondence, and made all adjustments with the wholesale houses. On the day mentioned, Miller signed Hatter's name to the mortgage sued on, covering the entire stock of drugs and other goods, by himself as agent. This was done after consulting the sons of Hatter, and under the apprehension that the agent of the plaintiff, armed with a verified petition and bond as he was, would immediately sue out a writ of attachment, and cause it to be levied on the property. The competency of Miller and his wife as witnesses, under section 4604 of the Code, is exhaustively argued by the appellant,

but, as the appellees ignore the point, and submit the case on
the theory that they might testify, we pass that question. Each
party relies on the evidence of Miller, which is confirmed by
that of his wife, and we set it out *in extenso*. He testified:
"During the first and second weeks of his sickness, I went
up to see him [Hatter] almost every day, and sometimes twice
a day. Sometimes, during the first part of his sickness, something came up that I wanted to talk to him about. A claim
had come in that I couldn't meet. I went to see him. I told
him I didn't like to trouble him, because I knew he wasn't in
a condition to be troubled about business, but if he did not feel
able to talk to tell me so. He said he could talk to me a little
then, and we talked a little about the claim. He told me to
make some collections, to sue if I thought best, to make the
customers give their notes, and turn these in, or to work
things to the best advantage, and to do anything I could to
keep the business going. 'Come up when you can and see me,
and I will talk to you when I can; but in the meantime,' he
says, 'go ahead, and do the business just as though it was your
own.' He said that he knew that there were a great many
debts to be paid, and things weren't in very good condition,
but to go ahead, and do the best I possibly could, and that
whatever I did would be all right until he got well; and he
said, 'If I don't get well, it will be all right anyhow.' " It
will be observed that the special duty of Miller was to "keep
the business going." To this end he was given very general
powers. If the execution of the mortgage was included within
these, it is a valid instrument. *Richmond v. Greeley,* 38
Iowa, 666. The authority is not expressly given, and cannot
be implied unless practically indispensable to the accomplishment of the object of his agency. This is the rule with respect
to the making of promissory notes. *Whiting v. Stage Co.,*
20 Iowa, 557; *Miller v. House,* 67 Iowa, 737; *Paige v. Stone,*
43 Am. Dec. 420; Mechem Agency, section 389 *et seq.*; 1 Am.
& Eng. Enc. Law, 1022, 1032. And it must be applied with
strictness to the giving of chattel mortgages. The evidence
plainly indicates the purpose of Hatter to have been that the

business continue a going concern. This appears from his suggestions with reference to raising money. But observation teaches that the execution of a chattel mortgage on the stock of a retail merchant is ordinarily quite as effective in putting an end to his business as the levy of a writ of attachment. In *Dispatch Line of Packets v. Bellamy Mfg. Co.,* 12 N. H. 205, Chief Justice Parker remarked: "It is not carrying on the business of the company to pledge or mortgage the machinery used by the company, and thereby suspend its operation, or place them at the will and pleasure of a mortgagee." In *Taylor v. Labeaume,* 17 Mo. 338, an agent, having an entire management of a business of a lumber company, the members thereof living abroad, was held to have power to transfer lumber in trust in payment of the servants of the company. Only a part of its property was so disposed of, not enough to terminate its business. If the agent was permitted to do what the owner might have done, this must be construed with reference to carrying on his business, and not in respect to ending it. The mortgage, if valid, transferred the right of possession to the plaintiff. The mere fact that he did not exercise this right does not argue against the existence. Miller had the authority to sell in the ordinary course of trade, but, authority to mortgage cannot be inferred from that to sell. *Jeffrey v. Hursh,* 49 Mich. 31 (12 N. W. Rep. 898); *Wood v. Goodridge,* 52 Am. Dec. 771. As the mortgage transferred the right to the possession of the goods and fixtures in the store, and placed the operation of Hatter's business beyond the control of Miller, its execution was inimical to the very purpose of his agency. Clearly, under such circumstances, the authority to mortgage cannot be implied. AFFIRMED.

THOMAS CASCADEN, JR., Appellant, v. THE CITY OF WATER-
LOO, *et al.*

Wards of City: CHANGE: *Ordinances.* Code, title 5, section 641,
    authorizing the creating and changing of city wards, does not pro-
2 vide whether the power shall be exercised by ordinance or resolu-
8 tion. Section 680 provides that cities may make ordinances "for

earrying into effect and discharging the powers and duties conferred by this title." *Held*, that a change of the wards of a city must be by ordinance, and not by a resolution.

AMENDMENT OF ORDINANCE.   An ordinance fixing the wards of a city
3   can be amended or repealed only by another ordinance, and not by a resolution.

SAME.   Where an ordinance divides a city into four wards, a resolution changing two of them, and creating a fifth, is void under Code,
4   section 6-1, where it does not contain "the entire ordinance or section revised or amended," as required by such section

ADOPTION OF RESOLUTION.   A resolution of a city council not adopted
4   by a majority of the whole number of the council, as required by Code, section 683 is void.

Rights of Taxpayer of Town: INJUNCTIONS.   A taxpayer has a right of action to restrain a city from holding an election in a new
1   ward, claimed to have been illegally created, and from spending the public revenues in defraying the expenses thereof.

Appeal from Black Hawk District Court.—HON. A. S. BLAIR, Judge.

THURSDAY, DECEMBER 15, 1898.

PLAINTIFF, a taxpayer of the city of Waterloo, brings this action to restrain the defendants, the mayor and council of said city, from enforcing a certain resolution creating a new ward in said city.   Defendants' demurrer to plaintiff's petition was sustained, and, plaintiff electing to stand on his petition, judgment was rendered against him, from which he appeals.—*Reversed.*

Boies & Boies for appellant.

J. E. Williams, J. A. Mears, Courtright & Arbuckle, and *Alford & Gates* for appellees.

GIVEN, J.—I.   The petition filed March 16, 1898, and an amendment thereto, are, in substance, as follows: That the defendant city is a city of the second class; that the other defendants are the mayor and city council thereof, and that plaintiff is a resident of said city, is the owner of taxable real and personal property therein, and has been a taxpayer in said city for many years; that on the fourteenth day of September, 1896, an ordinance was duly adopted dividing said city into four wards, under which the defendant officers were duly elected; that on January 24, 1898,. said city council, by a vote of four for to two against (the other two members being absent), adopted a resolution creating an additional ward out of portions of the Third and Fourth, to be known as the Fifth ward. Said resolution provided: "That the necessary steps be taken at the next city election for the election of two councilmen from said Fifth ward, hereby created." It is alleged that said resolution is void for the reasons that it was not adopted by the required vote; that it does not contain the entire ordinance or sections attempted to be revised, amended, or repealed thereby, and was not passed in the manner required by law for the passage of ordinances, for that it was not read on three different days, nor the reading dispensed with, and was not passed by a majority of the whole council. It is further alleged that defendants will, unless restrained, proceed under said resolution to hold and cause to be held in said Fifth ward an illegal and unauthorized election, and will disburse the public revenues to which plaintiff has contributed in defraying the expenses thereof; that they will declare persons elected to be members of the city council, and entitled to compensation as such and as members of the board of equalization out of the public moneys, to which plaintiff has contributed and will hereafter contribute. Plaintiff prays for a decree enjoining such action, and for general relief. Defendants demurred to the petition upon the following grounds: "(1) The petition shows upon its face that the plaintiff is not entitled to the relief demanded, or to any relief. (2) No statements or allegations are contained in said petition to invoke the powers of or give jurisdiction to a court of equity. (3) The petition shows upon its face that the plaintiff has a speedy and adequate remedy at law. (4) The petition shows upon its face that the plaintiff has no interest in the subject-matter other and differently from any other citizen of the city or general public has, and for that reason said plaintiff cannot maintain this action." This demurrer was sustained generally.

II.   The first question discussed is whether the petition shows that plaintiff is entitled to maintain this action. It shows that he has contributed, and will, as a taxpayer, contribute to the city's revenues, and that, unless restrained, the defendants will proceed to carry out said illegal resolution, and to illegally pay the expenses thereof from said revenues; and these allegations we must, for the purpose of the demurrer, take as true.   Counsel for appellees say: "In this country the right of resident taxpayers to resort to equity to restrain municipal corporations or their officers from transcending their lawful powers in any mode which will injuriously affect the taxpayers, such as making unauthorized appropriations of corporate funds, or an illegal disposal of corporate property, or levying or collecting void or illegal taxes or assessments, is recognized in numerous cases, and is, perhaps, the prevailing doctrine on this subject; but this rule is one that has grown up in most of the states of the Union in recent years, and is really an exception to the general rule of equity, and only applies to prevent the illegal disbursement of corporate funds, or the illegal disposal of corporate property." Again, they say: "The rule that a taxpayer may maintain an action to enjoin a municipality or its officers from illegally disbursing or appropriating corporate funds, or disposing of corporate property has been followed by the courts of Iowa in numerous cases, nearly all of which are cited by appellant in his argument."   The claim is that this is not an action to restrain the using of the public funds to pay expenses in carrying out said resolution, and in compensating the persons elected, but to restrain defendants from fixing voting places, holding an election, and issuing certificates of election to persons elected.   We do not so view the petition.   It asks to restrain the carrying out of said resolution, not alone because it is illegal to do so, but because it is illegal, and in doing so the public revenue will be illegally expended.   The case is clearly within the rule that entitles a taxpayer to maintain an action to restrain an illegal disposal of the corporate funds. Of the cases cited we note *Brockman v. City of Creston,* 79 Iowa, 587; *Snyder v. Foster,* 77 Iowa, 638. This view of the petition answers appellees' contention that appellant's remedy is adequate at law, and that the matters alleged are not sufficient to call for equitable relief.

III.   The next question is whether the city council could create the new ward by resolution, appellant's contention being that it can only be done by ordinance. There is no dispute but that the city council had power to create the
1   new ward. Code, section 641. Appellant insists that the statute requires this power to be exercised by ordinance, and cites many authorities to the effect that, where the statute requires a power to be exercised in a particular manner, it cannot be exercised in any other. Of the cases cited we only mention *Ryce v. City of Osage,* 88 Iowa, 558; *Henke v. McCord,* 55 Iowa, 378; *Blanden v. City of Ft. Dodge,* 102 Iowa, 441; *Noyes v. Mason City,* 53 Iowa, 418. Appellees concede that such is the law, but contend "that the statutes, or rather the law, of this state does not require that wards be established by ordinance." This action being under the present Code, we turn to it to solve this question, only referring to prior legislation and decisions thereon so far as they aid in construing the present statute. The legislation in respect to cities and towns is largely, if not entirely, contained in title 5 of the present Code, which title is devoted entirely to that subject, and is divided into fourteen chapters. An examination of title 5 shows that municipal corporations are authorized to act by ordinance and by resolution,—sometimes by ordinance only, sometimes by resolution only, sometimes by ordinance or resolution. For instance, sections 640, 669, 675, 676, and paragraph 11 of section 668, require powers conferred to be exercised by ordinance; sections 628 and 810 allow the powers therein referred to to be exercised by resolution; and sections 619, 620, 751, 798, 799, 802, 811, 825, 836, 841, and 842 permit the powers therein referred to to be exercised by ordinance or resolution. Section 641,

which authorizes the creation and changing of wards, is silent as to whether that power shall be exercised by ordinance or resolution. Section 680 is as follows: "Municipal corporations shall have power to make and publish from time to time ordinances not inconsistent with the laws of the state for carrying into effect or discharging the powers and duties conferred by this title, and such as shall seem necessary and proper to provide for the safety, preserve the health, promote the prosperity, improve the morals, order, comfort and convenience of such corporations and the inhabitants thereof, and to enforce obedience to such ordinances by fine not exceeding one hundred dollars, or by imprisonment not exceeding thirty days." Section 482 of the Code of 1873 was the same as this section 680, except that the word "title" is used therein instead of "chapter," as in this section. This change was necessitated by the rearrangement of the titles and chapters, and leaves the effect the same, the word "chapter" in section 482 being quite as broad in its application as the word "title" in the present Code. Appellant's contention is that, the power to establish and change wards conferred by title 5, section 680, requires that it shall be exercised by the enactment of an ordinance. There being no direct provision as to whether the power conferred by section 641 shall be exercised by ordinance or by resolution, we are called upon to construe said section 680 in the light of other provisions of the title, and of prior decisions, and say whether this power can only be exercised by ordinance. The two instances referred to in which the council may act by resolution are in proposing a change of name of the corporation, and submitting the same to a vote of the people (section 628), and in declaring it advisable to make street improvements and sewers (section 810). Said sections authorizing action by ordinance or resolution relate to annexation of territory, the acceptance of dedicated streets, etc., the changing of water courses, the reconstruction of street improvements or sewers, the levy of special assessments for street and sewer improvements, the correction of informal or irregular assessments, for the issu-

ance of street improvements and sewer certificates, and for
the payment of the costs of street improvements or sewers. It
is also provided as to ordinances that "no ordinance shall contain more than one subject, which shall be clearly expressed
in its title; and that no ordinance or section thereof shall be
revised or amended unless the new ordinance contain the
entire ordinance or section revised or amended, and the former ordinance or section to be repealed." Section 681.
"Ordinances of a general or permanent nature and those for
the appropriation of money shall be fully and distinctly read
on three different days, unless three-fourths of the council
shall dispense with the rule." Section 682. Section 686
requires all ordinances to be recorded in a book kept for that
purpose, and to be authenticated by the signature of the presiding officer and the clerk; "and all ordinances of a general
or permanent nature, and those imposing any fine, penalty, or
forfeiture, shall be published," etc. There are no such provisions with respect to resolutions, and it is manifest that
much greater care is required in forming, adopting, publishing, and preserving ordinances than resolutions, and especially
so as to such as are of a general or permanent nature. Ordinances are of a general nature when general in their
application, and of a permanent nature when their provisions,
unless repealed, will continue in force indefinitely. It will
be observed that in the instances wherein action by resolution, or by resolution or ordinance, is authorized, the
power exercised is not of a general or permanent nature;
that the ordinance or resolution is not general to all
in its application, and does not continue in force indefinitely, but only until its purposes are accomplished. The
power to divide the city into wards is certainly a power
of a general and permanent nature, for, when exercised,
it applies to all alike, and, unless repealed, continues
in force indefinitely. In *McManus v. Hornaday*, 99 Iowa,
508, the question was whether the grade of a street established
by ordinance of the city of Keokuk could be changed by resolution. That city exists under a special charter, which authorizes the city council to make and publish ordinances upon

certain subjects, among which are "such laws and ordinances as to them shall seem necessary to provide for the safety, preserve the health, promote the prosperity and improve the morals, order, comfort and convenience of said city and the inhabitants thereof." Section 680 of the Code not only so provides, but also provides for the enactment of ordinances "for carrying into effect or discharging the powers and duties conferred by this title." The power to establish and change wards, as we have seen, is conferred by that title. After holding that the council of the city of Keokuk had power to change the grade of the street, we held that it could "only be legally exercised by the enactment and publication of ordinances." It is true, in that case there was no provision for exercising any of the powers conferred by resolution, and it is equally true that in this way there is no express authority for creating or changing wards by resolution. We have said in that case, "We do not think that a matter of such importance to property owners as the establishment of grades was intended to be exercised by the mere passage of resolutions." Certainly the establishing or changing of wards in a city is of equal importance. *Merchants' Union Barb-Wire Co. v. Chicago, B. & Q. Ry Co.*, 70 Iowa, 106, is cited. In that case the city of Des Moines had, in 1866, granted to defendant by ordinance the right to construct its track and side tracks upon Vine street, "but requiring that upon the part of the street whereon plaintiff's lots abutted the defendant shall build its track on the north side." In May, 1874, the city, by resolution, authorized the defendant to construct another track in said street opposite plaintiff's property. The first question considered was whether, in view of the restriction contained in the first grant, the city could grant further privileges. It is said: "In our opinion, the ordinance simply grants the right of way in the north half of the street, and is not a restriction in the nature of a prohibition against the occupancy of the south side. That side was left by the ordinance just as whole a street as before the ordinance was passed." The third paragraph of that opinion holds that the grant of the right of way in streets is simply a permission, and that: "There exists no necessity for expressing this grant of authority by ordinance, as the statute (Code 1873, section 464) conferring authority upon a city to authorize or forbid the construction of railway tracks in its streets does not prescribe the manner of exercising the authority, whether by ordinance, resolution, or vote duly recorded. The statute being silent upon this subject, the authority may be exercised by resolution duly passed, or vote duly taken, appearing in the proper record of the city." Notwithstanding said section 464 is included in chapter 10 of title 4 of the Code of 1873, no reference is made in this opinion to said section 482 of that title and chapter. That section, as we have seen, provided for carrying into effect the powers conferred by that chapter by making and publishing ordinances. If it may be said that this second grant or right of way in Vine street could be made by resolution, still we are of the opinion that a matter of such general and permanent nature as the establishment of wards was not intended by the legislature to be made in any less definite and enduring· manner than by ordinance. There are a number of Iowa cases bearing more or less directly upon the question, but, regarding the holding in *McManus v. Hornaday* as directly applicable and controlling, we need not refer further to these citations. Our conclusion is that the creating or changing of the boundaries of wards must be by ordinance.

. IV. The question whether an ordinance can "be amended, repealed, or suspended by resolution or vote" is suggested, but not determined, in *Merchants' Union Barb-Wire Co. v. Chicago, B. & Q. Ry. Co., supra.*

3   Surely, when the statute requires that the power conferred must be exercised by ordinance, and it has been thus exercised, the ordinance can only be amended, repealed, or suspended by ordinance. In amending, repealing, or suspending such an ordinance the council act under the same authority as authorized the adoption of the prior ordinance. Another potent reason is that ordinances of a general or permanent nature are required to be published in a certain

manner, and thereafter stand as the law, of which all must take notice. Resolutions are not required to be so published, and, therefore, the public would not be informed of amendments, repeals, or suspensions of ordinances made by resolution. We conclude that ordinances of a general or permanent nature cannot be amended, repealed, or supended by resolution, but by ordinance only.

V. It will be observed that there was an ordinance fixing the boundaries of the four wards, and that by this resolution the boundaries of two of these wards were changed, and a fifth ward created. Thereby it was sought to revise and amend the ordinance. If an ordinance might be revised, repealed, or amended by resolution, this resolution is not effective for that purpose, as it does not "contain the entire ordinance or section revised or amended," as required

4   by section 681, and, therefore, the ordinance remains in full force. Another reason why this resolution cannot be effective is that it was not adopted by concurrence of a majority of the whole number of the council, as required by section 683. Our conclusion upon the whole record is that the court erred in sustaining the demurrer to plaintiff's petition, and the judgment is, therefore, REVERSED.

BLANCHE DEVIER, *et al.*, v. THE ECONOMIC LIFE ASSOCIATION, Appellant.

Appealable Order: An order for the production of books and papers is not within Code 1873, section 3164, subds. 1, 4, giving the right of appeal from an order affecting a substantial right where such order determines the action, or prevents a final judgment from which an appeal may be taken, and from an intermediate order involving the merits, and materially affecting the final judgment.

REVIEW. Under Code 4656 which authorizes the same consequences for failure to obey a rule to produce books and papers that follow a refusal to appear and testify and section 4668 which provides that upon a failure to appear and testify the court may order, subject to reconsideration during the term, that the pleadings shall be deemed true if the pleader shows he could not have personal knowledge of the transaction, a judgment can not be had without a showing of lack of such knowledge even if it be assumed that the trial judge has, after such showing, no discretion, which this court is not willing to say.

Appeal from Clinton District Court.—HON. P. B. WOLFE, Judge.

THURSDAY, DECEMBER 15, 1898.

ACTION to recover upon two policies of life insurance. Both parties appeal from certain intermediate orders of the court. The appeal of defendant having been first perfected, it will be denominated the "appellant."—*Affirmed.*

Hayes & Schuyler for appellant.

Murray & Farr and *Ellis & Ellis* for appellees.

WATERMAN, J.—Plaintiffs sued as beneficiaries named in two policies of insurance issued by defendant company upon the life of one Hugh W. Devier, deceased. They alleged that the policies were in the possession of defendant. Thereafter, on June 5, 1897, the defendant filed a motion to compel plaintiffs to set out the terms of the contract. On August 5 following, plaintiffs filed a petition praying for an inspection of the books and papers of defendant company. Pending the hearing of this application the court sustained defendant's motion, and ordered plaintiffs to set out the particulars of the contracts. September 22 plaintiffs amended their petition, but not in the respects asked. With the record in this condition, on September 25 the court overruled defendant's exception to the application for the inspection of books and papers, and ordered the production of such documents; and from this order the defendant appeals. No appeal lies from such an order. *Cook v. Railroad Co.*, 75 Iowa, 169.

After defendant's appeal, and on October 4, 1897, plaintiffs filed a motion for judgment on the ground of the non-compliance of defendant with the order of the court which required it to permit an inspection to be made of books and papers. This motion was overruled, and it is from this action of the court that plaintiffs appeal. On December 4, 1897, the plaintiffs amended their petition, and set out the matters required by the order of court made on defendant's motion on September 8. The order for the production of the books and papers, as appears, was made before the present Code went into effect. The ruling on the application for judgment was entered on October 4, 1897. Both parties treat the matter as governed by the Code of 1897. Inasmuch as its provisions are substantially the same as the Code of 1873 on the same subject, it is immaterial to which we refer, so we shall follow counsel, and treat the case as though governed by the present Code. Section 4656 provides that, if a party fails to obey a rule requiring a production of books or papers for inspection, "the same consequences shall ensue as if the party had failed to appear and testify when subpœnaed by the party now calling for the books and papers." And in section 4668 it is provided that, when a party fails to obey a subpœna, if the other party "shows by his own testimony or otherwise that he could not have personal knowledge of the transaction, the court may order his pleadings to be taken as true; subject to be reconsidered during the term of the court." We are not willing to say that the trial court has no discretion under this section. But, however that may be, plaintiffs did not make the showing required,—of want of personal knowledge,—and for this reason their request for judgment was properly overruled. Defendant's appeal will be dismissed, and on plaintiff's appeal the action of the trial court is AFFIRMED.

STATE OF IOWA v. FRANK SHERMAN, Appellant.

Assault to Rape: KNOWLEDGE OF PROSECUTRIX' AGE   Under Code 1873, section 3873, providing that, "if any person assault a female
1   with intent to commit rape, he shall be punished," etc., defendant need not have known that she was under such age, in order to sustain a conviction for such assault

EVIDENCE. Where defendant caused a female under the age of consent to lie on the ground and unbotton her clothing, for the
2 purpose and with the intent of having sexual intercourse with
her, it was an assault with intent to commit rape.

INCLUDED OFFENSE: *When submitted.* Where the evidence shows
3 defendant guilty of the crime charged, or of none at all, an instruction as to lower degrees of crime is unnecessary.

INSTRUCTIONS. Where the jury are plainly charged as to the degree
of evidence necessary to convict, a refusal to charge that, if
4 they should reject the testimony of the State's only witness, they
must find for the defendant, is harmless.

Appeal from Cass District Court.—HON. N. W. MACY,
Judge.

THURSDAY, DECEMBER 15, 1898.

INDICTMENT for rape on a female under the age of thirteen years. Verdict of guilty and a judgment thereon. The
defendant appealed.—*Affirmed.*

John Hudspeth for appellant.

Milton Remley, Attorney General, *C. A. Meredith,*
County Attorney, and *Jesse A. Miller,* for the State.

GRANGER, J.—I. When the indictment was returned
the "age of consent" was thirteen instead of fifteen years, as
at present. The court instructed the jury on the question of
an assault with intent to commit rape, as being included in the
crime charged in the indictment, and of this complaint is
made, it not appearing that defendant had actual knowledge
of the age of the prosecutrix; and appellant's claim is that
there must not only be the intent to commit rape, but it must
be intent to do so on a female under the age of thir-
1   teen years. A female under the age of thirteen years
is not competent to consent to sexual intercourse,
nor can she consent to an assault for that purpose. *State
v. Grossheim,* 79 Iowa, 75; *State v. Carnagy,* 106 Iowa,
483. It is not necessary that the defendant should be shown

to have knowledge that the female was under the age of thirteen years, to sustain a conviction for an assault with intent
to commit rape. The crime does not depend upon the knowledge of defendant of the fact that the child was under that
age, but upon the fact of the assault. *State v. Newton*, 44
Iowa, 45; *State v. Grossheim, supra*. Code 1873, section
3873, provides: "If any person assault a female with intent
to commit rape, he shall be punished by imprisonment in the
penitentiary not exceeding twenty years." There is no provision of the law defining, as a specific crime, an assault with
intent to commit rape on a female under the age of thirteen
years. An assault on any female, with intent to commit rape,
makes the offense charged in the section quoted; and the punishment, whatever may be the age of the person assaulted, is
as provided in that section. The law simply requires that
there shall be an assault with intent to commit rape on a
female. The crime of rape itself, as to the different offenses
prescribed, is made to depend on different facts, as the indictment may show the age to be above or below that which marks
the distinction. Not so as to an assault with intent to commit rape. If, then, the law requires, in such a case as this,
that the jury must find that the female was under the age of
thirteen years, to sustain a conviction for an assault with
intent to commit rape,—which question we need not and do
not decide, for the court so instructed,—it is no more important that the defendant shall have knowledge of the age, than
that he should have such knowledge in a case of rape, to sustain a conviction where the indictment charges the female to
be under the age of thirteen. Conceding that as to both cases
there must be proof of the age, to convict of an intent to commit a particular crime, the intent need not be as to other facts
than those necessary to convict of the crime itself; and, as
we have said,—and the rule is not questioned,—in case of
rape, as charged in this indictment, knowledge of the age need
not be shown. Appellant has cited authorities and quoted
extensively general rules, as to the element of intent in crimes,
about which there is no controversy; but they do not apply

here, in the sense claimed for them.⌡ It will be well, in this immediate connection, to dispose of another question, largely controlled by what we have said. The court said to the jury, on the question of an assault with intent to commit

2   rape, after defining an "assault:" "If you find from the evidence that the defendant at the time and place in question asked or caused the said Minnie Blood to lie down upon the ground and disarrange or unbutton her clothing, for the purpose of having sexual intercouse with her, that would constitute an assault; and if, in addition to such facts you further find that it was the defendant's intention in so doing to carnally know her, and you further find that the said Minnie Blood at that time was under the age of thirteen years, and nothing further be shown, then the defendant is guilty of an assault with intent to commit rape, and should be convicted accordingly." Nothing but actual sexual intercourse was necessary, to follow the acts described as an assault, to constitute rape upon a female of that age. If so, and if the acts specified were done with intent to have such intercourse, then the conclusion must follow that it was an assault with intent to commit rape.   .

II.   The court did not submit to the jury the question of a simple assault, and error is assigned because of the failure. It was not error. In *State v. Cater*, 100 Iowa, 501, we said, as touching the lower degrees of a crime charged,

3   and referring to Code 1873, sections 4465, 4466, that they had "no application when the facts show that the defendant is either guilty of the crime charged, or not guilty of any crime, and that in such a case it is not incumbent on the court to charge as to the lower grades of the crime. See that case for a collection of the cases so holding in this state. The holding is decisive of the present assignment in this case. If there was not an assault with intent to commit rape, there was no crime committed. No other conclusion could properly be arrived at from the evidence.

III.   The defendant asked the court to instruct the jury that if, for any reason, it should reject the testimony of Min-

nie Blood as to defendant's alleged carnal knowledge of her,
and relations with her, then its verdict should be for
4   the defendant. The instruction could well have been
given, because there is no evidence, aside from that of
Minnie Blood, that could sustain a verdict in the case; but,
while such a conclusion was not stated in that way, the jury
was plainly told the degree of evidence necessary to convict,
and the defendant's rights were well and amply guarded
against a conviction except upon evidence to satisfy it beyond
a reasonable doubt.

Several other questions are argued, that we need not discuss, as they are covered by what we have said, or are not
doubtful, under the authorities of this state. The verdict has
full support in the evidence, and the judgment will be
AFFIRMED.

THE STATE OF IOWA v. ALONZO ROBBINS, Appellant.

Transcript in Criminal Case: ALLOWANCE AT COUNTY'S EXPENSE:
Abuse of discretion. Where accused is convicted of murder in
the first degree, and assigns fifteen grounds for a new trial,
which is refused, a refusal of the trial court to grant a transcript
at the expense of the county—under Code, section 254, providing
that if defendant has perfected an appeal from a judgment
against him, and satisfies a judge of the Court from which the
appeal is taken that he is unable to pay for the transcript, such
judge may order the same made at the expense of the county—on
the ground that the Court feels that defendant has had a fair
trial, is an abuse of discretion.

Appeal from Lee District Court.—HON. HENRY BANK, JR.,
Judge.

THURSDAY, DECEMBER 15, 1898.

THIS case is by leave submitted on a typewritten abstract,
which shows as follows: An indictment charging the defendant with murder in the first degree, signed: "A true bill. P.
M. Mathews, Foreman of the Grand Jury,"—was returned
and filed October 11, 1897. October 13, 1897, the defend-

ant pleaded not guilty. R. M. Marshall was appointed to
defend, and by consent the case was continued. At the December term, 1897, trial was had, and on December 30 the jury
returned its verdict, as follows: "We, the jury, find the
defendant guilty of murder in the first degree, as charged in
the indictment, and direct that he be punished by imprisonment in the penitentiary at hard labor for life. Wm. Adams,
Senior, Foreman." On January 3, 1898, the defendant filed
his motion for a new trial, assigning fifteen separate grounds
therefor, which are set out at length in the abstract. On January 7, 1898, this motion was overruled, and judgment of
imprisonment in the penitentiary at Ft. Madison for the term
of his natural life rendered against the defendant. On January 7, 1898, the defendant caused notice cᶜ appeal to be
served. On March 7, 1898, defendant made application for
an order for a transcript of the shorthand notes at the expense
of the county, as follows: "State of Iowa, Lee County—ss.:
I, Alonzo Robbins, being first duly sworn, depose and say that
I am defendant in above-entitled cause; that at the December
term, 1897, of this court, I was convicted of murder in the
first degree, and sentenced to the penitentiary for life; that I
desire to take an appeal in this cause; that I have no money
with which to pay for a transcript; that at the time of my trial
I had no money, and the court appointed an attorney to manage the case for me at the expense of the county; that I have
no money at the present time, and no property or assets of any
kind or description; that I am wholly unable to pay for a
transcript, and, unless the court grants me a transcript at the
expense of the county, I will be unable and cannot take an
appeal in this case. Wherefore, I respectfully ask the court
to grant me a transcript at the expense of the county, that
I may be able to have my cause reviewed by the supreme court.
Alonzo Robbins." "Subscribed and sworn to before me by
Alonzo Robbins this second day of February, 1898. F. M.
Ballinger, Notary Public." On the fourteenth day of May,
1898, judgment was rendered by Henry Bank, Jr., J., overruling said application "on the ground that the only question

in the trial was the question as to the defendant's sanity, and the court feels that the defendant had a fair trial on that question, and the jury found him guilty, and, the matter being discretionary with the court, the motion is therefore overruled." On May 19 following, the defendant caused notice of appeal from the judgment overruling said application to be duly served.—*Reversed.*

Frank M. Ballinger, for appellant.

Milton Remley, Attorney General, and *Hubert Remley* for the State.

GIVEN, J.—I. On the twenty-seventh day of September, 1898, the appellant served and filed an additional abstract, which shows that on September 20, 1898, Henry Bank, Jr., J., who tried the case and heard the said application, certified that the affidavit of defendant set out in the certificate, and which is the same shown in the abstract as quoted above, was all the evidence introduced at the hearing of said application. To said additional abstract is appended the certificate of the attorney for appellant that said additional abstract, together with the original abstract, "constitute the evidence, and all of the evidence, offered at or during, or which had reference to, the hearing of defendant's application for a transcript at the county's expense." Appellee's counsel move to strike this additional abstract upon the grounds that it was not filed until after appellee's argument; that it is not a bill of exceptions, and was not filed in the court below, or made a part of the record. The filing of this additional abstract was no doubt suggested by the claim of counsel for the state in their argument that the original abstract was not certified by either the judge, reporter, or attorney as containing all the record or all the evidence. It will be observed that this additional abstract discloses nothing more than what was contained in the original, except that it certifies that the only evidence upon which said application was heard was the affidavit of the appellant, which, as we have seen, appears at length in the original abstract. We have the certificate of counsel in effect that said affidavit constitutes all the evidence upon which the application was heard; therefore, if we strike the certificate of the judge, we still have the fact before us that said affidavit was all the evidence offered upon the hearing of said application. We conclude that the motion should be sustained, but, as we are required to consider cases like this without regard to technical errors or defects which do not affect substantial rights of the parties, we may proceed to consider the only question presented by this appeal, namely, whether the court erred in refusing said application for an order for a transcript at the expense of the county. See Code, section 5462.

II. This application is made under section 254 of the Code, which contains the following: "If a defendant in a criminal cause has perfected an appeal from a judgment against him, and shall satisfy a judge of the court from which the appeal is taken that he is unable to pay for the transcript of the evidence, such judge may order the same made at the expense of the county." Counsel discuss the question whether, the judge being satisfied that the appellant is unable to pay for a transcript, it is imperative upon him to grant an order. The difference between the prior statute (section 3777, Code 1873), as construed in *State v. Waddle*, 94 Iowa, 748, and the present statute, is pointed out, and authorities cited as to when permissive language will be held to be imperative. Appellant also contends that, conceding that it was discretionary with the judge whether or not to grant this order, there was such an abuse of that discretion as to call for a reversal. In the view we take of this last contention, it is unnecessary that we consider the first. There can be no question that, if the grounds stated for a new trial are well taken, the new trial should have been granted; and it is equally clear that a transcript of the evidence is indispensable to a full consideration of the defendant's appeal from the judgment of conviction. The learned judge, holding it to be discretionary with him, refused the order, not because he was not satisfied that the appellant is unable to pay for the transcript, but for the reason that there was but one question in the case, namely, the sanity of the defendant, "and the court feels that the defendant had a fair trial on that question." We are justified in concluding from the record that appellant is unable to pay for the transcript, and that the trial judge was satisfied of that fact. Now, conceding that it was discretionary with the judge, notwithstanding defendant's inabilty to pay for the transcript, to say whether or not the order should be granted, we inquire whether there was an abuse of that discretion, and we do so mindful of the superior opportunities of the trial judge to know as to the nature of the case. In *State v. Waddle, supra,* wherein a like application was made under the former statute, it is said: "He [the judge] is conscious of the character of the case, the nature of the testimony, the severity of the punishment, and of all the facts and circumstances surrounding the case; and we must presume that his discretion was wisely exercised." The severity of the punishment is recognized as proper to be considered. In that case the punishment was imprisonment in the county jail for a limited time; in this it is imprisonment in the penitentiary for life. No doubt the trial judge had felt that the appellant had had a fair trial, and the same is true in every case wherein a defendant's motion for a new trial is overruled. If it were otherwise, a new trial would be granted. It will not do to say that, because the judge is satisfied that the defendant has had a fair trial, he shall be denied the right of appeal; yet that is the effect of the ruling on this application. A transcript of the evidence is necessary to a prosecution of defendant's appeal. He is unable to pay for it, and therefore, if not furnished at the expense of the county, unable to procure it. The spirit of our law is not only to secure to the accused a full and fair trial in the lower court, but also a full review of his case on appeal to this court. In view of the severity of the punishment, the grounds assigned for a new trial, the necessity for a transcript of the evidence, the inability of the defendant to pay therefor, and his right to a review of the case on appeal in this court, we conclude that the exercise of a sound discretion required that the order for a transcript at the expense of the county should have been made. The judgment upon this application is reversed, and the case remanded for judgment sustaining the application. REVERSED.

C. L. TRENERY, Appellant, v. THOS. GOUDIE.

Wages: RIGHT TO RECOVER OF STAKE-HOLDER. One who wagered money cannot recover his share of the stakes from the stake holder, whatever the outcome, unless, before payment to the other wagering party, the former repudiated the transaction and notified the stake-holder not to pay the money; and his recovery is defeated if he merely gave notice not to pay the wager until further notice.

Appeal from Plymouth District Court.—HON. J. F. OLIVER, Judge.

THURSDAY, DECEMBER 15, 1898.

ACTION for money had and received. From a judgment in favor of defendant, plaintiff appeals.—*Affirmed.*

Zink & Roseberry for appellant.

McDuffie & Keenan for appellee.

WATERMAN, J.—Plaintiff and one Boyle made a wager upon the result of an election, and placed the stakes in the hands of defendant. It is alleged that Boyle lost the wager, but that defendant, before the result of the election was known, and notwithstanding he was notified by the plaintiff not to do so, paid the money over to said Boyle. This action is to recover plaintiff's share of the stakes. The evidence establishes that the count of the judges of election showed that the candidate upon whose success Boyle had bet had received the largest vote. In a contest thereafter, the other candidate was awarded the certificate of election. On the strength of the first returns, defendant gave the stakes to Boyle. He claims that he acted in good faith in paying the money to Boyle, for he believed at the time that Boyle was entitled to it. However this may be, we have nothing to do with the question of who won the wager. Courts will not take cognizance of such transactions to that extent. The rights of plaintiff here are no greater than if he were the admitted loser. In cases of this kind the plaintiff cannot recover the amount at stake because he won it, nor is he entitled to any part of it as a wager. His right in the courts begins only when he repudiates the original transaction. If, before the money was paid to Boyle, the plaintiff repudiated the wager, and notified the defendant of the fact, and warned him not to pay over the amount of plaintiff's money in his hands, then he can recover; otherwise not. We do not find that plaintiff ever revoked the wager. On the contrary, he expressly recognized it, and the only warning given defendant was that he should not treat Boyle as the winner without further notice. This was not enough to give plaintiff a claim on the stake-holder. *Okerson v. Crittenden*, 62 Iowa, 297. In the cited case the plaintiff claimed to have won the wager, and his demand for the whole amount of the stakes was held not to be a repudiation of the transaction, and a right of recovery was denied. In that case, too, the determination of the stake-holder as to who was entitled to the fund was, in effect, held to be conclusive. This we believe to be a correct rule in every case where the decision is made after the happening of the event upon which the wager is laid.

II. We may say further that this notice, such as it was, was not given until the money had been paid over. This fact alone would defeat a recovery. *Adkins v. Fleming*, 29 Iowa, 122; *Thrift v. Redman*, 13 Iowa, 25; *Shannon v. Baumer*, 10 Iowa, 210. Plaintiff claims, as we have said, that the money was paid over before the happening of the event that was the subject of the wager. It is true that defendant, after he received the stakes placed them in the safe of Boyle to await the result of the election; but we do not find that he relinquished his rights or surrendered his duties as stake-holder until after the announcement of the vote. We are not inclined to lay down any rule, in order to meet the alleged hardship of plaintiff's case, that will invite to the courts controversies of this character. It is well for those who indulge in this amusement to understand that they must depend more upon honor than upon law for their protection. AFFIRMED.

F. H. PIERSON v. THE INDEPENDENT SCHOOL DISTRICT OF HAWARDEN, IOWA, Appellant.

School Districts: ACTION ON CLAIMS AGAINST: *Presentation.* Under Code, section 2780, requiring that claims against a school district must be first presented to the board of directors before suit can be maintained, where the petition founded on such a claim did not allege presentation, and plaintiff's evidence affirmatively showed that it was only proposed to the president of the board of directors to arbitrate the claim, a verdict for the district should have been directed.

MOTION IN ARREST OF JUDGMENT. Such objection may be taken by motion in arrest, under Code, section 2650, providing that, if the petition entitled plaintiff to no relief whatever, objection may be taken by motion in arrest.

Appeal from Sioux District Court.—HON. WILLIAM HUTCHINSON, Judge.

THURSDAY, DECEMBER 15, 1898.

THE claim for damages contained in the petition is based on the employment of the plaintiff as janitor for one year, and the breach of such contract by discharging him within four months without cause. There is no allegation in the petition of the presentation of this claim to the board of directors of the defendant, though the failure so to do is expressly averred in the answer. The other issues need not be stated. Trial to jury, verdict and judgment for plaintiff, and defendant appeals.—*Reversed.*

W. H. Palmer and *J. B. Van Dyke* for appellant.

Hutchinson & Plank and *P. D. Van Oosterhout* for appellee.

LADD, J.—As a condition precedent to the maintenance of an action against a school district, the claim on which it is based must be presented to the board of directors. *Spencer Dist. Tp. v. Riverton Dist. Tp.,* 56 Iowa, 88. Omission to do so appeared on the face of the petition, and, under the practice prior to the enactment of chapter 96, Acts Twenty-fifth General Assembly, the defect would be deemed waived by failure to demur. *Weir Furnace Co. v.Independent School Dist. of Seymour,* 99 Iowa, 116. Sections 2650 and 2651 of the Code of 1873 were amended by that chapter after the cited case had been tried. As amended, these sections appear as 3563 and 3564 of the Code. Under the present statutes, an objection to the petition, not raised by answer or demurrer, is not deemed waived. *Pardey v. Town of Mechanicsville,* 101 Iowa, 266; *McClain v. Capper,* 98 Iowa, 148. No evidence was offered by the plaintiff tending to show that the claim had been presented or a demand made, and when the defendant sought to bring out, on cross-examination, that this had not in fact been done, the court ruled it to be immaterial, and that the question would "not be submitted to the jury whether there was a demand filed by the plaintiff." The evidence so elicited showed that the claim had never been presented, and that Oel-richs, representing the plaintiff, merely proposed arbitration to the president of the board. Such claims must be audited and allowed by the board of directors, and not by the president, and until it has been presented, and the board has had an opportunity to act upon it, no suit can be maintained. Code, section 2780; *Spencer Dist. Tp. v. Riverton Dist. Tp., supra.* As the petition did not so allege, and the evidence showed affirmatively that this had not been done, the motion to direct a verdict for the defendant at the close of the evidence introduced by the plaintiff should have been sustained. *Seaton v. Hinneman,* 50 Iowa, 397; *Smith v. Railway Co.,* 59 Iowa, 73. The same point was well taken in the motion in arrest of judgment. *Rabe v. Sommerbeck,* 94 Iowa, 656; *Linden v. Green,* 81 Iowa, 368. As what we have said disposes of the case, other matters argued require no attention. REVERSED.

JOHN L. THERME V. KATE BETHENOID, Appellant.

Homesteads. A grantee of land subject to a life reservation of use and
4 rents acquires no homestead right, as against a subsequent
creditor, by occupancy through sufferance of a life tenant.

Transcript Judgments: SALE. Where there was a valid judgment,
1 based on a transcript from a justice court, and the execution,
levy, and sale are made in pursuance of it, as shown by introducing the filing entry and a sheriff's deed containing the usual re-
2 citals, the fact that through mistake a second entry of the filing
of the transcript was erroneously made does not invalidate the
sale.

MONEY JUDGMENT: *Presumptions.* The fact that there was no word
or dollar mark attached to the figures in the columns for "Costs"
and "Amount of Judgment" in the judgment docket entry
creates no inference that it was not a money judgment.

Appeal from Van Buren District Court.—HON. ROBERT
SLOAN, Judge.

THURSDAY, DECEMBER 15, 1898.

PLAINTIFF, claiming title under a sheriff's deed issued in
pursuance of a sale made on execution against Mark Bethenoid, defendant's husband, brings this action to recover possession of lots 2, 3, and 4, block 16, in the town of Farming-
ton. Defendant answered, denying that plaintiff had a valid
title; alleging as reasons that said execution was not issued
upon a valid judgment, that the property was exempt, as the
homestead of her husband and of herself, and because her husband had previously conveyed the property to her, and that
she had thereafter occupied it as her homestead. Plaintiff
replied, joining issue on the allegations in the answer; and the
case was transferred to, and tried as in, equity, and decree .
rendered in favor of the plaintiff. Defendant appeals.—
Affirmed.

Starr & Calhoun and *Bernard Dolan* for appellant.

Wherry & Walker for appellee.

GIVEN, J.—I. The facts necessary to be noticed are these: A Mrs. Dickey conveyed the property in question to Mark Bethenoid. This deed is not in evidence, but it otherwise appears that it was executed as early as the year 1886. The defendant testified, without objection: "I always understood that my husband's deed from Mrs. Dickey was subject to the reservation to her of the use, rents, and benefit during her life. Mrs. Dickey died October 16, 1890." The defendant and her husband and family moved into the house with Mrs. Dickey, with her consent, in 1886, and after residing therein for one year went elsewhere to live, and did not again occupy the property until December 6, 1890, since which time the defendant and her family have been in continuous possession. The property was rented for at least a part of the time between 1887 and the death of Mrs. Dickey, in 1890; Mrs. Dickey collecting the rents and controlling the property. On July 23, 1892, Mark Bethenoid conveyed the property by warranty deed to the defendant, and in April, 1894, went to France for the benefit of his health, where he died in 1895 or 1896.

It is upon these facts that defendant's claim of title is based. The plaintiff's is based upon the following facts:

August 3, 1885, Fred Hummelkee obtained a judgment against Mark Bethenoid before a justice of the peace for twenty-five dollars and ten cents, and two dollars and forty cents costs. Judgment Docket No. 6, page 100, of the district court, is in evidence, and shows as follows:

"No, 8,032. The names of plaintiff and defendant in judgment, direct and inverse, and—

Kind of Action.	Date of Filing.	Date of Judgment.	Amount of Judgment.	Costs.
Transcript from J. P.	August 12, 1888.	August 3, 1885.	25.10	2.40

It was upon a judgment based on the filing of a transcript that the execution was issued. The transcript is indorsed: "7805· Transcript, Fred Hummelkee vs. Mark Bethenoid, filed September 24, 1887. W. B. Flemming, Clerk. App. D. No. 5,260. Paid fifty cents by plaintiff."

Appearance Judgment and Execution Docket, No. 5, page 260, shows as follows:

"No. 7905. The names of the parties plaintiff and defendant, direct and inverse, and—

Kind of Action.	Date of Filing	Date of Judgment.	Amouut of Judgment.	Costs.
Transcript from J. P.	Sept. 24, 1887.	August 3, 1885.	25.10	2.40

Hummelkee obtained but one judgment against Bethenoid before the justice of the peace, and that was on August 3, 1885, and for twenty-five dollars and ten cents and two dollars and forty cents costs. The justice's docket shows but one transcript, and that was made September 21, 1887. It is evident that, for some reason that does not appear, these two entries were made of the same transcript.

II. By filing the transcript the judgment became the same as a judgment in the district court, and a lien upon real estate of the judgment defendant within the county, and was no longer enforceable as a judgment of the justice's court. That there was a valid judgment in the district court against Mark Bethenoid is not disputed, but the contention is that the entry of the filing of the transcript August 12, 1888, having been preceded by the filing September 24, 1887, is void, and that the execution issued with reference to that filing is therefore also void. There was a valid judgment against Mark Bethenoid, and the execution, levy, and sale were made in pursuance of that judgment; and the fact that, through inadvertence or otherwise, a second entry of the filing of the transcript was erroneously made, does not invalidate the sale. Appellant says there is no evidence of a judgment, and therefore the execution and deed are void; but appellant furnishes the evidence in introducing the filing of September 24, 1887, of a valid judgment. The plaintiff introduces his deed from the sheriff, containing the usual recitations; and from these we must presume the proceedings to be regular, and the fact of this second entry of the filing of the transcript does not overcome that presumption. So far as appears, the deed only shows a general execution issued December 19, 1894, on a judgment recovered in the district court in favor of Hummelkee against Bethenoid, and has no reference to the second entry made of the filing of the transcript. There being a valid judgment, we conclude that the execution and sale are referable to that judgment.

III. It will be observed that there is no word or dollar mark in the entries quoted above, expressly showing that the figures "25.10" and "2.40" are of dollars and cents; and it is therefore contended that the record fails to show a money judgment. No one can doubt from the reading of the entries, that the judgment is for money, and money only.

3

IV. As to defendant's claim to homestead, it is entirely clear that this judgment became a lien prior to the occupancy of the premises as a homestead. The first occupation by defendant and her family was by the suffrance of Mrs. Dickey, who had reserved the rents and use of the property during her lifetime; hence it was not until her death, in October, 1890, that defendant or her husband could have acquired a homestead right. This judgment became a lien upon whatever interest Mark Bethenoid had in the property prior to his conveyance to the defendant, and prior to the time that either had acquired a homestead right in the property. Therefore she took no right by the conveyance, as against this judgment. Our conclusion is that the decree of the district court is correct, and it is therefore AFFIRMED.

4

STATE OF IOWA v. BETSY SMITH, Appellant.

106 70
136

Accomplices: CONSPIRACY. Defendant was charged with and convicted of murder. The court charged that if defendant and others conspired to kill, and another gave poison with deadly effect in pursuance of the conspiracy, defendant was guilty of murder. *Held,* the instruction is proper though no conspiracy
1 was averred in the indictment, because the offense involved in the trial and found by the conviction was murder and not con-
2 spiracy, and Code, 1873, section 4814 abolishes the distinction between principals and accessories. In this case, the testimony circumstantially established conspiracy.

INSTRUCTIONS. Scoville was a witness for the State and M. for the defendant, both being her alleged accomplices. The court charged that if S. aided, assisted or abetted defendant in giving the poison, defendant could not be convicted on the testimony of S. *only,* unless there was corroboration tending to connect defendant which showed more than the mere death by poison, that unless there was more corroboration than this there could be no conviction on the testimony of S. *alone,* that if the jury found S. was not an accomplice, that her testimony was true and that it connected defendant, there might be a conviction on her testimony. The jury was also told that, on corroboration, it might consider the death and its cause, in connection with all the facts and circumstances shown which connected defendant with the death and that if such facts and circumstances corroborated the testimony of S. which tends to connect defendant with the crime charged there might be a conviction upon the testimony of S. so corroborated *alone,* if her testimony warrants conviction. *Held,*

a In the absence of request, the charge sufficiently defines accomplice.

b It was not necessary to instruct on the effect of a conspiracy between S. and C. The only question was whether S. and de-
4 fendant conspired. If defendant did not so conspire and S. and C. alone committed the crime, defendant was innocent and the relations sustained by S. and C. were wholly immaterial.

c It was not error to use the words "Alone" and "Only" because
5 the statute on corroboration, Code, 1873, section 4559, sanctions them by implication.

SAME. Where a witness for accused testifies that she and another did the murder and that defendant was innocent, it is unneces-
6 sary to charge that she must be corroborated, especially in the absence of request.

Evidence. Where concert of action as to a murder appears or may be
7 found, the treatment of deceased while living, by alleged conspirators is admissible on the trial of one of them for the murder.

SAME. Where an attempt was made to murder deceased a year before he was finally killed, and there is evidence connecting
accused, his wife, therewith, it may be shown, in contradiction of
8 her statement that she had no connection therewith, that, shortly
before such attempt, she tried to rent rooms, stating that they
would be occupied by herself and daughter alone.

CROSS-EXAMINATION. Where an inquiry as to a prior attempt to
murder deceased had become material, and an alleged accomplice, who confessed to having finally killed deceased, testified
9 for accused, it was discretionary with the court to permit a
cross-examination as to the prior attempt, though witness had
not testified in reference thereto on direct examination.

Speedy Trial: DISCHARGE OF DEFENDANT. Where delay in trial is
due to continuances obtained by defendant and her claims of ill
10 health she is not entitled to a discharge under section 4614 of the
Code of 1873.

Appeal from Polk District Court.—HON. W. F. CONRAD,
Judge.

. THURSDAY, DECEMBER 15, 1898.

DEFENDANT is accused of the crime of the murder of
her husband by the administration of poison. Two trials have
been had, the first resulting in a verdict of guilty, upon which
she was sentenced to imprisonment for life, and the second, in
a like verdict and sentence. Appeal was taken to this court
from the first conviction, and the case was reversed. See 102
Iowa, 656. This appeal is from the second conviction.—
Affirmed.

F. B. Huckstep and *Dale & Bissell* for appellant.

Milton Remley, Attorney General; *W. H. Redman,*
Assistant Attorney General, and *James A. Howe,* County
Attorney, for the State.

DEEMER, C. J.—The facts are quite fully stated in the
opinion filed on the first appeal, and need not be repeated

here, except in so far as it may be necessary to an understanding of the matters decided.

I.   The trial court instructed the jury, in effect, that if defendant gave, or was a party to the giving of, a deadly poison to Michael Smith, and if she did so knowingly and feloniously, then the jury might find her guilty. It further charged that if some person or persons other than defendant gave the poison, and if defendant and such other person or persons conspired and agreed together to kill said Smith, and if, in carrying out such conspiracy, they acted in concert to accomplish their end, and if the poison was administered by one of them, then the giving of the poison was the act of all, and each was equally guilty with the other. The indictment is in a single count, and in the usual form of such presentments. No conspiracy or confederation is charged.

Appellant contends that the portion of the charge above referred to is erroneous, for the reason that defendant cannot be convicted of conspiracy unless charged with that offense. If

1   defendant had been convicted of that crime, there would be much force in appellant's position. She was not convicted of that offense, however, but of murder; and the real question is whether there is a variance between the allegations and the proof. It must be remembered in this connection that our Code (1873, section 4314) abolishes the distinction between accessory before the fact and principal, and provides that all persons concerned in the commission of a public offense, whether they directly commit the act, or aid and abet its commission, though not present, may be indicted, tried, convicted and punished as principals. In construing this section, we have frequently held that all persons concerned in the commission of the offense, including aiders and abettors, are guilty as principals, and may be charged and held as such. *State v. Brown*, 25 Iowa, 561; *State v. Thornton*, 26 Iowa, 79; *State v. Stanley*, 48 Iowa, 221; *State v. Comstock*, 46 Iowa, 265; *State v. Hessian*, 58 Iowa, 68; *State v. Pugsley*, 75 Iowa, 742; *State v. Munchrath*, 78 Iowa, 268; *State v. Baldwin*, 79 Iowa, 714; *State v. Smith*, 100 Iowa, 1. Now, a conspirator such as the one referred to by the court in

its instructions is one who aids and abets the commission of
a crime, and he may be charged and convicted as a principal.
State v. McCahill, 72 Iowa, 111; *State v. Shelledy*, 8 Iowa,
477; *State v. Munchrath* and *State v. Smith, supra.*

Again, it is contended that there was no evidence upon
which to base these instructions. While it is true that there
is no direct evidence of a conspiracy between some of the parties who are said to have had connection with the homi-
2   cide, yet the facts and circumstances are such as to
justify a jury in finding concert of action between
defendant and one or both her daughters, and there was no
error in giving the charge. That a conspiracy or concert of
action may be proven by circumstances is a proposition so
elementary that no citation of authorities is needed to support it.

Further, it is said that the instruction with reference to
conspiracy is erroneous and misleading. This contention is
without merit, and the criticism is captious and hypercritical.

Another point made is that a conspiracy must be proven,
and defendant's connection therewith established, before the
acts, conduct, or declarations of the other conspirators can be
received in evidence. This may be true, but there is nothing
in the instructions to the contrary.

II.   Cora McCamley is defendant's daughter, and Ellen
Scoville is her sister. The latter was used as a witness by the
state, and gave evidence showing defendant's connection with
the offense charged. The former was a witness for the defendant, and testified that she and the Scoville woman administered the poison, and that defendant had nothing to do
with it. There was also other evidence tending to show that
Mrs. Scoville was directly connected with the commis-
3   sion of the offense. The court instructed that, if Ellen
Scoville aided, assisted, or abetted defendant in giving
the poison, then she would be an accomplice, and left it to the
jury to determine whether or not she did so act. It further
instructed that, if the jury found she was an accomplice, the
defendant could not be convicted on her testimony *"only,"*
unless she was corroborated by such other evidence as would

tend to connect the defendant with the commission of the offense. The charge continues as follows: "And the corroboration is not sufficient if it merely shows the commission of the offense or the circumstances thereof. And in this case you are instructed that mere proof of the death of the deceased, Michael Smith, from poison, is not such corroboration as would justify a conviction upon the testimony of the said Ellen Scoville *alone*, if you find she was an accomplice in causing the death of said Michael Smith. But if you fail to find that Ellen Scoville was an accomplice as heretofore defined, then if you believe her testimony to be true, and you find it connects the defendant with the commission of the crime, then it would be sufficient to connect the defendant with the commission of the crime without further testimony." Instruction No. 12: "But, upon this question of corroboration of an accomplice, you are further instructed that you have a right to consider the death of the deceased, the cause of said death, in connection with all the facts and circumstances, if any, shown or disclosed by the evidence, which tend to connect the defendant with causing said death of deceased; and if you find that the facts and circumstances, if any, shown or disclosed by the evidence, corroborate the testimony of the witness Ellen Scoville tending to connect the defendant with the commission of the crime charged, then you are entitled to convict said defendant upon the evidence of said Ellen Scoville so corroborated *alone*, if you believe the said witness, and if you further find that her evidence warrants such conviction." At defendant's request, the jury, in answer to special interrogatories, found that Ellen Scoville was an accomplice to the death of Michael Smith.

Several complaints are lodged against these instructions. It is argued that the one defining an accomplice is erroneous, because it did not authorize the jury to find Mrs. Scoville an accomplice of Cora McCamley, and did not instruct on this theory. In answer to this contention it may be said: (1) That the instruction is correct as far as it goes, and, if defendant desired that further light be given on the subject of Mrs. Scoville's being an accomplice, it was her duty to ask it. (2) We have already called attention to the instruction relating to defendant's connection with the offense as a conspirator, and there said that the jury was told, in effect, that defendant was guilty as principal if she conspired or confederated with others to commit the crime, although she did not administer the poison with her own hand. With this in mind, the jury could not have been misled by the instructions complained of. The mere fact that Mrs. Scoville may have been an accomplice with Cora McCamley was of no importance. The question was as to her connection with the defendant in the commission of the offense. If Cora McCamley and Ellen Scoville alone committed the crime, defendant was not guilty, and under such circumstances the fact that Mrs. Scoville was an acomplice was wholly irrelevant to any issue in the case.

Further objection is made to these instructions because of the use of the words "only" and "alone," which we have italicized to indicate the point more clearly. The language of the statute is that "a conviction cannot be had upon the testimony of an accomplice unless corroborated by other evidence which shall tend to connect the defendant with the commission of the offense; and the corroboration is not sufficient if it merely show the commission of the offense or the circumstances thereof." Code 1873, section 4559. We do not think the use of the words referred to vitiated the instructions. They are implied in the statute itself.

Some other objections are made to certain sentences used in these instructions. If these statements stood alone, there would be some ground for the complaints; but, when read in connection with the other parts thereof, they are not erroneous. Taken as a whole, these instructions fully and clearly state the law on the subject. We need not do more than refer to the rule that instructions should be considered together in arriving at their intent and meaning. Sentences and paragraphs can be culled out of nearly every set of instructions which, considered alone, would be erroneous, but when taken in connection with all the instructions, or all that is said on any given subject, they are found to be correct. Most of the criticisms passed upon the charge are fully answered by these suggestions.

III.   Error is assigned on the court's failure to instruct that defendant could not be convicted on the evidence of Cora McCamley alone, if the jury found she was an accomplice.

Miss McCamley was a witness for the defendant, and

6   testified, as we have heretofore observed, that she and the Scoville woman administered the poison, and that defendant had nothing to do therewith. It is hard to believe that it was the duty of the court to instruct that she must be corroborated. But, aside from this, the defendant asked no such instruction, and is not therefore in position to complain of the omission.

IV.   Appellant complains of the court's failure to instruct that corroboration of both Cora McCamley and Ellen Scoville was required in the event the jury found they were accomplices in the commission of the crime. Much that is said in the last preceding division of this opinion is applicable to this contention. Defendant offered Cora McCamley as a witness worthy of credit. This witness made no claim that she was an accomplice. If found to be such, it must have been from other evidence than her own. As defendant vouched for the truthfulness of Cora McCamley, no instruction as to corroboration of her evidence was necessary. See *Johnson v. State*, 4 G. Greene, 65, which gives one of the reasons why an accomplice must be corroborated.

V.   Some of the rulings on the admission and rejection of evidence are complained of. By reference to the former opinion filed in this case, it will be seen that the deceased, Michael Smith, received a gunshot wound about a year before his death, which made him wholly blind, and that it was con-

7   tended by the state that defendant had some connection therewith. At the last trial the same claim was made, and, from the evidence adduced, the jury may have found the defendant, Cora McCamley, and Ellen Sco-

ville were all concerned in various efforts made to put Michael
Smith out of the way. One of the witnesses for the state was
asked how the members of the family, Cora McCamley and
Mrs. Scoville, treated him (Michael Smith) in her (defendant's) presence. The witness answered: "Cora seemed to
treat him as rough as Mrs. Smith. I have heard Cora abuse
him and swear at him. I never saw Mrs. Scoville mistreat
him. She is the only one I saw do anything for him while I
was there." In view of the other evidence tending to show
concert of action on the part of defendant and her relatives,
and bearing in mind the evidence as to the treatment of
the deceased for some time prior to his death, it is manifest
that this evidence was admissible.

Defendant was a witness in her own behalf, and she testified, among other things, that she had no connection with the
shooting of her husband. On cross-examination she was asked
if she had not a short time before the shooting
8   attempted to rent rooms for herself and daughter, and
had not stated during the negotiations that they would
be occupied by herself and daughter alone. She denied having made any such statements. The state, in rebuttal, offered
the testimony of those parties with whom defendant had
her negotiations, in which they stated that she had made such
representations. Appellant contends that this was a wholly
irrelevant and collateral matter, and that the evidence ought to
have been excluded. We do not think so. While the evidence
so offered might not have been of much weight, it was properly admitted for the purpose of impeachment on a matter
which was material, because it tended in some degree, at
least, to show that defendant was expecting some mishap to
her husband. Cora McCamley, who, as we have said, was a
witness for the defendant, stated that she and the Scoville
woman administered the poison; that her mother had nothing to do with it; and that she did not know of her mother's
desire to be rid of deceased. She was subjected to a thorough
cross-examination, and, as she was a self-confessed murderess,
it was quite important that she be tried by all the tests known

to the skillful cross-examiner in order to determine the truthfulness of her story. She was asked by counsel for
9   the state regarding the shooting of her father. This
was objected to as not cross-examination. Now, while
it is true that she had given no testimony upon her direct
examination regarding this matter, yet we do not think that
the trial court abused its discretion in permitting this kind
of cross-examination. The case is a very peculiar one in many
of its aspects, and it is quite evident that this witness assumed
responsibility for the murder in order to shield her mother.
In answer to these questions, she denied having stated to one
McNutt and to a Mrs. Leach that her mother had some connection with the shooting of deceased. We have already seen
that the shooting of Michael Smith and defendant's connection therewith were material inquiries, and the witness was
therefore subject to impeachment by showing that she had
made contradictory statements with reference thereto. The
evidence given by McNutt, in rebuttal, with reference to
admissions made by the McCamley woman, was properly
received.

Some other errors are assigned on the admission and
rejection of evidence. None of them are of sufficient importance to demand separate consideration, and we answer them
with the simple statement that we find no error.

VI. The first opinion, reversing this case, was filed
October 5, 1897. The state gave notice of filing a petition
for rehearing, but no petition was ever filed. *Procedendo* was
returned to the district court December 10, 1897. On March
23, 1898, counsel filed a motion in the district court to have
defendant returned from the penitentiary to Polk county, for
a retrial. The motion was sustained, and on April 9, 1898,
defendant was returned for trial. Thereupon, and on the
thirteenth day of April, defendant asked an order for a medical examination to determine whether she could be
10   present during the trial. While this motion was pending, defendant filed another motion for discharge,
under section 4614 of the Code of 1873, which is as follows:

"If a defendant indicted for a public offense, whose trial has not been postponed upon his application, be not brought to trial at the next regular term of the court in which the indictment is triable after the same is found, the court must order it to be dismissed unless good cause to the contrary be shown." The terms of court in Polk county began September 6 and November 7, 1897, and January 3, March 7 and May 2, 1898. Defendant's motion to discharge was overruled, and of this complaint is made. The statute quoted was evidently designed to enforce the constitutional provision giving to defendants in criminal prosecutions the right to a speedy trial. It was was not intended as a sword for offense, but as a shield for defense to those who are accused of crime. Now, the trial court was justified in finding from the showing made in support of and in resistance to this motion that the delay in bringing the case on for trial was due to an agreement, or to requests made by her attorney from time to time for a continuance, and to representations made by him and others that his client was unable, on account of physical infirmity, to appear for trial. We say the court may have found this from the evidence, and it will be presumed it did so find, if that be necessary to sustain the ruling, for we must accept his conclusions upon this point if sustained by any evidence from which they could reasonably be found. In the case of *State v. Arthur*, 21 Iowa, 322, we held that if failure of trial in accordance with the provisions quoted was due to defendant's request or conduct, or if the cause is continued without objection on his part, and without demand for a trial, he is not entitled to a dismissal under the statute. There is no such showing as will justify us in reversing the order made by the trial court refusing the discharge.

VII. Lastly, it is insisted that the verdict is not supported by the evidence, and that the accomplice Ellen Scoville was not sufficiently corroborated. The case has been twice tried, each time resulting in a verdict and judgment of guilty as charged. That deceased died from arsenical poisoning seems too clear for serious dispute. If the witness Ellen

Scoville is to be believed, there is no doubt whatever that defendant is guilty of the offense charged.   There was also other evidence strongly tending to connect defendant with the commission of the crime.   The salient features of the case are stated in the first opinion, and we need not repeat them, as the evidence for the state was practically the same at each trial.   Indeed, the case was, by agreement, tried largely upon the evidence adduced upon the former hearing.   There is ample evidence to support the verdict, and we should not interfere. We have examined the whole record with care, and find no prejudicial errors.   AFFIRMED.

STATE OF IOWA v. N. J. HENGEN, Appellant.

Embezzlement: VENUE.   Defendant living in P. county, contracted with an installment house doing business in that county to travel and sell goods for it, for which he was there to account.   The goods were sent from P. county to the defendant in other counties, and there sold, and the proceeds converted.   *Held*, that the venue of a prosecution for embezzlement was properly laid in P. county.

103
140

Appeal from Polk District Court.—HON. W. F. CONRAD, Judge.

FRIDAY, DECEMBER 16, 1898.

THE defendant, indicted for and convicted of the crime of embezzlement, appeals.—*Affirmed.*

Spurrier & Maxwell for appellant.

Milton Remley, Attorney General, for the State.

LADD, J.—The evidence tended to show that Pattee, as manager of the installment house of W. A. Edwards, of Des Moines, in Polk county, and the defendant, there entered into an oral contract by the terms of which the latter agreed to travel and sell goods for Edwards in certain counties of Iowa other than Polk, and to account or report to Edwards at Des

Moines by mail every Saturday night, and inclose therewith the leases taken for goods sold or cash received therefor. These leases ran from Edwards to the purchaser, permitted payment in installments, and were conditioned that title should not pass until the price was fully paid. Some of the goods were delivered by Pattee to the defendant at Des Moines; others —and most of them—were shipped to him in Dallas, Boone, and Carroll counties, and from these localities he made reports at different times. The general agent demanded an accounting in Carroll, and also in Dallas county. This the defendant failed to make, and insisted on making settlement with Pattee at Des Moines. When he reached Des Moines, he was unable to account for the property received. The evidence tends to show that he appropriated goods of Edwards, delivered or sent to him, valued at two hundred and thirteen dollars. If it be conceded that the goods were delivered by Edwards to the defendant as his agent in Polk county, or were sent from there to him elsewhere, and upon the agreement that he was to account for them to Edwards, in Polk county, and he failed to do so when this was demanded, and it appears that he fraudulently converted the same to his own use by selling and appropriating the proceeds in some other county, had the district court of Polk county jurisdiction to try him for such offense? In other words, was the venue properly laid in Polk county? Our statute provides that "when a public offense is committed partly in one county and partly in another, or when the acts or effects constituting or requisite to the consummation of the offense occur in two or more counties, jurisdiction is in either county, except as otherwise provided by law." Code, section 5157. The venue can always be laid in the county where the conversion actually took place, but it is often as difficult to determine where as it is when that happened. This is especially true of an agent who travels as salesman from town to town through several counties. The authorities agree that, if the transaction constituting the offense extends through different counties, that in which the conversion took place has not the exclusive juris-

diction. 1 Bishop Criminal Procedure, 61; 7 Enc. Pl. &
Prac. 412. But, unless some essential element constituting
the crime of embezzlement occurred in Polk county, the venue
could not properly be laid therein. The establishment of the
contract creating the fiduciary relation, and the duty to
account for the property received, is quite as necessary for
conviction as proof of the conversion. In *Reg. v. Murdock,
Dennison & P.,* Crown Cas. 298, money was received by the
accused in Derbyshire, though both parties lived at Nottingham. Upon inquiry concerning the money at the latter place,
Murdock admitted having spent it, and the venue was held to
be there; Talfourd, J., remarking: "My opinion is, the
offense was completed when the prisoner refused to account
to his master at Nottingham." In *Reg. v. Rogers,* 3 Q. B. 28,
the sending of a letter by the defaulting employe, in effect
denying the receipt of the money from another county, where
he had collected it, to his employers, and its receipt by them
in that in which it was his duty to account, and where both
resided, gave jurisdiction in the latter county. In these cases
the judges assigned different reasons for their conclusion, and,
in the last, Huddleton, B. dissented. The demand and refusal
must be regarded, however, only as evidence of conversion,
and not essential to constitute the crime. *State v. Brooks,* 85
Iowa, 366; *Hollingsworth v. State,* 111 Ind. 289 (12 N. E.
Rep. 490); *State v. Mims,* 26 Minn. 191 (2 N. W. Rep. 492).
If this were not so, the offender might prevent the completion
of the offense by flight. And it follows that, if the conversion is made complete by the appropriation of the property
in one county, the mere demand and refusal would not add
to it in any way, and thereby aid in conferring jurisdiction in
the place of such demand. If there were no evidence of such
a conversion elsewhere, it might be inferred to have been at
the place where the demand is made, in event the duty to there
account existed. *Reg. v. Murdock, supra; Campbell v. State,*
35 Ohio St. 70. In the last case the defendant was shown to
have had the money of his principals in the county where it
was his duty to account, and the fact that he expended it in

another county was held to be no defense.   In *State v. Bailey*,
50 Ohio, 636 (36 N. E. Rep. 233) the defendant was
employed by Hood Bros. Co., in Toledo, Lucas county, to sell
goods for cash or on the installment plan in Fremont, San-
dusky county, but to report in person or by letter to the firm
at Toledo at the end of each week.   Part of the goods were
delivered to him in Toledo, and others sent to him at Fremont.
After working some time, he caused a letter to be written and
mailed to them, saying his sales were small; he was discour-
aged, but would await their further orders.   He had sold the
goods on hand, and spent part of the proceeds there, and afterwards the remainder in Buffalo, N. Y., to which place he
immediately absconded.   The court, in holding the venue to
be in Lucas county, said, through Bradbury, C. J.: "It is the
defendant's duty to account, together with his neglect or
refusal to do so, that constitutes the fraudulent breach of duty.
A demand at a place when and where he owes no duty is, of
itself, not enough.   The defendant's obligation was to account
to his employers at Toledo, in Lucas county.   This obligation
pressed upon him with equal force whether he was within or
without the county.   His refusal, neglect, or omission to discharge this duty may be as clearly manifested by silence and
the circumstances of his absence, or by letter, as by spoken
words, unless there is some magic in personal presence.   That
the presence of the offender within the county when a crime
is committed is not always necessary to give jurisdiction is a
settled principle.   *Norris v. State*, 25 Ohio St. 217.   The
question is by no means free from difficulty, but we think the
weight of authority, as well as of reason, authorizes us to hold
that the making of the contract in Lucas county, the express
duty it imposed upon the defendant to account weekly to his
employer there, either in person or by letter, together with the
fact that he did report to them falsely by letter, which they
received, constituted such integral and essential parts of the
transaction as entitle venue to be laid in Lucas county."   The
case at bar is like that from which we have quoted, and we
are inclined to follow it.   The defendant lives in Polk county,

where the contract was made, and from whence he received the property. He agreed to account to his employer at Des Moines. His failure or neglect or refusal to do so elsewhere would not amount to conversion, for he owed no such duty to his employer. That he fully realized this was shown by his insistency on settling with Pattee at Des Moines. Whether there or elsewhere, his obligation to account for the property at that place continued, and his failure to do so when then requested at that place was a clear breach of duty he owed to his principal. The existence of the contract, and the breach of the particular duty it imposed, were essential elements of the transaction constituting the embezzlement. See 7 Enc. Pl. & Prac. 412; *State v. Small*, 26 Kan. 209; *State v. Whiteman*, 9 Wash. 402 (37 Pac. Rep. 659); McClain Criminal Law, section 650. We do not overlook the case of *People v. Murphy*, 51 Cal. 376, announcing a contrary rule, but deem that adopted as having better support in authority and reason. The judgment is AFFIRMED.

MARIA J. BADER, *et al.*, v. AUGUSTUS L. DYER, *et al.*, Appellants.

Tenants in Common. Where a deed is to a husband and wife, they hold as tenants in common, and not an estate by the entirety,
2 under Code, section 2923, which provides that conveyances to two or more in their own right create a tenancy in common.

ADVERSE POSSESSION. Where a tenant in common had sole possession of land for thirty years, using it as his own, and knowing the co-tenancy existed, but making no public claim of entire ownership,
3 his possession was not adverse, and limitations did not run against his co-tenants, who had no knowledge of the co-tenancy or that the husband was making adverse claim to the whole estate.

SAME: *Husband and wife.* Where land was conveyed to a husband
3 and wife, who occupied it together and jointly shared the profits, the husband's possession was not adverse to the wife's.

HARMLESS ERROR. An error in finding that a tenant in common had
4 conveyed his interest in land was not prejudicial, it being found that the interest was reconveyed to him.

Deeds: MISTAKE: *Evidence.* The fact that the husband paid most
of the price is not conclusive that the wife's name was inserted in
1 a deed as a grantee by mistake, especially where the wife contributed substantially, helped improve and where the husband had
read, recorded and kept the deed, in silence.'

Appeal: CORRECTION OF RECORD BELOW. An erroneous record can-
4 not be first assailed on appeal.

Appeal from Clinton District Court.—HON. P. B. WOLFE,
Judge.

FRIDAY, DECEMBER 16, 1898.

ACTION in equity for the partition of real estate. There
was a hearing on the merits, and a decree for the plaintiffs.
The defendants appeal.—*Affirmed.*

D. A. Wynkoop for appellant Dyer.

Murray & Farr for appellant Anderson.

Hayes & Schuyler and *Thomas & Thomas* for appellees.

ROBINSON, J.—On the twenty-ninth day of May, 1855,
John H. Armitage and Martha Armitage executed to Augustus
L. Dyer and Elizabeth M. Dyer a warranty deed which purported to convey to the grantees a tract of 160 acres of land, in
Clinton county, for the consideration of one thousand one
hundred and twenty dollars. During the same year a small
house was built upon the land, and the grantees, who were
husband and wife, moved upon it, and made it their home
until December, 1864, when the wife died intestate and without issue. The husband lived upon the land about twenty
years after the death of his wife, and then moved to Maquoketa. He continued in possession of the land, however, until
January, 1896, when he conveyed his interest therein to Jesse
A. Anderson, and received a mortgage thereon for the purchase price, which he now holds. Three brothers and two sisters of Mrs. Dyer survived her, and the sisters and one brother
are the plaintiffs. The defendants are the husband and his

grantee, Anderson, who was a brother of Mrs. Dyer. D. H. Anderson, who was the third brother, has executed a quitclaim deed for the land to Dyer, and is not made a party to the action. The plaintiffs claim that each of them is entitled to an undivided one-tenth of an undivided one-half of the land described; that Jesse A. Anderson and D. H. Anderson were entitled to like shares; and that Dyer was entitled to but an undivided three-fourths of the entire tract. The defendants allege that all the land was purchased and owned by Dyer, and that Mrs. Dyer's name was inserted in the deed therefor erroneously and by mistake, and that the mistake was not discovered until the conveyance to Jesse A. Anderson was made. Other defenses are also pleaded. The district court found and adjudged that each plaintiff was entitled to the share claimed, or to an undivided one-twentieth of the entire tract of land; that Jesse A. Anderson was the owner of the remainder; that the premises could not be divided equitably; and ordered a sale thereof, and that the defendants pay the costs of witnesses and reporter's fees.

I.   Much evidence was submitted in regard to the property owned by Mr. and Mrs. Dyer, respectively, and as to the sources from which the money paid for the land in controversy was obtained. Their parents lived in Virginia. They were married there, and came to this state in the year 1853. The husband had some property which he had obtained from his father and by his labor, which he converted into money, and claims to have brought to this state about $400 in money and some other personal property. His wife also had a small amount of property, which she received from her father. She was a glove maker and tailoress, and made gloves and clothing for others, and derived considerable revenue from that source. In June, 1854, they purchased eighty acres of prairie land and ten acres of timber for one hundred and fifty dollars, and in October of the same year the eighty-acre tract was sold for five hundred and fifty dollars, and a contract for the land in controversy was made. The five hundred and fifty dollars so received and three hundred and fifty dollars borrowed by Dyer constituted the first payment on the land, and he claims to have paid the remainder of the purchase price, and to have repaid the money borrowed from his share of his father's estate. He received from that source, in the year 1855, about one thousand dollars. Improvements were made upon the land to the value of about six thousand dollars. It is probable that the larger part of the purchase price of the land was paid from the resources of Dyer, but, if that be true, it does not follow that a mistake was made by inserting in the deed the name of the wife as one of the grantees. It is probable that she contributed a substantial amount to the purchase price and to the cost of the improvements, nearly all of which were made during her lifetime, and it was proper and commendable to give her an interest in the land. The Armitages resided in Indiana, and the land in question was purchased of them through their agent, named Beard, who resided near the Dyers, in Clinton county. The deed was executed in Indiana, acknowledged there before a justice of the peace, and sent to Beard, who delivered it to Dyer. When the deed was first received, Beard called Dyer's attention to the fact that a certificate showing the official character of the justice had not been attached, and the deed was returned to Indiana for a certificate of that character. The presumption is that Dyer read the deed when he received it, and knew that his wife was named as grantee. It was not, and is not, usual in conveying land to a husband to insert the name of his wife as a grantee unless that is required by the contract of purchase. It is true that Dyer testifies that he first learned of or was informed that the deed in question was drawn to himself and his wife jointly in January, 1896, but the claim is unreasonable. He could read and write. The deed was examined when it was received. He kept it in his possession for several weeks and then had it recorded. After it was recorded it was returned to him, and ever since has been in his possession. We are satisfied that the deed was drawn as intended, and that he knew how it was drawn when he received it.

II. It is claimed, if a mistake in the deed in question be not shown, that it created in Dyer and his wife an estate by the entirety, which passed to him on the death of his wife, according to the rule of the common law. But section 2923 of the Code provides that "conveyances to two or more in their own right create a tenancy in common, unless a contrary intent is expressed." That was the law of this state when the conveyance in question was made. Code 1851, section 1206. The effect of a conveyance to the husband and wife, under that provision as it appeared in the revision of 1860, was determined in the well-considered case of *Hoffman v. Stigers,* 28 Iowa, 302, and held to vest in them an estate in common, and with that decision we are content

III. It is next contended that Dyer held possession of the land in question from the time the deed was delivered to him until January, 1896, under a claim of absolute and exclusive ownership adverse to all others, and that the claims of the plaintiff are barred by the statute of limitations. It is also insisted that the plaintiffs have been so grossly negligent in asserting their claims that a court of equity should not give its aid to enforce them. It is well settled that the seizin and possession of one of several tenants in common are the seizin and possession of all. It was said in *Burns v. Byrne,* 45 Iowa, 285, "that the seizin and possession of one tenant in common are the seizin and possession of the others. One can never be disseized by another without actual ouster. By actual ouster is not meant a physical eviction, but a possession attended with such circumstances as to evince a claim of exclusive right and title, and a denial of the right of the other tenants to participate in the profits. An actual ouster, and consequent adverse possession, might be inferred from sole possession, and an exclusive reception and enjoyment of the rents and profits, with the knowledge and implied acquiescence of the other tenant in common, for the period of ten years." The rule of that case has been followed frequently

in this state. See *Kinney v. Slattery*, 51 Iowa, 353 ; *Hume
v. Long*, 53 Iowa, 299 ; *Killmer. v. Wuchner*, 74 Iowa,
359; *Moore v. Antill*, 53 Iowa, 612. There is not the
slightest ground for claiming that the possession of
Dyer during the lifetime of his wife was adverse to her nor
that it was exclusive. So far as the facts are disclosed by the
record, they occupied the premises together and jointly shared
in its benefits. After the death of his wife, Dyer was in the
sole possession of his farm until January, 1896. It does not
appear that any of the plaintiffs had knowledge of the condition of the title until the farm was sold to Jesse A. Anderson.
They were then asked to execute to Dyer quitclaim deeds in
order to perfect his title. It thus appears that we have a case
where one tenant in common had the sole use and possession
of the subject of the tenancy, and knew that such tenancy
existed, for more than thirty years, while his co-tenants had
no knowledge of the tenancy nor of their rights. It is true
that in many cases the statute of limitations will begin to run
against the owner of real property, or of an interest therein,
even though he may not have any actual knowledge of the
adverse possession and claim of the person in whose favor the
statute runs ; but that rule does not apply to tenants in common who have no knowledge of and no reason to know that
the tenant in possession is holding adversely to them under a
claim of right. The evidence in this case shows that the plaintiffs knew, or must be charged with knowing, that Dyer, after
the death of his wife, occupied and used the property as his
own ; and had he claimed title adverse to them, and had they
known or had sufficient reason to know that fact, they would
be barred by the statute of limitations from now recovering
any interest in the land. But there is no evidence that he pub-
licly or openly claimed the entire ownership of the land until
the year 1896. It is not shown that he rented it and appropriated the rents after he moved to Maquoketa, but the claim
and proof are that he continued in possession of it. Had he
rented the land after he moved to Maquoketa, and appropriated the rents to his own use, a different question might have

been presented. *Moore v. Antill*, 53 Iowa, 612; *Burns v. Byrne*, 45 Iowa, 285.

But it is the rule that one tenant in common is not liable to his co-tenant "for mere use and occupation of the entire lands, without any agreement with the others to pay rent and without any demand from them for possession, or refusal to surrender possession, and without his having rent for such premises from a third person." *Reynolds v. Wilmeth*, 45 Iowa, 693. Since the possession held by Dyer was presumptively for his co-tenants as well as for himself, and not adverse to them, the burden is on him to show that it was adverse for the requisite length of time to give him title as against them, and that they knew, or had sufficient reason to know, the true character of his possession; but that he has failed to do. He has not shown any claim of ownership which was known to the plaintiffs, or which, in the exercise of ordinary care, they would have known, prior to January, 1896, inconsistent with his rights as a tenant in common in possession, and he has therefore failed to establish title in himself by virtue of adverse possession under a claim of entire ownership. Our conclusion finds support in the following authorities: *Lapeyre v. Paul*, 47 Mo. 590, in which it is said that, for the purpose of an ouster by a tenant in common, "there must be outward acts of exclusive ownership of an unequivocal character, overt and notorious, and of such a nature as by their import to impart information and give notice to the co-tenants that an adverse possession and an actual disseizin are intended to be asserted against them"; *Colman v. Clements*, 23 Cal. 245, in which it is said: "The possession of one tenant in common is presumed to be the possession of all, and, in order to rebut this presumption and make the possession adverse, it must be shown that the possession was with the intent to hold adversely, and such intent must be indicated by acts calculated to exclude the co-tenant." See, also, *Warfield v. Lindell*, 30 Mo. 281 (38 Mo. 561); *Dubois v. Campau*, 28 Mich. 304; *Thornton v. Bank*, 45 Me. 161; *Colburn v. Mason*, 25 Me. 435; *Parker v.*

Proprietors, 3 Metc. (Mass.) 91; *Mansfield v. McGinnis*, 86 Me. 118 (29 Atl. Rep. 956); *McClung v. Ross*, 5 Wheat. 116; 1 Am. & Eng. Enc. Law (2d Ed.) 801; 11 Am. & Eng. Enc. Law (1st Ed.) 1112.

IV.   The defendant Jesse A. Anderson has taken a separate appeal, and complains of the action of the district court in finding that his share and that of D. H. Anderson in the property in question had been conveyed to Dyer, and in finding that Jesse A. Anderson was represented by counsel. The record shows that the defendant Anderson was represented in the district court by an attorney, and that the answer filed by him admitted that D. H. Anderson had conveyed his interest in the land to Dyer. If the record is erroneous, it should have been corrected in the district court. It cannot be assailed here for the first time. If the district court erred in finding that Jesse A. Anderson had conveyed his interest to Dyer, the error was without prejudice, as the court found that the interest was reconveyed to Jesse A. Anderson. The pleadings showed that D. H. Anderson did not have any interest in the property. If that was not true, Jesse A. Anderson cannot complain of the error. The decree of the district court is sustained by the evidence, and appears to be correct. It is therefore AFFIRMED.

4

SARAH J. GOLDTHORP, *et al.*, v. ED. GOLDTHORP, Appellant.

Wills: CONTEST: *Competency of opinion evidence.* Where on the issue of the mental condition of the testatrix, after such preliminary questions were asked of a witness as to show his acquaintance with and knowledge of the testatrix, justifying an opinion as to her mental condition. a question which, for aught that appears, called for an independent statement of fact not based on the preliminary testimony, was properly excluded.

1

MISCONDUCT OF COUNSEL. On the trial before a jury on an issue as to the mental condition of testatrix, a witness having stated that she had a remarkable mind, counsel for proponent said, "I agree with you; I have known her most of her life." *Held*, to be improper and something which might be prejudicial.

2

Appeal from Dubuque District Court.—HON. J. L. HUSTED,
Judge.

FRIDAY, DECEMBER 16, 1898.

THE issues in this case arise by objections to the probate
of the will of Alice Goldthorp, deceased, on the application of
proponents. ˙ The grounds of objection are: First, unsoundness of mind of the testatrix; and, second, undue influence.
At the conclusion of the evidence the court, on motion of
proponents, directed a verdict in their favor, and the contestant appealed.—*Reversed.*

R. W. Stewart for contestant.

D. E. Lyon and *Henderson, Hurd, Lenehan & Keisel*
for proponents.

GRANGER, J.—I.   This cause was before in this court,
and is reported in 94 Iowa, at page 336. The questions settled
on that appeal were as to the admission and exclusion of evidence.   Questions of the same character and presented on this
appeal, and also the right of the court to take the case from
the jury by directing a verdict for proponents. A reference
to the case, as before reported, will give a better insight into
the contentions presented at this time.

II.   As the case must go back for another trial, it would
be unwise, nor would it be desired, that we should comment
on the force or effects of parts of the evidence to show the
reason for our conclusion. If only the question of unsoundness of mind, or mental incapacity, was involved, we should
not disturb the ruling of the court, for we think, as the case is
presented by the record, a finding of a want of testamentary
capacity could not be sustained. But on the question of undue
influence we are agreed that the case presents a question of
fact for the jury on the testimony as admitted on the trial. It
should not be understood, from what we have said, that on
a retrial the inquiry will be limited to the single question of

undue influence, for it is a law case, and our holding is only
that the court erred in sustaining the motion to direct a verdict.   In view of a new trial, it may be well for us to notice
briefly some points in dispute as to the admission of evidence.
Mrs. Butler, a granddaughter of decedent, was a witness for
contestant, and, after showing an acquaintance and knowledge of her that would justify an opinion as to her mental
condition at that time, under our holding on the former appeal,
she was asked on her direct examination this question: "You
may now state whether or not Mrs. Goldthorp during that
summer, and especially in August, 1883, was of strong or
weak mind."   The question was excluded, we assume, as
incompetent.   George W. Cocker was a witness for the proponent, and, after such preliminaries as to show him competent to speak of her mental condition, he was asked how she
appeared as to being a woman of strong or weak mind.   This
question was admitted against an objection that it was incompetent.   One Morgan was also a witness for proponent, and
the following appears in the record: "Q.   Well, what I
want to ask you is, look at Mrs. Goldthorp just as you would
used to see her, and talk to her, and taking her manner and
appearance and style of conversation, what do you say as to
whether she was of a strong or a weak mind? (Objected to
as incompetent; no foundation laid for testimony.   Overruled.   Contestant excepts.)   A.   I should say she was a
remarkable woman.   Q.   In what way?   A.   Vigorous.   Q.
What do you say about her mind?   A.   I should think she
had a most remarkable mind for a woman of her age; the
most remarkable mind for a woman of her age that I ever
saw."   As we understand contestant, he does not claim that
the questions to Cocker and Morgan were not proper, but he
does claim that the rulings are inconsistent, the court excluding his questions, and permitting like questions by
the proponent. There is this difference: The question by proponent clearly makes the opinion asked for
depend on the facts shown as a basis for the question, while
that of contestant is not clearly so, if, indeed, it may not be

said to call for an independent answer as to the fact inquired about.   The question itself makes no reference to what the witness had testified to, and, while the purpose of the question might have been to have it answered as if the reference had been made, the uncertainty should operate against the questioner rather than the other party.   The question was clearly incompetent, unless based on the facts necessary to be shown to make it competent.   Such is the rule as to non-expert evidence of such character.   See opinion on former appeal. There does not appear to be error in these rulings.   These views dispose of numerous other similar complaints.

III.   There is a complaint that the court to an unwarranted extent suggested and aided proponent in the examination of witnesses, and in a way to prejudice contestant, and the complaint has quite a strong support in the record.   It also appears in the case of the examination of a witness for proponent that he said of Mrs. Goldthorp: "I should think she had a most remarkable mind for a woman of her age; the most remarkable mind for a woman of her age that I ever saw."   One of the counsel for proponent said, "I agree with you," and added, "I have known her most of her life."   The case was taken from the jury, and, likely, no prejudice resulted because of the interference by the court, or the remarks of counsel, and we notice them to avoid a recurrence on another trial.   The prejudice to result from such a remark by an attorney in a case, who is respected by the jurors, is very manifest.   What we say as to the interference by the court should not be misapprehended.   We do not discourage timely suggestions and aids by the court in the conduct of a trial, and we well understand the emergencies that call for interference in many trials, and this case is one by no means free from them.   The ground of complaint is in the manner the right was exercised, so that the character of the questions asked by the court, and the remarks in connection therewith, would likely be misunderstood by the jury to the prejudice of a party.   The record abounds with complaints, most of which are without merit.

We think of no others that need be noticed in view of a new trial. The judgment is REVERSED.

J. F. HILL, *et al.*, v. JAMES DENNEY, *et al.*, Appellants.

Fraudulent Conveyance: LIEN. It is indicated that an attachment at
1 law may sufficiently invoke equity in cases where else, the proceeding at law must remain wholly ineffectual.

SAME. At any rate it must be plead and proven in order to take a
2 mortgage out of the way of the attachment that the debtor's property, over and above the mortgage is insufficient to satisfy the debt.

Appeal from Johnson District Court.—HON. M. J. WADE, Judge.

FRIDAY, DECEMBER 16, 1898.

ACTION in equity to cancel a mortgage which is alleged to have been fraudulently executed. A demurrer to the petition was overruled, and the defendants, having elected to stand upon their demurrer, appeal.—*Reversed.*

Cash & Coldren and *Remley, Ney & Remley* for appellants.

No appearance for appellee.

ROBINSON, J.—The petition shows that there are twelve plaintiffs; that about the sixteenth and eighteenth days of December, 1896, they commenced their several actions in the district court of Johnson county against the defendant James Denneny, to recover severally upon his obligations, all of which existed prior to August 4, 1896, and upon each of which he is justly indebted to the party seeking to recover upon it; that in each action a writ of attachment was issued and levied upon a quarter section of land in Johnson county, which is described; that, on the date last specified, James Denneny and his wife, for the purpose of defrauding his creditors, and without consideration, executed a mortgage upon

the land to the defendant Lawrence Denneny, Sr., the father
of James; that the mortgage has been recorded · and that on
the fifteenth day of December, 1896, a pretended assignment
of the mortgage was executed by the mortgagee to his wife, the
defendant Harriet Denneny, and recorded. The petition further alleges that there was no consideration for the assignment; that it was made to defraud the creditors of James
Denneny; that, by virtue of the levies made under the writ
mentioned, the several plaintiffs acquired liens on the land
described; and that their actions are still pending. The petition asks that the mortgage be canceled, set aside, and declared
not to be a lien on the land. The demurrer alleges that the
facts stated in the petition do not entitle the plaintiffs to the
relief demanded.

The appellants contend that the demurrer should have
been sustained, for the reason that the plaintiffs did not
acquire a lien or interest in the land, by virtue of their writs,
which a court of equity will enforce. Inasmuch as the
question thus presented is of great importance, we
regret that the argument for the appellants covers less
than a printed page, and that we are without any argument
for the appellees. In the case of *Buchanan v. Marsh*, 17 Iowa,
494, the plaintiffs sought to recover on a foreign judgment,
and to restrain, pending the suit, the alienation of certain
real estate alleged to be owned by the judgment debtor, but
to have been purchased in the name of his wife with the intention of defrauding his creditors. This court said that "the
rule is, as far as we know, without exception, that the creditor must have completed his title at law, by judgment (if not
by execution), before he can question the disposition of the
debtor's property.　*　*　*　The reason for the rule is that,
until the creditor has established his title or his debt by the
judgment of a court, he has no right to interfere; for, unless
he has a certain claim upon the property of the debtor, he
has no concern with his frauds." It was accordingly held that
the temporary injunction granted was properly dissolved. It
was said in *Goode v. Garrity*, 75 Iowa, 713, that "until a creditor in some manner obtains a lien on his debtor's property, or

has exhausted his remedies at law, or done what is equivalent thereto, he cannot question in equity a fraudulent conveyance or incumbrance of his property made by such debtor, and have the same set aside." What was thus said was based upon the fact that a lien upon the property sought to be reached had not been obtained. In the case of *Clark v. Raymond*, 84 Iowa, 251, the right of the plaintiff to have a receiver appointed to take possession of certain land alleged to have been conveyed by the defendant, J. M. Raymond, to defraud his creditors was involved. The application was based upon an action on a promissory note of said Raymond, in which an attachment had been issued and levied upon the land. It was said that the attachment did not create a lien as against J. M. Raymond, because he had no legal interest in the property. and that, in case of judgment against him and sale thereunder, it would be necessary to set aside the conveyance alleged to be fraudulent to give to the plaintiff title. It was said, further, that as a general rule, a creditor's bill cannot be maintained until judgment has been obtained in the principal action, and that it must be shown that the judgment defendant is insolvent, and that the debt cannot be collected on execution. The real point determined, however, was that an attaching creditor, whose claim is not in judgment, is not entitled to have appointed a receiver of attached realty alleged to have been conveyed by the debtor to defraud his creditors. The case was again before us on a second appeal (86 Iowa, 661), and we again said that the attachment alone created no lien upon the land, and held that the plaintiff was not entitled to a receiver, because she had failed to show any right to or interest in the property which she could not enforce by ordinary methods and process. The plaintiffs in *Faivre v. Gillman*, 84 Iowa, 573, sought to recover judgment against an alleged debtor, and to have a conveyance of land alleged to have been made by her without consideration, when of unsound mind, set aside; that, if her personal property proved to be insufficient to pay the plaintiff's claim, so much of the real estate be sold as should be necessary to pay the claim. Other relief was also asked. It was held that there was a misjoinder of causes of action, and it was also said that, as the plaintiffs were not judgment creditors, they were not entitled to maintain a creditors' bill. In the case of *Boggs v. Douglass*, 89 Iowa, 150, we said that "it is the well-settled rule in this state that the levy of an attachment upon real estate which the attachment debtor has conveyed to another to defraud his creditors, unless followed by supplemental proceedings, creates no lien upon the property so attached." What supplemental proceedings, in such a case would be effectual to establish a lien, was a question not involved and not determined. The rule of the cases cited was again approved in *Ware v. Delahaye*, 95 Iowa, 667. In the case of *Taylor v. Branscombe*, 74 Iowa, 534, some statements were made which seem to be in conflict with the rule stated in the cases cited. It is to be observed, however, that the defendants in that case were non-residents of this state. The judgment debtor, by means of a fraudulent conveyance, had divested himself of all interest in the land which he could have asserted against his grantee. An action at law, aided by attachment, would have been wholly ineffectual, and the plaintiff would have been without remedy had he been restricted to proceedings at law. The action was commenced in equity, and was aided by attachment, and the right to proceed by that method was sustained. It would have been a reproach to our jurisprudence had there been no remedy in such a case.

It will be ascertained by a careful examination of the cases cited that none of them hold that an action in equity in aid of an attachment at law cannot be maintained where it is made to appear that the proceedings at law will be wholly insufficient to give the relief demanded if the aid of a court of equity be not also given. The case of *Goode v. Garrity* involved the attachment of notes and accounts; the case of *Clark v. Raymond* involved the appointment of a receiver; the case of *Faivre v. Gillman* was determined upon the misjoinder of causes and parties; and the case of *Boggs v. Douglass* merely decided that the levy of an attachment upon land conveyed by the attachment debtor to defraud his creditors did not create a lien unless followed by supplemental proceedings. In the case of *Buchanan v. Marsh,* an injunction to restrain the alienation of property, alleged to have been conveyed to the wife of the debtor to defraud his creditors, was denied; but it did not appear that the plaintiff would have been without remedy if the injunction had not been allowed. In several of the cases referred to, however, language was used which would lead logically to the conclusion that an attaching creditor had no right to maintain a proceeding in equity, before judgment, in aid of his attachment, to reach property fraudulently conveyed. Whether that was the rule prior to the enactment of section 3899 of the Code, we do not

2   find it necessary to determine. But, if it was not the rule, it was, at least, necessary to show that the relief which an action at law would afford would not be adequate, before a proceeding in equity could have been maintained. No showing of that kind is made by the petition in this case. It does not appear that the plaintiffs will be unable to realize the amounts due on their respective claims if the relief asked is not granted. It is not alleged that the debtor is insolvent. The value of the land, the amount of the mortgage, and the amounts claimed by the plaintiffs, are not shown. There is nothing in the petition to justify the conclusion that the interest of the debtor in the land subject to the mortgage is not sufficient to satisfy the claims of the plaintiffs, or that they may not be satisfied from other property owned by him. We conclude that the petition does not show that the plaintiffs are entitled to any relief in this action, and that the demurrer should have been sustained. It must be understood that what we have said is not intended to indicate the proper practice under section 3899 of the Code. The order of the district court overruling the demurrer is REVERSED.

STATE OF IOWA, *ex rel.,* STANFORD DOUD, Appellant, v. J. H. COUNCIL, *et al.*

Incorporation of Town: COURT AND JUDGE. Under McClain's Code, sections 569, 570 providing for application to the district court for the incorporation of a town, and the appointment by the court of commissioners to call an election to determine the question of incorporation, the application must be presented to the court, and the order of appointment issued by it, and not by the judge.

Estoppel by Recital in Decree: PARTIES. One not a party to proceedings to incorporate a town is not prevented, by a recital in the order appointing commissioners to call an election, that the proceedings were had before the court, from showing they were had before the judge.

Appeal from Marion District Court.—HON. J. H. HENDERSON, Judge.

FRIDAY, DECEMBER 16, 1898.

Quo warranto proceedings to test the right of the defendants to exercise the functions of members of the town council of the incorporated town of Bussey, in Marion county. The trial court sustained a demurrer to the petition, and plaintiff appeals.—*Reversed.*

Geo. W. Crozier for appellant.

L. N. Hayes for appellees.

DEEMER, C. J.—The short facts recited in the petition are that the defendants are unlawfully and illegally holding office as members of the town council of the town of Bussey, for the reason that the town was never legally incorporated. It is charged that no petition of the inhabitants of the territory proposed to be incorporated was ever presented to the district court of Marion county, no commissioners were ever appointed by said court to hold the election to determine the question of incorporation, no persons were ever appointed commissioners by the district court, and no proceedings of record were ever had in the district court of Marion county for the incorporation of the territory, and no order of record was ever made by any court of record incorporating said town or territory, or authorizing any persons to hold an election to determine the question of incorporation. It is conceded in the petition that while the district court of Marion county was in session a petition in due form was presented to Hon. J. H. Henderson, judge of said court, and that an order was signed by the said judge, finding the petition sufficient, and appointing commissioners to call an election and give notice as provided by law. And it is further conceded that the commissioners so appointed called an election, and that at said election a majority of the votes cast was in favor of incorporation, and that the result of said election was duly reported to the clerk of the district court of Marion county. It is further conceded that at an election called for the purpose of selecting members of the town council the defendants, and each of them, received a majority of the votes cast. But it is charged that the petition for incorporation was not filed in or presented to the district court, or entered upon any docket or record of said court, nor was any trial or proceeding had thereon, or entered of record in said court. It is further charged that the order made by Judge Henderson was not an order of court, was not entered of record until some time after the election was held, and was then entered by the clerk in a book known as the "Complete Record," in the office of said clerk. It is also alleged that the election called and held by the commissioners, as well as the election for selecting members of the town council, was illegal, for the reason that no proceedings were pending for the appointment of the said commissioners, and no order was ever made by the court appointing the commissioners, or authorizing the election. Further; it is alleged that nothing was ever done or entered of record in the said district court in relation to said incorporation, except as heretofore stated, nor was the result of the aforesaid elections returned, filed, or indexed of record in the clerk's office of said

Marion county. The order signed by Judge Henderson is also in the record, and, aside from the signature of the judge, it appears to have been made by the district court. The demurrer is upon the ground that the facts stated in the petitoin do not entitle the plaintiff to the relief demanded, or to any relief whatever, for the reason that it appears that the town was legally incorporated, and that the defendants were the duly elected and qualified officers of said town.

The provisions of law relating to the incorporation of towns and cities are as follows: "When the inhabitants of any part of any county, not embraced within the limits of any city or incorporated town, shall desire to be organized into a city or incorporated town, they may apply by petition in writing, signed by not less than twenty-five of the qualified electors of the territory to be embraced in the proposed city or incorporated town to the district court of the proper county, which petition shall describe the territory proposed to be embraced in such city or incorporated town, and shall have annexed thereto an accurate map or plat thereof and state the name proposed for such city or incorporated town and shall be accompanied with satisfactory proofs of the number of inhabitants within the territory." "When such petition shall be presented the court shall forthwith appoint five commissioners who shall at once call an election of the qualified electors residing within the territory embraced within the limits as described and platted to be held at some convenient place within said limits," etc. See sections 569 and 570 of 1 McClain's Code, and sections 421 (as amended by Eighteenth General Assembly, chapter 79) and 422 of the Code of 1873. It will be observed that the petition must be presented to the district court, and that the court must appoint the commissioners. The distinction between a judge and a court is too familiar and too well understood to demand explanation. And a court may do many things which a judge cannot do. To give existence to a court, there must be present the officers constituting it,—the judge. or judges, and probably the clerk authorized to record the action of the court. Time must also be regarded, for the offi-

cers of the court must be present at the time and place
appointed by law. *Hobart v. Hobart*, 45 Iowa, 501. These
propositions are not seriously controverted by appellees.
Their claim is that the facts stated show that the petition
was presented to, and an order made by, the court—not by the
judge. To this we cannot lend our assent. True it is that the
order recites that it was made by the court, but this is
2   not conclusive. The relator was not a party to the
original proceedings, and is not bound thereby, unless
the statutes were strictly followed. He may prove, if he can,
that, notwithstanding the recital in the order, the proceedings
were had before the judge, and were therefore illegal. He
has charged that they were so had, and, if he is able to prove
his charge, he is entitled to the relief demanded. Appellees
rely upon the case of *Tracy v. Beeson*, 47 Iowa, 155. An
examination of that case, however, will show that it is clearly
distinguishable. There it appeared that a decree had in fact
been rendered by the court, but for some reason it had not
been entered upon the records by the clerk. After the decree
had in fact been rendered, but before it was recorded, the
court ordered a reference of the case. Pending the reference
the clerk entered the decree, which had been signed by the
judge, upon the records of his office. Appeal was taken from
the order of reference, and it was held that it was not proper
to make such order when the files showed that the cause had
been fully submitted to and determined by the court, and
contained a full and formal decree signed by the judge thereof.
In the opinion it is said that failure to record the decree was
not such an omission as to necessitate a retrial, and that it
was the province of the court to order the clerk to perform
the purely ministerial duty of recording the decree at any
time. Were it not for the distinct allegation in the petition
in the case at bar that the district judge, and not the district
court, made the order, the case might be considered parallel.
As the district court did not make the order, there was nothing to record. We are of opinion that the demurrer was
improperly sustained, and the judgment is REVERSED.

SUPPLEMENT.

[This case did not reach me in time to be published in its chronological order.—Reporter.]

STATE OF IOWA, Appellant, v. T. J. SHEA, P. W. CRAWFORD, ANTON VOLGER, THEODORE BAUER, JOHN SCHULTE, JOSEPH K. KAUFMANN, A. A. CULLEN and JOHN W. HALPIN.

Officers: INCREASING SALARY: *Charter Construed.* Dubuque city charter (Acts Sixth General Assembly, chapter 210, section 5,) provides that no alderman shall vote "on any question in which he is
1 ⌐ directly or indirectly interested." Certain aldermen, constituting the majority of the council, voted as such to increase their salaries. *Held*, that such act constituted an indictable offense, under Code, 1873, section 3966, providing that, "when the performance of any act is prohibited by any statute, and no penalty for the violation of such statute is imposed, the doing of such act is a misdemeanor," and section 3967, which provides a punishment for such misdemeanor, making it an indictable offense.

SAME. That no injury resulted to any individual and no money was drawn from the treasury by reason of the vote of the aldermen to
4 increase their salaries in violation of Laws Sixth General Assembly, chapter 210, section 5. does not relieve the aldermen from criminal responsibility by reason of such vote.

SAME. The power conferred upon a city council by Laws Sixth General Assembly, chapter 210, to fix the salaries and compensation of "all" officers of the city not fixed by the act, does not authorize the council to fix the salaries of its present members; but they can
2 only fix it for those who subsequently become members, in view of section 5, providing that no alderman shall vote in the council upon any question in which he is directly or indirectly interested.

SAME. Thus construed, the several provisions of such charter are not in conflict, and, consequently, the aldermen so voting were not
3 excused from criminal liability on the ground that they acted judicially, and could not be held liable for errors or mistakes.

Appeal from Dubuque District Court.—HON. C. M. WATERMAN, Judge.

FRIDAY, OCTOBER 8, 1897.

DEFENDANTS were indicted for willful and corrupt misconduct in office. A demurrer to the indictment was sustained, and the state appeals.—*Reversed.*

Milton Remley, Attorney General, *M. C. Matthews,* County Attorney, and *William Graham* for the State.

Alphons Matthews and *James E. Knight* for appellees.

DEEMER, J.—The indictment charges the defendants, who were members of the city council of the city of Dubuque, with having wrongfully, unlawfully, and corruptly voted to increase their salaries as aldermen of the said city from the sum of three hundred dollars, which had been the annual salary of aldermen for about ten years prior to April 24, 1895, to the sum of five hundred dollars for the year 1895, in violation of a section of the charter of said city, which provides that "neither shall any alderman vote in said council upon any question in which he is directly or indirectly interested." Laws Sixth General Assembly, chapter 210, section 5. The indictment further charges that the city of Dubuque is a municipal corporation, acting under a special charter, and that the defendants, who are a majority of the aldermen of said city, and who were at the time convened as a city council, did willfully, unlawfully, knowingly, and corruptly vote in favor of increasing their salaries, and did by their said vote carry the question, and increase their salaries, as aforesaid, in violation of the section of the charter before quoted, and in violation of their duties as aldermen. There are six grounds of demurrer, but the principal reasons urged in support of the rulings of the trial court are: (1) That the vote was authorized, and therefore did not constitute a crime; (2) that in voting the salary, defendants acted in a judicial or quasi judicial capacity, and are not criminally liable for any error or mistake in their interpretation of the charter. Section 5, chapter 210, Acts Sixth General Assembly, being a part of the charter of the city, provides for the election of two aldermen from each ward, and then enacts the following: "No member of the city council shall be directly or indirectly interested in the profits of any contract or job for the city, and to become so interested when elected, or being so interested, shall be deemed a vacation of said office. Neither shall any alderman vote in said council upon any question in which he is directly or indirectly interested." In the Code 1873, section 3966, we find the following general statute: "When the performance of any act is prohibited by any statute, and no penalty for the violation of such statute is imposed, the doing of such act is a misdemeanor." This is followed by section 3967, which provides a punishment for such a misdemeanor, making it an indictable offense. The defendants place much reliance upon section 7 of the charter (Laws Sixth General Assembly, chapter 210), which, among other things, gives the city council power, and makes it its duty, "to establish and fix the salaries and compensation of all officers of said city not fixed by this act;" and upon section 2 of the charter, which recognizes aldermen as officers of the city. The section of the charter first quoted, taken in connection with the statutes before referred to, seems to clearly cover such a state of facts as is set forth in the indictment; for it is expressly provided in the charter that no alderman shall vote in the council upon any question in which he is directly or indirectly interested. The indictment charges that each of the defendants as councilmen, voted to increase his own salary. It is contended, however, that section 7 of the charter authorized the council to fix the salaries of all officers of the city, and that, in doing the acts complained of, the defendants were performing a duty; or, if this be not true, that the council was required to construe the sections of the charter before set out, and in so doing it was acting in a judicial or quasi judicial capacity, and that none of the members of that body can be held liable, either civilly or criminally, for mistake or error in the construction of the charter. We do not think that section 7 authorizes the council to fix its own salary. Section 5 says it may not do so, if the members are directly or indirectly interested. That they are directly interested must be conceded. What, then, is the proper construction of this charter? It seems to us that the two provisions were meant to stand and be construed together, and that the council can fix the salary of the members of that body when they are not directly interested; that is to say, they can fix it for those who subsequently become members of the council, but cannot vote affirmatively upon a proposition either to increase or diminish their own compensation. Application of the ordinary and well-

3   known rules of construction leads inevitably to this conclusion. It is said, however, that these two sections of the charter are in conflict; that the defendants were required to determine under which one they would act, and that in so doing they were acting judicially, and cannot be held liable for any error or mistake. The argument is based upon a false premise. There is no conflict in these sections. Both can stand, and be construed so as to give effect to each. Defendants were presumed to know the law, and it will be assumed that they put a proper interpretation upon the provisions of the charter relating to their duties and disabilities. That criminal laws should be strictly construed is conceded, and it is also true that all doubts concerning the interpretation of penal statutes are to be resolved in favor of the accused. But the statute is broad, and covers the performance of every act prohibited by statute for the violation of which no penalty is provided. The charter is explicit in saying that no alderman shall vote upon any question in which he is directly or indi-

4   rectly interested. There is no room for doubt or for construction. See *State v. Conlee*, 25 Iowa, 237. It is not necessary that any injurious consequences should have resulted from the misconduct of the officers. The crime consists in a perversion of their powers and duties to the pur-

poses of fraud and wrong; and they are punishable, although no injury resulted to any individual, and no money was drawn from the treasury, by reason of the vote to increase the salaries. As bearing upon this question, see *State v. Van Auken,* 98 Iowa, 674; Wharton Criminal Law, section 2514; *Duty v. State,* 9 Ind. App. 595 (36 N. E. Rep. 655); *People v. Bogart,* 3 Parker Cr. R. 143.

Other grounds of the demurrer are disposed of by what is said in *State v. Conlee, supra.*

The trial court erroneously sustained the demurrer, and its decision is REVERSED.

APPENDIX

Notes of Cases Not Otherwise Reported

FLORA SHERMAN v. W. C. DAVENPORT, Sheriff, Appellant.

CONVEYANCE WITHOUT CONSIDERATION: *Good between parties.*

Appeal from Woodbury District Court.—HON. SCOTT M. LADD Judge.

WEDNESDAY, MAY 11, 1898.

ACTION at law for the conversion of seven head of cows. Defendant denied the conversion, and further pleaded that he sold the same under execution as the property of one William Sherman, and that William Sherman was the owner thereof prior to the sale. Trial to a jury. Verdict and judgment for plaintiff, and defendant appeals.— *Affirmed.*

T. F. Bevington and *M. B. Davis* for appellant.

J. A. Prichard for appellee.

DEEMER, C. J.—Appellant contends that the court erroneously submitted to the jury the question of fraud in the sale of the animals by William Sherman to his wife, Flora. He claims that there was no such issue, and that, if there was, the court erred in some of the instructions relating thereto. We agree that no such issue was in the case, and may concede that some of the instructions relating to fraud in the sale of personal property were erroneous. Yet it is difficult to see how appellant was prejudiced thereby. The error, if any, was favorable to appellant, and the fault in the instructions was without prejudice.

II. The defendant, as sheriff of Woodbury county, levied upon the property on the tenth day of December, 1895. Prior to that time, and on or about March 8, 1894, William Sherman, the defendant in execution, executed a bill of sale conveying the cows in dispute to his wife, the appellee herein. This bill of sale was duly acknowledged and filed for record before the levy of the execution. Appellee says that the consideration for the transfer was a loan made to her husband before her marriage   The court instructed that "if the bill of sale was delivered to plaintiff for some other purpose than in payment of money

(741)

borrowed from her by William Sherman, and that said borrowed money, if any, was not the consideration for the delivery of said bill of sale, then said bill of sale is void, and you should find for the defendant." The court further instructed that the burden was upon plaintiff to establish the execution of the bill of sale, which she had done, and upon defendant to show that the bill of sale was void, either because not based upon the consideration claimed, or because made with intent to hinder, delay, or defraud creditors. These instructions were, if anything, more favorable to defendant than the pleadings and evidence would warrant. The bill of sale vested the legal title in appellee, and, although not based upon any consideration, was good as between the parties thereto, and all others except creditors who may have been defrauded thereby. There was, as we have seen, no issue of fraud in the case. The verdict has support in the evidence, and the judgment is AFFIRMED.

LADD, J., took no part.

GAYETTA L. TREGO, Appellant, v. LYDIA M. STUDLEY, *et al.*, Appellees.

DOWER: *Payment of liens.* A balance of personal property paid over by executors to the widow under a will giving her a life use of all real and personal property should not, in proceedings for the assignment of dower, be applied in payment of a mortgage on the land.

Appeal from Buchanan District Court.—HON. J. J. TOLERTON, Judge.

THURSDAY, MAY 12, 1898.

THIS is an action to secure the admeasurement of plaintiff's dower. There was a decree setting off her interest, but charging it with the sum of three hundred and seventy dollars and sixty-three cents. From the action of the court in thus subjecting her interest to the payment of this amount, the plaintiff appeals.—*Modified.*

Cook & Leach for appellant.

E. E. Hasner for appellees.

WATERMAN, J.—The plaintiff took, by devise from her husband, a life estate in certain real estate in Buchanan county. It is admitted that the will does not bar plaintiff's right to a dower interest, also, in said land. This action was brought for the purpose of having her dower interest assigned. At the time of the death of plaintiff's husband, there was a mortgage upon said land amounting to one thousand eight hundred and fifty dollars, and it still stands unpaid. The will gave plaintiff the use during life of all real and personal property, with a devise over to others of any remainder. On the settlement of the estate, there was a balance of three hundred and seventy dollars and sixty-three cents in the hands of the executors, which, under order of court, they paid to plaintiff, and they were then discharged. It is now claimed, as we understand it, that this three hundred and seventy dollars and sixty-three cents should be applied in payment, *pro tanto*, of the principal of the mortgage. This seems to have been the reason for the trial court's action in charging it as a lien upon the widow's dower interest. It is elementary that a life tenant cannot be charged with the payment of the principal of an incumbrance upon the estate, but only with keeping down interest. Plaintiff was entitled to the possession and use of this money, at least. She rightfully received it from the executors. Being under no obligation to make any payment on the principal of this mortgage, we cannot understand why it was charged against her share. The decree below provided "that the mortgage now on said premises amounts to $1,850, no part of which is chargeable upon said homestead of plaintiff; that one-third in fee simple, belonging to Gavetta L. Trego, after deducting the homestead, is chargeable with $370.63 of said mortgage, being the money which plaintiff received from the executors of said Seth D. Trego, deceased, and it is further charged with its *pro rata* share of the balance of said mortgage, to-wit: $1,479.37," etc. The decree should be changed in this respect: It should charge the dower interest of the plaintiff, exclusive of her homestead, with its proportionate share of the mortgage of one thousand eight hundred and fifty dollars, and it should not be charged with the money received by plaintiff from the executors. As thus modified, it will be AFFIRMED.

FRANC C. ELLIS v. MARTHA E. SANFORD Appellant, and JULIA K. HOWES.

APPEAL: REVIEW: *Finding of fraud.* A finding of fraud by the trial court will be reversed on appeal where the evidence as it appears in the record is insufficient to show fraud and it is apparent that the trial judge based his decision largely upon "facts and circumstances transpiring upon the trial," which are not presented to the appellate court.

Appeal from Polk District Court.—HON W. A. SPURRIER, Judge.

THURSDAY, MAY 26, 1898.

In March, 1895, defendant, Julia K. Howes, became a judgment debtor of the plaintiff. Prior to that time she was the owner of certain real estate described in the petition, and conveyed the same to her co-defendant Sanford. This action is brought, asking that the conveyance be adjudged void as to plaintiff, because made to defraud her in the collection of her judgment. The district court gave judgment for plaintiff, and defendant Sanford appealed.—*Reversed.*

Barcroft & McCaughan for appellant.

Dunshee & Allen and *A. P. Smith* for appellee.

GRANGER, J.—The controlling question is as to the fraud charged which is denied. The district court presented an opinion showing its reasons for the conclusion, from which it is apparent that the fact of fraud was so doubtful that it could not be sustained, except for "facts and circumstances transpiring upon the trial." Among the facts so relied upon by the district court is that of the husband of Mrs. Sanford being present in the court during the trial, "taking an exceedingly active part in the direction and management of her case." It seems that he had been her agent in the transactions charged as fradulent, and other transactions. Judging from the record, much importance and weight must have been given to this and other matters at the trial, that do not appear in the record, and could not well be made to appear. Independent of such considerations, we regard the evidence as insufficient to sustain the claim of fraud. Mr. Sanford was not a witness, and the court seems to have been of the opinion that he should have been made one by Mrs. Sanford, to explain matters favorable to her, if true; and because of this failure, and an evident impression, because of Sanford's interest at the trial, that he could have made such explanations, the court has assumed what was not otherwise proven. This situation fairly appears from the opinion. As the record is presented here, we have not the facts that in part induced the conclusion of the district court; and, as we have said, the evidence, as it appears here, is not a showing of fraud. It is a question of fact, and we will not discuss the evidence. The judgment must stand REVERSED.

JANE E. SPANGLER, *et al.*, v. JAMES L. BEAVER, *et al.*

SHERIFF'S FEES: *Subpoena and Order*: On a motion for change of venue for prejudice of the trial judge, the court ordered persons signing affidavits in support hereof to appear for cross-examination, and directed that subpoenas should be served on such of them as the adverse party should indicate to the clerk. The clerk issued "an order to appear for cross-examination," in which he recited the above order, and notified the person named therein to appear in court and submit to cross-examination on a day stated. *Held*, that this order amounted to no more than a subpoena, and that the sheriff was entitled only to the fees provided for service of subpoenas, for serving the same.

Appeal from Linn District Court —HON. WILLIAM P. WOLF, Judge.

FRIDAY, MAY 27, 1898.

ISSUE was joined in an action for partition of certain real estate. Thereupon defendants applied for a change of forum on the ground of the prejudice of the presiding judge, supporting the application by the affidavits of the defendants and about three hundred others. On the application of the plaintiffs, the court entered an order for the cross-examination of affiants, in these words: "And it is further ordered by the court that the affiants signing affidavit for a change be cited to appear before this court on November 18, 1895, at 9 o'clock A. M., for examination touching the matter stated in respective affidavits, and that subpoenas be served accordingly on such of them as the adverse party shall indicate to the clerk." On the twelfth day of November, 1895, the clerk issued the following "order to appear for cross-examination" to the persons addressed: "You are each of you hereby notified that in the matter of the application for change of venue in the above-entitled proceedings and cases the said court has made and entered an order requiring you to appear in court, and submit to cross-examination touching the matters and things sworn to by you in your affidavit in support of said motion for a change of venue; and in pursuance of the said order you are hereby ordered and commanded to be and appear in said district court at Marion, Iowa, on Monday, November 18, 1895, at 9 o'clock in the forenoon. And hereof fail not at your peril." This was served by the sheriff on sixty-nine persons, and in his return he charged as fees for serving one hundred and thirty-eight dollars, or two dollars for each service, and the costs therefor were taxed accordingly by the clerk On the eighteenth day of January, 1896, the plaintiffs and defendants joined in a motion to retax costs, asking that the sheriff be allowed only twenty cents for serving each person, instead of two dollars, as taxed. This motion being overruled, the plaintiffs and defendants appeal.—*Reversed.*

Hubbard & Dawley, Charles E. Wheeler, J. W. Jamison, and *Chas. A. Clark & Son,* for appellants.

Charles W. Kepler. for appellees.

LADD, J.—The entry was an order, within the meaning of section 3842 of the code. It fixed the time when affiants might be required to appear, and limited the number to those the adverse party should indicate to the clerk. On these only subpoenas were to be severed. The order did not require affiants to appear in court. It was never served on any one, nor was this required. To have done so, the certified copy of the journal entry, and not the clerk's interpretation of it, should have been used. The clerk issued an order of his own making, which, however, amounted to no more than a subpoena. True, it included certain information which he might, though not bound to, give. It was proper for the court to say in what way affiants might be brought before it, and, having done so, the officers were limited to that method. As the sheriff did not serve an order of the court, he is not entitled to compensation for such a service. The paper the court directed might be served, and which was in fact served, was a subpoena. The sheriff was entitled to thirteen dollars and eighty cents only for service and two dollars and eighty cents for mileage. The motion to retax ought to have been sustained.—*Reversed.*

JANE GILLETT v. JENNIE C. McFARLAND and C. M. BROWN, Executors of the Estate of SAMUEL McFARLAND, Deceased, Appellants,

STATUTORY ATTORNEY'S FEES: *Executor and Administrator*: Attorney's fees may be allowed against a decedent's estate upon the establishment in the district court, of a claim based upon a promisory note containing the usual provision for attorney's fees where the claim was duly prepared and filed within six months, and not allowed and plaintiff employed an attorney to give the notice and prosecute the claim who filed the required affidavit for attorneys on the day the notice was served and appeared and prosecuted the claim to judgment.

Appeal from Keokuk District Court.—HON. A. R. DEWEY, Judge.

SATURDAY, OCTOBER 8, 1898.

THIS is a proceeding for the establishment of a claim against an estate. Judgment was rendered establishing the claim in the sum of seven hundred and twenty-five dollars and eleven cents, as a claim of the third class, and ordering the same to be paid. It was also ordered that statutory attorney's fees be taxed in favor of plaintiff's attorney. Defendant's appeal.—*Affirmed.*

C. M. Brown for appellants.

D. T. Flockman and *T. C. Legoe* for appellee.

PER CURIAM.—No reason appears for questioning the correctness of the judgment in allowing the claim. Appellant's complaint is against the allowance of attorney's fees. The claim was duly prepared and filed within the six months, and the executors having failed to allow or disallow it, plaintiff served notice as required, and defendants appeared and resisted the claim. The claim not being allowed, plaintiff employed an attorney to give the notice and to prosecute the claim. The attorney filed the required affidavit for attorney's fees on the day the notice was served, and appeared and prosecuted the claim to judgment, and appears in this court. The claim is upon a promissory note containing the usual provision for attorney's fees, and we discover no reason why the fee was not properly allowed.—AFFIRMED.

LAURINDA J. DEPEE, Appellant, v. GRAND LODGE OF A. O. U. W., of Iowa, Defendant, and OTIS B. DEPEE, Appellee, v. GRAND LODGE OF A. O. U. W., of Iowa, Defendant.

INSURANCE: *Change in beneficiary.* While a by-law of a beneficial association which provides the manner in which a change of beneficiary may be made cannot be taken advantage of by parties claiming the insurance, yet such claimant may question whether a change in beneficiary has, in fact, been made.

APPEAL: *Finding in law action.* The finding of the trial court will not be disturbed when supported by the evidence.

Ruling below necessary. On the trial of a law action, errors assigned on the admission or rejection of evidence cannot be considered in the absence of rulings thereon.

Appeal from Woodbury District Court.—HON. F. R. GAYNOR, Judge.

FRIDAY, OCTOBER 21, 1898.

THIS is a contest between Laurinda J. Depee and Otis B. Depee over the avails of a certificate of membership in the Grand Lodge A. O. U. W., issued to one Alonzo Depee, the husband of Laurinda J. Each claims to be the beneficiary named in the certificate. The lodge makes no defense to the proceeding, but stands ready to pay the amount due to him who is found to be entitled thereto. The trial court found that Otis B. Depee is the rightful beneficiary, and entitled to the fund, and Laurinda J. Depee appeals.—*Affirmed.*

Hallam & Stevenson for appellant.

Lynn & Foley for appellee.

Henderson & Berry for defendant.

DEEMER, C. J.—The original certificate, issued in the year 1878, made appellant the beneficiary. Appellee contends, and the lower court found, however, that Alonzo Depee made a change of beneficiary some time in the year 1890, and directed the lodge to issue a new certificate, making Otis B. Depee, his brother, the beneficiary. On the back of the original certificate, under date of December 11, 1890, appears what purports to be a revocation of the direction as to payment, and an order directing payment to be made to Otis B. Depee, signed, "A. L. Depee." It is conceded by all parties that Alonzo Depee did not personally sign this revocation and order. Appellee contends, however, that it was signed by E. E. Wells or D. A. Winne, and that whichever one signed it in the name of A. L. Depee did so with authority. He also contends that appellant had no interest in the original certificate, and that the change of beneficiary, although irregular, cannot be questioned by any one except the lodge.

It may be conceded that a by-law pointing out the manner in which a change of beneficiary may be made is directory, and cannot be taken advantage of by parties claiming the insurance; but it is, nevertheless, true that the holder of the certificate must have, in fact, made a change in order to defeat the original beneficiary. Whether Alonzo Depee did this or not is the controlling question in the case. The action is at law, and the finding of the court to which the case was submitted has the force and effect of a verdict of a jury. Witness Winne testified in effect, that he wrote the order for the change, and affixed the name of A. L. Depee thereto; and he further said that he did so by authority of the assured. There are many things tending to discredit his evidence, but he was upon the witness stand before the trial court, and the presiding judge was better able than we are to judge of the truthfulness of his testimony. If his testimony be accepted, then the judgment awarding the proceeds of the certificate to Otis B. Depee is correct.

The rules relating to the force and effect to be given the findings of a court or the verdict of a jury in a law action are so well understood that we need not reiterate them here. The judgment has support in the evidence, and we cannot interfere.

As the court made no ruling on the admission and rejection of evidence, the errors assigned thereon cannot be considered. The judgment is AFFIRMED.

STATE OF IOWA v. WILLIAM McKEAVITT, MORGAN CHASE, E. J. TRAVIS, and J. A. CARMICKLE, Appellants.

LARCENY: EVIDENCE OF VALUE: FORM OF QUESTIONS: COMPETENCY.

Appeal from Linn District Court.—HON. H. M. REMLEY, Judge.

THURSDAY, DECEMBER 15, 1898.

DEFENDANTS were indicted, tried, and convicted of the crime of stealing two hogs, one sheep, and one ram, and from the sentence imposed they appeal.—*Reversed.*

John M Hughes for appellants.

Milton Remley, Attorney General and *J. M. Grimm*, County Attorney for the State.

DEEMER, C. J.—The state offered evidence to show that the ram was a full-blooded Cotswold, worth in the market at Cedar Rapids thirty dollars, and that he was bought and used by the prosecuting witness for breeding purposes. Defendants produced witnesses to show the value of the animal, and to one of them propounded the following questions: "Did you know the market value of that kind of a ram in and about Cedar Rapids about the fifteenth day of December, 1897?" To this an objection was sustained. He was then asked: "Do you know the value of full-blooded Cotswold rams?" An objection to this question was also sustained Questions of similar import were propounded to other witnesses, and objections thereto were sustained, the court evidently being of opinion that the questions called for the value of the animal as mutton. It is evident that the questions which we have set out do not call for that kind of an answer. One witness stated that he was a butcher, and that he was in the business of buying sheep, cattle, and hogs. Another said that he was a stock buyer, and knew the market value of sheep, as he bought them in a speculative way. He was then asked if he knew the market value of the ram, and the court refused to allow him to answer. It is manifest that these rulings were erroneous. And, as the value of the property was a material ingredient of the offense, the errors were highly prejudicial. The judgment is REVERSED.

A. J. McDERMOTT v. F. ABNEY, Appellant.

CONTRACTS. A written memorandum of agreement, as assented to by one of the parties, but not signed by him, is admissible against him to prove the contract.

MEASURE OF RECOVERY. Where defendant in an action to recover a real estate broker's commission admits having agreed to pay a commission, and plaintiff claims the agreement was for a specific sum, the measure of damages is the agreed commission, and not the value of the services.

HARMLESS ERROR. In a suit on an agreement of which an unsigned memorandum has been made, an instruction referring to the memorandum as a written contract is harmless, since the contract is the basis of recovery, whether it be written or oral.

APPEAL: *Abstract.* An abstract will not be stricken because it does not contain all the evidence, where it contains everything essential to enable the court to pass on the errors urged. .

ADDITIONAL ABSTRACT: *Costs.* Where appellees' additional abstract contains matters not required to pass on the questions argued, its cost, except as to that portion containing necessary matter, will be taxed to him.

Appeal from Calhoun District Court.—HON. Z. A. CHURCH, Judge.

SATURDAY, DECEMBER 17, 1898.

THE petition is in two counts. In the first the plaintiff alleges that the defendant orally agreed to pay him two per cent. commission if he should find a customer with whom the defendant might exchange certain property, and, as to the other property, a similar agreement was reduced to writing, to which the defendant's name was attached, at his request, by plaintiff. In the second count, recovery is sought on a *quantum meruit.* The answer is a general denial. Trial to jury; verdict and judgment for plaintiff; and defendant appeals.—*Affirmed.*

M. R. McCrary and *Brown McCrary* for appellant.

W. E. Gray for appellee.

PER CURIAM. As the abstract contains everything essential to enable the court to pass upon the errors argued, the motion to strike because it does not contain all the evidence must be overruled. The motion to tax the cost of the appellee's abstract to him is sustained, except as to the two pages containing the ninth instruction, for the reason it is not an abstract of the evidence, but a printed transcript of the testimony of certain witnesses, not required in order to pass upon the questions argued. If the written memorandum was assented to, as stating the agreement, it was admissible in evidence, though not signed. The petition alleged the transaction as claimed by the plaintiff, and this was set out in the instructions, and the plaintiff's recovery limited thereto. That the court referred to the memorandum as a written contract was not material, because, whether construed to be written or oral, it might serve, if assented to, as a basis of recovery.

In several instructions the court advised the jury under what circumstances recovery might be had on a *quantum meruit,* but finally withdrew the second count of the petition, and directed the allowance of the commission or nothing. As the plaintiff testified that a commission was agreed upon, and the defendant admitted that he had agreed to pay a commission, this was the true measure of damages, and the jury could not have misunderstood it. There are no doubtful questions involved in the case, and the judgment is AFFIRMED.

J. H. POWERS, Appellant, v. A. WINTERS *et al.*

INJUNCTIONS: *Continuance.* Code, section 2405, provides that where a continuance of an application for injunction to restrain liquor selling is had at the instance of the defendant, a temporary injunction shall issue. *Held,* that where defendant, at the hearing, elects to take testimony by depositions, thus necessitating a continuance, a temporary injunction does not issue as a matter of right.

Appeal from Chickasaw District Court.—HON. A. N. HOBSON, Judge.

SATURDAY, DECEMBER 17, 1898.

THE action is in equity by J. H Powers for an injunction to restrain A. Winters and another, defendants, from conducting a saloon, and the petition makes it appear that they are so engaged in violation of law. At the appearance term the defendants answered by a general denial. The following then appears: "New Hampton, Iowa, December 8, 1897. In case No. 2,721, J. H. Powers vs. A. Winters and others, the case was called up by the attorney for the plaintiff, and before the case was reached for trial in the regular order, and attorneys for the defendants elected to have the testimony taken in the form of depositions. It is ordered by the court that the testimony be so taken, and that the case be tried upon depositions, and the case continued by the court on account of the foregoing order. Plaintiff demands that a temporary writ of injunction issue against the defendant on account of the foregoing order. The court refuses to grant the temporary injunction on account of the foregoing order, to which the attorney for the plaintiff excepts. The court states that this term of court will necessarily adjourn to-morrow on account of a term of court which will convene in Fayette county on Monday next, and that on account of lack of time, and the court having other matters to attend to, refuses to have a hearing upon the question of a temporary injunction, upon evidence, on account of lack of time at this term of court. The court states to the attorney for the plaintiff that application for hearing upon a temporary injunction can be presented in vacation at such time as the court is not otherwise engaged, and that it will be passed upon, and time for hearing fixed, at that time. To all of which the plaintiff excepts. A. N. Hobson, Judge." From the order refusing a temporary injunction, the plaintiff appealed. *Affirmed.*

J. H. Powers, in pro. per.

Springer & Clary, for appellees.

GRANGER, J.—Appellant's claim for a temporary injunction rests on a part of section 2405 of the Code, and we quote part of the section, including the particular provision relied on, as follows: "Whenever a nuisance is kept, maintained or exists, as defined in this chapter, any citizen of the county may maintain an action in equity to perpetually enjoin and abate the same. In such action the court or a judge in vacation, shall upon the presentation of a petition therefor, allow a temporary writ of injunction without bond, if it shall be made to appear to the satisfaction of the court or judge, by evidence in the form of affidavits, depositions, oral testimony or otherwise, as the plaintiff may elect, unless the court or judge, by previous order, shall have directed the form and manner in which it shall be presented, that the nuisance complained of exists. Three days' notice in writing shall be given the defendant of the hearing of the application, and if then continued at his instance, the writ as prayed shall be granted as a matter of course." Appellant's view is that, when defendants elected to take their testimony by deposition, it necessitated a continuance of the cause, and hence the continuance was at their instance; so that, as a matter of right, he was entitled to a temporary injunction. The petition asks for a temporary writ, and that it be made perpetual on final hearing. No other application for a temporary writ was made, nor was the matter of such a writ suggested until after the continuance of the cause, when such a writ was demanded because of the continuance. Appellant states, as the only question in this court, as follows: "Should the court have granted a temporary injunction when the defendant elected to have his testimony taken in the form of depositions, and the court conceded the request?" The depositions to be taken had no reference to an application for a temporary injunction, but to the final trial, involving the right to a permanent injunction. It does not appear that when the order was made that, in effect, continued the cause, the parties contemplated any inquiry into a right to a temporary injunction that was continued, but the cause on its merits. Now, looking to the section, as quoted, and it will be seen that the granting of the temporary writ as a matter of course follows a continuance of an application for a temporary writ. It will be seen that it applied as well to a hearing before a judge in vacation as the court. The language, summarized, is: "In such action the court, or a judge in vacation, shall, upon the presentation thereof, allow a temporary writ of injunction without bond, if it shall be made to appear to the satisfaction of the court or judge * * * that the nuisance complained of exists. Three days' notice in writing shall be given the defendant of the hearing of the application, and, if then continued at his instance, the writ as prayed shall be granted as a matter of course." We think there was no application pending to bring the case within the statute. Judgment is AFFIRMED.

INDEX

ABORTION—See Crim. Law, [6].

ABSTRACT IN DISTRICT COURT—See Costs, [2].

ACCEPTANCE—See Checks, [1], [3]; Sales, [1], [3].

ACCIDENTS—See Insurance, [6].

ACCOMPLICES—See Crim. Law, [1], [31].

ACTIONS—

1. **Parties—Bank and Cashier**—Where a cashier, for his bank, cashes a check upon the undertaking of third persons that the check should be honored by the drawee, he may bring suit as cashier to recover on the check and said incidental agreement, without joining his bank as plaintiff.—Leach v. Hill, 171.

2. **Same**—The possibility that controversies respecting boundary lines may arise between the owners of other lots of the tier, similar to that involved in the action, does not make them proper parties to an action respecting boundary lines, between the owners of two adjoining lots of the tier.—Klinker v. Schmidt, 70.

2a   **Transfer to Equity**—It was error to transfer the cause to the equity side of the court.—*Idem.*

3   **Election**—In an action where the plaintiff alleges that he purchased a lot of the defendants which they falsely represented to be a certain number and that he took a conveyance from them by that description, which does not cover the land contracted for, by reason of which he seeks a rescission of the sale and a recovery of damages, he will not be required to elect between a claim on the covenants of the deed or for damages because of fraud and misrepresentation.—Watson v. Bartholomew, 576.

4   **Indorsement in Blank**—Early told Sisson that S. should buy cattle for him and that he would provide funds for the payment of checks for cattle drawn by Sisson in the latter's name. S. gave such a check to Hill, who endorsed it to plaintiff, in blank, with intent thereby to transfer all his rights growing out of his selling the cattle. *Held*, this endorsement gave plaintiff the right to sue Early on said agreement with Sisson.—Leach v. Hill, 171.

Small figures refer to subdivisions of Index. The others to page of report.

ADJUDICATION—See CRIMINAL LAW, [23], [24], [26], [27], [28]; JUDGMENTS, [1]; PRACTICE SUP. CT., [62].

1. **Homesteads**—An action was brought to restrain sale because the property to be sold was a homestead. A temporary injunction ordered became ineffective through failure to file bond, and a permanent injunction granted was set aside. But a finding in the decree that the property was a homestead was never set aside or appealed from. Notwithstanding this finding there was a sale after the permanent injunction was set aside, and a sheriff's deed resulted. *Held*, the finding of homestead concluded parties and privies and said decree did not estop the setting up of the homestead right in an action to set the deed aside.—McClelland v. Bennett, 74.

2. **Estoppel by Recital**—One not a party to proceedings to incorporate a town is not prevented, by a recital, in the order appointing commissioners to call an election.—State of Iowa v. Council, 731.

ADVERSE POSSESSION—See DEDICATION, [2]; TENANTS IN COMMON, [2], [3].

AFFIDAVITS—See PRAC. SUP. CT., [4].

AGENCY—See INSURANCE, [16], [19], [20]; PRACTICE, [10]; TAXATION, [7], [8].

1. **Principal and Agent**—Plaintiff testified to conversations he had with persons in the home office of the company. He could not state positively that they were officers or agents, but the company acted in accordance with statements made by those persons to plaintiff. *Held*, no prejudice resulted.—Brock v. Insurance Company, 30.

2. **SAME**—A merchant's son-in-law, who managed the business as agent, and bought and paid for stock, and who, on the principal's becoming sick, was told to do the best he could, and to make collections and take notes for outstanding accounts and apply them on a certain claim and "to work things to the best advantage and to do anything he (the agent) could to keep the business going," had no authority to execute a chattel mortgage on the stock.—Edgerly & Co. v. Cover, 670.

3. **Landlord and Tenant**—The authority of an agent to make a lease does not imply an authority to cancel it.—Faville v. Lundvall & Co., 133.

ALIENS—See ESTATES [2], [3].

ALTERATION—See BILLS AND NOTES [1].

AMENDMENTS—See INSUR. [4]; MUN. CORP. [6], [7]; PLEAD. [1], [4]; PRACT. SUP. CT. [66].

AMOUNT IN CONTROVERSY—See Pract. Sup. Cr. [25].
APPEAL—See Pract. Sup. Ct.
ARGUMENT—see Pract. Sup. Ct. [10].
ASSAULT—See Crim. Law [3].
ASSESSMENT—See Cities and Towns [1] to [6].
ASSIGNMENT—See Sales [1].
ASSUMPTION—See Deeds [1], [4].

ATTACHMENTS—See Fraudulent Conveyance, [9]; Instructions, [13], [14]; Judgments, [1]; Mortgages, [1].

1. Damages—Evidence as to the relative condition of trade at the approach of holidays as compared with other seasons of the year, is reversible error where the attachment debtor's trade was not interfered with by the levy.—Hooker v. Chittenden, 321.

2. Same—Depreciation of real property while under levy is not, in the absence of change of possession, recoverable on the attachment bond.—Tisdale v. Mayor, 1.

3. Same—Mental suffering resulting from the wrongful and malicious suing out of a writ of attachment does not entitle to compensatory damages.—Idem.

4. Pleading—An averment of the use of attached property and that it was the only mill equipment of the kind in town and doing a substantial business does not state ultimate and material facts.—Idem.

5. Second Attachment—Defendant's property was attached, and placed in the custody of the sheriff. Plaintiff levied a subsequent attachment, and the property was sold for the benefit of both creditors. Held, that defendant was not entitled to recover on the second attachment bond the difference between the sum realized from the sale of his interest in the property and the value of such interest at the time of the levy, since the measure of damages was only legal interest on the surplus, during the time it was wrongfully held by virtue of plaintiff's attachment —Emerson & Co. v. Converse, 330.

ATTORNEYS—See Certiorari, [2].

ATTORNEY FEES—See Estates, [1]; Practice Sup. Cr. [31].

Deposition—Plaintiff is not entitled to have the expenses of his counsel incurred in attending at three different places in the state to take the deposition of a witness in an equity cause, before it was finally secured, taxed as costs.—Grapes v. Grapes, 316.

BANKS—See Actions, [1].
BILL OF EXCEPTIONS—See Pract. Sup. Cr. [15] to [19], [48], [56].

Small figures refer to subdivisions of Index. The others to page of report.

plead that the note was without consideration, had been transferred to plaintiff and by him sued to cheat defendant. *Held.*

a That the firm's indorsement did not tend to show that the firm had delivered the note to plaintiff for collection.

b Defendant could not show that plaintiff had purchased the note as agent for a third person, who afterwards delivered it to him for collection.

c One to whom a note is endorsed for collection may sue thereon.—Lehman v. Press, 389.

3. Negotiability—A note otherwise negotiable is not rendered non-negotiable in Iowa by a provision in it authorizing an attorney to appear at any time and confess judgment thereon, on the ground that the time of payment is thereby rendered uncertain.—Tolman v. Janson, 455.

BOARDS—See CERTIORARI, ¹; OATHS.

BONA FIDE PURCHASER—See BILLS AND NOTES, ², ³, ⁴.

BOOKS OF ACCOUNT—See EVID. ⁹⁸.

BUILDING AND LOAN ASSOCIATIONS—See USURY, ¹, ².

Foreclosure—A building and loan association may recover the interest, premium and dues maturing after the commencement of and before judgment in a suit to foreclose a mortgage and to cancel shares of stock pledged as collateral security, under Acts Twenty-sixth General Assembly, chapter 85, section 9.—Loan Association v. Johnston, 218.

BURDEN OF PROOF—See RAILROADS, ¹⁶.

CANCELLATION—See FRAUDULENT CONVEYANCE, ¹.

Facts which are held sufficient to cancel a conveyance because of fraud practiced upon a woman seventy years old by one in whom she placed confidence and who obtained same upon grossly inadequate consideration.—Bruguier v. Pepin, 432.

CARLISLE TABLES -See EVID. ⁷.

CERTIORARI.

1. Review The action of the state board of medical examiners in revoking the certificate of a practicing physician cannot be cured by *certiorari* proceedings, where it did not proceed without opportunity to defend or unreasonably. *Certiorari* is not available to review the sufficiency and competency of testimony.—Traer v. State Board of Med. Examiners, 559.

2. ATTORNEYS. A disbarred attorney, whose right to appear in and prosecute an action brought by him as trustee is denied, cannot maintain *certiorari* proceedings to review the decision.—Wilson v. Remley, 583.

Small figures refer to subdivisions of Index. The others to page of report.

CHANGE OF VENUE—See PRACTICE SUP. CT., 49.
CHARACTER—See CRIM. LAW, 10.

CHECKS—See ACTIONS, 1.

1. **Oral Acceptance**—An oral agreement by a banker to accept checks drawn upon him is binding as to checks drawn within a reasonable time notwithstanding the drawer had no funds in the bank at the time of the promise or at the time the checks were drawn, where a third person who did have funds in the bank had agreed to provide funds to meet such checks.—Leach v. Hill, 171.

2. *Same*—Where checks are given for the purchase of stock by stock buyers, seventy days is not an unreasonable time for a promise to accept future checks, to be binding.—*Idem.*

3. FUTURE CHECKS—*Jury Question*— Plaintiff testified that he telephoned defendant, inquiring whether thereafter checks drawn by S., a live stock buyer, would be paid, and the response was "It will be O. K. to cash checks from S. to the amount of stock he gets" Defendant testified that this response was an inquiry as to specific checks. *Held,* that the jury was warranted in finding that it referred to future checks.—*Idem.*

CITIES AND TOWNS—See CRIMINAL LAW, 52, 53, 54, 55; DAMAGES, 3; DRAINS; FRAUDULENT CONVEYANCE, 3; MUNICIPAL CORPORATIONS, 1, 2, 3, 4; NEGLIGENCE, 3, 4; PLEA AND PROOF, 4; TAXATION, 1.

1. **Assessment**—Under Acts Twenty-fifth General Assembly, chapter 7, section 12, providing that an assessment for a street improvement, "shall be a lien upon the property abutting the street" on which the improvement is made, and that it "shall be limited to the lot or lands bounding or abutting on such street;" where a tract has been platted into lots the platted boundary lines must control, and the assessment must be limited to the lot or parcel of ground which actually abuts on the street, and cannot be extended to a contiguous point though, the latter, with the abutting lot constitute a single tract, and is used jointly for a single purpose, as a residence, and fronts on the street to be improved.—Smith v. City of Des Moines, 590.

2. SAME—A special assessment for street improvement is not void because erroneously made against the owner as well as against the property.—*Idem.*

3. *Certificates*—The holder of a special assessment certificate cannot be prevented from intervening in an action to enjoin the collection of the assessment, and asking for the enforcement of his lien, on the ground that the city has elected to

---

Small figures refer to subdivisions of Index. The others to page of report.

have the property sold by the county treasurer and that such election was final.—*Idem.*

4. FRAUDULENT CONVEYANCE—The levy of an assessment for street improvements cannot be defeated by a conveyance made to evade it.—*Idem.*

5. Incorporation of Town—*Court and Judge*—The application to incorporate and have election commissioners appointed must be presented to the court, and the order of appointment issued by it, and not by the judge.—State of Iowa v. Council, 781.

CLAIMS—See ESTATES, [1]; PRACTICE, [17].
CLERK AND REPORTER—See PRACT. SUP. CT. [19], [73].
COMMISSIONS—See DAMAGES, [3].

CONFLICT OF LAWS.

In an action on a note made in a foreign state, the laws of another state concerning provision for power of attorney to confess judgment on a note will be presumed to be the same as those of Iowa.—Tolman v. Janson, 455.

CONFRONTATION—See CRIM. LAW, [47].
CONSPIRACY——See CRIM. LAW, [1], [11], [31].
CONSTABLES—See JURISD. [1].
CONSTRUCTION—See EVID. [22]; LAND. AND TEN. [1], MORTG. [3].

CONTEMPT—

NEWSPAPER ARTICLE—During an *adjournment* in a cause on trial, an editor handed two jurors a copy of his paper to which one of the jurors was a subscriber. It had an article on the pending trial, headed "A put up job;" and in which the arrest, the apparent conclusiveness of the evidence and public indignation were referred to. It then stated that a revulsion of feeling had set in and that, now, "the majority of the sensible, thinking people took very little stock in the story told by the parties chiefly interested." It named the jurors, belittled the talk of the county attorney, and exalted that of defendant's counsel. Neither the proceedings nor the evidence were given, but a set of derogatory innuendoes and an inferential statement that the witnesses were in a deal to convict defendant. The two jurors read the article and one of them read part of it aloud in the jury room while the jury was deliberating. *Held*, this was contempt within Code, 4460, which inhibits contemptuous and insolent behavior towards a court "while engaged in the discharge of a judicial duty."—Field v. Thornell, 7.

CONTINUANCES—See page 751.

CONTRACTS Continued

right to withhold payment was reserved until such liens, claims or demands were settled or released. *Held,*

a. The right to reserve exists so long as such claims remain unpaid and is not limited to demands for which a mechanic's lien might be established.

b Money borrowed by a contractor and used in payment of labor and material furnished in the construction of a building is a debt for such money and not for labor and material, within the meaning of the contract provision.

c The owner may require claimants to interplead and establish their demands against the fund although the contractor has assigned the amount due to some of them.

d A material man who interpleads to establish his claims against the fund due the contractor is not precluded from asserting his rights under a provision of the building contract by the fact that he had taken an assignment from the contractor of any balance due him.—Ind. School Dist. v. Mardis, 295.

8a. **Harmless Error**—In a suit on an agreement of which an unsigned memorandum has been made, an instruction referring to the memorandum as a written contract is harmless, since the contract is the basis of recovery, whether it be written or oral. —McDermott v. Abney, 749.

9. **Joint Liability**—A wife who owned a farm and was present at the negotiations which led up to a contract with the plaintiffs is a proper party defendant in an action for breach, where the agreement was drawn and signed in her presence and both she and her husband orally promised to give their joint note for the subject of the contract.—Thompson & Son, v. Brown, 367.

10. **Quantum Meruit**—*Pleading*—One prevented from the completing of a contract, who sets out his contract as a recital of fact and seeks to recover the reasonable value of work done and material furnished instead of the contract price, does not sue upon the contract but upon a *quantum meruit.*—*Idem.*

11. **Sales**—PERSONAL LIABILITY—The grantee is not personally liable for repairs on the premises made under a contract with the grantor, even where he stipulated for such repairs in the contract of purchase.—Des Moines Savings Bank v. Goode, 568

12. **LIENS**—A plumbing company. which, after request of one engaged in the business of buying, improving and selling real estate, did work for him on credit on property which it knew he had sold cannot upon discovery of his insolvency enforce a mechanic's lien against the grantee or owner with neither of whom it sustained contract relations, and for whom the debtor did not act as agent.—*Idem.*

Small figures refer to subdivisions of Index. The others to page of report.

CONVERSION—See FACTORS, [1].
CORPUS DELICTI—See CRIM. LAW, [15].
CORROBORATION—See CRIM. LAW, [14], [15], [23], [24].

COSTS—See DRAINS; PRACT. [19]; PRACT. SUP. CT. [19], [20], [21].

Apportionment—*Review*—A person deeded land to another as security, and the grantee deeded the land to a bank as security for a debt of his own. The grantor asked an accounting and a reconveyance against the grantee and the bank. Plaintiff's deed was found to be intended as security for a certain sum found due thereon, and the grantee was decreed a lien for the amount thereof, which judgment was to inure in favor of the bank as its interest might appear, and both deeds were decreed to be cancelled, and it was ordered that the lien of the bank should be inferior to the lien of the officers and others entitled to costs, except the costs to which plaintiff and members of his family were entitled. *Held*, that it was, in effect, an apportionment of costs, which would not be disturbed.—Grapes v. Grapes, 816.

2.   SAME—The cost of making an abstract of evidence for use in the trial court, is not an item taxable as costs.—*Idem.*

COUNTIES—See DRAINS; EVIDENCE, [8], [9]; MECHANIC'S LIENS, [1]; TAXATION, [1].

1.   Paupers—PHYSICIANS—A county is liable for medical services rendered a pauper patient at the request of township trustees although it had a regularly employed physician to attend the poor, when his contract did not extend to the township in question, even though the patient was afterwards removed to another township covered by the contract —Taylor v. Woodbury County, 502.

2.   SAME—A physician, summoned to attend a pauper, called in another to assist in the performance of a surgical operation, but no claim was made against the county except by the former. *Held*, that such employment not being a delegation of authority, the county was liable.—*Idem.*

8.   CERTIFICATE OF TRUSTEES—A certificate by township trustees that medical services to a specified value were rendered a pauper patient at their request is binding on the county, in the absence of fraud.—*Idem.*

4.   *Same*—A physician was summoned unofficially by the trustees of a township to attend a pauper, and after the services were rendered the trustees officially signed a certificate that the physician acted on their official request. *Held*, that such

certificate was, in the absence of fraud, binding on the county. —*Idem.*

5. RATIFICATION. A county cannot defend an action to recover for medical services rendered a pauper patient, on the ground that the plaintiff's services were not authorized by the township trustees when they thereafter sanctioned them by written certificate.—*Idem.*

6. **Medical Aid**—*Liability.* The board has power to contract with a physician for attendance upon the county poor; and the trustees cannot employ a physician other than the one contracted with by the board and charge the county his services to a pauper without proof that the county physician was either incompetent or inconvenient of access.—Lacy v. Kossuth County, 16.

7. INFECTIOUS DISEASE—A county health physician is not required by virtue of his appointment to treat persons suffering with an infectious disease professionally, but the township board has power to employ a physician to treat an infected person; and such physician may recover, if the patient be a pauper, for the services so performed, from the county, even though the board of supervisors may have a contract with another physician to treat all paupers of the county.—*Idem.*

COURT AND JUDGE—See ADJUD. [2]; CITIES, [5].
COURT AND JURY—See CRIM. LAW, [46], [47], [48].
COURTS—See EM. DOM. [1], [2], [3].
CREDITOR'S BILL—See FRAUD. CONV. [3] to [7].

CRIMINAL LAW—See NEW TRIAL, [9]; PRACTICE, [1]; PRACTICE SUP. CT. [19], [20], [46].

Abortion—See [6], *post.*

1. **Accomplices**—See [31], *post—Conspiracy*—Defendant was charged with and convicted of murder. The court charged that if defendant and others conspired to kill, and another gave poison with deadly effect in pursuance of the conspiracy, defendant was guilty of murder. *Held,* the instruction is proper though no conspiracy was averred in the indictment.—State of Iowa v. Smith, 701.

2. **Assault to Rape**—*Knowledge of Prosecutrix' Age*—Defendant need not have known that prosecutrix was under age of consent in order to sustain a conviction for such assault.—State of Iowa v. Sherman, 684.

3. ELEMENTS—It is not an essential element of the crime, that the defendant intended to accomplish his purpose in spite of any resistance where the prosecutrix is a child under the age of consent.—State of Iowa v. Carnagy, 483.

Small figures refer to subdivisions of Index. The others to page of report.

Small figures refer to subdivisions of Index. The others to page of report.

VOL. 106 Ia—49

priate the property to his own use is harmless.—State of Iowa v. Minor, 642.

Libel—See [7],[8],[9] *ante*; [47] to [51] *post*.

46. COURT AND JURY—An instruction in a prosecution for libel that the jury, in exercising the authority conferred upon them, to determine the law as well as the facts, should reflect whether from their habits of thought, their study, and experience they were better qualified than the court to judge of the law, and that they should not reject the court's view of the law, unless they have a deep and confident conviction that the court is wrong, and they are right, is proper.—State of Iowa v. Heacock, 191.

47. SAME—It is the duty of the court to instruct the jury in a prosecution for libel in regard to the law, notwithstanding that authority.—*Idem.*

48. SAME—That authority does not require them to determine all legal questions which may arise on the trial, *e. g.*, the sufficiency of the indictment, the qualifications of jurors and the admissibility of evidence, but only such matters as they may consider in deliberating upon a verdict.—*Idem.*

49. EVIDENCE—The testimony of defendant charged with libel as to what he meant by the article in question is properly excluded where the language of the article is not ambiguous.—*Idem.*

50. INDICTMENT—An indictment for libel, charging that the writing was printed and circulated to injure prosecutor "and others," and that it tended to provoke prosecutor "and others" to wrath etc., where it clearly shows that the alleged libel was directed against prosecutor and was designed to provoke him to wrath, is not defective.—*Idem.*

51. Manslaughter—EVIDENCE—*Sentence*—Deceased was insulting, threatening and violent towards accused, and was endeavoring to provoke a quarrel, which accused tried to avoid. Deceased pressed the quarrel so that they came together, and accused stabbed deceased four times with a pocket knife, causing death. There was some evidence that deceased had a razor, but none that he used it. Both were drunk, but had been friendly and on good terms, and accused assisted to carry deceased to his home. *Held*, that a verdict of manslaughter was warranted, but that sentence should be reduced from six to three years.—State of Iowa v. Copeland, 102.

Murder—See [12], [16] *ante*.

52. Officers—INCREASING SALARY—Dubuque city charter (Acts Sixth General Assembly, chapter 210, section 5,) provides that

Small figures refer to subdivisions of Index. The others to page of report.

DAMAGES—See ATTACHMENT, [1], [2], [3], [5]; CONTRACTS, [6]; EMINENT DOMAIN, [4], [5]; MUNICIPAL CORPORATIONS, [2]; PRACTICE SUP. CT [55]; RAILWAYS, [1]; TELEGRAMS, [2].

1. **Future Suffering**—To authorize an allowance for future pain, inconvenience and impairment of enjoyment, in an action for personal injuries, the evidence must show that such consequences are reasonably certain to continue, and evidence which merely shows that they may continue is not sufficient.—Ford City of Des Moines, 94.

2. **Measure**—In an action to recover for the removal of ground protecting the plaintiff's property and the diversion of water so that it washed away his land, an instruction which authorizes the jury to allow as damages the difference between the value of the premises prior to such wrongful acts and their value afterwards is erroneous where such acts occurred four years before the trial, since the depreciation might have been due in part to other causes than the defendant's acts.—Podhaisky v. City of Cedar Rapids, 543.

3. SAME—Where the defendant in an action to recover a real estate broker's commission, admits having agreed to pay a commission, and plaintiff claims the agreement was for a specific sum, the measure of damages is the agreed commission, and not the value of the services.—McDermott v. Abney, 749.

DEATH—See DEEDS, [3].

DEDICATION.

1. **Evidence**—Though the board of supervisors has no jurisdiction to locate a street in an incorporated town, yet, in an action against the town for injury to land included in a highway thus located, it may be shown, on the question of dedication, that plaintiff acquiesced in its being so used, that the highway was laid out at his instance and with his approval, and a record of the board showing that he filed a petition with it, asking for the location of a public highway on said land, is admissible on whether plaintiff intended to dedicate such land to the public use.—Philbrick v. University Place, 352.

2. **Revocation**—*Adverse possession*—Adverse possession under a claim of right for more than ten years, of a portion of a plat of land designated thereon as a street, constitutes a revocation of the dedication as against the owner of lots situated on that plat.—Uptagrafft v. Smith, 385.

3. SAME—A dedication of land for a public street is revoked where it was never accepted and the general public has acquiesced in the action of the grantor in using and occupying the alleged

street as lots for a period of more than ten years during most
of which time taxes were levied upon the land and paid, and
the town subsequently incorporated, including the land in
question, has raised no objection to the action of the grantor.
—*Idem.*

DEEDS.

1. **Assumption of Mortgage**—PAROL VARIANCE—While a *party*
to a deed may not contradict its recitals as to consideration by
parol evidence, no one but a party is under such disability.
Hence, where a deed was left blank as to grantee, one whose
name was inserted as grantee by him to whom the blank deed
was made, may show, in a suit to charge him with a mortgage assumed by recital in the deed, that, under an agreement with the first grantee, the person whose name was inserted
was not to assume said mortgage.—Logan v. Miller, 511.

2. **Blank**—GRANTEE—*Contracts*—A deed executed in blank as to the
grantee confers authority on the real grantee to contract for the
sale of the lands, and to fill in his own grantee's name.—*Idem.*

3. **Delivery**—The delivery of a deed after the grantor's death to a
purchaser in possession of the premises by one with whom the
grantor has deposited it with directions to make such delivery
upon payment of the balance of the purchase price, is upon
fulfillment of the condition, valid and effectual and relates
back to the first delivery.—Dettmer v. Behrens, 585.

4. **Equity Jurisdiction**—A grantee of lands need not go into
equity to avail himself of a defense against personal liability
for a mortgage which his deed recites he assumes, where the
deed had been executed in blank to a preceding grantee, and
by him filled in with the present owner's name, on a sale made
for a different consideration.—Logan v. Miller, 511.

5. **Mistake**—*Evidence*—The fact that the husband paid most of
the price is not conclusive that the wife's name was inserted in
a deed as a grantee by mistake.—Bader v. Dyer, 715.

6. **Mortgage**—*Evidence*—Agreement of grantee that if he does not
sell the property, and grantor pays a certain debt within a year,
he will convey the property back, does not make the deed a
mortgage.—Robertson v. Moline Stoddard Co., 414.

7. REDEMPTION—A creditor to whom real estate has been conveyed by an absolute deed for the purpose of securing a debt
cannot redeem the property from a sale on foreclosure after
nine months from the date of sale.—*Idem.*

8. **Possession**—*Injunction*—One in possession of land under a
deed effective only as a mortgage, and having a plain remedy

at law, if entitled to protection, was not entitled to an injunction restraining the purchaser of such property at a sale on foreclosure of a prior mortgage, from interfering with such possession.—McDonald v. Second National Bank, 517.

DEFAULTS—See PRACT. ² to ⁵; PRACT. SUP. CT. ⁶².
DELIVERY—See DEEDS, ³.
DEMURRER—See CRIM. LAW, ²³ to ²⁷; PRACT. SUP. CT., ⁵¹.
DEPOSITIONS—See ATTY. FEES; PRACT. SUP. CT., ²⁴; page 751.
DESCENT AND DISTRIBUTION—See ESTATES, ², ³.
DESERTION—See HOMESTEADS, ⁴.
DISCRETION—See EVID , ⁶.

DIVORCE.

Evidence held insufficient to warrant a divorce to a husband though there was testimony that the wife had beaten and abused him.—Schaffer v. Schaffer, 492.

SAME—And held insufficient to give the wife a divorce on account of cruel and inhuman treatment.—Blair v. Blair, 269.

DOCTORS—See CERTIORARI, ¹; COUNTIES, ¹ to ⁷; EVID. ⁶, ⁸, ⁹.

DOWER—See ESTATES. ⁴.

DRAINS.

County Board—TOWNS AND CITIES—Under Code, 1873 section 1207, authorizing the board of supervisors of counties having a population of five thousand inhabitants to construct "ditches or drains * * * in such county whenever the same will be conducive to the public health, convenience or welfare." the power of the board is not territorially restricted to portions of a county outside of the limits of incorporated towns.—Aldrich v. Paine, 461.

ELECTION OF REMEDIES—See PRACTICE ⁶.

ELECTIONS—See ACTIONS, ²; MUNICIPAL CORPORATIONS, ¹⁰.

1. Ballot—Under Code, section 1122, an election of candidates for municipal offices, by a majority of ballots cast, is not invalidated by the fact that the mayor and council, without authority, changed one ticket on the ballot by heading it "democratic," which change was without fraud and deceived no one, where the election officers accepted those, and refused to use the ballots prepared by the recorder who was rightfully authorized to prepare them.—State of Iowa v. Bernholtz, 157.

2. SAME—Code, section 1121, prohibiting any "but ballots provided in accordance with the provisions of this chapter " from being

counted, intends that no ballot of the voter's choosing, but only those furnished by the proper officials to the voter, shall be counted.—*Idem.*

EMBEZZLEMENT—See CRIMINAL LAW, ⁵.

EMINENT DOMAIN—See INSTRUCTIONS, ¹, ⁷; MUN. CORP. ⁹.

1. **Courts**—REVIEW—The determination of the city council as to the amount of land necessary to be taken for a proposed sewer outlet is subject to review by the courts.—Bennett v. City of Marion, 628.

2. **SAME**—The decision of city council as to the amount of land necessary to be taken for a proposed sewer outlet will not be interfered with on appeal if the land sought to be taken will to some extent conduce to the public use, but any abuse of power will be restrained.—*Idem.*

3. **SAME**—A city, while allowed to determine for itself whether a sewer outlet shall be constructed in a certain locality, should not be permitted to fix arbitrarily on *ex parte* consideration the amount of land to be taken therefor, but the land owner should be allowed to controvert allegations of the application by answer or other pleadings.—*Idem.*

4. **Damages**—The jury in assessing damages for land condemned by the municipality for a sewer outlet may consider the effect upon the value of the remainder of the landowner's property, or to what extent he will be inconvenienced in the use of it.—*Idem.*

5. **SAME**—The measure of damages for property condemned by a city for a sewer outlet is the difference between the fair market value of the whole tract immediately before the taking of the part condemned and the fair market value of the remainder immediately after the taking, less any advantage to the owner on account of the improvements.—*Idem.*

EQUITY JURISDICTION—See PRACTICE, ³⁴.

ESTATES—See HOMESTEADS, ³, ⁵.

1. **Attorney's Fees**—*Executor and Administrator*—Attorney's fees may be allowed against a decedent's estate upon the establishment in the district court, of a claim based upon a promissory note containing the usual provision for attorney's fees where the claim was duly prepared and filed within six months, and not allowed and plaintiff employed an attorney to give the notice and prosecute the claim who filed the required affidavit for attorney's fees on the day the notice was served and appeared and prosecuted the claim to judgment.—Gillett v. McFarland, 746.

2. Descent and Distribution—ALIENS—*Next of Kin*—Code, 1873, section 2457, does not entitle claimants who are children of a sister of an intestate's father to inherit, when the mother through whom they claimed was disqualified because a non-resident alien, although such ancestor had died before claimant and before the intestate, and though said children are the nearest relatives of the intestate, all parties to this action being citizens of the United States.—Meier v. Lee, 304.

3. TREATIES—A non-resident alien is not empowered to acquire or inherit an interest in lands in Iowa by virtue of the treaty of 1783 between the king of Sweden and the United States providing that the subjects of the contracting parties in the respective states, although unnaturalized, may dispose of and inherit *goods and effects.—Idem.*

4. Dower—PAYMENT OF LIENS—A balance of personal property paid over by executors to the widow under a will giving her a life use of all real and personal property should not, in proceedings for the assignment of dower, be applied in payment of a mortgage on the land.—Trego v. Studley, 742.

5. Estoppel—*Estates, Widow*—Where, after a widow sued her husband's executor for the amount due on a certificate of deposit as her individual property, she applied for a year's support, stating that she was seventy-eight year's of age, unable to work, and had to be cared for by a nurse, and that all she possessed in her own right was involved in the suit, and the allowance was made and paid from the money due on the certificate, these facts did not amount to an election to treat the certificate as assets of the estate so as to estop her claim to it, where she did not ask that the allowance be paid out of the certificate and stated in the application that same was her property.--Owen v. Christensen, 894.

ESTOPPEL—See ESTATES, [5]; HIGHWAYS, [2]; INSURANCE, [22]; MECHANIC'S LIEN, [14]; PRACTICE, [5].

EVIDENCE—See CRIMINAL LAW, [6], [7], [9], [10], [13], [15], [18], [49], [51]; DEDICATION, [1]; HOMESTEADS, [6]; INSTRUCTIONS, [2]; INSURANCE, [1], [4], [7]; LANDLORD AND TENANT, [6]; MUNICIPAL CORPORATIONS, [2], [3], [4]; RAILROADS, [2]; SALES, [2]; TELEGRAMS, [4]; WILL CONTEST, [16].

1. Admission—A letter written by an insurance agent to its general adjuster that the premises had been let and sublet, and the subtenant had left them about three hours before the fire, is not an admission of their occupancy.—Stoltenberg v. Continental Ins. Co. 565.

2. Best—TRANSCRIPT—A certified transcript of documents filed in the office of the clerk is under Code, 1873, section 3702, evidence

Small figures refer to subdivisions of Index. The others to page of report.

execution, levy, and sale are made in pursuance of it, the fact
that through mistake a second entry of the filing of the transcript was erroneously made does not invalidate the sale.—
Therme v. Bethenoid, 697.

EXEMPTIONS—See HOMESTEADS, ².

1. **Pension Money**—One seeking to establish an exemption in
   property alleged to be partly paid for with pension money
   must show, not only that such money was invested in the property, but also the exact amount invested.—Lee v. Grim, 37.

2. **SAME**—One owning loan association stock bought real property.
   For the purchase price he gave a mortgage on said property
   and pledged said stock. Some pension money was used in
   payments made on the stock, and the buyer intended to mature
   it and pay the mortgage with pension money. *Held*, that the
   proceeds of selling the real property on execution were not
   exempt, where the purchaser agreed, as part of the purchase
   price, to pay the loan and remove all clouds and liens, and the
   seller still retains the stock.—*Idem*.

EXPERT TESTIMONY—See WILL CONTEST, ¹⁵.

FACTORS.

1. **Lien**—*Conversion*—A factor's lien for commission and advances
   is waived where, after having consented that the owner might
   sell the goods himself, and after learning of a sale by the latter,
   the factor made a sale to a third person, it appearing that both
   the owner and the purchaser secured by him expressed their
   willingness to pay the factor's charges.—M. M. Walker Co., v.
   Produce Co., 245.

2. **JURY QUESTION**—The case should have gone to the jury on the
   question of waiver of the lien and the sufficiency of the tender.
   —*Idem*.

FALSE REPRESENTATIONS—See INSUR. ⁹.
FEES—See SHERIFFS.
FELLOW SERVANTS—See RAIL. ⁶.
FINAL JUDGMENT—See CRIM. LAW, ³⁶.
FIXTURES—See SALES, ⁴ to ⁶; TEN. AT WILL, ¹; TRESPASS.
FORECLOSURE—See BUILD. & LOAN ASSOC ; DEEDS, ⁷; MORTGAGES,
    ³, ⁴, ⁵; PRACT. SUP. CT., ²³, ²⁴.
FORGERY—See CRIM. LAW, ¹⁷.
FORMER ADJUDICATION—See ADJUD.
FORMER ACQUITTAL—See CRIM. LAW, ²².
FRAUD—See CANCELLATION; EXECUTIONS; PLEA AND PROOF, ¹;
    PRACT., ²².

discrepancy as to the amount of such credit. The son testified that he kept deeds executed in blank by his wife, in his office, and the quitclaim, with the nominal consideration written in, was the only one on hand at the time. *Held,* insufficient to establish fraud on the part of the son in contracting for the improvements.—Des Moines Savings Bank v. Goode, 568.

8. SAME—A conveyance by a son to his father is not shown to have been fraudulent because the grantee states that the consideration was eight thousand dollars, while the grantor testified that it was nine thousand, when the former's evidence was taken by deposition in the absence of his books of accounts.—*Idem.*

9. Lien—It is indicated that an attachment at law may sufficiently invoke equity in cases where else, the proceeding at law must remain wholly ineffectual.—Hill v. Denneny, 726.

10. SAME—At any rate it must be plead and proven in order to take a mortgage out of the way of the attachment that the debtor's property, over and above the mortgage is insufficient to satisfy the debt.—*Idem.*

11. Subsequent Creditors—Where a conveyance from a husband to a wife is not made to hinder or defraud subsequent creditors it will not be set aside in favor of such a creditor, although made without adequate consideration, and where a wife paid for property largely with her own labor, the fact that her husband contributed his labor towards the purchase will not give his subsequent creditors a claim against the property.—King & Co. v. Wells, 649.

12. SAME—The fact that notes transferred by a wife as her separate property in payment of land had been made payable to her husband for convenience will not give the husband's creditors a claim against the land, where they were not misled by the fact.—*Idem.*

FURNITURE—See JURY QUESTION, ¹, ².

GARNISHMENT.

A judgment will not be rendered against a garnishee upon his answer, where it is left in reasonable doubt whether he is chargeable or not.—Kerr v. Edgington, 68.

GRADES—See INSTRUCT, 6, MUN. CORP., ¹ to ⁵; PLEA AND PROOF, ⁴.
HARMLESS ERROR—See CONTRACTS, ⁸a, CRIMINAL LAW, ¹⁰, ²⁰, EVIDENCE, ¹¹, ¹², ¹³; INSTRUCTIONS, ¹¹, ¹²; INSURANCE, ¹⁶; PRACTICE SUP. CT., ²³, ²⁴; PRACTICE, ⁴; RAILROADS, ³; TENANTS IN COMMON, ⁴; WILL CONTEST, ¹¹, ¹².

HIGHWAYS.

1. Abandonment—*Estoppel*—Non-user will not operate to discontinue a lawfully established highway unless accompanied by such long continued adverse possession or transfer of the land by purcha-e and sale as to demand that the public should be estopped from asserting the right to re-open it.—Bradley v. Appanoose County, 105.

2. SAME—One who has agreed that a highway which he has fenced up and cultivated may be re-opened is estopped from asserting any right to the land where public expenditures have been made upon it in reliance on such agreement.—*Idem.*

HOMESTEADS—See ADJUDICATION, [1]; PRACTICE SUP. CT. [11].

1. Homesteads—*Abandonment*—Judgments rendered were not liens upon a homestead. Owner left it to reside with his daughter without intending to return, neither did he return. Within three days *after* leaving, he deeded the property to the daughter in consideration of her agreement to furnish him a home and support for life. *Held*, the homestead was abandoned and the lien of the judgment attached before said transfer by deed.—Chambers v. Jackson, 6.

2. SAME—A homestead will be deemed abandoned where the owner removed therefrom with the intention of selling it as he expected to do, although he intended to return to it if he could not make a sale.—Conway v. Nichols, 858.

3. Decedents—The homestead of a testatrix who leaves neither husband or children surviving her, is subject to the payment of any claims established against her estate.—Dettmer v. B·hrens, 585.

4. Deserting Wife—*Occupancy by Husband*—A wife who chooses to live apart from her husband is not entitled to any benefit from the homestead property set off in land owned by her, but the husband has full right during his occupancy to cultivate it.—Ehrck v. Ehrck, 614.

5. Estate—CREDITORS—Creditors cannot complain that a testatrix sold her homestead for a certain sum, to be paid her during life, and left a deed thereof with the depositary of her will to be turned over to the purchaser upon the payment of a specified additional sum.—Dettmer v. Behrens, 585.

6. Evidence—QUIETING TITLE—The burden is upon plaintiff in a suit to quiet title against the apparent lien of a judgment against his grantor, which the latter at one time occupied as a homestead, to overcome the presumption created by latter's being of the homestead.—Conway v. Nichols, 858.

Small figures refer to subdivisions of Index. The others to page of report.

7. **Life Tenant**—A grantee of land subject to a life reservation of use and rents acquires no homestead right, as against a subsequent creditor, by occupancy through sufferance of a life tenant —Therme v. Bethenoid, 697.

8. **Selection**—Where a wife living apart from her husband selects a homestead in lands owned by her, her selection will not, in the absence of evidence of bad faith on her part in making it, be set aside, and the selection of the husband adopted, though the wife's selection is from the roughest and most unproductive portion of the tract and cut off from convenient access to a highway.—Ehrck v. Ehrck, 614.

HUSBAND AND WIFE—See CONTRACTS, *; HOMES, *, *; TRUSTS; TEN IN COMMON.

HYPOTHETICAL QUESTIONS—See WILL CONTEST, [13], [14].

IMPEACHMENT—See EVID. [15] to [21].

INCLUDED OFFENSES—See CRIM. LAW, [37].

INCORPORATION—See ADJUD., *; CITIES AND TOWNS, *.

INCREASE—See MORTGAGES, *.

INCUMBRANCE.

How Created—A person who takes title to property as security for a loan made to one of its owners and executes to the other owner a note showing her interest in the premises, thereby creates an incumbrance upon the property.—Grapes v. Grapes, 816.

INDECENT EXPOSURE—See CRIM. LAW, [22].

INDICTMENT—See CRIM. LAW, [21], [23], [24], [25], [27], [30], [60].

INDORSEMENTS—See ACTIONS, *; BILLS AND NOTES, [7].

INFANTS—See RAIL. [13].

INJUNCTION

—See CITIES AND TOWNS, *; DEEDS, *; JUDGMENTS, *, *; MUNICIPAL CORPORATIONS, [10]; PRACT. SUP. CT. [70]; page, 751.

1. **Motion to Dissolve**—A motion to dissolve an injunction directed to the injunction as a whole, will be denied if the injunction is good as to any part.—Brady v. Crittenden, 840.

2. **Replevin**—*Injunction pendente lite*—An answer in replevin denied plaintiff's right to possession in certain articles; alleged that the articles were not included in the mortgage under which plaintiff claimed possession, nor in the writ under which they were taken; that some of them were exempt, and that the balance were placed with him for repairs, his occupation being that of a jeweler; and asked for a return thereof, for damages for their detention, and for an injunction restraining their sale. *Held*, since, under Code 1873, section 3226, prohibiting counterclaims in actions of replevin and entitling defendant to recover the property and damages for its recovery, his answer

was an "action by ordinary proceedings, within section 3386, providing that "in all cases of * * * injury, where the party injured is entitled to maintain and has brought an action by ordinary proceedings, he may in the same cause pray and have a writ of injunction * * * against * * * continuance of such * * * injury."—*Idem.*

INSOLVENCY—See EVIDENCE, 25; MECHANICS' LIENS, 9.

INSTRUCTIONS—See CONTRACTS, 3*a*; CRIMINAL LAW, 31, 33, 35, 36, 38, 39, 45, 46, 47; EVIDENCE, 19, 21; JURY QUESTION, 2; NEW TRIAL, 3; PRACTICE, 13; PRACTICE SUP. CT., 15, 54, 55, 56, 59; RAILROADS, 3, 4, 6, 14; TELEGRAMS, 4.

1. An instruction not to allow damages for a possible misuse of land condemned for a sewer outlet, nor to assume that it will be made a nuisance, "or otherwise inconvenience plaintiff or lessen the value of his premises, except as hereinbefore explained," is too restrictive, where no explanation precedes.— Bennett v. City of Marion, 628.

2. **Applicability**—An instruction that if a municipal corporation negligently constructed a sidewalk, one who sustained injuries from a fall caused by its unevenness may recover if free from contributory negligence, is erroneous where there is no evidence that the city was negligent in constructing the sidewalk.—Barce v. City of Shenandoah, 426.

3. SAME—An instruction "that it is a violation of law for any person to threaten with intent to compel another by threats to do an act against his or her will" is reversible error in an action by a woman to recover for physical and other injuries alleged to have been induced by threats.—Botkin v. Cassady, 334.

4. PLEADING—An instruction in an action upon a promissory note that if the indorser authorized or consented to a waiver of demand and protest and guarantee the note he is estopped denying liability thereon, is properly refused where the plaintiff did not plead waiver or estoppel and did not rely upon an oral waiver of demand and protest, instead, declaring on a written waiver.—Benjamin v. Flitton, 417.

6. **Construed**—An instruction which explains that an ordinance adopted prior to a change of grade complained of, was admitted in evidence to show whether or not the plaintiff's means of convenient access to his property were increased by grades which that ordinance established, does not tell the jury, in effect, that the means of access were increased, and that only the extent of the increase is to be determined.— Morton v. City of Burlington, 50.

Small figures refer to subdivisions of Index. The others to page of report.

15. SAME—Refusal of an instruction in an action for a miscarriage
and other injuries alleged to have been induced by threats, that
if the plaintiff was suffering from uremia which might have
brought on such injuries or if they might have occurred without the action complained of, she could not recover is reversible error, where she had previously had a miscarriage which
might have caused the one in question and had been doing
work which might have produced such a result.—Botkin v.
Cassady, 834.

INSURANCE—See AGENCY, ¹, EVID., ¹, ¹⁴; MECHANIC'S LIENS, ⁴.

1. Accident Insurance—In an action by an assignee upon a certificate of membership for the payment of a weekly indemnity
in case of accidental injury to the insured, the by-laws of the
defendant association are admissible in evidence to show that
the plaintiff's assignor was suspended and not entitled to benefits and that the action was not brought within the time limited
by the by-laws which are stated to be a part of the certificate,
although not indorsed thereon or attached thereto and the
plaintiff's assignor had no actual knowledge of their contents —
Fitzgerald v. Accident Association, 457.

2. CHANGE IN BENEFICIARY—While a by-law of a beneficial association which provides the manner in which a change of beneficiary may be made cannot be taken advantage of by parties
claiming the insurance, yet such claimant may question
whether a change in beneficiary has, in fact, been made.—
Depee v. Grand Lodge A. O. U. W., 747.

8. CONSTRUCTION OF POLICY—The insured in a policy of accident
insurance providing indemnity for injuries "immediately,
wholly and continuously disabling (him) from transacting any
of the duties pertaining to his occupation as a merchant" is
not entitled to indemnity during the time he was able to perform some of the work pertaining to such occupation, although
there were many of the duties incident to it that he could not
perform—McKinley v. Insurance Co., 81.

4. CONTRACTS—_Amendment of Constitution_**—**An amendment of
articles of incorporation and by-laws of an insurance association, limiting the indemnity to death effected through or by
external, violent, or accidental means, does not affect existing
certificates issued while the constitution provided for indemnity whenever the death of a member occurred from an accidental cause with certain exceptions, where the constitution
does not authorize an amendment binding a member to any
change in the contract without his assent.—Carnes v. I. S. T.
M. Association, 281.

INTOXICATING LIQUORS—See LAND. AND TENANT, ⁴, ⁶; PRACTICE SUP. CT. ²⁹; page 751.

1. **Tax**—The requirement of Acts Twenty-tifth General Assembly, chapter 62, section 9, that the board of supervisors at the regular meeting in September shall levy an annual tax upon premises used for the sale of liquors is directory. and the fact that levy was not made until December will not invalidate it when the delay did not prejudice the person assessed.—Hubbell v. Polk County, 618.

2. **PRESUMPTIONS**—It will be presumed in support of the validity of a tax that it was levied at a regular meeting of the board of supervisors where that is an essential requirement and the contrary is not shown.—*Idem.*

3. **REBATE**—One against whose property used for the sale of intoxicating liquors the annual tax of six hundred dollars has been levied is not entitled to a remission of the tax for the balance of the year where the sales were suspended after continuing about nine months —*Idem.*

JUDGMENTS—See CRIMINAL LAW, ²⁶, ⁵⁰; EXECUTION SALE, ²; HOMESTEAD, ⁶; PRACTICE, ²; PRACTICE SUP. CT ²⁸.

1. **Conclusiveness**—Code, 1873, section 3011, provides that when judgment is rendered for the plaintiff in attachment, the court shall apply to the judgment the proceeds of perishable property attached. or shall order a sale of attached property not yet sold. Plaintiff recovered judgment in an action where attached property was sold as perishable, and the judgment contained no reference to the proceeds, and plaintiff thereafter moved for an order applying the proceeds to his judgment, which motion was denied. No appeal was taken, and the sheriff paid over the proceeds to the judgment debtor. *Held*, in an action by the judgment creditors against the sheriff and sureties for conversion, that the motion was a part of the former judgment. which had become final by failure to appeal, and hence determined plaintiff's rights in the attached property.—Second National Bank v. Haerling. 505.

2. **BY CONSENT**—The fact that the record contains no evidence does not justify an assumption that the judgment therein was entered by consent.—Cooper v. Disbron, 550.

8. **Equitable Relief as to**—Tne fact that a void judgment has been satisfied by execution will not prevent the restraining of its enforcement.—Heath v. Halfhill, 131.

4. SAME—Where a judgment is restrained and the judgment defendant awarded damages, the court has no power, over the objection of the judgment creditor, to order money collected on the judgment by garnishment to be refunded to a garnishee who was not a party to the suit to restrain.—*Idem.*

5. **Money Judgment**—*Presumptions*—The fact that there was no word or dollar mark attached to the figures in the columns for "Costs" and "Amount of Judgment" in the judgment docket entry creates no inference that it was not a money judgment. —Therme v. Bethenoid, 697.

JUDICIAL NOTICE—See CRIM. LAW, ⁵⁷, ⁶⁴.

JURISDICTION—See DEDICATION, ¹.

1. **Constables**—*Liability*—An officer is not liable for a levy under an execution regular on its face, issued on a judgment void only for want of jurisdiction of defendant, even where he had notice of the defect when making the levy, unless he acted with improper motives.—Heath v. Halfhill, 131.

2. **Justice of the Peace**—A justice of the peace does not acquire jurisdiction of a defendant, residing in another county, although the latter appears and files a counter claim.—*Idem.*

8. SAME—A justice is not liable for renewing in good faith an execution on a judgment void only for want of jurisdiction of defendant, even where he made the renewal with notice of the defect.—*Idem.*

JURORS—See NEW TRIAL, ¹⁰; PRACT., ¹⁸.

JURY—See FACTORS, ¹; MASTER AND SERVANT; NEW TRIAL, ⁸.

JURY QUESTION---See BILLS AND NOTES, ¹; CHECKS, ³; NEGLIGENCE, ¹, ³; PRACTICE SUP. CT., ³³; RAILROADS, ⁷, ¹², ¹³; TELEGRAMS, ¹, ³; TENANTS AT WILL, ¹.

1. What is "furniture in a store," or what articles are legitimately a part of a stock of goods of a peculiar nature, or what tools a particular artisan uses, is for the jury.—Brody v. Chittenden, 840.

2. "FURNITURE" DEFINED—On an issue whether certain articles kept in a place of business were covered by a mortgage of "furniture," an instruction that the appliances, implements, instruments, and like articles used in carrying on the business conducted at the place would not be furniture was error.— Brody v. Chittenden, 524.

JUSTICE OF THE PEACE—See JURISD. ², ³.

LACHES—See PRACT. ⁴.

Small figures refer to subdivisions of Index.   The others to page of report.

Small figures refer to subdivisions of Index. The others to page of report.

MASTER AND SERVANT—See PLEA AND PROOF, ²; RAIL.¹⁴, ¹⁶.

Negligence—*Jury Question*—Plaintiff was injured by the falling of a scaffold on which he was working as a bricklayer, in pursuance of a contract of hiring made between his father and defendant. The father testified that, when the contract was made, defendant agreed to build the scaffold, which was corroborated by others, and denied by defendant, who claimed that he contracted with the father to furnish the man, and that the building of the scaffold was part of the employment. *Held*, that the question whether defendant agreed to build the scaffold was for the jury.— Eller v. Loomis, 276.

MECHANIC'S LIENS—See CONTRACTS, ⁸, ¹²; INSURANCE, ⁹, ¹⁰.

1. **Claims Against County**--A Claim for material furnished for a county building must be filed with the county auditor, even where the board of supervisors appoint one member of the board a superintendent for the building, and direct the auditor to draw warrants for work on the building on his order. While the supervisor is a public officer, the law does not authorize him by virtue of his office to issue an order for payment of public money.—Green Bay Lumber Co. v. Thomas, 420.

2. **Contractual Relation**—Where the grantor, as part of the contract of sale, undertakes to repair the premises, and after the conveyance contracts therefor with a third person having knowledge of the conveyance, and who does the work on the grantor's personal credit, the property is not subject to a mechanic's lien for such repairs.—Des Moines Savings Bank v. Goode, 568.

3. INSOLVENCY—It is not a sufficient reason for establishing a lien against property owned by a third person, for plumbing work done at the request and upon the credit of one engaged in the improvement and sale of real estate, that such person is insolvent and therefore indifferent as to whether personal judgment is obtained against him.—*Idem.*

4. **Equitable Interests**—The interest of an equitable owner of land may be subjected to a mechanic's lien. Smith v. Insurance Co., 225.

Small figures refer to subdivisions of Index. The others to page of report.

did not amount to a fraud which would destroy its mechanic's lien.

b But while this evidence negatives such fraud it does not establish that a mistake was in fact made in the application of the payment.

c So, while a judgment for the sum due after such change was made, might properly be rendered against the contractor, for the reason that debtor and creditor may change the application of a payment at will, as between themselves, such change will not be allowed to deprive other sub-contractors of any portion of the fund subject to their liens, and as to them, the representation, by which the contractor obtained the change, are mere hearsay.—Green Bay Lumber Co. v. Thomas, 420.

11. MISTAKE—An inadvertent failure to give proper credits in a statement for a mechanic's lien does not render it unjust and untrue within the contemplation of the Code of 1873, section 2133.—Ewing & Jewett v. Stockwell, 26.

12. Sub-Contractor—The owner is not protected against a sub-contractor's lien, to the extent of payments made to the contractor in anticipation of the time of payment specified in the contract, with knowledge of the sub-contractor's claim.—Green Bay Lumber Co. v. Thomas, 154.

13. ESTOPPEL OF—Where a sub-contractor represented to the owner, before settlement with the principal contractor, that he would not look to the owner for payment for materials furnished, he is estopped from claiming a lien as to part of an installment due at that time to the principal contractor, which was paid by the owner to other sub-contractors on the strength of such representation.—*Idem.*

MINORS—See SURETIES.
MISCONDUCT—See NEW TRIAL, [4] to [10]; PRAC. [7]; PRACT. SUP. CT. [57].
MISJOINDER—See MORTGAGES, [5].
MISTAKE—See DEEDS, [5]; MECH. LIENS, [11].
MODIFICATION—See PRACT. SUP. CT. [21], [29].

MORTGAGES—See DEEDS, [1], [4], [6], [7], [8]; LANDLORD AND TENANT, [3], [4], REMAINDER.

1. Attachment—Where an attachment of mortgaged property is made before the giving of a second mortgage, but the deposit to secure the prior mortgage is not made until afterwards, the lien of the attachment is superior to that of the second mortgage, always an apparent lien; and if it develops on such contest that the first mortgage is invalid, the lien of the attachment is prior to the second mortgage as to all the

Small figures refer to subdivisions of Index. The others to page of report.

6.   **Future Increase**—A chattel mortgage purporting to cover certain mares and all increase of said mares, includes foals born *after* the execution of the mortgage and not alone those in existence at the time of its execution.—Hopkin's Fine Stock Co. v. Reid, 78.

7.   **Liens**—*Priorities*—A mortgage executed on corporate property prior to the time a contractor furnished labor and material, and which was thereafter discharged of record, is not entitled to priority as a continuing lien by reason of an unrecorded written agreement that the corporate bonds secured by a trust deed should be sold and creditors including the mortgagee paid with the proceeds, and the rule that the lien of the mortgage is presumed to continue until the debt is paid, notwithstanding any change in the evidence of the debt, has no application—Sioux City E. S. Co. v. S. C. & L. E. Ry. Co., 573.

MUNICIPAL CORPORATIONS—See EVIDENCE, [23]; TAXATION, [1].

1.   **Grade**—*Implied Extension*—While it may be true that changing grade at a corner, of necessity, amounts to a change for some distance from the corner, such rule will not be extended to a holding, that where a grade is established on two streets which cross a third, the same grade is made by implication on that portion of the street crossed which lies between the two said streets which cross it.—Morton v. City of Burlington, 50.

2.   **EVIDENCE**—*Damage*—The immediate surroundings of plaintiff in an action against a city for damages from a change of grade in the street in front of it, and the effect upon it, if any, of bringing the streets on either side to grade, may be considered by the jury in determining how much and in what way the work complained of affects the property. If there is any benefit, it bears on recovery —*Idem.*

3.   **SAME**—One who has contracted with a municipal corporation to grade a street cannot recover therefor without showing the amount of grading he has done, under a contract which reserved to the city the right to change the grade and thus increase or diminish the amount of grading to be done and provided that if such amount was changed the compensation to be paid therefor should be increased or diminished in proportion to such change. Hence, it was error to deny defendant's motion for

---

Small figures refer to subdivisions of Index.   The others to page of report.

NEGLIGENCE—See MASTER AND SERVANT; RAILROADS, [7], [8], [9], [10], [11], [12], [13]; TELEGRAMS, [1].

1. Contribution—*Jury Question*—One is, as matter of law, guilty of contributory negligence precluding recovery for a fall caused by the uneven condition of the sidewalk, where she knew the exact condition of the walk, having passed over it frequently and having frequently fallen at the very same place, and, though walking rapidly, nothing had occurred to distract her attention.—Barce v. City of Shenandoah, 426.

2. HIGHWAY—A pedestrian who knows that a part of a street crossing is sloping, slippery with ice and snow and dangerous, but who uses no care to avoid the peril although he might easily have done so, cannot recover for injuries sustained by a fall.—Marshall v. City of Belle Plaine, 508.

3. Sidewalks—*Jury Question*—Evidence is admissible that a walk sloped five feet in forty and that it had no cleats or hand rail, and where it also appears that the walk was not constructed according to any plan adopted by the city, but built as a temporary expedient to be used until the street was brought to grade, it becomes a jury question whether the city was negligent in constructing and permitting the walk to remain as it was at the time of an accident.—Ford v. City of Des Moines, 94.

4. SEVERAL CAUSES OF INJURY—A city is not relieved from liability for injuries sustained by falling upon a sidewalk which was established at too steep a grade, because the icy condition of the walk, for which it was not responsible. contributed to the accident. It was for the jury to say whether danger from snow should have been provided for when a sloping walk was built. —*Idem*.

NEW TRIAL—See PRACTICE SUP. CT. [40].

1. Exceptions—*Amendment*—Under Code, 1873, section 2789, providing that either party may take and file exceptions to the instructions within three days after verdict, a party who does not except to instructions when given or within three days after verdict, waives objections, and cannot urge them by way of amendment to a motion for a new trial, filed by leave of court, after the expiration of the three days.—Turley v. Griffin, 161.

2. SUFFICIENCY—An exception to the granting of a new trial is sufficient for a review of that ruling though the new trial was granted on a ground presented in an amendment to the motion which was filed by leave of court, without exception to the permission to file it.—*Idem*.

10. *Same*—The mere fact that a material prosecuting witness treated two of the jurors to beer, in a saloon, before any deliberation on the verdict was commenced, is not sufficient to show that the jurors were guilty of misconduct.—State of Iowa v. Minor, 642.

11. Motion for—*What is*—Plaintiff filed a motion to set aside a general verdict and certain special verdicts for defendant, and to have rendered a judgment for himself on a special verdict in his favor, stating as reasons therefor certain grounds appro_ priate for a motion for a new trial, none of which would authorize the court in sustaining this motion. *Held*, where plaintiff has not asked for a new trial, the record was in a condition which precluded a determination whether a new trial could have been granted.—Hooker v. Chittenden, 321.

12. *Same*—The mere fact that such motion was designated in the judgment as a motion for new trial does not authorize the conclusion that it was treated as a motion for new trial, in the lower court.—*Idem*.

18. Newly Discovered Evidence—A new trial on the ground of newly discovered evidence is properly refused where the witness who is to give such evidence was so connected with the transaction in regard to which he would testify that ordinary diligence would have suggested inquiries of him before the trial but no such inquiries were made, and no excuse is given for not making them.—Benjamin v. Flitton, 417.

NEWLY DISCOVERED EVIDENCE—See NEW TRIAL, [12].
NON-USER—See HIGHWAYS, [1].
NOTES AND BILLS—See BILLS AND NOTES; INSTRUCT. [9]; PRACT. [19].
NOTICE—See COSTS, [2].
NUNC PRO TUNC ORDER—See PRACT. SUP. CT., [6].

OATHS.

CONSTRUCTION OF STATUTE—*Board of Medical Examiners*—The provision of Acts Twenty-first General Assembly, chapter 104, that the president or any member of the board of state medical examiners may administer oaths and take testimony in relation to matters pertaining to their official duties is not exclusive and does not prevent consideration by the board of evidence not so taken.—Traer v. State Board of Med. Examiners, 559.

OBJECTIONS—See PLEA AND PROOF, [4].
OFFICERS—See CRIM. LAW, [44] to [56]; OIL INSPECTORS; SHERIFFS.

OIL INSPECTORS.

SALARY—Under Acts Twenty-fourth General Assembly, chapter 52, section 3, authorizing a deputy oil inspector to retain service fees earned by him, up to fifty dollars per month, and twenty-five per cent. thereafter, not to exceed one hundred dollars per month, where one inspector died in the middle of the month, and his successor filled out the time, two salaries of one hundred dollars each are not authorized, and this, though the fees for each month were sufficient to warrant them.—State of Iowa v. Dyer, 640.

OPENING CASE—See PRACT. [11].

ORDINANCE—See MUN. CORP., [5] to [8].

PAROL VARIANCE—See DEEDS, [1], [4]; EVID. [26].

PARTIES—See ACTIONS, [1], [2]; ADJUD. [5]; EXECUTIONS; JUDGMENTS, [4].

PARTITION—See PRACT. [12].

PARTNERSHIP—See FRAUD. CONV. [11].

1. Dissolution—*Contract Construed*—Under a dissolution agreement of a law firm, the partners were each to do his share of work on all unfinished business, one partner retaining the office with the firm papers. The other was not to be required to keep an office, but, for the purpose of finishing the business, was to be 'allowed to "use such office and supplies and employes therein." The "expenses and earnings and profits and emoluments of all the business" were to be "equally divided between the parties hereto." *Held*, that the expenses referred to were court expenses and special expenses in the cases, and not ordinary office expenses, which were to be borne by the partner retaining the office.—Varnum v. Winslow, 287.

2. LIMITATION OF ACTIONS—An action to recover *for a breach of the terms of an agreement for the dissolution of a partnership* is not barred because five years have elapsed from the date of the dissolution, although an accounting is asked.—*Idem.*

PAUPERS—See COUNTIES, [1] to [7].

PENSIONS—See EXEMPTIONS, [1], [2].

PERSONAL INJURY—See DAMAGES, [1]; INSTRUCT. [2], [15]; PLEA AND PROOF, [2].

PLATS.

VACATION—An addition cannot be replatted so as to vacate certain streets therein, where lots, though not abutting on the streets attempted to be vacated, have been sold under the original plat, unless all the owners of the lots in the plat join in vacating the street, as required by Code, 1873, section 563.—Uptagrapft v. Smith, 385.

PLEA AND CHARGE—See PRACTICE, [12].

Small figures refer to subdivisions of Index. The others to page of report.

806 INDEX.

PLEA AND ISSUE--See PRACTICE, ¹⁴.

PLEA AND PROOF—See RAILROADS, ⁴, ⁵.

1. **Fraud**—Where a widow sued her husband's executor for property she claimed in her own right, the proceeds of a farm he had conveyed to her, evidence that plaintiff did not have the means to buy the farm from her husband was inadmissible, there being no charge of fraud.—Owen v. Christensen, 394.

2. **General Denial**—*Custom*—Where an action is based on injuries caused by the falling of a scaffolding, the defense that there was a custom of bricklayers to build their own scaffolds is not available under general denial.—Eller v. Loomis, 276.

3. **Mental Anguish**—Where allegations as to mental anguish caused by threats were coupled with allegations as to physical injury, and damages were asked in a gross sum, the petition did not present a case for a recovery for mental anguish alone.—Botkin v. Cassady, 834.

4. **Objections**—Where plaintiff pleads that a grade fixed by an ordinance was wrongfully changed, the court will not assume that a later ordinance authorized the grade change complained of, by sustaining objections to evidence tending to show that the grade was changed after improvements were built with reference to it.—Morton v. City of Burlington, 50.

PLEADING—See INSTRUCTIONS, ⁴; INSURANCE, ³⁴.

1. **Amendment**—*Verification*—An unverified amendment may be permitted, which alleges that a contract to drill a well was made for the benefit of one defendant, and that she knew it was being drilled on her land, where the petition alleges that she had agreed to pay for the work; and this, though both petition and answer are verified.—Thompson & Son v. Brown, 367.

2. **Denial by Law**—The law operates as a denial of an affirmative defense pleaded in the answer·—Kinkhead v. Harvesting Machine Co., 222.

3. **Matter in Avoidance**—*Reply*—Facts relied upon by plaintiff in an action for the recovery of the price paid for a machine, to avoid the effect of the plea of acceptance of the machine after knowledge of its condition as a waiver of the warranty, must be set up in the reply by way of avoidance of the plea.—*Idem.*

4. **Surprise**—A party cannot complain of surprise because the court permitted an amendment to the petition to be filed on the day of the trial, when it contained nothing of which evidence might not have been given under the original petition.—Thompson & Son v. Brown, 367.

PRAC. Continued   TO   PRAC. SUP. CT.

certain portion of plaintiff's recovery be ordered paid to one who was not a party to such action, and that plaintiff be required to reconvey to defendants.—*Idem.*

22. SAME—Where plaintiff alleged, that defendants falsely represented such lot as described by a certain number, and that the lot was described by such number in the conveyance which he received from them, but that such description did not cover the lot purchased, the court erred in transferring the cause to the equity docket —*Idem.*

23. WAIVER—Where an action to foreclose several mortgages on real estate situated in different counties, was brought in one of such counties, all objections, on the ground of such misjoinder of actions were waived by failure of the mortgagors to appear and move therein.—McDonald v. Second National Bank, 517.

24. *Same*—A decree of foreclosure was not invalid for want of jurisdiction where a portion of the mortgaged property was situated in a different county from that in which the action was brought, and such action was *in personam* as well as *in rem*, and the mortgagors entered no appearance therein, as their right to insist on a trial in the other county was waived by their default.—*Idem.*

PRACTICE SUPREME COURT—See COSTS, ¹; CRIMINAL LAW. ⁶⁶; EMINENT DOMAIN, ²; NEW TRIAL. ¹, ¹¹, ¹²; TAXATION, ³,⁴,⁵.

1. Abstracts—See ⁴⁴, *post*—*Affirmance*—The requirement that abstract be filed thirty days before the second term, after appeal is perfected, is mandatory, and does not conflict with the requirement of other rules directing service of abstract at least thirty days before hearing day and docketing fifteen days before the trial term.—Newberry v. Getchell, etc., Company, 140.

2. EXTENSION—TIME OF APPLICATION—An extension of time wherein to file abstract, cannot be granted after the time by rule has expired.—*Idem.*

3. NOTICE OF APPLICATION—Notice should be given of an application to extend the time for filing an abstract.—*Idem.*

4. GROUNDS—An extension of time in which to prepare a case for submission will be granted where the delay is occasioned by unforeseen demands upon an attorney's time and no injury will be caused the other party; but where he has no reasonable grounds for believing he can submit the case in time or knows that he cannot do so, it is his duty to so inform his client, or obtain assistance.—*Idem.*

PRAC. SUP. CT. Continued

Attorney's Fee—See [21] *post.*
Bill of Exceptions—See [46] *post.*

14. The evidence rulings and exceptions will not be stricken from the abstract where the bill of exceptions contains the direction to the clerk to copy the shorthand reporter's report of the trial in full as extended, certified, and signed by such reporter, because the clerk was not directed to copy the original notes.—Manatt v. Scott, 203.

15. IDENTIFICATION—Instructions are sufficiently identified in the bill of exceptions by referring to them as filed in the case by their numbers and as duly indorsed by the presiding judge.—*Idem.*

16. JURISDICTION—The filing of a bill of exceptions is not necessarily jurisdictional.—Newbury v. Lumber Mfg. Co., 140.

17. SHORTHAND REPORT—The evidence is properly preserved of record if the notes certified by the judge and reporter were filed within the time given to file bill of exceptions, although the transcript is not filed until the time had elapsed.—Hopkins Fine Stock Co. v. Reid, 78.

18. STRIKING—Where a bill of exceptions was not signed until after the time given to prepare and file it, it will be stricken out.—*Idem.*

Change of Venue—See [46], *post.*
Clerk and Reporter—See [39], *post.*
Conflict—See [50], *post.*
Correction of Record—See [32], *post.*

19. Costs—CRIMINAL APPEALS—*Printing*—Code, section 5462, that if a judgment in a criminal case is reversed or modified in favor of defendant, he shall be entitled to the cost of printing applies to a case decided on appeal after the section took effect, although the printing was done before that day.—State of Iowa v. Dorland, 40.

20. TAXATION—The cost of printing may be taxed against the county, on motion, in the supreme court, in the main case.—*Idem.*

21. ATTORNEY'S FEES—Attorney's fees for defending a petition to modify a decree cannot be taxed against a petitioner.—Denby v. Fie, 299.

22. RE-TAXATION BELOW—A party failing to move for a re-taxation of costs in the trial court cannot complain of the taxation of costs, on appeal.—Young v. Goodhue, 447.

Demurrer—See [51], *post.*
Depositions—See [34], *post.*

Small figures refer to subdivisions of Index. The others to page of report.

Small figures refer to subdivisions of Index. The others to page of report

VOL. 106 Ia—52

72. CLERK's FEES—A clerk who accepts service of a notice of appeal containing an admission that the provisions of McClain's Code, section 4408, relating to security for his fees have been complied with, thereby waives a compliance with such statute. —Varnum v. Windslow, 287.

PRESUMPTIONS—See BILLS AND NOTES, *; CONFLICT OF LAWS; INSUR. 14.

PRINCIPAL AND AGENT—See INSUR. 10, 20.

PRIORITIES—See MECH. LIEN, *; MORTGAGES, 7, 8.

PRIVILEGE—See EVID. 29.

PROBATE LAW—See USURY, 8.

PUBLIC IMPROVEMENTS—See CITIES AND TOWNS, 1, 2.

RAILROADS.

1. Damages—EXCESSIVE VERDICT—A verdict of seven thousand dollars awarded a child injured by a passenger coach which was backed across the street will not be disturbed where pain and suffering was an element of damages in addition to the actual disfigurement and loss of actual earning capacity.— Allen v. Ames & C. Ry. Co., 602.

2. Evidence—HARMLESS ERROR—Admission of evidence that parents of plaintiff, a six-year-old boy, carefully endeavored to guard against his having to cross by himself a railroad track where he was injured, on the way from school, is harmless error, where the jury was charged that it was plaintiff's want of care contributing to the injury which would bar recovery, and thus, inferentially, that the parents' care was immaterial. —*Idem.*

3. Instructions—An instruction which contains an unqualified statement that if an employee was killed by reason of a defective appliance the master is liable, is erroneous where it ignores the defense of contributary negligence and waiver interposed by the master.— Ford v. C. R. I. & P. Ry. Co., 85.

4. PLEA AND PROOF—In an action for injury by a defective cattle guard, contributory negligence is an affirmative defense and plaintiff need not plead or prove freedom from contributory negligence. Plaintiff may rely on the denial interposed by law, or he may deny the contribution or confess and avoid, with or without denial. And where plaintiff simply files denial, it is error to submit whether defendant could have avoided the injury by reasonable care after discovering the contributory negligence of plaintiff. Such issue should have been expressly pleaded by plaintiff, after defendant asserted contributory negligence.—*Idem.*

Small figures refer to subdivisions of Index. The others to page of report.

but it was for plaintiff to prove that allegation and not for defendant to negative it.

c While the jury is also told that knowledge of danger is admitted and that this constitutes a waiver, this is not said with reference to burden of proof; nor is it said to be admitted that such knowledge existed without objection and promise of amendment, and therefore, it cannot be known but that the jury held such knowledge not to constitute a waiver because defendant had failed to prove the absence of protest and promise to repair.   .

d If the jury did not so understand it, the charge was contradictory. It said, then, that defendant should prove a fact, and also, that the same fact was admitted.—Ford v. C., R. I. and P. Ry. Co., 85.

15. **Risks of Employment**—A locomotive firemen assumes the risk of being overcome by the heat while in a position over the boiler for the purpose of oiling the machinery, which position he is obliged to assume because of the defective condition of the automatic lubricator.—Stockwell v. C. & N. W. Ry. Co., 63.

16. SAME—What will constitute the ordinary care which a master is bound to exercise in inspecting and repairing appliances furnished to his servants depends somewhat upon the danger to be reasonably apprehended from the defective condition of such appliances and the opportunity which the servant has of discovering such condition.—*Idem.*

17. **Statute Penalty**—LIMITATION OF ACTION—An action to recover damages for excessive freight charges under laws Twenty-second General Assembly, chapter 28, is for a statutory penalty within Code, 1873, section 2529, subdivision 1, limiting actions for the recovery of statutory penalties to two years.—Baker Wire Co. v. C. & N. W. Ry. Co., 289.

RAPE—See CRIM. LAW, [19], [20], [33], [61]; PRACTICE, [1].

RATIFICATION—See COUNTIES, [5].

REAL PROPERTY.

License—WATERS—Where, with the owner's acquiescence, waste waters from a leased portion of a tract were conducted across the other part for eight years, first by being turned upon the lands, then through a ditch built by the lessee, who paid the owner an annual rental for the land occupied by it, and then through an underground drain, the lessee had a license for the term of the lease to conduct such waters across the land which was not a mere right, revocable at the pleasure of the lessor.—Hansen v. Co-operative Creamery, 167.

REFORMATION.

Evidence--A note contained the printed promise to pay the principal five years after date, with interest payable annually until paid; also a written recital that "this note is payable in installments of eight dollars or more per month, with interest on the amount paid." The two makers and the scrivener, who was the partner of the payee, testified that the agreement was that during the five years no payments were required other than the monthly installments, with interest thereon. Other witnesses testified to corroborative circumstances. The payee had accepted monthly payments during the first year. The only evidence to support payee's contention that interest was payable annually was that of himself, and the fact that the makers knew of the printed clause making it so payable. The makers claimed to have understood the written clause to prevail. *Held*, that the note should be reformed so as to make it conform to the makers' contention.--Turpin v. Gresham, 187.

REMAINDERS.

Mortgages--LIFE ESTATE--The interest of the remaindermen in real property, under a recorded conveyance, cannot be defeated by the action of the life tenant in suffering a mortgage upon the property to be foreclosed through her fault and conveying the property to third persons after receiving a quitclaim deed from the purchaser at the judicial sale.--Werner v. Dolan, 855.

SALES--See CONTRACTS, [11]; EVIDENCE, [12]; MECHANIC'S LIENS, [9].

1. ACCEPTANCE--*Warranty*--A purchaser is liable for the agreed price of goods accepted by him without objections after opportunity of inspection, in the absence of a warranty intended to survive acceptance.--Schopp v. Taft & Co., 612.

2. **Evidence**—In an action to recover the purchase price of strawberries, defended on the ground that the goods were not of a character and quality ordered, a receipt given by the defendant to the railway company for the car and its contents after partial inspection which stated "received above O. K." is admissible.—*Idem.*

3. **License**—*Abandonment by Sale*—A sale of corn cribs constructed on land under a bare license or permission from the owner operates as a revocation of the license or tenancy at will.—Fisher & Knorr v. Johnson, 181.

4. **FIXTURES**—*Personal Property*—Corn cribs constructed upon the land of another under his bare license of permission remain personal property.—*Idem.*

5. **Vendor and Purchaser**—*Notice*—A purchaser of land with notice that corn cribs thereon were claimed by a third party, in possession acquires no better claim to the cribs than his vendor had.—*Idem.*

6. **FIXTURES**—A purchaser of land is not entitled to an injunction restraining a third person from removing a fence inclosing the land, where the fence was erected by the latter under an agreement with the vendor permitting its removal, and the purchaser knew of such agreement at the time he paid the purchase money.—Jones v. Cooley, 165.

SEDUCTION—See CRIM. LAW, [14], [46], [48], [62], [63].
SELF DEFENSE—See CRIM. LAW, [64].
SENTENCE—See CRIM. LAW, [61], [63].

SHERIFF'S FEES.

Subpoena and Order—On a motion for change of venue for prejudice of the trial judge, the court ordered persons signing affidavits in support hereof to appear for cross-examination, and directed that subpoenas should be served on such of them as the adverse party should indicate to the clerk. The clerk issued "an order to appear for cross-examination," in which he recited the above order, and notified the person named therein to appear in court and submit to cross-examination on a day stated. *Held*, that this order amounted to no more than a subpoena, and that the sheriff was entitled only to the fees provided for service of subpoenas, for serving the same.—Spangler v. Beaver, 744.

SIDEWALKS—See INSTRUCT., [2]; NEGLIG., [1], [3], [4].
SPECIAL INTERROGATORIES—See PRACT. SUP. CT., [18], [67].
STATUTE PENALTY—See RAIL., [17].
STOCK OF GOODS—See JURY QUESTION, [1].

Small figures refer to subdivisions of Index. The others to page of report.

STREET RAILWAYS—See TAX., ⁴.
STREETS—See NEGLIGENCE, ².
SUICIDE—See INSUR., ⁴,⁷.

SURETIES—See CONTRACTS, ¹,⁸.

Infants—A surety upon the promissory note of a minor is not liable thereon where the minor upon attaining majority disaffirmed the contract and returned the property for the purchase price of which the note was given.—Keokuk County State Bank v. Hall, 540.

TAXATION—See INTOXICATING LIQUORS, ¹, ².

1. County—CITIES AND TOWNS—The authority given the county board to levy a tax of not more than one mill on the dollar "of the assessed value of the taxable property in their county" for a county road fund, gives the right to so tax property in a city or town of the county, though no part of the sum raised is expended in said municipality or intended to be so expended.— C., R. I. & P. R'y Co. v. Murphy, 43.

2. Deed—*Presumptions*—The fact that a tax deed was issued is *prima facie* evidence that notice of the expiration of the period of redemption was given.—Young v. Goodhue, 447.

8. Equalization—APPEAL TO DISTRICT COURT—On appeal from the decision of the board of equalization upon an assessment, the district court has jurisdiction to strike from the assessment three lots described by the assessor which were not the property of the corporation assessed and to include two parts of lots which were its property, where the board of equalization failed to act upon the corporation's request to make such correction and such parts of lots were in fact included in the valuation but were by mistake described as the three lots.—C. R. & M. C. R'y Co. v. Cedar Rapids, 476.

4. SAME—The board of equalization assessed only that portion of a street railroad which lay within the city. The company applied to the board to have a misdescription of part of such property corrected, and, on refusal, appealed to the district court. On the appeal the city sought to have the property outside the city added to the assessment. *Held*, that, as the district court had no power to make an original assessment, it could not make such addition, as that issue was not raised by the appeal.—*Idem.*

5. To SUPREME COURT—The supreme court will change an assessment, to the amount which the weight of evidence shows most nearly represents the actual value of the property assessed.— *Idem.*

Small figures refer to subdivisions of Index. The others to page of report.

6. **Street Railway Defined**—A railway was constructed within a city, and also along a highway to a neighboring town. It was operated at first by steam, but afterwards by overhead trolly. It was built and operated under Acts Eighteenth General Assembly, chapter 32, relating expressly to street railways, and authorizing their extension beyond the limits of the city. It carried a small amount of freight and some express matter between the towns. *Held,* that it was a street railway, and therefore not within Code, 1873, section 1317, providing for the assessment of railways for taxation by the state executive council, but subject to taxation by the local assessors.—*Idem.*

7. **Title**—PURCHASER—*Agency*—An agent who has in his possession money of his principal wherewith to pay taxes on property owned by the former cannot through his neglect to do so obtain a valid tax title as against the principal, neither can such title be acquired by a purchaser who buys at a tax sale, through such agent. —Young v. Goodhue, 447.

8. **SAME**—Where a purchaser at foreclosure sale gives an agent money to pay the taxes on the premises, which he neglects to do, a valid tax title against said principal cannot rest on the facts, that a creditor of the agent furnished him money to bid in the land at tax sale, that he did so, that he assigned the certificate to his creditor as security and that said creditor quit-claimed to an association of which said agent was an officer, taking back a mortgage which was simply a change of security.—*Idem.*

TAXPAYER--See MUNICIPAL CORPORATIONS, [10].

TELEGRAMS.

1. **Delivery**—NEGLIGENCE—*Jury Question*—In an action against a telegraph company for damages for failure to promptly deliver a message, the evidence showed that the message reached its destination at eight o'clock A. M., and was delivered on the same day at one thirty P. M ; that the message was urgent; that the company's messenger made several attempts to find the addressee down town, and went to his office twice for that purpose but did not leave a notice under the door or visit his residence, which was within the company's free delivery limits, where the addressee was all the forenoon. *Held,* sufficient to sustain a finding of negligence.--Hendershott v. Western U. T. Co., 529.

2. **DAMAGES**—PROXIMATENESS—Damages sought against a telegraph company for the death of a valuable horse, alleged to be due to the defendant's delay in the delivery of a message are within the contemplation of the contract and not too

remote where both the receiving and sending parties knew from the nature of the dispatch that promptness was required. —*Idem*.

8.   JURY QUESTION—A telegraph message reading "Bravo is sick; come and fetch Miller at once," was sent to plaintiff. There was a delay of about five hours in its delivery. Bravo was a valuable horse of plaintiff, at a training stable about twelve miles from plaintiff's home. Miller was a veterinary surgeon. The evidence shows that the horse was taken sick about seven A. M.; that if Miller had reached the horse about five or six hours earlier, his chances for recovery would have been greater; and that in all reasonable possibility the horse would have been saved, had it been treated five or six hours earlier. *Held*, sufficient to sustain a finding that the delay in the delivery of the message was the proximate cause of the death of the horse.—*Idem*.

4.   Evidence—INSTRUCTIONS—*Issue*—The burden of proof is on the plaintiff to show by a preponderance of the evidence that in all reasonable possibility the cause of the death of the horse was the failure to deliver the message in due time, and the sole issue is whether the death is attributable to delay in treatment caused by the failure to deliver the message. Hence, an instruction that negligence in the surgeon's treatment of the animal after the dispatch was received is imputable to the plaintiff, is erroneous.—*Idem*.

TENANCY AT WILL.

1.   *Jury Question*—Consent that corn cribs constructed on land under a bare license from the owner may remain thereon after their sale to a third person may be inferred from the fact that they remain on the land with the knowledge of the owner and without objection on his part for such a length of time and under such circumstances that objection might have been expected if the owner of the land did not assent.—Fisher & Knorr v. Johnson, 181.

2.   Removal of Buildings—An agreement that structures erected upon land by permission or license of the owner may be removed by the person making them will be implied in the absence of any interest of the latter in enhancing the value of the land or of other facts or circumstances showing an intention that the structure should not be removed.—*Idem*.

TENANTS FOR LIFE--See HOMESTEADS, '; REMAINDERS.

TENANTS IN COMMON.

1. Where a deed is to a husband and wife, they hold as tenants in common, and not an estate by the entirety, under Code, section 2923, which provides that conveyances to two or more in their own right create a tenacy in common.—Bader v. Dyer, 715.

2. **Adverse Possession**—Where a tenant in common had sole possession of land for thirty years, using it as his own, and knowing the co-tenancy existed, but making no public claim of entire ownership, his possession was not adverse, and limitations did not run against his co-tenants, who had no knowledge of the co-tenancy or that the husband was making adverse claim to the whole estate.—*Idem.*

3. HUSBAND AND WIFE—Where land was conveyed to a husband and wife, who occupied it together and jointly shared the profits, the husband's possession was not adverse to the wife's.—*Idem.*

4. **Harmless Error**—An error in finding that a tenant in common had conveyed his interest in land was not prejudicial, it being found that the interest was reconveyed to him.—*Idem.*

TENDER—See PRACT., 19.
THREATS—See INSTR., 3; PLEA AND PROOF, 2.
TOOLS—See JURY QUEST., 1.
TRANSCRIPT—See CRIM. LAW, 46; EVID. 2, 3; EXECUTION SALE, 6.
TRANSFER—See PRACT., 34.
TRANSFER TO EQUITY—See ACTIONS, 2, PRACT., 20, 21.
TREATIES—See ESTATES, 2.

TRESPASS.

Removal by Trespasser—A trespasser who makes erections on the land of another cannot remove the structures erected.—Fisher & Knorr v. Johnson, 181.

TRUSTEES—ACTIONS, 1.

TRUSTS.

Evidence—Where a wife allowed her husband to use her property in his business, expecting that she would be compensated therefor, and he invested it in real estate in his own name,—there being no understanding that the title should be taken in her name,—and no claim that her property was used to pay for property taken in his name without her knowledge or consent, there is no constructive trust, nor a resulting trust.—Shupe v. Bartlett, 654.

Small figures refer to subdivisions of Index. The others to page of report.

USURY.

1. **Building Association**—A loan by a building and loan association to one of its members, made while Code, 1873, section 1185, authorizing such associations to collect from their members such premiums bid for the right of priority it taking loans as its by-laws might adopt was in force, is not usurious because the contract provides for the payment of premiums which were bid for the loan by the secretary under the authority of the borrower.—Loan Association v. Johnston, 218.

2. Same—In the absence of evidence to the contrary, a stipulation in a mortgage to a building and loan association requiring the borrower to pay a premium will be presumed to have been made under a bid to enable him to obtain a right of precedence in taking the loan as authorized by the Code, rather than a device to cover up a usurious transaction, where the borrower in his application, authorized the secretary of the association to bid such a premium, that he might have such precedence.—*Idem.*

3. **National Banks**—A trustee who gave his individual note to a bank to obtain money to purchase a mortgage on trust property for its protection, which instrument he assigned to the bank as security, cannot maintain an action under United State Revised Statutes, section 5198, to recover back usurious interest exacted, is, since it was not paid by him within the meaning of the statute, although he advanced sums for that purpose for which the heirs repaid him.—Parde v. Iowa State National Bank, 845.

4. Same—A note, the amount of which is computed in the amount loaned together with a sum illegally added thereto as usurious interest and which bears interest at the highest lawful rate is usurious, and the interest wrongfully exacted may be recovered where the note was paid in full.—*Idem.*

5. Assignment—The right conferred by the United States Revised Statutes section 5198, upon a debtor from whom usurious interest has been exacted by a national bank or his legal representatives, to recover back twice the amount is personal and cannot be transferred by an ordinary sale or assignment.—*Idem.*

6. Custom—Under the laws of Iowa limiting interest to six per cent. per annum in the absence of an agreement for a higher rate, the charging of ten per cent. upon a depositor's overdraft, arrived at by balancing the account monthly computed on the aggregate amount of the overdraft approximating the nearest hundred for the month, on the basis of thirty days to

Small figures refer to subdivisions of Index   The others to page of report.

• the month, is usury under the United States revised statutes, 5197, which authorizes national banks to charge interest at the ·rate allowed by the state in which such banks are located, and the said charge of ten per cent. cannot be legalized by a custom of banks which permits it.—Talbot v. First National Bank, 861.

7. RECOVERY BACK—*Limitation of Statute*—A national bank charged usurious interest. It was included in a note which was not otherwise tainted with usury. This note was secured by trust deed, and on foreclosure of the deed the said excessive interest was deducted by the decree. *Held,*

   a The action provided by United States Revised Statute 5198, allowing the recovery back of usurious interest applies only to cases in which such interest has been actually paid. In this case this was not done, for as said interest was left out of the judgment, no property could have been sold under it to pay what was not in the judgment.

   b This action having been begun more than two years after said note was given is barred by United States Revised Statute 5198 which allows it within two years "from the time the usurious transaction occurred."—*Idem.*

8. Renewals—The payment of usurious interest upon a note taints all the subsequent notes given in renewal of it with usury.— Pardoe v. Iowa State National Bank, 845.

VACATION— See PLATS.
VENDOR AND VENDEE—See CONTRACTS ¹¹, MECH. LIENS, ².
VENUE—See CRIM. LAW, ⁵.
VERDICT—See PRAC., ¹⁶; RAIL, ¹.
VETERINARIES—See EVID., ²⁹.

WAGERS.

RIGHT TO RECOVER OF STAKE-HOLDER—One who wagered money cannot recover his share of the stakes from the stake-holder, whatever the outcome, unless, before payment to the other wagering party, the former repudiated the transaction and notified the stake-holder not to pay the money; and his recovery is defeated if he merely gave notice not to pay the wager until further notice.—Trenery v. Goudie, 693.

WAIVER—See CONTRACTS, ²; INSURANCE, ¹⁹, ²⁰, ²¹, ²²; PLEADING, ⁴: PRACTICE, ⁹,¹⁵,²²; PRACTICE SUP. CT., ⁸,²⁶,⁷¹.
WARRANTY—See SALES, ¹.
WATERS—See REAL PROP.
WELLS—See CONTRACTS.
WIDOWS—See ESTATES, ⁴.

Small figures refer to subdivisions of Index. The others to page of report.

Small figures refer to subdivisions of Index. The others to page of report

VOL. 106 Ia—53

AUTHORITIES CITED

IN THE OPINIONS REPORTED IN THIS VOLUME.

S

T

W

CASES CITED

IN THE OPINIONS REPORTED IN THIS VOLUME.

D

E

F

H

I

R

S

Trask v. Trask .... 90 Iowa, 318.... 589
Trawick v. Martin Brown Co.. 79 Tex. 460; 14 S. W. Rep. 564.... 4
Trego v. Studley ....106 Iowa, —.....................357
Trout v. Trout................. 44 Iowa, 471....................657
Trust Co. v. Day............. ... 63 Iowa, 459. 521
Trustees v. Hill. .... 12 Iowa, 462 ....398, 456, 541
Tucker v. Lake ....— N. H. —; 29 Atl. Rep. 406....523
Tuffree v. State Center......... 57 Iowa, 538..................429
Tubeville v. State............. 56 Miss. 798..................487
Turner v. Hine.............. 87 Iowa, 500....... ....148, 152
Turner v. Turner.............. 85 N. J. Eq, 487................216
Twedy v. Fremont County..... 99 Iowa, 721 21
Tyler v. Langworthy.......... 87 Iowa, 555 301

U

Union Building Association v.
  Rockford Ins. Co............ 83 Iowa, 647 209
Utley v. Merrick.............. 11 Met. (Mass.) 302............. 25

V .

Vannest v. Fleming.......... 79 Iowa, 688 170
Viele v. Insurance Co.......... 26 Iowa, 9 599
Villiage of St. Johns v. Board..111 Mich. 609; 70 N. W. Rep. 131.. 21

W

Waller v. Insurance Co........ 64 Iowa, 101 383
Waller v. Waller.............. 76 Iowa, 513 207
Walton v. Mandeville......... 56 Iowa, 597 180
Walton v. Wray.............. 54 Iowa, 531 184
Walsh v. Insurance Co..... ... 80 Iowa, 133 459
Warfield v. Lindell............ 30 Mo. 281....................721
Ware v. Delahaye............ 95 Iowa, 667 .... 500, 729
Waterbury v. Railway Co..... 104 Iowa, 32....................510
Waterhouse v. Black .... 87 Iowa, 317..................325
Waterman v. Whitney .... 11 N. Y. 157...................211
Watson v. Chesire............. 18 Iowa, 202 178
Watson v. Phelps.............. 40 Iowa, 482... 450
Watson v. Williams........... 36 Miss. 331................... 11
Webster v. Hunter.... ...... 50 Iowa, 215 457
Weidert v. Insurance Co....... 19 Or. 261; 24 Pac. Rep. 242......568
Weigen v. Insurance Co ....104 Iowa, 410 260
Weir Furnace Co. v. Ind Dis. of
  Seymour .... 99 Iowa, 116 696
Weis v. Morris....... .....102 Iowa, 827 22
Welch v. Spies.................103 Iowa, 389 370
Wellborn v. Weaver............ 17 Ga. 267; 63 Am. Dec. 235......588
Wellor v. Goble.............. 66 Iowa, 113 298
Wells v. Railway Co........... 56 Iowa, 520 88
Wheelright v. Wheelright ..... 2 Mass. 447, 3 Am. Dec. 66.....589
Whicher v. State.............. 2 Wash.St.286; 26 Pac.Rep.268..486
White v. Abstract Co.......... 96 Iowa, 843 149
White v. Smith.............. 54 Iowa, 233 130
Whiting v. Stage Co.,......... 20 Iowa, 557 672
Wilcox v. McCune............. 21 Iowa, 294 301
Wilgus v. Gettings .... 21 Iowa, 178 184
Willits v. Railway Co.......... 80 Iowa, 531 93
Wilson v. State................. 73 Ala, 527....................127
Windland v. Deeds .... 44 Iowa, 98....................280

Y

Z

STATUTES CITED, CONSTRUED, ETC.,

IN THE OPINIONS REPORTED IN THIS VOLUME.